PART II
THE THERAPEUTIC DIALOGUE: COMMUNICATION AND RELATIONSHIP-BUILDING SKILLS

3   Empathic Presence and Responding – Building a Mutual Understanding

WMH20 EGN3

Gerar
Robe

The   per

A Clie

Third EM

CENGAGE

Australia • Brazil • Canada • Mexico • Singapore • United Kingdom • United States

***The Skilled Helper: A Client-Centred Approach*, 3rd EMEA Edition**
US authors: Gerard Egan, Robert J. Reese
Adapter: Helen Nicholas

Publisher: Annabel Ainscow

List Manager: Virginia Thorp

Development Editor: Hannah Jones

Marketing Manager: Laura Lichtensteiger

Senior Content Project Manager: Phillipa Davidson-Blake

Manufacturing Buyer: Elaine Bevan

Typesetter: Lumina Datamatics

Cover Design: Varpu Lauchlan

Cover Image: © MirageC/Getty Images

For product information and technology assistance, contact us at **emea.info@cengage.com**

For permission to use material from this text or product and for permission queries, email **emea.permissions@cengage.com**

British Library Cataloguing-in-Publication Data

A catalogue record for this book is available from the British Library.

ISBN: 978-1-4737-7491-9

Cengage Learning, EMEA
Cheriton House, North Way
Andover, Hampshire, SP10 5BE
United Kingdom

Cengage Learning is a leading provider of customized learning solutions with employees residing in nearly 40 different countries and sales in more than 125 countries around the world. Find your local representative at: **www.cengage.co.uk**

To learn more about Cengage platforms and services, register or access your online learning solution, or purchase materials for your course, visit **www.cengage.co.uk**

Printed in the United Kingdom by Ashford Colour Press Ltd.
Print Number: 02   Print Year: 2022

BRIEF CONTENTS

CONTENTS

PREFACE

In this new third edition of the EMEA adaptation of Egan's *The Skilled Helper*, all of the useful themes developed over the past 40 years stay intact, including: the primacy of client focus; the importance of life-enhancing client outcomes; the collaborative client–helper alliance; a problem-management and opportunity-development approach; the essential communication skills needed for effective client–helper dialogue; an emphasis on the values that drive the helping process, the importance of diversity. One of the important updates to this edition is a new co-author, Jeff Reese, who brings with him a strong research background.

The Power of Basics™

The popularity of *The Skilled Helper* lies in 'the power of basics', a phrase that has been trademarked by the author to keep it uncorrupted. The basics in this edition remain the same, but with better ways of designing, developing and delivering them, for instance by using fresh, more contemporary examples to illustrate them. Basics are the foundations needed by the skilled helper and are powerful but often ignored, even in the training of helpers. The basics here are called the 'key ingredients of successful therapy'. Both this phrase and 'the power of basics' have been used in this edition, as this reflects the target audience and linguistic conventions of students and helpers across the UK, Europe, South Africa and the Middle East. *The Skilled Helper* has always emphasised the basics of effective therapy and has ignored the fads and 'the next big thing' in the helping industry. This edition names, simplifies, clarifies and organises these basics more effectively.

Overview

The book has four parts. Part I deals with the key ingredients, the 'power of basics' approach, the role of the therapist, the importance of the helping relationship and the values that drive the entire helping process. Part II focuses exclusively on the communication skills therapists need to engage in a collaborative, outcome-focused dialogue with clients. Part III deals in detail with the problem-management and opportunity-development approach. Part IV includes useful counselling skills exercises for helpers to practise with, and an annotated extract of a counselling conversation.

The book uses a version of the 'common factors' approach to understanding successes in therapy. The common factors research is a search for 'what works' in therapy (Duncan, Miller, Wampold & Hubble, 2010), that is, those key ingredients and the 'power of basics' that are essential to successful therapy no matter which approach(es) to therapy the helper uses. For instance, research shows, not surprisingly, that a strong working alliance or therapeutic relationship between client and helper contributes greatly to the successful outcomes in therapy. In this book, these factors are called 'the ingredients of successful therapy'.

The ingredients that are pulled together include and move a bit beyond the ones described by Duncan *et al.* (2010). Naming them and describing what they have to offer clients provides greater crispness and focus to the problem-management and opportunity-development approach to therapy outlined in this book.

The approach in this edition underscores the importance of the CDOI (client-directed, outcome-informed) movement in the helping professions (Bohart & Tallman, 2010). Life-enhancing outcomes for clients constitute the backbone of therapy. In this edition there is a heightened emphasis on clients and all that they bring with them to the therapeutic encounter and on the importance of 'keeping the client in the driver's seat' throughout the helping process.

Feedback – client to self, client to helper, helper to client and helper to self, together with the give-and-take discussions these forms of feedback evoke – is presented as one of the basics for successful therapy. This kind of feedback has always been a theme in previous editions, but research has demonstrated how essential it is to successful therapy. Feedback on progress towards desired outcomes and on how each session contributes (or does not contribute) to progress belongs in every session.

The Standard Problem Management Model, which is found, directly or indirectly, in practically every form of therapy, organises all the skills, methods and themes of successful helping. The problem-management process is not about schools of psychology, interesting theories or the latest fads. It is about people with problem situations and unused opportunities. This process – broadly speaking, a contextual cognitive-behavioural-emotive approach to therapy – is presented as a valid treatment approach in itself. It is also a tool of psychotherapy integration. Effective therapists appreciate the power of both goal setting and planning even when the troubled person, or the world at large, does not.

Effective decision making (and its shadow side) lies at the heart of problem management and opportunity development and, therefore, at the heart of therapy. It is now included as one of the key ingredients of successful therapy and the main 'power of basics'. Therapists help clients make various decisions throughout the helping process. Effective helpers understand both the bright and dark side of decision making and become guides as troubled people muse about, make, glide towards, flirt with, reflect on or fall into decisions – or attempt to avoid them. They also help clients explore the possible unintended consequences of the decisions they are making. Because decision making has a deep shadow side, the more therapists understand its inner workings the better.

The essential uncertainties associated with human behaviour play an important role in therapy and require helping approaches that are both rigorous and flexible. Both client-focused rigour and client-focused flexibility in the use of models, methods and skills permeate the chapters of this book.

This edition further promotes the concept of 'personal culture', the way that each individual lives out the beliefs, values and norms of the larger social culture. Diversity at the individual client level takes precedence over any particular form of diversity such as multicultural diversity. The personal culture of each individual client includes his or her incorporation and expression of ethnic and cultural themes, together with all the other forms of diversity in his or her makeup. If social culture is 'the ways *we* do things', then personal culture refers to 'the way I do things' as a member of any given culture.

The clinical use of research findings demonstrates that therapists do not have to choose between evidence-based practice and practice-based evidence. If we are client-focused, then there is room for both evidence-based practice and practice-based evidence. Either-or gives way to both-and. The problem-management process is used as a 'browser' to search for a wide range of therapeutic methods and adapt them to the needs of this client. Client-need drives the process.

The tendency of the helping industry to avoid the term 'challenge' is noted. There is increased focus on *invitations* to clients to engage in self-challenge and the concept of helper self-challenge is covered. Therapy is presented as a form of positive challenge in itself. If therapy is to make a difference, it must be different from what happens in everyday life. Some form of challenge is part of this difference.

COVID-19

It is worth noting that during the editing of this edition of *The Skilled Helper*, the Coronavirus (COVID-19), an international pandemic, affected the world on a global scale. As the world went into lockdown, practitioners were not able to conduct face-to-face sessions with clients and had to adapt to offering remote and online sessions. Several regulatory bodies came together to produce guidance, information and webinars for their members on how to conduct effective video therapy. Task forces were formed to discuss the issues surrounding COVID-19 and their professional members. The British Psychological Society produced a webinar series to support their members with working online (www.bps.org.uk/news-and-policy/free-webinar-gives-top-tips-effective-video-therapy). The Psychological Society of South Africa produced a podcast series on COVID-19 on their PsyCAST medium (www.psyssa.com/psycast/); a multi-stakeholder initiative for South African health care workers and a special edition of their Psytalk in March 2020 (psytalk.psyssa.com/current-issue/). Resources for professionals were collated, for example the British Psychological Society produced a number of useful documents on how to talk to children about the situation; parenting while self-isolating; and documents to support their members (www.bps.org.uk/responding-coronavirus).

Researchers and professional bodies began to study the psychological impact of COVID-19 on individuals and journals were sending out calls for papers on research about the impact of COVID-19 on individuals' physical and mental health. There was a surge of research survey requests for participants to rate the impact of COVID-19 on their mental and physical well-being. Lee (2020) published a Coronavirus anxiety scale and, with the emergence of more research, there is no doubt that further studies will be focused on the impact for a while to come. There is a current gap in the literature on the impact of COVID-19 on therapists and helpers. These findings will be important for the future. The move from face-to-face sessions with clients to online video sessions can cause therapists to become tired and drained. Little research has been conducted in this area. During this time, self-care has been highlighted as essential for therapists and clients, especially those with pre-existing anxiety disorders and mental health issues. Within physical isolation, helpers from different backgrounds are needing to work in new and often innovative ways with clients, as well as focusing more on their own self-care in order to provide their services. Working from home has become the new norm, with therapists and clients having to juggle their many roles within a home environment. It will be interesting to see what research comes out of this global pandemic and what we can learn from the literature.

CONTRIBUTING AUTHOR

Dr Helen Nicholas
Counselling Psychologist and Practitioner Psychologist

Helen Nicholas is a registered practitioner and counselling psychologist with the Health and Care Professions Council (HCPC), a British Psychological Society (BPS) chartered psychologist and Eye Movement Desensitisation and Reprocessing (EMDR) therapist. She is a senior lecturer at the University of Worcester, United Kingdom, where she teaches on the BSc Counselling Psychology, MSc Counselling and MSc EMDR courses.

Helen holds a Doctorate (PsychD) in psychotherapeutic and counselling psychology from the University of Surrey and currently works in academia, as well as in independent private practice in Somerset (HCN Psychology). She is the immediate past chair of the BPS, Division of Counselling Psychology (DCoP) and has held a variety of voluntary positions in the BPS and DCoP over the last six years. Helen currently sits on the training committee for counselling psychology, the BPS ethics committee and the professional practice board and is a fitness to practice panel member for the HCPC.

Helen has a wide range of experience working in settings such as the NHS, adult mental health, old age psychiatry, research, the voluntary sector, private hospitals and in academia. She specialises in working across the lifespan with adolescents, adults and older adults and has a particular interest in depression, anxiety, trauma and neurodegenerative diseases. She is widely published in the fields of Alzheimer's disease, Dementia, Personality traits, work–life balance and counselling psychology, and divides her time between teaching, research and independent practice.

ACKNOWLEDGEMENTS

The content of this Europe, Middle East and Africa edition is predominantly adapted from the eleventh edition of *The Skilled Helper: A Problem-Management and Opportunity-Development Approach to Helping,* by Gerard Egan and Robert J. Reese but also includes some examples adapted from the following Cengage Learning EMEA textbooks:

Burnard, P., *Counselling Skills for Health Professionals Fourth Edition* (2005)

Bayne, R., Jinks, G., Collard, P. & Horton, I., *The Counsellor's Handbook: A Practical A-Z Guide to Integrative Counselling and Psychotherapy Third Edition* (2008)

Crawford, R., Brown, B. & Crawford, P., *Storytelling in Therapy* (2004)

Finlay, L., *The Practice of Psychosocial Occupational Therapy Third Edition* (2004)

Stewart, W., *An A-Z of Counselling Theory and Practice Fifth Edition* (2013)

Full copyright details and acknowledgements will appear in the aforementioned publications.

The publisher would also like to thank the following reviewers for their helpful and insightful comments in developing this new edition:

Annelize Bonthuys, North West University, South Africa

Maria Dempsey, University College Cork, Ireland

Lungile Mabundza, University of Swaziland, Swaziland

Beth Moran, University of Plymouth, UK

Lindi Nel, University of the Free State, South Africa

Edmarie Pretorius, University of the Witwatersrand, South Africa

Paula Beesley, Leeds-Beckett University, UK

Laetitia Petersen, University of Witwatersrand, South Africa

Tasneemah Cornlissen-Nordien, University of Stellenbosch, South Africa

Mark Hoelterhoff, Edinburgh University, UK

CENGAGE

Teaching & Learning Support Resources

Cengage's peer-reviewed content for higher and further education courses is accompanied by a range of digital teaching and learning support resources. The resources are carefully tailored to the specific needs of the instructor, student and the course. Examples of the kind of resources provided include:

 A password-protected area for instructors with, for example, a test bank, PowerPoint slides and an instructor's manual.

 An open-access area for students including, for example, useful weblinks and glossary terms.

Lecturers: to discover the dedicated teaching digital support resources accompanying this textbook please register here for access:
cengage.com/dashboard/#login

Students: to discover the dedicated learning digital support resources accompanying this textbook, please search for *The Skilled Helper: A Client-Centred Approach*, Third EMEA Edition on: **cengage.co.uk**

BE UNSTOPPABLE!

Learn more at **cengage.co.uk**

PART I
LAYING THE
FOUNDATIONS

Although the centrepiece of this book is a problem-management and opportunity-development framework that encompasses all the ingredients of successful helping (Part III) and the communication and relationship-building skills needed to engage in the client–helper dialogue (Part II), it is also essential to emphasise from the outset that a client-centred approach to helping is key. The term 'client-centred', first used by Carl Rogers (1951), refers to the notion that it is the clients themselves who are best able to decide how to find the solutions to their problems in living, and is a prevalent theme in effective helping across the world, including within the United Kingdom, Europe, South Africa and the United States.

In Part I, Chapter 1 outlines the nature and goals of helping and the ingredients of successful helping together with a snapshot of the problem-management and opportunity-development framework that organises these ingredients. It introduces the term 'power of basics', to highlight the key ingredients needed in successful therapy in order to practise competently. Chapter 2 focuses on the helping relationship and the values that drive it, one of the basics. Both chapters highlight the client-centred and outcome-focused nature of helping espoused in this book.

CHAPTER 1: Successful Helping – An Introduction

CHAPTER 2: The Helping Relationship

CHAPTER 1
SUCCESSFUL
HELPING – AN
INTRODUCTION

Chapter Contents

- Formal and Informal Helpers: A Very Brief History

- What Helping Is About

- The Ingredients of Successful Helping

- Embracing and Befriending the Uncertainties Inherent in Helping

- Moving from Smart to Wise: Managing the Shadow Side of Helping

FORMAL AND INFORMAL HELPERS: A VERY BRIEF HISTORY

Throughout history, people the world over have held a deeply embedded conviction that, under the proper conditions, some of us are capable of helping others come to grips with problems in living. This conviction, of course, plays itself out differently in different cultures, but it is still a cross-cultural phenomenon. Today this conviction is often institutionalised in a variety of formal helping professions. In Western cultures, counsellors, psychiatrists, psychologists, social workers and ministers of religion, among others, are counted among those whose formal role is to help people manage the distressing problems of life.

A second set of professionals, although they are not helpers in the formal sense, also help people in times of crisis and distress. Included here are organisational consultants, dentists, doctors, lawyers, physician associates, support workers, nurses, midwives, health visitors, social workers, probation officers, teachers, managers, pastoral support staff in schools and universities, supervisors, police officers and practitioners in other service industries. Although these people are specialists in their own professions, there is still some expectation that they will help those they serve to manage a wide variety of problem situations. For instance, teachers teach English, history and science to students who are growing physically, intellectually, socially and emotionally, and struggling with developmental tasks and transitions in their lives. Teachers may help adolescents' transition into the emerging adulthood phase of development (Arnett, 2000). Teachers are, therefore, in a position to help their students, in direct and indirect ways, explore, understand and deal with the problems of growing up. Managers and supervisors in work environments help workers cope with problems related to job performance, career development, interpersonal relationships in the workplace, returning back to work after periods of illness and a variety of personal problems that affect their ability to do their jobs. This book is addressed directly to the first set of professionals and indirectly to the second.

To these professional helpers can be added any and all who try to help others come to grips with problems in living: relatives, friends, acquaintances and even strangers (on buses, trains and aeroplanes). In fact, only a small fraction of the help provided on any given day comes from qualified helping professionals. Informal helpers – bar staff, beauticians and hairdressers are often mentioned – abound in the social settings of life. Friends and family help one another through troubled times. Parents need to manage their own marital problems while helping their children grow and develop. Indeed, most people grappling with problems in living seek help, if they seek it at all, from informal sources (Heller, Swindle, Pescosolido and Kikuzawa, 2000). In the end, of course, all of us must learn how to help ourselves cope with the problems and crises of life. Sometimes we do this on our own, but at other times we seek help from mostly informal sources. This book is about the basic ingredients of successful helping. It is designed to assist you in becoming a better helper no matter which category you fall into.

WHAT HELPING IS ABOUT

Helping is first and foremost about the person seeking help. Let's call the person seeking or needing help a client rather than patient to avoid, at least for the time being, the dispute relating to the use of the medical model in helping (Wampold, 2010a, 2010b). To determine what helping is about, it is useful to consider (1) why people seek – or are sent to get – help in the first place and (2) what the principal goals of the helping process are.

The Power of Basics

The basic working knowledge, competencies and skills that people need to engage in any human endeavour effectively are, of course, an important ingredient in the helping profession. But because they are basic, they are often overlooked, taken for granted or dismissed. For instance, the basic working knowledge and skills people need to live effective social lives – interpersonal communication and relationship-building skills – fall into this category.

Many people think they have these foundation and basic skills when, in fact, they do not. In most societies these skills are not named or described in a direct way, nor are they taught. People may be expected to 'know what these skills are' and 'pick them up' along the way. Some people are able to do this, but many are not. Organisations may expect their employees to be 'good communicators', but they do not say what they mean by that term and often go on to recruit people who are not good communicators. These organisations tend to do little to help their employees develop these key skills; many see the basics as boring. In truth they are powerful, an important foundation and a key ingredient in our interactions with others.

I believe that *The Skilled Helper* has been successful over the years precisely because it focuses, not on the 'latest thing' or on any particular model, method or approach to counselling and therapy but on the basic working knowledge and skills that helpers need to do a competent job. Having the key ingredients and foundation are important when embarking on a career in a helping profession. This edition will focus on highlighting these key foundational skills and the 'power of basics' in our interactions with clients.

Clients with problem situations and unused opportunities

Many people become clients because, either in their own eyes or in the eyes of others, they are involved in problem situations that they are not handling well or are currently struggling with. Others seek help because they feel they are not living as fully as they might or up to their personal values at the time (Harris, 2008). Many come because of a mixture of both. Therefore, clients with problem situations and unused opportunities constitute the starting point and the primary focus of the helping process.

Problem situations Clients come for help because they have crises, troubles, doubts, difficulties, frustrations or concerns. Often called 'problems' or 'issues' generically, they are not problems in a mathematical sense because these problems usually cause emotional turmoil and often have no clear-cut solutions. It is probably better to say that clients come not with problems but with problem situations, issues or difficulties – that is, with complex and messy problems that they are not currently handling well. These current issues are often poorly defined. Or, if they are well defined, clients still don't know how to handle or solve them. Or clients feel that they do not have the resources or resilience needed to cope with them adequately. If they have tried previous coping strategies or solutions, they have not worked this time.

All of us face problems in life. Problem situations arise in our interactions with ourselves, with others and with the social settings, organisations and institutions of life. Clients – whether they are hounded by self-doubt, tortured by unreasonable fears, grappling with the stress that accompanies serious illness, addicted to alcohol or drugs, involved in failing marriages, suffering from postnatal depression, fired from jobs because of personal behaviour, office politics or disruptions in the economy, confused or abused in their efforts to adapt to a new culture, returning from some battlefield with the psychological ravages associated with war, ostracised due to political and government upheaval in their home country, suffering from a catastrophic loss, imprisoned because of child abuse, struggling with a midlife crisis, lonely and out of community with no family or friends, battered by their spouses or victimised by racism – all face problem situations that move them to seek help. In some cases, these problem situations move others – such as teachers, supervisors, the legal system – to refer people who are not managing their problems very well to helpers or even mandate that they seek help.

Even people with devastating problem situations can, with help, handle these situations more effectively. Consider the following example.

> Lisa, aged 58, living in Bedford in the UK, suffered three devastating losses within six months. Her only daughter, who lived on the other side of the country in Cornwall, died suddenly of a heart attack. Her daughter was only 28. Shortly after, Lisa lost her job in a redundancy movement by her employer stemming from poor sales performance in difficult market conditions. Finally, her husband, who had been ill for about four years, died of cancer. Although she was not destitute, her financial condition could not be called comfortable, at least not by British middle-class standards. One of her two sons was married with a family of his own and the other lived in Switzerland. The unmarried son, a banker for an international bank with headquarters in Geneva, travelled extensively and was not always easy to contact.
>
> After her husband's death, Lisa became agitated, confused, angry and depressed. She also felt guilty. First, because she believed that she should have done 'more' for her husband. Second, because she also felt strangely responsible for her daughter's early death. Finally, she was terribly afraid of becoming a burden to her sons. At first, retreating into herself and withdrawing from friends, she refused help from anyone. But eventually she responded to the gentle persistence of the local vicar. She began attending a support group at the church. A psychologist facilitated the group and helped her interaction within the group. She slowly began to accept help from the other group members and her sons. She began to realise that she was not the only one who was experiencing a sense of loss and began to understand the reasons for her emotions. She became part of the 'grieving family', the group members helping each other cope with the turmoil they were experiencing. She began relating with some of the members of the group outside the group sessions and this helped fill the social void she experienced when she had been made redundant. Eventually, through contacts within the group, she got another job. Gradually her depression eased and, despite some persistent anxieties, she found a kind of peace.

Note that help came from many quarters. Her newfound solidarity with her family, the church support group, the active concern of the vicar, the informal chats with the psychologist and positive-thinking interactions with her new friends helped Lisa enormously. Furthermore, because she had always been a resourceful person, the help she received enabled her to tap into her own unused strengths.

It is important to note that none of this 'solved' the losses she had experienced. Indeed, the goal of helping is not to 'solve' problems but to help the troubled person manage them more effectively or even to transcend them by taking advantage of new possibilities in life. Problems have an upside. They are opportunities for learning.

Missed opportunities and unused potential   Some clients come for help not because they are dogged by problems like those listed earlier but because their coping strategies are not as effective as they would like them to be. And so clients' missed opportunities and unused potential constitute a second starting point for helping. Most clients, like the rest of us, have resources they are not using or opportunities they are not developing. People who feel locked in dead-end jobs or bland marriages, who are frustrated because they lack challenging life goals, who feel guilty because they are failing to live up to their own values and ideals, who want to do something more constructive with their lives or who are disappointed with their uneventful interpersonal lives – such clients come to helpers not to manage their problems better but to live more fully.

It is not a question of what is going wrong but of what could be better. It has often been suggested that most of us use only a small fraction of our potential. Most of us are capable of dealing much more creatively with ourselves, with our relationships with others, with our work life and, generally, with the ways in which we involve ourselves with the social settings of our lives. Consider the following case.

> After ten years as a helper in several mental-health centres around Birmingham in the United Kingdom, Sameena was experiencing compassion fatigue and burnout. In the opening interview with a counsellor, she berated herself for not being dedicated enough. Asked when she felt best about herself, she said that it was on those relatively infrequent occasions when she was asked to assist in providing help for other mental-health centres that were experiencing problems, having growing pains or reorganising. The counsellor helped her explore her potential as a consultant to human-resource organisations and make a career adjustment. She enrolled in an organisation development programme at a local university. In this programme she learned not only a great deal about how organisations work (or fail to work) but also how to adapt her skills to organisational settings. Sameena stayed in the helping field, but with a new focus and a new set of skills.

In this case, the counsellor helped the client manage her problems (compassion fatigue, burnout and guilt) by helping her identify, explore and develop an opportunity (a new career). The helper was a catalyst; Sameena took the lead.

Helping clients identify and develop unused potential and opportunities can be called a 'positive psychology' goal. Seligman and Csikszentmihalyi (2000) called for a better balance of perspectives in the helping professions. In their minds, too much attention is focused on pathology and too little on what they call 'positive psychology': 'Our message is to remind our field that psychology is not just the study of pathology, weakness and damage; it is also the study of strength and virtue. Treatment is not just fixing what is broken; it is nurturing what is best' (p. 7). They and their fellow authors discuss such positive topics as subjective well-being, happiness, hope, optimism, the capacity for love, forgiveness, civility, nurturance, altruism, an appreciation of beauty and art, responsibility, self-determination, courage, perseverance, moderation, future mindedness, originality, creativity, talent, a civic sense, spirituality and wisdom. Traditionally, this has not been the ordinary language of the helping professions.

Seligman and Csikszentmihalyi's challenge has stimulated a great deal of theory, research, debate and practical programmes for helping clients identify and tap into unused resources and opportunities (Biswas-Diener & Dean, 2007; Carr, 2004; Diener & Biswas-Diener, 2008a, 2008b; Dykens, 2006; Ince, 2009; Peterson, 2006; Seligman, 2004; Seligman, Steen, Park, & Peterson, 2005; Siegel & Allison, 2009; Simonton & Baumeister, 2005; Snyder & Lopez, 2005, 2006). Helping is not just about 'fixing', but about enabling clients to design and redesign their lives. Ince (2009), in a Harvard Medical School Special Health Report, refers to positive psychology as 'the science of satisfaction' (p. 2). Obviously, both fixing and redesigning have a place in helping, and one often melds into the other. Effective counsellors help clients choose the mix that is best for them. The 'materials' of designing/redesigning are the often overlooked resources within the client – strengths, values, beliefs, pools of resilience that currently lie unnoticed. Sometimes it is better to help clients transcend problems than to work through them. Positive psychology suggests ways of doing just that.

You will find the positive psychology research and literature useful in striking a balance with your clients. But, because there is a human tendency to turn what is useful into a fad, a note of caution is appropriate. Positive psychology is not an 'everything's going to be all right' approach to life. Richard Lazarus (2000) put it well:

> "However, it might be worthwhile to note that the danger posed by accentuating the positive is that if a conditional and properly nuanced position is not adopted, positive psychology could remain at a Pollyanna level. Positive psychology could come to be characterised by simplistic, inspirational, and quasi-religious thinking and the message reduced to 'positive affect is good and negative affect is bad'. I hope that this ambitious and tantalising effort truly advances what is known about human adaptation, as it should, and that it will not be just another fad that quickly comes and goes." (p. 671)

Ongoing research (McNulty & Fincham, 2012) challenges the often-inflated claims made in the name of positive psychology. And this is only right. However, at its best, helping by whatever name (counselling, therapy, psychotherapy) engenders in clients hope for a better life. Clients with hope are more likely to achieve life-enhancing goals. There is a more detailed discussion of hope in Chapter 9 in Part III. Clients are encouraged to increase their levels of resilience in order to cope more effectively with life's challenges. This may include learning to regulate their emotions (Gross, 2014).

The three principal outcome-focused goals of helping

A great deal of the helping literature focuses on the models, methods and skills of helping. Less of it focuses on outcomes. That is a pity, because helping should be mainly about life-enhancing outcomes for clients. Duncan, Miller and their associates (2010) and a growing number of researchers and practitioners are working to introduce a better balance into the helping professions. They talk about client-directed and outcome-informed (CDOI) helping. As indicated earlier, the primary focus of helping is the client with unmanaged problem situations and/or unused resources, strengths and opportunities. But because helpers do not solve or manage clients' problems, it is essential to help clients become agents of change in their own lives. And change means life-enhancing *outcomes* in terms of problems managed and opportunities spotted and developed.

Fifteen-year-old Jordan was a victim of internet bullying at his university in Pretoria, South Africa. A small group of his classmates who thought he was a 'sissy' or a 'homo' used the internet, social media and mobile phones to torment and humiliate him. Jordan, actually a very decent teenager, was embarrassed and confused. He did not know who was doing this or why. He became chronically anxious, stopped going out with friends and curtailed his social life in other ways. Once the perpetrators saw that they had Jordan on the run, they increased the frequency of their attacks. Only when he finally begged his parents to let him go to a different university did they realise what was happening. Jordan's parents moved into action. First, they provided whatever support they could by talking with Jordan. Next, they arranged a meeting with a counsellor at the university who began to help Jordan manage his humiliation and anxiety. Then they had a meeting with the university vice chancellor. The vice chancellor made an announcement stating that cases of internet bullying were in progress and that data were being gathered to share with parents of the offenders and, if necessary, the police. The internet bullying stopped – or went deeper underground – almost immediately. The universities' trustees came out with a strong no-tolerance statement about bullying in all its forms. But its members also began to discuss how to implement such a policy without turning the university into a police state. 'It's about time,' one of the parents said. Things exploded when a couple of research articles on bullying and other forms of adolescent aggression in universities and other higher education establishments, mostly psychological and social, hit the headlines (Faris & Ennett, 2011; Faris & Felmlee, 2011). Psychological and social aggression, primed by the internet, seemed to be much more widespread in this environment than anyone realised. The research showed that over half the students in the study either engaged in aggression, were victims of aggression or fell into both camps.

There were some constructive outcomes. Because of his parents' support and the counsellor's help, Jordan's anxieties eased. A couple of his friends took him aside and confessed that they knew what was happening but didn't have the courage to do anything about it. Jordan came to realise that university life had an 'edge' to it and that he had to deal with it. And he still had some good friends, including the parents of some of his classmates and some of the adults in the neighbourhood. His parents did not become overprotective but both they and Jordan sensed a better, more mutual relationship. The university began to search for ways of taking these issues seriously and provided additional mental-health services and awareness campaigns across the campuses.

Jordan ended up with a better sense of himself and of the darker side of communal life, a more secure environment, decreased anxiety and more supportive relationships with his parents and some of his friends. He got his life back. The bullies may not have had a change of heart but they did get some kind of wake-up call.

As we have seen, clients come to helpers primarily because they want or need to manage specific problem situations more effectively and/or develop unused opportunities in order to live life more fully. This is the first goal of helping. But counselling, done right, can help them achieve two other goals. Let's take a look at all three. Read what follows and then return to Louis' case and see if you can find elements of all three goals.

Goal One: Life-enhancing outcomes for the client *Help clients manage their problems in living more effectively and develop unused or underused resources and opportunities more fully at the service of life-enhancing outcomes.*

Helpers are successful to the degree to which their clients – through client–helper interactions – see the need to manage specific problem situations and develop specific unused resources and opportunities more effectively. Notice that I stop short of saying that clients actually end up managing problems and developing opportunities better. Although counsellors help clients achieve valued outcomes, they do not control those outcomes directly but guide the client through options. In the end, clients can choose to live more effectively or not.

A corollary to Goal One suggests that helping is about *constructive change* that leads to life-enhancing results, outcomes, accomplishments and impact. Satisfaction, symptom reduction, constructive change as perceived by self and/or others, and end-point improved functioning have all been studied as positive outcomes of therapy (Lunnen, Ogles, & Pappas, 2008). All of these outcomes point to an improved life on the part of the client. Helping is an '-ing' word: it includes a series of activities in which helpers and clients engage. These activities, however, have value only to the degree that they lead to valued outcomes in clients' lives. Ultimately, statements such as 'We had a good session,' whether spoken by the helper or by the client, must translate into more effective living on the part of the client. If a helper and a client engage in a series of counselling sessions productively, something of value will emerge that makes the sessions worthwhile. Unreasonable fears will disappear or diminish to manageable levels, self-confidence will replace self-doubt, addictions will be conquered, an operation will be faced with a degree of equanimity, a better job will be found, a couple will breathe new life into their marriage, a battered wife will find the courage to leave her husband, or a man embittered by institutional racism will regain his self-respect and take his rightful place in the community.

The British Association for Counselling and Psychotherapy phrased it as such:

> "Therapy is time set aside by you and the therapist to look at what has brought you to therapy. This might include talking about life events (past and present), feelings, emotions, relationships, ways of thinking and patterns of behaviour. The therapist will do their best to help you to look at your issues, and to identify the right course of action for you, either to help you resolve your difficulties or help you find ways of coping. Talking about these things may take time, and will not necessarily all be included in one session."
> (Retrieved from www.bacp.co.uk/media/2637/bacp-what-is-counselling-psychotherapy-c2.pdf)

The Psychological Society of South Africa expresses similar sentiments:

> *"The discipline of psychology is concerned with mental processes (like learning, reasoning, motivation & emotion) and behaviour, and the relationship between these processes. The study of psychology is concerned with how people feel, think, learn, understand, perceive, act and interact with others. This understanding allows psychologists to help people with emotional and behavioural difficulties within a number of contexts including individual psychotherapy, family and group psychotherapy, as well as therapeutic interventions within organisational contexts."*
> *(Retrieved from www.psyssa.com/public-interest/what_is/)*

Regulatory and profession bodies outline their aims, values and codes of conduct that members must adhere to (e.g. The British Psychological Society, 2018; Psychological Society of South Africa, 2007), as well as their strategic plan; for example, many professional and regulatory bodies for psychologists, therapists and counsellors. The focus is often on integrity, competence, respect and dignity. The PsySSA states that

> *"Psychologists consult with, refer to, and cooperate with, other professionals and institutions to the extent needed to serve the best interests of their patients, clients, or other recipients of their services."*
> *(Retrieved from www.psyssa.com/wp-content/uploads/2016/12/SOUTH-AFRICAN-PROFESSIONAL-CONDUCT-GUIDELINES-IN-PSYCHOLOGY-2007-PsySSA_updated_01-12-2016pdf.pdf)*

Clients often need help in finding solutions to problems, alleviating distress and working collaboratively with the helper to aid their recovery. The British Psychological Society (BPS) describes counselling psychologists as follows:

> *"Counselling psychologists deal with a wide range of mental health problems concerning life issues including bereavement, domestic violence, sexual abuse, traumas and relationship issues. They understand diagnosis and the medical context to mental health problems and work with the individual's subjective psychological experience to empower their recovery and alleviate distress."*
> *(Retrieved from careers.bps.org.uk/area/counselling)*

Helping is about constructive change that makes a substantive difference in the life of the client.

The kind of results discussed in this book can be perceived by clients and people who interact with clients, such as family, friends, peers and co-workers. Kazdin (2006), who works with families and children, emphasises the importance of moving beyond change based on statistical significance and even clinically significant change, to change that has palpable impact on clients' daily lives. Here Kazdin provides some examples of outcomes that make a difference in the everyday life of a child with 'conduct disorder' and the lives of those who interact with him:

> *"For example, one can see that the child no longer beats up a parent, teacher, or siblings; has stopped running away from home; does homework for the first time; no longer steals from neighbours; no longer brandishes a knife with younger siblings or peers; interacts appropriately with an infant sibling (e.g., talk, gentle play) rather than physically abusing him or her; and becomes only mildly upset during a tantrum at home without any of the usual property destruction."* (p. 47)

The need for 'palpable' results is not new. Effective helpers have realised this throughout the history of helping. Thirty years ago, Driscoll (1984) saw this clearly in his work with Andrea N., a battered woman.

The mistreatment had caused her to feel that she was worthless even as she developed a secret superiority to those who mistreated her. These attitudes contributed in turn to her continuing passivity and had to be challenged if she was to become assertive about her own rights. Through the helping interactions, she developed a sense of worth and self-confidence. This was the first outcome of the helping process. As she gained confidence, she became more assertive; she realised that she had the right to take stands, and she chose to challenge those who took advantage of her. She stopped merely resenting them and did something about it. The second outcome was a pattern of assertiveness, however tentative in the beginning, that took the place of a pattern of passivity. When her assertive stands were successful, her rights became established, her social relationships improved and her confidence in herself increased, thus further altering the original self-defeating pattern. This was a third set of outcomes. As she saw herself becoming more and more an 'agent' rather than a 'patient' in her everyday life, she found it easier to put aside her resentment and the self-limiting satisfactions of the passive-victim role and to continue asserting herself. This constituted a fourth set of outcomes. The activities in which she engaged, either within the helping sessions or in her day-to-day life, were valuable because they led to these valued outcomes. (1984, p. 64)

Andrea needed much more than 'good sessions' with a helper. She needed to focus on and work towards outcomes that made a difference in her life.

Goal Two: Learning how to help oneself   *Help clients become better at helping themselves in their everyday lives.*

Clients often are poor problem solvers, or whatever problem-solving ability they have tends to disappear in times of crisis or personal challenge. What G. A. Miller, Galanter and Pribram (1960) said many years ago is, unfortunately, probably just as true today.

> "In ordinary affairs we usually muddle about, doing what is habitual and customary, being slightly puzzled when it sometimes fails to give the intended outcome, but not stopping to worry much about the failures because there are still too many other things still to do. Then circumstances conspire against us and we find ourselves caught failing where we must succeed – where we cannot withdraw from the field, or lower our self-imposed standards, or ask for help, or throw a tantrum. Then we may begin to suspect that we face a problem... An ordinary person almost never approaches a problem systematically and exhaustively unless he or she has been specifically educated to do so." (pp. 171, 174)

Many people in our society are still not 'educated to do so'. And if many clients are poor at managing problems in living, they are equally poor in identifying and developing opportunities and unused resources. We have yet to find ways of making sure that our children develop what most consider to be essential 'life skills', such as problem management, opportunity identification and development, sensible decision making and the skills of interpersonal relating.

It is no wonder, then, that clients – often poor problem solvers to begin with – often struggle when crises arise. If the second goal of the helping process is to be achieved – that is, if clients are to go away better able to manage their problems in living more effectively and develop opportunities on their own – then helpers need to impart the working knowledge and skills clients need to move forward. As Nelson-Jones (2005) puts it, 'In the final analysis the purpose of using counselling skills is to enable clients to become more skilled in their own right... Counsellors are only skilled to the extent that they can be successful in skilling clients' (p. 14). That is, helping at its best provides clients with tools to become more effective self-helpers. Therefore, although this book is about a process helpers can use to help clients, more fundamentally it is about a problem-management and opportunity-development process that clients can use to help themselves. This process can help clients become more effective problem situation managers and opportunity developers, better decision makers and more responsible 'agents of change' in their own lives. Helpers need to work with clients, collaboratively fostering their autonomy and ensuring that the decisions made are best suited to their needs.

Goal Three: Developing a prevention mentality   *Help clients develop an action-oriented prevention mentality in their lives.*

Just as doctors want their patients to learn how to prevent illness through good nutrition and healthy activities, just as dentists want their patients to engage in effective oral hygiene and healthy eating to prevent tooth decay, so skilled helpers want to see their clients anticipate problem situations rather than merely manage them, however successfully, once they have arisen. In marriage and other relationships the economics of prevention are extraordinary. In healthcare every pound, euro, rand or dollar spent in prevention saves, by some estimates, ten in cure. People who develop good nutrition and exercise habits not only avoid a host of physical complaints but also enjoy energy levels that can be poured into other life-enhancing activities. But prevention is fundamentally problematic. If we are good at it, bad things *don't happen*. If we get sick, we can see, touch and sometimes literally taste cure. But the benefits of prevention are often invisible. The very materiality of cure makes it more attractive, or at least more noticeable, than prevention. While it's true that some people thoroughly enjoy a good workout and glorify in making healthy eating and calorie counting a focus of their dietary habits, many others don't. Prevention is invaluable, but we must help clients work at making it attractive for themselves.

Counselling provides an opportunity for helping clients embark on the prevention path.

> Take the case of South African couple Kagiso and Baruti. Four years into their marriage they found themselves sitting unhappily with a marriage counsellor, pointing fingers at each other. With the help of the counsellor they began, painfully, to come to grips with problems dealing with financial decisions, sexual relations and child rearing (three children). The counsellor pointed to how, over the years, they both had experienced 'pinches' – small annoyances – in their interactions. For instance, Kagiso noticed that Baruti was rather generous in buying small things for himself, but expressed mild resentment when she did the same. But she said nothing. On the other hand, Baruti thought that Kagiso at times was less spontaneous, less 'into it', in their sexual relations, but still resented it whenever she thought he was giving another woman a second glance. But he said nothing. The problem was that both of them 'saved up' the pinches until they erupted, or even exploded, into 'crunches' – major blow-ups in their relationship. And the number of crunches had begun to grow.

The original pinch–crunch model is from Sherwood and Glidewell (1973) but an internet search will reveal ways in which this has been used in other areas as well as a number of variations of this very useful prevention-focused conflict-management model.

The counsellor helped the clients do three things. First, he helped them diffuse and manage their most acute problem situation, which dealt with childcare. Second, he not only taught them the rudiments of the problem-management and opportunity-development approach to counselling he was using (the one that is described and illustrated in this book), but helped them use this process to manage some of the financial problems they faced. He pragmatically 'walked them through' the model as a way of providing them with a set of skills they could use on their own in the future. They used the model to deal with financial problems. Third, from a prevention point of view, he helped them see that ignoring or 'saving up' pinches almost inevitably led to crunches. In talking with them separately, he discovered that they both had a reasonably solid set of communication skills. But, strangely enough, they did not use these skills when talking with each other. He showed them how they could use their communication skills to defuse the pinches that creep into relationships. He made them aware that negotiating is not restricted to country-to-country relationships or to what opposing political parties do as a last resort. In fact, fair-minded negotiation is part of everyday communal living. The counsellor introduced the clients to resources which they then used.

THE INGREDIENTS OF SUCCESSFUL HELPING

Here we take up the question of the basic *factors* or *elements* or *ingredients* found in successful helping. Success is defined as life-enhancing outcomes for clients. While naming and describing each ingredient is important, these ingredients are interactive and dynamic in actual helping encounters. In practice they overlap. The purpose of this book is to bring them alive through descriptions, examples and discussions. The term 'common factors' has been used by many helpers and writers to designate the essential ingredients of successful therapy and, over the past ten years, a great deal of research has been done to ferret them out (Duncan, 2010; Duncan, Miller, Wampold, & Hubble, 2010; Norcross, 2011a, 2011b; Wampold, 2010a, 2010b). Even though the elements presented here are for the most part research-based, they go beyond the 'usual' lists. That's why I use the term 'ingredient' rather than 'factor' – and so not everyone would agree that the list outlined here is the right list, developed in the right order, with the right evidence. What Miller, Hubble, Duncan and Wampold (2010) say of the common factors is true of the set of ingredients outlined here. That is, they are 'not invariant, proportionally fixed, or neatly additive. Far from it, they are interdependent, fluid, and dynamic' (p. 34).

I set out the reasoning behind my inclusions and let you and the profession itself be my judge. But that is currently the nature of the helping industry. The social sciences deal with human behaviour which is often messy, disordered and difficult to predict. And so debate, sometimes acrimonious, is part and parcel of the helping professions. There will always be a degree of uncertainty about the findings of the social sciences. Indeed the place of uncertainty in the helping profession is discussed later in this chapter. Actually, we have already seen the first ingredient, the life-enhancing outcomes clients seek. The rest of the ingredients are:

- The client and the contextual factors of the client's life
- The person of the therapist
- The helping relationship
- The therapeutic dialogue between client and helper
- Two-way feedback between client and helper
- The model or method of treatment and the assumptions behind it
- The standard problem-management process as a human universal
- Decision making as a human universal
- The beliefs, values, norms, ethics and morality that drive human behaviour.

All of these ingredients, separately or in combination, are useful to the degree that they contribute to life-enhancing outcomes for the client. The pages of this book are filled with examples of life-enhancing outcomes. So we turn our attention to the ingredients that both individually and collectively lead to or produce these outcomes. Each ingredient will be described here and then explored and illustrated throughout this book. Let's start with an overview of a case.

David, a British soldier, was a veteran of two wars. His first stint was in Iraq, his second in Afghanistan. His tour in Afghanistan ended abruptly after his squad was ambushed near the Pakistani border. Two of his best friends were killed. David escaped with relatively minor injuries. Minor physical injuries, that is. When he first returned to base he seemed to be all right but about a month later the dam broke. Not only did the full range of post-traumatic stress disorder (PTSD) symptoms flood through him off and on – nightmares, flashbacks, bouts of anxiety and depression, irritability, insomnia, social avoidance, trouble concentrating, feeling emotionally numb – but he also began ruminating and agonising over his pre-military life, especially poor decisions he had made. For instance, after secondary school he decided to join the army instead of going to university. During his first year in the army he broke up with his girlfriend, believing that 'the military and deeper relationships did not mix'. He let himself 'drift away from God'. It's not that he led an immoral life, rather his 'beliefs became twisted'. This caused feelings of guilt. Early on he was told that all of this was probably only temporary. But that was not the case. He had his 'good days', but various PTSD symptoms kept popping up 'for no reason at all'. He returned to the United Kingdom, but whilst on sick leave back in his home town, found relationships with family and friends 'difficult'. Army doctors decided that he was not fit to continue to serve in the army. An honourable discharge was arranged. Many of David's symptoms persisted. Some grew worse. For instance, he began thinking that he could have done something to prevent the deaths of his friends, and this increased the burden of guilt. While he did not entertain suicidal thoughts, he did wonder about servicemen who had taken their own lives. How bad could things get? He knew that he could never take his own life, but he began to understand why people do take their lives. What he saw ahead of him was a life of misery. He resisted all but intermittent help – 'I'm no psycho' – and, reluctantly and intermittently, took some medication for both anxiety and depression. Finally, at the urging of a military doctor he agreed to seek psychological help – 'I'll try anything.' Well, almost anything. David does not want to get involved with a military therapist because he wants to distance himself from the military – 'I want to leave all that behind.' He believes that working in a military setting would for him be part of the problem rather than part of the solution.

So David and Laura, who works in a mental health clinic associated with a Christian hospital near where David lives, become client and helper. Because the hospital is near an army camp, Laura has seen a number of soldiers, but none with David's background.

We will continue to review and expand this case as we explore and explain the key ingredients of successful helping.

The client and the contextual factors of the client's life

The client in his or her search for life-enhancing outcomes is the first and most important 'ingredient' in the therapeutic process (Bohart & Tallman, 2010). However, much of therapy research has focused on the model or method of treatment. What clients themselves bring to the party, however substantial, has been short-changed. This is odd, because research shows that clients, together with what they bring to therapy, are responsible for most of the success or failure in the helping endeavour (Corey & Corey, 2016; Duncan, 2010; Orlinsky, Rønnestad, & Willutzki, 2004).

What do clients bring to the helping encounter? They arrive with their version of humanity in all its simplicity and all its complexity. They bring with them their beliefs, values, background, upbringing and interpretation of life situations. Here are some of the things clients may bring with them, in no particular order:

- The problem situations, issues, concerns, in various degrees of severity, for which they are seeking help
- Successful or failed attempts to manage problem situations and/or exploit unused opportunities
- The past to the degree that it is affecting them positively or negatively in the present
- Their general life expectations and aspirations, however realistic or distorted, and associated disappointments
- Their skills, strengths and resources
- Their general emotional state
- Their hopes, fears and expectations regarding therapy
- Their degree of openness to and readiness for change
- Their willingness to work at change
- Whatever reluctance or resistance they feel
- Their ability to engage in a collaborative relationship
- Their sense of right and wrong, their personal ethics, their approach to morality
- Their cultural beliefs, values and norms of behaviour, especially their particular version of their dominant culture and its impact on their behaviour
- The entire range of their relationships together with all the associated ups and downs, especially the relationships related to their current problem situations
- Their level of interpersonal communication skills
- Their blind spots
- External factors that stand in the way of progress
- External factors that support constructive change.

This is just a partial list, but all of it is relevant to David's situation. Since people are complex, it is important for helpers to identify factors that are key for each client. Or even better, it is important for clients, often with the help of a therapist, to discover the key factors that have an impact on their problem situations. *In the end the quality of the client's participation in the therapeutic endeavour is the major determinant of outcome.* So David needs a therapist who can help him give his best to the therapeutic process. Clients are or should be in the driver's seat with respect to managing problem situations in everyday life. It is essential that therapists help them get into the driver's seat and stay there throughout the helping process. Therefore, for the reasons outlined by Duncan and Sparks (2010), if there are any heroes (an overused and misused word) in the therapeutic endeavour, they are the clients rather than the therapists. David is responsible for life-enhancing change. His helper is a catalyst for that change.

Irish writer Brian Keenan, who was held hostage in Beirut between 1986 and 1990, described his experiences in 1991 in the following words, soon after the release of his friend and fellow hostage John McCarthy:

"Each man must find within himself the various methods to contain and control the pain and confusion within. There are no ready-made answers. It is a slow process of rediscovery, where denial or flight from the inward turmoil is the antithesis of self-healing. We go that road alone. We may be helped but we cannot be pushed or misdirected. We each have the power within us to re-humanise ourselves. We are our own self-healers."

The person of the therapist

A great deal of research focuses on different kinds of client problems and different kinds of treatment for these problems. It is the stuff of abnormal psychology. But, strange to say, over the years relatively little research has been done on the key capabilities and characteristics of the therapist (Beutler *et al.*, 2004). Nevertheless, we do know some key things. We know that the person of the therapist is more important than the method of treatment (Crits-Christoph *et al.*, 1991, 2006; Miller, Hubble, Duncan, & Wampold, 2010; Wampold & Brown, 2005; Barber, Muran, McCarthy & Keefe, 2013). We also know that some therapists are better than others (Okiishi, Lambert, Nielsen, & Ogles, 2003). But the real question is: What makes some more effective than others? Wampold (2011), in a review of what research says about therapists, comes up with a list of characteristics, which I have adapted. An effective therapist:

- Has a solid set of interpersonal skills and through them expresses acceptance, warmth and empathy. These are discussed and illustrated in Part II.
- Acts in such a way as to build trust with clients. 'This person understands me. I believe this person can help me.'
- Does his or her part to develop a collaborative working alliance with clients and come to an agreement with them on the goals of helping.
- Understands the client's condition and can provide a plausible explanation for the source of the client's distress.
- Understands both the client and the client's problem situation in every relevant context – cultural, social, economic, political and so forth.
- Has a flexible helping approach or treatment plan and communicates this approach clearly to the client.
- Is believable, persuasive and convincing without robbing the client of his or her autonomy or dignity.
- Collaborates with clients in monitoring their progress and their views of the helping process.
- Establishes a formal or informal feedback system.
- Makes adjustments to the therapeutic process based on an evolving understanding of the client's problem situation, formal or informal feedback and signs of client reluctance or resistance.
- Helps clients, despite their difficulties, to develop a realistic sense of possibility, hope and optimism.
- Does not avoid difficult issues related to the client's problems or to the client–helper relationship, but handles them tactfully.
- Understands self, and injects self into the therapeutic dialogue only to the degree that this helps and does not distract the client. More will be said about helper self-disclosure in Part II.
- Knows best research related to the client: the client's personality, the client's problems, the social context and possible treatments for the client.
- Is committed to professional self-improvement. Understands the best the helping industry has to offer and makes it available to the client.
- Has a solid grasp of the key ingredients of successful therapy and, through collaboration with the client, knows how to tailor and orchestrate them at the service of client outcomes.

There are a lot of items on this list and there is no one right way of mixing and matching them to the client's needs. Because there is no 'right' or 'perfect' set of characteristics, let me take the role of client and answer that question for myself, that is, let me personalise the list. What kind of therapist would I want? So I tell you that I have chosen Laura, a counsellor I know. You ask 'Why Laura?' Here is my response.

I have chosen Laura because she understands and can deal competently with all the factors being outlined and illustrated here as key ingredients in successful helping. However, she works with me in adapting these ingredients to my needs rather than to her theories. She has no preset formula. She is smart and she is competent, but she does not shove either her intelligence or her competence down my throat. She is a pro but wears her professionalism lightly. Her professional skills are there to serve me. For her, helping is not just a job. I don't know whether she sees it as a vocation, but I do know that she is totally there all the time. She respects me and is street-smart. I feel secure with her; I'm in good hands. She has excellent communication skills, including the ability to

(Continued)

help me communicate when my own communication skills fail me. The values that drive her behaviour emerge in the way she conducts herself, but she takes pains to understand my values and to help me see how they drive my behaviour. She neither cudgels nor coddles me. But she does invite me to explore the unintended consequences of both my past decisions and the ones I am about to make. I like her invitational stance, knowing that I want a catalyst, not an advice-giver. The problem-management framework outlined in this book floats seamlessly in the background. It's the geography of helping. We collaborate. We are a team, a unit. She is not afraid of work and assumes that I am willing to work at managing my problems. She is not a heroic figure. Sometimes she makes mistakes, but she readily admits them and works with me in reversing them. Right from the beginning she points out how important it is to establish a good working relationship. She explains the value of feedback. At the end of each session we evaluate what we have accomplished. What went right? What went wrong? How can we do better? At the beginning of each session we review what kind of progress I have made in managing my problem situation or some aspect of it. For us, feedback is a two-way street. The work we are engaged in is about life-enhancing outcomes. If I seem lax, she invites me to review my commitment. This is not her demand but rather my need. We explore the incentives I have for creating a better life for myself. We talk about obstacles that stand in the way of a better life or obstacles that I put in the way. We are honest with each other.

This is the kind of therapist I would like. Others would rather have a different mix of ingredients. For instance, in one study (Murphy, Cramer & Lillie, 1984), clients who were mainly from the lower socioeconomic class wanted advice, signs of real interest in their problems, encouragement and reassurance, understanding, and the instillation of hope from their helpers. But the principle remains: within reason, work with the client to tailor the ingredients of therapy to his or her needs and preferences. As we shall see throughout this book, this does not mean indulging the client.

If you are interested in becoming a therapist, you may want to read an article by Barry Duncan (2011) entitled 'What Do Therapists Want?' He first answers this question by saying, 'It's certainly not money or fame.' That's interesting in a society whose media scream at us every day that life is about money and fame. He cites a study (Orlinsky & Rønnestad, 2005) that provides some answers that are both sobering and uplifting: 'Therapists stay in the profession, not because of material rewards or the prospect of professional advancement, but because – above all – they value connecting deeply with clients and helping them improve. On top of that the clinicians interviewed consistently reported a strong desire to continue learning about their profession…' (p. 40). They found satisfaction in deepening their sense of themselves, their clients, the profession and the world. Therapists-to-be have much to mull over as they choose the helping professions. Cooper, Norcross, Raymond-Barker and Hogan (2019) outlined therapist directedness and the emotional intensity wants of laypersons and mental health professionals in a systematic review of clients' psychotherapy preferences.

The helping relationship

According to the research, the second most important ingredient in helping (after client factors) is the quality of the relationship between client and helper (Muran & Barber, 2010; Norcross, 2011a, 2011b). Generally speaking, if client and helper are a collaborative team, the three goals or outcomes listed at the beginning of this chapter are more likely to be achieved. The therapist's intelligence and competencies mentioned earlier come alive and produce results only to the degree that they are channelled into the establishment and development of a collaborative client–helper relationship. Furthermore, while the therapist can do a great deal to see that this happens, it will not happen unless clients do their part. So it is up to the client *and* the therapist in their dialogue to orchestrate the mix of ingredients that best leads to targeted life-enhancing outcomes.

The American Psychological Association Interdivisional Task Force on Evidence-Based Therapy Relationships, chaired by John C. Norcross (Norcross, 2010, 2011a, 2011b; Norcross & Wampold, 2011), came up with a range of conclusions regarding the client–helper relationship. Instead of a list of findings, here is how these findings might influence Laura directly and David indirectly. Laura says to herself:

David and I should make building and focusing our relationship a top priority. Focus means making sure that our emerging relationship is contributing to the main work at hand, namely David's dealing with the problematic issues of his life. Our relationship will contribute more to David's search for life-enhancing outcomes than any helping approach I take. I have to make sure that David understands the problem-management approach I will be taking. I have to do my best in helping him see its value and buy into it. I have to be open to adapting my approach to his needs and do so without compromising my professional standards. I don't own the approach. David and I own it together. I have to make sure that David, if he so chooses, has a say in everything. Any therapeutic approach or programme will lose its power if the relationship is poor. I will suggest programmes or parts of programmes that have been demonstrated to work with clients to, say, alleviate anxiety and/or depression, but David and I must be co-owners and collaborative implementers of these programmes. We both need to understand, at some level of consciousness, that the relationship pervades every aspect of the treatment. My skills come to life only through the relationship. David is not an anaesthetised patient undergoing an appendectomy where skills and techniques are of paramount importance. I deliver my skills and techniques through the relationship. So I cannot take even a PTSD treatment programme that has been demonstrated to be effective and apply it like a technician, even a skilled technician. There are many things I need to do to make this relationship work, especially understanding David from his point of view, even when I think that he might profit from challenging his point of view. And there are things I must avoid, such as hostile interchanges, critical comments, rejection and blame. I must continually remind myself that no one formula fits every client. I have had some clients who felt short-changed when I failed to challenge them. Other clients have resented even tactful invitations on my part to self-challenge. Everything I do must help David become a partner.

The members of the Task Force also issued a caution. Given the complexity of the moving parts in the helping process, their findings should be taken with a pinch of salt: 'Readers are encouraged to interpret these findings in the context of the acknowledged limitations of the Task Force's work.' Cautions like that could be issued for all the findings of the social sciences. So Laura needs to remain flexible and take her cues from David. Given its importance, the helping relationship is addressed in greater detail in Chapter 2.

Communication skills at the service of dialogue

At the heart of any relationship is communication. Helpers need a range of communication skills to become collaborators with their clients. The chapters in Part II outline and illustrate such skills as attending, listening, understanding what clients are saying about themselves, responding to clients with understanding, helping clients explore their concerns more fully, helping them stay focused, and helping clients develop new perspectives on their problem situations and unused opportunities. Conversations between helpers and their clients should be a therapeutic or helping dialogue (Knapp, 2007; Paré & Lysack, 2004; Seikkula & Trimble, 2005). Interpersonal communication competence means not only being good at the individual communication skills outlined in Part II of this book but also marshalling them at the service of dialogue. The elements of dialogue are addressed in Part II of this book.

It would be helpful if clients had the communication skills outlined in Part II and the ability to weave them into constructive dialogues with their helpers. This is often not the case. In fact, many clients are in trouble precisely because they do not know how to establish and maintain healthy interpersonal relationships which are nourished by effective communication. What do helpers do when their clients are poor communicators? They use their communication skills to help clients engage in dialogue. And they do this without ever becoming condescending. Precisely how to do this will be explained and illustrated in Part II.

Two-way feedback between client and helper

Feedback is a critical factor in the helping dialogue (Janse, De Jong, Van Dijk, Hutschemaekers & Verbraak, 2017; Miller, Duncan *et al.*, 2006). In therapy, two things need to be monitored carefully and continually – progress towards life-enhancing client outcomes and the degree to which therapy sessions are contributing to these outcomes. As to the sessions themselves, these are the kinds of questions that need to be asked: How are we doing? What is going right? What mistakes are we making? How can we make these sessions more productive? What do we need to do to improve our collaboration? As to the client's progress in managing problem situations and developing opportunities, these are the kinds of questions that need to be asked: Overall, what does progress look like? What progress am I making in terms of getting to the heart of the problem situation? To what degree do I understand what the resolution of the problem situation should look like? What are my goals? How can I clarify these goals? What actions must I take to achieve these goals? How do I start moving in the right direction? What obstacles am I running into, and how am I dealing with them? What do I need to do to persist in achieving the life-enhancing outcomes I say I want?

These two kinds of feedback have been studied thoroughly (Duncan, 2010; Lambert, 2010a, 2010b), and Duncan and his colleagues have developed and researched a simple feedback system based on two brief surveys, one given at the beginning of each session and the other administered towards the end of each session. The first survey asks the clients to rate themselves in four broad categories – personal well-being; how things are going with family and other close relationships; how things are going with work, school and other relationships such as friends; and an overall category called a general sense of well-being. The survey given at the beginning of the first session helps 'jump-start' the helping process and acts as a kind of baseline against which between-session progress is determined. The second survey, scored towards the end of each session, deals with within-session satisfaction. In this survey clients indicate what has gone right and what needs further attention in the session itself by rating four broad categories – degree of satisfaction with the helping relationship itself; the degree to which the session addressed the right topics and focused on the clients' goals; how well the approach to treatment fits the clients' needs; and overall satisfaction with the session. Ideally, the surveys stimulate collaborative dialogue, help keep the client in the driver's seat and make both the sessions and the client's between-session behaviour more productive in terms of problem-managing outcomes. Client feedback has been attributed to more effective treatment (Janse *et al.*, 2017) and beneficial in specific client groups (Schuman, Slone, Reese & Duncan, 2015).

At one point during the first session Laura explains the importance of feedback to David and then goes on to describe the survey system outlined above and suggests that they use it. David looks at the forms and then dismisses them, saying 'I don't think so. It's too much like playing games.' Laura does not try to convince David to use the forms, but decides to make feedback a more seamless part of the dialogue. About five minutes before the end of the session, she asks, 'How do you think we're doing?' David hesitates and then says pleasantly, 'You're the expert. How do you think we're doing?' She realises that David is not completely convinced that therapy is a good idea. So she shares what she thinks are the highlights of the session and does so in such a tentative way that David adds a few comments of his own. She ends by saying, 'So I think we're still feeling our way.' David hesitates again and then says, 'That's about right. We're both feeling our way.' Laura believes that feedback is essential but is not going to shove a formal system down David's throat. She does, however, make another suggestion, one that had proved useful in other cases. She suggests to David a 'buddy' arrangement similar to those in support programmes like Alcoholics Anonymous. Like David, he would be someone who has returned from the wars in Iraq and Afghanistan, who had many of the problems that David is facing, but who has come out 'the other side' in pretty good shape. For David this would be another voice, another relationship that could well be, not therapy, but therapeutic. David says that he will think about it. But it remains an option.

At the beginning of each session Laura explores with David his sense of the progress towards problem-managing outcomes (or the lack thereof) he is making and what they both need to do to facilitate progress. At the end of each session she helps David review the session, what he has learned and what he needs to do 'out there'. Miller *et al.* (2010) see these two kinds of feedback as a way of saying, indirectly, to the client: 'Your input is crucial; your participation matters. We invite you to be a partner in your care. We respect what you have to say, so much so that we will modify the treatment to see that you get what you want' (p. 424). In the fourth session David says, 'You know, we're not using the forms, but we are doing the feedback thing. It helps. So I don't care whether we use the forms or not. It's working for me.'

Most of the research on feedback deals with feedback provided by clients. What about feedback from the helper to the client? For instance, should helpers provide feedback to their clients with respect to the quality of their collaboration in the helping sessions or with respect to their between-session behaviour? Feedback in this sense is a form of challenge to the client. Does such feedback take the client out of the 'driver's seat' or is it an invitation to take the 'wheel' more fully? Is challenge or even an invitation to self-challenge a form of criticism? I deal with challenge or invitations to self-challenge more fully in Part II. Helping, I will say there, is inescapably a form of social influence. It is a two-way social-influence endeavour that does not take the client out of the driver's seat any more than it makes a helper the victim of a client's whims. In my view, clients who are never invited to challenge themselves are being short-changed.

The treatment approach and its methods and techniques

There are dozens (by some counts, hundreds) of different approaches to helping. Which one is the right one? To answer that question, consider the following situation. There are ten therapists. Each of these helpers espouses one of the following approaches to therapy: behaviour therapy, rational-emotive-behaviour therapy, narrative therapy, emotion-focused therapy, reality therapy, person-centred therapy, brief dynamic therapy, cognitive-behavioural therapy, existential-humanistic therapy, relational-cultural therapy. Each of the ten therapists has ten clients. Each set of ten clients has more or less the same mix of problem situations with a similar range of degrees of severity. That is, the ten groups are comparable. What these therapists have in common, however, is that all ten are equally successful, that is, all hundred clients are successful in managing, within reason, the problem situations of their lives. All the therapeutic encounters lead to life-enhancing outcomes for the clients. If this is the case, then it cannot be said that the principal vehicle of success was the treatment approach because there were ten different approaches.

Instead of asking, 'Which approach to therapy is the most effective one?', it is better to ask, 'What do successful therapists have in common?' My answer is this: all successful helpers have the ability to tailor the essential ingredients of successful therapy outlined in this chapter to their clients and to work collaboratively with them. Although the research says that it is not the treatment method that is the main driver of success (Wampold, 2010a, 2010b), this does not mean that it is not important. The treatment model helps organise and give focus to both the client's and the helper's resources. Of course, the model or approach must have substance and face validity, that is, it must 'make sense', it must look like it might work. The therapist must believe in the model and be both skilled and comfortable in its use. The client in his or her own way must see the approach as reasonable and collaborate with the therapist in its execution. But execution involves all the ingredients of successful therapy. Take David. Studies on what researchers call 'bona fide' psychotherapies for treating PTSD (Shapiro, 1995; Benish, Imel & Wampold, 2007) show that even though each approach has merit, for any given client one approach may be better than others. Tailoring is essential because clients with PTSD symptoms are not homogeneous. Each client is different.

Problem management: A human universal and a common factor

What treatment approach is highlighted in this book? The answer is simple: an approach which is embedded in every other approach, an approach with which clients are already familiar, and an approach that can be used as a tool to borrow helpful treatments from any other approach. Sounds too good to be true. So let me explain.

This approach, what I call the Standard Problem-Management Framework, poses four questions clients need to ask themselves in their search for life-enhancing outcomes:

- **What's going on?** 'What are the problems, issues, concerns, or undeveloped opportunities I should be working on?' This involves helping clients spell out his or her *current picture*.
- **What does a better future look like?** 'What do I want my life to look like? What changes would help manage my problem situation and develop unused opportunities? What goals do I need to pursue to manage my problem situation?' This involves helping clients paint their *preferred picture*.

- **How do I get there?** 'What do I need to do to make the preferred picture a reality? What plan will get me where I want to go? What actions will get me started on the right path?' The plan outlines the actions clients need to take to create a better future. This is the *way forward*.

- **How do I make it all happen?** 'How do I turn planning and goal setting into the kind of action that leads to the solutions, results, outcomes or accomplishments that have the impact I'm looking for? How do I get going and persevere until I manage my problems and develop my unused opportunities?' The Action Arrow indicates the broad and specific actions clients must take to produce the changes they want. This is the *ongoing challenge of implementation*.

These questions are in a logical sequence, but don't let the logical sequence fool you. A logical sequence is not necessarily the way things happen in life. These four questions, turned into three logical 'stages' and an 'implementation arrow' in Figure 1.1, provide the basic framework for the helping process. The term 'stage' is placed in quotation marks because it has sequential overtones that are misleading. In practice the three stages overlap and interact with one another as clients struggle to manage problems and develop opportunities. And, as we shall see in Part III, helping, like life itself, is not as logical as the models used to describe it.

FIGURE 1.1 **Key problem-management questions.**

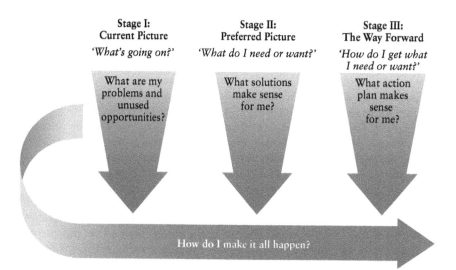

Embedded in people   Around the world, everyone faces problems in living and everyone has overlooked and unused life-enhancing opportunities. The advantage of a problem-management and opportunity-development approach to helping, which is also wholly client-centred, is that it is easily recognised across the world. That is, the standard problem-management process seems to be what McCrae and Costa (1997) call a 'human universal' or what Norenzayan and Heine (2005), in a stimulating article, call a 'psychological universal'. Its logic seems to be embedded in human beings. People don't so much *learn* the problem-management process; rather they *recognise* it. In essence it's already there. It is, to use Orlinsky and Howard's (1987) term, a 'generic' model or framework for helping. Sometimes, when I explain this approach, people say, 'Oh, I know that.' Of course they know that; its logic is wedded to their bones. The problem is that too many people who say they know it never really use it. It is not part of their lives.

Many years ago, before presenting an earlier version of the helping process outlined in this book to some 300 college students and faculty members in Tanzania, I said, 'All I can do is present to you the helping process I teach and use. You have to decide whether it makes sense in your own culture.' At the end of the three-day seminar they said two things. First, the communication skills used in the helping process would have to be modified somewhat to fit their culture. Second, the problem-management helping process itself was very useful.

Since then, this scene has been repeated – in conferences and training events many others and I have presented – over and over again on every continent. The approach, presented in detail in Part III, spells out, in a flexible, step-by-step fashion, a common way human beings think about constructive change. This kind of cross-cultural validation is, as Norenzayan and Heine note, at the heart of universality: 'A compelling case for universality can be made when a phenomenon is clearly identifiable in a large and diverse array of cultures' (2005, p. 769). Of course, the Standard Model as outlined here and explored in detail later has to be adapted both to different cultural settings and to different individuals within those settings. This demands the kind of diversity sensitivity discussed in Chapter 2. Universal psychological processes together with their cultural variations help make counselling both effective and efficient.

Embedded in therapy   While few models or approaches to helping talk explicitly about problem solving or problem management and the flip side, opportunity identification and development, all treatment approaches use problem-management concepts and language either directly or indirectly. That is, they talk about identifying and exploring problems or problem situations, they discuss the issue of unused strengths and other resources, they talk about goals and the action strategies or plans needed to achieve goals, they point out the difficulties inherent in carrying out plans and suggest ways of overcoming these difficulties. Therefore, in my thinking, the standard problem-management and opportunity-development process is one of the 'common factors' in helping. That is, some form of it is found in all successful helping.

In Part III, I use this problem-management framework as the primary approach to treatment and to organise the key ingredients of successful therapy outlined in this chapter. Chapter 7 reviews in some detail my version of the Standard Problem-Management Framework. There are many different versions. Some, unfortunately, leave out the Stage-II question: 'What kind of future do I want?' The shortened version – 'What is my problem and what can I do about it?' – loses the richness of imagining a better future. This truncated version works if the problem is, let's say, a broken refrigerator. The desired outcome is clear. Problems in human behaviour are different. A couple in marriage therapy can spend time exploring their problems but ultimately need to ask themselves, 'If we want to be married, what kind of marriage do we want?' Then they can ask themselves, 'Well, what do we have to do to create that kind of marriage?' It would be helpful to read Chapter 7 after finishing Chapter 1 to get a feeling for the problem-management process at the heart of this book.

Decision making: A psychological universal and a common factor

If we review any given day of our lives, we realise that we make many decisions, most of them of small or intermediate importance – what to eat for breakfast, whether to return the call of an annoying relative, what to say to the children when you know they are going to ask you if they can stay out late with their friends, when to tell your spouse that you have to go on an unplanned business meeting, and the decisions the two of you will have to make before you go. Life also has its big decisional moments. Shall I pursue other relationships when my spouse seems to have lost interest in me? At age 80, which treatment, if any, should I choose for prostate cancer that has been described as 'somewhat aggressive'? Shall I give up trying to get my spouse to stop smoking? Shall I screw up the courage to tell my boss that his style is belittling? We are decision makers. So are our clients. When they come to us, they often learn that they have to make some difficult decisions or that they have to deal with the fallout from poor past decisions. They come when they are afraid to decide at all.

Helping as a problem-management and opportunity-development process is decision rich or decision fraught. Choose your term. The two are often written about together (Adair, 2010). Because problem management deals with options, decision making, that is, choosing from among options, is at the heart of helping. Clients have to decide many things: to come for help in the first place (unless mandated, say, by a court), to choose to talk about certain issues but not others, to determine what issue or set of issues they want to work on, to set goals, to make plans, to find the strength, courage and resources to implement these plans, to tell you when the helping process is working and when it is not, to persevere until they get what they have come for. Clients come to therapy with a decision-making style. Understanding how they make decisions will help you become a catalyst for change.

What follows are the bare essentials of what may be called the Newtonian, or rational, approach to decision making (Baron, 2001; Galotti, 2002; Hammond, Keeney, & Raiffa, 1999; Harford, 2008; *Harvard Business Essentials*, 2006; Hastie & Dawes, 2001; Hoch & Kunreuther, 2004). But don't be fooled. Later on we will see that decision making in everyday life and in helping can come closer to the complexity and messiness of relativity and quantum mechanics.

Problem identification and information gathering   The starting point is some issue, concern or problem. The first rational task is to gather information related to the particular issue or concern. It is essential to describe or 'frame' the issue being considered accurately. A patient who learns that he or she has cancer must understand the nature of the disease before he or she can decide what treatment to choose. What kind of cancer is it? How aggressive is it? What is the most likely progression of the kind of cancer I have? What are the treatments like? What will they accomplish? What are the side effects? What are the consequences of not having them? What would another doctor say? In a word, what *options* are available? And there is a whole range of ways in which he or she might gather this information – internet searches, books and articles, talking to doctors, talking to patients who have undergone treatment or who have refused treatment. Many patients today routinely mount extensive internet searches on their medical conditions in order to make better-informed decisions. This does not mean that the information they gather provides ready-made answers.

Problem identification in therapy is different from problem identification in medicine and many other areas of life. The problems themselves are often murky. If applied to David, we have the following picture. David comes to realise that being a loner, being out of the community, is an important part of the problem situation. So in his mind he gathers the information he needs to make a decision about what kind of social life he would like. Before he went into the army he was relatively gregarious. For the most part he enjoyed being with both family and friends. But he is a bit of an introvert. So he was not happy when he socialised too much. He said yes to too many invitations. He also realised that when he did socialise, he was relatively passive. But this meant that others would make the decisions: for instance, what to talk about, where to go and so forth. This did not sit well. In the army David had a few very good friends. They did things together. They counted on one another. They had common interests and talked about them when they got a chance to relax. David assembled a lot of information about his social life, including the fact that he did not like being a loner. Somewhat of an introvert – that was all right, but a loner – no. So David continues in this way to gather information related to his social life. He says to himself (but perhaps not in these words): 'In the army I was in community. Now I'm out of community. That's not good for me.'

Analysis   The next rational step is processing the information. This includes analysing, thinking about, working with, discussing, meditating on and immersing oneself in the information. Just as there are many ways of gathering information, so there are many ways of processing it. Effective information processing leads to a clarification and an understanding of the range of possible choices. 'Now, let's see, what are the advantages and disadvantages of each of these choices?' is one way of analysing information. This approach assumes that the decision maker has criteria, whether objective or subjective, for comparing alternatives.

David analysed the information he gathered. He took an upside-downside approach. For instance, the upside of being relatively passive in social situations meant that people did not 'invade' his space, he felt free to leave if any given gathering was doing nothing for him because people were not counting on his contributions, and he could daydream at will. But as soon as he said these things to himself, he realised how self-centred this kind of 'upside' was. He was more of a parasite than a contributor. Choosing to be passive was going beyond 'being a bit of an introvert'. But there was an upside to being a bit of an introvert. Yes, he said to himself, 'I can listen well, think about what's being said, and then make some kind of intelligent contribution to the conversation.' He discusses the results of his analysis with Laura.

Making a choice   Finally, decision makers need to make a choice – that is, commit themselves to some internal or external action that is based on the analysis. Anita says, 'After thinking about it, I have decided to sue for custody of the children.' And, as the fullness of the choice includes an action, she adds: 'I had my lawyer file the custody papers this morning.' There are also rational 'rules' that can be used to make a decision. For instance, one rule, stated as a question, deals with the consequences of the decision: 'Will it get me everything I want or just part?' Values also enter the picture because, from one point of view, values are criteria for making decisions. 'Should I do X or Y? Well, what are my values?' The woman suing for the custody of the children says to herself, at least implicitly, 'I value fairness. I'm not going to try to extort a lot of money for childcare. I'll make reasonable demands.'

In one session David says, 'I've become a loner, but I can't stay that way. It's deadly. I wasn't a loner in Afghanistan. It would have been deadly there. If my buddies could see me now they wouldn't recognise me. But to tell the truth, I've become comfortable, not happy, but comfortable being a loner. I bother no one. No one bothers me.' This is the beginning of a decision to get back into community even though he does not have a clear idea of what community would look like or how he would go about doing it. That is another phase of the problem-management process.

Follow-through   Real decision making ends in action. In therapy this means problem-managing and/or opportunity-developing action that leads to life-enhancing outcomes. Otherwise decision making is just wishful thinking. As a first step David decides to take up an offer Laura had made early in therapy of talking with someone who has gone through the kinds of experiences he has had in Iraq and Afghanistan with the same crippling effects but who has come out the other side. At the time she made the offer, he said that he would 'think about it'. When he thinks of getting back with family or friends, he realises he does not want to get involved on a superficial level. Small talk and all that. Having some kind of 'buddy' (he hated that word) had substance to it and fitted in with what he was trying to do. It could be the beginning of 'normalisation', but his kind of normalisation.

There are many different versions of the standard, rational decision-making process. However, in Part III you will see that the rational process of decision making described here is not the stuff of everyday life. Decision making casts a large shadow and you will do well to understand what lies in that shadow. People frequently do themselves in by the way they go about making decisions, even very important decisions (Kahneman, 2012; Lehrer, 2009).

While you don't want to make decisions for your clients, you do want to help them make life-enhancing rather than life-limiting decisions. You want to help them face up to decisions they are trying to avoid. You want to help them explore the possible consequences – good or bad – of decisions they have made or that they are in the process of making. Furthermore, you as a helper will have many options in the way you interact with clients. Understanding what influences you in making these decisions is a key form of helper self-knowledge.

The beliefs-values-norms-ethics-morality factors that drive human behaviour

If helping is to be a social-civilising and not just an individual-enhancement process, it must be value-driven and ethical. Therefore, morality and ethics constitute one of the key ingredients of therapy. I have been criticised by some for not including a more extensive section on ethics in this book. My contention has been that ethics is so important that any kind of abbreviated overview would send the wrong message. I cannot imagine a helper training programme that did not include a complete course on ethics. And beyond the bare bones of the codes supplied by the British Association for Counselling and Psychotherapy, the European Association for Counselling, various counselling associations in South Africa and the American Counselling Association, there are many excellent texts on ethics in the helping professions (Knapp, 2012; Welfel, 2013). So let me lay out the reasoning behind my decision.

The beliefs, values, norms, ethics and morality package presents an intellectual challenge to the helping professions (Mikulincer & Shaver, 2012). While the helping professions are trying vigorously to demonstrate that they are driven by the rigorous methods of science, it is also true that beliefs, values, norms, ethics and morality, and the cultures in which they are embedded, are not scientific terms. The social sciences can study these phenomena as forms of human behaviour, but although science can demonstrate the societal usefulness of shared patterns of behaviour, science cannot prove their 'validity'. By definition, science can neither prove nor disprove the existence of God together with the moral injunctions that stem from religious belief systems, but that does not stop both scientists and religion-minded people from trying. I once watched a TV debate between an internationally well-known scientist who is a committed atheist and an outspoken Christian apologist. At one point the atheist conceded, 'Well, of course, everyone needs a moral compass', at which point social pragmatism entered the debate while science flew out the window.

Counselling associations want psychological treatments to be based on science, but they all also promote strict ethical codes. For many people this is not an issue. They find the basis for ethics and morality in religion and culture. Judaism, Christianity and Islam all have extensive moral codes. But these codes, while similar, do have differences. Injunctions such as 'Do not kill' are found in all three, but there are variations. Others turn to cultures for moral codes. Culture can be defined as the interactive shared beliefs, values and norms shared by the members of a group, but, because cultures differ, there are differences in their respective moral codes. For instance, while one culture condemns revenge, another might, under certain circumstances, see it as a duty. Still others look beyond both religion and culture and see the emergence of morality among human beings as a bio-social-evolutionary phenomenon (Brooks, 2012; Churchland, 2011; Wilson, 1993).

Still others turn their back on all this theory and take an even more pragmatic approach. If the world's seven billion people (and the number is increasing every day) are to live in some kind of harmony and lead a decent life (however defined), common-sense rules and regulations are needed. Many individuals will sense the need for such a pragmatic moral code and do their best to live up to it. And there are laws meting out punishments for those who are caught not living up to this code. So in many ways beliefs, values, norms, ethics and principles of morality are not givens but choices. In the end there is a common conclusion: rules and regulations, whatever their source, are necessary to contain the 'fallen angels' of our nature and make social life liveable.

There is a way to transcend rather than manage or solve the issues outlined here, a way that avoids the negativity often associated with ethics and morality. Handelsman, Knapp and Gottlieb (2009) review the work being done on 'positive ethics': 'Positive ethics shifts the emphasis from following rules and avoiding discipline to encouraging psychologists to aspire to their highest ethical ideals' (p. 105). This, they contend, makes for better ethical decision making. Moving beyond the 'First, do no harm' approach, Corey (2008) makes a distinction between 'mandatory' and 'aspirational' ethics. Aspirational ethics focuses on doing what is in the best interests of clients, a sentiment in keeping with the radical client-centred nature of helping: 'Ethics is a way of thinking about becoming the best practitioner possible' (p. 37). Grappling with ethical decision making is part and parcel of life for both you and your clients. Beliefs, values, behavioural norms, ethics and morality permeate the helping process. Positive ethics offers a way of grappling on the higher ground.

EMBRACING AND BEFRIENDING THE UNCERTAINTIES INHERENT IN HELPING

At first glance it seems odd to include uncertainty among the ingredients of successful therapy. Uncertainty is not in itself an ingredient. Rather, uncertainty pervades all of the ingredients that have been mentioned so far. Helpers who understand the uncertainties associated with the helping professions and their processes are in a better position to help clients deal with the uncertainties of their lives. The social sciences want to be included in the STEM group – science, technology, engineering, mathematics. Indeed, the social sciences have elements of all four. In research they use the methodologies of the 'hard' sciences to the degree that this is possible. They borrow and use various technologies such as video and the internet in helping clients. Therapists, in some sense, help clients redesign or 're-engineer' their lives. And mathematics and statistics have a large role. None of this, however, changes the nature of human behaviour. The social sciences, let's say economics or political science, study various forms of individual and group behaviour, but the kind of probability associated with human behaviour differs radically from the probability associated with the 'hard' sciences. Research in counselling and psychotherapy draws its conclusions but these conclusions are permeated with different kinds of uncertainties. Researchers routinely outline these uncertainties or hesitations at the end of articles. So it is often difficult to translate these conclusions into methods practitioners can use. Consider the conclusions offered by the Task Force on the therapeutic relationship outlined earlier. They are very broad and are not easy to translate into practice. Or they sound like common sense, things we knew even without the research.

So, back to the ingredients of successful helping. Each of the ingredients brings its own uncertainties. Here is a brief review.

The client and the contextual factors of the client's life

David, like the rest of us, is a complex human being and complexity breeds uncertainty. There are many issues that he could explore. Which factors from his past are having a negative impact in the present? Does he need to confront his problems head-on or is it better for him to find ways around them? What outcomes does he want beyond relief from both depressive moods and anxiety? To what degree are PTSD symptoms just that, symptoms, and other underlying issues really key? But neither David nor Laura can afford to be overwhelmed by the natural complexity of human beings. With Laura's help, David has to determine what the key issues are and what he is going to do about them.

The therapist

Laura brings her own culture, personality and approach to helping the process. She uses the cognitive-behavioural social-emotional problem-management approach outlined here and described in detail in Part III to organise her thinking about therapy and her interactions with her clients. She also uses this problem-management process as a kind of 'browser' to explore other approaches and draw from them methods and skills that are useful for clients. She organises them within the problem-management framework. So, like many therapists, she is eclectic in her approach but with an eclecticism that is organised, client-centred and outcome-oriented. The richness of her understanding of the helping process is a positive factor. But this richness involves complexity and therefore uncertainty. The uncertainty comes from the fact that methods and skills need to be adapted to the needs of each client. She needs to understand David before enlisting his help to adapt any particular PTSD treatment programme to his needs. PTSD is not a disease but a package of interrelated dysfunctional elements or symptoms. David is David, not his symptoms.

The helping relationship

All relationships have the potential for complexity and uncertainty. The helping relationship is a particular kind of relationship. It has to be established relatively quickly and must, from the beginning, be focused on client-enhancing outcomes, but it is always a work in progress. Collaboration is a two-way street. If done well, it reduces uncertainty. David and Laura keep adjusting to each other. Laura has entered into any number of these relationships, while, in a sense, everything is new to David. This makes things somewhat uncertain. Adding to the uncertainty is the fact that right now he is a person who is 'out of community'. To what degree is he capable of establishing the kind of collaborative relationship needed in therapy? Therefore, helping David get into the driver's seat and helping him stay there could possibly breed more uncertainty.

The therapeutic dialogue

Communication is at the heart of relationship building. Yet we live in a society that does not take these skills seriously enough to incorporate them into our formal and informal curriculum. Research also shows that many, if not most people, believe that they are better at interpersonal communication than they really are. The communication skills needed to engage effectively in dialogue are described and illustrated in Part II. As you will see, this is a relatively complex set of skills. Becoming competent in dialogue is no easy task. If David does not have all these skills, then Laura can use her skills to help him engage in a dialogue. But this adds another note of uncertainty. Furthermore, uncertainty is part of the nature of dialogue. If either party knows the outcome of the conversation before the conversation starts, they may well have a conversation but it will not be a dialogue. Dialogue means that the parties involved 'co-create' the outcomes. Laura is not treating David's PTSD. The two of them are collaborating in an endeavour to make his life more liveable.

Two-way feedback between client and helper

Feedback needs to be given, explored, confirmed and acted upon by both client and helper. Yet the role of feedback in therapy has been slow to be recognised and studied. Actually, monitoring the quality of the helping sessions and the progress the client is making reduces uncertainty for both client and helper.

It is an opportunity to 'clear things up'. That is why Duncan and his associates use very simple feedback surveys. What is important is not the survey itself but the kinds of consciousness raising and exploration it promotes. There is also uncertainty about feedback from the helper to the client. Does this rob clients of their autonomy? Is this a kind of power play or one-upmanship helpers are trying to avoid?

The model or method of treatment and the assumptions behind it

Laura realises that there are dozens, indeed hundreds, of different approaches to helping. All claim to be effective. But, as mentioned earlier, she can use the problem-management framework to suggest methods and treatments drawn from a wide range of approaches. In her practice this isn't a 'let's-try-this-and-see-what-happens' approach. The fact that she knows many different evidence-based approaches does not clutter her mind because she uses the problem-management framework to organise them. And although she makes sure that David understands what is on offer, she also makes sure that she does not dump any of this complexity on David.

The standard problem-management process as a human universal

Even though most approaches to treatment use, directly or indirectly, problem-management language, the profession as a whole has not openly recognised its importance in therapy. You are more likely to find research in problem management in business schools than in psychology departments. The fact that David is in some way familiar with the problem-management process that Laura suggests they use helps to cut down on complexity and uncertainty. The problem-management process provides a map, but of course the map is not the territory. Laura knows both the map and the territory well because of her experience. But now David and the context of his life constitute the territory. They have to chart a course together and agree on course changes as they move along. Even when a general direction is set, the journey itself will take twists and turns. The general direction of their journey together must be set by mutual agreement, but how to get there needs to be worked out. Sometimes the destination itself needs to be altered. There are starts and stops. A degree of uncertainty pervades the entire process. That's why collaboration and feedback are so important.

The fact that there are dozens of different evidence-based approaches to anxiety, depression and the whole range of PTSD symptoms is a possible source of uncertainty. However, Laura uses the problem-management framework as browser, sorter and organiser to tap into approaches that make sense for David.

Decision making as a human universal

Decision making, although on the surface a rational process of choosing between reasonably well-researched alternatives (Galotti, 2002), has many pitfalls (Ariely, 2010a, 2010b; Chabris & Simons, 2010; Kahneman, 2012; Kahneman, Lovallo & Sibony, 2011; March, 1994; Van Hecke, 2007; Watts, 2011). In his book, *Thinking, Fast and Slow*, Nobel Laureate Daniel Kahneman (2012) describes two systems people use to make decisions. System One is fast, intuitive and emotional. He describes the capabilities, faults and biases of fast thinking. People are strongly influenced by their intuitive impressions, so it is important to know when we can trust our intuitions. People brag about 'following their gut' even though it is often the road to disaster. Although System Two, slow thinking, is more deliberative and logical, it can lead to life-enhancing decisions. David followed his gut when he quickly decided to leave the army and this proved to be a life-enhancing decision. When he summarily dismissed Laura's offer of a simple survey-driven feedback system, his fast-thinking approach did him no favours.

Decision making tends to be a process that is both rational and irrational, with these two dimensions intermingled like toffee-ripple ice cream. We work with clients to help them crawl out of the decisional pits into which they have fallen or to help them from falling into these pits in the first place. David admits that he made a mistake by cutting himself off from family and friends when he returned from Afghanistan, so one of his goals is to get back into community. He has to reconstruct this part of his life. Wanting to get back into community is a decision in itself and the 'how' of doing this requires any number of decisions. What kind of community of family and friends does he want? How should he go about reconnecting or making new connections? It will become evident that David (and clients in general) will not move in a linear fashion through the rational decision-making process outlined earlier. Problem management and decision making are often circuitous journeys.

What David is like as a decision maker is a key factor in this therapeutic endeavour. It seems that he too often gets caught up in the common irrationalities that plague decision making. He seems to make decisions, even important ones, quickly, with little internal debate or reflection. Both little and big decisions get the same treatment. Is this a deep-seated pattern, or is it temporary? To what degree might this interfere with the range of decisions, both big and little, required by the problem-management process? Laura believes that it would be quite useful to help David get in touch with and review what kind of decision maker he is.

The beliefs-values-norms-ethics-morality factors

As we saw earlier, this package has its own complexities. In an *American Psychologist* article, Rogerson and his associates (2011) add fuel to the fire. They discuss the role of 'non-rational' processes in ethical decision making. They take issue with current ethical decision-making models, seeing them as overly rational and based on faulty or inadequate assumptions. These models, they say, ignore non-rational factors such as context, the decision maker's perceptions, relationships and emotions. Ethics, they suggest, need to be re-conceptualised.

The beliefs-values-norms-ethics-morality package pervades all of David's and Laura's interactions. As to religion, David could be called a semi-lapsed fundamentalist. He is no longer a churchgoer, but aspects of the basic fundamentalist package cling to his psyche, if not his bones. They are part of the person he is. In one session, out of the blue as it were, David says, 'You know, I pray sometimes, especially if I get angry.' Laura sees this as a positive sign, recalling research on the value of prayer in controlling anger and aggression (Bremner, Koole & Bushman, 2011). For her, the issue is not a belief system but what works.

Decisions tend to be driven by beliefs and values. Therefore, as decisions are being made, it is important that David and Laura focus on what underpins them. When David says that he was 'perhaps too hasty' in turning his back on his family and pre-war friends, he may be saying he feels guilty. Laura realises that he feels 'out of the community', but it is not yet clear what he means by community.

Given all these variables, it is essential that Laura and David work together to ferret out and deal with key issues, such as guilt and being 'out of the community'. When David faces, explores and deals with such issues, turning problems into opportunities, a better future, moderate or substantive, can rise from the ashes of the past. But David will always be David. Helping is about managing problems in living and developing unused opportunities, not personality transformation. David is an expert in David, knowing himself, however incompletely, from the inside out. Like all of us he has blind spots which contribute to the complexity–uncertainty dyad, but he, rather than textbooks on abnormal psychology, is still the best source of knowledge about David. Laura, as an expert, has dealt with all these complexities before, but David is the decision maker. She can help David find his way through these inevitable uncertainties and not be paralysed by them.

Let's end this section on uncertainty on a positive note. Duncan (2010) highlights the upside of uncertainty: 'As frightening as it feels, uncertainty is the place of unlimited possibilities for change. It is this indeterminacy that gives therapy its texture and infuses it with the excitement of discovery. This allows for the 'heretofore unsaid,' the 'aha moments,' and all the spontaneous ideas, connections, conclusions, plans, insights, resolves and new identities that emerge when you put two people together in a room and call it psychotherapy' (pp. 154–155). Orlinsky and Rønnestad (2005) show that the helper's tolerance for complexity and uncertainty is a vital factor in therapy. Perhaps 'tolerance' is the wrong word. Therapists and, at least eventually, clients need to befriend and embrace uncertainty, distil it, learn from it. The world of human behaviour will always be full of uncertainties. Lakeman (2014) also highlights that adopting an unknowing stance helps to foster the therapeutic relationship.

MOVING FROM SMART TO WISE: MANAGING THE SHADOW SIDE OF HELPING

Let me add one more dimension of uncertainty. More than intelligence is needed to establish a constructive client–helper relationship and use the problem-management framework and skills outlined in this book well – smart is not smart enough. The helper who understands and uses the framework together with the processes, skills and techniques that make it work might well be smart, but he or she must also be wise. Effective helpers understand the limitations not only of helping theories, frameworks and models, but also of helpers, the helping profession, clients and the environments that affect the helping process. It is one thing to understand and factor in the 'known unknowns' described in the section on uncertainties. It is another to understand and deal with the 'unknown unknowns' that lurk in the background of all human endeavours, including helping. The latter unknowns constitute what I call the 'shadow side' of life. The shadow side of helping can be defined as:

> *All those things that often adversely (and sometimes constructively) affect the helping relationship, process, and outcomes, in substantive ways but that are not identified and explored by helper or client or even the profession itself.*

All human endeavours have their shadow side. Companies and institutions are plagued with internal politics and are often guided by covert or vaguely understood beliefs, values and norms that do not serve the best interests of the business, its customers, its employees or its shareholders. In the worldwide financial crisis that has plagued the world, lots of seamy things were going on in the shadows for years before the financial system began to implode. The helping professions, too, have their shadow side. Helping models are flawed; helpers are sometimes selfish, lazy and even predatory, and they are prone to burnout. Clients are sometimes selfish, lazy and predatory, even in the helping relationship itself.

Shadow-side challenges, managed wisely, can provide benefits. Consider the following analogy. The shadow side of helping is a kind of 'noise' in the system. Scientists have discovered that sometimes a small amount of noise in a system, called 'stochastic resonance', makes the system more sensitive and efficient. In the helping professions, noise in the guise of the debate around what makes helping both effective and efficient can ultimately benefit clients. But sometimes the noise gets too loud.

There are not just debates but also conflicts close to internecine wars in the helping professions. For instance, the debate on the 'correct' approach to diversity and multiculturalism brings out some of the best and some of the worst in the helping community. Accusations, however subtle or blatant, of cultural imperialism on the one side and 'political correctness' on the other fly back and forth. The debate on whether or how the helping professions should take political stands or engage in social engineering generates more heat than light. No significant article is published about any significant dimension of counselling without a barrage of often testy replies.

What happened to learning from one another and integration? The search for the truth gives way at times to the need to be right. It is not always clear how all of this infighting serves the needs of clients. Indeed, clients are often enough left out of the debate. Just as many businesses today are reinventing themselves by starting with their customers and markets, so the helping professions should continually reinvent themselves by looking at helping through the eyes of clients.

If the world were completely rational, we would run out of clients. Not to worry, however, because many clients cause their own problems. People knowingly head down paths that lead to trouble. Life is not a straight road; often it is more like a maze. It often seems to be a contradictory process in which good and evil, the comic and the tragic, cowardice and heroism are inextricably intermingled. In the pages of this book the helping relationship and process are described and illustrated unapologetically in very positive terms. They are described as they might be or even should be, not as they always are.

Wise helpers are idealistic without being naive. They also know the difference between realism and cynicism and opt for the former. If helpers don't know what's in the shadows, they are naive. If they believe that shadow-side realities win out more often than not, they are cynical. Helpers should be neither naive nor cynical about themselves, their clients or their profession. I describe a cynic as someone who has given up but who, unfortunately, has not yet shut up. Wise helpers pursue a course of positive and compassionate realism. They see the journey 'from smart to wise' as a never-ending one. And they do not neglect the 'smart' part of helping or of everyday living. They continually get better at 'separating sense from nonsense', the subtitle of John Ruscio's (2005) book *Critical Thinking in Psychology*, an excellent exploration of the value of critical thinking.

The Skilled Helper is by no means a treatise on the shadow side of helping. Rather, its intent is to get helpers to begin to think about the shadow side of the profession and its professionals. There are signs that the helping professions are beginning to explore their shadow side. An example of that is the book *What Therapists Don't Talk About and Why* (Pope, Sonne & Greene, 2006). These authors explore myths and taboos that they see as standing in the way of effective helping. This is a start. Of course, you may not agree with what they have to say, but it is a stimulus to deeper thinking about the helping professions and to professional dialogue and debate. In my opinion the helping professions need to become, in a positive way, more self-critical. I doubt that science will ever eradicate the shadow side of life.

CHAPTER 2
THE HELPING
RELATIONSHIP

Chapter Contents

- The Helping Relationship

- The Values that Drive the Helping Relationship

- Respect as the Foundation Value

- Empathy as the Primary Orientation Value

- Proactive Appreciation of Diversity

- Self-Responsibility as an Empowerment-Focused Value

- A Bias for Action as an Outcome-Focused Value

- Shadow-Side Realities in the Helping Relationship

THE HELPING RELATIONSHIP

This chapter addresses how to behave towards clients. It contains many suggestions, but don't get lost in the detail. One way of proceeding is to read this chapter thoughtfully but quickly. Then re-read it as you move through Parts II and III of this book.

Although theoreticians, researchers and practitioners alike, not to mention clients, agree that the relationship between client and helper is important, there are significant differences as to how this relationship is to be characterised and played out in the helping process. Some stress the relationship itself, whereas others highlight the work that is done through the relationship. Some use the term 'relationship', while others prefer the term 'working alliance'. Although researchers define terms such as 'relationship' and 'alliance' differently, certain themes such as 'collaboration' dominate. Even then, what collaboration looks like differs from author to author. Recall the notion of 'uncertainty' discussed in Chapter 1. The purpose of this section is not to reconcile differences but to give helpers a clinical 'feel' for what a good relationship looks like, together with some of the behaviours that contribute to the helping partnership. There is no one right way of developing a helping relationship. Even though there are fundamental principles, you and each client have to co-discover and co-develop the 'right way' for that encounter.

An enormous amount of research on the nature of the helping relationship has been done over the past ten years (Norcross, 2011a, 2011b), although, unsurprisingly, some of its findings are contradictory. The basic findings of an APA Task Force and the clinical principles that stem from it were alluded to in Chapter 1. No attempt is made in this chapter to dissect all that research and provide a critical review. Rather, this chapter tries to answer a few basic questions in light of all this research. What do helpers need to know about the relationship? What do clients need to know? How can counsellors help clients enter a collaborative relationship? What needs to be done to make sure that the relationship serves life-enhancing outcomes for clients? In my view, the research findings often do no more than confirm common sense, which, admittedly, is not a 'scientific' term. But clients certainly understand the term 'common sense'. And if you think of the words related to the term – discretion, levelheadedness, practicality, prudence, sense, wisdom, street-smart, acumen, judgement, care, caution, circumspection and the like – you get the idea. Admittedly, one person's common sense need not be another's. And common sense might be misnamed because, as some say, it isn't that common.

The importance of the relationship itself

All of us establish relationships of one kind or another throughout our lives. One way of looking at any relationship, including a helping relationship, is to consider what each party 'brings to the table', as it were, and how these offerings interact. Both helper and client have a set of personality traits and personal cultures (discussed later in this chapter) that affect how they go about establishing and maintaining relationships. If helper and client had met at, let us say, a party or conference before therapy began, the relationship would be a result of what each would 'bring to the party'. That is, neither would be acting from a role – the helper role or the client role. The point is that the helping relationship can be affected by the package of human elements each brings to the helping encounter. Norcross (2011a, 2011b) puts it simply: 'Remember: The relationship is far broader and inclusive than the [working] alliance alone' (p. 120). It follows that the better both clients and helpers understand themselves in terms of how they establish and maintain relationships, the better they might be in establishing a working alliance in therapy. The word 'might' is important here.

Knox and Cooper (2015) write about several levels of relating as clients seek help for a variety of reasons. This connectedness, relational depth and therapeutic component adds to the flavour of the therapeutic relationship and will be determinate on the type of therapeutic relationship formed between helper and client.

Most approaches to therapy affirm the importance of the helping relationship, but not in the same way. In a different mode, Carl Rogers (1951, 1957; Kirschenbaum, 2009), one of the great pioneers in the field of counselling, emphasised the quality of the relationship in representing the humanistic-experiential approach to helping (see Kelly, 1994, 1997). Rogers claimed that the unconditional positive regard, accurate empathy and genuineness offered by the helper and perceived by the client were both necessary and often sufficient for therapeutic progress. Through this highly empathic relationship, counsellors, in his eyes, helped clients to understand themselves, liberate their unused resources and manage their lives more effectively. Rogers' work started the widely discussed client-centred approach to helping (Rogers, 1965).

On the other hand, in psychoanalytic or psychodynamic approaches, 'transference' and 'countertransference' – the complex and at first unconscious interpersonal dynamics between helper and client that are rooted in the client's and even the helper's past – are central. Resolving these often murky dynamics, some say, is intrinsic to successful therapeutic outcomes. Rogers considered the empathic helping relationship a facilitative condition, not a 'problem' in itself to be explored and resolved.

The relationship as a means to an end

Some see the helping relationship as very important but still as a means to an end. This makes sense because life-enhancing client outcomes, as noted in Chapter 1, are what helping is all about. The cognitive-behavioural tasks of the helping process are accomplished, as Tursi and Cochran (2006) have noted, in a person-centred relational framework. In this view, a good relationship is practical because it enables client and counsellor to do the work called for by whatever helping process is being used. Practitioners using cognitive and behavioural approaches to helping, such as the manualised treatments discussed in Part III, although sensitive to relationship issues, tend towards this means-to-end view. Overstressing the relationship, they say, is a mistake because it obscures the ultimate goal of helping: managing problem situations and developing life-enhancing opportunities. This goal won't be achieved if the relationship is poor, but if too much focus is placed on the relationship itself, both client and helper can be distracted from the real work to be done.

The relationship as a working alliance

'The alliance refers to the quality and strength of the collaborative relationship between client and therapist' (Norcross, 2010, p. 120). Although the term 'working alliance' has a long history and a number of different interpretations (Horvath *et al.*, 2011), it can be used to bring together the best of the empathic-relationship-in-itself and the relationship-as-means-to-achieving-desired-outcomes. Bordin (1979) defined the working alliance as the collaboration between the client and the helper based on their agreement on the goals and tasks of counselling. Horvath and his associates (2011) add a dynamic-process touch: 'The alliance represents an emergent quality of partnership and mutual collaboration between therapist and client ... Its development can take different forms and may be achieved quickly or nurtured over a longer period of time ...' (p. 11).

The collaborative nature of helping   In the working alliance, helpers and clients are collaborators. Helping is not something that helpers do to clients; rather, it is a process that helpers and clients work through together (Frankel, 2007). Helpers do not 'cure' their patients. Both have work to do in the problem-management and opportunity-development stages and tasks, and both have responsibilities related to outcomes. Outcomes depend on the competence and motivation of the helper and the client, and on the quality of their interactions. Helping is a two-person team effort in which helpers need to do their part and clients theirs. If either party refuses to play, or plays incompetently, then the entire enterprise can fail. A positive therapeutic alliance has been found to be one of the best predictors in therapy (Horvath *et al.*, 2011; Knox & Cooper, 2015).

Bachelor, Laverdière, Gamache and Bordeleau (2007), digging down into the heart of collaboration, found three different types of client collaboration – active, mutual and therapist-dependent, although the last of these three might better be called cooperation rather than collaboration. Active clients see themselves 'as playing a significant role, or at least as making a difference, as to whether the work moves forward or not' (p. 181). The mutual-type client 'acknowledges his or her role in the work of therapy and positive change but also views (and in some cases explicitly expects) the therapist to play an equally active role' (p. 183).

As to dependent-collaborative clients, 'collaboration refers to change-inducing or otherwise beneficial therapist interventions' (p. 184). The researchers found that a third of clients fall into this last category. *The Skilled Helper* will provide plenty of grist for the mill of your mind to determine what precisely collaboration means and the role it plays in the helping process.

Guiding principles for alliance behaviour   Because the term 'working alliance' is a concept, an abstraction, it takes on life and clinical significance through the behavioural principles that make it a reality. Here are some alliance-focused principles:

- *Alliances emerge.* Don't try to build an alliance. Rather, make sure that everything you do in using, for instance, the problem-management process briefly mentioned in Chapter 1 and described in detail in Part III, or any other approach to treatment, contributes to a spirit of collaboration and partnership. When David and Laura interact constructively, say, in exploring David's tendency to run away from closer interpersonal relationships, the alliance 'emerges' and grows.

- *Track the client's evolving needs and wants.* Make an effort to understand the client's preferences and modulate accordingly. Remember that both of you are on a collaborative search for the right relationship. When David summarily rejects the survey approach to monitoring the helping process and outcomes, Laura doesn't push the issue. There are other ways to get feedback. And some clients need to get comfortable with the relationship before adding what they might see as 'extras'.

- *Focus on resources.* Make sure that you are getting in touch with not just the client's problems and concerns but also the resources and expectations the client brings to the helping endeavour. Effective helpers begin focusing on the client's strengths right from the beginning. Right from the start Laura says to herself, 'This guy seems to have a lot going for him, but I'm not sure if he is in touch with his considerable resources.'

- *Don't be surprised at differing views of the relationship.* Your view of how the relationship is evolving may not be the same as the client's view, especially in the early stages of the relationship. Look for cues indicating the state of the relationship throughout the helping endeavour.

- *Ups and downs are common.* Do not be surprised about ups and downs in the relationship. That happens in everyday life. For example, a client might get an insight that is upsetting ('I've really be acting like a fool in my family life'). You might think that you've done something wrong. Even when you're the cause of some kind of negative reaction, this does not mean that the relationship is in trouble. When Laura invites David to look at the consequences of being 'out of community', David sulks. Both of them have to work at re-establishing equilibrium. Horvath and his colleagues (2011) see these ups and downs as 'normal' variations, which, if 'attended to and resolved, are associated with good treatment outcomes' (p. 15).

- *Expect and deal with client negativity.* Therapy is hard work for clients. When they get frustrated, they often enough lash out at their therapists. When David is frustrated by the fact that he keeps dreaming about the attack in which his buddies were killed, he interrupts Laura: 'Laura, you know nothing, I mean nothing, about war and you never will. So stop pretending.' Laura has been responding empathically to what David has been saying, but her empathy is seen as ignorance. But, given the fact that their relationship has been growing stronger, she does not internalise David's remarks. Rather, she tries to learn from them.

The communication and relationship-building skills essential to all of the above are outlined and illustrated in Part II.

Getting off to a good start

Burnard (2005, p. 120) refers to 'an eight-stage map' as one way of looking at the client–helper relationship, and the first stage of this is 'meeting the client', which offers some useful guidance to the helper. When the client meets the helper for the first time, each is sounding out the other and setting tacit ground rules for the relationship. In a sense, both the client and helper are 'on their best behaviour'. This is an important part of the larger helper–client relationship in that it sets the tone for the whole dialogue. The skilled helper will set the client at ease in this stage and encourage them to gently spell out their reasons for talking to the helper. It is likely that both parties will experience some anxiety in this phase of the relationship: the client will want to be seen in a good light by the helper, and the helper will be keen to ensure that the client feels comfortable in their company. According to Burnard's model, this then leads into the two subsequent stages of 'Stage two: discussion of surface issues' and 'Stage three: revelation of deeper issues'.

Miller *et al.* (2006, p. 5) noted that 'research has found that client change occurs earlier rather than later in the treatment process, and that the client's subjective experience of meaningful change in the first few sessions is critical. If improvement in the client's subjective sense of well-being does not occur in the first few sessions, then the likelihood of a positive outcome significantly decreases.' They go on to review the evidence for this finding. If that is the case, then helpers, in collaboration with their clients, need to establish the kind of alliance that supports such change relatively quickly, if possible. DeFife and Hilsenroth (2011), in reviewing the evidence on effective therapeutic relationships, identified three areas related to helping clients and therapists get off to a good start.

First, help clients develop *positive expectancies* related to both the helping process and its outcomes. How can helpers do this?

- By using all the relationship-building skills presented in Part II. For instance, Laura comes across as attentive, honest and flexible. This helps David say to himself, perhaps subconsciously, 'I think that I can work with her.'
- By providing a model or framework that helps clients understand the problems they are facing. Early on, Laura gives her take on the PTSD framework, but personalises it by tailoring it to David's symptoms.
- By sharing the problem-management process detailed in Part III of this book, but describing it in terms of some of the issues David has highlighted. For instance, she helps him explore some of the issues from a different perspective. 'It seems that sometimes your thinking gets a bit twisted. It's you, but it's not really your kind of thinking.'
- By suggesting that there are specific ways of handling his symptoms. Laura says, 'There are ways of helping you deal with both anxiety and depression, but we, you and I, need to find the programmes that are best for you.'
- By helping patients develop confidence in the treatment process. The fact that David agrees to try the 'buddy' approach is a positive sign. He says to himself, 'Here's a guy who has been through it all and has come out the other side.'
- By discussing the kind of commitment and work that is needed both in the sessions themselves and in everyday life. Laura says, 'I can't say that all of this will be easy. You will have to be convinced that the payoff is worth it.'
- By 'normalising' the client's problems and concerns. David needs to see that, given what he has seen and gone through in both Iraq and Afghanistan, the problems that are plaguing him can be expected. No one escapes unscathed. It is a question of degree.

Second, help clients understand and move into the *role* of a proactive and committed client. How do you help them do that?

- By helping clients understand the essential details of the helping process, including frequency of meetings, meeting length, work between sessions and the like. Laura does this and adds, 'But remember, you can ask any kind of question you want. If you have any objections, bring them up. If you think we are headed in the wrong direction, say so. What we are doing has to make sense to you.' It is important for the helper to understand what works for each client.
- By providing a brief overview of what the sessions *could* be like. The overview should be simple, but not simplistic, and clear. Continue to reinforce the notion that David is in the driver's seat and that there is flexibility in the session plans. For instance, after describing what sessions could look like, Laura adds, 'I can help you see the different potential options, but you will be making the decisions as we move along. We will look at what works for you.'
- By making sure that the client understands the collaborative nature of that role. Laura says, 'Notice that I use "we" a lot. During the time we spend together you will probably make any number of decisions. My role is to help you make choices that are best for you.'
- By providing some idea of the issues to be discussed. Laura says, 'My job is to help you explore issues that will make a difference in your life. I'll help you, but you're the agenda setter.' In summary, Laura wants to find ways of helping David move into the driver's seat right from the start and become autonomous in his decision making.

Third, emphasise *goal formation* and highlight its *collaborative* nature. Life-enhancing outcomes chosen by the client constitute the goal of helping. Collaborative goal setting is addressed in detail in Part II of this book.

There are a lot of guidelines in these lists. Which ones are the most important? The answer is simple: the ones that make a difference in the client's life. It is impossible to predict which ones will make a difference in *this* client's life. Client and helper have to work that out together through the process of their interaction (Jacobs, 2012). It is extremely important in all of this not to dump too many decisions on the client right from the start. Simplicity helps.

Keeping the client's point of view and preferences centre stage

Burnard (2005) usefully reminds us that,

> "Central to client-centred helping is the notion that given the space and time, we are the best arbiters of what is and what is not right for us. We can listen to other people but in the end we, as individuals, have to decide upon our own courses of action."

The client is the expert on themselves and the helper provides the framework and model of this exploration. Bedi (2006) has expressed concern that the research community has, in reality, given too much attention to therapists' views of the helping relationship, to the neglect both of clients' views and the client-centred approach. There are two key questions: First, what kind of relationship does the client want? Clients can differ widely in this regard. Second, what does the therapist need to do to help the client become a collaborating partner in the helping process? Ackerman and Hilsenroth (2003) presented a comprehensive examination of therapists' personal attributes and in-session activities that positively influence the therapeutic alliance. These attributes include flexibility, honesty, respect, trustworthiness, confidence, warmth, interest and openness. Techniques that helped the alliance include exploration, reflection, noting past therapy success, accurate interpretation, facilitating the expression of affect and paying attention to the client's experience. Bedi's (2006) study showed that clients appreciated the nature of the helping setting, helper's self-presentation and body language, non-verbal gestures, emotional support and care, honesty, validation, guidance, challenging, helper's education, helper's appreciation of client self-responsibility and good session administration. Duff and Bedi (2010) found that clients appreciate even 'seemingly small, strengths-fostering behaviours such as making encouraging statements, making positive comments about the client, and greeting the client with a smile' can contribute, perhaps disproportionately, to alliance building. Bedi, Davis and Arvay (2005) point out that helpers need to be trained in client-focused behaviours, especially in programmes that overstate the importance of treatment methods. Arnold and Boggs (2020) outline the importance of relationship skills in health communications within the nursing profession, and this can be applied to other helping professions.

For you, the helper, all of this is essential background knowledge. Tailoring what the research shows as important to the individual client is essential, and personalising this to your client is an important part of the relationship. Don't get lost in the kind of detail found in these pages. Rather, reflect on it and then proceed to develop your own natural style and way of working with your clients. Parts II and III of this book are filled with examples of tailoring the relationship to the client.

The relationship as a forum for relearning

Even though helpers don't 'cure' their clients, the relationship alone can be therapeutic. In the working alliance, the relationship itself is often a forum or a vehicle for social-emotional relearning (Mallinckrodt, 1996). Effective helpers model attitudes and behaviour that help clients challenge and change their own attitudes and behaviour. It is as if clients were to say to themselves (although not in so many words), 'She [the helper] obviously cares for and trusts me, so perhaps it is all right for me to care for and trust myself.' Or, 'He takes the risk of challenging me. To tell the truth, I need to be challenged. So what's so bad about challenge when it's done well?' Or, 'I came here frightened to death by relationships and now I'm experiencing a non-exploitative relationship that I cherish.' Furthermore, protected by the safety of the helping relationship, clients can experiment with different behaviours during the sessions themselves. The shy person can speak up, the reclusive person can open up, the aggressive person can back off, the overly sensitive person can ask to be challenged and so forth. Positive outcomes are often related to a strong therapeutic relationship and helpers who can offer clients a high and consistent level of empathy work at relational depth (Knox & Cooper, 2015).

Clients can then transfer what they are learning to other social settings. It is as if clients might say to themselves, 'He [the helper] listens to me so carefully and makes sure that he understands my point of view even when he thinks I should reconsider it. My relationships outside would be a lot different if I were to do the same.' Or, 'I do a lot of stuff in the sessions that would make anyone angry. But she doesn't let herself become a victim of emotions, either her own or mine. And her self-control doesn't diminish her humanity at all. That would make a big difference in my life.' The relearning dynamic, however subtle or covert, is often powerful. In summary, needed changes in attitudes, emotional expression and behaviour often take place within the sessions themselves through the relationship.

Relationship flexibility

The idea that one kind of perfect relationship or alliance fits all clients is a myth. Different clients have different needs, and those needs are best met through different kinds of relationships and different modulations within the same relationship. One client may work best with a helper who expresses a great deal of warmth, whereas another may work best with a helper who is more objective and businesslike. Some clients come to counselling with a fear of intimacy. If helpers communicate a great deal of empathy and warmth right from the beginning, these clients might be put off. Once the client learns to trust the helper, stronger interventions can be used. Effective helpers use a mix of styles, skills and techniques tailored to the kind of relationship that is right for each client (Knox & Cooper, 2015; Clarkson, 2003; Lazarus, 1993; Mahrer, 1993). And they remain themselves while they do so.

If clients and helpers are collaborators, can we talk about who should take the lead? Does the one who has something to say at any given moment take the lead? Duncan, Miller and Sparks (2004; see also Duncan & Sparks, 2010; Duncan *et al.*, 2010) answer that question in a way that many would consider radical:

> *"Data from 40 years of outcome research provide strong empirical support for privileging the client's role in the change process (Hubble, Duncan & Miller, 1999). In short, clients, not therapists, make therapy work. As a result, therapy should be organised around their resources, perceptions, experiences and ideas. ... need only take direction from clients: following their lead; adopting their language, world view, goal, and ideas about the problem; and acknowledging their experiences with, and inclinations about, the change process." (pp. 11–12)*

This view is radical because it moves at least one step beyond Carl Rogers' client-centred approach. And, if up to now we have said that there is 'no one right way' to relate to a client, we would have to change it to 'there is no one right way to put the client in the driver's seat'. Obviously, thinking about the helping relationship continues to evolve.

Finally, don't be discouraged if a fully collaborative relationship does not pop up immediately. Keep on doing the right things, but remember that what you think is most important may not be what the client thinks. At one point David says, 'I keep thinking that I should see you as my mum or teacher or nurse or something and I'm a kid or a student or a patient. But I don't really feel that way.' Laura replies, 'So it's taking a bit of time getting a fix on what this relationship is about.' David: 'Yeah, that's it. This is something new for me. I'm not quite there yet.'

Breakdowns in client–helper relationships do happen, so it is essential to know how to get back on track. Eubanks-Carter, Muran and Safran (2010) outline ways of dealing with challenges, misunderstandings, impasses, deterioration, stress and threats to the relationship. They point out how these 'ruptures', as they call them, can be transformed into opportunities for change and growth. Ruptures can be a great way for the helper and client to explore their interaction further. Gilbert and Leahy (2007) state that 'the goal of working with ruptures is not simply to repair them so that therapy can continue with a strengthened alliance but rather to help patients understand how they construe events and how that construal impacts their interactions with others'. People build relationships through conversations and behaviour. This chapter outlines how we should behave towards clients. Part II outlines what successful conversations with clients look like. The communication and relationship-building skills, including the skill of immediacy, needed to handle ruptures are detailed in Part II.

THE VALUES THAT DRIVE THE HELPING RELATIONSHIP

One of the best ways to characterise a helping relationship is through the values that permeate and drive it. The relationship is the vehicle through which values come alive. Expressed concretely through working-alliance behaviours, values play a critical role in the helping process. But the uncertainties associated with the beliefs-values-norms-ethics-morality package outlined in Chapter 1 cloud the issue.

The ethical codes adopted by psychological and counselling associations across the world, and other bodies in the helping professions worldwide, provide a clear set of values and a detailed list of norms guiding the interactions between helpers and clients. These codes dissipate many of the uncertainties associated with the beliefs-values-norms-ethics-morality package, but they do not eliminate them. Ethical uncertainties and conflicts will always bedevil the helping process. In this section we review the values that many people (including me) believe 'should' drive the helping process, but you will not find universal agreement on the 'right' package. In the end, you have to come up with a set of values that make sense to you and your clients and that keep you in compliance with both the codes mentioned earlier and the laws of the land.

Borrowing from Argyris (Argyris, 1980; Argyris & Schön, 1974), values can be seen as 'mental maps' which define how to act in situations. However, even though people have values (behavioural maps), they do not always use them. So clients (like the rest of us) have both 'espoused' values, which are like ideals, and 'values-in-use', that is, behavioural maps they use more or less consistently to make decisions and guide behaviour. Often enough there is a split between espoused values and action on the part of either helper or client that adds a note of uncertainty to the helping process. Moreover, some values-in-use lead to life-limiting rather than life-enhancing outcomes.

Values as tools of the trade

Values-in-use are not just mental states. They are tools that guide decision making. They give rise to client-enabling helping behaviour. Helpers might say to themselves during a session with a difficult client something like this:

> This client needs to come to grips with her arrogant, I'm-always-right attitude. It distorts her decisions and poisons her relationships. It keeps her mired in her problems. How I give her feedback or, perhaps better, how I invite her to challenge herself is important. On the one hand, I don't want to damage our relationship; on the other, I value genuineness and openness. I don't want to belittle her, but I owe it to her to help her see herself as others see her. But I have to do this in the right way and at the right time. How can I help her 'discover' this dimension of her behaviour?

Values help counsellors make decisions on how to proceed. Helpers without a set of working values are adrift. Those who don't have an explicit set of values have an implicit or 'default' set that may or may not serve the helping process. Therefore, reviewing the values that drive your behaviours as a helper is not optional. Harris (2008, 2009) has adapted a model on values from Tobias Lundgren that can be used with clients. The 'bull's eye worksheet' can help to clarify clients' values to ensure that helpers are working with what is important for clients at the time. The worksheet can be downloaded free (thehappinesstrap.com/upimages/Long_Bull%27s_Eye_Worksheet.pdf)

Determining the values inherent to successful helping

Helping-related values, like your other values, cannot be handed to you on a platter. Much less can they be shoved down your throat. Therefore, this chapter is meant to stimulate your thinking about the values that should drive helping. In the final analysis, as you sit with your clients, only those beliefs, values and norms that you have made your own will make a difference in your helping behaviour.

Of course, this does not mean that you will invent a set of values different from everyone else's. Tradition is an important part of value formation, and we all learn from the rich tradition of the helping professions. And so, in the following pages, five major values from the tradition of the helping professions – respect, empathy, a proactive appreciation of diversity, self-responsibility together with client empowerment, and a bias towards action – are translated into a set of norms. Respect is the foundation value; empathy is the value that orients helpers in every interaction with their clients; an appreciation of diversity is a value that opens you up to the world as it is; client empowerment is the value that highlights self-responsibility; a bias towards action is an outcome-focused value. These values serve as a starting point for your reflection on the values that should drive the helping process. Don't just swallow them: analyse, reflect on and debate them. Come up with your own values package.

RESPECT AS THE FOUNDATION VALUE

Respect for clients is the foundation on which all helping interventions are built. Respect is such a fundamental concept that, like most such concepts, it eludes definition. The word comes from a Latin root that includes the idea of 'seeing' or 'viewing'. Indeed, respect is a particular way of viewing oneself and others. If it is to make a difference, respect cannot remain just an attitude or a way of viewing others. Ideally, helpers and their clients 'matter to one another' (Rayle, 2006). Carl Rogers (1957) early on saw the importance of respect, calling it 'positive regard' (p. 101) and adding the notion of non-possessive warmth towards, and affirmation of, the client. Latter-day research (Farber & Doolin, 2011) links these behaviours to successful client outcomes. Here are some norms that flow from the interaction between a belief in the dignity of the person and the value of respect.

Behaviours showing disrespect

Here are some things not to do lest you show disrespect to clients.

Do no harm   This is the first rule of the physician and the first rule of the helper (Lilienfeld, 2007; Rhule, 2005). Yet some helpers do harm, either because they are unprincipled or because they are incompetent. Helping is not a neutral process – it is for better or for worse. In a world in which such things as child abuse, domestic violence and exploitation of workers are much more common than we care to think, it is important to emphasise a non-manipulative and non-exploitative approach to clients. Berk and Parker (2009) outline the impact of inappropriate psychotherapy and behaviours and state that the 'therapist style is a major influence on outcome and adverse events'. They go on to state that the 'therapist who is exploitative, overly narcissistic, patronizing, uncaring, inattentive, or unable to establish some congruence with the patient and their world, may be expected to create a lack of fit and an adverse outcome'.

Do not rush to judgement   You are not there to judge clients or to force your values on them. You are there to help them identify, explore, review and challenge the consequences of the values they have adopted. Let's say that a client during the first session says somewhat arrogantly, 'When I'm dealing with other people, I say whatever I want when I want. If others don't like it, well, that's their problem. My first obligation is to myself, being the person I am.' Irked by the client's attitude, a helper might respond judgementally by saying, 'You've just put your finger on the core of your problem. How can you expect to get along with people with this kind of self-centred philosophy?' However, another counsellor, taking a different approach, might respond, 'So being yourself is one of your top priorities and being totally frank is, for you, part of that picture.' The first counsellor rushes to judgement; the second neither judges nor condones. At this point she merely tries to understand the client's point of view and let him know that she understands – even if she realises that the client would benefit from exploring the perhaps unintended consequences of such a philosophy.

Behaviours showing respect

These are the kinds of behaviour through which you show respect to clients.

Become competent and committed   Master whatever model of helping you use. Get good at the basic problem-management and opportunity-development framework outlined in this book and the skills that make it work. There is no place for the 'caring incompetent' in the helping professions. It would be great to say that everyone who graduates from some kind of helping training programme is not only competent but also increases their competence over their career. Unfortunately, this is not the case. It is therefore vitally important for helpers to keep up to date with current research in their field, to attend workshops, courses and events in order to continue their professional development. There is an ethical obligation for helpers to develop personally and professionally throughout their career.

Be genuine   Gelso (2011; Moore & Gelso, 2011) and others (Kolden *et al.*, 2011) make a difference between the 'real' relationship and the alliance described earlier. Gelso (2009) has defined the real relationship as the 'personal relationship existing between two or more people as reflected in the degree to which each is genuine with the other, and perceives and experiences the other in ways that befit the other' (pp. 254–255). That is, the relationship is real to the degree it is empathic (explained later) and not phony. But there are various types of phoniness. If I pretend to like you but really don't, I'm being phony. The point is that phoniness is incompatible with respect. Another type of phoniness is to overstress your professional role. When I am with a client, I am there as a helper, a catalyst, an encourager, a collaborator and so forth. I am not there primarily as a member of my profession, an expert, the one with the answers and so forth. The client's success is my success. You are competent to the degree the client improves.

Make it clear that you are 'for' the client   The way you act with clients will tell them a great deal about your attitude towards them. Your manner should indicate that you are 'for' the client, that you care for him or her in a down-to-earth, non-sentimental way. It is as if you are saying to the client, 'Working with you is worth my time and energy.' Respect is both gracious and tough-minded. Being for the client is not the same as taking the client's side or acting as the client's advocate. 'Being for' means taking clients' points of view seriously even when they need to be challenged. Respect often involves helping clients place demands on themselves. Of course, this kind of 'tough love' in no way excludes appropriate warmth towards clients.

Assume the client's goodwill   Work on the assumption that clients want to work at living more effectively, at least until that assumption is proved false. As we shall see later, the reluctance and resistance of some clients, particularly involuntary clients, is not necessarily evidence of ill will. Respect involves entering clients' world to understand their reluctance and a willingness to help clients work through it.

Keep the client's agenda in focus   Helpers should pursue their clients' agendas, not their own. Here are three examples of helpers who lost clients because of lack of appreciation of their agendas. One helper recalled, painfully, that he lost a client because he had become too preoccupied with his theories of depression rather than the client's painful depressive episodes. Another helper, who dismissed as either trivial or irrelevant a client's bereavement over a pet that had died, was dumbfounded and crushed when the client made an attempt on her own life. The loss of the pet was the last straw in a life that was spiralling downwards. A third helper, a white male counsellor who prided himself on his multicultural focus in counselling, went for counselling himself when a Hispanic client quit therapy, saying, perhaps somewhat unfairly, as he was leaving, 'I don't think you're interested in me. You're more interested in Anglo-Hispanic politics.'

EMPATHY AS THE PRIMARY ORIENTATION VALUE

One critical way of showing respect is empathy, the ability to understand the client from his or her point of view and, when appropriate, to communicate this understanding to the client. Put simply, it involves an understanding and feeling for the mental states and emotions of another person and, I would add, how the person's context influences his or her thinking and feeling. The empathic person experiences the other in context. Although empathy is a rich concept in the helping professions, it has been a confusing one. The literature covering many different perspectives is overwhelming (Batson, 2011; Coplan & Goldie, 2012; Decety, 2012; Elliott *et al.*, 2010, 2011; Farrow & Woodruff, 2007; Gordon, 2007; Trout, 2009), with both philosophers and psychologists, theoreticians and practitioners vying for our attention. Different theoreticians and researchers have defined it in different ways. Some see it as a personality trait, a disposition to feel what other people feel or to understand others 'from the inside', as it were. In this view some people are by nature more empathic than others. Others see empathy not as a personality trait but as a situation-specific state of feeling for, and understanding of, another person's experiences. The implication is that helpers can learn how to bring about this state in themselves because it is so useful in the counselling process. Still others, building on the specific state-of-feeling approach, have focused on empathy as a process with stages. For instance, Barrett-Lennard (1981) identified three phases – empathic resonance, expressed empathy and received empathy. Carl Rogers (1975) talked about sensing a client's inner world and communicating that sensing.

This book tries to simplify things for the helper. This chapter deals with empathy as a basic value that informs and drives all helping behaviour. Chapter 3 in Part II deals with empathy as a communication skill.

A brief overview of empathy

All theoreticians, researchers and practitioners agree on one thing: Empathy is important both in everyday life and in helping.

Is empathy even possible? Can a helper really understand a client who is very different from himself or herself? Can a normal person understand a person with bipolar disorder? Can a Hispanic male counsellor understand a middle-class female South-African–British client? The practical answer is yes (Hatcher *et al.*, 2005). That is, clients working with helpers who espouse the value of empathy as delineated here and who have the communication competence described in Part II can feel understood. Answering the philosophical question underlying the clinical question is another matter.

A rich concept, perhaps too rich for a scientist A number of authors look at empathy from a value point of view and talk about the behaviours that flow from it. Sometimes their language is almost lyrical. For instance, Kohut (1978) said, 'Empathy, the accepting, confirming, and understanding human echo evoked by the self, is a psychological nutrient without which human life, as we know and cherish it, could not be sustained' (p. 705). In this view, empathy is a value, a philosophy, or a cause with almost poetic overtones. Covey (1989), naming empathic communication one of the 'seven habits of highly effective people', said that empathy provides those with whom we are interacting with 'psychological air' that helps them breathe more freely in their relationships. Goleman (1995, 1998) puts empathy at the heart of emotional intelligence. It is the individual's 'social radar' through which he or she senses others' feelings and perspectives and takes an active interest in their concerns.

The importance of empathy early in life The WAVE Trust, an international charity dedicated to advancing public awareness of the root causes of violence and the means to prevent and reduce it in society, commissioned research that came up with an extraordinary finding: 'Empathy is the single greatest inhibitor of the development of propensity to violence. Empathy fails to develop when parents or prime carers fail to attune with their infants' (Hosking & Walsh, 2005, p. 20). In their research the definition of empathy is important. The researchers define empathy as what takes place when 'the observed experiences of others come to affect our own thoughts and feelings in a caring fashion. Empathy entails the ability to step outside oneself emotionally and to be able to suppress temporarily one's own perspective on events to take another's' (p. 20). To 'attune' to a child means 'attempting to respond to his or her needs, particularly emotionally, resulting in the child's sense of being understood, cared for, and valued' (p. 20).

Children should not only be the recipients of empathy, but they should also learn how to express empathy towards others. Kennedy (2008) argues for the importance of teaching children to be empathic towards others. Unless they both experience and express empathy, children are in danger of becoming self-centred, prone to aggressive and cruel behaviour, and unable to feel or express remorse – a quasi-sociopathic interpersonal style. This happens when parents are unavailable physically and/or emotionally, when they are overindulgent and when children are exposed to violent media. Kennedy urges parents to talk to their children about the emotions of others, model empathic communication and behaviour, help children understand the need to make amends when they have harmed others, expose children to the less fortunate, allow children to feel useful forms of unhappiness such as frustration from not getting their way, and shield them from media with violent content.

Empathy as a two-way street

Pedersen, Crethar and Carlson (2008) show how helpers can increase their competence by moving beyond a traditional 'this-individual-helper-trying-to-understand-this-individual-client' approach to empathy. Empathy at its best is relationship oriented. For instance, Zaki, Bolger and Ochsner (2008) demonstrate that empathic accuracy depends on how both parties to a conversation communicate. Pedersen and his colleagues explore the many ways that cultural similarities and differences influence relationships in the counselling process and how important it is for helpers to become less focused on individuals and more focused on relationships.

Janet Clark (2003a, 2003b) has re-conceptualised empathy in a similar way. Like Pedersen and his colleagues, her definition of culture is very wide, including traits and characteristics that make individuals different from one another. She uses ethnographic concepts and principles (Goldstein, 1994; Green, 1995; Leigh, 1998) to focus on the individual client's unique frame of reference, rather than on a cultural group's frame of reference. She highlights some of the principal differences she sees between traditional one-way individualistic empathy and diversity-oriented two-way relationship empathy, what Pedersen and his colleagues call 'inclusive cultural empathy'. Empathy is a lived skill that needs to be cultivated through the helper's self-awareness. Stephany (2015) lists some useful ways in which helpers can develop their empathy skills through reflective journaling, mindfulness, obtaining feedback from others, mindful listening and many more:

- While the client's reality is knowable, the helper's understanding is always partial and fallible.
- Helpers need to be attuned not only to underlying mental states and feelings but also to the cultural meaning of the client's words.
- Relationship empathy is not just person-centred but encompasses the key contexts of the client's life.
- The complex sociopolitical environment and status of the client ('social location') is often a key part of context.
- When it comes to the client's cultural uniqueness, the helper is not an expert but a learner.
- The client's inductive understandings of self and the world are more important than the helper's deductive understandings (from theory, research and practice) about the client.
- Empathy is not something unilaterally offered by the helper, rather something that is mutually produced through dialogue.
- Self-awareness of such things as cultural bias on the part of the helper is not sufficient; ongoing introspection or self-reflexivity regarding ideas, fears, mistakes, confusion, breakthroughs and obstacles that arise in the helping sessions is essential.

Empathy as radical commitment

Empathy as a value is a radical commitment on the part of helpers to understand clients as fully as possible in three different ways. First, empathy is a commitment to work at understanding each client from his or her point of view together with the feelings surrounding this point of view and to communicate this understanding whenever it is deemed helpful. Second, it is a commitment to understand individuals in and through the context of their lives. The social settings, both large and small, in which they have developed and currently 'live and move and have their being' provide routes to understanding. Third, empathy is also a commitment to understand the dissonance between the client's point of view and reality. Understandably, providing feedback on this third type of empathy is a sensitive issue that will be discussed in detail in Part II. There is nothing passive about empathy. Empathic helpers respectfully communicate the kinds of understanding outlined in this paragraph to their clients and generally take an active interest in their concerns. Respectful empathy is very important when interacting with clients who are different from you in any respect – personally, socially, culturally and so forth (Wang et al., 2003). And, as we shall see in Chapter 3, the communication of empathy is also one of the best ways of helping clients remain in the driver's seat.

PROACTIVE APPRECIATION OF DIVERSITY

Dealing knowledgeably and sensitively with diversity (Muran, 2006) and that particular form of diversity called multiculturalism is part of both respect and empathy and is related to client empowerment. However, diversity is given special attention here because of its importance in itself and because of the emphasis currently being placed on diversity in all areas of society. The most important feature of the focus on diversity and multiculturalism is that they highlight the importance of client factors as *the* essential ingredient of successful therapy. It is not about the myriad forms of diversity. It is not about culture. *It's about clients*.

Helpers' self-awareness of biases, stereotypes, values and views play a key role in relating to clients. There has been an explosion of literature on diversity and multiculturalism over the past few years (Bernal & Domenech Rodriguez, 2012; Hays, 2008, 2009; Lewis, Lewis, Daniels & D'Andrea, 2010; Ponterotto, Casas, Suzuki & Alexander, 2010; Smith, Domenech Rodriguez & Bernal, 2011). A simple search on the website of an internet bookseller yielded over 16,000 entries. A dictionary of multicultural psychology (L. E. Hall, 2005) runs to more than 170 pages. Entire journal issues are dedicated to it (for instance, see *Journal of Counselling and Development*, 86, Summer, 2008). So I hesitate to cite references to books and articles that should be read.

There is both an upside and a downside to this avalanche. One plus is that helpers are forced to take a look at the blind spots they may have about diversity, including ethnic and cultural diversity, and to take a deeper look at the world around us. Another plus is that there is evidence that 'exposure to multiple cultures [and to all forms of diversity, I would add] in and of itself can enhance creativity' (Leung, Maddux, Galinsky & Chiu, 2008, p. 169). One minus is that the form of diversity called multiculturalism runs the danger of becoming a fad that spawns an industry that may focus attention away from the needs of individual clients. Putnam (2007) has discovered another, at least short-term, minus. His research has shown that the more diverse a community, the less likely its inhabitants are to trust anyone, from the next-door neighbour to the town mayor. This is probably true also on the individual level. He goes on to point out that, in the long term, diversity can be enriching, but this does not happen automatically. Mere contact is not enough (Dixon, Durrheim & Tredoux, 2005). Communities and individuals need to work at it. Nothing is free. Perhaps maintaining a 'curious stance' will enable the helper to focus on the client's values and needs.

Culture, personal culture and values

Because culture is the form of diversity that receives most of the attention, it is important to understand what the term means. Bronfenbrenner (1977) called it the 'largest and most controlling of the systems' on both the individual and societal level. Once more, there are many different definitions of culture, but helpers need definitions that can be translated into practice. Values are central to culture, but culture is more than values. The fuller notion of culture is, briefly, this: *Shared beliefs and assumptions* interact with *shared values* and produce *shared norms* that drive *shared patterns of behaviour*. Culture is usually not applied directly to individuals but rather to societies, institutions, companies, professions, groups, families and the like. However, counsellors don't deal immediately and directly with societies but with individuals and small groups of individuals such as families. So, if we apply this basic culture framework to an individual, it goes something like this:

- Over the course of life, individuals develop *assumptions and beliefs* about themselves, other people and the world around them. For instance, Johan, a client suffering from post-traumatic stress disorder (PTSD) stemming from racist gang activity in his Durban neighbourhood and a brutal attack he suffered, has come to believe that the world is a heartless place.

- In addition, *values* – what people prize – are picked up or inculcated along the path of life. Johan, because of dangers he encounters in his community, has come to value or prize personal security.

- Assumptions and beliefs, interacting with values, generate *norms of behaviour*, the 'dos and don'ts' we carry around inside ourselves. For Johan one of these is: 'Don't trust people. You'll get hurt.'

- These norms drive *patterns of internal and external behaviour* and these patterns of behaviour constitute, as it were, the bottom line of personal or individual culture – 'the way I live my life'. For Johan this means being in a state of defensive alert whenever he is with people. It also means not taking chances with people. He tends to be a loner.

Because no individual is an island, personal cultures do not develop in a vacuum. The beliefs, values and norms people develop are greatly influenced by the groups to which they belong. That said, individuals within any given culture can and often do personalise the beliefs, values and norms of the cultures in which they live. People within the same culture tailor these beliefs, values and norms in different ways (Massimini & Delle Fave, 2000). Individuals are not cultural carbon copies. Individuals from the same social culture often differ widely in their personal cultures. Effective helpers come to understand both the cultural background of their clients and the personal culture of each individual client. For instance, Johan has many of the cultural characteristics of his family, his ethnic group, his neighbourhood, his school and his socioeconomic class, but he is not a carbon copy of any of these cultures. His mix is unique.

Because patterns of behaviour constitute the 'bottom line' of culture, a popular definition of societal, institutional and familial culture is 'the way we do things here'. This definition applied to the individual client is 'the way I choose to live my life'. Helpers, too, although influenced by the cultures of the various helping professions, have their personal cultures as helpers, that is, 'the way I do helping'. Inevitably, the helper's social-personal-professional culture interacts with the client's for better or for worse.

The spirit of these principles needs to permeate the discussion of diversity and multiculturalism and its implications for helping practice.

Imagine the case of Sunita, an Indian girl, who is married to Patrick, an IT consultant from Ireland, and who now live together in Wiltshire in the United Kingdom. They come to a marriage counsellor because they are having problems aligning their culturally different belief systems on what marriage should be like. Their helper, Monika, is a Polish-born British citizen whose parents immigrated to the United Kingdom 30 years ago. Many clients come to helpers because they are having difficulties in their relationships with others or because relationship difficulties are part of a larger problem situation. Therefore, understanding clients' different approaches to developing and sustaining relationships is important.

Guisinger and Blatt (1994) put this in a broader multicultural perspective: 'Western psychologies have traditionally given greater importance to self-development than to interpersonal relatedness, stressing the development of autonomy, independence and identity as central factors in the mature personality. In contrast, women, many minority groups and non-Western societies have generally placed greater emphasis on issues of relatedness' (p. 104). Helping Sunita and Patrick, individuals from different cultures, achieve the right balance between the two depends on understanding what the 'right balance' means in any given culture and what 'right balance' means in their personal cultures. Monika's challenge is to put Clark's principles into practice. When the values of different cultures clash (Knapp and VandeCreek, 2007), which set of values is to prevail? Multiculturalism solves some problems and raises others (Johnston, 2015).

Helper competencies related to client diversity

Diversity competence refers to both the knowledge and the skills needed to relate to and communicate effectively with people who differ from us in any significant way. Cross-cultural competence gets most of the attention (Constantine & Sue, 2008; Daniel, Roysircar, Abeles & Boyd, 2004; Fraga, Atkinson & Wampold, 2004; Worthington, Soth-McNett & Moreno, 2007), but other forms of diversity are just as important. Over the years people have drawn up a variety of lists outlining specific cross-cultural competencies (La Roche & Maxie, 2003). Hefty handbooks offering 'the theoretical background, practical knowledge and training strategies needed to achieve multicultural competence' (Pope-Davis, Coleman, Liu & Toporek, 2004) are being published. In addition, there are dozens – or by now hundreds – of highly detailed research studies offering further insights into multicultural competence (see Darcy, Lee & Tracey, 2004). Multicultural counselling competence is usually conceptualised as including awareness of one's own culture, biases and values; knowledge about social and cultural influences on individuals; and skills for applying this knowledge in counselling. But it seems that there is no universal agreement as to the 'right' package of multicultural competencies (Kiài Kitaoka, 2005). Here are a few broad guidelines for developing a style in counselling that honours the best in diversity, including multicultural diversity.

Understand and appreciate diversity   Although clients have in common their humanity, they differ from one another in a whole host of ways – abilities, accent, age, attractiveness, colour, developmental stage, disabilities, economic status, education, ethnicity, fitness, gender, group culture, health, national origin, occupation, personal culture, personality variables, politics, problem type, religion, sexual orientation, social status – to name some of the major categories. Hays (2007, 2009) offers a framework she calls ADDRESSING – an acronym for Age, Developmental and acquired Disabilities, Religion, Ethnicity, Socioeconomic status, Sexual orientation, Indigenous heritage and Gender – to help therapists better recognise, understand and address diversity and multiculturalism in a multidimensional way.

It is worth stating here that this book is aimed at helpers across some multiculturally diverse international regions, including the United Kingdom, South Africa, Europe and parts of the Middle East. Further still, clients within any of those given regions vary enormously in their ethnic, sociocultural, economic, religious, family and sexual orientation backgrounds, and it is an important helper skill to appreciate this.

Bearing this in mind, we all differ from one another in hundreds of ways. And who is to say which differences are key? This presents several challenges for helpers. For one, it is essential that helpers understand clients and their problem situations contextually. For instance, a life-threatening illness might be one kind of reality for a 20-year-old and quite a different reality for an 80-year-old. Homelessness is a complex phenomenon. A homeless client with a history of drug abuse who has dropped out of university is far different from a drifter who hates homeless shelters and resists every effort to get him to go to one.

The Emmaus Movement, an international charity which targets homelessness in 36 countries across Europe, Africa, Asia and America, fully appreciates this. The work that the members do varies depending on the needs of the country that they work in, but all are focused on helping others and avoiding the despair and sense of helplessness associated with homelessness. See further www.emmaus.org.uk.

Although it is true that over time helpers can come to understand a great deal about the characteristics of the populations with whom they work – for instance, they can and should understand the different development tasks and challenges that take place over the life span, and, if they work with the elderly, they can and should grow in their understanding of the challenges, needs, problems and opportunities of the aged – still, it is impossible to know everything about every population. Read a hefty abnormal psychology text or the *DSM-V*. It soon becomes clear that it is impossible to become an expert on every syndrome discussed there. This impossibility becomes even more dramatic when the combinations and permutations of characteristics are taken into consideration. How could a South African, middle-class, highly educated, younger, urban, atheist, female psychologist possibly understand a poor, unemployed, homeless, middle-aged, uneducated, lapsed-but-anxious-Catholic male, born of migrant workers, the father a Mexican, the mother a Polish immigrant? Indeed, how can anybody fully understand anybody else? If the legitimate principles relating to diversity were to be pushed too far, no one would be able to understand and help anybody else.

Challenge whatever diversity blind spots you may have   Because helpers often differ from their clients in many ways, there is often the challenge to avoid diversity-related blind spots that can lead to inept interactions and interventions during the helping process. For instance, a physically attractive and extroverted helper might have blind spots with regard to the social flexibility and self-esteem of a physically unattractive and introverted client. Much of the literature on diversity and multiculturalism targets such blind spots. Counsellors would do well to become more self-aware and to understand their own cultural values and biases. They should also make every effort to understand the worldviews of their clients. Helpers with diversity blind spots are handicapped. Helpers should, as a matter of course, become aware of the key ways in which they differ from their clients and take special care to be sensitive to those differences.

Tailor your interventions in a diversity-sensitive way   Both a practical understanding of diversity and self-knowledge need to be translated into appropriate interventions. The way a Hispanic helper challenges a Hispanic client may be inappropriate for a white client and vice versa. The way a younger helper shares his or her own experience with a younger client might be inappropriate for an older client and vice versa. Client self-disclosure, especially more intimate disclosure, might be relatively easy for a person from one culture, but very difficult for a client from another culture. In this case, interventions that call for intimate self-disclosure may be seen as inappropriate by such a client. If you are a middle-class helper helping a poor client, check your assumptions about poverty carefully. If you are dealing with a client with some disability, do not feel sorry for him or her, but try to see the world from his or her perspective.

Remember that individual or personal cultures within the same social culture differ. When people, however jokingly, say to me, 'I know you Irish', I tend to think that they know little about the Irish and nothing about me. The fact that a client may be from a culture that is more open to self-disclosure does not mean that he or she is open. He or she may be frightened to death by it. In sum, check all your assumptions about groups of people at the door. This gay person may be proud of his or her sexual identity, while another gay person might feel ashamed or guilty. Take clients as the individuals they are.

Work with individuals   The diversity principle is clear: the more helpers understand the broad characteristics, needs and behaviours of the populations with whom they work – the many different groups within South Africa, the different socioeconomic groups within the United Kingdom, the different religions within the Middle East, the different cultures within Europe, diabetics, the elderly, drug addicts, the homeless, people diagnosed with HIV, people terminally ill with cancer, you name it – the better positioned they are to adapt these broad parameters and the counselling process itself to the individuals with whom they work. But, whereas diversity focuses on differences both between and within groups, helpers interact with clients as *individuals*. As Satel (1996) pointed out: 'Psychotherapy can never be about celebrating racial diversity because it is not about groups; it is about individuals and their infinite complexity' (p. A14). Your clients are individuals, not cultures, subcultures or groups. Remember that category traits can destroy understanding as well as facilitate it. In the end, focus on forms of diversity and cultural factors that are relevant to *this* client with *this* set of problems. Otherwise you will get lost in the weeds. Worse, you will lose the client.

Of course, individuals often have group characteristics, but they do not come as members of a homogeneous group because there are no homogeneous groups. One of the principal learnings of social psychology is this: there are as many differences, and sometimes more, within groups as between groups (see Weinrach & Thomas, 1996, pp. 473–474). This middle-class black male is this individual. This poor Asian woman is this person. In a very real sense, a conversation between identical twins is a cross-cultural event because they are different individuals with differences in personal assumptions, beliefs, values, norms, patterns of behaviour and even immune systems (Brenner, 2003). Genetics and group culture account for commonalities among individuals, but personhood and personal cultures emphasise each person's uniqueness. Finally, valuing diversity is not the same as espousing a splintered, antagonistic society in which one's group membership is more important than one's humanity. On the other hand, valuing individuality is not the same as espousing a 'society of one'. This would make counselling and other forms of human interaction impossible.

Take George, a client you are seeing at your new helper job in Johannesburg, for the first time. He is bright, well spoken, gay, black, poorly educated, lower-middle-class, slight of build, indifferent to his Catholic heritage, unemployed, good-looking, honest, and confused because he feels 'defeated'. At his age, 26, life should be opening up, but he feels that it is closing down. He feels trapped. Understand this individual in any way you can, but work with George.

Specific multicultural competencies

The National Centre for Cultural Competence at Georgetown University has adapted a cultural framework from a monograph developed by Cross and his colleagues (1989) for helpers. It is called the Cultural Competence Continuum and has six stages: cultural destructiveness, cultural incapacity, cultural blindness, cultural pre-competence, cultural competence and cultural proficiency. Cultural competence includes 'acceptance and respect for difference, continuing self-assessment, careful attention to the dynamics of difference, continuous expansion of knowledge and resources, and adaptation of services to better meet the needs of diverse populations'. I like the fact that it uses the language of diversity rather than the narrower language of culture.

Here is my adaptation of a list of multicultural competencies outlined and illustrated by Hansen, Pepitone-Arreola-Rockwell and Greene (2000). This is one of dozens of views on cultural competence and was chosen somewhat randomly. I have changed the language, separated what the authors have grouped, grouped what the authors have separated, introduced ideas from different authors, added thoughts of my own, and thereby introduced my own bias. My own bias, of course, is that diversity, especially diversity as represented in personal culture, is the key concept and that culture, important as it certainly is, is one among many key diversity factors. As a counsellor, I must engage the personal culture of each client I see:

- Be aware of your own personal culture, including your cultural heritage, and how you might come across to people who differ from you culturally and in a host of other ways.
- Be aware of the personal-culture biases you may have towards individuals and groups other than your own.
- As a counsellor, be aware of both ways in which you are like any given individual and ways in which you differ. Both can aid or stand in the way of the helping process.
- Come to understand the values, beliefs and worldviews of groups and individuals with whom you work.
- Come to understand how all kinds of diversity, cultural and otherwise, contribute to each client's dynamic makeup.
- Be aware of how sociopolitical influences such as poverty, oppression, stereotyping, stigmatisation, discrimination, prejudice and marginalisation might have affected groups and individuals with whom you are working, no matter what their culture might be. Culture is one among many targets of such abuse. Any sort of diversity – such as age, education and disability – can become targets of these negative behaviours.
- Realise that mainstream Western psychological theory, methods of inquiry, diagnostic categories, assessment procedures and professional practices might not fit other cultures or might need some adaptation. Be aware that some of these factors might not even fit people from Western cultures that well because of within-culture diversity and other diversity factors beyond culture.
- Get to know the basics of family structure and gender roles of groups with whom you work. Remember that there can be great differences within any given culture. Culture does not automatically mean homogeneity.
- Develop an understanding of how people in different cultures understand and deal with illness, including mental illness, and how they feel about help-seeking behaviour. Remember also that people in the same culture have wide differences in this regard because of their personal cultures.
- Establish rapport with and convey empathy to clients in culturally sensitive ways. Extend this sensitivity to the personal cultures of all clients. Be especially careful not to think that people from your own culture are all alike. You are establishing rapport and expressing empathy to individuals, not cultures or other forms of diversity.
- Recognise and appreciate cultural and personal-culture differences in interaction styles and language differences, including non-verbal communication, between yourself and your clients. Remember that people in the same culture communicate and interact in a whole range of ways.
- When clients tell their stories, recognise which issues are culture-specific and which are more related to universal human experience. If a young person is having some problems with his parents, realise that having problems with parents is close to a universal experience. In the words of a Jacques Brel song, 'Who is the child without complaint?' Parents aren't perfect. On the other hand, since parent–child relations differ widely from culture to culture, the specific twists of the problem are often culturally conditioned. But within-culture differences can also play a big role here.
- Design non-biased treatment interventions and plans for clients that factor in key cultural and personal-culture variables.
- Initiate and explore issues of difference between yourself and your clients when this is appropriate. Remember that culture is only one difference. In the end, your interactions with your clients are a personal culture to personal culture affair.
- Assess your own level of cross-cultural and personal-culture competence and strive to improve in all the areas outlined earlier.

In other words, work with your clients the way they are, but don't feel the need to apologise for who you are. Keep it simple. If we add up all the principles relating to cultural competence found in the psychological literature, we begin to get dizzy. Collins, Arthur and Wong-Wylie (2010) outline 13 steps involving over 60 questions in a 'cultural audit' to be used by practitioners. To me this is a step too far.

Stuart (2004), noting that it 'is easy to endorse the principle of culturally sensitive practice, it is often much harder to make it a reality' (p. 3), has written an excellent article on ways of avoiding either overvaluing or undervaluing key cultural-competence behaviours in encounters with clients. When it comes to culture, complexity is the name of the game. He notes that no one is the repository of a 'pure' culture.

Everyone belongs to multiple groups – nation, region, gender, religion, age cohort and occupation, to name a few – each of which exerts a different cultural influence that may be congruent, complementary, or in conflict with any of the others. Every influence is interpreted by each person, who decides whether and, if so, how personal beliefs should respond to each of these influences. Therefore, every individual is a unique blend of many influences. Whereas culture helps to regulate social life, specific beliefs are products of individuals' minds. Because of this complexity, it is *never* safe to infer a person's cultural orientation from knowledge of any group to which he or she is believed to belong.

Stuart's article is an excellent introduction to the cultural-competence issue. He neither overstates nor understates the importance of culture in the helping process. He emphasises the overarching importance of diversity beyond cultural diversity. His 12 practical suggestions for achieving multicultural, and I would add diversity, competence may not be the last word, but they constitute an excellent starting point.

SELF-RESPONSIBILITY AS AN EMPOWERMENT-FOCUSED VALUE

Robert Zoellick (2009), the president of the World Bank (who was succeeded by Jim Yong Kim in July 2012 and subsequently David R. Malpass who began his five-year term in 2019), when reviewing the problems the world faces at the beginning of a new century, mused on how the first half of the 21st century should be defined. He dismissed such terms as 'the Age of Reversal', 'the Age of Intolerance' and 'the Age of Decline'. Instead he opted for a more positive term – 'the Age of Responsibility'. Client responsibility assumes that the client has the power to do what is right for self and others. The second and third goals of helping outlined in Chapter 1 – helping clients develop a problem-management and opportunity-development approach to life and a preference for prevention rather than cure – are both empowerment skills. However, helpers do not empower clients. Rather they help clients discover, acquire, develop and use the power they have at the service of constructive life change – that is, they help clients identify, develop and use resources that will make them more effective agents of change both within the helping sessions themselves and in their everyday lives (Strong, Yoder & Corcoran, 1995).

William Stewart (2013, p. 399) gives us a useful example of this. The client, Paula, has gone to see a helper because she *thinks* she wants a separation from her marriage but isn't quite decided yet. This is her story.

I came to England from the West Indies to train as a nurse at the age of 18. At 21, I married Charles, from Nigeria. We have been married 25 years and have two daughters who are 24 and 22. My religious upbringing and culture calls for and expects obedience to my husband. My professional training, particularly in social work, challenges many of my beliefs and values, and I feel increasingly imprisoned in a marriage which has long since lost its meaning to me. At the same time, the prospect of separation fills me with great fear. I need help with gaining some power and control over my feelings and so enabling me to decide what is the best course of action.

The helper's role is not to advise Paula what to do, but instead to help her identify, develop and use the resources available to her so that she can empower herself to make a constructive life change, whatever that actual change might be.

The opposite of client empowerment is client dependency (Abramson, Cloud, Keese & Keese, 1994; Bornstein & Bowen, 1995), deference (Rennie, 1994) and client oppression (Salmon, 2017; McWhirter, 1996). Because helpers are often experienced by clients as relatively powerful people and because even the most egalitarian and client-centred of helpers do influence clients, it is necessary to come to terms with social influence in the helping process.

Helping as a social-influence process

People influence one another every day in every social setting of life. E. R. Smith and Mackie (2000) consider it one of eight basic principles needed to understand human behaviour. William Crano (2000) suggests that 'social influence research has been, and remains, the defining hallmark of social psychology' (p. 68). Parents influence each other and their children. In turn they are influenced by their children. Teachers influence students and vice versa. Bosses influence subordinates and vice versa. Team leaders influence team members, and members influence both one another and the leader. The world is abuzz with social influence. It could not be otherwise. Rashotte (2006) makes a difference between social influence and power plays:

> *"Social influence is defined as change in an individual's thoughts, feelings, attitudes, or behaviours that results from interaction with another individual or a group. Social influence is distinct from conformity, power, and authority. ... Social influence, however, is the process by which individuals make real changes to their feelings and behaviours as a result of interaction with others who are perceived to be similar, desirable, or expert."* (p. 4426)

Clients tend to dislike social influence they see as a form of power because power too often leads to manipulation and oppression (McCarthy & Frieze, 2002).

Years ago, Strong (1968) wrote an article entitled 'Counselling: An interpersonal influence process' that proved to be very influential. From then on, helping as a social-influence process received a fair amount of attention in the helping research literature, a lot of it stemming from Strong's original article (Dorn, 1986; Heppner & Claiborn, 1989; Heppner & Frazier, 1992; Houser, Feldman, Williams & Fierstien, 1998; W. T. Hoyt, 1996; McCarthy & Frieze, 1999; McNeill & Stolenberg, 1989; Strong, 1991; Tracey, 1991). In 1980, Corrigan and his associates did an extensive review of the research. They opened by saying that 'virtually all human relationships involve persons attempting to influence each other' (p. 395). Forty pages later they end with the curt conclusion that 'counsellors are influential'. But how? And to what purpose? In a recent review of social influence in therapy Perrin and his colleagues (2010) suggest that the, relatively speaking, more recent emphasis on diversity and multiculturalism has done much to reduce helpers' tendency to overly influence their clients and has created a new perspective 'in which the top-down aspect of social influence by therapists towards clients is de-emphasised and a more interactive, reciprocal and collegial influence process is given renewed emphasis' (p. 451).

The skimpy research tells us what we probably already know. Social influence is pervasive in human interactions and, understandably, it pervades the helping professions. The point here is that helpers can influence clients without robbing them of self-responsibility. Even better, they can exercise their trade in such a way that clients are, to use a bit of current business jargon, 'empowered' rather than oppressed, both in the helping sessions themselves and in the social settings of everyday life. There is a growing and quite diverse literature and debate on the role of social justice in the helping professions (Daniels & D'Andrea, 2007; Goodman *et al.*, 2004; Jencius, 2010; Kenny, Horne, Orpinas & Reese, 2009; C. C. Lee, 2007; Ratts, Toporek & Lewis, 2010; Shallcross, 2010; Smith, Reynolds, Rovnak & Thibault, 2010). One of the themes in this literature is the potential power imbalance in helping relationships, with the helper being 'one up', although this supposition, too, has been challenged (Zur, 2008). At any rate, the properly 'empowered' client, that is, a client whose resources for self-regulation and improvement are recognised and appreciated, faces another challenge – the exercise of self-responsibility.

Imagine a continuum. At one end lies 'directing clients' lives' and at the other 'leaving clients completely to their own devices'. Thaler and Sunstein (2008) suggest that the latter is impossible. 'In many situations, some … agent *must* make a choice that will affect the behaviour of other people. There is, in those situations, no way of avoiding nudging in some direction, and whether intended or not, these nudges will affect what people choose' (p. 10). Helping is one of those situations. Somewhere along that continuum is 'helping clients make their own decisions and act on them'. Most forms of helper influence will fall somewhere in between the extremes. Preventing a client from jumping off a bridge moves, understandably, to the controlling end of the continuum. On the other hand, simply accepting and in no way challenging a client's decision to put off dealing with a troubled relationship because he or she is 'not ready' moves towards the other end. As Hare-Mustin and Marecek (1986) noted, there is a tension between the right of clients to determine their own way of managing their lives and the therapist's obligation to help them live more effectively.

Norms for empowerment and self-responsibility

Helpers don't self-righteously 'empower' clients. That would be patronising and condescending. In a classic work, Freire (1970) warned helpers against making helping itself just one more form of oppression for those who are already oppressed. Effective counsellors help clients discover, develop and use the untapped power within themselves. Here, then, is a range of empowerment-based norms, some adapted from the work of Farrelly and Brandsma (1974).

Start with the premise that clients can change if they choose   Clients have more resources for managing problems in living and developing opportunities than they – or sometimes their helpers – assume. The helper's basic attitude should be that clients have the resources both to participate collaboratively in the helping process and to manage their lives more effectively. A belief that clients have it within themselves to pursue what is best for them, given the correct information, is key in the therapeutic empowering relationship. These resources may be blocked in a variety of ways or simply unused. The counsellor's job is to help clients identify, free and cultivate these resources. The counsellor also helps clients assess their resources realistically so that their aspirations do not outstrip their resources.

Do not see clients as victims   Even when clients have been victimised by institutions or individuals, don't see them as helpless victims. The cult of victimhood is already growing too fast in society. Even if victimising circumstances have diminished a client's degree of freedom – the abused spouse's inability to leave a deadly relationship, for example – work with the freedom that is left.

Rowan Bayne in the third edition of *The Counsellor's Handbook* (Bayne, Jinks, Collard & Horton 2008, pp. 65–66) also warns against seeing clients as victims. She makes a useful reference to the 'drama triangle' (Karpman, 1968) and how it is very important that clients who perceive themselves to be in the 'Victim' role are helped to escape this by having their self-esteem and self-sufficiency increased, even if they seem to be resisting and the helper is finding it hard not to see the client as a victim. Otherwise the client stays in their 'Victim' role, even within the helping relationship.

Don't be fooled by appearances   One counsellor trainer in a meeting with his colleagues dismissed a reserved, self-deprecating trainee with the words, 'She'll never make it. She's more like a client than a trainee.' Fortunately, his colleagues did not work from the same assumption. The woman went on to become one of the programme's best students. She was accepted as an intern at a prestigious mental-health centre and was hired by the centre after graduation.

Share the helping process with clients   Both implicit and explicit contracts govern the transactions that take place between people in a wide variety of situations, including marriage (in which some but by no means all of the provisions of the contract are explicit) and friendship (in which the provisions are usually implicit). If helping is to be a collaborative venture, then both parties must understand what their responsibilities are. Perhaps the term 'working charter' is better than 'contract'. It avoids the legal implications of the latter term and connotes a cooperative venture.

To achieve these objectives, the working charter should include, generically, the issues covered in Chapters 1, 2 and 7 – that is, (1) the nature and goals of the helping process, (2) an overview of the helping approach together with some idea of the techniques to be used, (3) a sense of the flexibility built into the process, (4) how this process will help clients achieve their goals, (5) relevant information about yourself and your background, (6) how the relationship is to be structured and the kinds of responsibilities both you and the client will have, (7) the values that will drive the helping process and (8) procedural issues. 'Procedural issues' refers to the nuts and bolts of the helping process, such things as where sessions will be held and how long they will last. Procedural limitations should also be discussed – for instance, ground rules about whether the client can contact the helper between sessions. Ordinarily we won't contact each other between sessions, unless there is some kind of emergency or we prearrange it for a particular purpose. Manthei and Miller (2000) have written a practical book for clients on the elements of a working charter. There is some evidence that charters also work with the seriously mentally ill (Heinssen, Levendusky & Hunter, 1995).

Helping should not be a 'black box' for clients. They have a right to know what they are getting into (Heinssen, 1994; Heinssen, Levendusky & Hunter, 1995; Hunter, 1995; Manthei & Miller, 2000). How to clue clients into the helping process is another matter. Helpers can simply explain what helping is all about. A simple pamphlet outlining the stages and steps of the helping process can be of great help, provided that it is in language that clients can readily understand. Just what kind of detail will help will differ from client to client. Obviously, clients should not be overwhelmed by distracting detail from the beginning. Nor should highly distressed clients be told to contain their anxiety until helpers teach them the helping process model. Rather, the details of the process can be shared over a number of sessions. There is no one right way. Reis and Brown (2006) created a short video for clients entering therapy. The video introduces the overall goals of therapy and shows clients how they might best benefit from it. So use your imagination. In my opinion, however, clients should be told as much about the helping process as they can reasonably assimilate.

Help clients see counselling sessions as work sessions Helping is about client-enhancing change and empowerment. Therefore, counselling sessions deal with exploring the need for change, determining the kind of change needed, creating programmes of constructive change, engaging in change 'pilot projects' and finding ways of dealing with obstacles to change. This may entail setting agendas within sessions, goals and homework tasks that clients would need to engage in. This is work, pure and simple. This search for, and implementation of, solutions can be arduous, even agonising, but it can also be deeply satisfying, even exhilarating. Helping clients develop the 'work ethic' that makes them partners in the helping process can be one of the helper's most formidable challenges. Some helpers go so far as to cancel counselling sessions until the client is 'ready to work'. Helping clients discover incentives to work is, of course, less dramatic and hard work in itself.

Become a coach or consultant to clients Helpers can see themselves as coaches or 'expert consultants' (Mee-Lee, McLellan & Miller, 2010, p. 403) engaged by clients (or third parties) to help them face problems in living more effectively. Coaches and consultants in the business world adopt a variety of roles. They listen, observe, collect data, report observations, teach, train, provide support, challenge, advise, offer suggestions and even become advocates for certain positions. But the responsibility for running the business remains with those who hire the consultant. Therefore, even though some of the activities of the coaches or consultant can be seen as quite challenging, the decisions are still made by managers. Coaching and consulting, then, are social-influence processes, but collaborative ones that do not rob managers of the responsibilities that belong to them. In this respect, it is a useful analogy to helping. The best clients, like the best managers, learn how to use their coaches or consultants to add value in managing problems and developing opportunities.

Accept helping as a natural, two-way influence process Tyler, Pargament and Gatz (1983) moved a step beyond the consultant role in what they called the 'resource collaborator role'. Seeing both helper and client as people with defects, they focused on the give-and-take that should characterise the helping process. In their view, either client or helper can approach the other to originate the helping process. The two have equal status in defining the terms of the relationship, in originating actions within it and in evaluating both outcomes and the relationship itself. In the best case, positive change occurs in both parties.

Helping is a two-way street. Clients and therapists change one another in the helping process. Even a cursory glance at helping reveals that clients can affect helpers in many ways. For instance, Wei-Lian has to correct Timothy, his counsellor, a number of times when Timothy tries to share his understanding of what Wei-Lian has said. For instance, at one point, when Timothy says, 'So you don't like the way your father forces his opinions on you', Wei-Lian replies, 'No, my father is my father and I must always respect him. I need to listen to his wisdom.' The problem is that Timothy has been inadvertently basing some of his responses on his own cultural assumptions rather than on Wei-Lian's. When Timothy finally realises what he is doing, he says to Wei-Lian, 'When I talk with you, I need to be more of a learner. I'm coming to realise that Chinese culture is quite different from mine. I need your help.'

Focus on learning instead of helping   Although many see helping as an education process, it is probably better characterised as a learning process. Effective counselling helps clients get on a learning track. Both the helping sessions themselves and the time between sessions involve learning, unlearning and relearning. Howell (1982) gave us a good description of learning when he said that 'learning is incorporated into living to the extent that viable options are increased' (p. 14). In the helping process, learning takes place when options that add value to life are opened up, seized and acted on. If the collaboration between helpers and clients is successful, clients learn in very practical ways. They have more 'degrees of freedom' in their lives as they open up options and take advantage of them.

Do not see clients as overly fragile   Neither pampering nor brutalising clients serves their best interests. However, many clients are less fragile than helpers make them out to be. Helpers who constantly see clients as fragile may well be acting in a self-protective way. Driscoll (1984) noted that early in the helping process, too many helpers shy away from doing much more than listening. The natural deference many clients display early in the helping process (Rennie, 1994) – including their fear of criticising the therapist, understanding the therapist's frame of reference, meeting the perceived expectations of the therapist and showing indebtedness to the therapist – can send the wrong message to helpers. Clients early on may be fearful of making some kind of irretrievable error. This does not mean that they are fragile. Reasonable caution on your part is appropriate, but you can easily become overly cautious. Driscoll suggested that helpers intervene more right from the beginning – for instance, by reasonably challenging the way clients think and act and by getting them to begin to outline what they want and are willing to work for.

There are cultural differences in the ways people approach self-responsibility. Consider Taiwanese university students. They tend to see help-seeking as a sign of weakness, even as a cause for shame; informal is more acceptable than formal help; the situation has to be quite serious before they think of seeking help; and they are reluctant to seek help from strangers (Lin, 2002). Typical convictions about dealing with problem situations are found in such sayings as 'God helps people who help themselves' and 'Solve problems on my own' (p. 51). It is also important to note that this kind of self-reliance differs greatly from the kind of individualism found in Western societies. You will find different convictions about self-responsibility in other cultures. In the end, of course, what matters is this client's approach to self-responsibility.

Conscientiousness

Another rich source for understanding and developing self-responsibility is the growing literature on conscientiousness (Bogg & Roberts, 2004; Friedman & Martin, 2011; Hill *et al.*, 2011; B. W. Roberts, Walton & Bogg, 2005). '*Conscientiousness* refers to individual differences in the propensity to follow socially prescribed norms for impulse control, to be task- and goal-oriented, to be planful, to delay gratification, and to follow norms and rules' (Bogg & Roberts, 2004, p. 887). While some would see this as a definition of a dull person, others would relate it to social-emotional intelligence and maturity. We do not know whether conscientiousness as a trait is genetically and/or neurologically determined, whether it is the product of personal and social development, or whether it can be acquired and fostered through personal choice and effort. But all the research shows that conscientious people live longer and healthier lives. And I am sure that further research will show other personal and social benefits. Of course, there is *that* question: is conscientiousness genetic, environmental or simply a choice? From what I read, probably some of each.

Self-responsibility, self-regulation, self-control

Self-regulation or self-control (Hoyle, 2010) is a key component of self-responsibility, although one wonders how much of it gets into everyday life. Baumeister and his colleagues (2006) define self-regulation as 'a highly adaptive, distinctively human trait that enables people to override and alter their responses, including changing themselves so as to live up to social and other standards' (p. 1773). Yet despite the personal and social value of self-control, most of us have been exposed to people, including or especially children, with seemingly little or no self-control. It can be maddening. An endless number of cases can be found in the popular literature. In one controversial book, Druckerman (2012) suggests that French children are better behaved than American children because French parents do not indulge their children as much. Indeed, self-indulgence or being indulged by others often leads to trouble. When these behaviours become part of the culture, society is in trouble.

If we are honest with ourselves, our own lack of self-control at times gets us into trouble. So it should not be surprising to find that lack of self-regulation and self-control is often at the heart of the problem situations clients share with us. While self-indulgence and its sibling self-absorption (McKenzie & Hoyle, 2008) can be damaging, self-control and self-regulation can be learned. Baumeister and his colleagues (2006) found evidence that efforts to maintain self-control are psychologically costly ('ego depletion'), but that regular exercises in self-regulation can produce improvements in self-regulation akin to the strengthening of a muscle. Van Dellen, Hoyle and Miller (2012) make a distinction between self-regulation and self-control. They present and test a theory in which self-control is distinguished from broader acts of self-regulation when it is both effortful and conscious. So self-control for them is a subset of self-regulation marked by effort and consciousness. Completing a self-regulatory task depleted resources only when it required sustained effort. But they, too, contend that self-control can be learned. Van Dellen and Hoyle (2010) found evidence that self-control can be 'contagious'. Watching someone exercise self-control makes it easier to exercise self-control later. Even thinking about a friend with good self-control helps people stay in control. Helping clients find ways of staying in control is more useful than merely getting them to recognise habits of self-indulgence and challenging these habits.

The point of all of this is that many of your clients will have issues with self-regulation and self-control. If they are to take responsibility for themselves – if they are to get into and stay in the driver's seat – they may need your help in struggling with self-control.

A BIAS FOR ACTION AS AN OUTCOME-FOCUSED VALUE

If life-enhancing outcomes are central to helping, then the behaviour that leads to these outcomes is also central. In the end, clients must engage, directly or indirectly, in the kind of internal (thinking) and external (action) behaviour that creates these outcomes.

The need for behavioural activation

Behavioural activation (BA), sometimes called 'activity scheduling', is a type of treatment for depression that adheres to this principle. It was devised years ago (Jacobson *et al.*, 1996), and has recently experienced a renaissance of sorts (Coffman *et al.*, 2007; Cuijpers, van Straten & Warmerdam, 2007; Hopko *et al.*, 2003; Hunnicutt-Ferguson, Hoxha & Gollan, 2012; Lazzari, Egan & Rees, 2011; Moss *et al.*, 2012). I'll explain the 'of sorts' part shortly. BA targets both inertia and avoidance. BA 'is based on the premise that increased activity and the resulting contact with positive consequences is sufficient for the reduction of depressive symptoms and the subsequent increase of positive thoughts and feelings' (Hopko *et al.*, 2003, p. 461).

BA involves helping clients monitor mood and daily activities, identifying activities that they experience as rewarding, identifying and scheduling pleasant ideas, increasing the number of pleasant activities, increasing positive interactions with the environment, moving from easier to more difficult behaviours and tasks, and rewarding progress and reviewing and maintaining gains. In a word, helping clients move into *action*, beyond inertia, beyond avoidance. 'Activity scheduling is an attractive treatment for depression, not only because it is relatively uncomplicated, time-efficient and does not require complex skills from patients or therapist, but also because this meta-analysis found clear indications that it is effective' (Cuijpers, van Straten & Warmerdam, 2007, p. 318). I referred to a renaissance 'of sorts' earlier. A real renaissance would involve a greater emphasis on the need for clients to act on their own behalf with respect to *all* problem situations. BA is not limited to depression. An action component is needed in all problem-management situations.

The overall goal of helping clients become more effective in problem management and opportunity development was mentioned in Chapter 1. That means helping them become more effective 'agents' in the helping process and in their daily lives – doers rather than mere reactors, preventers rather than fixers, initiators rather than followers.

> Lawrence was liked by his superiors for two reasons. First, he was competent – he got things done. Second, he did whatever they wanted him to do. They moved him from job to job when it suited them. He never complained. However, as he matured and began to think more of his future, he realised that there was a great deal of truth in the adage, 'If you're not in charge of your own career, no one is.' After a session with a career counsellor, he outlined the kind of career he wanted and presented it to his superiors. He pointed out to them how this would serve both the company's interests and his own. At first they were taken aback by Lawrence's assertiveness, but then they agreed. Later, when they seemed to be side-tracking him, he stood up for his rights. Assertiveness was his bias for action.

The doer is more likely to pursue 'stretch' rather than merely adaptive goals in managing problems. The doer is also more likely to move beyond problem management to opportunity development. Bandura (1991, 2006), focusing on 'human agency', suggests that the helping professions do not emphasise 'personal agency' enough. Angus and Kagan (2007) link empathy and action. They say that when helpers respond with empathy to clients who talk about what they have done to bring about positive change in their lives, they encourage clients' sense of personal agency. They call this 'empathic validation' (p. 373).

Action and discretionary change

If clients are to become more effective agents in their lives, they need to understand the difference between discretionary and non-discretionary change. Non-discretionary change is mandated change. If the courts say to a divorced man negotiating visiting rights with his children, 'You can't have visiting rights unless you stop drinking', then the change is non-discretionary. There will be no visiting rights without the change. In contrast, a man and wife having difficulties with their marriage are not under the gun to change the current pattern. Change here is discretionary. 'IF you want a more productive relationship, THEN you must change in the following ways.'

The fact of discretionary change is central to mediocrity. If we don't have to change, very often we don't. We need merely to review the track record of our New Year's resolutions. Unfortunately, in helping situations, clients often see change as discretionary. They may talk about it as if it were non-discretionary, but deep down a great deal of 'I don't really have to change' pervades the helping process. 'Other people should change; the world should change. But I don't have to.' This is not cynical. It's the way things are. The sad track record of discretionary change is not meant to discourage you but to make you more realistic about the challenges you face as a helper and about the challenges you help your clients face.

A pragmatic bias towards client action on your part – rather than merely talking about action – is a cardinal value. Effective helpers tend to be active with clients and see no particular value in mere listening and nodding. They engage clients in a dialogue. During that dialogue, they constantly ask themselves, 'What can I do to raise the probability that this client will act on his or her own behalf intelligently and prudently?' I know a man who years ago went 'into therapy' (as 'into another world') because, among other things, he was indecisive. Over the years he became engaged several times to different women and each time broke it off. So much for decisiveness.

Real-life focus

If clients are to make progress, they must 'do better' in their day-to-day lives. The focus of helping, then, is not narrowly on the helping sessions and client–helper interactions themselves, but on clients managing their day-to-day lives more effectively. A friend of mine in his early days as a helper exulted in the 'solid relationship' he was building with a client until in the third interview she stopped, stared at him, and said, 'You're really filled with yourself, aren't you? But, you know, we're not getting anywhere.' He had become so lost in relationship building that he forgot about the client's pressing everyday concerns. In working with difficult clients, Hanna (2002) has developed a model of change that highlights the importance of clients as 'active agents' (p. 11). The behaviourist view of human beings, he suggests, has overemphasised mechanistic and deterministic factors in human behaviour. This view short-changes clients. As Bohart and Tallman (1999) have put it, 'Clients in varying degrees can solve their own problems, come up with their own ideas, and actively contribute to the therapy process' (p. xiv). The view taken here is that they not only can, but they must.

SHADOW-SIDE REALITIES IN THE HELPING RELATIONSHIP

All sorts of things can go wrong in the helper–client relationship, just as they can go wrong in any relationship. Here is a sample.

Helpers' and clients' flaws

Helping relationships often enough fall short of the ideals outlined in this chapter. Helpers' motives are not always as pure as they are portrayed in this book. For instance, helpers find clients attractive or unattractive. There is nothing wrong with this. However, they must be able to manage closeness in therapy in a way that furthers the helping process (R. S. Schwartz, 1993). They must deal with both positive and negative feelings towards clients lest they end up doing silly things. They may have to fight the tendency to be less challenging with attractive clients or not to listen carefully to unattractive clients. Some helpers are not very committed even though they are in a profession in which success demands a high degree of commitment. Finally, although, like other people, helpers get into trouble, often they don't use the tools of their trade to get themselves out of trouble – 'Don't do as I do; do as I say.'

Clients, too, have their tendencies. Some have unrealistic expectations of counselling (Tinsley, Bowman & Barich, 1993), whereas others trip over their own distorted views of their helpers. In such cases, helpers have to manage both expectations and the relationship. Clients often enough play games with themselves, their helpers and the helping process. Helpers sometimes seduce their clients and clients seduce their helpers, although not necessarily sexually. Hidden agendas are pursued by both helper and client. The helping relationship itself can end up as a conspiracy to do nothing. Much has been written on the power dynamic within therapy that can cause unintentional harm; however, it is still an under-explored area (Zur, 2015; Bystedt *et al.*, 2014).

Neither helpers nor clients are usually heroic figures. They are human beings with all-too-human tendencies. We have begun to talk openly about human defects, our own and our clients', without descending into cynicism. Needleman (2007) asks why people repeatedly violate their most deeply held values and beliefs. Hollis (2007) asks why good people do bad things and explores the darker side of our humanity as he looks for answers. Ford (2008) asks the same question and suggests ways of stopping being our own worst enemies. Martinez-Lewi (2008) discusses ways of freeing ourselves from the narcissism of our lives. We do not have to look far – sometimes this side of the end of our nose – to find the dark side of humanity. The trick is being neither naive nor cynical about yourself or your clients.

Incompetent helpers

Some helpers are competent; others are not. Incompetent helpers pass themselves off as professionals and work outside their competencies. There are good and bad helpers, just as there are good and bad teachers, good and bad social workers, good and bad managers, good and bad police officers, good and bad ministers and so forth. Helpers who underestimate the severity of clients' problems, experience interpersonal difficulties with clients, use poor techniques, overuse any given technique or disagree with clients over helping methodology can make things worse rather than better. Helpers working outside their areas of competencies, or who are not fit to practise in their field, risk causing harm to clients. Regulatory bodies within each helper's profession will have a policy on professional performance standards and a procedure if a client makes a complaint about the helper.

Clients, aided and abetted by their helpers, work on the wrong issues. Helpers fail to keep up with developments in the profession. They end up using helping methods that are not likely to benefit their clients. Helping is continued even though it is going nowhere. The list goes on. And therefore, it should not come as a surprise that there is evidence that therapy sometimes not only does not help but also actually makes things worse. That is, some helping leads to negative outcomes.

Even the competent and committed have their lapses. As noted by Luborsky and his associates (1986):

- There are considerable differences between therapists in their average success rates.
- There is considerable variability in outcome within the caseload of individual therapists.
- Variations in success rates typically have more to do with the therapist than with the type of treatment.

Although helping can and most often does work, there is plenty of evidence that ineffective helping also abounds. Helping is a potentially powerful process that is all too easy to mismanage. It is no secret that because of inept helpers, some clients get worse from treatment. Helping is not neutral; it is 'for better or for worse'. The late Albert Ellis (1984) claimed that inept helpers are either ineffective or inefficient. Even though the inefficient may ultimately help their clients, they use 'methods that are often distinctly inept and that consequently lead these clients to achieve weak and unlasting results, frequently at the expense of enormous amounts of wasted time and money' (p. 24). Because studies on the efficacy of counselling and psychotherapy do not usually make a distinction between high-level and low-level helpers, and because the research on deterioration effects in therapy suggests that there are a large number of low-level or inadequate helpers, the negative results found in many studies are predictable. Finally, comparatively little has been written about how helpers deal with failures in therapy (Stewart, Chambless & Chambless, 2008).

We now move on to Part II (communication and relationship-building skills) and Part III (the problem-management/opportunity-development framework). The spirit and themes of Chapters 1 and 2 will pervade these sections.

PART II
THE THERAPEUTIC DIALOGUE: COMMUNICATION AND RELATIONSHIP-BUILDING SKILLS

Given the importance of the therapeutic relationship and alliance highlighted in Chapters 1 and 2, the communication and relationship-building skills that helpers need to engage in the behaviours outlined in Chapter 2 are described and illustrated in Part II. These skills are among the key ingredients of successful helping. Moreover, therapists with good communication skills can help clients who have lower levels of these skills engage more collaboratively and effectively in the helping process.

Chapter 3 highlights and illustrates the importance of building an empathic presence and ensuring that you engage in therapeutic *dialogue* together with the client, including the essential communication skills of *tuning in*, *attending* and *active listening*.

Chapter 4 outlines and illustrates how *probing and summarising* can help clients engage more fully in the helping process.

Chapter 5 considers the role of *challenge* and *client-self challenge* in therapy. The importance of helping clients move beyond blind spots and develop *new perspectives* that serve life-enhancing outcomes is highlighted. Chapter 6 focuses on how the helper can self-challenge themselves, and to overcome client resistance.

CHAPTER 3
EMPATHIC PRESENCE AND RESPONDING – BUILDING A MUTUAL UNDERSTANDING

Chapter Contents

- Becoming Competent and Confident in Responding with Empathy: Principles and Guidelines

- Tactics for Responding with Empathy

- A Case: Tumi, the Client and Carlos, the Helper

- The Shadow Side of Responding

THE IMPORTANCE OF COMMUNICATION SKILLS IN HELPING

There is a great deal of research on the importance of the helping relationship together with, as we have seen, suggestions on how to develop and maintain a solid helping relationship. There does seem to be a taken-for-granted attitude towards effective communication in many societies, including our own. Over the years the following mini-drama has played out when I address large audiences. I say, 'Given the importance of good relationships in almost every facet of society, how important is it for your children to develop a solid set of communication and relationship-building skills? Rate this on a range from 1 through 100.' Inevitably the scores are near (and sometimes surpassing!) 100. Then I say, 'Here's my next question. How do we and our society in general make sure that our children develop these skills?' Then the humming and hawing begins. Ultimately, the answer seems to be, 'We more or less leave it to chance'.

And so a solid set of communication skills on the part of helpers constitutes a key ingredient to successful helping. However, the communication skills outlined in these chapters are not special skills peculiar to helping. Rather, they are extensions of the kinds of skills all of us need in our everyday interpersonal transactions (Adler, Proctor & Towne, 2007; Canary, Cody & Manusov, 2008; DeVito, 2011, 2013; West & Turner, 2009; Wood, 2009). Ideally, helpers-to-be would enter training programmes with this basic set of interpersonal communication skills in place, and training would simply help them build on and adapt the skills to the helping process. Unfortunately, this is often not the case. Training or retraining in communication skills is the norm when it comes to 'therapeutic communication' (Knapp, 2007). These communication skills need to become 'second nature' to helpers. People like Carl Rogers (1951, 1957, 1965), Bob Carkhuff (1987) and Allen Ivey (Ivey, Ivey, Zalaquett & Quirk, 2012), to name a few, have been trailblazers in developing and humanising communication skills and integrating them into advances in the helping process. Their influence is seen throughout this book.

The chapters in Part II outline and illustrate the following skills: attending (empathic presence), listening, understanding what clients are thinking and saying about themselves, responding to clients with understanding, helping clients explore their concerns more fully, helping them to stay focused, and helping clients challenge themselves to develop new perspectives on their problem situations and unused opportunities. The manual (Egan & Reese, 2018) that accompanies this text, *Exercises in Helping Skills*, provides opportunities for extensive practice in all the communication skills discussed in these chapters.

It would be helpful if clients had the communication skills outlined here and the ability to weave them into constructive dialogues with their helpers. Once more, this is often not the case. In fact, many clients are in trouble precisely because they do not know how to establish and maintain healthy interpersonal relationships which are nourished by effective communication. In the following chapters, you will find suggestions for helping clients with poor communication skills engage in dialogue.

DIALOGUE-FOCUSED INTERACTIONS WITH CLIENTS

Interpersonal communication competence means not only being good at the individual communication skills outlined in this and following chapters, but also marshalling them at the service of dialogue (Paré & Lysack, 2004; Seikkula & Trimble, 2005). There are four requirements for true dialogue (Egan, 2013).

Turn taking

Dialogue is interactive. You talk, then I talk. In counselling this means that, generally speaking, monologues on the part of either client or helper don't add value. Endless stories on the part of clients and equally endless lectures on the part of helpers have no place in counselling. Monologues breed isolation. Dialogue demands engagement. Turn taking opens up the possibility for mutual learning. Helpers learn about their clients and base their interventions on what they come to understand through the give-and-take of the dialogue. Clients come to understand themselves and their concerns more fully and learn how to face up to their problems and unused opportunities.

Connecting

Have you ever witnessed (or engaged in) a conversation when the two parties keep talking past each other? Alternating monologues have no place in therapy. Ideally, what either client or helper says in the conversation should be connected in some way to what the other has said. The helper's responses should connect to the client's remarks and, ideally, clients should connect with what their helpers are saying. That is, helper and client need to engage each other if their working alliance is to be productive. They need to actively listen to one another and respond in terms of what they think the other person is saying. Later in Part II we will demonstrate what you can do to help clients who are not up to speed in their ability to connect.

Mutual influencing

In true dialogue the parties are open to being influenced by what the other person has to say. This echoes the social-influence dimension of counselling discussed in Chapter 2. Helpers influence their clients, and open-minded helpers learn from and are influenced by their clients. In fact, it is impossible for clients to remain in the driver's seat without influencing their helpers. In very real ways clients and helpers continually challenge one another to be open to new learning. Fowers and Davidov (2006, 2007) suggest that the virtue of 'openness to the other' and dialogue keep multicultural diversity and other forms of diversity from descending into chaos. The pairing of the two keeps both client and helper on track.

Co-creating outcomes

Good dialogue and trust lead to outcomes that benefit both parties. As we have seen, counselling is about results, accomplishments and outcomes. The job of the counsellor is neither to tell clients what to do nor merely to leave them to their own devices. The counsellor's job is to act as a catalyst for the kind of problem-managing dialogue that helps clients find their own answers. In true dialogue, neither party should know exactly what the outcome will be. If you know what you're going to tell a client or if the client has already made up his or her mind what he or she is going to say and do, the two of you may well have a conversation, but it is probably not a dialogue. Only clients can change themselves. Helpers influence and facilitate change through effective dialogue. Co-creation of outcomes still leaves clients 'in the driver's seat'.

Although individual communication skills are a necessary part of communication competence, dialogue together with the collaboration it fosters is the integrating mechanism. This means dialogue informed by and permeated with the values outlined in Chapter 2. Effective dialogue is both respectful and empathic, helps clients better understand and own their problems, and helps them engage in problem-managing change. Exploitative dialogue is a contradiction in terms.

VISIBLY TUNING IN: THE IMPORTANCE OF EMPATHIC PRESENCE

During some of the more dramatic moments of life, simply being with another person is extremely important. If a friend of yours is in hospital, just your being there can make a difference, even if conversation is impossible. Similarly, being with a friend who has just lost his wife can be very comforting to him, even if little is said. Your empathic presence is comforting. Most people appreciate it when others listen and pay attention to them. By the same token, being ignored is often painful: the averted face is too often a sign of the averted heart. Given how sensitive most of us are to others' attention or inattention, it is paradoxical how insensitive we can be at times about paying attention to others.

Helping and other deep interpersonal transactions demand a certain robustness or intensity of presence. Geller and Greenberg (2012) see therapeutic presence as a 'foundational therapeutic stance that supports deep listening and understanding of the client in the moment'. Attunement and involvement with clients is an essential ingredient to the therapeutic relationship (Erskine, 2015). Visibly tuning in to others contributes to this presence. It is an expression of empathy that tells clients that you are with them, and it puts you in a position to listen carefully to their concerns. Your attention can be manifested in both physical and psychological ways. Because non-verbal behaviour can play an important part in empathic communication, let's start by briefly exploring non-verbal behaviour as a channel of communication.

Non-verbal behaviour as a channel of communication

Some people limit their interpersonal effectiveness by failing to recognise and read the non-verbal messages of others and/or fail to use non-verbal behaviour to send or modulate messages to others (Manusov, 2005; Manusov & Patterson, 2006). For instance, Terrence does not see the signs of boredom in others when he engages in endless monologues. And Cynthia wonders why others remain unaffected by what she says, but she does not use non-verbal behaviour to give zest to her messages. Over the years both researchers and practitioners have come to appreciate the importance of non-verbal behaviour both in daily life (Burgoon, Guerrero & Floyd, 2009; Knapp & Hall, 2010; Pease & Pease, 2006) and in counselling (Mehrabian, 1972, 1981; Philippot, Feldman & Coats, 2003; Richmond, McCroskey & Hickson, 2012; Weitz, 1974). Riggio and Feldman (2005) have edited a book that looks at non-verbal behaviour in a wide variety of settings. And there is the *Journal of Nonverbal Behavior* with theory- and research-based articles in all areas of non-verbal behaviour. Although the literature dealing with non-verbal behaviour in all the settings of life is vast, only a few key principles are outlined here to get you started. Highlen and Hill (1984) pointed out why the understanding and use of non-verbal behaviour is important. Non-verbal behaviours regulate conversations, communicate emotions, modify verbal messages, provide important messages about the helping relationship, give insights into self-perceptions and provide clues when clients (or counsellors) are not saying what they are thinking. This area has taken on even more importance because of the multicultural nature of helping. David Givens (2008) of the Center for Nonverbal Studies has published an online non-verbal dictionary of gestures, signs and body language cues. To assume that non-verbal behaviours mean the same thing across cultures is not only wrong but sometimes dangerous as well. Watch what you do with your hands in different cultures.

The face and body are extremely communicative. We know from experience that even when people are together in silence, the atmosphere can be filled with messages. Sometimes clients' facial expressions, bodily motions, voice quality and physiological responses communicate more than their words do. The following factors, on the part of both helpers and clients, play an important role in the therapeutic dialogue:

- Bodily behaviour, such as posture, body movements and gestures
- Eye behaviour, such as eye contact, staring, eye movement
- Facial expressions, such as smiles, frowns, raised eyebrows and twisted lips
- Voice-related behaviour, such as tone of voice, pitch, volume, intensity, inflection, spacing of words, emphases, pauses, silences and fluency
- Observable autonomic physiological responses, such as quickened breathing, blushing, paleness and pupil dilation

- Physical characteristics, such as fitness, height, weight and complexion
- Space, that is, how close or far a person chooses to be during a conversation
- General appearance, such as grooming and dress.

People constantly 'speak' to one another through their non-verbal behaviour. Even not communicating is communication in itself – think about it. Have you experienced the 'silent treatment' from someone at work? Or perhaps someone's words and non-verbal communication don't seem to match. Effective helpers learn this 'language' and how to use it effectively in their interactions with their clients. They also learn how to 'read' relevant messages embedded in the non-verbal behaviour of their clients. Clients' non-verbal behaviour will be addressed later in this chapter.

Helpers' non-verbal behaviour Before you begin interpreting the non-verbal behaviour of your clients, take a look at yourself. You speak to your clients through all the non-verbal categories outlined earlier. At times your non-verbal behaviour is as important as, or even more important than, your words. Your non-verbal behaviour influences clients for better or for worse. Clients read in your non-verbal behaviour cues that indicate the quality of your presence to them and may even 'test' your reaction to a smaller issue before feeling confident in disclosing something they find more difficult. Attentive presence can invite or encourage them to trust you, open up and explore the significant dimensions of their problem situations. Half-hearted presence can promote distrust and lead to clients' reluctance to reveal themselves to you. Clients may misinterpret your non-verbal behaviour. For instance, you may be comfortable with the space between you and your client, but it is too close for the client. Or remaining silent might in your mind mean giving a client time to think and reflect on what has been said, but the client might feel embarrassed or pressurised into saying something. Part of listening, then, is being sensitive to clients' reactions to your non-verbal behaviour.

Effective helpers are mindful of, but not preoccupied with, the stream of non-verbal messages they send to clients. Reading your own bodily reactions is an important first step. For instance, if you feel your muscles tensing as the client talks to you, you can say to yourself, 'I'm getting anxious here. What's going on? And what non-verbal messages indicating my discomfort am I sending to the client?' Again, you probably would not use these words. Rather you read the signals your body is sending you without letting them distract you from your client.

You can also use your body to censor instinctive or impulsive messages that you feel are inappropriate. For instance, if the client says something that instinctively angers you, you can control the external expression of the anger (for instance, a sour look) in order to give yourself time to reflect. Such self-control is not phoney because your respect for your client takes precedence over your instinctive reactions. Not dumping your annoyance or anger on your clients through non-verbal behaviour is not the same as denying it. Becoming aware of it is the first step in dealing with it.

In a more positive vein, you can 'punctuate' what you say with non-verbal messages. For instance, Sophia is especially attentive when Jacomina talks about actions she could take to do something about her problem situation. She leans forward, smiles, nods and says 'uh-huh'. She uses non-verbal behaviour to reinforce, let's say, Jacomina's intention to act constructively in renewing contact with a couple of key friends.

On the other hand, don't become preoccupied with your body and the qualities of your voice as a source of communication. Rather, learn to use your body instinctively as a means of communication. Being aware of and at home with non-verbal communication can reflect an inner peace with yourself, the helping process and your clients. Your non-verbal behaviour should enhance rather than stand in the way of your working alliance with your clients.

Although the skills of visibly tuning in can be learned, they will be phoney if they are not driven by the attitudes and values such as respect and empathy discussed in Chapter 2. Your mindset – what's in your heart – is as important as your visible presence. If you are not actively interested in the welfare of your client or if you resent working with a client, subtle or not-so-subtle non-verbal clues will colour your behaviour. I once mentioned to a doctor my concerns about an invasive diagnostic procedure he intended to use. The doctor said the right words to reassure me, but his physical presence and the way he rushed his words said, 'I've heard this dozens of times. I really don't have time for your concerns. Let's get on with this.' His words were right but the real message was in the non-verbal messages that accompanied his words.

Guidelines for visibly tuning in to clients There are certain key non-verbal skills you can use to visibly tune in to clients. Some of these skills can be summarised in the acronym SOLER. Because communication skills are particularly sensitive to cultural differences, care should be taken in adapting what follows to different cultures. What follows is only a framework.

S: Face the client *Squarely*. That is, adopt a posture that indicates involvement. In Western culture, facing another person squarely is often considered a basic posture of involvement. It usually says, 'I'm here with you; I'm available to you.' Turning your body away from another person while you talk to him or her can lessen your degree of contact with that person. Even when people are seated in a circle, they usually try in some way to turn towards the individuals to whom they are speaking. The word 'squarely' here should not be taken too literally. 'Squarely' is not a military term. The point is that your bodily orientation should convey the message that you are involved with the client. If, for any reason, facing the person squarely is too threatening, an angled position may be more helpful. The point is not inches and angles but the quality of your presence. Your body sends out messages whether you like it or not. Make them congruent with what you are trying to do.

O: Adopt an *Open* posture. Crossed arms and crossed legs can be signs of lessened involvement with or availability to others. An open posture can be a sign that you're open to the client and to what he or she has to say. In Western culture, an open posture is generally seen as a non-defensive posture. Again, the word 'open' can be taken literally or metaphorically. If your legs are crossed, this does not mean that you are not involved with the client. But it is important to ask yourself, 'To what degree does my present posture communicate openness and availability to the client?' If you are empathic and open-minded, let your posture mirror what is in your heart.

L: Remember that it is possible at times to *Lean* towards the other. Watch two people in a restaurant who are intimately engaged in conversation. Very often they are both leaning forward over the table as a natural sign of their involvement. The main thing is to remember that the upper part of your body is on a hinge. It can move towards a person and back away. In Western culture, a slight inclination towards a person is often seen as saying, 'I'm with you, I'm interested in you and in what you have to say.' Leaning back (the severest form of which is a slouch) can be a way of saying, 'I'm not entirely with you' or 'I'm bored.' Leaning too far forward, however, or doing so too soon, may frighten a client. It can be seen as a way of placing a demand on the other for some kind of closeness or intimacy. In a wider sense, the word 'lean' can refer to a kind of bodily flexibility or responsiveness that enhances your communication with a client. And bodily flexibility can mirror mental flexibility.

E: Maintain good *Eye* contact. In Western culture, fairly steady eye contact is not unnatural for people deep in conversation. It is not the same as staring. Again, watch two people deep in conversation. You may be amazed at the amount of direct eye contact. Maintaining good eye contact with a client is another way of saying, 'I'm with you; I'm interested; I want to hear what you have to say.' Obviously, this principle is not violated if you occasionally look away. Indeed, you have to if you don't want to stare. But if you catch yourself looking away frequently, your behaviour may give you a hint about some kind of reluctance to be with this person or to get involved with him or her. Or it may say something about your own discomfort. In other cultures, however, too much eye contact, especially with someone in a position of authority, is out of order. I have learned much about the cultural meaning of eye contact from my Asian students and clients.

R: Try to be relatively *Relaxed* or natural in these behaviours. Being relaxed means two things. First, it means not fidgeting nervously or engaging in distracting facial expressions. The client may wonder what's making you nervous. Second, it means becoming comfortable with using your body as a vehicle of personal contact and expression. Your being natural in the use of these skills helps put the client at ease.

A counsellor trained in *The Skilled Helper* was teaching counselling to visually impaired students in the Royal National University for the Blind. Most of her clients were visually impaired. However, she wrote this about SOLER:

"In counselling students who are blind or visually impaired, eye contact has little or no relevance. However, attention on voice direction is extremely important, and people with a visual impairment will tell you how insulted they feel when sighted people are talking to them while looking somewhere else. I teach SOLER as part of listening and attending skills and can adapt each letter of the acronym [to my visually impaired students] with *the exception of the E. ... After much thought, I would like to change your acronym to SOLAR, the A being for 'Aim', that is, aim your head and body in the direction of your client so that when they hear your voice, be it linguistically or paralinguistically, they know that you are attending directly to what they are saying." (personal communication)*

This underscores the fact that people are more sensitive to how you orient yourself to them non-verbally than you might imagine. Anything that distracts from your 'being there' can harm the dialogue. The point to be stressed is that a respectful, empathic, genuine and caring mindset might well lose its impact if the client does not see these internal attitudes reflected in your external behaviours.

In the beginning you may become overly self-conscious about the way you visibly tune in, especially if you are not used to being attentive. Still, the guidelines just presented are just that – guidelines. They should not be taken as absolute rules to be applied rigidly in all cases.

Advances in the understanding of non-verbal behaviour

Ants and bees send signals to one another in swarms and hives and use these signals not only to 'talk' to one another but also to make life-enhancing 'decisions'. Of course, the signals are non-verbal. Current research (Buchanan, 2007, 2009; Pentland, 2008, 2010) indicates that people do the same thing. In therapy, these signals constitute part of the social influence dimensions of helping mentioned in Chapter 2. Pentland organises the 'honest signals' – they are 'honest' because they are largely automatic, autonomic and unconscious – that we send to one another into four categories – activity, interest, mimicry and consistency. Take activity. Both clients and helpers display more nervous energy when they become more active. Each party can pick up these signals. Or take interest. You can tell the level of interest ('skin in the game') people have in what they are doing by reading how attentive they are to each other. This attention enables them to anticipate when the other person has made his or her point and finds the opportune moment to jump in. Pentland and his colleagues have developed technologies that enable them to read and measure this signalling process. Honest signals are hard to fake, and they do influence the other person. The kind of person – the kind of helper – you are comes across through these signals and are read by your clients. Genuineness cannot be faked. The point here is that non-verbal signals are at the heart of dialogue and not just conversational niceties. The fact that signals are being sent, received and acted on 'in the shadows' adds a note of uncertainty to the dialogue, but, as Duncan noted in Chapter 1, uncertainty can add vigour to the helping process.

Avoiding myths about non-verbal behaviour

Richmond and McCroskey (2000) spell out the shadow side of non-verbal behaviour in terms of commonly held myths (pp. 2–3):

1 *Non-verbal communication is nonsense. All communication involves language. Therefore, all communication is verbal.* This myth is disappearing. It does not stand up to the scrutiny of common sense.

2 *Non-verbal behaviour accounts for most of the communication in human interaction.* Early studies tried to 'prove' this, but they were biased. Studies were aimed at dispelling myth number 1 and overstepped their boundaries.

3 *You can read a person like a book.* Some people, even some professionals, would like to think so. You can read non-verbal behaviour, verbal behaviour and context and still be wrong.

4 *If a person does not look you in the eye while talking to you, he or she is not telling the truth.* Tell this to liars! The same non-verbal behaviour can mean many different things.

5 *Although non-verbal behaviour differs from person to person, most non-verbal behaviours are natural to all people.* Cross-cultural studies give the lie to this. But it isn't true even within the same culture.

6 *Non-verbal behaviour stimulates the same meaning in different situations.* Too often the context is the key. Yet some professionals buy the myth and base interpretive systems on it.

Box 3.1 summarises, in question form, the main points related to being visibly tuned-in to clients.

BOX 3.1	Questions on Visibly Tuning in

- What are my attitudes towards this client?
- Am I fully present with this client?
- If I am not fully present, what is preventing me from being so?
- To what degree does my non-verbal behaviour indicate a willingness to work with the client?
- Am I aware of my non-verbal behaviour with this client?
- What attitudes am I expressing in my non-verbal behaviour?
- What attitudes am I expressing in my verbal behaviour?
- To what degree does the client experience me as effectively present, tuned-in and working with him or her?
- To what degree does my non-verbal behaviour reinforce my internal attitudes?
- In what ways am I distracted from giving my full attention to this client? What am I doing to handle these distractions? How might I be more effectively present to this person?

Turn to the *Exercises in Helping Skills* for opportunities to 'practise' the skill of visibly tuning in. And remember that every conversation you have is an opportunity to practise.

ACTIVE LISTENING: THE FOUNDATION OF UNDERSTANDING

Burnard (2005, p. 136) provides a useful summary of listening which all helpers can relate to. Burnard explains that listening is the process of 'hearing' the other person, which involves not only noting the things they say but also a whole range of other aspects of communication. Aspects of listening can include the following:

- **Linguistic aspects of listening:**
  - words
  - phrases
  - figures of speech
  - 'personal' and idiosyncratic forms of speech.

- **Paralinguistic aspects of listening:**
  - timing
  - volume
  - tone
  - pitch
  - 'ums' and 'ers'
  - fluency
  - range.

- **Non-verbal aspects of listening:**
  - facial expressions
  - gestures
  - touch
  - body position
  - proximity to the counsellor
  - body movement
  - eye contact.

Visibly tuning in to clients is not, of course, an end in itself. We tune in both mentally and visibly in order to listen to what clients have to say – their stories, complaints, points of view, intentions, proposals, decisions and everything else. Listening carefully to a client's concerns seems to be a concept so simple to grasp and so easy to do that one may wonder why it is given such explicit treatment here. Nonetheless, it is amazing how often people fail to listen to one another. Full listening means listening actively, listening accurately and listening for meaning. Listening is not merely a skill. It is a rich metaphor and essential for the helping relationship itself – indeed, for all relationships. I will attempt to tap into some of that richness here.

Active listening plays a key role in all human-service endeavours and interactions. Take the doctor–patient relationship, for instance. Patients have two central concerns about their doctors – their medical competence and knowledge, and their ability to relate and communicate. Listening, then, is an important medical skill. Hippocrates told aspiring doctors to 'listen to the patient, and the patient will tell you what is wrong'. Today, even though doctors use sophisticated high-tech diagnostic methods together with a hands-on approach in making their diagnoses, listening to patients is still an extremely important part of healthcare. If Hippocrates were living, I'm sure that he would still be giving the same advice to doctors.

As a further guidance in this matter, Burnard (2005, p. 142) has suggested that aids to effective listening can include:

- Attention focused 'out'
- Suspension of judgement by the helper
- Attention to the behavioural aspects of listening
- Comfortable seating
- Avoidance of interpretation
- Development of 'free floating' attention
- Judicious use of minimal prompts.

Forms of poor listening

Effective listening is not a state of mind, like being happy or relaxed. It's not something that 'just happens'. It's an activity. In other words, effective listening requires active work. Let's first take a look at the opposite of active listening. All of us have been, at one time or another, both perpetrators and victims of the following forms of inactive or inadequate listening.

Non-listening   Sometimes we go through the motions of listening but are not really engaged. At times we get away with it. Sometimes we are caught. 'What would you do?' Lucy asks her colleague, Kieran, after outlining a problem the university counselling centre is having with a sudden increase in requests for help. Embarrassed, Kieran replies, 'I'm not sure.' Staring him down, she says, 'You haven't been listening! Where have you been the last 10 minutes?' For whatever reason, he had tuned her out. Obviously no helper sets out not to listen, but even the best can let their mind wander as they listen to the same kind of stories over and over again, forgetting that the story is unique to this client. You may have had the experience of being distracted whilst 'listening' to a co-worker. When our minds are very 'chatty' or we have a lot on our mind, it may be more difficult for us to engage in active listening.

Partial listening   This is listening that skims the surface. The helper picks up bits and pieces, but not necessarily the essential points the client is making. The lovely South African saying 'picking up stompies' applies here. This is when we pick up fragments of the conversation and perhaps make up the rest of the conversation so that we form a more coherent story for ourselves. We will often get the story wrong, or get the wrong end of the stick. Misunderstandings can then occur. For instance, Janice's client, Dean, who is feeling desperate about a job search, is talking to her about a meeting with a recruiter that went terribly wrong. Janice only half listens. It seems that Dean is not that interesting. Dean stops talking and looks rather dejected. Janice tries to pull together the pieces of the story she did listen to. Her attempt to express understanding has a hollow ring to it. Dean pauses and then says in a dejected voice, 'Maybe I'm just going about my search in the wrong way. What can I do?' Partial listening can be worse than non-listening because it has an air of pretence about it. It's fake. This may also occur when the helper is distracted by events in their own life that are interfering with their ability to listen to the client.

Tape-recorder listening What clients look for from listening is not the helper's ability to repeat their words. Any kind of recorder could do that perfectly. People want more than physical presence in human communication; they want the other person to be present psychologically, socially and emotionally. Sometimes helpers fail to visibly tune in and listen; they are not totally present. Clients pick up on signs of non-listening and lack of total presence. How many times have you heard someone exclaim, 'You're not listening to what I'm saying.' When the person accused of not listening answers, almost predictably, 'I am too listening; I can repeat everything you've said', the accuser is not comforted. Usually clients are too polite or cowed or preoccupied with their own concerns to say anything when they find themselves in that situation. But it is a shame if your auditory equipment is in order, but you are elsewhere. Your clients want you, a live counsellor, not a recorder.

Rehearsing Picture Sid, a novice counsellor, sitting with Casey, a client who is talking about some 'wild dreams' he is having. Sid says to himself, 'I don't believe that it's possible to extract any kind of meaning from dreams. It's all speculation', failing to realise that Casey is really disturbed by his dreams. He can capture his client's strong emotion without resolving the meaning-of-dreams issue. Even when experienced helpers begin to mull over how they will respond to the client, they stop listening. On the other hand, effective helpers listen intently to clients and to the themes and core messages embedded in what clients are saying. They are never at a loss in responding. They don't need to rehearse. And their responses are much more likely to help clients move forward in the problem-management process. When the client stops speaking, they often pause to reflect on what he or she just said, and then speak. Pausing says, 'I'm still mulling over what you've just said. It seems to move the problem in a different direction. Let me see if I can put my finger on what you've just said.' Effective helpers pause, not because they have not listened or have nothing to say, they pause because they have listened and want to respond helpfully.

Empathic listening: Listening to clients' stories and their search for solutions

The opposite of inactive or inadequate listening is empathic listening, listening driven by the value of empathy. Empathic listening centres on the kind of attending, observing and listening – the kind of 'being with' – needed to develop an understanding of clients and their worlds. Although it might be metaphysically impossible to actually get 'inside' the world of another person and experience the world as he or she does, it is possible to approximate this.

Carl Rogers (1980) talked passionately about basic empathic listening – being with and understanding the other – even calling it 'an unappreciated way of being' (p. 137). He used the word 'unappreciated' because in his view few people in the general population developed this 'deep listening' ability and even so-called expert helpers did not give it the attention it deserved. A genuineness that comes with being with the client and listening intently to what is said is key to the therapeutic relationship. A helper who is real, genuine and personal is preferred by clients (Knox & Cooper, 2015). Here is his description of empathic listening, or 'being with':

> "It means entering the private perceptual world of the other and becoming thoroughly at home in it. It involves being sensitive, moment by moment, to the changing felt meanings which flow in this other person, to the fear or rage or tenderness or confusion or whatever that he or she is experiencing. It means temporarily living in the other's life, moving about in it delicately without making judgements." (p. 142)

Such empathic listening is selfless because helpers must put aside their own concerns to be fully with their clients. Of course, Rogers pointed out that this deeper understanding of clients remains sterile unless it is somehow communicated to them. Although clients can appreciate how intensely they are attended and listened to, they and their concerns still need to be understood. Empathic listening leads to empathic understanding, which leads to empathic responding.

Empathic participation in the world of another person requires a level of engagement. As a helper, you must be able to enter clients' worlds deeply enough to understand their struggles with problem situations or their search for opportunities with enough depth to make your participation in problem management and opportunity development valid and substantial. If your help is based on an incorrect or invalid understanding of the client, then your helping may lead him or her astray. If your understanding is valid but superficial, then you might miss the central issues of the client's life.

The following case will be used to help you develop a better behavioural feel for empathic listening.

Jacomina, a South African student in her third year at university, was raped by a 'friend' on a date. She received some immediate counselling from the university student pastoral support system and some ongoing support during the subsequent investigation. But even though she was raped, it turned out that it was impossible for her to prove her case. The entire experience – both the rape and the investigation that followed – left her shaken, unsure of herself, angry and mistrustful of institutions she had assumed would be on her side (especially the university and the legal system). When Sophia, a middle-aged and middle-class Greek social worker who was a counsellor for a health maintenance organisation (HMO), first saw her a couple of years after the incident, Jacomina was plagued by a number of somatic complaints, including headaches and gastric problems. At work, she engaged in angry outbursts whenever she felt that someone was taking advantage of her. Otherwise she had become quite passive and chronically depressed. She saw herself as a woman victimised by society and was slowly giving up on herself.

Sophia is a pro, so she doesn't have much of a problem with inadequate listening. She is an empathic listener par excellence. She is engaged by Jacomina's story and by what Jacomina is going through right now. Sophia knows she has to be with Jacomina every step of the way.

Focused listening: experiences, thoughts, behaviours, and affect   In many ways helping is a 'talking game'. Therefore, the kind and quality of talk are both crucial. Listening at its best is both focused and unbiased. Two forms of focus are offered here. First, the problem-management helping model itself, because it is not theory- or school-focused and helps counsellors organise what they are hearing without prejudice. Problem-management and opportunity-development dialogue is at the heart of helping. Helpers listen intently to clients' stories to help them search for solutions: that is, life-enhancing outcomes.

The second aid to focused listening is a particular view of personality. Pervin's (1996) definition of personality is 'the complex organisation of cognitions [thoughts], affects [emotion], and behaviours that gives direction and pattern (coherence) to the person's life' (p. 414). Rasmussen (2005), author of one of the books in a personality-guided therapy series (Everly & Lating, 2004; Farmer & Nelson-Gray, 2005; Harper, 2004; Magnavita, 2005), adds the notion of 'activating event' (p. 4) to Pervin's triad. Because clients tell their stories in terms of their experiences (activating events), thoughts, behaviours and emotions, we as helpers are listening to their personalities at work, as it were. More precisely, we are listening to both individual thoughts and patterns of thinking, to both individual behaviours and patterns of behaving, and to both individual emotions and patterns of emotionality – all stimulated by both internal and external experiences or events.

Stewart (2013, pp. 362–367) talks at length about the importance of understanding different personality types to be able to provide effective counselling and helping. He refers to the psychosynthesis research conducted by Roberto Assagioli (1888–1974), an Italian psychiatrist who broke away from Freudian orthodoxy in the early 20th century and developed an integrated approach to psychiatry which identified a number of core 'personality types' which could be used to help gain a better understanding of a client's subconscious through careful listening, and so how to ultimately help the client.

Clients' stories tend to be mixtures of clients' life experiences, thoughts, emotions and behaviours. Each client will come with their own story and narrative that the helper listens to and tries to understand from their point of view. Bricker, Glat and Stover (2007) claim that familiarity with this schema or framework fosters 'clinical mindfulness' and helps counsellors organise their work in order to keep therapy 'moving towards objective, recognisable goals'. They claim that the helper without any framework or schema for organising what clients are saying risks 'clinical drift' (all citations p. 25).

- **Experiences.** Clients talk about their *experiences* – that is, what has happened and is happening to them. If a client tells you that she was fired from her job, she is talking about her problem situation as an experience. Jacomina, of course, talked about being raped, belittled and ignored.

- **Thoughts.** Clients talk about the way they think and the *thoughts* that go through their head in order to make sense of their experiences. Jacomina shares her points of view about the rape and its aftermath. She thinks that her nationality worked against her.

- **Behaviour.** Clients talk about their *behaviour* – that is, what they do or refrain from doing. If a client tells you that he smokes and drinks a lot, he is talking about his external behaviour. If a different client says that she spends a great deal of time daydreaming, she is talking about her internal behaviour. Clients' behaviours can also be their chosen coping strategies such as avoiding a situation, withdrawing from social engagements or dissociating from traumatic events. Jacomina, for example, talked about pulling away from her family and friends after the rape investigation.

- **Affect.** Clients talk about their *affect* – that is, the feelings, emotions and moods that arise from or are associated with their experiences and both internal and external behaviour. If a client tells you how depressed they get after fights with their partner, they are talking about the mood associated with their experiences and behaviour. Jacomina talked about her shame, her feelings of betrayal and her anger. Often, our emotions are stored in the body (Van der Kolk, 2015). Think about your own body sensations when you are stressed, or under pressure at work or finding life difficult. Do your shoulders tense up, do you experience butterflies in your stomach, do you notice where you store your emotions in your body?

Of course, thoughts, actions and emotions are interrelated in the day-to-day lives of clients. And so they mix them together in telling their stories. Some clients are not aware of their emotions or their physical sensations when stressed. Consider this example. A client is talking to a counsellor in the personnel department of a large company. The client says in a very agitated way: 'I've just had one of the lousiest days of my life.' At this point the counsellor knows that something went wrong and that the client feels bad about it, but she knows relatively little about the specific experiences, thoughts and behaviours that have made the day such a horror for the client. However, the client continues.

> **CLIENT:** Toward the end of the day my boss yelled at me in front of some of my colleagues for not landing an order from a new customer [an experience]. I lost my temper [emotion] and yelled right back at him [behaviour]. He blew up and fired me on the spot [an experience for the client]. I really think that he's an idiot and the company should not tolerate people like him in supervisory positions [a thought, a point of view]. And now I feel awful [emotion] and am trying to find out if I really have been fired and, if so, if I can get my job back [behaviour]. I have every intention to fight this; it's unjust [a thought, a resolve, a point of view].

Now the counsellor knows a great deal more about the problem situation. Problem situations are much clearer when they are spelled out as specific experiences, thoughts, behaviours and feelings related to specific situations. Because clients spend so much time telling their stories, a few words about each of these elements are in order.

Listening to clients' experiences Most clients spend a fair amount of time, sometimes too much time, talking about what happens to them.

- 'I live in a society where there are "No Help Wanted" signs wherever I turn.'
- 'My blood boils whenever he shows up with that I've-done-nothing-wrong smile.'
- 'It's hard. Drugs are everywhere. They're too easy to get.'
- 'I get headaches a lot. They make it impossible for me to do anything.'

It is of paramount importance to listen to and understand clients' experiences. However, because experiences often dwell on what other people do or fail to do, experience-focused stories at times are usually incomplete and, often enough, tinged with – or flooded with – victimhood. The implication is that others – or the world in general – are to blame for the client's problems.

- 'She doesn't do anything all day. The house is always a mess when I come home. No wonder I can't concentrate at work.'
- 'He tells his little jokes, and I'm always the butt of them. He makes me feel bad about myself most of the time.' Some clients talk about experiences that are internal and out of their control.
- 'These feelings of depression come from nowhere and seem to suffocate me.'
- 'I just can't stop thinking of him.'

The last statement sounds like an action, but it is expressed as an experience. It is something happening to the client, at least to the client's way of thinking.

Burnard (2005, p. 147) provides the following example of a helper providing effective listening in practice:

Andrew is a GP in a busy city centre practice in Manchester. He gets repeated visits from a young woman, Sarah, whose husband has recently been killed on the M60 in a road traffic collision. Sarah often makes allusion to the problems of adjusting to her bereavement but presents with fairly minor physical ailments. Andrew gently suggests to her that it may be helpful if they talked about her loss in more detail and offers her an afternoon, booked appointment. At first she is reluctant to accept this, but later phones to make such an appointment. During the next few weeks, Andrew meets Sarah on a regular basis and listens to her. During these appointments, Andrew has to make very few verbal interventions: Sarah is able to describe and ventilate her feelings very easily, once she is offered the opportunity. She works through stages of anger, extreme sorrow and meaninglessness, and finally to some acceptance. During these stages, Andrew has to 'do' very little. His supportive attention and ability to listen, without making too many suggestions or offering too much advice, has been therapeutic in itself. He realises, however, that he has had to 'learn to listen'. Previously in his career, he tended to be a 'sentence finisher' for other people and has slowly learned to focus attention on other people and really listen to them.

One reason that some clients fail to manage the problem situations of their lives is that they are too passive or see themselves as victims, adversely affected by other people, by the immediate social settings of life such as the family, by society in its larger organisations and institutions such as government or the workplace, by cultural prescriptions or even by internal forces. They feel that they are no longer in control of their lives or some dimension of life. Therefore, they talk extensively about these experiences.

- 'Company policy discriminates against women. It's that simple.'
- 'The economy is picking up, but the kinds of jobs I want are already taken.'
- 'No innovative and creative teacher gets very far around here.'

Of course, some clients *are* treated unfairly; they are victimised by the behaviours of others in the social and institutional settings of their lives. Although they can be helped to cope with victimisation, full management of their problem situations demands changes in the social settings themselves. A counsellor helped one client cope with a brutal husband, but ultimately the courts had to intervene to keep him at bay.

For other clients, talking constantly about experiences is a way of avoiding responsibility: 'It's not my fault. After all, these things are happening to me.' A good illustration of this can be found in Karpman's drama triangle (Karpman, 2014), where he describes the positions taken by people as being either a victim, persecutor or rescuer. Sykes (1992), in his book *A Nation of Victims*, was troubled by the tendency of the United States to become a 'nation of whiners unwilling to take responsibility for our actions'. This statement is too broad, but whether the statement is true or not, counsellors must be able to distinguish 'whiners' from those who are truly being victimised. The point is that self-pity and whining do little to make things better. Helpers need both to respect clients' negative experiences and to help them move beyond them.

Listening to clients' thoughts and patterns of thinking   A lot goes on in clients' heads. Common ways in which clients share their thinking include sharing points of view, stating intentions, declaring decisions and offering proposals and plans. The helper needs to get inside the client's world, to see things from their point of view in order to truly understand their view and account of situations.

Clients' points of view   As clients tell their stories, explore possibilities for a better future, set goals, make plans and review obstacles to accomplishing these plans, they often share their points of view. A point of view is a client's personal estimation of something. A full point of view includes the point of view itself, the reasons for it, an illustration to bring it to life and some indication of how open the one holding the point of view might be to modifying it. If the client also expects others to adopt the point of view, then he or she is engaging in some form of selling or persuasion. But, realistically, the implication of a stated point of view often is: 'I think this way. Why don't other people think this way?' Or, 'This is my opinion and I don't care what other people think.' For instance, Marjorie, an 80-year-old woman, is talking to a counsellor about the various challenges of old age. At one point she says:

> My sister in Port Elizabeth [85-years-old] – Sis, we call her – is very ill. She's probably dying, but she wants to stay at home and spend her final days in the comfort of her own house. She has asked me to stay at her house and to take care of her. I think that's asking too much to ask me. I could use some help myself these days but she keeps calling me.

Marjorie's point of view is that her sister's request is not realistic because she herself needs some help to get by. But her sister has a different point of view – 'my needs trump yours' – and so persists in trying to persuade her to change her mind.

Points of view reveal clients' beliefs, values, attitudes and convictions. Clients may share their points of view about everything under the sun. You will need to listen to and understand the ones that are relevant to their problem situations or undeveloped opportunities. Let's return briefly to Jacomina and Sophia. Jacomina says:

> You just can't trust the system. They're not going to help. They take the easy way out. I don't care which system it might be. Church, government, the community, sometimes even the family. They're not going to give you much help. If you've got problems, then you become a problem to others.

Sophia listens carefully to Jacomina's point of view and realises how much it is influencing her behaviour. In Jacomina's case it's easy to see where the point of view comes from. But Sophia also knows that at some point Jacomina would benefit from exploring the consequences, however unintended, of that point of view. Jacomina's point of view may be one of the things that is keeping her locked in her misery. Points of view have power, but the power can be either self-enhancing or self-limiting.

Clients' intentions, proposals and plans   Clients provide a window into their thinking when they state intentions, offer proposals or make a case for certain courses of action – all problem-management behaviours. Consider Lydia. She is a single parent of two young children and a member of the 'working poor'. Her wages don't cover her expenses. The father of her children has long disappeared. She says to a social worker:

> I've been thinking of quitting my job. I'm making the minimum wage and with travel expenses and all I just can't make ends meet. I spend too much time travelling and don't see enough of my children. Friends look after them when I'm gone, but that's hit and miss and puts a burden on them. You know if I go on unemployment benefits I could make almost as much. And then I could pick up jobs that would pay me cash. I've got friends who do this. I believe I could make ends meet. My children and I would be better off. And I wouldn't be hassled as much.

Lydia is making a case, but stops short of announcing a decision. The case includes what she wants to do (quit her job and move into the 'alternate' work economy), the reasons for doing it (the inadequacy of her current work situation, the need to make ends meet) and the implications for herself and her children (she'd be less hassled and her children would see more of her and be better off).

Clients' decisions   Helping clients review the decisions they have made and make new decisions is one of the key ingredients of successful therapy. Clients often talk about decisions they are making or have already made. A client might say, 'I've decided to stop drinking. Cold turkey.' Or, 'I'm tired of being alone. I'm going to see if I can find someone on an online dating service.' Decisions usually have implications for the decision maker and for others. The client who has decided to quit drinking has his work cut out for himself, but there are implications for his spouse. For instance, she's used to coping with a drunk, but now she may have to learn how to cope with this 'new person' in the house.

Sharing a decision fully means spelling out the decision itself, the reasons for the decision, the implications for self and others, and some indication as to whether the decision or any part of it is open to review. For instance, Jacomina, talking with Sophia about future employment, says in a rather languid tone of voice, 'I'm not going to get any kind of job where I have to fight the woman thing. I'm tired of fighting. I only get hurt. I know that this limits my opportunities, but I can live with that.' Note that this is more than a point of view. Jacomina is more or less saying, 'I've made up my mind.' She notes the implication for herself – a limitation of job opportunities – and an implication for Sophia might be, 'So that's the end of it. Don't try to convince me otherwise.' Sophia hears the message and the implied command. However, she believes that some of Jacomina's messages need challenging. Decisions can be tricky. Often enough, how they are delivered says a great deal about the decision itself. Given the rather languid way in which Jacomina delivers her decision, Sophia thinks that it might not be Jacomina's final decision. This is something that has to be checked out. A dialogue with Jacomina about the reasons for her decision and a review of its implications can add value.

Listening to clients' behaviours and patterns of behaviour   All of us do things that get us into trouble and fail to do things that will help us get out of trouble or develop opportunities. Clients are no different.

- 'When he ignores me, I begin thinking of ways of getting back at him.'
- 'Whenever anyone gets on my case for having a father in prison, I let him have it. I'm not taking that kind of crap from anyone.'
- 'Even though I feel the depression coming on, I don't take the pills the doctor gave me.'
- 'When I get bored, I find some friends to party with and get wasted.'
- 'I have a lot of sexual partners and have unprotected sex.'

Some clients talk freely about their experiences and what happens to them, but seem more reluctant to talk about their behaviours. One reason for this is that it's hard to talk about behaviours without bringing up, at least indirectly, issues of personal responsibility, and clients may not want to admit their part in the behaviour.

Listening to the client's feelings, emotions and moods   Feelings, emotions and moods constitute a river that continually runs through us – peaceful, meandering, turbulent or raging – often beneficial, sometimes dangerous, seldom neutral. They are certainly an important part of clients' problem situations and undeveloped opportunities (Angus & Greenberg, 2012; Plutchik, 2001, 2003; Rottenberg & Johnson, 2007). In 2001, a new American Psychological Association journal, *Emotion*, entered the scene because of the recognition that emotion is fundamental to so much of human life. Books on emotional regulation are useful for helpers and their clients (Gross, 2014; Leahy, Tirch & Napolitano, 2011; Linehan, 2014). These very practical books tend to take a positive psychology approach to the experience, regulation and use of emotion in everyday life. Inevitably, there is the commercialisation of emotion highlighted by a veritable industry focused on 'anger management'. Some of the programmes are excellent; some are rubbish. Roffman (2004) rejects the notion of anger as a 'thing-to-be-managed' (p. 161) and looks on anger as a resource. Anyway, there is more to emotional life than anger.

There is a rich literature about emotional intelligence as a distinct kind of intelligence or ability (Ciarrochi & Mayer, 2007; Ciarrochi, Forgas & Mayer, 2006; Mayer & Salovey, 1997; Mayer, Roberts & Barsade, 2008; Salovey & Mayer, 1990). These studies differ from the writings about emotional intelligence in a broader sense (Egan, 2010, Chapter 1; Goleman, 1995, 1998), which spell out what social-emotional maturity looks like. This concept has its supporters and its detractors (Murphy, 2006). Here, however, the focus is on one's ability to make emotions life-enhancing. According to Mayer and Salovey (1997), emotional intelligence has four 'branches': accurately perceiving emotions in oneself and others; using emotions to facilitate thought and understanding; understanding emotional meanings; and managing one's emotions effectively. Clearly these are abilities that serve helpers well, enabling them to get a fix on their own emotions and to help clients deal with theirs. Mayer, Roberts and Barsade (2008) provide an excellent overview of the research on emotions.

Recognising key feelings, emotions and moods (or the lack thereof) is very important for at least three reasons. First, they pervade our lives. There is an emotional tone to just about everything we do. Feelings, emotions and moods pervade clients' stories, points of view, decisions and intentions or proposals. Second, they greatly affect the quality of our lives. A bout of depression can stop us in our tracks. A client who gets out from under the burden of self-doubt breathes more freely. Third, feelings, emotions and moods are drivers of our behaviour. As Lang (1995) pointed out, they are 'action dispositions' (p. 372). Clients driven by anger can do desperate things. On the other hand, enthusiastic clients can accomplish more than they ever thought they could. The good news is that we can learn how to tune ourselves in to our clients' and our own feelings, emotions and moods at the service of discovering how to regulate them.

Understanding the role of feelings, emotions and moods in clients' problem situations and their desire to identify and develop opportunities is central to the helping process. Emotions highlight learning opportunities:

- 'I've been feeling pretty sorry for myself ever since he left me.' This client learns that self-pity constricts her world and limits problem-managing action.
- 'I yelled at my mother last night and now I feel very ashamed of myself.' Shame may well be a wake-up call in this client's relationship with his mother.
- 'I've been anxious for the past few weeks, but I don't know why. I wake up feeling scared and then it goes away but comes back again several times during the day.' Anxiety has become a bad habit for this client. It is self-perpetuating. What can the client do to break through the vicious circle?
- 'I finally finished the mid-term assignment that I've been putting off for weeks and I feel great.' Here emotion becomes a tool in this client's struggle against procrastination.

The last item in this list brings up an important point. In the psychological literature, negative emotions tend to receive more attention than positive emotions. Now work is under way to study positive emotions and their beneficial effects. There are indications that we can use positive emotions to promote both physical and psychological well-being (Salovey, Rothman, Detweiler & Steward, 2000). There are indications that emotions can free up psychological resources, act as opportunities for learning and promote health-related behaviours. In managing problems and developing opportunities, social support plays a key role. As Salovey and his colleagues note, clients are more likely to elicit social support if they manifest a positive attitude towards life. Potential supporters tend to shun clients who let their negative emotions get the best of them.

Of course, clients often express feelings without talking about them. When a client says, 'My boss gave me a pay rise and I didn't even ask for one!', you can feel the emotion in her voice. A client who is talking listlessly and staring down at the floor may not say, in so many words, 'I feel depressed.' A dying person may express feelings of anger and depression without talking about them. Other clients feel deeply about things but do their best to hold their feelings back. But effective helpers can usually pick up on clues or hints, whether verbal or non-verbal, that indicate the feelings and emotions rumbling inside.

Clients' stories, points of view, decisions and expressed intentions or proposals for action are permeated by feelings, emotions and moods. Your job is to listen carefully to the ways in which they affect, colour and give meaning to words they are using. The meaning is not just in the words. It's in the full package. In order to name the range and subtleties of emotions that you are feeling and clients are expressing, you need the experience and the vocabulary to do so. Plutchik (2001, 2003) fills the bill with one of the widest ranges of emotions derived from and arranged around eight basic emotions and brightly-coloured graphics to organise the whole range. Take a look.

Listening for strengths, opportunities and resources If you listen only for problems, you will end up talking mainly about problems. And you will short-change your clients. Every client has something going for him or her. Your job is to spot clients' resources and help them invest these resources in managing problem situations and opportunities. If it is true that people generally use only a fraction of their potential (Maslow, 1968), then there is much to be tapped. For instance, a counsellor is working with a 65-year-old, successful businessman who, with his wife, has raised three children. The children are well educated and successful in their own right. The man is having difficulty coping with some health problems. The counsellor learns that the man was one of a group of poor inner-city boys in a longitudinal study. The boys had a mean IQ of 80 and a lot of social disadvantages (see Vaillant, 2000). As the counsellor listens to the man's story, he hears a history of resilience. The counsellor helps him review the strategies he used to cope as he was growing up. Energised by this, the man says, 'I never gave up then. Why should I start giving up now?'

One section of the positive psychology movement focuses on strengths, especially strengths that clients have but fail to use as they struggle with problem situations (Aspinwall & Staudinger, 2003; Peterson & Seligman, 2004). Just the list of the strengths examined in a book on 'positive psychological assessment', edited by Lopez and Snyder (2003), gives the reader a lift – hope, optimism, self-efficacy, problem-solving, internal locus of control, creativity, wisdom, courage, positive emotions, self-esteem, love, emotional intelligence, forgiveness, humour, gratitude, faith, morality, coping and well-being. Although we might long for a world in which striving for these virtues was a priority, listening for hints of any or all of these capabilities in our clients is a first step. Finally, all of these writers are committed to developing a science of human strengths. Poor counsellors listen just for problems; successful counsellors search out the client's resources.

Listening to clients' non-verbal messages and modifiers Carton, Kessler and Pape (1999) showed that the ability of people to read non-verbal messages is one factor in establishing and maintaining relationships. So once we have an understanding of our own non-verbal 'speech', we can turn to an exploration of clients' non-verbal behaviour. Clients send a steady stream of clues and messages through their non-verbal behaviour. Helpers need to learn how to read these messages without distorting or over-interpreting them. For instance, when Sophia says to Jacomina, 'It seems that it's hard talking about yourself', Jacomina says, 'No, I don't mind at all.' But the real answer is probably in her non-verbal behaviour, for she speaks hesitatingly while looking away and frowning. Reading such cues helps Sophia understand Jacomina better. Our non-verbal behaviour has a way of 'leaking' messages about what we really mean. The very spontaneity of non-verbal behaviours contributes to this leakage even in the case of highly defensive clients. It is not easy for clients to fake non-verbal behaviour (Wahlstein, 1991).

Besides being a channel of communication in itself, such non-verbal behaviour as facial expressions, use of gestures, body position and movement, proximity to the helper, touch in relation to the helper and voice quality often modifies and punctuates verbal messages in much the same way that periods, question marks, exclamation points and underlining punctuate written language. All the kinds of non-verbal behaviour mentioned earlier in this chapter can punctuate or modify verbal communication in the following ways:

- *Confirming or repeating.* Non-verbal behaviour can confirm or repeat what is being said verbally. For instance, once when Sophia responds to Jacomina with just the right degree of understanding – she hits the mark – not only does Jacomina say, 'That's right', but also her eyes light up (facial expression), she leans forward a bit (bodily motion) and her voice is very animated (voice quality). Her non-verbal behaviour confirms her verbal message.

- *Denying or confusing.* Non-verbal behaviour can deny or confuse what is being said verbally. When challenged by Sophia, Jacomina denies that she is upset, but her voice falters a bit (voice quality) and her upper lip quivers (facial expression). Her non-verbal behaviour carries the real message.

- *Strengthening or emphasising.* Non-verbal behaviour can strengthen or emphasise what is being said. When Sophia suggests to Jacomina that she ask her boss what he means by her 'erratic behaviour', Jacomina says in a startled voice, 'Oh, I don't think I could do that', while slouching down and putting her face in her hands. Her non-verbal behaviour underscores her verbal message.

- *Adding intensity.* Non-verbal behaviour often adds emotional colour or intensity to verbal messages. When Jacomina tells Sophia that she doesn't like to be confronted without first being understood and then stares at her fixedly and silently with a frown on her face, Jacomina's non-verbal behaviour tells Sophia that her feelings are intense.

- **_Controlling or regulating._** Non-verbal cues are often used in conversation to regulate or control what is happening. Let's say that, in a group counselling session, Nina looks at Tom and gives every indication that she is going to speak to him. But he looks away. Nina hesitates and then decides not to say anything. Tom has used a non-verbal gesture to control her behaviour.

In reading non-verbal behaviour – 'reading' is used here instead of 'interpreting' – caution is a must. We listen to clients in order to understand them, not to dissect them. But merely noticing non-verbal behaviour is not enough. Trainees can learn how to identify useful non-verbal messages, clues and modifiers by watching videotaped interactions, including their own interactions (Costanzo, 1992). Once you develop a working knowledge of non-verbal behaviour and its possible meanings, the next step is practice.

Because non-verbal behaviours can often mean a number of things, how can you tell which meaning is the real one? The key is the context in which they take place. Effective helpers listen to the entire context of the helping interview and do not become overly fixated on details of behaviour. They are aware of and use the non-verbal communication system, but they are not seduced or overwhelmed by it. Sometimes novice helpers will fasten selectively on this or that bit of non-verbal behaviour. For example, they will make too much of a half-smile or a frown on the face of a client. They will seize upon the smile or the frown and, in over-interpreting it, lose the person.

Burnard (2005, p. 137) advises us that it is much more effective on the part of the helper if they merely bring the client's attention to the way they are sitting or their facial expression, rather than offer an interpretation of it. He gives two examples to illustrate this. In the first, the helper offers an interpretation and an assumption.

HELPER: I notice from the way that you have your arms folded and from your frown that you are uncomfortable with discussing things at home.

In the second example the helper merely feeds back to the client what they have observed, and allows the client to clarify the situation:

HELPER: I notice that you have your arms folded and that you're frowning. What are you feeling at the moment?

Putting it all together: Listening to the client's integrated narrative

When clients talk about their concerns, they mix all forms of discourse – thoughts, stories, experiences, emotions, actions, evolving decisions, points of view, proposed actions, strengths, resources – together. This is the client's narrative. Some lessons from the narrative therapy movement (Angus & Greenberg, 2012; Angus & and McLeod, 2004; Brown & Augusta-Scott, 2006; Madigan, 2011; Payne, 2006; White, 2007) can help you help clients integrate this mix into a coherent story. Narrative therapy focuses on clients' understanding of their stories and how their experiences, thoughts, emotions and actions fit into the context of the story. This approach can help clients do three things: put 'untold' aspects of the client's past into the life narrative, emotionally enter and re-author their own stories and/or construct new meanings in old stories or find new meanings in stories that emerge during therapy. Whilst narrative therapy is often associated with philosophical theories such as constructivism and postmodernism, these issues are not relevant here.

At the beginning of therapy Sophia realises that Jacomina's story contains many self-limiting and even self-defeating themes. Later, Jacomina, with Sophia's help, begins to 're-author' her story, and new life-enhancing themes begin to emerge. For example, what follows came out through dialogue in one of

Jacomina's sessions with Sophia. However, for the sake of illustration, it is presented here in summary form in Jacomina's words. She is talking much more animatedly and maintains much more eye contact with Sophia than she usually does.

'A couple of weeks ago I met a woman at work who has a story similar to mine. We talked for a while and got along so well that we decided to meet outside of work. I had dinner with her last night. She went into her story in more depth. I was amazed. At times I thought I was listening to myself! Because she had been hurt, she was narrowing her world down into a little patch so that she could control everything and not get hurt anymore. I saw right away that I'm trying to do my own version of the same thing. I know you've been telling me that, but I haven't been listening very well. Here's a woman with lots going for her and she's hiding out. As I came back from dinner I said to myself you've got to change. So I want to revisit two areas we've talked about – my work life and my social life. I don't want to live in the hole I've dug for myself. I could see clearly some of the things she should do. So here's what I want to do. I want to engage in some little experiments in broadening my social life, starting with my family. And I want to discuss the kind of work I want without putting all the limitations on it. I want to start coming out of the hole I'm in. And I want to help my new friend do the same.'

Everything is here – a story about her new friend, including experiences, actions and feelings; points of view about her new friend; decisions about where she wants her life to go; proposals about experiments in her social life and in her relationship with her friend. The new narrative focusing on a different set of experiences, thoughts, emotions and actions begins to emerge. The point is this: developing frameworks for listening can help you zero in on the key messages your clients are communicating and help you identify and understand the feelings, emotions and moods that permeate them. The narrative construct helps you help clients integrate all these elements into a coherent picture.

While listening is important, there is no need to go overboard on listening. Remember that you are a human being listening to a human being, not a vacuum cleaner indiscriminately sweeping up every scrap of information. Effective dialogic listening helps both you and your client discover the kind of meaning needed to move forward in managing problem situations and spotting and developing life-enhancing opportunities.

Processing what you hear: The thoughtful search for meaning

As we listen, we process what we hear. The trick is to become a thoughtful processor. As we shall see a bit further along, there are many less-than-thoughtful ways of processing clients' stories, points of view and messages. But first, what does thoughtful processing look like? Here are some guidelines.

Understand clients through context   People are more than the sum of their verbal and non-verbal messages. Listening, in its deepest sense, means listening to clients themselves as influenced by the contexts in which they 'live, move, and have their being' (Cook, 2012). As mentioned earlier, it is important to interpret a client's non-verbal behaviour in the context of the entire helping session. It is also essential to help clients understand their stories, points of view and messages, and the emotions that permeate them through the wider context of their lives. Tiedens and Leach (2004), in their edited book *The Social Life of Emotions*, develop the theme that emotions cannot be understood independently of the social relationships and groups in which they occur. All the things that make people different – culture, personality, personal style, ethnicity, key life experiences, life events, education, travel, economic status and the other forms of diversity discussed in Chapter 2 – provide the context for the client's problems and unused opportunities. Key elements of this context become part of the client's story, whether they are mentioned directly or not. Effective helpers listen through this wider context without being overwhelmed by the details of it. There are a number of development frameworks that can help you take a contextual frame of reference with your clients (Arnett, 2000; Egan & Cowan, 1979; Qualls & Abeles, 2000). A graduate programme now in place for a number of years at the University of Michigan, called Personality and Social Contexts, explores the contexts in which people live out their lives and how these contexts influence their lives (DeAngelis, 2005).

To return to our previous example, Sophia tries to understand Jacomina's verbal and non-verbal messages, especially the core messages, in the context of Jacomina's life. As she listens to Jacomina's story, Sophia says to herself right from the start something like this:

> Here is an intelligent South African woman from a conservative Catholic background. She has been very loyal to the Church because it proved to be a refuge in the inner city. It was a gathering place for her family and friends. It provided her with a decent primary and secondary school education and a shot at university. She did very well in her studies. Initially university was a shock. It was her first venture into a predominantly white and secular culture. But she chose her friends carefully and carved out a niche for herself. Because studies were much more demanding, she had to come to grips with the fact that, in this larger environment, she was, academically, closer to average. The rape and investigation put a great deal of stress on what proved to be a rather fragile social network. Her life began to unravel. She pulled away from her family, her church and the small circle of friends she had at university. At a time when she needed support the most, she cut it off. After graduation she continued to stay 'out of community'. Now she is underemployed as a secretary in a small company. This does little for her sense of personal worth.

Sophia listens to Jacomina through this context without assuming that it needs to define Jacomina. The helping context is also important. Sophia needs to be sensitive about how Jacomina might feel about talking to a woman who is quite different from her and also needs to understand that Jacomina might well have some misgivings about the helping professions.

In sum, Sophia tries to pull together the themes she sees emerging in Jacomina's story and tries to see these themes in context. She listens to Jacomina's discussion of her headaches (experiences), her self-imposed social isolation (behaviours) and her chronic depression (feelings) against the background of her social history – the pressures of being religious in a secular society at school, the problems associated with being an upwardly mobile South African woman in a predominantly white male society. Sophia sees the rape and investigation as social, not merely personal, events. She listens actively and carefully, because she knows that her ability to help depends, in part, on not distorting what she hears. She does not focus narrowly on Jacomina's inner world, as if Jacomina could be separated from the social context of her life. Finally, although Sophia listens to Jacomina through the context of Jacomina's life, she does not get lost in it. She uses context both to understand Jacomina and to help her manage her problems and develop her opportunities more fully.

Identify key messages and feelings   Helpers must avoid information overload. A thoughtful search for meaning demands the identification of key factors; that is, key not to some theory but key to the purpose of helping. Sophia listens to what Jacomina has to say early on about her past and present experiences, thoughts, actions and emotions. She listens to Jacomina's points of view and the decisions Jacomina has made or is in the process of making. She listens to Jacomina's intentions and proposals. Jacomina tells Sophia about an intention gone awry and the emotions that went with it: 'When the investigation began, I had every intention of pushing my case, because I knew that some of the men on campus were getting away with murder. But then it began to dawn on me that people were not taking me seriously because I was a South African woman. First I was angry, but then I just felt numb …'. Later, Jacomina says, 'I get headaches a lot now. I don't like taking pills, so I try to tough it out. I have also become very sensitive to any kind of injustice, even in movies or on television. But I've stopped being any kind of crusader. That got me nowhere.' As Sophia listens to Jacomina speak, questions based on the listening frameworks outlined here arise in the back of her mind:

- 'To what degree are both involved in discovering what is really important?'
- 'How is the dialogue going?'
- 'What are the main points here?'
- 'What experiences and actions are most important?'

- 'What themes are coming through?'
- 'What is Jacomina's point of view?'
- 'What is most important to her?'
- 'What does she want me to understand?'
- 'What decisions are implied in what she's saying?'
- 'What is she proposing to do?'

The Duncan feedback surveys mentioned in Chapter 1 help Sophia enormously to come up with answers to these questions. The questions in the survey do not mimic these questions. Rather they open up a give-and-take feedback process that enables both helper and client to bring up issues that have not been discussed directly.

Hear the slant or spin: Don't avoid tough-minded listening and processing   This is the kind of listening needed in order to help clients explore issues more deeply and to identify blind spots that need to be tuned into new perspectives. Skilled helpers not only listen to clients' stories, points of view, decisions, intentions and proposals but also to any slant or spin that clients might give their stories. Although clients' visions of and feelings about themselves, others and the world are real and need to be understood, their perceptions are sometimes distorted.

For instance, if a client sees herself as ugly, her experience of herself as ugly is real and needs to be listened to and understood. If her experience does not square with the facts – if she is, in fact, nice looking – then this, too, must be listened to and understood.

Linda Finlay, in her book *The Practice of Psychosocial Occupational Therapy* (2004, p. 149), provides us with a useful case to illustrate this in practice.

Jennifer, the client, has sought the advice of a helper because she feels that she is fat and horrible. The helper, Rowena, can see that in reality Jennifer is both slim and attractive, but that even if Rowena stated this observation to Jennifer, it probably would not help Jennifer at the present time. Rowena explains to her mentor and supervisor: 'I don't think Jennifer wants reassurance from me as she is not currently in a mindset where she can take compliments on board. Even if I entered into evaluation of her physical appearance, however positive, this would give a message to Jennifer that I was judging her. Jennifer's perception is what is important here, and so my approach is to listen carefully to her and acknowledge her poor self-image, and then focus, as her helper, on how I might help her change her negative thinking.'

Rowena's mentor agrees that is the best approach for Rowena to show Jennifer that she is properly listening to and understanding her.

If a client sees himself as above average in his ability to communicate with others when, in reality, he is below average, his experience of himself needs to be listened to and understood, but reality cannot be ignored. Tough-minded listening includes detecting the gaps, distortions and dissonance that are part of the client's experienced reality.

Sophia realises from the beginning that some of Jacomina's understandings of herself and her world are not accurate. For instance, in reflecting on all that has happened, Jacomina remarks that she probably got what she deserved. When Sophia asks her what she means, she says, 'My ambitions were too high. I was getting beyond my place in life.' This is the slant or spin Jacomina gives to her career aspirations. It is one thing to understand how Jacomina might put this interpretation on what has happened; it is another to assume that such an interpretation reflects reality. To be client-centred, helpers must first be reality-centred.

Muse on what's missing   Clients often leave key elements out when talking about problems and opportunities. Having frameworks for listening can help you spot important things that are missing. For instance, they tell their stories but leave out key experiences, behaviours or feelings. They offer points of view but say nothing about what's behind them or their implications. They deliver decisions but don't give the reasons for them or spell out the implications. They propose courses of action but don't say why they want to head in a particular direction, what the implications are for themselves or others, what resources they might need or how flexible they are. As you listen, it's important to note what they put in and what they leave out. Reflecting on what is said as well as what has not been said is important in finding the meaning behind the words clients use. This continuous interpretation helps the psychologist formulate ideas about why this client is experiencing these issues at this point in time. Psychologists use the assessment process to formulate with the client (Johnstone & Dallos, 2006; Van Rijn, 2015).

For instance, when it comes to stories, clients often leave out their own behaviour or their feelings. Jacomina says, 'I got a call from an old girlfriend last week. I'm not sure how she tracked me down. We must have chatted away for 20 minutes. You know, catching up.' Because Jacomina says this in a rather matter-of-fact way, it's not clear how she felt about it at the time or feels now. Nor is there any indication of what she might want to do about it – for instance, stay in touch.

In another session Jacomina says, 'I was talking with my brother the other day. He runs a small business. He asked me to come and work for him. I told him no.… By the way, I have to change the time of our next appointment. I forgot I've got a doctor's appointment.' Sophia notes the experience (being offered a job) and Jacomina's behaviour or reaction (a decision conveyed to her brother refusing the offer). But Jacomina leaves out the reasons for her refusal or the implications for herself or her brother or their relationship and moves to another topic.

Note that this is not a search for the 'hidden stuff' that clients are leaving unsaid. We all leave out key details from time to time. Rather, because Sophia understands what full versions of stories, points of view and messages look like, she notes what parts are missing. She then uses her clinical judgement – a large part of which is common sense – to determine whether or not to ask about the missing parts. For instance, when she asks Jacomina why she refused her brother point-blank, Jacomina says, 'Well, he's a good guy and I'd probably like the work, but this is no time to be getting mixed up with family.' This is one more indication of how restricted Jacomina has allowed her social life to become. It may be that she has determined that support from her family is out of bounds. In later chapters you will find ways of helping clients fill out their stories with essential but missing details related to stories, points of view and messages.

Listening to oneself: The helper's internal conversation

The conversation helpers have with themselves during helping sessions is the 'internal conversation'. To be an effective helper, you need to listen not only to the client but also to yourself. Granted, you don't want to become self-preoccupied, but listening to yourself on a 'second channel' can help you identify both what you might do to be of further help to the client and what might be standing in the way of your being with and listening to the client. It is a positive form of self-consciousness.

I remember when this second channel did not work very well for me. A friend of mine who had been in and out of mental hospitals for a few years and whom I had not seen for over six months showed up unannounced one evening at my flat. He was in a highly excited state. A torrent of ideas, some outlandish, some brilliant, flowed non-stop from him. I sincerely wanted to be with him as best I could, but I was very uncomfortable. I started by more or less naturally following the guidelines of tuning in, but I kept catching myself at the other end of the couch on which we were both sitting with my arms and legs crossed. I think that I was defending myself from the torrent of ideas. When I discovered myself almost literally tied up in knots, I would untwist my arms and legs, only to find them crossed again a few minutes later. It was hard work being with him. In retrospect, I realise I was concerned for my own security. I have since learned to listen to myself, reflect on my own thoughts and to remain curious about the client on the second channel a little better. When I listen to my non-verbal behaviour as well as my internal dialogue, I interact with clients better.

Helpers can use this second channel to listen to what they are 'saying' to themselves, their non-verbal behaviour, and their feelings and emotions. These messages can refer to the helper, the client or the relationship.

- 'I'm letting the client get under my skin. I had better do something to reset the dialogue.'
- 'My mind is occupied with other things and has been wandering. I had better refocus on what the client is saying.'
- 'Here's a client who has had a tough time of it, but her self-pity is standing in the way of her doing anything about it. My instinct is to be empathic and nurturing but I need to talk to her about her self-pity. I have to go slowly and cautiously.'
- 'It's not clear that this client is interested in changing at this time. I need to test the waters.'

The point is that this internal conversation goes on all the time. It can be a distraction or it can be another tool for helping and analysing the situation. For example, if the helper feels preoccupied, it is worth thinking if this is the helper's distraction or the client's distraction. The terms transference and counter-transference are used in psychoanalytical psychotherapy to denote this relationship between the client's issues and the therapist's issues. Another way helpers can understand the client is in relation to the therapeutic relationship. For example, is the way the client relates to the helper in therapy similar to the way they relate to others? This can then be used to help the client see themes and patterns in their relationships. Highlighting this to a client can make for useful learning on both parts.

In one study, Fauth and Williams (2005) found that helpers' internal conversations were 'generally helpful rather than hindering from both the trainee and student-client perspectives' (p. 443). The client, too, is having his or her internal conversation. One intriguing study (Hill, Thompson, Cogar & Denman, 1993) suggested that both client and therapist are more or less aware of the other's 'covert processes'. This study showed that even though helpers knew that clients were having their own internal conversations and left things unsaid, they were not very good at determining what those things were. At times there are verbal or non-verbal hints as to what the client's internal dialogue might be. Helping clients move key points from their internal conversations into the helping dialogue is a key task and will be discussed in Chapters 4 and 5.

LISTENING TO THE 'POWER OF BASICS' OF SUCCESSFUL THERAPY

We end by considering how listening relates to the key ingredients of successful therapy outlined in Chapter 1.

Listening to the client

We strive to give our full attention to our clients and to listen carefully to what they see as important, their stories, their expectations, their resources, their degree of collaboration, their struggles with obstacles, their ability to express their concerns, their reactions to their helpers, their willingness or hesitation to be in the driver's seat, the outcomes they are looking for, their understanding of and willingness to participate in the mode of treatment being used, the emotions they express, their uncertainties and hesitations, the contextual factors that affect their problems, used opportunities and participation. Sophia listens carefully to the signs of hope in what Jacomina says and does, especially her 'tiny steps' towards moving back into community. Laura listens to how David emphasises how helpful his phone and internet interactions with Peter, his PTSD 'buddy', are. In fact, David keeps intimating that he is getting more from his 'buddy' arrangement (mentioned in Chapters 1 and 2) than from the helping sessions themselves. Laura realises that this is useful for their feedback sessions.

Listening to ourselves as therapists

We listen to the ways we impact our clients, our own uncertainties and hesitations, how we are being affected by the client, the difficulties that arise, the mistakes we make, our own emotions, how genuine we are, the effectiveness of our treatment method – and we do all this without becoming preoccupied with ourselves. Laura comes to grips with the fact that David's relationship with Peter seems to be producing better or more results than David's relationship with her. She does so by recognising that client outcomes are the bottom line, no matter how they are achieved. She knows her relationship to David is solid. If his relationship with Peter is 'better' in some sense of the term, so be it. The relationship is not an end in itself. Sophia, listening to all Jacomina's resources, feels that she needs to encourage Jacomina to move even more aggressively into the driver's seat because Jacomina is showing signs of wanting to do so.

Listening to the relationship

Effective helpers listen carefully to the relationship-in-progress to discover which factors are working and which need attention; to the kind and quality of collaboration being developed; to the quality of the dialogue; to the ways they and their clients are influencing each other; to any 'bumps in the road' that arise;

to the ways in which the bumps or ruptures are handled. Laura sees cues indicating that David sees her as an authority figure to be managed rather than as a helper-collaborator-catalyst. When she asks, 'How are you doing?' she inevitably gets a response such as 'I am doing just fine' or something like that. He keeps her at arm's length. Because there is every sign that he is making progress, she hesitates to push the issue. Good outcomes trump ideal relationships.

Listening to the flow of communication and dialogue

Helpers listen to how effectively they and their clients are collaborating through dialogue. Listening to how clients respond to what they say, counsellors learn how to tailor their communication to the needs of clients. Helpers also listen to clients to discern their clients' abilities as communicators. They then use their own communication skills unobtrusively to help clients engage as fully as possible in the dialogue. Sophia recognises Jacomina's communication skills as a resource to be used to get back into community. David is clumsier as a communicator. He has a tendency to see conversations, at least conversations with Laura, as a power game. Laura is not bothered because she has no need to be 'one up' in any relationship. Furthermore, there seems to be little one-upmanship in David's relationship with Peter. So it's a question of leaving well-enough alone, at least for the time being.

Listening to the two-way feedback between client and helper

Helpers listen carefully to both formal and informal feedback with respect to both progress towards outcomes and quality of sessions. And they muse on it thoughtfully. Sophia uses the formal feedback from Duncan's surveys to explore any problematic issue. Laura listens carefully to all the 'messages' being sent by David during their sessions. She 'hears' his defensiveness and muses on what she might be doing to cause it. She learns more about the progress he is making by debriefing his sessions with Peter. And that progress seems to be substantial.

Listening to the flow of the method of treatment

Helpers look for signs that clients understand and can collaborate on the method of treatment. They listen for difficulties the client might have with any part of the treatment. In the case of both Jacomina and David, the method of treatment is the problem-management process outlined in Part III. So their helpers listen to how they grasp and use the problem-management framework – telling their stories and exploring their concerns, what kind of outcomes they are looking for and how they explore ways of achieving these outcomes. Helpers also look for clues as to clients' level of commitment to the work involved in achieving outcomes. Neither Jacomina nor David has any issues with the framework, though Jacomina understands the language better and uses the process more proactively.

Listening to the decisions being made

Helpers listen to the overall decision-making style of their clients – for instance, whether they are, in Kahneman's sense (2012), 'fast' or 'slow' decision makers and fast or slow with respect to the right issues. Helpers look for signs that their clients have some idea of the consequences, intended or unintended, of the decisions they are making. Jacomina tends to be more thoughtful in making decisions but does not always review the consequences of her decisions. David is abrupt. Sometimes his decisions seem to come out of nowhere – for instance, his immediate rejection of feedback surveys, but, as it turned out, not the feedback process itself. Laura believes that his 'fast' decision-making style can get him into trouble and wonders how to broach the issue with him. Helpers are also in touch with their own decision-making style in the flow of decisions involved in responding to clients. Sophia wonders whether she tries to influence Jacomina (and other clients) too much. Laura wonders whether she should be more forceful at times.

Helpers need to listen to or stay in touch with their own decision-making style. Responding to clients involves a whole series of decisions. Ongoing research on 'naturalistic' or 'adaptive' decision making (Klein, 1998, 2008, 2011; Schraagen, Militello, Ormerod & Lipshitz, 2008) shows that the kind of 'fast' decisions experts such as firefighters and airline pilots make on the spot makes sense under two conditions. They must be skilled and experienced. In the give-and-take of the helping process, counsellors and therapists need to be skilled, experienced and principled. However, in the end, uncertainty will always haunt decision making and helpers need to be prepared for the 'complexity and ambiguity' Klein sees at the heart of important decisions. David, in spite of his defensiveness, knows in his heart that Laura is skilled, experienced and principled.

Listening to the key assumptions, beliefs, values, norms, ethical issues and moral issues in play

The elements of this package, which includes culture, often permeate clients' stories either directly or indirectly or are key issues in and of themselves. Jacomina's religious sensitivities are often an important subtext in her narrative. Rediscovering what she really believes and values is a resource for recovery. David, from a fundamentalist background, struggles with a religious culture he has set aside but whose elements influenced him in his tours of Iraq and Afghanistan and still play a role in his recovery. He has a lot of 'musts/shoulds' from his upbringing, some of which help and some of which stand in the way of progress. Loyalty to the church turned into loyalty to company, platoon and squad – all with mixed feelings. The fact that he lived while his friends died leaves him with a sense of betrayal. He does not think that he has betrayed anyone or any group, but this does not eradicate his sense of betrayal. So helpers need to listen carefully to the assumptions, beliefs, values, norms, ethical challenges and moral issues, and focus on what their clients see as key. Which themes emerge as important, as influential?

THE SHADOW SIDE OF LISTENING: FORMS OF DISTORTED LISTENING

Listening as described here is not as easy as it sounds. Obstacles and distractions abound. Some relate to listening generally. Others relate more specifically to listening to and interpreting clients' non-verbal behaviour. As you will see from your own experience, the following kinds of distorted listening permeate human communication. They also insinuate themselves at times into the helping dialogue. Sometimes more than one kind of distortion contaminates the helping dialogue. They are part of the shadow side because helpers never intend to engage in these kinds of listening. Rather, helpers fall into them at times without even realising that they are doing so. But they stand in the way of the kind of open-minded listening and processing needed for real dialogue. Here are some forms of distorted listening.

Filtered listening

It is impossible to listen to other people in a completely unbiased way. Through socialisation we develop a variety of filters through which we listen to ourselves, others and the world around us. As Hall (1977) noted: 'One of the functions of culture is to provide a highly selective screen between man and the outside world. In its many forms, culture therefore designates what we pay attention to and what we ignore. This screening provides structure for the world' (p. 85). We need filters to provide structure for ourselves as we interact with the world. But personal, familial, sociological and cultural filters introduce various forms of bias into our listening and do so without our being aware of it.

The stronger the cultural filters, the greater the likelihood of bias. For instance, a white, middle-class helper probably tends to use white, middle-class filters in listening to others. Perhaps this makes little difference if the client is also white and middle class, but if the helper is listening to an Asian client who is well-to-do and has high social status in his community, to an African American mother from an urban ghetto or to a poor white subsistence farmer, then the helper's cultural filters might introduce bias. Prejudices, whether conscious or not, distort understanding. Like everyone else, helpers are tempted to pigeonhole clients because of gender, race, sexual orientation, nationality, social status, religious persuasion, political preferences, lifestyle and the like. Helpers' self-knowledge is essential. This includes ferreting out the biases and prejudices that distort listening.

Evaluative listening

Most people, even when they listen attentively, listen evaluatively. That is, as they listen, they are judging what the other person is saying as good/bad, right/wrong, acceptable/unacceptable, likeable/unlikeable, relevant/irrelevant and so forth. Helpers are not exempt from this universal tendency. The following interchange takes place between Jacomina and a friend of hers. Jacomina recounts it to Sophia as part of her story.

> **JACOMINA:**   Well, the rape and the investigation are not dead, at least not in my mind. They are not as vivid as they used to be, but they are there.
>
> **FRIEND:**   That's the problem, isn't it? Why don't you do yourself a favour and forget about it? Get on with life, for God's sake!

Evaluative listening gives way to advice giving. It might well be sound advice, but the point here is that Jacomina's friend listens and responds evaluatively. Clients should first be understood, then, if necessary, challenged or helped to challenge themselves. Evaluative listening, translated into advice-giving, will just put clients off. Indeed, a judgement that a client's point of view, once understood, needs to be expanded or transcended, or that a pattern of behaviour, once listened to and understood, needs to be altered, can be quite useful. That is, there are productive forms of evaluative listening. It is practically impossible to suspend judgement completely. Nevertheless, it is possible to set one's judgement aside for the time being in the interest of understanding clients, their worlds, their stories, their points of view and their decisions 'from the inside'.

Stereotype-based listening

I remember my reaction to hearing a doctor refer to me as the 'hernia in 304'. We don't like to be stereotyped, even when the stereotype has some validity. The very labels we learn in our training – paranoid, neurotic, sexual disorder, borderline – can militate against empathic understanding. Books on personality theories provide us with stereotypes: 'He's a perfectionist.' We even pigeonhole ourselves: 'I'm a Type A personality.' Although in this case the stereotype is often used as an excuse.

In psychotherapy, diagnostic categories can take precedence over the clients being diagnosed. Helpers forget at times that their labels are interpretations rather than understandings of their clients. You can be 'correct' in your diagnosis and still lose the sense of the person. In short, what you learn as you study psychology may help you organise what you hear, but it may also distort your listening. To use terms borrowed from Gestalt psychology, make sure that your client remains 'figure' – in the forefront of your attention – and that models and theories about clients remain 'ground' – knowledge that remains in the background and is used only in the interest of understanding and helping this unique client.

Fact-centred rather than person-centred listening

Some helpers ask clients many informational questions, as if clients would be cured if enough facts about them were known. It's entirely possible to collect facts but miss the person. The antidote is to listen to clients contextually, trying to focus on themes and key messages. Sophia, as she listens to Jacomina, picks up what is called a 'pessimistic explanatory style' theme (Peterson, Seligman & Vaillant, 1988). Clients with this style tend to comment negatively on unfortunate events, saying such things as, 'It will never go away', 'It affects everything I do' and 'It is my fault.' Sophia knows that the research indicates that people who fall victim to this style tend to end up with poorer health than those who do not. There may be a link, she hypothesises, between Jacomina's somatic complaints (headaches, gastric problems) and this explanatory style. This is a theme worth exploring. A person's 'locus of control' will determine to what extent they feel they have control over their lives, external situations and the decisions they make.

Sympathetic listening

Because most clients are experiencing some kind of misery and because some have been victimised by others or by society itself, helpers tend to feel sympathy for them. Sometimes these feelings are strong enough to distort the stories that clients are telling. Consider this case:

> Liz was counselling Ben, a man who had lost his wife and daughter to an earthquake. Liz had recently lost her husband to cancer. As Ben talked about his own tragedy during their first meeting, she wanted to hold him. Later that day she took a long walk and realised how her sympathy for Ben had distorted what she heard. She heard the depth of his loss, but, reminded of her own loss, only half heard the implication that his loss now excused him from getting on with his life.

Sympathy has an unmistakable place in human relationships, but its 'use', if that does not sound too inhuman, is limited in helping. In a sense, when I sympathise with someone, I become his or her accomplice. If I sympathise with my client as she tells me how awful her husband is, I take sides without knowing what the complete story is. Expressing sympathy can reinforce self-pity, which has a way of driving out problem-managing action.

Interrupting

I am reluctant to add 'interrupting', as some do, to this list of shadow-side obstacles to effective listening. Certainly, when helpers interrupt their clients, by definition, they stop listening. And interrupters often say things that they have been rehearsing, which means that they have been only partially listening. My reluctance, however, comes from the conviction that the helping conversation should be a dialogue. There are benign and malignant forms of interrupting. The helper who cuts the client off in mid-thought because he has something important to say is using a malignant form. But the case is different when a helper 'interrupts' a monologue with some gentle gesture and a comment such as, 'You've made several points. I want to make sure that I've understood them.' If interrupting promotes the kind of dialogue that serves the problem-management process, then it is useful. Still, care must be taken to factor in cultural differences in storytelling.

One possible reason counsellors fall prey to these kinds of shadow-side listening is the unexamined assumption that listening with an open mind is the same as approving what the client is saying. This is not the case, of course. Rather, listening with an open mind helps you to learn and understand. Whatever the reason for shadow-side listening, the outcome can be devastating because of a truth philosophers learned long ago – a small error in the beginning can lead to huge errors down the road. If the foundation of a building is out of kilter, it is hard to notice with the naked eye. But by the time construction reaches the ninth floor, it begins to look like the leaning tower of Pisa. Tuning in to clients and listening both actively and with an open mind are foundation counselling skills. Ignore them and dialogue is impossible.

INTRODUCTION TO RESPONDING SKILLS AND THE IMPORTANCE OF EMPATHIC RELATIONSHIPS

Helpers listen to clients both to understand them and their concerns and to respond to them in constructive ways. The logic of listening includes, as we have seen, tuning in to clients both physically and psychologically, listening actively, processing what is heard contextually and identifying the key ideas, messages or points of view the client is trying to communicate – all at the service of understanding clients and helping them understand themselves. Listening, then, is a very active process that is at the heart of understanding.

Responding skills

Helpers don't just listen; they also respond to clients in a variety of ways. They respond by sharing their understanding, checking to make sure that they've got things right, probing for clarity, summarising the issues being discussed and helping clients challenge themselves in a variety of ways. Of course, this is not a one-way street. Helpers respond to clients and clients respond to helpers in the give-and-take of the therapeutic dialogue.

The value of inclusive empathy (Pedersen *et al.*, 2008; Clark, 2003a, 2003b) and the other values discussed in Chapter 2 should permeate all responding to clients. Counsellors use the responding skills of empathy, probing, summarising and facilitating client self-challenge described in Chapters 3–5 not only to help clients tell and explore their stories but also in every stage and task of the problem-management framework covered in Part III. That is, helpers use all the communications skills outlined in Part II to help clients explore possibilities for a better future, set goals, develop plans for achieving goals and turn all this planning into problem-managing and opportunity-developing action.

In the following dialogue, a young girl, Rebecca, is talking to her social worker, who is providing the role of a helper, about the situation she is facing at home – the social worker's responses to her clearly illustrate an example of the nature of developing empathy:

REBECCA: I don't know, I just don't seem to be getting on with people.

SOCIAL WORKER: When you say people?

REBECCA: I mean my parents. They don't have any idea.

SOCIAL WORKER: They don't have any idea about you?

REBECCA: No, they think that I want to stay at school and go to university and everything. Well I do, in a way. But I wish they wouldn't push me all the time! They think they have to tell me how to do things all the time.

SOCIAL WORKER: It's as if they want to push you in a certain direction and you're not sure whether or not you want to go that way.

REBECCA: That's exactly it! I don't know what I want to do anymore! They push me so much that I don't know what I want!

SOCIAL WORKER: And that's upsetting you?

REBECCA: Yes, a lot . . . . I get upset easily these days and I'm sure it's got a lot to do with what's happening at home.

In this example, the two people become closely involved in the conversation and the social worker, rather than directing the conversation in a particular way, follows the thoughts and feelings that Rebecca expresses. Empathy is developed through this following process and through a willingness to listen to both what is said and what is implicit in what is being said. An intuitive ability is just as important in empathy as is technical skill.

I said earlier that the communication skills in helping situations are not special therapeutic skills. Rather they are skills that should characterise everyday interactions of ordinary people, even though, unfortunately, this is not the case. The ability to express empathy, the topic in this chapter, is important because we all want to be understood and we function better when we are understood. In day-to-day conversations, responding with empathy is also a tool of civility. Making an effort to get in touch with your conversational partner's frame of reference sends a message of respect. Therefore, empathic responses play an important part in building relationships.

Empathic relationships

In everyday life, understanding does not necessarily have to be put into words. Given enough time, people establish empathic relationships with one another in which understanding is communicated in a variety of rich and subtle ways without necessarily being put into words. A simple glance across a room as one spouse sees the other trapped in a conversation with a person he or she does not want to be with can communicate worlds of understanding. The glance says, 'I know you feel caught. I know you don't want to hurt the other person's feelings. I can feel the struggles going on inside you. But I also know that you'd like me to rescue you as soon as I can do so tactfully.' Signalling, discussed in this chapter, plays an important role in the communication of empathy.

People with empathic relationships often express empathy in actions. An arm around the shoulders of someone who has just suffered a defeat expresses both empathy and support. I was in the home of a poor family when the father came bursting through the front door shouting, 'I got the job.' His wife, without saying a word, went to the refrigerator, got a bottle of beer with a makeshift label on which 'Champagne' had been written, and offered it to her husband. Beer never tasted so good.

On the other hand, some people enter caringly into the world of their relatives, friends and colleagues and are certainly 'with' them but don't know how to communicate understanding through words or feel the need to do so. When a wife complains, 'I don't know whether he really understands', she is not necessarily saying that her relationship with her husband is not mutually empathic. She is more likely saying that she would appreciate it if he were to put his understanding into words from time to time.

The therapeutic alliance should be an empathic relationship. The skill and practice of communicating empathy to clients should not be an 'add on' ('she's good at communicating empathy'), but should flow naturally from this relationship. What Pedersen and his associates (2008) call 'inclusive cultural empathy', mentioned in Chapter 2, should permeate every facet of the dialogue between helper and client. This is not heroic but human. The 'technology' of communicating empathy outlined in this chapter is humanised through the relationship. Empathy is a two-way street (Zaki, Bolger & Ochsner, 2008). Clients must be willing to reveal themselves and helpers must be ready to understand. Another way of looking at the fullness of empathy is this. At one level there is, ideally, a verbal dialogue as described earlier between client and helper. But at another level there should also be an ongoing *social-emotional* dialogue between helper and client. This makes the relationship real and genuine. Goleman and Boyatzis (2008) in an article on social intelligence and the biology of leadership put it this way:

> "The salient discovery is that certain things leaders do – specifically, exhibit empathy and become attuned to others' moods – literally affect both their own brain chemistry and that of their followers. Indeed, researchers have found that the leader-follower dynamic is not a case of two (or more) independent brains reacting consciously or unconsciously to each other. Rather, the individual minds become, in a sense, fused into a single system." (p. 76)

Articles of both Goleman and Boyatzis, and Zaki, Bolger and Ochsner, use neuroscience to flesh out our understanding of empathy. In some non-hokey sense my being is communing with yours and yours with mine when we engage in empathic dialogue. This affects the quality and substance of the words we use. While it is possible to learn the skill and technology of responding with empathy, the exercise of that skill is hollow outside an empathic relationship. The technology of communicating empathy described in this chapter must be seen through this lens.

Empathic responding: A wide view of empathy

Empathy, we are told, is back in favour in intellectual circles (Elliott, Bohart, Watson & Greenberg, 2011; Stueber, 2010). Hopefully in the helping professions it has never been out of favour. Some now see empathy not just as a value and skill, but as a mode of treatment in itself (Slattery & Park, 2011). Empathic responding, in the view taken in this book, is based on empathic listening and involves sharing with clients your non-judgemental understanding of what they are thinking and feeling. Rogers (1980) described empathy in this way (as quoted in Elliott and his colleagues' article, p. 133):

> *"Empathy is the therapist's sensitive ability and willingness to understand the client's thoughts, feelings and struggles from the client's point of view. [It is] this ability to see completely through the client's eyes, adopt his frame of reference ... (p. 85). It means entering the private perceptual world of the other ... being sensitive, moment by moment, to the changing felt meanings which flow in this other person... It means sensing meanings of which he or she is scarcely aware..."* (p. 142)

We will revisit Rogers' last sentence in Chapter 5 when we talk about helping clients get in touch with these 'meanings'. That said, empathy is not an interpretation, but is derived from the client's frame of reference. It signals your desire to understand how clients see themselves, others and the world. It is a way of checking the accuracy of the listening and thoughtful processing mentioned earlier. It also signals your desire to put clients first and collaborate with them in their efforts to manage the problem situations of their lives. It is a natural outcome of the value of empathy discussed in Chapter 2. Norcross (2010) puts it this way:

> *"Empathy is linked to outcomes because it serves a positive relationship function, facilitates a corrective emotional experience, promotes exploration and meaning creation, and supports clients' self healing."* (p. 119)

Arthur Clark (2007) devotes an entire book to empathy in counselling and therapy. In Part 2 of his book he outlines the important role empathy plays in 13 different methods of treatment. He has also come up with a wider view of empathy (Clark, 2010a) that possibly affects the purity of the concept outlined earlier. He describes three kinds of empathy: subjective, interpersonal and objective. In his view *subjective* empathy 'enables a counsellor to momentarily identify with a client through intuitive reactions, and fleetingly imagine and experience what it is like to be a client' (p. 349). This kind of understanding of the client comes from the understanding of oneself and one's exposure in reality or in imagination to experiences similar to those of the client. When a client discusses an issue, such as struggling with perfectionism, the helper may briefly recall his or her own struggle with the same issue, or be able to view the client's struggle through their eyes. The counsellor is not necessarily distracted by what he or she experiences. Rather it adds something to his or her understanding of the client. *Objective* empathy arises from what a counsellor has learned from various sources, including his or her own experience or from reputable theories and research findings. As Rema, a counsellor, listens to Benjamin's story, she begins to see the outline of an obsessive-compulsive disorder. This, tentatively, adds to her understanding of Benjamin. Both subjective and objective empathy provide the counsellor with some kind of understanding of the client, but it is usually not the kind of understanding that is shared either immediately or directly with the client. Rema is hardly going to say, 'Aha, a classic obsessive-compulsive syndrome!'

The kind of empathy described and illustrated in this chapter is *interpersonal* empathy, the ability to get inside a client's frame of reference and understand what the client is thinking and feeling, together with the ability to communicate this understanding without prejudice to the client. If the client feels understood, he or she is more likely to 'move forward' in the helping process in a number of ways. It can lead to such outcomes as the strengthening of the therapeutic alliance, a deeper understanding of self, a better grasp of the problem situation, a clearer idea of what the desired outcome of the problem-management process should be and so forth. That said, both subjective and objective empathy can either contribute to and facilitate interpersonal empathy or, conversely, stand in the way. Empathy and the therapeutic relationship is a process and needs to be nurtured.

When a counsellor, let's say Jeff, is personally struck by what Susan is saying, this can help him get inside Susan's frame of reference or cause him to be distracted from her story. When Clarissa realises that Ted's story fits in with the findings of a research project in which she is engaged, this, too, can complement what Ted is saying about himself. But it could also cause her to miss something unique about Ted. The helper needs to stay focused on the client rather than get distracted by their own agenda. Or interests.

Consider this example. A counsellor, Sacha, has his first meeting with a client, Mariah, who has just lost her husband. He had a heart attack while driving and either the heart attack or the resulting crash killed him. She has two teenage sons. The meeting takes place about a week after the funeral. Here is part of their conversation:

> **SACHA:** First of all, I'd like to express my sorrow for your loss. So sudden. I lost my wife like that three years ago.
>
> **MARIAH (pauses):** My loss. Well. . . (she says this very softly, pauses, and then up straight, she leans forward and continues in a stronger voice). Tragic? Of course. His loss? Yes. But it wouldn't be right to call it my loss. The last years have not been very nice.
>
> **SACHA:** The two of you were not getting along. . . at all.
>
> **MARIAH:** At all. . . I don't know when our marriage died. I'm sure he blamed me. But for the last three years he has been going out with other women. Gambling. There's no use going into all of it. He still supported us, financially, that is. It's been a nightmare, but it's over. Fate intervened.
>
> **SACHA:** You're relieved. . . . Maybe more than relieved?
>
> **MARIAH:** I am totally relieved. But just saying straight out like that makes me feel. . . . What's the word I'm looking for?
>
> **SACHA:** Sounds like you don't want to say 'guilty'.
>
> **MARIAH:** No I don't. . . I'm more than relieved. I'm free. There's something like hope in the air. I still feel that I'm trampling on his grave. . . . No, that's not it.
>
> **SACHA:** Well, you are free to reconstruct your life. Perhaps the hope part means that's what you want to do.
>
> **MARIAH:** That's just what I want to do. There's a lot of hard work ahead of me.

Sacha makes two mistakes. One relates to self-disclosure, subjective empathy. This was not inappropriate at that time as it was their first meeting and he had not listened to her story first. This led him to have objective empathy, his second mistake. He reverted to the 'grieving widow' stereotype and this seemed to have been based more on his own experience rather than that of the client. Once he caught himself doing this, he was able to refocus his attention on the client and listen intently to what she had to say. She responded to his brief empathic responses by telling her story, expressing emotions that *she* feels, and looking towards the future.

This hardly means that subjective and objective empathy are always out of order. Rather they should be complementary to interpersonal empathy, not central. The literature on empathy is infuriatingly rich. There is no such thing as one pure approach to empathy. The approach taken in this chapter is based primarily on having the needs of the client drive the helping process. If we remember that clients and their concerns are of primary importance, we can learn to instinctively relate elements of both subjective and objective empathy to the kind of interpersonal empathy that immediately serves the needs of the client. Or we can let our own experiences, together with the theories and research findings of our profession, distract us from what clients need. But that would not be professional. This chapter highlights the importance of empathy but keeps the focus on the client.

THE THREE DIMENSIONS OF RESPONDING SKILLS: PERCEPTIVENESS, KNOW-HOW AND ASSERTIVENESS

Before we begin our exploration of empathy as a communication skill, here is a caution that applies to this and to the rest of the chapters of this book. There will be a kind of anatomy lesson in each chapter. For instance, in this chapter we are going to take the process of responding with empathy apart and look at the pieces. There will also be anatomy lessons in probing, summarising, facilitating client self-challenge, goal setting, action-plan design and implementation. The purpose of the anatomy lesson is to give you a deeper understanding of the processes involved in helping. Of course, the parts will be reassembled to give you a feeling for the skill-in-action. This process of breaking a skill down into its component parts is hardly restricted to counselling. People do this in learning how to fix an automobile engine, design a dress, swing a golf club, analyse a company's balance sheets, give a talk or get in touch with fundamental particles that make up the universe. Learning bit by bit is not always 'fun' (whatever that is), but it is often the price to pay for competence.

The communication skills involved in responding to clients have three dimensions: perceptiveness, know-how and assertiveness. Here is what these three look like in responding with empathy.

Perceptiveness

Feeling empathy for others is not helpful if the helper's perceptions are not accurate. But empathy, as used here, is much more than a feeling for the other person and, therefore, accuracy is more complicated than one would first think. Ickes (1993, 1997; Mast & Ickes, 2007) defined 'empathic accuracy' as 'the ability to accurately infer the specific content of another person's thought and feelings' (1993, p. 588). According to Ickes (1997), this ability is a component of success in many walks of life:

> *"Empathically accurate perceivers are those who are consistently good at 'reading' other people's thoughts and feelings. All else being equal, they are likely to be the most tactful advisors, the most diplomatic officials, the most effective negotiators, the most electable politicians, the most productive salespersons, the most successful teachers, and the most insightful therapists."* (p. 2)

The assumption is, of course, that such people are not only accurate perceivers but they can also weave their perceptions into their dialogues with their constituents, customers, students and clients. Helpers do this by sharing empathic responses with their clients. An empathic response involves accurately communicating one's understanding of another person from that person's point of view. Clinically, however, it is accurate only if it is perceived to be accurate by the client (Hodges, 2005). The understanding, the communication of that understanding and the client's view of the accuracy are all components. Accuracy is a relationship thing that is subject to all the uncertainties involved in the relationship.

From one point of view your responding skills are only as good as the accuracy of the perceptions on which they are based. Consider the difference between these two examples:

> Beth is counselling Ivan in a community mental health centre. Ivan is scared to talk about an 'ethical blunder' that he made at work. Beth senses his discomfort but thinks that he is angry rather than scared. She says, 'Ivan, I'm wondering what's making you so angry right now.' Because Ivan does not feel angry at the moment, he says nothing. In fact, he's startled by what she says and feels even more insecure. Beth takes his silence as a confirmation of his 'anger'. She tries to get him to talk about it.

Beth's perception is wrong and therefore disrupts the helping process. She misreads Ivan's emotional state and tries to engage in a dialogue based on her flawed perception. Contrast this to what happens in the following example:

> Mario, a manager, is counselling Enrique, a relatively new member of his team. During the past week, Enrique has made a significant contribution to a major project, but he has also made one rather costly mistake. Enrique's mind is on his blunder, not his success. Mario, sensing Enrique's discomfort, says, 'Your ideas in the meeting last Monday helped us re-conceptualise and reset the entire project. It was a great contribution. That kind of "outside the box" thinking is very valuable here. (He pauses.) I'd also like to talk to you about Wednesday. Your conversation with Acme's purchasing agent on Wednesday made him quite angry. (He pauses briefly once more.) Something tells me that you might be more worried about Wednesday's mistake than delighted with Monday's contribution. I just wanted to let you know that I'm not.' Enrique is greatly relieved. They go on to have a useful dialogue about what made Monday so good and what could be learned from Wednesday's blunder.

Mario's perceptiveness and his ability to defuse a tense situation lay the foundation for a positive dialogue.

The kind of perceptiveness needed to be a good helper comes from basic intelligence, social intelligence, experience, reflecting on your experience, developing wisdom and, more immediately, tuning in to clients, listening carefully to what they have to say, and thoughtfully and objectively processing what they say. Perceptiveness is part of social-emotional maturity. Finally, empathic accuracy is important, but it is not a thing in itself. Rather it is something you do *with* the client. The *effort* to be accurate may not always lead to perfect accuracy, but it can lead to a collaborative discussion with the client that produces the kind of shared understanding that helps the client move forward.

Know-how

Once you are aware of what kind of response is called for, you need to be able to deliver it. For instance, if you are aware that a client is anxious and confused because this is his first visit to a helper, it does little good if you don't know how to translate your perceptions and your understanding into words. Let's return to Ivan and Beth for a moment.

Ivan and Beth end up arguing about his 'anger'. Ivan finally gets up and leaves. Beth, unfortunately, takes this as a sign that she was right in the first place. The next day Ivan goes to see his minister. The minister sees quite clearly that Ivan is scared and confused. His perceptions are right. He says something like this: 'Ivan, you seem to be very uncomfortable. It may be that whatever is on your mind might be difficult to talk about. But I'd be glad to listen to it, whatever it is. But I don't want to push you into anything.' Ivan blurts out, 'But I've done something terrible.' The minister pauses and then says, 'Well, let's see what kind of sense we can make of it.' Ivan hesitates a bit, then leans back into his chair, takes a deep breath and launches into his story.

The minister is not only perceptive but also knows how to address Ivan's anxiety and hesitation. It's as if the minister, however unconsciously, says to himself, 'Here's a man who is almost exploding with the need to tell his story, but fear or shame or something like that is paralysing him. How can I put him at ease, let him know that he won't get hurt here? I need to recognise his anxiety and offer an opening.' He does not use these words, of course, but these are the kinds of sentiment that instinctively run through his mind. This chapter is designed to help you develop the know-how needed to communicate accurate empathic understanding.

Assertiveness

Accurate perceptions and excellent know-how are meaningless if they remain locked up inside you. They need to become part of the therapeutic dialogue. For instance, if you see that self-doubt is a theme that weaves itself throughout a client's story about her frustrating search for a better relationship with her estranged brother but fail to share your hunch with her, you do not pass the assertiveness test. Consider this example:

Nina, a young counsellor in the Centre for Student Development, is in the middle of the first session with Antonio, a graduate student. During the session, he mentions briefly a very helpful session he had the previous year with Carl, a middle-aged counsellor on the staff. Carl has accepted an academic position at the university and is no longer involved with the Centre. Nina realises that Antonio is disappointed that he couldn't see Carl and might have some misgivings about being helped by a new counsellor – a younger woman. She has faced sensitive issues like this before and would not be offended if Antonio were to choose a different counsellor. During a lull in the conversation, she says something like this: 'Antonio, could we take a time-out here for a moment? I think you might be a bit disappointed to find out that Carl is no longer here. Or at least I probably would be if I were in your shoes. You were just more or less assigned to me, and I'm not sure the fit is right. Maybe you can give that a bit of thought. Then, if you think I can be of help, you can schedule another meeting with me. But you're certainly free to review who is on staff and choose whomever you want.'

In this case, perceptiveness, know-how and assertiveness all come together. This is not to suggest that assertiveness is an overriding value in and of itself. To be assertive without perceptiveness and know-how is to court disaster. These three dimensions of responding skills apply to all the communication skills discussed in Part II and their use in all the stages and tasks of the problem-management helping process.

RESPONDING WITH EMPATHY

Although many people may 'feel empathy' for others – that is, they are motivated in many different ways by the value of empathy described in Chapter 2 – the truth is that few know how to put empathic understanding into words. And so responding with empathy as a way of communicating understanding during conversations remains, unfortunately, a relatively improbable event in everyday life. Perhaps that's why it is so powerful in helping settings. When clients are asked what they find helpful in counselling sessions, being understood gets top ratings, in part because so many of them have an unfulfilled need to be understood. They don't find it in their everyday life.

The basic formula

Some say that trying to teach counsellors how to respond with empathy is 'rigid and wooden'. I believe that empathy can be taught, but all communication skills come to life, are personalised and become part of one's interpersonal relationship style only through genuine day-to-day use. Helpers can learn the theory about empathy but need to put it into practice to really develop their skills. This comes with time and experience. Hopefully, this chapter avoids the 'rigid and wooden' critique as successfully as others who have developed therapeutic communication training programmes.

Basic empathic understanding can be expressed in the following stylised formula:

You feel... [here name the correct emotion expressed by the client]
Because... [here indicate the correct experiences, thoughts and behaviours that give rise to the feelings].

> For instance, Leonardo is talking with a helper about his arthritis and all its attendant ills. There is pain, of course, but more to the point, he can't get around the way he used to. At one point the helper says, 'You feel bad, not so much because of the pain, but because your ability to get around – your freedom – has been curtailed.'
>
> Leonardo replies, 'That's just it. I can manage the pain. But not being able to get around is killing me. It's like being in prison.'
>
> They go on to discuss ways in which Leonardo, with the help of family and friends, can get out of 'prison' more often – that is, become more mobile – together with ways of coping with both the pain and the boredom of his 'prison' time.

The formula – 'You feel... because...' – is a basic beginner's tool to get used to the concept of responding with accurate empathy but needs to be developed with practice. It focuses on the key points of clients' stories, points of view, intentions, proposals and decisions, together with the feelings, emotions and moods associated with them. This basic formula is used in the following examples. For the moment, ignore the fact that it might sound a bit stylised. Ordinary human language will be substituted later. In the first example, a divorced mother with two young children is talking to a social worker about her ex-husband. She has been talking about the ways he has let her and their children down. She ends by saying:

> **CLIENT:** I could kill him! He failed to take the children again last weekend. This is three times out of the last six weeks.
>
> **HELPER:** You feel furious because he keeps failing to hold up his part of the bargain.
>
> **CLIENT:** I'm not even sure that he's taking our 'bargain' seriously. I just have to find some way to get him to do what he promised to do. What he told the court he would do.

His not taking the children according to their agreement [an experience for the client] infuriates her [an emotion]. The helper captures both the emotion and the reason for it. And the client moves forward in terms of thinking about possible actions she could take.

In the next example a woman who has been having a great deal of gastric and intestinal distress is going to have a colonoscopy. She is talking with a hospital counsellor the night before the procedure.

> **PATIENT:**   God knows what they'll find when they go in. I keep asking questions, but they keep giving me vague answers.
>
> **HELPER:**   You feel troubled because you believe that you're being left in the dark.
>
> **PATIENT:**   In the dark not just about my body. It's my life! If they'd only tell me. Then I could prepare myself better.

They go on to discuss what she needs to do to get the kind of information she wants. The accuracy of the helper's response does not solve the woman's problems, but the patient does move a bit. She gets a chance to vent her concerns, she receives a bit of understanding and she says why she wants more information. This perhaps puts her in a better position to ask for a more open relationship with her doctors. An alternate way to this basic formula is a more tentative statement such as 'It sounds like you are feeling …'. This may help to engage the client in open dialogue about these feelings and emotions.

Respond accurately to clients' feelings, emotions and moods

The importance of feelings, emotions and moods in our lives was discussed earlier. Helpers need to respond to clients' emotions in such a way as to move the helping process forward. This means identifying key emotions the client either expresses or discusses (helper perceptiveness) and weaving them into the dialogue (helper know-how), even when they are sensitive or part of a messy situation (helper courage or assertiveness). Do you remember the last time you as a consumer got a problem resolved with a good customer service representative? He or she might have said something like this to you: 'I know you're angry right now because the package didn't arrive, and you have every right to be. After all, we did make you a promise. Here's what we can do to make it right for you …'. Rather than ignoring the customer's emotions, good customer service reps face up to them as helpfully as possible. Here are some guidelines:

Use the right family of emotions and the right intensity   In the basic empathy formula, 'You feel…' should be followed by the correct family of emotions and the correct intensity.

> *Family.* The statements 'You feel hurt', 'You feel relieved' and 'You feel enthusiastic' specify different families of emotion.
>
> *Intensity.* The statements 'You feel annoyed', 'You feel angry' and 'You're furious' specify different degrees of intensity in the same family (anger).

The words 'sad', 'mad', 'bad' and 'glad' refer to four of the main families of emotion, whereas 'content', 'quite happy' and 'overjoyed' refer to different intensities within the glad family.

Distinguish between expressed and discussed feelings   Clients both express emotions they are feeling during the interview and talk about emotions they felt at the time of some incident. For instance, consider this interchange between a client involved in a child custody proceeding and a counsellor. She is talking about her husband.

CLIENT (calmly):   I get furious with him when he says things, little snide things, that suggest that I don't take good care of the children.

HELPER: You feel especially angry when he intimates that you're not a good mother.

The client isn't angry right now. Rather, she is talking about the anger. The following example – a woman is talking about one of her colleagues at work – deals with expressed rather than discussed feelings.

CLIENT (enthusiastically):   I threw caution to the wind and confronted him about his sarcasm and it actually worked. He not only apologised but behaved himself the rest of the trip.

HELPER: You feel great because you took a chance and it paid off.

Clients don't always name their feelings and emotions. However, if they express emotion, it is part of the message and needs to be identified and understood.

Read and respond to feelings and emotions embedded in clients' non-verbal behaviour   Often helpers have to read clients' emotions – both the family and the intensity – in their non-verbal behaviour. In the following example, a student comes to you, sits down, looks at the floor, hunches over and speaks haltingly:

CLIENT: I don't even know where to start. (He falls silent.)

HELPER: It's pretty clear that you're feeling miserable. Maybe we can talk about why.

CLIENT (after a pause):   Well, let me tell you what happened. . . .

You see that he is depressed and his non-verbal behaviour indicates that the feelings are quite intense. His non-verbal behaviour reveals the broad family ('You feel bad') and the intensity ('You feel very bad'). Of course, you do not yet know the experiences, thoughts and behaviours that give rise to these emotions.

Be sensitive in naming emotions   Naming and discussing feelings and emotions threaten some clients. Cultural sensitivities and personal sensitivities within a culture differ widely. If this is the case, it might be better to focus on experiences, thoughts and behaviours and proceed only gradually to a discussion of feelings. The following client, an unmarried man in his mid-30s who has come to talk about 'certain dissatisfactions' in his life, has shown some reluctance to express or even to talk about feelings.

CLIENT (in a pleasant, relaxed voice):   You won't believe it! My mother is always trying to make a little kid out of me. And I'm 35! Last week, in front of a group of my friends, she brought out my rubber boots and an umbrella and gave me a little talk on how to dress for bad weather (laughs).

COUNSELLOR A: It might be hard to admit it, but I get the feeling that deep down you were furious.

CLIENT: Well, I don't know about that. Anyway, at work. . . .

COUNSELLOR A: (pushes the emotion issue and is met with some resistance. The client changes the topic.)

COUNSELLOR B (in a somewhat lighthearted way):   So she's still playing the mother role – to the hilt, it would seem.

CLIENT (with more of a bite in his voice):   And the hilt includes not wanting me to grow up. But I am grown up . . . well, pretty grown up. But I don't always act grown up around her.

Counsellor B, choosing to respond to the 'strong mother' issue rather than the more sensitive 'being kept a kid and feeling really lousy about it' issue, gives the client more room to move. This works, for the client himself moves towards the more sensitive issue – his playing the child, at least at times, when he's with his mother.

Some clients are hesitant to talk about certain emotions. One client might find it relatively easy to talk about his anger but not his hurt. The following client is talking about his disappointment at not being chosen for a special team at work.

> **CLIENT:** I worked as hard as anyone else to get the project up and running. In fact, I was at the meeting where we came up with the idea in the first place. . . . And now they've dropped me.
>
> **COUNSELLOR A:** So you feel really hurt – left out of your own project.
>
> **CLIENT (hesitating):** Hmm. . . . I'm really ticked off. Why shouldn't I be?

Here is a client with lots of ego. He doesn't like the idea that he has been 'hurt'. Counsellor B takes a different tack.

> **COUNSELLOR B:** So it's more than annoying to be left out of what, in many ways, is your own project.
>
> **CLIENT:** How could they do that? It is more than annoying. It's . . . well . . . humiliating.

Counsellor B, factoring in the client's ego, sticks to the anger, allowing the client himself to name the more sensitive emotion. Contextual listening – in this case listening to the client's emotions through the context of the pride he takes in himself and his accomplishments and his relationships at work that have gone wrong – is part of social intelligence. However, being sensitive to clients' sensitive emotions should not rob counselling of its robustness. Too much tiptoeing around clients' 'sensitivities' does not serve them well. Remember what was said earlier. Clients are not as fragile as we sometimes make them out to be.

Use variety in responding to clients' feelings and emotions   Because clients express feelings in a number of different ways, helpers can communicate an understanding of feelings in a variety of ways.

> *By single words.* You feel good. You're depressed. You feel abandoned. You're delighted. You feel trapped. You're angry.
>
> *By different kinds of phrases.* You're sitting on top of the world. You feel down in the dumps. You feel left in the lurch. Your back's up against the wall. You're really on a roll.
>
> *By what is implied in behavioural statements.* You feel like giving up (implied emotion: despair). You feel like hugging him (implied emotion: joy). Now that you see what he's been doing to you, you almost feel like throwing up (implied emotion: disgust).
>
> *By what is implied in experiences the client is discussing.* You feel you're being dumped on (implied feeling: victimised). You feel you're being stereotyped (implied feeling: resentment). You feel you're at the top of her list (implied feeling: elation). You feel you're going to get caught (implied feeling: fear). Note that the implication of each could be spelt out: You feel angry because you're being dumped on. You resent the fact that you're being stereotyped. You feel great because it seems that you're at the top of her list.

Because ultimately you must discard formulas and use your own language – words that are yours rather than words from a textbook and words that make sense to the client – it helps to develop a variety of ways of communicating your understanding of clients' feelings and emotions. It keeps you from being wooden in your responses.

Consider this example: The client tells you that she has just been given the kind of job she has been looking for over the past two years. Here are some possible responses to her emotion.

> *Single word.* You're really happy.
>
> *A phrase.* You're on cloud nine.
>
> *Experiential statement.* You feel you finally got what you deserve.
>
> *Behavioural statement.* You feel like going out and celebrating.

With experience, you can extend your range of expression at the service of your clients. Providing variety will become second nature.

Neither overemphasise nor underemphasise feelings, emotions and moods Some counsellors take an overly rational approach to helping and almost ignore clients' feelings. Others become too preoccupied with clients' emotions and moods. They pepper clients with questions about feelings and at times extort answers. To say that feelings, emotions and moods are important is not to say that they are everything. The best defence against either extreme is to link feelings, emotions and moods to the experiences, thoughts and behaviours that give rise to them.

Respond accurately to the key experiences, thoughts and behaviours in clients' stories

Key experiences, thoughts and behaviours give rise to clients' feelings, emotions and moods. The 'because...' in the empathic-response formula is to be followed by an indication of the experiences, thoughts and behaviours that underlie the client's feelings. In the following example, the client, a graduate student in law school, is venting his frustration.

> **CLIENT (heatedly):** You know why he got an A? He took my notes and disappeared. I didn't get a chance to study them. And I never even confronted him about it.
>
> **HELPER:** You feel doubly angry because not only did he steal your notes, but you let him get away with it.

The response specifies both the client's experience (the theft) and his behaviour (in this case, a failure to act) that give rise to his distress. His anger is directed not only at his classmate but also himself.

In the following example, a mugging victim has been talking to a social worker to help cope with his fears of going out. Before the mugging, he had given no thought to urban problems. Now he tends to see menace everywhere.

> **CLIENT:** This gradual approach of getting back in the swing seems to be working. Last night I went out without a companion. First time. I have to admit that I was scared. But I think I've learned how to be careful. Last night was important. I feel I can begin to move around again.
>
> **HELPER:** You feel comfortable with the one-step-at-a-time approach you've been taking. And it paid off last night when you regained a big chunk of your freedom.
>
> **CLIENT:** That's it! I know I'm going to be free again. . . . Here's what I've been thinking of doing. . . .

The client is talking about success in implementing a course of action. The helper's response recognises the client's satisfaction and also how important it is for the client to feel both safe and free. The client moves on to describe the next phase of his programme.

Another client, after a few sessions spread out over six months, says something like this about the progress she is making in rebuilding her life after a devastating car accident. She's back at work and has been working with her husband at rebuilding their marriage.

> **CLIENT (talking in an animated way):** I really think that things couldn't be going better. I'm doing very well at my new job, and my husband isn't just putting up with it. He thinks it's great. He and I are getting along better than ever, even sexually, and I never expected that. We're both working at our marriage. I guess I'm just waiting for the bubble to burst.
>
> **HELPER:** You feel great because things have been going better than you ever expected – and it seems almost too good to be true.
>
> **CLIENT:** Well, a 'bubble bursting' might be the wrong image. I think there's a difference between being cautious and waiting for disaster to strike. I'll always be cautious, but I'm finding out that I can make things come true instead of sitting around waiting for them to happen as I usually do. I guess I've got to keep making my own luck.

This client talks about her experiences, attitudes and behaviours, and expresses feelings, the flavour of which is captured in the helper's response. The response, capturing as it does both the client's enthusiasm and her lingering fears, is quite useful because the client makes an important distinction between reasonable caution and expecting the worst to happen. She moves on to her need to make things happen, to become more of an agent in her life.

In the following example, the client, a 45-year-old male construction worker, married, with four children between the ages of 9 and 16, has been expressing concerns about his children.

CLIENT: I don't consider myself old-fashioned, but I think children these days suffer from overindulgence. We keep giving them things. We let them do whatever they want. I fall into the same trap myself. It's just not good for them. I don't think we're preparing them for what the world is really like.

COUNSELLOR: So you see the 'do-what-you-want' and 'free-lunch' messages as a lot of hogwash. It's going to backfire and your children could end up getting hurt.

CLIENT: Right. . . . But I'm not in control. My children can get one set of messages from me and then get a flood of contradictory messages outside, and from TV, and the internet. . . . I don't want to be a tyrant. Or come across as a killjoy. That doesn't work anyway. At work I see problems and I take care of them. But this has got me stymied.

COUNSELLOR: So the whole picture seems pretty gloomy right now. You're not exactly sure what to do about it. You handle problems at work. But it's a lot harder to do something about societal problems that could hurt your children. What have you tried so far? What works, even a little? And what doesn't work?

Once the counsellor communicates understanding of the client's point of view, he (the client) moves on to share his sense of helplessness. The helper realises, however, that the client probably has tried some approaches to managing this problem situation. It could be that he is not as helpless as he makes himself out to be.

In the next example, the client, who is hearing-impaired, has been discussing ways of becoming, in her words, 'a full-fledged member of my extended family'. The discussion between client and helper takes place through a combination of lip reading and signing.

CLIENT (enthusiastically): Let me tell you what I'm thinking of doing. . . . First of all, I'm going to stop fading into the background in family and friends' conversation groups. I'll be the best listener there. And I'll get my thoughts across even if I have to use props. That's how I really am . . . inside, you know, in my mind.

HELPER: Sounds exciting. You're thinking of getting right into the middle of things. . . where you think you belong. You might even try a bit of drama.

CLIENT: And I think that, well, socially, I'm pretty smart. So I'm not talking about being melodramatic or anything. I can do all this with finesse, not just barge in.

HELPER: You'll make it all natural. . . . Draw me a couple of pictures of what this would look like.

The client comes up with a proposal for a course of action that will help her take her 'rightful place' in conversations with family and friends setting her agenda. The helper's response recognises her enthusiasm and sense of determination. They go on to have a dialogue about practical tactics.

When clients announce key decisions or express their resolve to do something, it's important to recognise the core of what they are saying. In the following example, a client being treated for social phobia has benefited greatly from cognitive-behavioural therapy. For instance, in uncomfortable social situations he has learned to block self-defeating thoughts and to keep his attention focused externally – on the social situation itself and on the agenda of the people involved – instead of turning in on himself.

CLIENT (emphatically):   I'm not going to turn back. I've had to fight to get where I am now. But I can see how easy it could be to slide back into my old habits. I bet a lot of people do. I see it all around me. People make resolutions and then they peter out.

HELPER: Even though it's possible for you to give up your hard-earned gains, you're not going to do it. You're just not.

CLIENT: But what can I do to make sure that I won't? I'm convinced I won't, but. . . .

HELPER: You need some ratchets. They're the things that keep roller-coaster cars from sliding back. You hear them going click, click, click on the way up.

CLIENT: Ah, right! But I need psychological ones. . . .

HELPER: And social ones. . . . What's kept you from sliding back so far?

This client is in the implementing-the-action-programme stage. In a positive psychology mode, the counsellor focuses on his successes. They go on to discuss the kind of 'ratchets' he needs to keep him from backsliding.

BECOMING COMPETENT AND CONFIDENT IN RESPONDING WITH EMPATHY: PRINCIPLES AND GUIDELINES

While helpers need competence in communication skills in general, they especially need competence in communicating empathy to their clients. Active listening is wasted without empathic responding. If empathic responding is not part of your everyday communication skills, you have a problem because if they are 'dragged out' to be used in helping, they can sound phoney. Then essential genuineness is out the window. Here are a number of principles that can guide you as you respond with empathy. Remember that these guidelines are not formulas to be followed slavishly.

Use empathic responses throughout the helping process

Responding with empathy is useful at every stage and in every task of the helping process. Communicating and checking understanding is always helpful. Here are some examples of helpers responding with empathy at different stages of the problem-management process covered in Part III.

Problem clarification and opportunity identification   A teenager in his third year of high school has just found out that he is moving with his family to a different city. A school counsellor responds, 'You're miserable because you have to leave all your friends. But it sounds like you may even feel a bit betrayed. You didn't see this coming at all.' The counsellor realises that he has to help his client pick up the pieces and move on, but sharing his understanding helps build a foundation to do so. The teen goes on to talk in positive terms about the large city they will be moving to and the opportunities it will offer. At one point the school counsellor responds, 'So there's an upside to all this. Big cities are filled with things to do. You like theatre and there are loads there. That's something to look forward to.'

Discovering and evaluating options for a better future   A woman has been discussing the trade-offs between marriage and career. At one point her helper says, 'There's some ambivalence here. If you marry Jim, you might not be able to have the kind of career you'd like. Or did I hear you half say that it might be possible to put both together? Sort of get the best of both worlds.' The client goes on to explore the possibilities around 'getting the best of both worlds'. It helps her greatly in preparing for her next conversation with Jim.

Choosing actions to accomplish goals   A man has been discussing his desire to control his cholesterol level without taking a medicine, the possible side effects of which worry him. He says that it might work. The counsellor responds, 'It's a relief to know that sticking to the diet and exercise might mean that you won't have to take any medicine ....Hmm .... Let's explore the "might" part. I'm not exactly sure what your doctor said.' The helper recognises the client's aversion to taking medications, but then seeks further clarification.

Programme implementation issues   A married couple has been struggling to put into practice a few strategies to improve their communication with each other. They've both called their attempts a 'disaster'. The counsellor replies, 'OK, so you're annoyed with yourselves for not accomplishing even the simple active-listening goals you set for yourselves.... Let's see what we can learn from the "disaster"' (said somewhat lightheartedly). The counsellor communicates understanding of their disappointment in not implementing their plan, but, in a more positive vein, focuses on what they can learn from the failure.

Responding with empathy is a mode of human contact, a relationship builder, a conversational lubricant, a perception-checking intervention and a mild form of social influence. It is always useful. Driscoll (1984), in his common-sense way, referred to empathic responses as 'nickel-and-dime interventions that each contribute only a smidgen of therapeutic movement, but without which the course of therapeutic progress would be markedly slower' (p. 90). Because empathic responses provide a continual trickle of understanding, it is a way of providing support for clients throughout the helping process. It is never wrong to let clients know that you are trying to understand them from their frame of reference. Of course, thoughtful listening and processing can lead to empathic responses that are much more than 'nickel-and-dime' interventions. Clients who feel they are being understood participate more effectively and more fully in the helping process. Because responding with empathy helps build trust, it paves the way for the helper to use stronger interventions, such as inviting clients to engage in self-challenge.

Respond selectively to core client messages

It is impossible to respond with empathy to everything a client says. Therefore, as you listen to clients, make every attempt to identify and respond to what you believe are core messages – that is, the heart of what the client is saying and expressing, especially if the client speaks at any length. Sometimes this selectivity means paying particular attention to one or two messages even though the client communicates many. For instance, a young woman, in discussing her doubts about marrying her companion, says at one time or another during a session that she is tired of his sloppy habits, is not really interested in his friends, wonders about his lack of intellectual curiosity, is dismayed at his relatively low level of career aspirations and resents the fact that he faults her for being highly ambitious.

> **COUNSELLOR:**   The picture you paint doesn't look that promising, but the mismatch in career expectations is especially troubling.
>
> **CLIENT:** You know, I'm beginning to think that Jim and I would be pretty good friends, even because we're so different. But partners? Maybe that's pushing it.

In this example, the counsellor's empathic response helps the client herself to identify what is core. The counsellor follows her lead. In the spirit of inclusive empathy, the counsellor believes that she can take the lead in exploring her relationship. After all, it is *her* relationship. His summary empathic response at the end allows her to question the direction in which she and her friend are headed. Of course, because clients are not always so obliging, helpers must continually ask themselves as they listen, 'What is key? What is most important here?' and then find ways of checking it out with the client. This helps clients sort out things that are not clear in their own minds.

Responding to what is key sometimes means focusing on experiences *or* actions *or* feelings rather than all three. Consider the following example of a client who is experiencing stress because of his wife's poor health and concerns at work.

CLIENT: This week I tried to get my wife to see the doctor, but she refused, even though she fainted a couple of times. The children had no school, so they were underfoot almost constantly. I haven't been able to finish a report my boss expects from me next Monday.

HELPER: It's been a lousy week all the way around.

CLIENT: As bad as they come. When things are lousy both at home and at work, there's no place for me to relax. I just want to get the hell out of the house and find some place to forget it all. . . . Almost run away, . . . But I can't. . . . I mean I won't.

Here the counsellor chooses to emphasise the feelings of the client, because she believes that his feelings of frustration and irritation are what is uppermost in his consciousness right now. This helps him move deeper into the problem situation – and then find a bit of resolve at the bottom of the pit.

At another time or with another client, the emphasis might be quite different. In the next example, a young woman is talking about her problems with her father.

CLIENT: My dad yelled at me all the time last year about how I dress. But just last week I heard him telling someone how nice I looked. He yells at my sister about the same things he ignores when my younger brother does them. Sometimes he's really nice with my mother and other times, too much of the time, he's just awful – demanding, grouchy, sarcastic.

HELPER: The inconsistency is really getting to you.

CLIENT: Absolutely! It's hard for all of us to know where we stand. I hate coming home when I'm not sure which 'dad' will be there. Sometimes I come late to avoid all this. But that makes him even madder.

In this response, the counsellor emphasises the client's experience of her father's inconsistency. It hits the mark and she explores the problem situation further.

Respond to the context, not just the words

A good empathic response is based not just on the client's immediate words and non-verbal behaviour. It also takes into account the context of what is said, everything that 'surrounds' and permeates a client's statement. This client may be in crisis. That client may be doing a more leisurely 'taking stock' of where he is in life. You are listening to clients in the context of their lives. The context modifies everything the client says.

Consider this case. Jeff, a white teenager, is accused of beating a black youth whose car stalled in a white neighbourhood. The beaten youth is still in a coma. When Jeff talks to a court-appointed counsellor, the counsellor listens to what Jeff says in light of Jeff's upbringing and environment. The context includes his family, the people he interacts with in his neighbourhood, the racist attitudes of many people in his blue-collar neighbourhood, the sporadic violence there, the fact that his father died when Jeff was in primary school, a somewhat indulgent mother with a history of alcoholism, easy access to drugs, the 'cultural voices' he has listened to with regards to ethnic groups and the cultural voices he has listened to at school and at church. Jeff is what he is in part because of all the cultural influences in his life. The following interchange takes place.

> **JEFF:** I don't know why I did it. I just did it, me and these other guys. We'd been drinking a bit and smoking up a bit – but not too much. It was just the whole thing.
>
> **HELPER:** Looking back, it's almost like it's something that happened to you rather than something you did, and yet you know, somewhat bitterly, that you actually did it.
>
> **JEFF:** More than bitter! I've screwed up the rest of my life. It's not like I got up that morning saying that I was going to bash someone that day.

The counsellor's response is in no way an attempt to excuse Jeff's behaviour, but it does factor in some of the environmental realities. Later on he will help Jeff challenge himself to decide whether he is to remain a victim of his environment in terms of the prejudices he has acquired, gang membership, family history and the like or whether he has the convictions, the will and the guts to do something about it.

Use empathic responses as a mild social-influence process

Because helpers cannot respond with empathy to everything their clients say, they are always searching for core messages. They are forced into a selection process that influences the course of the therapeutic dialogue. So even responding with empathy can be part of the social-influence dimension of counselling mentioned in Chapter 2. Helpers believe that the messages they select for attention are core primarily because they are core for the client. But helpers also believe, at some level, that certain messages *should* be important for the client.

In the following example, an incest-victim-turned-incest-perpetrator is in prison awaiting trial. In a session with a counsellor he is trying to exonerate himself by blaming what happened to him in the past. He has been talking so quickly that the helper finds it difficult to interrupt. Finally, the helper, who has a pretty good working relationship with the client, breaks in.

> **HELPER:** You've used some strong language to describe yourself. Let me see if I have it right. You said something about being 'structurally deformed'. I believe you also used the term 'automatic reactions'. You describe yourself as 'haunted' and 'driven'.
>
> **CLIENTS:** Well . . . I guess it's strong language. . . . Makes me sound like a psychological freak. Which I'm not.

The helper wants the client to listen to himself. So his 'let me get this straight' response is a kind of challenge, but he uses the client's own words. The helper could also seek to clarify what was said by 'let me see if I have understood this ...'. His response breaks the client's chain of thinking. It hits the mark because the client pulls himself up short. Of course, helpers need to be careful not to put words in a client's mouth and may need to seek clarification or highlight inconsistencies in the client's story.

Use empathic responses to stimulate movement throughout the helping process

While responding with empathy is an excellent tool for building the helping relationship, it also acts as a stimulus at every stage and step of the process. When clients are understood, they tend to move forward, however 'moving forward' is defined. Responding with empathy helps clients move forward early on if it helps clients explore a problem situation or an undeveloped opportunity more realistically. Later, empathy helps clients identify and explore possibilities for a better future, craft change agendas or explore their degree of commitment to an agenda. Once goals are set, empathy helps clients clarify action strategies and set out an action plan. In the action phase, helpers use empathy to help clients identify obstacles to action, overcome them and accomplish goals.

In the following example, a young woman visits the student services centre at her university to discuss an unwanted pregnancy.

> **CLIENT:** And so here I am, two months pregnant. I don't want to be pregnant. I'm not married, and I don't even love the father. To tell the truth, I don't even think I like him. Oh, Lord, this is something that happens to other people, not me! I wake up thinking this whole thing is unreal. Now people are trying to push me towards abortion.
>
> **HELPER:** You're still so amazed that it's almost impossible to accept that it's true. To make things worse, people are telling you what to do.
>
> **CLIENT:** Amazed? I'm stupefied! Mainly, at my own stupidity for getting myself into this. I've never had such an expensive lesson in my life. But I've decided one thing. No one, no one is going to tell me what to do now. I'll make my own decisions.

After the helper's empathic response, self-recrimination over her lack of self-responsibility helps the client make a stand. She says she wants to capitalise on a very expensive mistake. It often happens that empathic responses that hit the mark put pressure on clients to move forward. So responding with empathy, even though it is a communication of understanding, is also part of the social-influence process.

Use empathic responses as a way of bridging diversity gaps

This principle is a corollary of the preceding two. Empathic responses based on effective tuning in and listening constitute one of the most important tools you have in interacting with clients who differ from you in significant ways. Responding with empathy is one way of telling clients that you are a learner and that you are interested in understanding them better. Or rather you are interested in helping them understand themselves. Scott and Borodovsky (1990) referred to empathic listening as 'cultural role-taking'. They could have said 'diversity role-taking'. In the following example, a younger white male counsellor is talking with an elderly African American woman who has recently lost her husband. She is in hospital with a broken leg.

> **CLIENT:** I hear they try to get you out of these places as quick as possible. But I seem to be lying around here doing nothing. Jimmy [her late husband] wouldn't even recognise me.
>
> **HELPER:** It's pretty depressing to have this happen so soon after losing your husband.
>
> **CLIENT:** Oh, I'm not depressed. I just want to get out of here and get back to doing things at home. Jimmy's gone, but there's plenty of people around there to help me take care of myself.
>
> **HELPER:** Getting back into the swing of things is the best medicine for you.
>
> **CLIENT:** Now you've got it right. What I need right now is to know when I can go home and what I need to do for my leg once I get there. I've got to get things in order. That's what I do best.

The helper makes assumptions that might be true for him but don't seem to be true for her. Perhaps *he* would like the luxury of being cared for in a hospital. If he were to lose his wife, he would be depressed and not want to get back to work quickly. Perhaps he does not have a community of family and friends that would rally around him. Her personal culture has no place for just lying around. She's taking her problems in her stride and counting on her social system and a return to everyday household life to keep her going. The helper's second response hits the mark and she outlines some of the things she wants. There will be times when helpers do get things wrong and it is at these times that if the therapeutic relationship is strong, the client will feel comfortable expressing this.

Recover from inaccurate understanding

Although helpers should strive to be accurate in the understanding they communicate, all helpers can be inaccurate at times. You may think you understand the client and what he or she has said, only to find out, when you share your understanding, that you were off the mark. Therefore, responding with empathy is a perception-checking tool. If the helper's response is accurate, the client often tends to confirm its accuracy in two ways. The first is some kind of verbal or non-verbal indication that the helper is right. That is, the client nods or gives some other non-verbal cue or uses some assenting word or phrase such as 'that's right' or 'exactly'. This happens in the following example, in which a client who has been arrested for selling drugs is talking to his probation officer.

> **HELPER:**   So your neighbourhood makes it easy to do things that can get you into trouble.
>
> **CLIENT:**   You bet it does! For instance, everyone's selling drugs. You not only end up using them, but you begin to think about pushing them. It's just too easy.

On the other hand, when a response is inaccurate, the client often lets the counsellor know in different ways. He or she may stop dead, fumble around, go off on a different tangent, tell the counsellor 'That's not exactly what I meant' or even try to get the helper back on track. Helpers need to be sensitive to all these cues. In the following example, Ben, a man who lost his wife and daughter in a train crash, has been talking about the changes that have taken place since the accident.

> **HELPER:**   So you don't want to do a lot of the things you used to do before the accident. For instance, you don't want to socialise much anymore.
>
> **BEN (pausing a long time):**   Well, I'm not sure that it's a question of wanting to or not. I mean that it takes much more energy to do a lot of things. It takes so much energy for me just to phone others to get together. It takes so much energy sometimes being with others that I just don't try.
>
> **HELPER:**   It's like a cinema of a man in slow motion – it's so hard to do almost anything.
>
> **BEN:**   Right. I'm in low gear, grinding away. And I don't know how to get out of it.

Ben says that it is not a question of motivation but of energy. The difference is important to him. By picking up on it, the helper gets the interview back on track. Ben wants to regain his old energy but he doesn't know how. His 'lack of energy' is most likely some form of depression. And there are a number of ways to help clients deal with depression. This provides an opening for moving the helping process forward.

If you are intent on understanding your clients, they will not be put off by occasional inaccuracies on your part. If the relationship is solid, clients will read your intent and not just the degree of your accuracy. In a sense there is no such thing as perfect accuracy or the right kind of accuracy or the right degree of accuracy (Biesanz & Human, 2010; Lewis & Hodges, 2011). Recovering from a failure to understand the client accurately, but recovering from inaccuracy, is something that you and your client do together. It can be a relationship-building interaction, part of the give-and-take of therapy.

TACTICS FOR RESPONDING WITH EMPATHY

The principles just outlined provide strategies for responding with empathy. Here are a few hints – tactics, if you will – to help you improve the quality of your responses.

Give yourself time to think

Beginners sometimes jump in too quickly with an empathic response when the client pauses. 'Too quickly' means that they do not give themselves enough time to reflect on what the client has just said in order to identify the core message being communicated. Watch video clips of competent helpers. They often pause and allow themselves to assimilate what the client is saying.

Use short responses

As I have said before, I find that the helping process goes best when I engage the client in a dialogue rather than give speeches or allow the client to ramble. In a dialogue the helper's responses can be relatively frequent, but lean and trim. In trying to be accurate, the novice helper is often long-winded, especially if he or she lets the client go on and on before responding. Again, the question 'What is the core of what this person is saying to me?' can help you make your responses short, concrete and accurate.

Gear your response to the client, but remain yourself

If a client speaks animatedly, telling you how he finally got his partner to listen to his point of view about a new venture, and you reply accurately but in a flat, dull voice, your response is not fully empathic. This does not mean that you should mimic your clients, go overboard or not be yourself. It means that part of being with the client is sharing in a reasonable way in his or her emotional tone. Consider this example:

12-YEAR-OLD CLIENT: My teacher started picking on me from the first day of class. I don't fool around more than anyone else in class, but she gets me any time I do. I think she's picking on me because she doesn't like me. She doesn't yell at Bill Smith, and he acts funnier than I do.

COUNSELLOR A: This is a bit perplexing. You wonder why she singles you out for so much discipline.

Counsellor A's language is stilted, not in tune with the way a 12-year-old speaks. Here's a different approach.

COUNSELLOR B: You're mad because the way she picks on you seems unfair.

On the other hand, helpers should not adopt a language that is not their own just to be on the client's wavelength. An older counsellor using 'hip' language or slang with a young client sounds ludicrous. Box 3.2 summarises factors that go into effective empathic responding.

BOX 3.2	**Suggestions for Responding with Empathy**

- Remember that empathy is a value, a way of being, which should permeate the relationship and every aspect of your dialogue with the client.
- Your empathic responses should flow naturally from your empathic relationship with the client.
- Be aware that empathic responding is a way of influencing your client.
- Don't get lost in your communication skills; keep the big picture in mind.
- Respond to the client-in-context and the part diversity plays in that context.
- Tune in carefully, both physically and psychologically, and listen actively to the client's point of view.
- Make every effort to set your judgements and biases aside and walk in the shoes of the client.
- As the client speaks, listen especially for cultural voices and core messages.
- Pay attention to both verbal and non-verbal messages and their context.
- Use frequent but short responses that highlight the client's core messages.
- Be flexible and tentative in your responses so that the client does not feel pinned down.
- Move gradually towards the exploration of sensitive topics and feelings.
- After an empathic response, attend carefully to cues that either confirm or deny the accuracy of your response.
- Take special care when the client's personal culture differs considerably from your own.
- Note signs of client stress or resistance; try to judge whether these arise because you are inaccurate or because you are too accurate in your responses.
- Make sure that your responses are helping the client remain focused on the clarification of key issues.
- Keep in mind that the communication skill of responding with empathy, however important, is just one tool at the service of the overall goals of helping.
- Use empathy in every stage and task of the helping process.

A CASE: TUMI, THE CLIENT AND CARLOS, THE HELPER

Here is an example to bring the use of empathy to life. The case, though real, has been disguised and simplified. It is not a session-by-session presentation. Rather, it illustrates ways in which one client was helped to ask and answer for herself the four fundamental problem-management questions outlined in Chapter 1 and at the heart of Part III. The client, Tumi, is voluntary, verbal and, for the most part, cooperative. Here is the background.

Tumi, 30, is a single black woman from South Africa. Tumi and her parents emigrated to the UK shortly after her brother was killed in a road traffic accident when he was five years old. They settled in Leeds where her father's sister, husband and sons lived. Both their sons are married and have begun families of their own.

There is no extended South African community in Leeds. Tumi's father managed to establish a moderately successful car dealership but he could not find the kind of job that interested him. Tumi, who graduated from Leeds University with a degree in business, has worked full time at her father's car dealership. She began working there part time early in secondary school and continued to do so in her university years.

Tumi has always lived at home, even during her years at Leeds University in the same city. In school she came across as bright and enthusiastic. She had a bit of a temper, but usually kept it under control except for an occasional ironic, but not cynical or sarcastic, remark. Her fellow pupils liked her and her slightly mordant sense of humour, but she socialised very little with them. Outside of work, she spends her time at home or with her family, including her aunt and uncle who live a few miles away.

The precipitating event was a car accident. A drunk driver without insurance hit Tumi's car early one morning as she drove to work. She suffered a broken collar bone and some rather serious lacerations. She did well in a physical rehabilitation programme, but the accident proved to be quite a psychological jolt. She experienced some classic PTSD symptoms but seemed to recover fairly quickly from them. As part of her recovery she took a trip to South Africa and spent three months living with relatives in Durban and visiting other relatives in smaller towns. It was during this trip that she began to think more broadly about the direction of her life. This was proving to be more disquieting than the accident and its immediate consequences.

Tumi wants some kind of help, so she gets in touch with the instructor in the one psychology course she took at the university. He suggests a couple of names, one a man, the other a woman, and adds, 'Tumi, I wouldn't suggest anyone that I would not go to myself. I think you'll get some good help from either of these.' Tumi chooses Carlos, a married counsellor with two children, because she thinks that his cultural background, though different from hers, might be an asset because she has some cultural issues. Tumi also wants to face the challenge of talking about her personal issues with a man. So Carlos and Tumi have a brief orientation meeting at the university. Tumi briefly shares the background outlined earlier, including the accident and the fact that she has some newly discovered concerns about her life. Carlos briefly explains his approach to helping (which is the approach taken in this book), emphasising the collaborative nature of helping and indicating that she is always 'in the driver's seat'. She asks a few questions about his approach and gets some clarity about Carlos's phrase 'being in the driver's seat'. Carlos also notes they are both from mixed-culture backgrounds but admits to knowing little about South African culture. In this regard, he says, he'll be a learner. Carlos comes away with the impression that Tumi is an intelligent woman with 'spirit'. Tumi's take is that Carlos is decent, personable and full of common sense.

Here is an excerpt from one of Carlos's sessions with Tumi. This session takes place after Tumi has a conversation with her father about her future. Tumi called Carlos and cancelled a session right after her meeting with her father, saying she did not 'feel well'. Carlos suspected that the meeting did not go well, but left it to her. About five days later she called and said that she wanted another session as soon as he could schedule one. She came in, sat down and looked very dispirited. Once more, Carlos helps Tumi tell her story and explore her reactions to it. The following gives you the flavour of their session.

CARLOS: You and I tried to prepare for the meeting with your dad, but it didn't seem to go well.

TUMI (after pausing): Not well? It was a total disaster! I don't think it could have been worse.

CARLOS: Tell me what made it so bad.

TUMI: He listened for a little while, then cut me off. He said that he was shocked by my talking like that. He didn't want to hear anything about my career. 'You've already got a good job', he said. He asked me what was wrong with me. It was as if he was a completely different person. Not the father I thought I knew. (Tumi pauses, looks away and slowly shakes her head; she seems to be on the verge of tears.)

CARLOS: So, worse than you ever imagined.

TUMI: Yes. He said that I was ungrateful. He asked me where I was getting these ideas. He said that all of this would shock my mother. He couldn't believe that I began thinking of all of this in earnest when I visited South Africa. 'What did they do to you there?' he asked me. 'How could you misinterpret what you saw and heard there?' He sounded so harsh! He's been distant at times, but never really harsh.

CARLOS: As far as he was concerned, you stepped out of line and that was totally unacceptable.

TUMI: That's it! In his eyes I was totally out of line. . . . I was so shocked at the time that I don't remember feeling anything. . . . But after I left, it all came crashing down on me. I went back to my room and literally cried myself to sleep. Exhausted.

CARLOS: And bewildered?

TUMI: In many different ways. My whole world came crashing down. What I thought were dreams turned into sins. I almost threw up. All of a sudden I felt that I had been letting my parents down. Living some kind of lie. At the same time I felt that I had not been doing anything wrong. What I was trying to do would help my parents. I'm sorry. I was so out of it I had to cancel our appointment. I think they half know that I'm seeing some kind of counsellor. I guess they suppose that it is a medical thing. Now I think that they would be horrified to know what I am talking about here.

(Continued)

> **CARLOS:** Feeling that you have done something terribly wrong and at the same time that you haven't done anything wrong. And even talking with me is some kind of betrayal. It's really bewildering.
>
> **TUMI:** Yes, but I'm not betraying anyone. It's the opposite of betrayal. . . I'm so glad I have someone to talk to. . . I don't know what I'd do if I didn't. I don't care what they think.

Carlos's empathic presence and responding helps Tumi tell and in some way even relive her story. She goes on to talk about her feelings of isolation. She feels trapped. She's depressed. She begins to realise that she has been at least 'semi-depressed' for a long time. She wonders if it would have been better if she had never begun to think about a 'bigger' life for herself. Home had been a comfortable, if not comforting, place. Now what would it be? She is confused. She thought she had recovered from the trauma of the car accident, but now she thinks she might have just 'covered it over'. Everything needs to change, but she can't see how anything can change. She feels that she's back at 'square one'. By the end of the session, however, she finds herself unexpectedly composed. It has all flooded out, but now, as she says resolutely as she departs, 'I just have to deal with it.'

Duncan (2010) sums this chapter up well:

> *"Empathy, therefore, is work. You can't take it for granted; instead you have to sort out what the client finds empathic, what engages the client in the work. But it is really worth the effort."* (p. 134)

THE SHADOW SIDE OF RESPONDING

Some helpers are poor communicators without even realising it. Many responses that novice or inept helpers make are really poor substitutes for accurate empathic responses. Consider the following example, which includes a range of such responses. Rami is a middle-aged man who has been caught up in the economic collapse. His immediate problem is that his house is being foreclosed. His wife, who until recently did not work outside the home, works as a cashier in a supermarket. He has one son in university and another who is about to graduate from high school. His extremely constrained financial condition means that the older son will have to transfer to a state school or even drop out of university. His younger son has no chance of going to the university of his choice. This is his second visit to a counsellor in a mental health clinic. In the first session he said he wanted to 'talk through' some issues relating to the 'financial transition' he was going through. He was in very difficult financial straits, but appeared to be managing fairly well under the circumstances. In this session, after talking about a number of transition issues, he begins speaking in a rather strained voice and avoids eye contact with the counsellor.

> Something else is bothering me a bit . . . More than a bit. It's driving me crazy. The reason I'm in such a desperate position is that a partner of mine, seeing the crash coming, robbed me blind. And I mean blind. I didn't see it coming. He manipulated the finances of our partnership and without going into the details I found myself high and dry. (He pauses) I trusted him. I thought we were more than partners. I thought we were friends. To make things worse, everything he did to defraud me was either impossible to prove or legal. He's ruined me. Worse, he's ruined my family. But I think I've found a way of getting back at him. It won't get my money back, but the honour of my family will be restored. Right now that's all I can think of. I wasn't born or raised here. Back home I'd probably be bound to hunt him down and kill him. That I wouldn't do. But I've hunted him down financially and found ways of doing him in. And I wouldn't be doing anything illegal. No one will know who did it.

Rami pauses and looks at a piece of art on the wall. What would you do or say? The following are some possibilities that are better avoided.

No response

It can be a mistake to say nothing, although cultures differ widely in how they deal with silence (Sue & Sue, 1990). In Western culture, generally speaking, if the client says something significant, respond to it, however briefly. Otherwise, the client may think that what he or she has just said doesn't merit a response. Don't leave Rami sitting there stewing in his own juices.

Distracting questions

Some helpers, like many people in everyday life, cannot stop themselves from asking questions. Instead of responding with empathy, a counsellor might ask something like, 'Are you sure there is no way to get your money back?' 'Did you confront him?' Responses like these ignore Rami's key messages and the feelings he has expressed and focuses rather on the helper's mistaken agenda to get more information.

Clichés

A counsellor might say, 'Given the greed that has crept into our culture, I'm not at all surprised that things like this happen.' Or 'The workplace these days is so competitive. It's not uncommon for things like this to come up.' This is cliché talk. It turns the helper into an insensitive instructor and must sound dismissive to the client. Clichés are hollow. The helper is saying, in effect, 'You don't really have a problem at all because a lot of this stuff goes on.' Clichés are a very poor substitute for understanding.

Interpretations

For some helpers, interpretive responses based on their theories of helping seem more important than expressing understanding. Such a counsellor might say something like, 'Rami, have you ever thought that revenge will cure nothing and probably make things worse? Revenge is a way of selling yourself short.' Here the counsellor fails to respond to the client's feelings, sounds moralistic, ignores key messages (such as the meaning of revenge in Rami's culture) and is dismissive.

Advice

In everyday life, giving unsolicited advice is extremely common. It happens in counselling, too. For instance, a counsellor might say to Rami, 'Hey, focus on your financial and family concerns. Do what you probably do best. It's a business problem. How many different ways can you solve it?' Advice-giving at this stage is out of order and, to make things worse, the advice given has a cliché flavour to it. Furthermore, advice-giving robs clients of self-responsibility. That said, in some cultures clients expect helpers to give advice. Expecting to get advice may also be part of any given client's personal culture. In these cases there are ways of giving advice that elicits the client's collaboration. I might say something like this: 'Let's see. If I were in a situation like yours, here are some of the options I might be thinking about, though, on the spot, I can't say what I'd really do.' After sharing the options, I would ask the client if any of them made sense to him.

Parroting

Responding with empathy does not mean merely repeating what the client has said. Such parroting is a parody of responding with empathy. Re-read what Rami said, then evaluate the following response.

COUNSELLOR: So, Rami, your so-called friend read the economy right, devised his dirty little plan and pulled it off before you even began to realise what was happening. As you looked at the whole mess, you realised there was little you could do financially. You and your family were already done in. And in the culture you come from, that kind of rotten behaviour calls for a strong response. You don't want to get into more trouble than you're already in, but there's one thing you can do. You can get your revenge. That's not going to save you financially, but somehow or other it will put things back in balance, at least some kind of social balance. And there's some satisfaction to that.

Most of this is accurate, but it sounds awful. Mere repetition or restatement or paraphrasing carries no sense of real understanding of, no sense of being with, the client. Real understanding, because it passes through you, should convey some part of you. Parroting doesn't. To avoid parroting, tap into the processing you've been doing as you listened, consider what is key, come at what the client has said from a slightly different angle, use your own words, note the emotion, but don't say too much. Remember the saying: 'The person who says too much says nothing.'

Agreement and sympathy

Responding with empathy is not the same as agreeing with the client or being sympathetic. An expression of sympathy has much more in common with pity, compassion, commiseration and condolence than with empathic understanding (Clark, 2010b). Although in many cultures these are fully human traits, they are not particularly useful in counselling. Sympathy denotes agreement, whereas empathy denotes understanding and acceptance of the person of the client. At its worst, sympathy is a form of collusion with the client. Note the difference between Counsellor A's response to Rami and Counsellor B's response.

> **COUNSELLOR A:**   Boy, I can see that it's really hard to tell a story like this. As a successful businessman, you're probably saying to yourself, 'How did I ever let this happen to me?' I know I'd feel awful. It's even worse for someone who is as self-confident as you usually are.
>
> **RAMI (pauses):**   I guess so.

Rami does not respond very enthusiastically to collusion talk. He's struggling. He wants some help. The helping process does not move forward. Counsellor B takes a different approach.

Counsellor B's response hits a key issue and helps Rami look at both issues that are tearing him apart. Give a critique of Counsellor B's response and then formulate your own.

> **COUNSELLOR B (pauses):**   I'm trying to think what I would do. I think I'd be torn between getting my family back on track and seeing justice done.
>
> **RAMI:**   I am torn. I've got clashing emotions. But the need to get even is so strong right now. I never thought of this guy's dirty tricks as both an insult to my family and stealing from them. So the thought of giving up on my family seems awful.

Faking it

Clients are sometimes confused, distracted and in a highly emotional state. All these conditions affect the clarity of what they are saying about themselves. Helpers may fail to pick up what the client is saying because of the client's confusion or because clients are not stating their messages clearly. Or the helpers themselves have become distracted in one way or another. In any case, it's a mistake to feign understanding. Genuine helpers admit that they are lost and then work to get back on track again. A statement like 'I think I've lost you. Could we go over that once more?' indicates that you think it important to stay with the client. It is a sign of respect. Admitting that you're lost is infinitely preferable to such clichés as 'uh-huh', 'um' and 'I understand.' On the other hand, if you often catch yourself saying that you don't understand, then you'd better find out what is standing in the way. In any case, faking it is never a substitute for competence.

If you catch yourself making any of these mistakes, then find a way to recover. Helpers are not immune from mistakes. In her book *Learning from Mistakes in Clinical Practice*, Carolyn Dillon (2003) categorises common mistakes and demonstrates how helpers can learn from them. She describes the 'signals' clients send to helpers indicating a mistake is being or has been made. Effective helpers recognise these signals and act on them.

CHAPTER 4
THE ART OF PROBING
AND SUMMARISING

Chapter Contents

NUDGING

In Chapter 2 it was noted that all attempts to help others involve, to one degree or another, influencing them. Helpers influence their clients. The trick is to influence them to do such things as discussing difficult problems, developing new life-enhancing perspectives on themselves, others and the world, working on the right issues, exploring possibilities for a better future, choosing and committing themselves to problem-managing goals, exploring ways of achieving these goals and engaging in the kind of effective and efficient action needed to accomplish all of this – to influence them, certainly, but without robbing them of their freedom and autonomy. Thaler and Sunstein (2008), in a fascinating and useful book entitled *Nudge*, call this kind of influence 'libertarian paternalism'. The influence part is, in some sense, paternalistic and the freedom part is libertarian. Paternalism does not necessarily connote coercion, whether physical or psychological. And libertarian in the sense in which they use the term certainly does not mean 'Do whatever you want'.

In their book, Thaler and Sunstein (2008) talk about 'choice architects', that is, someone who 'has the responsibility for organising the context in which people make decisions' (p. 3). Because decision making is one of the key ingredients of successful therapy, it is important to explore the role helpers play in organising the context in which clients make decisions. Because helpers cannot help but influence their clients, they are choice architects. Treatment models, including the Skilled Helper framework itself, together with the methods and communication skills that make it work, provide different kinds of choice architecture. In the hands of savvy and principled helpers, the model, methods and skills of any treatment approach can be used as 'nudges'. Thaler and Sunstein describe a nudge as 'any aspect of the choice architecture that alters behaviour in a predictable way without forbidding any options' (2008, p. 6). Of course, the predictability referred to is the predictability of the social rather than the physical sciences. For instance, we have already seen that an empathic response to a client can constitute a nudge in two ways. First of all, because helpers cannot reply empathically to everything a client says, their selective responding is a form of influence. Second, empathic responses tend to influence clients to explore the issue being discussed more broadly or deeply. But, while empathic responses might well (but not necessarily) influence clients, they do not pin clients down. Nudges have power, but it is 'gentle'. In the hands of skilful helpers, nudges lead to collaboration rather than standing in the way of it. Skilful nudging does not overwhelm clients. It keeps clients at the centre of the decision-making process. As we shall see, the next two communication skills, probing and summarising, are often used as nudges. Their 'gentle power', rightly used, can be of great benefit to clients. There is a skill and art in nudging, probing and steering the client in a gentle yet effective way.

THE ART OF PROBING

In most of the examples used in the discussion of sharing empathic responses, clients have explored themselves and their behaviour relatively easily. Obviously, this is not always the case. Although it is essential that helpers respond with empathy when their clients do reveal themselves, it is also necessary at times to nudge, encourage or prompt clients to explore their concerns when they fail to do so spontaneously. Therefore, the ability to use prompts and probes well is another important communication skill. If sharing empathic responses is the lubricant of dialogue, then probes provide often-needed nudges. Probes may be challenging for the client but useful in raising their self-awareness. Susan and Tim had gone to couples' therapy as they had been arguing more lately. Tim mentioned that Susan 'never' praises him for anything he does. Susan stated that she found it hard to express her thanks for what Tim does. By exploring this, Susan was able to understand that her difficulty with expressing praise and thanks was due to her harsh upbringing where she did not receive this validation from her parents. Susan and Tom were able to work on their communication and empathy skills with each other.

Prompts and probes are verbal and sometimes non-verbal tactics for helping clients talk more freely and concretely about any issue at any stage of the helping process. For instance, counsellors can use probes to help clients identify and explore opportunities they have been overlooking, to clear up blind spots, to translate dreams into realistic goals, to come up with realistic plans for accomplishing goals and for working through obstacles to action. Probes, judiciously used, provide focus and direction for the entire helping process. We start with prompts.

Verbal and non-verbal prompts

Prompts are brief verbal or non-verbal interventions designed to let clients know that you are with them and to encourage clients to talk further.

Non-verbal prompts   Counsellors' various non-verbal behaviours can have the force of probes. For example, a client who has been talking about how difficult it is to make a peace overture to a neighbour with whom he or she is at odds says, 'I just can't do it.' The helper says nothing but, rather, simply leans forward attentively and waits. The client pauses and then says, 'Well, you know what I mean. It would be very hard for me to take the first step. It would be like giving in. You know, weakness.' They go on to explore how such an overture, properly done, could be a sign of strength rather than weakness. Such things as bodily movements, gestures, nods, eye movement and the like can be used as non-verbal prompts or nudges.

Vocal and verbal prompts   You can use such responses as 'um', 'uh-huh', 'sure', 'yes', 'I see', 'ah', 'okay' and 'oh' as prompts, provided you use them intentionally and they are not simply a sign that your attention is flagging, that you don't know what else to do or that you are on automatic pilot. In the following example, the client, a 33-year-old married woman, is struggling with perfectionism both at work and at home.

> **CLIENT (hesitatingly):**   I don't know whether I can 'kick the habit', you know, just let some trivial things go at work and at home. I know I've made a contract with myself. I'm not sure that I can keep it.
>
> **HELPER:**   Um. (The helper utters this briefly and then remains silent.)
>
> **CLIENT (pauses then laughs):**   Here I am deep into perfectionism and I hear myself saying that I can't do something! How ironic. Of course I can. I mean it's not going to be easy, at least at first.

The helper's 'Um' prompts the client to reconsider what she has just said. Prompts should never be the main course, but they are useful condiments in the therapeutic dialogue.

Different forms of probes

Used judiciously, probes help clients name, take notice of, explore, clarify or further define any issue at any point in the helping process. Probes are designed to provide clarity and to move things forward. They take different forms.

Statements   One form of probe is a statement indicating the need for further clarity. For instance, a helper, talking to a client who is having problems with his 25-year-old daughter who is still living at home, says, 'It's still not clear to me whether you want to challenge her to leave the nest or not.' The client replies, 'Well, I want to, but I just don't know how to do it without alienating her. I don't want it to sound like I don't care about her and that I'm just trying to get rid of her.' Probes in the form of statements often take the form of the helper's confessing that he or she is in the dark in some way. 'I'm not sure I understand how you intend…', 'I guess I'm still confused about…'. This kind of request puts the responsibility on clients without accusing them of failing to cough up the truth.

Requests   Probes can take the form of direct requests for further information or more clarity. A counsellor, talking to a woman living with her husband and her mother-in-law, says, 'Tell me what you mean when you say that three's a crowd at home.' She answers, 'I get along fine with my husband, I get along fine with my mother-in-law. But the chemistry among the three of us is very unsettling.' This is helpful new information. Obviously requests should not sound like commands. 'Come on, just tell me what you are thinking.' Tone of voice and other paralinguistic and non-verbal cues help to soften requests.

Questions   Direct questions are perhaps the most common type of probe. Whether they should be that common or not is a different issue.

- 'How do you react when he flies off the handle?'
- 'In situations like that, what keeps you from making a decision?'
- 'Now that the indirect approach to getting him to provide for the children is not working, what might Plan B look like?'

Consider this case. A client has come for help in controlling her anger. With the help of a counsellor she comes up with a solid programme. In the next session, the client gives signs of backtracking. The counsellor says, 'You seemed enthusiastic about the programme last week. But now, unless I'm mistaken, I hear a bit of hesitancy in your voice. Or am I just hearing things?' The client responds, 'Well, after taking a second look at the programme, I'm afraid it will make me look like a wimp. My fellow workers could get the wrong idea and begin pushing me around.' The counsellor says, 'So there's something about yourself and your style of relating at work that you don't want to lose.' When the client responds, 'That's right' the counsellor asks, 'What might that be?' The client hesitates for a moment and then says, 'Spunk!' The counsellor replies, 'Well, maybe there's a way of keeping your spunk without giving in to outbursts that get you in trouble.' They go on to discuss the practical differences between assertiveness and aggression.

Single words or phrases that are, in effect, questions or requests   Sometimes single words or simple phrases are, in effect, probes. A client talking about a difficult relationship with her sister at one juncture says, 'I really hate her.' The helper responds simply and unemotionally, 'Hate.' The client responds, 'Well, I know that hate is too strong a term. What I mean is that things are getting worse and worse.' This kind of clarity helps. Another client, troubled with irrational fears, says, 'I've had it. I just can't go on like this. No matter what, I'm going to move forward.' The counsellor replies, 'Move forward to ...?' The client says, 'Well ... to not indulging myself with my fears. That's what they are, a form of self-indulgence. From our talks I've learned that it's a bad habit. A very bad habit.' They go on to discuss ways of controlling such thoughts.

Whatever form probes take, they are often, directly or indirectly, questions of some sort. Therefore, a few words about the use of questions are in order.

Using questions effectively

Helpers, especially novices and inept counsellors, tend to ask too many questions and don't leave enough gaps and silences in the conversation for clients to reflect and think. When in doubt about what to say or do, they ask questions that add no value. It is as if gathering information were the goal of the helping interview. On the other hand, questions, judiciously used, can be an important part of your interactions with clients. The helping relationship is a process, so you will not be able to get all the information from your client in your first interaction with them. Here are two guidelines.

Do not ask too many questions   When clients are asked too many questions, they feel grilled, and that does little for the helping relationship. Furthermore, many clients instinctively know when questions are just fillers, used because the helper does not have anything better to say. I have caught myself asking questions the answers to which I didn't even want to know. Let's assume that the helper is working with Rolly, an inmate in a state facility for young offenders. He is doing time for burglary and drug use. Because he is difficult to work with and blames everything on his dysfunctional family, the counsellor out of frustration ends up asking a whole series of questions:

- 'When did you first feel caught in the messiness of your family?'
- 'What did you do to try to get away from their influence?'
- 'What could you do differently?'
- 'What kind of friends did you have?'
- 'Why did you do that?'

These questions are no more than a random search for information, seemingly through nosiness, and the value of which is not clear. Rolly is an expert in evading questions like this. He has been grilled by professionals many times. When he tires of being questioned, he just clams up or says 'I don't know.' Helping that turns into question-and-answer sessions tends to go nowhere.

Ask open-ended questions   As a general rule, ask open-ended questions – that is, questions that require more than a simple yes or no or similar one-word answer. Not, 'Now that you've decided to take early retirement, do you have any plans?' but, 'Now that you've decided to take early retirement, how do you see the future? What plans do you have?' Counsellors who ask closed questions find themselves asking more and more questions. One closed question leads to another. Of course, if a specific piece of information is needed, then a closed question may be used. A career counsellor might ask, 'How many jobs have you had in the past two years?' The information is relevant to helping the client draw up a resumé and a job-search strategy. Of course, occasionally, a sharp closed question can have the right impact. For instance, a client has been outlining what he was going to do to get back at his 'ungrateful' son. The counsellor asks, 'Is getting back at him what you really want?' Rhetorical questions like this are a form of challenge. If the client responds by saying, 'You're damn right I do', then you know more about the intensity of his feelings. And you know you're facing a tricky issue. In general, though, open-ended questions in moderation can help clients fill in what is missing at every stage of the helping process.

Guidelines for using probes

Here, then, are some suggestions that can guide you in the use of all probes, whatever form they may take.

Use your ongoing feedback system as a way of probing   Whether you use surveys such as Duncan's or some other way of systematically getting feedback from the client on both progress towards and the achievement of outcomes and quality of therapy sessions, the feedback system is an excellent opportunity for probing. Consider these two brief examples. In the first example, Letta is a single mother who lost her fairly well-paying job during the 2008 economic disaster. She was a 'hip' drinker when times were good but turned into a problem drinker when things turned sour. She spent what she earned on her lifestyle so there was no financial cushion when things went south. She felt sorry for herself and spent a lot of time railing against all the usual suspects everyone was blaming for the financial crash. In the first session she understandably rated herself rather low on the how-are-you-doing-individually scale. Her rating went up significantly in the second session because she thought that counselling was the answer. But here in the third session she rates herself lower than she did in the first session.

HELPER: I see the 'individually' score has taken a hit, Letta. What's the message? . . . I think I might be reading it in your face and posture.

LETTA: I felt so good after the last session. I was fired up. My hopes were high, they were flying. I was going to take my life back. But two days later I received a couple of default notices. My boss told us we would all have to take a cut in pay. And my boyfriend described me as 'scary'. My world collapsed, I collapsed. I just don't know how I'm going to recover.

HELPER: So, for a while you soared, then the crash.

LETTA (emphatically):   I was shot down!

HELPER: Shot down?

LETTA: Yes, I was attacked on all sides. Bank, work, boyfriend. Even the children ganged up on me.

HELPER: You said your hopes soared. Tell me more about that.

LETTA: Well, I thought it was going to be easy to pull everything together. I just felt so good. Now I'm thinking that I can't pull this off at all. It's just too much. It's going to take so much work. Budgets, working out repayment schedules, an austerity programme. I have to create a whole new lifestyle.

HELPER: The misery is very real. But let's put it aside for a moment. What good might come from all of this? What could you mine from it?

LETTA (pauses):   Nothing! (The helper remains silent) . . . (in a more subdued voice) I suppose I could become more realistic. . . . Come back to earth.

(Continued)

HELPER: OK. Let's see what this 'realism' might look like.

They go on to draw a picture of what a more 'realistic' lifestyle might look like. Letta gradually relaxes as they discuss possibilities.

The second example deals with the survey at the end of the session. Letta rates the 'overall' category higher than the other two sessions.

HELPER: Well, Letta, what made this session work for you?

LETTA: One very bittersweet word – realism.

HELPER: OK. How did that work?

LETTA: It triggered something in me. I hate self-centred people and all of a sudden I saw myself as self-centred (she stops).

HELPER: I'm not sure about the interplay between 'realism' and 'self-centred' and your score for the session.

LETTA: One lesson from the financial crash is that we were all – well, many of us – were living beyond our means. Maybe our whole society, government and all. Like a national self-centredness. I feel that I'm a fairly intelligent person. But all that was stupid. The dose of realism during this session was very good for me, especially because we went about it in a constructive way

This session opened the door to progress, to life-enhancing outcomes. During the dialogue realism was defined in terms of concrete possibilities. This edged Letta away from the brink of 'impossible' and she recaptured some of her enthusiasm, but perhaps a more realistic brand.

Use probes to help clients engage as fully as possible in the therapeutic dialogue   As noted earlier, many clients do not have all the communication skills needed to engage in the problem-managing and opportunity-developing dialogue. Probes are the principal tools needed to help all clients engage in the give-and-take of the helping dialogue. The following exchange takes place between a counsellor at a church parish centre and a parishioner who has been struggling to tell her story about her attempts to get her insurance company to respond to the claim she filed after a car accident.

CLIENT: They just won't do anything. I call and get the cold shoulder. They ignore me and I don't like it!

HELPER: You're angry with the way you're being treated. And you want to get to the bottom of it. . . . Maybe it would be helpful to review what you've done so far.

CLIENT: Well, they sent me forms that I didn't understand very well. I did the best I could. I think they were trying to show that it was my fault. I even kept copies. I've got them with me.

HELPER: You're not sure you can trust them. . . . Let's see what the forms look like. . . .

The forms turn out to be standard claims forms. The fact that this is the client's first encounter with an insurance company and that she has poor communication skills gives the counsellor some insight into what the phone conversations between her and the insurance company might have been like. By sharing empathic responses and using probes, he gets her to see that her experience might well be normal. The outcome is that the client gets help from a fellow parishioner who has filled in insurance forms a number of times.

Use probes to help clients achieve concreteness and clarity   Probes can help clients turn what is abstract and vague into something concrete and clear – something you can get your hands on and work with. In the next example, a man is talking about an intimate relationship that has turned sour.

CLIENT: She treats me badly, and I don't like it!

HELPER: Tell me what she actually does.

CLIENT: She talks about me behind my back. I know she does. Others tell me what she says. She also cancels dates when something more interesting comes up.

HELPER: That's pretty demeaning. . . . How have you been reacting to all this?

CLIENT: Well, I think she knows that I have an idea of what's going on. But we haven't talked about it much. Well, not at all.

In this example, the helper's probe leads to a clearer statement of the client's experience and behaviour. By sharing empathic responses and using probes, the helper discovers that the client puts up with a great deal because he is afraid of losing her. He goes on to help the client deal with the psychological 'economics' of such a one-sided relationship. It is important to understand the facts of the situation from the client's point of view and then use your own understanding to see if there is a match. If the client's view and yours do not match, then this may identify something to explore. For example, in the above example, exploring the client's part in the interaction with her colleague.

In the next example, a man who is dissatisfied with living a somewhat impoverished social life is telling his story. A simple probe leads to a significant revelation.

CLIENT: I do funny things that make me feel good.

HELPER: What kinds of things?

CLIENT: Well, I daydream about being a hero, a kind of tragic hero. In my daydreams I save the lives of people whom I like but who don't seem to know I exist. And then they come running to me but I turn my back on them. I choose to be alone! I come up with all sorts of variations of this theme.

HELPER: So in your daydreams you play a character who wants to be liked or loved but who gets some kind of satisfaction from rejecting those who haven't loved him back. I'm not sure I've got that right.

CLIENT: Well . . . yeah . . . I sort of contradict myself. . . . I do want to be loved but I guess I don't do very much to get a real social life. It's all in my head.

The helper's probe leads to a clearer statement of what's going on in the client's head. Helping the client explore his fantasy life could be a first step towards finding out what he really wants from relationships and what he needs to do to get it.

The next client has become the breadwinner since her husband suffered a stroke. Someone takes care of her husband during the day.

CLIENT: Since my husband had his stroke, coming home at night is rather difficult for me. I just. . . . Well, I don't know.

HELPER: It sounds like it really gets you down. . . . What's it like?

CLIENT: When I see him sitting immobile in the chair, I'm filled with pity for him and the next thing I know it's pity for myself and it's mixed with anger or even rage, but I don't know what or whom to be angry at. I don't know how to focus my anger. Good God, he's only 42 and I'm only 40!

In this case, the helper's probe leads to a fuller description of the intensity of the client's feelings and emotions, her sense of desperation. In each of these cases, the client's story gets more specific. Of course, the goal is not to get more and more detail. Rather, it is to get the kind of detail that makes the problem or unused opportunity clear enough to see what can be done about it.

Use probes to explore and clarify clients' points of view, intentions, proposals and decisions Clients often fail to clarify their points of view, intentions, proposals and decisions. For instance, a client might announce some decision he or she has made. But the decision itself is unclear, and the reasons behind it and the implications for the client and others are not spelled out. In the following case, the client has had a bad automobile accident while driving under the influence (DUI). Luckily he was the only one hurt. He is recovering physically, but his psychological recovery has been slow. The accident opened up a Pandora's Box of psychological problems that were not being handled – for instance, a lack of self-responsibility. A counsellor has been helping him work through some of these issues. The following exchange takes place between them during an early session.

> **CLIENT:** I don't think that the laws around driving under the influence should be as tough as they are. I'm scared to death of what might happen to me if I ever had an accident again.
>
> **COUNSELLOR:** So you feel you're in jeopardy. . . . I'm not sure why you think that the laws are too tough?
>
> **CLIENT:** Well, they bully us. One little mistake and bingo! Your freedom goes out the window. Laws should make people free.
>
> **COUNSELLOR:** Well, let's explore this a little. Hmm, let's say all laws on driving under the influence were dropped. Then, starting from zero, you were asked to start adding ones that make sense. Where would you start?

The counsellor knows that the client is running away from taking responsibility for his actions. Using probes to get him to spell out the implications of his point of view on DUI laws is the beginning of an attempt to help the client face up to himself.

In a later session, the client talks about the legal ramifications of the accident. He has to go to court.

> **CLIENT:** I've been thinking about this. I'm going to get me a really good solicitor and fight this thing. I talked with a friend, and he thinks he knows someone who can get me off. I need a break. It might cost me a bundle. After all, I messed up someone's property a bit, but I didn't hurt anyone.
>
> **COUNSELLOR:** What's the best thing that could happen in court?
>
> **CLIENT:** I'd get off scot-free. Well, maybe a slap on the wrist of some kind. A warning.
>
> **COUNSELLOR:** And what's the worst thing that could happen?
>
> **CLIENT (a long pause):** I haven't given that a lot of thought. I don't really know much about the laws or the courts or how tough they might be. That sort of stuff. But with the right solicitor. . . .
>
> **COUNSELLOR:** Hmm. I'm trying to put myself in your shoes. . . . I think I'd try to find out how cases like mine tend to go in court. . . . I'd like to know that before spending a lot of money on a defence solicitor. What do you think?

The counsellor is using probes to help the client explore the implications and potential consequences of a decision he's making.

The state has very tough DUI laws. In the end, because the client's blood-alcohol level was so high, his licence is suspended for six months, he is fined heavily and he has to spend a month in prison. All of this is very sobering. The counsellor visits him in prison and they talk about the future.

> **CLIENT:** I feel like I've been hit by a train.
>
> **COUNSELLOR:** You had no idea that it would be this bad.
>
> **CLIENT:** Right. No idea. . . . I know you tried to warn me in your own way, but I wasn't ready to listen. . . . Now I have to begin to put my life back together. Though I don't feel like it.
>
> **COUNSELLOR:** But now that you've had the wake-up call, a horrible wake-up call, it might make sense to start piecing the future together. What do you think?
>
> **CLIENT:** I've been thinking. One thing I want to do is to make some sort of apology to my family. They're hurting as bad as I am. I feel so awkward. I know how to act in cocky mode, but humble mode I'm not used to. Do I write a long letter? Do I wait and just apologise through my actions? Do I take each one of them aside? I don't know, but I've just got to do it.
>
> **COUNSELLOR:** Somehow you have to make things right with them. Just how, well that's another matter. Maybe we could start by finding out what you want to accomplish through an apology, however it's done.

Here we find a much more sober and cooperative client. He proposes, roughly, a course of action. The counsellor supports his need to move beyond past stupidities and present misery. It's about the future, not the past. The counsellor's last statement is a probe aimed at giving substance and order to the client's proposal. It asks the client, what do you want to accomplish?

Use probes to help clients fill in missing pieces of the picture   Probes further the therapeutic dialogue by helping clients identify missing pieces of the problem-management puzzle – thoughts, experiences, behaviours and feelings that would help both clients and helpers get a better fix on the problem situation or some unused opportunity; discovering possibilities for a better future; or coming up with a plan of action. In the following example, the client is at odds with his wife over his mother-in-law's upcoming visit.

> **HELPER:** I realise now that you often get angry when your mother-in-law stays for more than a day. But I'm still not sure what she does that makes you angry.
>
> **CLIENT:** First of all, she throws our household schedule out and puts in her own. Then she provides a steady stream of advice on how to raise the children. My wife sees this as an 'inconvenience'. For me it's a total family disruption. When she leaves, there's a lot of emotional cleaning up to be done.

Just what the client's mother-in-law does to get him going has been missing. Once the behaviour has been spelled out in some detail, it is easier to help him come up with some remedies. Still missing, however, is what he does in the face of his mother-in-law's behaviour. The helper continues:

> **HELPER:** So when she takes over, everything gets turned upside down. . . . How do you react in the face of all this turmoil?
>
> **CLIENT:** Well. . . well. . . I guess I go silent. Or I just get out of there, go somewhere and fume. After she's gone, I take it out on my wife, who still doesn't see why I'm making such a fuss.

So now it's clear that the client does little to change things. It is also obvious that he is a little taken aback by being asked how he handles the situation.

In the next example, a divorced woman is talking about the turmoil that takes place when her ex-husband visits the children. It has some similarities with the case we've just seen.

> **HELPER:** The Sundays your husband exercises his visiting rights with the children end in his taking verbal potshots at you, and you get these headaches. I've got a fairly clear picture of what he does when he comes over and how it gets to you, but it might help if you could describe what you do.
>
> **CLIENT:** Well, I do nothing.
>
> **HELPER:** So last Sunday he just began letting you have it for no particular reason. Or just to make you feel bad.
>
> **CLIENT:** Well. . . not exactly. I asked him about increasing the amount of the child-support payments. And I asked him why he's dragging his feet about getting a better job. He's so stupid. He can't even take a bit of sound advice.

Through probes the counsellor helps the client fill in a missing part of the picture – her own behaviour and the way she communicates with her ex-husband. She keeps describing herself as total victim and her ex-husband as total aggressor. That doesn't seem to be the full story. Her behaviour contributes to this ongoing drama. She can't change his behaviour directly, but she can start to understand her part in the interaction and experiment with changing her own behaviour to influence a different outcome.

Use probes to help clients get a balanced view of problem situations and opportunities In their eagerness to discuss an issue or make a point, clients often describe one side of a picture or one viewpoint. Remember, it is their experience, from their point of view. Some clients need to be nudged into thinking about the impact of their behaviour on others. Probes can be used to help them fill out the picture and explore the wider picture for themselves. In the following example, the client, a manager who has been saddled with a bright, highly ambitious and aggressive young woman who plays politics to further her own interests, has been agonising over his plight.

> **COUNSELLOR:** I've been wondering whether you see any upside to this; any hidden opportunities?
>
> **CLIENT:** I'm not sure what you mean. It's just a disaster.
>
> **COUNSELLOR:** Well, you strike me as a pretty bright guy. I'm wondering if there are any lessons for you hidden in all this.
>
> **CLIENT (pausing):** Oh, well, you know I tend to ignore politics around here, but now it's in my face. Where there are people, there are politics, I suppose. I think she's being political to serve her own career. But I don't want to play her game. There must be some other kind of game or something that would let me keep my integrity. The days of avoiding all of this are probably over.

The problem situation has a flip side. It is an opportunity for re-thinking and learning. As such, problems are incentives for constructive change. The client can learn something through all this. It's an opportunity to come to grips with the male–female dynamics of the workplace and a chance to explore 'positive' political skills.

Use probes to help clients move into more beneficial stages of the helping process Probes can be used to help clients engage in dialogue about any part of the helping process – telling their stories more fully, surfacing blind spots, setting goals, formulating action strategies, discussing obstacles to action and reviewing actions taken. Many clients do not easily move into whatever stage of the helping process might be most useful for them. Probes can help them do so. In the following example, the counsellor uses a probe to help a middle-aged couple, Sean and Fiona, who have been complaining about each other, to move on to some kind of problem-managing action. Besides complaining, they have talked vaguely about 'reinventing' their marriage, a term used in some kind of marriage encounter group they attended. For instance, they have hinted at doing more things in common.

COUNSELLOR: What kinds of things do you like doing together? What are some possibilities?

FIONA: I can think of something, though it might sound stupid to you (she says with a glance towards her husband). We both like doing things for others, you know, caring about other people. Before we were married, we talked about spending some time in the Peace Corps together, though it never happened.

SEAN: I wish we had. . . . But those days are past.

COUNSELLOR: Are they? The Peace Corps may not be an option, but there must be other possibilities. (Neither Fiona nor Sean says anything.) I tell you what. Here are a couple of pieces of paper. Jot down three ways of helping others. Do your own list. Forget what your spouse might be thinking.

The counsellor uses probes to get Sean and Fiona to brainstorm possibilities for some kind of service to others. This moves them away from tortuous problem exploration towards opportunity development.

The next client has been talking endlessly about the affair her husband is having. Her husband knows that she knows.

COUNSELLOR: You've said you're not going to do anything about it because it might hurt your son. But doing nothing is not the only possible option. Let's just name some of them. Who knows? We might find a gem.

CLIENT: Hmm. . . . I'm not sure I know.

COUNSELLOR: Well, you know people in the same predicament. You've read novels, seen movies. What are some of the standard things people do? I'm not saying do them. Let's just review them.

CLIENT: Hmm. . . . Well, I knew someone in a situation like this who did an outrageous thing. She knew her teenage daughter was aware of what was going on. So one night at dinner she just said, 'Let's all talk about the affair you're having and how to handle it. It's certainly not news to any of us.'

COUNSELLOR: All right, that's one possible way. Let's hear some more

This primes the pump. The counsellor uses a few more probes to put a number of possibilities on the table. The focus on action brings energy to the session.

In the following example, Jill, the helper, and Justin, the client, have been discussing how Justin is letting his impairment – he has lost a leg in a car accident – stand in the way of his picking up his life again. The session has bogged down a bit.

JILL: Let's try a bit of role play. I'm going to be Justin for a while. You're going to be Jill. As my counsellor, ask me some questions that you think might make a difference for me. Me, that is, Justin.

JUSTIN (pausing a long time):   I'm not much of an actor, but here goes. . . . 'Why are you taking the coward's way out? Why are you on the verge of giving up?' (His eyes tear up.)

Jill gets Justin to formulate the probes. It's her way of asking Justin to 'move forward' and take responsibility for his part of the session. Justin's 'probes' turn out to be challenges, almost accusations, certainly much stronger than anything Jill, at this stage, would have tried. However painful this is for Justin, it's a breakthrough.

Use probes to invite clients to challenge themselves   In Chapter 3 we saw that even sharing empathic responses can act as a mild form of social-influence or challenge. We also saw that effective responses often act as probes. That is, they can be indirect requests for further information or ways of steering a client towards a more productive stage of the helping process. And, as you have probably noticed in the examples used in this chapter, probes can edge much closer to outright invitations to self-challenge. Many probes are not just requests for relevant information. They often place some kind of demand on the client to respond, reflect, review or re-evaluate. Probes can serve as a bridge between communicating understanding to clients and helping them challenge themselves. The following client, having committed himself to standing up to some of his mother's possessive ways, now shows signs of weakening in his resolve.

> **HELPER:** The other day you talked of 'having it out with her' – though that might be too strong a term. But just now you mentioned something about 'being reasonable with her'. Tell me how these two differ.
>
> **CLIENT (pausing):** Well, I think you might be witnessing a case of cold feet. . . . She's a very strong woman.

The counsellor helps the client revisit his decision to 'get tough' in some decent way with his mother and, if this is what he really wants, what he can do to strengthen his resolve. Using probes as mild forms of challenge is perfectly legitimate provided you know what you are doing.

The relationship between sharing empathic responses and using probes

The trouble with dealing with skills one at a time is that each skill is taken out of context. In the give-and-take of any given helping session, however, the skills must be intermingled in a natural way. In actual sessions, skilled helpers continually tune in, listen actively and use a mix of probes and empathy to help clients clarify and come to grips with their concerns, deal with blind spots, set goals, make plans and get things done. There is no formula for the right mix. That depends on the client, client needs, the problem situation, possible opportunities and the stage of the helping process.

Here is a basic guideline about sharing empathic responses and using probes. After using a probe to which a client responds, respond with empathy to what the client has to say. Check your understanding. Be hesitant to follow one probe with another. The logic of this is straightforward. First, if a probe is effective, it will yield information that needs to be listened to and understood. Second, an empathic response, if accurate, tends to place a demand on the client to explore further. It puts the ball back in the client's court.

In the following example, the client is a young Chinese British woman whose father died in China and whose mother is now dying in the United Kingdom. She has been talking about the not uncommon subservience of Chinese women and her fears of slipping into a form of passivity in her British life. She talks about her sister, who gives everything to her husband without looking for anything in return. The first counsellor sticks to probes.

> **COUNSELLOR:** To what degree is this self-effacing role rooted in your culture?
>
> **CLIENT:** Well, being somewhat self-effacing is certainly in my cultural genes. And yet I look around and see many of my European counterparts adopt a very different style; a style that frankly appeals to me. But last year, when I took a trip back to China with my mother to meet my half-sisters, the moment I landed I wasn't British. I was totally Chinese again.
>
> **COUNSELLOR A:** What did you learn there?
>
> **CLIENT:** That I am Chinese!

The client says something significant about herself, but instead of responding with understanding, the helper uses another probe. This elicits only a repetition, with some annoyance, of what she had just said. Now a different approach:

> **COUNSELLOR B:** You learned just how deep your cultural roots go.
>
> **CLIENT:** And if these roots are so deep, what does that mean for me here? I love my Chinese culture. I want to be Chinese and British at the same time. How to do that, well, I haven't figured that out yet. I thought I had, but I haven't.

In this case, an empathic response works much more effectively than another probe. Counsellor B helps the client move forward.

In the next example, a single middle-aged woman working in a company that has reinvented itself after a downturn in the economy still has a job, but the pay is much less and she is doing work she does not enjoy. She does not have the computer and internet-related skills needed for the better jobs. She feels stuck, stressed and depressed.

> **CLIENT:** Well, I suppose that I should be grateful for even having a job. But now I work longer hours for less pay. And I'm doing stuff I don't even like. My life is no longer mine.
>
> **HELPER:** So the extra pressure and stress make you wonder just how 'grateful' you should feel.
>
> **CLIENT:** Precisely. . . . And the future looks pretty bleak.
>
> **HELPER:** What could you change in the short term to make things more bearable?
>
> **CLIENT:** Hmm. . . . Well, I know one way. We all keep complaining to one another at work. And this seems to make things even worse. I can stop playing that game. It's one way of making life a bit less miserable.
>
> **HELPER:** So one way is to stop contributing to your own misery by staying away from the complaining chorus. . . . What might you start doing?
>
> **CLIENT:** Well, there's no use sitting around hoping that what has happened is going to be reversed. I've been really jolted out of my complacency. I assumed with the economy humming again I'd find things easy. The economy may be humming, but jobs, good jobs, are still scarce. But I'm still young enough to acquire some more skills. And I do have some skills that I haven't needed to use before. I'm a good communicator, and I've got a lot of common sense. I work well with people. There are probably some jobs around here that require those skills.
>
> **HELPER:** So, given the wake-up call, you think it might be possible to take unused skills and reposition yourself at work.
>
> **CLIENT:** Repositioning. Hmm, I like that word. It makes a lot of pictures dance through my mind. . . . Yes, I need to reposition myself. For instance. . .

This combination of empathic responses and probing gets things moving. Instead of focusing on the misery of the present situation, the client names a few possibilities for a better future.

You should be careful not to become either an empathic response 'machine', grinding out one after another, or an 'interrogator', peppering your clients continually with needless probes. All responses to clients, including probes and challenges, are empathic if they are based on a solid understanding of the client's core messages and points of view. All responses that build on and add to the client's remarks are implicitly empathic, which cuts down on the need to share a steady stream of empathic responses. Box 4.1 summarises guidelines for using probes.

BOX 4.1	Guidelines in Using Probes

- Keep in mind the goals of probing. Use probes to:
  - Help clients engage as fully as possible in the therapeutic dialogue.
  - Help non-assertive or reluctant clients tell their stories and engage in other behaviours related to managing their problems and developing opportunities.
  - Help clients identify experiences, behaviours and feelings that give focus to their stories.
  - Help clients become more self-aware.
  - Help clients open up new areas for discussion.
  - Help clients explore and clarify stories, feelings, points of view, decisions and proposals.
  - Help clients understand their part in others' behaviours and their interactions.
  - Help clients to be as concrete and specific as possible.
  - Help clients remain focused on relevant and important issues.
  - Help clients move on to a further stage of the helping process.
- Use probes to provide nudges or mild challenges to clients to examine the way they think, behave and act, both within helping sessions and in their daily lives.
- Make sure that probing is done in the spirit of empathy.
- Use a mix of statements, open-ended questions, prompts and requests, not questions alone.
- Follow up a successful probe with an empathic response rather than another probe.
- Use whatever judicious mixture of empathic responses and probing is needed to help clients clarify problems, identify blind spots, develop new scenarios, search for action strategies, formulate plans and review outcomes of action.

THE ART OF SUMMARISING: PROVIDING FOCUS AND DIRECTION

The communication skills of visibly tuning in, listening, responding with empathy and probing need to be orchestrated in such a way that they help clients focus their attention on issues that make a difference. The ability to summarise and to help clients summarise the main points of a helping interchange or session is a skill that can be used to provide both focus and challenge.

When to use summaries

Brammer (1973) listed a number of goals that can be achieved by judicious use of summarising – 'warming up' the client, focusing scattered thoughts and feelings, bringing the discussion of a particular theme to a close and prompting the client to explore a theme more thoroughly. There are certain times when summaries prove particularly useful: at the beginning of a new session, when the session seems to be going nowhere and when the client needs a new perspective.

At the beginning of a new session   Using summaries at the beginning of a new session, to help the client focus on what they have managed to do since your last session. This will also help clients who are uncertain about how to begin. It also prevents clients from merely repeating what has already been said before and focuses their attention to what might be useful for you both to explore together this session. It puts clients under pressure to move on and to be future focused. Consider this example: Liz, a social worker, begins a session with a rather overly talkative man by summarising the main points from the previous session. This serves several purposes. First, it shows the client that she had listened carefully to what he had said in the last session and that she had reflected on it after the session. Second, the summary gives the client a jumping-off point for the new session. It gives him an opportunity to add to or modify what was said. Finally, it places the responsibility for moving forward on the client. The implied sentiment of the summary is: 'Now where do you want to go with this?' Summaries put the ball in the client's court and give them an opportunity to exercise initiative. Of course, if you are getting feedback from clients at the beginning and at the end of each session, the flow from session to session will be much smoother.

During a session that is going nowhere   Helpers can use a summary to give focus to a session that seems to be going nowhere. One of the main reasons sessions go nowhere is that helpers allow clients to keep discussing the same things over and over again instead of helping them either go more deeply into their stories, focus on possibilities and goals or discuss strategies that will help clients get what they need and want. For instance, Anaya is a coach, consultant and counsellor who is working with the staff of a shelter for the homeless in Johannesburg. One of the staff members is showing signs of burnout. In a second meeting with Anaya, she keeps going over the same ground, talking endlessly about stressful incidents that have taken place over the last few months. At one point Anaya provides a summary.

> **ANAYA:**   Let's see if I can pull together what you've been saying. The work here, by its very nature, is stressful. You've mentioned a whole string of 'incidents' such as being hit by someone you were trying to help, or the heated arguments with some of your co-workers. But I believe you've also suggested that you know that these are the kinds of things that happen in these places. Shelters are prone to them. They are part of the furniture. They're not going to stop. But they can be very punishing. At times you wish you weren't here. But if you're going to stay and if these kinds of incidents are not going to stop, maybe some questions might be, 'How do I cope with them? How do I do my work and get some ongoing satisfaction from it? What changes can we make around here that might lessen the number of these incidents?'

The purpose of the summary here is to help the client move beyond 'poor me' and find ways of coping with this kind of work. The challenge in places like shelters is creating a supportive work environment, developing a sense of organisational and personal purpose, promoting the kind of teamwork that fits the institution's mission and fostering a culture of coping strategies.

When the client needs a new perspective   Often when scattered elements are brought together, the client sees the 'bigger picture' more clearly. In the following example, a man who has been reluctant to go to a counsellor with his wife has, in a solo session with the counsellor, agreed to a couple of sessions 'to please her'. In the session, he talks a great deal of his behaviour at home, but in a rather disjointed way.

> **COUNSELLOR:**   I'd like to pull a few things together. You've encouraged your wife in her career, especially when things are difficult for her at work. You also encourage her to spend time with her friends as a way of enjoying herself and letting off steam. You also make sure that you spend time with the children. In fact, time with them is important for you.
>
> **CLIENT:**   Yeah. That's right.
>
> **COUNSELLOR:**   Also, if I have heard you correctly, you currently take care of the household finances. You are usually the one who accepts or rejects social invitations, because your schedule is tighter than hers. And now you're about to ask her to move because you can get a better job in London.
>
> **CLIENT:**   When you put it all together like that, it sounds as if I'm running her life. . . . She never tells me I'm running her life.
>
> **COUNSELLOR:**   Maybe we could talk a little about this when the three of us get together.
>
> **CLIENT:**   Hmm. . . . Well, I'd . . . hmm . . . (laughs). I'd better think about all of this before the next session.

The summary provides the client with a mild jolt and an opportunity to go away and think about this between sessions. He realises that he needs to face up to the 'I am making many decisions for her, and some of them are big' theme implied in the summary. Helping clients develop new perspectives is the focus of Chapter 5.

In the following example, the client is a 52-year-old man who has been talking about a number of problems he is experiencing. He has come for help because he has been 'down in the dumps' and can't seem to shake it.

> **HELPER:**   Let's take a look at what we've seen so far. You're down – not just a normal slump; this time it's hanging on. You worry about your health, but you check out all right physically, so this seems to be more a symptom than a cause of your slump. There are some unresolved issues in your life. One that you seem to be stressing a lot is the fact that your recent change in jobs means that you don't see much of your old friends anymore. Because you're single, this leaves you, currently, with a rather bleak social life. Another issue – one you find painful and embarrassing – is your struggle to stay young. You don't like facing the fact that you're getting older. A third issue is the way you – to use your own word – 'over-invest' yourself in work, so much so that when you finish a long-term project, suddenly your life is empty.
>
> **CLIENT (pauses):**   It's painful to hear it all that badly, but that about sums it up. I've suspected I've got some screwed-up values, but I haven't wanted to stop long enough to take a look at it. Maybe the time has come. I'm hurting enough.
>
> **HELPER:**   One way of doing this is by taking a look at what a better future would look like.
>
> **CLIENT:**   That sounds interesting, even hopeful. How would we do that?

The counsellor's summary hits home – somewhat painfully – and the client draws his own conclusion. Care should be taken not to overwhelm clients with the contents of the summary. Nor should summaries be used to 'build a case' against a client. Helping is not a judicial procedure. Perhaps the foregoing summary would have been more effective if the helper had also summarised some of the client's strengths. That would have provided a more positive context.

Getting the client to provide the summary

Summaries can be useful when clients don't seem to know where to go next, either in the helping session itself or in a real-world action programme. In cases like this, helpers can, of course, use probes to help them move on. Summaries, however, have a way of keeping the ball in the client's court. Moreover, the helper does not always have to provide the summary. Often it is better to ask the client to pull together the major points. This helps the client own the helping process, pull together the salient points and move on. Because this is not meant to test clients, the counsellor should provide clients whatever help they need to stitch the summary together.

In the following example, the client, who has lost her job and her boyfriend because of her alcohol-induced outbreaks of anger, has been talking about 'not being able to stick to the programme.' The counsellor asks her to summarise what she's been doing and the obstacles she has been running into. With the help of the counsellor, she stumbles through a summary. At the end of it she says, 'I guess it's clear to both of us that I haven't been doing a very good job sticking to the programme. On paper, my plan looked like a snap. But it seems that I don't live on paper.' The client then uses the counsellor to help her take a couple of steps back. She begins to review goals, plans, obstacles and execution.

TUMI AND CARLOS REVISITED

Carlos, of course, uses probes throughout his dialogue with Tumi as a way of helping her get greater depth and clarity about the key issues she is discussing. In the following exchange he helps Tumi review her encounters with people her age during her visit to South Africa. He suspects that she might find implications or guidelines for a better future for herself. Here is an excerpt from one of their sessions.

CARLOS: It might be useful to review what you learned during your trip to South Africa. There might be some hints on how to fashion your own future here.

TUMI: Given what I've read about South Africa, I expected a lot of people to be, well, depressed: there is a lot of poverty there.

CARLOS: But you discovered that they have their own kind of freedom.

TUMI: Exactly. The young people wanted greater freedom, but they were almost always positive. They criticised the government a lot, just as we do. They criticised their leaders for being too conservative and too controlling. But they didn't criticise religion itself. And they wanted a better economic future. But they didn't just complain like some young people here do. They talked about ideas. Talking about better ways of doing things excited them. And they loved their culture. They didn't seem constrained by it. In a way they seem to feel freer than I do. To tell you the truth I didn't experience the kind of miserable life that is reported in the press here.

CARLOS: This sounds so positive. Even their complaining sounds positive.

TUMI: Don't get me wrong. I'm not saying that everything was perfect.

CARLOS: That's a good point. You don't want to idealise what you experienced there, but it spoke to you in some strong way.

TUMI: That's just it! It spoke to me. It was positive but it made me think of what is lacking in my own life.

CARLOS: The contrast hit you. The 'cultural ghetto' feeling.

TUMI: And it is a feeling. The young people I met talked positively about family life even though they found some of it constraining. They were energised by their families and communities. I envied them because they had a community of friends. The families I visited were alive. I don't have a community of friends. Home for me has never been lively. And it's even worse now after the conversation with my father. I envy the young people I met even more.

CARLOS: So finding or creating your version of what you experienced over there is central to the future you'd like to create for yourself.

TUMI: Yes, exactly. When I talk to you about the future I always feel better. Even now after the disastrous conversation with my father

Carlos uses a combination of empathy and probing to help Tumi explore other issues in her life such as her relationship with her mother and how that plays out in the task of creating a better future for herself. As a way of helping Tumi reset the system after her disastrous conversation with her father, Carlos suggests that she summarise what has happened and what she has learned up to this point. Because his suggestion comes near the end of their session, she suggests that she think about this between sessions and begin the next session with her summary. What follows is the flavour of the summary which emerges from their dialogue.

CARLOS: Well, Tumi, where do we stand today?

TUMI: I'd like to talk about the key things I've learned so far and use them as a jumping-off point for getting my life in order. First of all, I think I have been naive in my attempt to carve out a future for myself. All that has happened has made me both more realistic and more determined; yet also more fearful.

CARLOS: So you're wiser now, but with your eyes wide open what you see is daunting.

TUMI: Yes, the challenges scare me. I have a huge dilemma. I want to create a full life for myself both with respect to career and to social life, but what I want and what my parents want clash. They see my desire to create a different life for myself as betrayal. They're older now and my father's health is in question. It's a kind of culture clash inside me – the independent citizen who wants to move on versus the dutiful daughter who knows what she has to do. But I know that's too simplistic.

(Continued)

CARLOS: Or it may be a simple framework for getting a clear picture of the elements that are in conflict.

TUMI: Yes, something like a tool or a map.

CARLOS: What are the main features of the 'social life' issue?

TUMI: The equation is wrong. My home life plus my work life equals my social life. I don't have friends my own age. I don't have a friendship community. I'd like to have friends of all ages. That's what I liked about South Africa. I don't have any intimate friends, either women or men. Some of the conversations I have with you I should be having with friends. And my extended family is a bit of a mess. My aunt is very nice, but she is very busy being a grandmother. And my upwardly mobile cousins have bought too much into the consumer culture. This leaves me cold.

CARLOS: So the balance between work and social life is wrong and needs some immediate attention. Anything on the positive side?

TUMI: Well, I do feel secure at home and at work. But it's kind of a lifeless security. This may sound self-serving, but the most positive thing about the social picture is my desire for a more engaging community of some kind. I loved my brief fling with an expanded social life in South Africa. People are good for me and I'm good for them.

CARLOS: So you're ready to go. What about your friend Jim?

TUMI: I found out that Jim's getting divorced. We get along well, but he's not the one. I'm not sure there will ever be a 'one'.

They go on to review the main features of Tumi's career aspirations and where she stands with respect to them. She talks about what it is like being a 'cultural hybrid'. Tumi concludes by reviewing her main challenge.

TUMI: Right now something in me says that I can't follow my heart in either my social life or my work life without in some sense abandoning my parents. And I don't want to abandon them. I don't think I can.

CARLOS: So the search is on its way to do both career and social life without abandoning them. Where does 'not always pleasing them' fit into the picture?

The issues are fairly clear. Tumi pretty much knows what she wants but at the moment can't see how she can get what she wants. Figuring this out is the challenge.

THE SHADOW SIDE OF COMMUNICATION SKILLS: ESSENTIAL, BUT NOT EVERYTHING

Up to this point we have been dealing with basic communication skills. In Chapter 5, we will consider advanced communication skills and processes dealing with helping clients move beyond blind spots to the kind of new perspectives that lead to life-enhancing outcomes and the actions needed to get there. But first, let's look again at the shadow side of communication skills.

Communication skills as necessary but not sufficient

Some training programmes and helpers tend to over-identify the helping process with the communication skills – that is, with the tools, critical tools, that serve it. Being good at communication skills is not the same as being good at helping. Moreover, an overemphasis on communication skills can turn helping into a great deal of talk with very little action – and few outcomes that make a difference in clients' lives.

Communication skills are essential, of course, but they still must serve both the process and the outcomes of helping. These skills certainly help you establish a good relationship with clients. And a good relationship is the basis for the kind of social-emotional re-education that has been outlined earlier. But you can be good at communication, good at relationship building, even good at social-emotional re-education and still short-change your clients, because they need more than that. Some who overestimate the value of communication skills tend to see a skill such as responding with empathy as some kind of 'magic bullet'. Others overestimate the value of information gathering. This is not a broad indictment of the profession. Rather, it is a caution for beginners. Goal setting is important in focusing the client on their future.

The helping relationship versus helping technologies

On the other hand, some practitioners underestimate the need for solid communication skills. There is a subtle assumption that the 'technology' of their approach, such as treatment manuals, suffices. They listen and respond through their theories and constructs rather than through their humanity. They become technologists instead of helpers. They are like some medical doctors who become more and more proficient in the use of medical technology and less and less in touch with the humanity of their patients.

Some years ago I spent 10 days in a hospital (an eternity in these days of managed care). The staff were magnificent in addressing my medical needs. But the psychological needs that sprang from my anxiety about my illness were not addressed at all. Unfortunately, my anxieties were often expressed through physical symptoms. Then those symptoms were treated medically. Out of frustration I asked the young doctor who was debriefing me about the staffing conference in which my case was reviewed. 'When you have conferences during which patients are discussed, do you say, "Well, we've thoroughly reviewed his medical status and needs. Now let's turn our attention to what he's going through. What can we do to help him through this experience?"' The resident said, 'No, we don't have time.' Don't get me wrong. These were dedicated, generous people who had my interests at heart. But they ignored many of my needs. Having healthcare psychologists involved in such staffing sessions is a step in the right direction. I am glad to say that in more recent visits to the same medical centre I had startlingly different experiences. It was obvious that the medical profession's relatively new focus on relationships skills had become part of the centre's culture.

DEVELOPING PROFICIENCY IN COMMUNICATION SKILLS

Understanding communication skills and how they fit into the helping process is one thing. Becoming proficient in their use is another. Some trainees think that these 'soft' skills should be learned easily and fail to put in the kind of hard work and practice that makes them 'fluent' in them. Doing the exercises in communication-skills manuals and practising these skills in training groups can help, but that isn't enough to make these skills second nature. Tuning in, listening, processing, sharing highlights and probing that are trotted out, as it were, for helping encounters are likely to have a hollow ring to them. These skills must become part of your everyday communication style and stem from a commitment to empathic relationships.

After providing some initial training in communication skills, I tell students, 'Now, go out into your real lives and get good at these skills. I can't do that for you.' In the beginning, it may be difficult to practise all these skills in everyday life, not because they are so difficult, but because they are relatively rare in conversations. Take responding with empathy. Listen to the conversations around you. If you were to use an unobtrusive counter, pressing a button every time you heard someone engage in an empathic response, you might go days without pressing the button. But you can make empathic responding a reality in your own life. And those who interact with you will often notice the difference. They probably will not call it empathy. Rather, they will say such things as 'She really listens to me' or 'He takes me seriously.' Helpers can practise reflective work with families and friends in order to polish their skills.

On the other hand, you will hear many probes, usually in the form of questions, in everyday conversations. People are much more comfortable asking questions than providing understanding. However, many of these probes tend to be aimless. Worse, many will be disguised criticisms. 'Why on earth did you do that?' Learning how to integrate purposeful probes with empathy demands practice in everyday life. Life is your lab. Every conversation is an opportunity.

These skills have a place in all the human transactions of life, including business transactions. When businesses are asked what competencies they want to see in job applicants, especially for managerial positions, communication and relationship-building skills are inevitably at or near the top of the list. I once ran a training programme on these skills for an accounting firm. Although the director of training believed in their value in the business world, many of the account managers did not. They resisted the whole process. I got a call one day from one of them. He had been one of the more notable resisters in one of the training groups. He said, 'I owe you this call.' 'Really?' I replied with an edge of doubt in my voice. 'Really', he said. He went on to tell me how he had recently called on a potential client, a man whose company was dissatisfied with its current audit firm and looking for a new one. During the interview, the account executive said to himself, 'Since we don't have the slightest chance of getting this account, why don't I amuse myself by trying these communication skills?' In his phone call to me he went on to say, 'This morning I got a call from that client. He gave us the account, but in doing so he said, "You're not getting the account because you were the low bidder. You were not. You're getting the account because we thought that you were the only one that really understood our needs." So, almost literally, I owe you this call.' I forgot to ask him for a share of the fee.

CHAPTER 5
FACILITATING CLIENT SELF-CHALLENGE: FROM NEW PERSPECTIVES TO NEW BEHAVIOUR

Chapter Contents

- Self-Challenge: The Basic Concept

- Inviting Clients to Challenge the Blind Spots at the Root of Dysfunctional Thinking, Emotional Expression and Behaviour

- Specific Skills for Helping Clients Challenge their Blind Spots and Move to New Perspectives

SELF-CHALLENGE: THE BASIC CONCEPT

Helping is about change, and change entails making choices. Chapters 5 and 6 are about helping clients make life-enhancing choices. These chapters present a form of 'choice architecture' mentioned in Chapter 4. Inviting clients to challenge themselves in a variety of ways is a stronger form of the kind of 'nudging' discussed in that chapter. How do we 'frame' therapy in such a way that clients discover and tap into resources within and around themselves? Helping clients place demands on themselves can be one of most important things helpers can do. Although little current research on therapy focuses on making choices and self-challenge, over the course of history the human race has developed a vast literature dealing with finding and tapping into the best in ourselves – from the Bible to the latest articles on creating a healthy physical, psychological, social, value-laden and moral lifestyle for oneself. It would be hubris to think that the human-development wisdom of the ages must now be subjected to randomised clinical trials before it can be incorporated into therapeutic practice. This in no way discounts the value of evidence-based practice. Rather it highlights the need to balance evidence-based practice with the kind of practice-based evidence that has evolved over the centuries. Invitations to self-challenge and for self-discovery are about helping clients bring the good, the better and even the best within themselves to bear on problem situations and unused opportunities. These chapters highlight the value of self-challenge and demonstrate how therapists can help clients engage in self-challenge and in the process highlight and promote self-responsibility, self-discovery and self-determination.

Life at all levels is full of conflict, and conflict involves challenging. In some areas of life, failure to challenge can have devastating consequences. For instance, when nurses and technicians do not challenge mistakes surgeons are making in the operating room, they fail to prevent needless damage to patients, hospitals and the surgeons themselves. Therefore, many hospitals are making concerted efforts to encourage open discussions and whistleblowing, so that no one there needs to agree with the statement, 'In the operating rooms here, it is difficult to speak up if I perceive a problem with patient care' (Carter, 2006, p. 5). In one survey, 60 per cent of respondents agreed with this statement. Too much is at stake not to challenge and even report near misses (ICO, 2018).

Helpers can use the communication skills we have reviewed so far to help clients engage in reality testing. Clients who don't know how to engage in self-challenge or who simply do not do it for whatever reason are doing themselves no favour. Reasonable self-challenge is part of maturity. The values of self-responsibility and a bias towards action outlined in Chapter 2 demand some form of self-challenge. Consider Belinda, a mother with three young children aged between 7 and 12. She is seeing a counsellor because raising three children, being a good partner with her husband, tending to a widowed mother with health problems and holding a very demanding part-time job have become too much for her. She has sleepless nights, loses her temper with the children and then indulges them as a way of saying 'I'm sorry', and feels guilty for neglecting her mother. She is especially concerned about her 'wild' children and has this to say about her parenting in the second counselling session.

'This morning I read an article that struck a very painful chord. It talked about how many middle-class parents raise their children. On the one hand, they want their children to be independent and think for themselves, you know, be responsible, but then they do everything for them. And they overprotect them. Gene and I do that and now we have self-centred children that expect us to do everything for them. They start nagging me as soon as I get home. Sometimes I begin to think that they don't care about anyone but themselves. And we've done that to them.'

Belinda engages in self-challenge. The article she read was very challenging but she was able to recognise herself in it. Rearing her children lies at the heart of Belinda's problem situation. When she gets home, she gets her husband to read the article. He agrees that both of them should attend the counselling sessions.

Such self-initiated self-challenge is ideal, but it's not what usually happens. Because helping at its best is a constructive social-influence process, some form of challenge is central to helping. This does not signal a movement from the pro-client stance taken in this book. Rather it highlights the need for collaboration in making self-challenge part of the helping process. The reality is simple. All effective helping is some kind of mixture of support and challenge. If they are going to manage their problem situation, Belinda and her husband will have to both support and challenge themselves and each other, and both support and challenge their children. Finding the right mixture is essential because challenge without support is harsh and unjustified; support without challenge can end up being empty and counterproductive.

Martin (1994) put it well when he suggested that the helping dialogue may add the most value when it is perceived by clients as relevant, helpful, interested, supportive and 'somehow inconsistent (discordant) with their current theories of themselves and their circumstances' (pp. 53–54). The same point is made by Trevifio (1996) in the context of cross-cultural counselling.

> *"Certain patterns of congruency and discrepancy between client and counsellor facilitate change. There is a significant body of research suggesting that congruency between counsellor and client enhances the therapeutic relationship, whereas discrepancy between the two facilitates change. In a review of the literature on this topic, Claiborn (1982, p. 446) concluded that the presentation of discrepant points of view contributes to positive outcomes by changing 'the way the client construes problems and considers solutions'." (p. 203)*

Challenge adds that discordant note. Note that the term 'challenge' rather than the harder-edged term 'confrontation' is used here. Most people see both confronting and being confronted as unpleasant and unhelpful experiences. But, at least in principle, they more readily buy the softer but still edgy option of challenge. Self-challenge and self-discovery has a more productive and constructive ring to it. Finn (2005) stresses compassion and firmness, pointing out that at times 'we must say difficult things to clients in plain non-judgemental language, which forces us to develop courage and wisdom' (p. 29). Or perhaps we should say that clients at times 'must say difficult things' to themselves and come to terms with some important issues that they may not have been aware of. If we can help them do so, we are adding value, and significant and life-changing potential.

Because people make choices based on their beliefs-values-norms-ethics-morality package discussed in Chapter 1, helpers must listen carefully to these drivers of behaviour. They must also help clients understand how these drivers are influencing their decisions. It is not that helpers challenge clients' drivers, but they can help clients become aware of these drivers and explore the consequences of their use. Belinda and her husband had, perhaps unknowingly, bought into a philosophy of parenting that proved to have unwanted consequences, that is, consequences that they themselves did not want. They wanted to change their behaviour, but they needed help in discovering how.

The goals of challenging

The ultimate goal of helping is a set of life-enhancing and problem-managing client outcomes. The overall goal of challenging is to help clients do some reality testing and invest what they learn from this in creating a better future for themselves.

> *Help clients challenge themselves to change ways of thinking, expressing emotions and acting that keep them mired in problem situations and prevent them from identifying and developing opportunities.*

It is especially important to help clients challenge self-defeating *patterns* of thinking, expressing emotion and behaving (Wei & Ku, 2007). A parallel goal is more positive. It deals with new perspectives and translating these new perspectives into new ways of acting. It goes something like this:

> *Become partners with your clients in helping them challenge themselves to find possibilities in their problems, to discover unused strengths and resources, both internal and external, to invest these resources in the problems and opportunities of their lives, to spell out possibilities for a better future, to find ways of making that future a reality, and to commit themselves to the actions needed to make it all happen.*

As idealistic as this might sound, it contains the spirit of the counsellor's role as 'catalyst for a better future'.

Target areas of self-challenge

Given the two goals just outlined, some forms of self-challenge involve self-criticism, while others involve self-enhancement. Chang (2008) has edited a book that asks and attempts to answer such questions as: Is self-enhancement good or bad? Is self-criticism good or bad? Under what conditions is either of these good or bad? What do helpers do about all of this? It is worth reading before you commit yourself to helping clients challenge themselves.

Counsellors should help clients challenge whatever stands in the way of understanding and managing problem situations or identifying and developing life-enhancing opportunities. Identifying their barriers to change, obstacles they put up and patterns in their life can all be very useful for change. Exploring clients' underpinning values and beliefs that drive their behaviour may provide them with insight into how to change. The following are some of the main targets of self-challenge:

- Self-defeating mindsets, such as prejudice
- Patterns, themes and barriers to change
- Self-limiting internal behaviour, such as dysfunctional thinking styles and daydreaming
- Self-defeating expressions of feelings and emotions, such as flying off the handle and jumping to conclusions
- Dysfunctional external behaviour, such as putting people down and criticising others
- Distorted understanding of what the world is really like
- Discrepancies between thinking and acting
- Unused strengths and resources
- The predictable dishonesties of everyday life.

A final category, helping clients challenge themselves to participate fully in the helping process, is discussed later. Here are a few examples in each of these categories.

Self-defeating mindsets   Mindsets here refer to more or less permanent states of mind. They include such things as assumptions, attitudes, beliefs, values, bias, convictions, inclinations, norms, outlook, points of view, unexamined perceptions of self/others/the world, preconceptions and prejudices. Let's revisit Tumi and Carlos.

> Carlos realises that Tumi has a number of unexplored assumptions, beliefs and norms that are rooted in the family culture. Even when she talks about her career aspirations, the subtext seems to be that she would like to move ahead to the degree that her family culture would permit such movement. But she never says this directly. Carlos also knows that her personal culture has been influenced by her educational experiences in the United Kingdom. Her ambitions, though contained, are typically British. Culturally, she is a hybrid, but Carlos is not sure how these two sets of cultural 'voices' play out against each other. It's not his place to take sides, but he thinks that inviting her to explore her beliefs and assumptions in that regard would help her make decisions in the area of career and in personal relationships. Her painful conversation with her father about her desires to move ahead in the business is a sign that such self-exploration is perhaps overdue.

Mindsets, whether productive or problematic, tend to drive external behaviour – or at least leak out into external behaviour. The principle is clear: invite clients to transform outmoded, self-limiting mindsets and perspectives into self-enhancing and liberating new perspectives that drive problem-managing and opportunity-developing action. Here are examples dealing with two kinds of mindsets – prejudices and self-limiting beliefs and assumptions.

Prejudices   Candace is having a great deal of trouble with a colleague at work who happens to be Jewish. As she grew up, Candace picked up the idea that 'Jews are treacherous business people'. The counsellor invites her to re-think this prejudicial stereotype. Her colleague may or may not be treacherous, but, if he is, it's not because he's Jewish. Separating the individual from the prejudicial stereotype helps Candace think more clearly. But it is now clear that Candace has two problems – her troubled relationship with her colleague at work and her prejudice. She has discovered that her problem with her colleague is not his Jewishness, but she may also need to discover that in troubled relationships often both parties contribute to the mess. She realises that she has to go back and examine her behaviour and the degree to which it has been affected by her prejudice.

Self-limiting beliefs and assumptions   Albert Ellis (Ellis, 2004; Ellis & Ellis, 2011) developed a rational-emotional-behavioural approach (REBT) to helping. He claimed that one of the most useful interventions helpers can make is to challenge clients' irrational and self-defeating beliefs. Clients (and the rest of us) have a way of talking themselves into these dysfunctional beliefs. Some of the common beliefs that Ellis saw as getting in the way of effective living are these:

- *Being liked and loved.* I must always be loved and approved by the significant people in my life.
- *Being competent.* I must always, in all situations, demonstrate competence, and I must be both talented and competent in some important areas of life.
- *Having one's own way.* I must have my way, and my plans must always work out.
- *Being hurt.* People who do anything wrong, especially those who harm me, are evil and should be blamed and punished.
- *Being danger-free.* If anything or any situation is dangerous in any way, I must be anxious and upset about it. I should not have to face dangerous situations.
- *Being problemless.* Things should not go wrong in life and, if by chance they do, there should be quick and easy solutions.
- *Being a victim.* Other people and outside forces are responsible for any misery I experience. No one should ever take advantage of me.
- *Avoiding.* It is easier to avoid facing life's difficulties than to develop self-discipline; making demands of myself should not be necessary.
- *Tyranny of the past.* What I did in the past, and especially what happened to me in the past, determines how I act and feel today.
- *Passivity.* I can be happy by being passive, by being uncommitted, and by just enjoying myself.

I am sure that you could add to the list. Ellis suggested that when these kinds of belief are violated in a person's life, he or she tends to see the experience as terrible, awful, even catastrophic. 'People pick on me. I hate it. It shouldn't happen. Isn't it awful!' Such 'catastrophising', Ellis said, gets clients nowhere. It is unfortunate to be picked on, he says, but it's not the end of the world. Moreover, clients can often do something about the issues over which they catastrophise.

Take Allison, a widow in her early 60s, who is seeing a counsellor because of 'anxiety attacks'. A very stressful marriage ended suddenly the previous year when her husband died of a heart attack. At the time she felt angry, guilty and relieved. She felt guilty because he died at a time when they were having particularly serious disagreements. She wondered whether the arguments had precipitated the attack. But she was also angry because 'he left me holding the bag', that is, there was now no way to resolve the conflict. Still she was 'profoundly relieved that all of this is over'. The relationship together with all its stress was over, she was sure that he was 'in a better place' and she was free to redesign her life.

Her current anxiety is due to the fact that she has just had a cancerous intestinal polyp removed. There was no metastasis, so the prognosis is actually quite good. She will have to have tests from time to time to monitor the state of her colon, but she is in no immediate danger. Instead of rejoicing over the good news, she has begun catastrophising about the things that could go wrong. 'These are supposed to be the "golden years" and now I'm facing the possibility of a deadly disease! And I hate those tests!' Allison is working from the assumption that she should be problemless. 'These things shouldn't be happening to me!' The counsellor needs to help her challenge her dysfunctional beliefs.

Sternberg (2002, 2003) has explored self-beliefs that make otherwise smart people do stupid things. He has identified four fallacies in the thinking of such people.

- '*The egocentrism fallacy.* They think it's all about them. In planning their actions, they take into account their own interests, but no one else's.
- *The omniscience fallacy.* They may indeed know a lot about something. However, they start to think they know everything about everything.
- *The omnipotence fallacy.* They think that they are all-powerful – that they can do whatever they want.
- *The invulnerability fallacy.* They think that they can get away with whatever they do – that they will not be caught, or that even if they are, they will be able to get themselves out of any fix.' (Sternberg, 2003, p. 5)

The fact that in politics, the executive suite, the entertainment industry and sports these blind spots are displayed on the widescreen does not mean that the rest of us are exempt. In fact, no one is exempt.

Riso, du Toit, Stein and Young (2007) have edited a book that describes the kinds of maladaptive cognitive schemas and core beliefs that characterise a range of psychological disorders. The notion of 'schemas', which is relatively new, points not just to dysfunctional beliefs but also to ingrained systems of thinking that cause trouble. Clients can benefit from identifying and dealing with disordered, self-defeating patterns of thinking. Helping them do so can add a great deal of value.

Self-limiting internal behaviour   Some forms of thinking are actually behaviours. They are things we can choose to do or not do. Internally we daydream, pray, ruminate on things, believe, identify problems, review opportunities, make decisions, formulate plans, make judgements, question motives, approve of self and others, disapprove of self and others, wonder, value, imagine, ponder, create standards, fashion norms, mull things over, ignore, forgive, rehearse – we do all sorts of things internally. These are internal or cognitive behaviours, not just thoughts or things that happen to us. The helping principle is clear. If clients are to replace self-limiting and self-defeating internal behaviours with more creative ones, they may need some help. The ways in which internal behaviour can be self-limiting are legion. Consider a few examples.

> John daydreams a lot, seeing himself as some kind of hero whom others admire. Thinking about unrealistic success in his social life has taken the place of working for actual success. The new perspective: daydreaming is not all that bad. It's how you use it. With the help of a counsellor, John does not stop daydreaming, but he switches its focus. He daydreams about what a fuller social life might look like. This provides him with some practical strategies for expanding and enriching his interactions with others. He begins to try these out in behavioural experiments.
>
> Nadia, when given an assignment on a project, immediately begins to try to think of reasons why the project won't work. Then her internal behaviour spills out into external behaviour as she goes around telling everyone that the project should be changed or shelved. This annoys her colleagues. With the help of a supervisor, she sees how self-limiting her instinct to take things apart is. She lacks intellectual balance. So her supervisor helps her get into the habit of first trying to see what value the project or programme will add to the company and what she might do to improve it. She finds that after doing some of this more positive internal work, she engages her colleagues more constructively about the project. She finds better ways of critiquing projects. They listen to her, and she adds real value.

For some clients, developing new perspectives and changing their internal behaviour can be enormously helpful. It certainly works for Bella, a woman whose husband died two years ago. She is suffering from depression, not incapacitating, but still miserable. At one point she says:

BELLA: You know, I stopped wearing black a year ago. But. . . (She pauses for a long time.)

THERAPIST: But you're still wearing black inside?

In a flash, Bella had it. Not magic, but now she had the metaphor she needed. She knew that she could and should stop wearing black 'inside'. With just a couple more sessions with the therapist, Bella begins to move beyond the grieving that had come to be the hallmark of her life.

Carlos notices that Tumi has certain ways of thinking that conflict with her desire to create a more satisfying future for herself. She seems to think of herself as the 'dutiful daughter' who puts the needs and wants of her parents ahead of her own. This is not the same as being a naturally generous person who readily considers the needs and wants of others and balances them against his or her own needs. If she is to create a more fulfilling future for herself, she might benefit from exploring mindsets such as this.

Self-defeating expressions of feelings and emotions   Managing our emotions and the ways we express them is part of social-emotional intelligence. Some of our emotions are bottled up, some go on inside and others are quite visible. Sheila becomes depressed when her boss fails to notice the good work she is doing. She feels taken for granted. But at work she puts on a good face. On the other hand, Ira rants and raves about his 'stupid' boss to whoever will listen. Everyone, except his boss, knows where he stands.

Clients can be helped to face up to needless denial and bottling up of emotions, letting emotions run riot internally and self-defeating forms of emotional expression. In two studies Berking, Orth, Wupperman, Meier and Caspar (2008) found, perhaps unsurprisingly, that 'a focus on emotion-regulation skills may be important in the prevention and treatment of affect-related mental health problems' (p. 485). The question is: where do people acquire these skills in the course of growing up? Arthur flies off the handle whenever anyone suggests that a less acerbic interpersonal style would benefit him and his friends, relatives and colleagues at work. Arthur needs help in seeing the world as others see it. Cynthia lavishes praise on her two children in primary school without exploring the consequences of her behaviour. Praising makes her feel good, but what is it doing to her children? She needs to learn that praising is not an unadulterated good. A counsellor helps Ken realise that long periods of surfing the internet tend to trigger episodes of depression. Ken needs to get out and interact with people to maintain emotional balance.

Tumi has always presented herself as self-contained, that is, until her disastrous conversation with her father about her job aspirations. Even when she broke down and cried when telling Carlos about the conversations, she kept apologising for expressing her emotions and made repeated attempts to control herself. Emotional over-control may be part of the problem.

Dysfunctional external behaviour   External behaviour is the stuff people could see if they were looking. For some clients, their external behaviour constitutes trouble.

- When Achilles is with women at work, he engages in behaviour that others, including the courts, see as sexual harassment. He thinks he is just being 'friendly'.
- Consider Jake. He is not an alcoholic, but when he has a couple of drinks he tends to get mean, critical and argumentative. He thinks that he is merely helping others 'get the point'. So he would benefit from taking a closer look at both his thinking and his acting.
- Clarence, a self-doubting and overly cautious person, is very deferential around his manager. He does not realise that his manager interprets his deference as a 'lack of ambition'. Clarence's behaviour keeps him mired in a job he hates. But the manager says nothing because she would rather have a 'compliant and obedient' rather than an 'aggressive' employee.

Not doing something is also a form of behaviour. Clients often fail to make choices and engage in behaviours that would help them cope with problems or develop opportunities. When Clarence is offered an opportunity to update his skills, he turns it down. He also refuses a promotion, saying to himself, 'I don't want to get in over my head.' His self-defeating external behaviours are based on a self-defeating thought about himself. His manager sees him bypass these opportunities, but says nothing to him. She says to herself, 'Anyway, I've got a hard-working drone. That's something these days. I'll leave well-enough alone.'

Ryan is having trouble relating to his college classmates. He is aggressive, hogs conversations, tries to get his own way when events are being planned and criticises others freely. One of his friends, after a couple of drinks, gets very angry with Ryan and tells him off. 'Self-centred', 'arrogant' and 'pushy' are the kinds of words she uses. Ryan goes into a fit of misery. Later in the week he talks things through with the dorm prefect, an older student for whom he has a great deal of respect. Ryan begins to see how self-defeating his interpersonal style is. He goes on to work with one of the counsellors in the student services centre to do something about it. They discuss ways of being proactive and assertive rather than aggressive. His 'edge' has too much of an edge about it. He takes a course in interpersonal communication, belatedly learns the value of dialogue and finds plenty of incentives to invest what he learns in his interactions with his classmates, in his part-time job and at home.

Distorted understanding of the world   Clients' failure to see the world as it really is can keep them mired in problem situations and prevent them from identifying and developing opportunities. For instance, parents fail to notice signs indicating that their teenage son has started to use drugs. If at times we are blind to others and their needs – often those closest to us – we are also blind to their attitudes towards us and the impact of their behaviour on us. Take Sandra. She interprets her husband's being less insistent when it comes to having sex as a sign that 'he is finally coming to his senses'. So she is shocked when she learns, by accident, that he is having an affair. All of us have our areas of ignorance and naiveté. Some clients will not be open to acknowledging what they probably know already. Clients' failure to fully understand the environment in which they live and the impact it is having on them does not mean that they are stupid. Rather, like all of us, clients fail to notice things that are having a negative impact on their lives and on others. It is therefore important that the helper sees this from the client's world view and highlights these for the client to consider.

Discrepancies   Various kinds of discrepancies plague our lives. For instance, we don't always do what we say we're going to do. Just review last year's 'New Year's resolutions'. Discrepancies keep clients mired in their problem situations. Discrepancies can include the following:

- What clients think or feel versus what they say
- What they say versus what they do
- Their views of themselves versus the views that others have of them
- What they are versus what they claim they want to be
- Their stated goals versus what they actually accomplish
- Their expressed values versus their actual behaviour.

The list goes on. For instance, a helper might help the following clients challenge the discrepancies in their lives:

- Tom sees himself as witty and good at banter but his friends see him as biting and harsh.
- Minerva says that physical fitness is important, but she overeats and under-exercises.
- George says he loves his wife and family, but he is seeing another woman and stays away from home a great deal.
- Clarissa, unemployed for several months, wants a job, but she doesn't want to participate in a retraining programme.

Let's use the example of Clarissa to illustrate how the discrepancy between talking and acting can be challenged. Clarissa has just told the counsellor that she has decided against joining the retraining programme.

> **COUNSELLOR:**   At one time you thought that the retraining programme would be just the kind of thing you've been looking for.
>
> **CLARISSA:**   Well. . . . I don't know if it's the kind of thing I'd like to do. . . . The work would be so different from my last job. . . . And it's a long programme.
>
> **COUNSELLOR:**   So you feel the fit isn't good.
>
> **CLARISSA:**   Yes, that's right.
>
> **COUNSELLOR:**   Clarissa, I'm curious. You seemed so enthusiastic when you first talked about the programme. . . . (gently): What's going on?
>
> **CLARISSA (pauses):**   You know, I've gotten a bit lazy. . . . I don't like being out of work, but I've gotten used to it.

The counsellor sees a discrepancy between what Clarissa is saying and what she is doing by highlighting these inconsistencies. She is actually letting herself slip into a 'culture of unemployment'. Now that the discrepancy is out in the open, they can work together on how she wants to shape her future.

Unused strengths and resources   Clients' self-challenge should focus not just on problems but also on the 'possible self' that every client is. Helping clients get in touch with unexploited opportunities and unused or underused strengths and resources (Aspinwall & Staudinger, 2003; Tedeschi & Kilmer, 2005) can add a great deal of value. Some of these resources are client-based – for instance, talents, coping strategies and abilities not being used – and some are external – for example, failure to identify and use social support in managing problems or developing opportunities. Therapists can help clients ask themselves questions like this: 'What kind of unused strengths do I have? What can I do to unleash and marshal both internal and external resources?' 'What is stopping me?' We all have resources we fail to use; they need to be mined. Sometimes our coping strategies are not as helpful or effective, which may mean developing new coping strategies with clients.

Strengths are buried even in dysfunctional behaviour. For instance, Driscoll (1984) has pointed out that helpers can show clients that even their 'irrationalities' can be a source of strength. Instead of forcing clients to see how stupidly they are thinking and acting, therapists can help them find the logic embedded even in seemingly dysfunctional ideas and behaviours. Then clients can use that logic as a resource to manage problem situations instead of perpetuating them. A psychiatrist friend of mine helped a client see the 'beauty', as it were, of a very carefully constructed self-defence system. The client, through a series of mental gymnastics and external behaviours, was cocooning himself from real life. My friend helped the client see how inventive he had been and how powerful the system that he had created was.

The predictable dishonesties of everyday life   The 'predictable dishonesties of everyday life' refers to the distortions, evasions, games, tricks, excuse-making and smoke screens that keep clients (and ourselves) mired in their problem situations. All of us have ways of defending ourselves from ourselves, from others and from the world, and we will often run the same 'scripts' in life (Berne, 1961). We all have our little dishonesties. But they are two-edged swords. Although lies, whether white or not, may help me cope with difficulties – especially unexpected difficulties – in my interactions with others, they come with a price tag, especially if they become a preferred coping strategy. The masks that people wear in different situations can also prove difficult in other situations. Blaming others for my misfortunes helps me save face, but it disrupts interpersonal relationships and prevents me from developing a healthy sense of self-responsibility. The purpose of helping clients challenge themselves with respect to the dishonesties of everyday life, whether they take place in the helping sessions or are more widespread patterns of behaviour, is not to strip clients of their defences, which in some cases could be dangerous, but to help them cope with their inner and outer worlds more creatively.

Distortions   Some clients would rather not see the world as it is – it is too painful or demanding – and therefore distort it in various ways. The distortions are self-serving and can be a protective coping strategy that they have learned. Clients' past often plays a role in this. Let's look at some examples:

- At work Arnie is afraid of his supervisor and therefore sees her as aloof, whereas in reality she is a caring person. He is working out of past fears rather than current realities.
- Edna sees her counsellor in some kind of divine role, putting her on a pedestal and therefore makes unwarranted demands on him.
- Nancy sees her getting her own way with her friends as an indication of whether they really like her or not.
- Charles fails to express his feelings as he does not want to burden his wife and family.

Let's take a look at Nancy, who is married to Milan. They are experiencing some bumps in their marriage.

Nancy and Milan come from different cultures. They fought a great deal in the early years of their marriage, but then things settled down. Now, squabbles have broken out about the best way to bring up their children. Milan is not convinced that counselling is a good idea, so the counsellor is talking to Nancy alone. She has forbidden her 12-year-old son to bicycle to school because she doesn't want 'his picture to end up on a milk carton'. Milan thought that she was being extremely overprotective. One day he stalks out of the house, yelling back at her, 'Why don't you just keep him locked in his room?' Nancy and her counsellor have a session not long after this incident. Nancy is defending her approach to her son.

NANCY: Milan's just too permissive. Now that Jan is entering his teenage years, he needs more guidance, not less. Let's face it, the world we live in is dangerous.

COUNSELLOR: So from your point of view, this is not the time for letting your guard down. . . . Of course, I'm also making the assumption that Milan is not indifferent to Jan's welfare.

(Continued)

NANCY: Of course not! Good grief, he cares as much as I do. We just disagree on how to do it. 'Safe, not sorry' is my philosophy.

Hopefully, this gets rid of an implied distortion: 'I'm interested in my son's welfare, but his father isn't.' They continue their dialogue.

COUNSELLOR: Let's widen the discussion a bit. What other issues do you and Milan disagree on?

NANCY: Well, we used to disagree a lot. But we've put that behind us, it would seem. He leaves a lot of the home decisions to me.

COUNSELLOR: I'm not sure whether you both decided that you should make the decisions at home or if it just happened that way.

NANCY (slowly): I suppose it just happened that way. . . . I don't really know.

COUNSELLOR: I'm curious because he seems to be annoyed that you're the one making the decisions about how to bring up your son. . . .

NANCY (pausing): Like he wants to reassert himself. Take over again.

Another distortion. Perhaps Nancy feels the counsellor is getting too close to a sensitive issue that she thought was resolved long ago.

COUNSELLOR: You got a bit annoyed when I asked whether Milan was as committed to the children as you. . . . Because he cares as much as you do about his son, I'm wondering what the disagreement is really about.

NANCY: Like he's drawing a line in the sand, taking a stand on this one? Or what?

COUNSELLOR (caringly): I don't want to guess what's going through Milan's mind. . . . Maybe we could try once more to get him to come with you.

The counsellor has a hunch that the problem is as much about power and getting one's own way as it is about bringing up children. Nancy does seem to have trouble with her own 'little dishonesties'.

Games, Tricks and Smoke Screens   If clients are comfortable with their delusions and profit by them, they will obviously try to keep them. If they are rewarded for playing games, inside the counselling sessions or outside, they will continue a game approach to life (see Berne, 1964). Consider some examples:

Kennard plays the 'Yes, but. . .' game. He gets his therapist to recommend some things he might do to control his anger. He then points out why each recommendation will not work. When the therapist calls this game, Kennard says, 'Well, I didn't think you guys were supposed to tell clients what to do.' A more savvy helper might have sniffed out Kennard's tendency to play games much earlier.

Dora makes herself appear helpless and needy when she is with her friends, but when they come to her aid, she is angry with them for treating her like a child. When she tries this in an early session, her counsellor invites her to examine this 'helpless and needy' routine. Finding out the meaning behind a behaviour can be useful for the client. This can help identify the behaviour and the maintaining pattern so that the client can start to make the necessary changes.

The number of games we can play to avoid the work involved in squarely facing the tasks of life is endless. Clients who are fearful of changing will attempt to lay down smokescreens to hide from the helper the ways in which they fail to face up to life. Such clients use communication in order not to communicate. Therefore, helpers do well if they establish an atmosphere that discourages clients from playing games.

Excuses   Snyder, Higgins and Stucky (1983) examined excuse-making behaviour in depth. Excuse-making, of course, is universal, part of the fabric of everyday life (see also Halleck, 1988; Higginson, 1999; Snyder &

Higgins, 1988; Yun, 1998). Like games and distortions, it has its positive uses in life. Even if it were possible, there is no real reason for setting up a world without myths. On the other hand, excuse-making contributes a great deal to avoiding the problems of life. Clients, like the rest of us, routinely provide excuses for why they did something 'bad', why they didn't do something 'good' and why they can't do something they need to do.

For example, Roberto tells the helper that he has engaged in benign attempts to sabotage his wife's career 'for her own good' because she would 'get hurt' in the Anglo world. The counsellor helps him explore the alternative hypothesis that 'he is not ready' for the changes in style that his wife's career and behaviour were demanding from him.

> Before Roberto and Maria got married, they talked a great deal about the cultural difficulties they might face. He tended to adhere to traditional Latino culture, whereas she was much more open to what he saw as 'Anglo' attitudes and behaviour. For instance, she was especially concerned about cultural norms relating to the role of women in society. When asked about their differences, Roberto said he would enjoy being married to someone with a 'pioneer' spirit. Maria said that she thought that they had 'worked things out'. That was then. Now she has put herself through college, got a job, developed it into a career and assumed the role of both mother and co-breadwinner. She makes more money than Roberto. His woes include thinking that he is losing face in the community, feeling belittled by his wife's success and being forced into an overly 'democratic' marriage.

If Roberto is going to manage the conflict between himself and his wife better, he needs to challenge himself to review and make changes in some of the ways he thinks.

This only skims the surface of the games, evasions, tricks, distortions, excuses, rationalisations and subterfuges resorted to by clients (together with the rest of the population). Skilled helpers are caring and empathic, but they do not let themselves be conned. That helps no one.

In practice, these targets for challenge are often mixed together. Take Minerva who is depressed because of the lack of a social life. Because of a few traumatic past experiences, she believes that the world is filled with dishonest people (a self-limiting mindset). Whenever she meets someone new, she views that person's behaviour through this lens and thinks that he or she is guilty until proven innocent (internal behaviour in need of reform). Because she is always on guard, she comes across as cold and indifferent (inadequate management of feelings and emotions). Therefore, when she meets someone new, she is defensive and often questions that person's intentions and actions (external behaviour needing change). She also realises that when she meets someone new, she expects some kind of initial trust on the part of the other person even though she doesn't give it herself (a discrepancy). She looks for flaws in other people's character and when she finds them she pounces on them (a self-defeating game). She fails to see that even her closest friends are becoming uncomfortable around her (failure to see the world as it really is). In the counselling sessions, Minerva remains guarded and is slow to share what she really thinks (inadequate participation). To make things worse, Minerva doesn't seem to have a clue that this is what she is doing.

This section ends with a caution from Steven Hayes (Hayes & Smith, 2005; Hayes, 2007, 2008; Bach & Moran, 2008; Dewane, 2008; Harris, 2009; Luoma, Hayes & Walser, 2007) related to the pervasiveness of self-defeating thoughts and emotions. In an approach to helping he calls 'acceptance and commitment therapy' (ACT), he invites clients to step back from their endless war with 'bad' thoughts and feelings. Don't waste time and energy avoiding or confronting them. Rather embrace and defuse them with 'respectful attention'. Change your *relationship* with bad thoughts and feelings. Clients are encouraged to have 'psychological flexibility' in their thinking (Harris, 2009; Hayes, Strosahl & Wilson, 1999).

> *"For example, instead of disputing negative thoughts, patients learn to watch them mindfully and at enough distance to realise, in a visceral and not just analytical way, that they're just thoughts. Instead of getting rid of sadness, patients learn to detect how sadness feels in their body, how it tugs at their behaviour, how it ebbs and flows, and begin to feel at a deep level that they can carry sorrow with them while still living the life they want."* (Hayes, 2007, p. 48)

But then what? Hayes next helps clients determine what they want to live for and, in light of a focused sense of purpose, how they want to live. Befriending troublesome thoughts and feelings clears the way for the real work of life. As counsellors, 'we... can help our clients gain access to their deepest aspirations and turn a life lived in the present moment into a life *worth* living' (Hayes, 2007, p. 52). Therefore, ACT is a mildly directive approach to counselling. ACT therapists help clients place demands on themselves to reconstruct their lives. Hayes has written extensively about the research behind his approach.

INVITING CLIENTS TO CHALLENGE THE BLIND SPOTS AT THE ROOT OF DYSFUNCTIONAL THINKING, EMOTIONAL EXPRESSION AND BEHAVIOUR

Up to this point the discussion has focused on what needs to be challenged, the content, as it were. However, it is also necessary to consider the client's degree of awareness of self-limiting thinking, emotional expression and behaviour. Like the rest of us, clients don't always realise, or realise fully, how they are limiting themselves. That is, they have blind spots. Blind spots are part of the human condition. They are things we fail to see or choose to ignore that keep us from identifying and managing problem situations, or identifying and developing opportunities. Van Hecke (2007) explores ten common blind spots that get people in trouble – failure to think things through, always having the right answers, failure to pick up cues and clues and notice what's going on, lack of self-awareness, failure to explore one's biases, seeing the world through rigid categories, jumping to conclusions, failure to check things out, seeing coincidences as causes and failure to see the big picture and put things in context. She suggests that, while we readily see others' blind spots and the 'stupidities' they lead to, we remain ignorant of our own: 'When *others* seem dense to us, whatever we grasp seems so clear that we cannot fathom how they could have missed it' (p. 19). So our clients might well be quite perceptive when it comes to others but need help to sharpen their perceptions of themselves. Blind spots are obstacles to effective decision making.

Lack of awareness

Some blind spots appear to be unintentional, whereas others tend to be self-inflicted. Either way, they stand in the way of change. Blind spots come in a variety of flavours. Some things clients are simply not aware of. Becoming aware of them helps them know themselves better, and both cope with problems and develop opportunities. Serge was surprised when a fellow member of a self-help group called him 'talented'. He was brought up in a family that prized modesty and 'humility'. He never thought about himself as talented, creative or resourceful and had little idea how this lack of awareness had narrowed his life. His mindset stood in the way of change. Katya, on the other hand, was always positive. Because she always tried to look at the positive side of things, she 'exuded sunshine', as one of her friends put it. What she did not realise was that sometimes her exuberance was inappropriate because it stood in the way of facing problems squarely. One of her colleagues at work thought that Katya's positive nature was great but needed to be tempered by a dose of reality.

Katya had two friends, Mia and Casper. Mia had her own problems. For instance, she thought that her emotional outbursts were part of her sassy, punchy style. She did not realise that sometimes her colleagues at work wanted to strangle her. Casper didn't know that he had an acerbic communication style. If asked, he would describe himself as 'assertive, rational and logical'. The problem is that his 'assertiveness' made people shy away from him. And others around him saw his 'logic' as stubbornness. People avoided or ignored him. They were reluctant to disagree with anything he said. No wonder he was dissatisfied with his social life.

'Simple unawareness' is itself an elastic term. There are degrees. At one end is simple ignorance – 'He doesn't have a clue.' At the other end the ignorance is not so simple. Mia said of Casper, 'He probably has some idea that he's rubbing people up the wrong way; he's not totally in the dark.'

Failure to think things through

This is a very common human experience. We explore problems, examine opportunities, search for possibilities or formulate plans of action in an incomplete and haphazard way. Then we go on to base decisions on our flawed reasoning.

> Kim and Lea are both women who have lost a son in Iraq. They have long been both neighbours and friends, but recently have had some bitter encounters. Kim believes that the war was a mistake and that her son has died because of the 'politicians', whereas Lea believes that the war was essential for national security and that her son has died fighting for a very just cause. Their beliefs are so charged with emotion that neither has any feeling for the other's point of view. They are both so set in their convictions that they are willing to destroy their relationship, something that neither son would have wanted.

In this case, strong convictions made stronger by emotion keep them from thinking things through. In other cases, habit or laziness or thoughtlessness is the villain. Counsellors who challenge and help clients think key issues through provide an invaluable service.

Failure to explore the possible short- and long-term consequences of a dysfunctional pattern of behaviour is an all-too-common human experience. One client, let's call him Clancy, knew that he could get into trouble if he hung around a group of classmates who forgot about limits when they went out together 'to have a good time'. His mother cautioned him a number of times, but really did not know the full extent of the emerging problem. Individually you would see them as 'good children' more or less, but when they got together for 'enjoyment' a dysfunctional kind of 'groupthink' and 'group act' took over. At the beginning of one holiday weekend his mother cautioned him not to go out of town with his buddies and not to drink. He went out of town with them, got drunk, rubbished a hotel, 'pushed' a police officer and ended up in hospital, being given two years of probation by a judge and expelled from his private high school – a life in shambles. It took one or two more incidents to bring him to his senses and, with the help of a counsellor very familiar with stories like his, he began to put his life back together. He's in pretty good shape now. A failure to see the consequences of dysfunctional behaviour messed up his life. Or did it teach him an invaluable life lesson?

Self-deception

Where does simple lack of awareness or failure to think things through end and self-deception start? There are things clients would rather not know, because, if they knew them, they would be challenged to change their behaviour in some way. So they'd rather stay in the dark. Goleman, who has written extensively about social and emotional intelligence, early on wrote a book called *Vital Lies, Simple Truths* (1985) on the psychology of self-deception and its pervasiveness in human life. Self-deception and the kind of social-emotional maturity outlined in his book *Emotional Intelligence* are incompatible.

Yet, as Eduardo Giannetti (1997) points out in *Lies We Live By: The Art of Self-Deception*, it is ubiquitous. 'How,' he marvels, 'do we carry out such feats as believing in what we don't believe in, lying to ourselves and believing the lie ...?' (p. viii). Stan thought that he could get away with flirting with other women even though he was engaged. 'It's just natural for a man' was his excuse. His fiancée saw his behaviour as insulting. When she called off the wedding, Stan painfully realised the price of his self-deception.

Choosing to stay in the dark

Ilia, recently released from prison, knows that she should have a clear understanding of the conditions of her probation, but chooses not to. When asked about the conditions, she says, 'I don't know. No one really explained them to me.' She knows that if she gets caught violating any of the conditions, she could go back to prison. But she puts that out of her mind.

Choosing to stay in the dark is a common human experience. It is as if someone were to say, 'I could find out, but I don't want to, at least not yet.' This act of keeping themselves intentionally unaware is termed 'ignorance of law' or, as Heffernan (2011) calls this, 'willful blindness':

"We make ourselves powerless when we choose not to know. But we give ourselves hope when we insist on looking. The very fact that willful blindness is willed, that it is a product of a rich mix of experience, knowledge, thinking, neurons, and neuroses, is what gives us the capacity to change it." (p. 247)

Lots of people, when they have physical symptoms such as pain in their guts, avoid thinking about it. This can be a life-threatening decision. Finding out whether the pain indicates something serious could be uncomfortable or even intolerable. Like the rest of us, clients often enough choose to stay in the dark.

When clients are being vague or evasive with their helpers, they may also be keeping something from themselves, something that would hurt to know or know more fully.

Knowing, not caring, and failing to see consequences

Clients sometimes know that their thinking, forms of emotional expression and acting are getting them into trouble or keeping them there, but they don't seem to care. We can use the term 'blind spot', at least in an extended sense, to describe this kind of behaviour because clients don't seem to fully understand or appreciate the degree to which they are choosing their own misery. Or they do not see the implications and consequences of not caring. Think of Clancy. Or consider Tanel. Tanel tells a counsellor that he knows nagging his wife to get a job even though there are two young children at home annoys his wife, but he keeps on anyway. 'I can't help it.' This creates a great deal of tension, but he continues to focus on his wife's reluctance to get a job rather than the negative consequences of his nagging. He has some idea of the pool of resentment that is building in his wife, but he persists. This case has not been resolved. How would you proceed with Tanel?

So, as you can see, the term 'blind spot' as used here is somewhat elastic. We are unaware, we deceive ourselves, we don't want to know, we ignore, we don't care or we know, but not fully, that is, we do not fully understand the implications or the consequences of what we know. But it's a good term. It has great face validity. As soon as you say 'blind spot', people generally know what you mean.

Helping clients deal with blind spots is one of the most important things you can do as a helper. For instance, if Lester has a prejudice and doesn't advert to it, he has a blind spot. If he has a prejudice but adverts to it only vaguely (though he probably does not refer to his attitude as a prejudice), then he is keeping himself in the dark. If he knows he is prejudiced and, when asked, says, 'Everyone I know is like that!', then he doesn't care and fails to explore the human meaning of prejudice. He is prejudiced, knows it, fosters it and lets it spill over into the way he deals with people. Lester has the full dysfunctional package.

Contrast this with Bernice. Initially she is unaware that she is prejudiced, becomes aware of her prejudice, tries to get rid of it as part of her internal mental furniture, refuses to act on it and even learns something about herself and the world as she does all this. She deals with her prejudice creatively. She has turned a problem into an opportunity. Helping clients deal with dysfunctional blind spots can prevent damage, limit damage already done and turn problems into opportunities. Box 5.1 outlines the kinds of questions you can help clients ask themselves in order to surface blind spots and develop new perspectives. In therapy, new perspectives are often called insights. Insight in the helping professions has a long and somewhat problematic history.

BOX 5.1	**Questions to Uncover Blind Spots**

These are the kinds of questions you can help clients ask themselves in order to develop new perspectives, change internal behaviour and change external behaviour:

- What problems am I avoiding?
- What opportunities am I ignoring?
- What am I getting from ignoring or avoiding this problem?
- What's really going on?
- What am I overlooking?
- What do I refuse to see?
- What don't I want to do?
- What unverified assumptions am I making?
- What if I saw this from another point of view?
- How am I being dishonest with myself?
- If others were honest with me, what would they tell me?

SPECIFIC SKILLS FOR HELPING CLIENTS CHALLENGE THEIR BLIND SPOTS AND MOVE TO NEW PERSPECTIVES

Self-challenge focuses on the kind of understanding that leads to constructive change. We do our clients a disservice if all that we do is help them identify and explore self-limiting blind spots. The positive part of self-challenge is helping clients transform blind spots into new perspectives and translate these new perspectives into more constructive patterns of both internal and external behaviour.

There are many positive names for this process of transforming blind spots into new perspectives: seeing things more clearly, getting the picture, getting insights, developing new perspectives, spelling out implications, transforming perceptions, developing new frames of reference, looking for meaning, shifting perceptions, seeing the bigger picture, developing different angles, seeing things in context, context breaking, re-thinking, getting a more objective view, interpreting, overcoming blind spots, second-level learning, double-loop learning (Argyris, 1999), thinking creatively, reconceptualising, discovering, having an 'ah-ha' experience, developing a new outlook, questioning assumptions, getting rid of distortions, relabelling and making connections. Some terms used to describe this process are 'frame breaking', 'frame bending' and 'reframing'. You get the idea. All of these imply some kind of cognitive restructuring that is needed in order to identify and manage both problems and opportunities. Developing new perspectives, although painful at times, tends to be ultimately prized by clients.

One way of helping clients challenge both internal and external actions is to help them explore the consequences of their actions. Let's return to Roberto. He has made some 'mild' attempts at sabotaging his wife's career. He refers to his actions as 'delaying tactics'.

HELPER: It might be helpful to see where all of this is leading.

ROBERTO: What do you mean?

HELPER: I mean let's review what impact your 'delaying tactics' have had on Maria and your marriage. And then let's review where these tactics are most likely ultimately to lead.

ROBERTO: Well, I can tell you one thing. She's become even more stubborn.

Through their discussion, Roberto discovers that his sabotage is working against rather than for him. He is endangering the marriage by keeping himself in the dark.

Effective helpers assume that clients have the resources to see themselves and the world in which they live in a less distorted way and to act on what they see. Another way of putting it is that skilled counsellors help clients move from what the Alcoholics Anonymous movement calls 'stinkin' thinkin'' to healthy thinking. And from 'stinkin'' emoting to constructive emotional expression. And from dysfunctional actions to healthy behaviour. Consider Carla. Facing menopause, she is lumbered with the outmoded view of menopause as a 'deficiency disease'. Without minimising Carla's discomfort and stress, a counsellor helps her see menopause as a natural developmental stage of life. Although it indicates the ending of one phase, it also opens up new life-stage possibilities. Looking forward to those possibilities rather than looking back at what she's lost helps Carla a great deal.

There are any number of ways in which counsellors can help clients engage in the kind of self-challenge that leads to perspectives that can help them change their behaviour, both internal and external. Some invitations to self-challenge tend towards the indirect end of the continuum, while others are more direct. Let's start with three indirect approaches: advanced empathy, that is, identifying and sharing the message behind the message, sharing information and helper self-disclosure.

Advanced empathy: Capturing the fuller message or the message behind the message

Recall the quote from Carl Rogers mentioned in Chapter 3. He said that empathy sometimes involves sensing meanings of which the client is scarcely aware. This is the fuller message or the message behind the message. I call sharing this added meaning 'advanced' empathy. For instance, Gordon gets angry when he talks about his interactions with his ex-wife, but as he talks, the helper hears not just anger but also hurt. It may be that Gordon can talk relatively easily about and express his anger but is reluctant to talk about his feelings of hurt. When you respond with basic empathy – provided, of course, that you are accurate – clients recognise themselves almost immediately: 'Yes, that's what I meant.' However, because responding with empathy to messages that are more covert (advanced empathy) digs a bit deeper, clients might not immediately recognise themselves in your response. And so they might experience a bit of disequilibrium. That's what makes advanced empathy a form of challenge. It invites clients to take a closer look at themselves and their behaviour. For instance, the helper says something like this to Gordon: 'It's pretty obvious that you really get steamed when she acts like that. ... But I thought I sensed, mixed in with the anger, a bit of hurt.' At that, Gordon looks down and pauses. He finally says, 'She can still get to me. She certainly can.' This appreciably broadens or deepens the discussion of the problem situation.

Here are some questions helpers can ask themselves to probe a bit deeper as they listen to clients:

- What is this person only half saying?
- What is this person hinting at?
- What is this person saying in a confused way?
- What covert message is behind the explicit message?

Note that advanced empathic listening and processing focuses on what the client is actually saying or at least expressing, however tentatively or confusedly. That is, it is not an interpretation of what the client is saying. Sharing advanced highlights is not an attempt to 'psych the client out'.

In the hands of skilled helpers, capturing and sharing the message behind the message focuses not just on the problematic dimensions of clients' thinking, emotional expression and behaviour, but also on unused opportunities and resources. Effective helpers listen for the resources that are buried deeply in clients and often have been forgotten by them. Consider the following example. The client, a soldier who has been thinking seriously about making the army his career, has been talking to a chaplain about his failing to be promoted. He has performed well in both Iraq and Afghanistan. As he talks, it becomes fairly evident that part of the problem is that he is so quiet and unassuming that it is easy for his superiors to ignore him.

SOLDIER: I don't know what's going on. I work hard, but I keep getting passed over when promotion time comes along. I think I work as hard as anyone else, and I work efficiently, but all of my efforts seem to go down the drain. I'm not as flashy as some others, but I'm just as substantial.

CHAPLAIN A: You feel it's quite unfair to do the kind of work that merits a promotion and still not get it.

SOLDIER: Yeah. . . . I suppose there's nothing I can do but wait it out. (A long silence ensues.)

Chaplain A tries to understand the client from the client's frame of reference. He deals with the client's feelings and the experience underlying those feelings. He responds with basic empathy. But the client merely retreats more into himself. Here's a different approach.

CHAPLAIN B: It's depressing to put out so much effort and still get passed by. . . . Tell me more about this 'not as flashy' bit. I'm curious. I wonder whether there is something in your style that might make it easy for others not to notice you, even when you're doing a good job.

SOLDIER: You mean I'm so unassuming that I could get lost in the shuffle? Or maybe it's the guys who make more noise, the squeaky wheels, who get noticed. . . . I guess I've never really thought of selling myself. That's not my style.

From the context, from the discussion of the problem situation, from the client's manner and tone of voice, Chaplain B picks up a theme that the client states in passing in the phrase 'not as flashy'. They go on to discuss how he might 'market himself' in a way that is consistent with his values. Advanced empathy can take a number of forms. Here are some of them:

Help clients make the implied explicit The most basic form of advanced empathy involves helping clients give fuller expression to what they are implying rather than saying directly. In the following example, the client has been discussing ways of getting back in touch with his wife after a recent divorce, but when he speaks about doing so, he expresses very little enthusiasm.

CLIENT (somewhat hesitatingly): I could wait to hear from her. But I suppose there's nothing wrong with calling her up and asking her how she's getting along.

COUNSELLOR A: It seems that there's nothing wrong with taking the initiative to contact her. After all, you'd like to find out if she's doing okay.

CLIENT (somewhat drearily): Yeah, I suppose I could.

Counsellor A's response might have been fine at an earlier stage of the helping process, but it misses the mark here, and the client does not move on.

COUNSELLOR B: You've been talking about getting in touch with her, but, unless I'm mistaken, I don't hear a great deal of enthusiasm in your voice.

CLIENT: To be honest, I don't really want to talk to her. But I feel guilty – guilty about the divorce, guilty about her going out on her own. Frankly, all I'm doing is trying to take care of her all over again. And that's one of the reasons we got divorced. I had a need to take care of her, and she let me do it, even though she resented it. That was the story of our marriage. I don't want to do that anymore.

COUNSELLOR B: What would a better way of going about all this be?

CLIENT: I need to get on with my life and let her get on with hers. Neither of us is helpless. (His voice brightens.) For instance, I've been thinking of quitting my job and starting a business with a friend of mine – helping small businesses to start their own business-oriented social networks. I think there's a great opportunity there.

Counsellor B bases her response not only on the client's immediately preceding remark but also on the entire context of his story. Her response hits the mark, and the client moves forward. As with basic empathic highlights, there is no such thing as a good advanced highlight in itself. Does the response help the client clarify the issue more fully so that he or she might begin to see the need to act differently?

Help clients identify themes in their stories   When clients tell their stories, often certain themes emerge. Thematic material might refer to feelings (such as hurt, depression, anxiety), thoughts (continually ruminating about a past mistake), behaviour (controlling others, avoiding intimacy, blaming others, overwork), experiences (being a victim; being seduced, punished, ignored, picked on), or some combination of these. Once you see a self-defeating theme or pattern emerging from your discussions, you can share your perception and help the client check it out.

In the following example, a counsellor trainee is talking with his supervisor. The trainee has four clients. In the past week, he has seen each of them for the third time. This dialogue takes place in the middle of a supervisory session.

SUPERVISOR: You've had a third session with each of four clients this past week. Even though you're at different stages with each because each started in a different place, you have a feeling, if I understand what you've been saying, that you're going around in circles with a couple of them.

TRAINEE: Yes, I'm grinding my wheels. I don't have a sense of movement.

SUPERVISOR: Any thoughts on what's going on?

TRAINEE: Well, they seem willing enough. And I think I've been very good at listening and sharing highlights. It keeps them talking.

SUPERVISOR: But this doesn't seem to be enough to get them moving forward. I tell you what. Let's listen to one of the tapes.

They listen to a segment of one of the sessions. The trainee turns off the recorder.

TRAINEE: Oh, now I see what I'm doing! It's all basic empathy with a few uh-huhs. And all the time I thought I was being pushy. But when I listen to the tape I realise I'm about as far from pushy as you can get.

SUPERVISOR: So what's missing?

TRAINEE: There are very few probes and nothing close to summaries or mild invitations to self-challenge. Certainly some probes would have given much more focus and direction to the session.

SUPERVISOR: Let me role-play the client as well as I can and see how you might redo the session.

They then spend about 15 minutes in a role-playing session. The trainee mingles some probes with basic highlights, and the result is quite different.

SUPERVISOR: How close did you get to challenging, even mild challenging?

TRAINEE: I didn't get there at all. . . . You know, I think that I see probes as invitations to self-challenge. And they are, at least to some degree. . . . The thread through all of this is 'playing it safe'. I think I'm playing it safe because I don't want to damage the client. I'm afraid to push.

The theme that the supervisor helps the trainee surface is a fear of 'being pushy', which explains his 'playing it safe' behaviour.

Help clients make connections that may be missing   Clients often tell their stories in terms of experiences, thoughts, behaviours and emotions in a hit-or-miss way. The counsellor's job, then, is to help them make the kinds of connections that provide insights or perspectives that enable them to move forward.

●   Her counsellor helps Chu Hua see that she is having difficulty developing strategies for her chosen goals because she is only half-heartedly committed to her goals. They revisit the goals she has set for herself to see how realistic and achievable they are.

- Owen says he has a 'problem with' pornography. He avoids the word 'addiction'. He says that his wife has found out and is very unhappy with his behaviour. When asked to describe his concern more fully he launches into a whole range of excuses as to why such behaviour is not that bad at all. His therapist gives a brief summary of what Owen has been saying, then adds, 'So I'm not sure whether you're saying that it's really your wife who has the problem.' Owen pauses for a while, then says, 'You know if the roles were reversed, if she was the one who was addicting herself to porn, I'd be mad as hell.' He pauses again, and the therapist says, 'Well, let's start over.' Wiping the therapy slate clean helps Owen a great deal. He begins to explore the implications of his addiction to porn.
- A therapist helps Joanna see the link between her ingratiating style and her inability to influence her colleagues at work.
- A supervisor helps Dieter, who works with an NGO on poverty issues in Kenya, see that the persistent anxiety he feels when working with tribal leaders is related to the perfectionist standards he constantly sets for himself, standards that are out of place in the Kenyan culture.

The following client, John, has a full-time job and is finishing the final two courses for his college degree. His father has recently had a stroke and is incapacitated. John talks about being progressively more anxious and tired in recent weeks. He visits his father regularly. He meets frequently with his mother, his two sisters and his two brothers to discuss how to manage the family crisis. Under stress, fault lines in family relationships appear. John does his best to be the peacemaker. He has deadlines for turning in papers for current courses.

JOHN: I don't know why I'm so tired all the time. And edgy. I'm supposed to be the calm one. I wonder if it's something physical. You know, what's happened to dad and all that. I never even think about my health.

COUNSELLOR: A lot has happened in the past few weeks: work; school; your dad's stroke; juggling schedules.

JOHN (interrupting): But that's what I'm good at: working hard; juggling schedules. I do that all the time. And I don't get tired and edgy.

COUNSELLOR: Add in your dad's illness. . . .

JOHN: You know, I could handle that, too. If I were the only one, you know, just me and mum, I bet I could do it.

COUNSELLOR: All right, so besides your dad's illness, what's different?

JOHN (slowly): Well, I hate to say it. It's the squabbling. We usually get on pretty well. We all like getting together. But the meetings about dad, they can be awful. I keep thinking about them at work. And the other evening when I was trying to write a paper for school, I was still annoyed with my older sister.

COUNSELLOR: So the family stuff is really a big deal and it's getting to you.

JOHN: I'm just not used to all that. I thought we'd rally together. You know, get support from one another. Sometimes it's just the opposite.

John handles the normal stress of everyday life quite well. But the 'family stuff' is acting like a multiplier. They go on to discuss what the family dynamics are like and what John can do to cope with them.

Share educated hunches based on empathic understanding   As you listen to clients, thoughtfully process what they say and put it all into context, you will naturally begin to form hunches about the message behind the message or the story behind the story. You can share the hunches that you feel might add value. The more mature and socially competent you become and the more experience you have helping others, the more 'educated' your hunches become. Here are some examples.

- *Helping clients see the bigger picture.* Hunches can help clients see the bigger picture. In the following example, the counsellor is talking with a client who is having trouble with his perfectionism. He also mentions problems with his brother-in-law, whom his wife enjoys having over. He and his brother-in-law argue, and sometimes the arguments have an edge to them. At one point the client describes him as 'a guy who can never get anything right'. Later the counsellor says, 'We started out by talking about perfectionism in terms of the inordinate demands you place on yourself. I wonder whether it could be "spreading" a bit. You should be perfect. But so should everyone else.' They go on to discuss the ways his perfectionism may be interfering with his social life.

- *Helping clients go a bit deeper.* Hunches can help clients see more clearly what they are expressing indirectly or merely implying. In this next example, the counsellor is talking to a client who feels that a friend has let her down: 'I think I might also be hearing you say that you are more than disappointed – perhaps even betrayed.' Because the client has been making every effort to avoid her friend, 'betrayal' rings truer than 'let-down'. She gets in touch with the depth of her feelings.

- *Helping clients see implications and draw conclusions.* Hunches can help clients draw logical conclusions from what they are saying. A manager is having a discussion with one of his team members who has expressed in a rather tentative way some reservations about one of the team's projects. At one point the manager says, 'If I stitch together everything that you've said about the project, it sounds as if you are saying that it was ill-advised in the first place and probably should be shut down. I know that might sound drastic and you've never put it in those words. But if that's how you feel, we should discuss it in more detail.'

- *Helping clients open up.* Hunches can help clients open up areas they are only hinting at. In this case, a school counsellor is talking to a senior in high school: 'You've brought up sexual matters a number of times, but you haven't pursued them. My guess is that sex is a pretty important area for you but perhaps pretty sensitive, too.'

- *Helping clients see things they may be overlooking.* A counsellor is talking to a client who probably has only six months to live. The man is unmarried and has never made a will. He has some money, but has expressed indifference to money matters. 'I'm financially lazy' is his theme. He adds, 'I'm ready to die.' Later in the session, the counsellor says, 'I wonder if your financial laziness has spread a bit. For instance, you live alone and, if I'm not mistaken, you haven't given anyone power of attorney in health matters either. That could mean that how you die will be in the hands of the doctors.' This helps the client begin to re-think how he wants to die. They even discuss finances. He may not be a slave to money, but whatever money he has could go to a good cause.

- *Helping clients own their stories.* Hunches can help clients take fuller ownership of partially owned experiences, behaviours, feelings, points of view and decisions. For example, a counsellor is talking to a client who is experiencing a lot of pain in a physical rehabilitation programme following an automobile accident. She keeps focusing on how difficult the programme is. At one point the counsellor says, 'You sound as if you have already decided to quit. Or I might be overstating the case. . . .' This helps the client enormously. She has been thinking of quitting but she has been afraid to discuss it. They go on to discuss her wanting to give up and her dread of giving up. When the counsellor finds out that she has never even mentioned the pain to the members of the rehabilitation staff, they discuss strategies for coping with the pain, including direct conversations with the staff about the pain.

Like all responses, hunches should be based on your understanding of your clients. If your clients were to ask you where your hunches come from – 'What makes you think that?' – you should be able to identify the experiential and behavioural clues on which they are based. Of course, responding with empathy is not a licence to draw inferences from clients' history, experiences or behaviour at will. Nor is it a licence to load clients with interpretations that are more deeply rooted in your favourite psychological theories than in the realities of the client's world. Constructive advanced empathy requires emotional intelligence and social competence on your part.

Information sharing

Sometimes clients are unable to explore their problems fully, set goals and proceed to action because they lack information of one kind or another. Information can help clients at any stage of the helping process. Early on, therapy helps some clients to know that they are not the first to try to cope with a particular problem. Later on, information can help them further clarify possibilities and set goals. In the implementation stage, information on commonly experienced obstacles can help clients cope and persevere.

The skill or strategy of information sharing is included under challenging skills because it helps clients develop new perspectives on their problems or shows them how to act. It includes both providing new information and correcting misinformation. In some cases, the information can prove to be quite confirming and supportive. For instance, a parent who feels responsible following the death of a newborn baby may experience some relief through an understanding of the earmarks of the sudden infant death syndrome. This information does not 'solve' the problem, but the parent's new perspective can help him or her handle self-blame.

In some cases, the new perspectives clients gain from information sharing can be both comforting and painful. Consider the following example.

> Adrian was a college student of modest intellectual means. He made it through school because he worked very hard. In his senior year, he learned that a number of his friends were going on to graduate school. He, too, applied to a number of graduate programmes in psychology. He came to see a counsellor in the student services centre after being rejected by all the schools to which he had applied. In the interview, it soon became clear to the counsellor that Adrian thought that many, perhaps even most, college students went on to graduate school. After all, most of his closest friends had been accepted in one graduate school or another. The counsellor shared with him the statistics of what could be called the educational pyramid – the decreasing percentage of students attending school at higher levels. Adrian did not realise that just finishing college made him part of an elite group. Nor was he completely aware of the extremely competitive nature of the graduate psychology programmes to which he had applied. He found much of this relieving but then found himself suddenly faced with what to do now that he was finishing school. Up to this point he had not thought much about it. He felt disconcerted by the sudden need to look at the world of work.

Giving information is especially useful when lack of accurate information either is one of the principal causes of a problem situation or is making an existing problem worse.

In some medical settings, doctors team up with counsellors to give clients messages that are hard to hear and to provide them with information needed to make difficult decisions. For instance, Doug, a 71-year-old accountant, has been given a series of diagnostic tests for possible prostate cancer. He finds out that he does have cancer, but now he faces the formidable task of choosing what to do about it. The doctor sits down with him and lays out the alternatives. Because there are many different options, including doing nothing, the doctor also describes the pluses and minuses of each. Later Doug has a discussion with a counsellor who helps Doug cope with the news, process the information and begin the process of making a decision. Helpers can also be asked to be involved in consultations where clients want to undergo cosmetic surgery procedures to rule out body dysmorphic disorder or in bariatric surgery to ensure that clients have the psychological support after surgery (Ristanto & Caltabiano, 2019).

There are some cautions helpers should observe in giving information. When information is challenging, potentially distressing or even shocking, be tactful and help the client handle the disequilibrium that comes with the news. Do not overwhelm the client with too much information. Make sure that the information you provide is clear and relevant to the client's problem situation. Don't let the client go away with a misunderstanding of the information. Be supportive; help the client process the information. Finally, be sure not to confuse information-giving with advice-giving. Professional guidance is not to be confused with telling clients what to do. Neither the doctor nor the counsellor tells Doug which treatment to choose. But Doug needs help with the burden of choosing.

Helper self-disclosure

Another route to helping clients challenge themselves involves your ability and willingness to share some of your own experiences, thoughts, behaviours and feelings with clients. The ups and downs of helper self-disclosure have been explored thoroughly (Barnett, 2011; Farber, 2006; Forrest, 2010; Henretty & Levitt, 2010; Kelly & Rodriguez, 2007; Myers & Hayes, 2006; Veach, 2011; Yeh & Hayes, 2011; Zur, Williams, Lehavot & Knapp, 2009). However, there is no single voice as to its value, its limitations and its dangers in therapy. In one sense counsellors cannot help but disclose themselves: 'The counsellor communicates his or her characteristics to the client in every look, movement, emotional response and sound, as well as with every word' (Strong & Claiborn, 1982, p. 173). This is the kind of indirect disclosure that goes on all the time. Effective helpers, as they tune in, listen, process and respond, try to track and manage the impressions they are making on clients.

Here, however, it is a question of direct self-disclosure. Research into direct helper self-disclosure has led to mixed and even contradictory conclusions. Henretty and Levitt (2010), in one of the most detailed reviews of the research, say that the problem starts with the definition of therapist self-disclosure: 'Multiple definitions of therapist self-disclosure render meaningful analysis of findings across studies difficult, if not impossible' (p. 69). Therefore, we can expect to run across contradictory findings. Some researchers have discovered that helper self-disclosure can frighten clients or make them see helpers as less well adjusted. Or, instead of helping, helper self-disclosure might place a further burden on clients. Other studies have suggested that helper self-disclosure is appreciated by clients. Some clients see self-disclosing helpers as 'down-to-earth' and 'honest'.

Direct self-disclosure on the part of helpers can serve as a form of modelling. Self-help groups such as Alcoholics Anonymous and other drug treatment programmes use such modelling extensively. Some would say that helper self-disclosure is most appropriate in such settings. This helps new members get an idea of what to talk about and find the courage to do so. It is the group's way of saying, 'You can talk here without being judged and getting hurt.'

Beth is a counsellor in a drug rehabilitation programme. She herself was a substance abuser for a number of years but, with the help of the agency where she is now a counsellor, she is clean and sober. It is clear to all people with addictions in the programme that the counsellors there were once substance abusers themselves and are not only rehabilitated, but also intensely interested in helping others both rid themselves of drugs and develop a kind of lifestyle that helps them stay drug-free. Beth freely shares her experience, both of being a drug user and of her rather agonising journey to freedom, whenever she thinks that doing so can help a client.

Other things being equal, counsellors who have struggled with addictions themselves often make excellent helpers in programmes like this. They know from the inside the games clients afflicted with addictions play. Sharing their experience is central to their style of counselling and is accepted by their clients. It helps clients develop both new perspectives and new possibilities for action. Such self-disclosure is challenging. It puts pressure on clients to talk about themselves more openly or in a more focused way.

Helper self-disclosure is challenging for at least two reasons. First, it is a form of intimacy and, for some clients, intimacy is not easy to handle. Therefore, helpers need to know precisely why they are divulging information about themselves. Second, the message to the client is, indirectly, a challenging 'You can do it, too', because revelations on the part of helpers, even when they deal with past failures, often centre on problem situations they have overcome or opportunities they have seized. However, done well, such disclosures can be very encouraging for clients.

In the following example, the helper, Rick, has had a number of sessions with Tim, a client who has had a rather tumultuous adolescence. For instance, he fell into the 'wrong crowd' and got into trouble with the police a few times. His parents were shocked, and his relationship with them became very strained. Rick believes it will be helpful to share some of his own experiences.

RICK: You know, Tim, I've had experiences like yours. It might be helpful to compare notes. In my junior year in high school I was expelled for stealing. I thought that it was the end of the world. My Catholic family took it as the ultimate disgrace. We even moved to a different neighbourhood in the city.

TIM: What did it do to you?

Rick briefly tells his story, one that includes setbacks not unlike Tim's. But Rick, with the help of a very wise and understanding uncle, was able to put the past behind him. He does not overdramatise the events. In fact, his story makes it clear that developmental crises are normal. How people interpret and manage them is the critical issue.

Current research does not give us definitive answers about helper self-disclosure or the amount of disclosure that may happen in sessions, but it does offer some common-sense guidelines. Because clients sometimes misinterpret helpers' self-disclosures and their intent, caution is in order. Psychotherapeutic schools will also differ in their approach to self-disclosure, often on a continuum, with some advocating no disclosure at all while others leave it up to the discretion of the therapist. Here are some useful guidelines to consider:

Make sure that your disclosures are appropriate   Sharing yourself is appropriate if it helps clients achieve treatment goals. Don't disclose more than is necessary. Helper self-disclosure that is exhibitionistic is obviously inappropriate. Jeffrey (2004) provides us some outrageous examples of inappropriate self-disclosure. One helper discussed her own problems with the father–daughter bond, her guilt at disappointing a parent, personal religious issues and her love life. The client switched to a therapist who said nothing about herself. Helper self-disclosure should be a natural part of the helping process, not a gambit. Rick's self-disclosure helps give Tim a different view of the 'bad things' that have happened. Rick's developmental perspective gives Tim a different lens, a new way of looking at his problem. But Rick also makes it clear that he is not trying to make excuses for Tim's behaviour.

Make sure that disclosures are culturally appropriate   (as advised by Barnett, 2011; Burkard *et al.*, 2006; Kim *et al.*, 2003.) Helper behaviours do not automatically transfer from one culture to another. For instance, Carlos is hesitant to talk about some of his dual-cultural experiences because he sees that Tumi's South African culture is far different from his Latin background. Many of her experiences have been negative, whereas most of his experiences have been positive. His Hispanic parents urged him to integrate with mainstream British culture. He spoke Spanish at home and had a deep appreciation of Latin culture. He had integrated the two cultures well. So he presented himself as Carlos, a person very content with his dual-heritage background.

Be careful of your timing   Timing is critical. Common sense tells us that premature or poorly timed helper self-disclosure can distract clients or turn them off. Rick's disclosures did not take place in the first meeting. He waited for a few sessions. However, once he saw a natural opening, he thought that sharing some of his own experiences would help. Experience teaches you what 'natural openings' look like.

Keep your disclosure selective and focused   Don't distract clients with rambling stories about yourself. Remember it's their therapy session and not yours. In the following example, the helper is talking to a first-year graduate student in a clinical psychology programme. The client is discouraged and depressed by the amount of work he has to do. The counsellor wants to help him by sharing his own experience of graduate school.

> **COUNSELLOR:**   Listening to you brings me right back to my own days in graduate school. I don't think that I was ever busier in my life. I also believe that the most depressing moments of my life took place then. On any number of occasions, I wanted to throw in the towel. I remember once towards the end of my third year when. . . .

It may be that selective bits of this counsellor's experience in graduate school would be useful, but he wanders off into a kind of reminiscing that meets his needs rather than the client's. In contrast, Rick's disclosure was selective and focused.

Don't disclose too frequently   Helper self-disclosure is inappropriate if it occurs too frequently. When helpers disclose themselves too frequently, clients may see them as self-centred, phony or immature. Or they may suspect that they have hidden motives. If Rick had continued to share his experiences whenever he saw a parallel with Tim's, Tim might have wondered who was helper and who was client.

Do not burden the client   Do not burden an already overburdened client. One novice helper thought that he would help make a client who was sharing some sexual problems more comfortable by sharing some of his own sexual experiences. After all, he saw his own sexual development as not too different from the client's. However, the client reacted by saying: 'Hey, don't tell me your problems. I'm having a hard enough time dealing with my own.' This novice counsellor shared too much of himself too soon. He was caught up in his own willingness to disclose rather than its potential usefulness to the client. In more extreme cases intimate disclosure might appear to be seductive.

Remain flexible Take each client separately. Adapt your disclosures to differences in clients and situations. When asked directly, clients say that they want helpers to disclose themselves, but this does not mean that every client in every situation wants it or would benefit from it. Even though Rick's disclosure to Tim was natural, it was a thoughtful decision on Rick's part.

Reviewers of Farber's (2006) book on self-disclosure in psychotherapy (Hamilton, Del Castillo & Stiles, 2007) conclude by saying that the 'reader comes away with the sense of having absorbed a great deal of information, yet (appropriately, in our view) having few definitive answers' (p. 362). Henretty and Levitt's (2010) extensive review of the research comes to the same conclusion. The broad principles and cautions outlined here will have to do for now, and, given the complexity of human nature, perhaps forever.

Now we turn to more direct approaches to challenge. Client self-responsibility is a key value in helping. Therefore, some version of Thaler and Sunstein's (2008) 'libertarian paternalism' is in order in just about every form of challenge. However, while some challenges are more direct than others, they still leave decision making where it belongs – in the hands of the client. Here are a few more direct approaches to client self-challenge.

Making suggestions and giving recommendations

This section begins with a few libertarian imperatives. Don't tell clients what to do. Don't try to take over their lives. Let clients make their own decisions. These imperatives flow from the values of respect and empowerment. Does this mean, however, that suggestions and recommendations are forbidden? Of course not. Some clients, more in some cultures than in others, expect or want explicit guidance. And guidance can be given in ways that do not rob the client of self-responsibility. As mentioned earlier, there is a natural tension between helpers' desire to have their clients manage their lives better and respecting their freedom. If helpers build strong, respectful relationships with their clients, then stronger and more direct interventions can make sense. In this context, suggestions and recommendations can stimulate clients to move to problem-managing action. Helpers move from counselling mode to guidance role. Research has shown that clients will generally go along with recommendations from helpers when the recommendations are clearly related to the problem situation, challenge clients' strengths and are not too difficult. Effective helpers can provide suggestions, recommendations and even directives without robbing clients of their autonomy or their integrity.

Here is a classic example of this from Cummings's (1979, 2000) work. Substance abusers came to him because they were hurting in many ways. He used every communication skill available to listen to and understand their plight:

> "During the first half of the first session the therapist must listen very intently. Then, somewhere in mid-session, using all the rigorous training, therapeutic acumen, and the third, fourth, fifth, and sixth ears, the therapist discerns some unresolved wish, some long-gone dream that is still residing deep in that human being, and then the therapist pulls it out and ignites the client with a desire to somehow look at that dream again. This is not easy, because if the right nerve is not touched, the therapist loses the client." (1979, p. 1123)

Cummings discovered that the desire for a better life was there, however faint or deeply buried, in most of his clients. So he shared both basic and advanced empathic highlights to let clients know that he understood their plight, their longings, but also their games. They came knowing how to play every game in the book. But Cummings knew all the games, too. Towards the end of the first session he told them they could have a second session – which they invariably wanted – only when they were 'clean'. That is, the time of the second session depended on the withdrawal period for the kind of substance they were abusing. They screamed, shouted 'foul', tried to play games, but he remained adamant. The directive 'Get clean, then return' was part of the therapeutic process. And most did return. Clean. Is this approach right for everyone? No approach is.

Suggestions, advice and directives need not always be taken literally. They can act as stimuli to get clients to come up with their own package. One client said something like this to her helper: 'You told me to let my teenage son have his say instead of constantly interrupting and arguing with him. What I did was make a contract with him. I told him that I would listen carefully to what he said and even summarise it and give it back to him. But he had to do the same for me. That has produced some useful monologues. But we avoid our usual shouting matches. My hope is to find a way to turn it into dialogue.' In everyday life, people feel free to give one another advice. It goes on all the time. But helpers must proceed with caution. Suggestions, advice and directives are not for novices. It takes a great deal of experience with clients and a great deal of savvy to know when they might work.

Stronger medicine: Confrontation

What about clients who keep dragging their feet and therefore keep themselves mired in their problem situations? Some clients who don't want to change or don't want to pay the price of changing simply terminate the helping relationship. However, those who stay stretch across a continuum from mildly to extremely reluctant and resistant (reluctance and resistance are taken up in Chapter 6). Or they may be collaborative on some issues but reluctant on others. For instance, Hester is quite willing to work on career development but very reluctant to work on improving interpersonal and work relationships, even though relationship building is an important part of the career package. Here is part of the dialogue with her coach:

> **HESTER:** Relationships? That's my private world. I deal with those privately.
>
> **COUNSELLOR:** I'm not sure whether you're saying that your relationships, whether personal or work-related, don't have an impact on your work and your career.
>
> **HESTER:** I'm not saying that. It's just nobody else's business.
>
> **COUNSELLOR:** And the forum in which you deal with relationship style and problems and the impact they have on your life?
>
> **HESTER:** I take care of that inside my head.
>
> **COUNSELLOR:** Well, that could mean that we are at a standstill in our conversation.
>
> **HESTER:** Why is that?

They go on to have a discussion about how making critical issues off limits affects a therapeutic dialogue.

If inviting clients to challenge themselves is at one end of the continuum, what's at the other? Where does respecting clients' right to be themselves stop and placing demands on them to live more fully begin? Because this is a values issue, different helpers give different answers. As a consequence, helpers differ, both theoretically and personally, in their willingness to confront. For instance, Lowenstein (1993) used what he called 'traumatic confrontation' (one wonders about the name) to challenge youths to face up to their dysfunctional behaviour. He gives the example of confronting a 12-year-old boy who had become involved in criminal activity after the disappearance of his father. At first the boy denied everything, but then decided to face up to the situation.

Patterson, Grenny, McMillan and Switzler (2004) suggest that 'crucial confrontations' are called for when people fail to live up to clear and realistic expectations that have been set up with them or for them: 'To confront means to hold someone accountable face to face' (p. 4). People who break promises, violate expectations or engage in bad behaviour should expect to be confronted. In counselling, confrontation focuses on the failure of someone to live up to his or her own expectations or the legitimate expectations of the culture or community, however defined, in which the person lives.

Helpers confront to 'make the case' for more effective living. Confrontation does not involve 'do this or else' ultimatums. More often it is a way of making sure that clients understand what it means not to change – that is, making sure they understand the consequences of persisting in dysfunctional patterns of behaviour or the cost of failing to seize opportunities. Confrontation, like strong medicine, is actually another way of caring for the client. But, like strong medicine, it needs to be used sparingly and carefully. Confrontation should be empathic and respectful, empower the client and lead to action. It should not be used by helpers to vent their frustrations on reluctant and resistant clients.

Encouragement

This section ends on a more positive note. If the whole purpose of challenging is to help the client move forward, and if encouragement (sugar) works as well as challenge (vinegar), then why don't we hear more about encouragement? The sugar–vinegar analogy is not exactly right, however, because many clients find invitations to self-challenge both refreshing and stimulating. Challenge certainly does not preclude encouragement. Encouragement itself is a mild form of challenge. It's a nudge. Furthermore, encouragement is a form of support and research shows that support is one of the main ingredients in successful therapy.

Rollnick and Miller (1995) introduced an approach to helping called 'motivational interviewing' (Arkowitz & Westra, 2008; Michael, Curtin, Kirkley, Jones & Harris, 2006; Miller & Rollnick, 1995, 2002, 2004; Moyers, Miller & Hendrickson, 2005; Rollnick, Miller & Butler, 2008; Rosengren, 2009). A simple internet search on 'motivational interviewing' reveals an extensive body of literature, including theory, research (Burke, Dunn, Atkins & Phelps, 2004) and case studies. Their original work focused on helping clients deal with addictive behaviour, but their methodology over the years has been adapted to a much wider range of human problems. Much of the literature highlights the main elements of a problem-management approach.

> *"Motivational interviewing is a directive, person-centred clinical method for helping clients resolve ambivalence and move ahead with change. It can be applied as a preparation for treatment, a freestanding brief intervention, an enduring clinical style, or a fallback approach when motivational obstacles are encountered."* (Miller & Rollnick, 2004, p. 299)

As such, it can be used at any stage or for any task in the problem-management framework. The values of respect, empathy, self-empowerment and self-healing are emphasised.

Because 'informing' clients about such things as the consequences of their behaviour is part of the motivational interviewing approach, it is an admittedly directive approach with a light touch. Norcross (2010) describes the approach as a 'person-centred directive therapy that relies on expressing empathy and rolling with the resistance to help clients explore and resolve their ambivalence about change' (p. 119). The spirit of encouragement rather than confrontation pervades the approach. Typically, clients (for instance, pregnant women who smoke or use alcohol) receive personal feedback on their problem area (such as how smoking has been affecting their lungs and the harmful impact smoking and drinking can have on the foetus). There are discussions of personal responsibility and advice on ways of managing the problem situation. Clients are encouraged to find the motives, incentives or levers of change that make sense to them and to use the change options that they find fit best. Intrinsic motives, that is, motives that clients have internalised for themselves ('I want to be free'), rather than extrinsic motives ('I'll get in trouble if I don't change'), are emphasised. Clients are also given help on identifying obstacles to change and ways of overcoming them. Empathy, both as a value and as a form of communication (empathic responses), is used extensively. Self-determination is at the heart of motivational interviewing (Vansteenkiste & Sheldon, 2006).

Common sense suggests that realistic encouragement be included among any set of helping skills. Like most of the skills we have been discussing, encouragement can be used at any stage of the helping process. Clients can be encouraged to identify and talk about their problems and unused opportunities, to review possibilities for a better future, to set goals, to engage in actions that will help them achieve their goals, and to overcome the inevitable obstacles. Effective encouragement is not patronising. It is not the same as sympathy, nor does it rob the client of autonomy. It respects the client's self-healing abilities and autonomy. It is a fully human nudge in the right direction.

CHAPTER 6
HELPER SELF-CHALLENGE AND OVERCOMING CLIENT RESISTANCE

Chapter Contents

- Guidelines for Effective Invitations to Self-Challenge

- The Challenges Related to Helping Clients Manage Reluctance and Resistance

- Guidelines for Helping Clients Move Beyond Reluctance and Resistance

- The Role of Negotiation in Challenge

- The Shadow Side of Helpers

Self-challenge applies as much to you the helper as it does to clients. Helpers need to continually challenge themselves to become more informed and effective in their profession. I have often been asked why I have published so many editions of *The Skilled Helper*. I assume that the same people would not think of asking the same question of professionals writing physics or medical texts. I say to myself, 'Don't people know that all professions develop over time? New theories, new research, new ways of doing things emerge all the time, even in the social sciences. What is it about psychology, and particularly psychotherapy, that makes them take such a static view?' Practitioners in the helping professions need to continually refresh and update their practices. A simple internet search will reveal many continuing-education (CE) requirements and an entire CE industry ready to service your needs. Continuing professional development is vital to keep your skills updated and to develop both professionally and personally, especially in the helping field.

Although helper self-challenge pertains to every aspect of the helping process, in this chapter we consider helper self-challenge in three areas – first, the challenges helpers face when they invite clients to engage in self-challenge (as outlined in Chapter 5); second, the challenges associated with helping reluctant and/or resistant clients; and third, the shadow side of helpers that relates to challenge in general.

GUIDELINES FOR EFFECTIVE INVITATIONS TO SELF-CHALLENGE

We start with the challenges helpers face as they invite their clients to engage in self-challenge. Your invitations to self-challenge might be on the mark (smart) and still be ineffective or even hurtful. All invitations should be permeated by the spirit of the client–helper relationship values discussed in Chapter 2; that is, they should be based on understanding of the client (not favourite theories), caring (not power games or put-downs), genuine (not tricks or games) and designed both to increase the client's self-responsibility (not expressions of helper control) and to help the client move into outcome-focused action (not endless discussions). Empathy should permeate every invitation to self-discovery and self-challenge. Clearly, inviting clients to self-challenge is not a skill that comes automatically. Helpers use all the communication and relationship-building skills discussed in Part II of this book. The following helper self-challenge principles constitute some basic guidelines for making the self-challenge invitations to clients discussed in Chapter 5 not just accurate but wise.

Keep the goals of invitations to client self-challenge in mind

Invitations to self-challenge must be integrated into the entire helping process. Keep in mind that the goal is to help clients develop the kinds of alternative perspectives, internal behaviour and external actions needed to achieve the three general outcomes discussed in Chapter 1. Of course, helpers need to guide clients to personalise these broad outcomes. Life-enhancing client outcomes remain the bottom line of helping, but the client has to discover and buy into any given set of outcomes for them to be effective and long lasting.

Chris, a therapist, is both politically and socially very conservative. He tends to invite his clients to challenge both thinking and behaving that is at odds with *his* values and principles. At times he moves beyond invitations to outright confrontation. He says to one young client, Abri, a drug user who has moved back home: 'You are probably not aware that you are operating out of a self-defeating philosophy. It seems to me that you are saying to yourself, however unconsciously, something like this: "I can do anything I want, but if I get into trouble, then you [that is, society] have to take care of me." If this is the case, you're always going to be at odds with your parents, yourself and society as a whole.' Fine – if this were a conversation between friends. But Chris is a helper, not a friend. What he says may be a true analysis of the client, but shoving the truth down clients' throats usually leads nowhere. Chris may think he is being clever by outlining his interpretation but this will not be well received by Abri and may even serve to distance her from the benefits of therapy. He *can* help Abri discover her philosophy of life and then explore the consequences, especially the unintended consequences, of that philosophy. He could even say, 'Abri, our philosophies of life are so different that I am probably not the best therapist for you.' Realising that you may not be the best fit for a client takes courage but it is far better than getting drawn into over-interpreting or over-analysing the client's situation.

Don't force clients to make decisions, but do provide 'choice structure'

Remember that choice structures do not force clients into any given decision. Rather they help clients see things in a different light and give them the freedom to make decisions that they otherwise would not have made (Corsini, 2011; Hagedorn, 2011). In the following excerpt, the counsellor is talking to a man who has discussed at length his son's ingratitude. There has been something cathartic about his complaints, but it is time to move on.

> **COUNSELLOR:** People often have blind spots in their relationships with others, especially in close relationships. Picture your son sitting with some counsellor. He is talking about his relationship with you. What's he saying?
>
> **CLIENT:** Well, I don't know . . . I guess I don't think about that very much. Hmm . . . . He'd probably say . . . well, that he loves me . . . . (pauses). And then he might say that since his mother died, I have never really let him be himself. I've done too much to influence the direction of his life rather than let him fashion it the way he wanted. Hmm . . . He'd say that he loves me but he has always resented my 'interference'.
>
> **COUNSELLOR:** So both love for you and resentment for all that control.
>
> **CLIENT:** And he'd be right. I'm still doing it. Only occasionally with him. He's on to my game. But I'm learning a couple of things. Being pushy is just part of my style. I do it instinctively. I'm just beginning to realise the negative impact it has at work. But I'm not sure that I'm ever going to change.

The counsellor provides a choice structure (suggesting that the client 'walk' a bit in his son's shoes) that enables the client to challenge himself with respect to the dysfunctional controlling aspects of his interpersonal style. He's just beginning to come to grips with the unintended negative consequences of that style. It would be nice if all clients were to respond so easily! Alternatively, the counsellor might have asked this client to list three things he thinks he does right and three things he thinks he should reconsider in his relationship with his son. The point is to be inventive with the probes and choice structures you provide clients with to help them challenge themselves.

Earn the right to invite clients to challenge themselves

Long ago Berenson and Mitchell (1974) claimed that some helpers don't have the right to invite clients to challenge themselves because they are not doing a good job keeping their own houses in order. They made a point worth exploring and also debating because it raises issues implied in the question, 'Is helping a profession or a vocation?' Here are some of the things you can do to earn the right to invite clients to challenge themselves.

First, develop a solid relationship   Challenge only after you have spent time and effort building a therapeutic rapport, therapeutic relationship and a solid foundation of trust with your client. If your rapport is poor or you have allowed your relationship with the client to stagnate, then challenge yourself to deal with the relationship more creatively. Can conservative Chris relate to liberal clients?

Invitations should spring from empathy. Effective challenge flows from accurate understanding. Only when you see the world through clients' eyes can you begin to see how their thinking, behaving and emotional expressions are getting them into trouble and keeping them there. Empathy is not an amenity; it should give substance to every helper response. If Chris always starts with his own world view, he diminishes his value to his clients.

Be open to invitations to challenge yourself   Hesitate to invite others if you deal poorly with the expressed or implied invitations others make to you both in counselling sessions and in everyday life. If you are defensive in the counselling relationship, in your relationship with supervisors or in your everyday life, your invitations might ring hollow. Model the kind of non-defensive attitudes and behaviour that you would like to see in your clients. Chris has a liberal-minded brother in another city. They don't see each other that often, but their phone conversations almost inevitably end in acrimony. He is capable of being empathic, but his preference for debate too often intervenes. A process of self-reflection can be useful in improving your skills as well as learning from your interactions with clients (Thompson & Thompson, 2008).

Work on your own life   How important is constructive change in your own life? Berenson and Mitchell claimed that only people who are striving to live fully according to their value system have the right to invite others to challenge themselves, for only such persons are potential sources of human nourishment for others. Perhaps we as helpers should ask ourselves such questions as, 'Why should others accept invitations to self-challenge from me? What remains unchallenged in my own life?' Helpers are often encouraged to undertake personal therapy in order to become more self-aware. They engage in continuing professional development, mindfulness, self-care and may even seek additional training in resilience to help themselves work more effectively with clients. A process of self-discovery and skill building can be useful when dealing with clients with complex needs.

You may disagree with any of the points Berenson and Mitchell make, but then you must still determine what gives you the right to invite clients to challenge themselves. If your approach to helping avoids challenge of any kind, then you avoid conflict, but your interactions with clients remain bland.

I have used the conservative-versus-liberal situation in one of the examples. Don't get me wrong. I am not choosing liberalism over conservatism or vice versa. The highly diverse world in which we live offers us all sorts of conflicting philosophies, beliefs, political systems, points of view, values, attitudes, opinions and approaches to ethics and morality. So, how well do you deal with diversity without surrendering your own beliefs and values in both your professional and everyday life?

Help clients be specific in their self-challenges

Inviting clients to challenge themselves on specific issues hits the mark. Vague challenges get lost and clients don't know what to do about them. Statements such as 'You need to pull yourself together', 'You need to grow up' and 'Just get on with it' might satisfy some helper need, such as the ventilation of frustration, but they do little for clients. Specific statements, on the other hand, can hit the mark. Equally, helpers need to be aware of their own values, cognitive biases, stressors and emotions in order to confidently work with clients. In the following example, the client is experiencing a great deal of stress both at home and at work.

HELPER: You say that you really want to spend more time at home with the children and you really enjoy it when you do, but you keep taking on new assignments at work, like the Eclipse project, that will add to your travel schedule. Maybe it would be helpful to talk a bit more about work–life balance.

CLIENT: Boy, there's that phrase! Work–life balance. The company talks a lot about it, but nothing much happens. I'm not sure there's anyone at work who's got the work–life balance right.

HELPER: You know what they say about career – 'If you're not in charge of your career, no one is.' It sounds like the same is true with work–life balance.

CLIENT: I hadn't thought about it like that . . . . But I'm afraid you're right. It's right where it belongs, I suppose, on my shoulders. I've been waiting for my family and my company to figure it out for me.

They go on to discuss the specifics that the client would like to see in the work–life balance package. Some helpers avoid clarity and specificity because they feel that they're being too intrusive. Often helping has to be intrusive to make a difference.

Be tentative but not apologetic in the way you invite clients to self-challenge

Tentative invitations are generally viewed more positively than strong, direct challenges. The principle is this: when your invitations are tentative, clients are more likely to *respond* rather than react. Deliver invitations as hunches that are open to review and discussion. If your invitations sound like accusations, your clients will react accordingly. Inviting clients to self-challenge is certainly not an opportunity to put clients in their place but an opportunity to explore together.

On the other hand, invitations that are delivered with too many qualifications – either verbally or through the helper's tone of voice – sound apologetic and can be easily dismissed by clients. I was once working in a career-development centre. As I listened to one of the clients, it soon became evident that one reason he was getting nowhere was that he was full of self-pity. When I shared this observation with him, I overqualified it. These are not my exact words, but it must have sounded something like this:

> **HELPER:** Has it ever, at least in some small way, struck you that one possible reason for not getting ahead, at least as much as you would like, could be that at times you tend to engage in a little bit of self-pity?

I still remember his response. He paused, looked me in the eye for what seemed to be an eternity, and said slowly, 'A little bit of self-pity?' When he paused again, I said to myself, 'I've been too harsh!' He continued, 'I *wallow* in self-pity.' He was waiting for the invitation. We moved on to explore what he might do to move beyond self-pity to constructive change. Clients may be stuck in the 'victim' role and exploring this with them can be a good opportunity to understand the reasons and meaning behind this.

Invite clients to challenge unused strengths rather than weaknesses

Many researchers in the positive psychology movement mentioned in Chapter 1 found that successful helpers tend to challenge clients' unused or underused strengths rather than their weaknesses. In this regard the positive psychology movement's emphasis on strengths (Dahlsgaard, Peterson & Seligman, 2005; Lopez, 2008; Peterson & Seligman, 2004; Wong, 2006) is just catching up to what Berenson and Mitchell said long ago. Individuals who over-focus on their failures find it difficult to change their behaviour. When they dwell too much on their shortcomings, they tend to belittle their achievements and withhold rewards from themselves even when they engage in life-enhancing behaviour. Life is always edgy.

Challenging strengths means helping clients explore the assets, coping strategies and resources they have but fail to use. In the following example, the helper is having a one-to-one session with a woman who is a member of a self-help group in a rape crisis centre. She is very good at helping others but is always down on herself.

> **COUNSELLOR:** Ann, in the group sessions, you provide a great deal of support for the other women. You have an amazing ability to spot a person in trouble and provide an encouraging word. And when one of the women wants to give up, you are the first to invite her to review her decision. You do it gently and forcibly at the same time. . . . But when Ann is dealing with Ann . . . .
>
> **ANN:** I know where you're headed . . . . I know I'm a better giver than receiver. I'm much better at caring than being cared about. I'm not sure why that is . . . . Or that it even matters. I'm sure this is not lost on the other members of the group . . . . This is the way I am. And have been for a long time. I think I've got some bad habits when it comes to dealing with myself. I'm so fearful of being self-indulgent.

The counsellor helps her place a demand on herself to use her rather substantial resources in her dealings with herself. Because she isn't self-indulgent, it's time to help her take a look at her resistance to being cared about.

Even adverse life experiences can be a source of strength and positive growth (Joseph, 2013). For instance, Park, Lechner, Antoni and Stanton (2009) have edited a book that explores how medical illness can lead to positive life change. McMillen, Zuravin and Rideout (1995) studied adult perceptions of benefit from child sexual abuse. Almost half the adults reported some kind of benefit, including increased knowledge of child sexual abuse, protecting other children from abuse, learning how to protect themselves from others and developing a strong personality – without, of course, discounting the horror of the abuse. Counsellors, therefore, can help clients 'mine' benefits from adverse experiences, putting to practical use the age-old dictum that 'good things can come from evil things'. People (including clients) are often more resilient than we make them out to be.

Help clients build on their successes

Effective helpers do not urge clients to place too many demands on themselves all at once. Rather, they help clients place reasonable demands on themselves and, in the process, help them appreciate and celebrate their successes. In the following example, the client, Anan, a student from the Middle East who has just finished a degree in business, is talking with a counsellor in the university placement centre. As a student, Anan always undersells himself and his achievements. The truth is that he has been an excellent student and deals with people very well. The only one he seems to be down on is himself. After each success in school and at university, he brightened up but soon retreated into his usual I'm-not-very-good mindset. He is talking to the counsellor about his misgivings about getting a job.

ANAN: I've had a few part-time jobs that didn't amount to much. The business world is looking for people with experience. I don't have any. So I think I just need a job, any job.

COUNSELLOR A: Anan, why do you keep underselling yourself? You keep referring to yourself as, well, almost damaged goods. No one's going to hire you if you keep doing that.

This counsellor emphasises the problem and browbeats the client. The following counsellor takes a different tack.

COUNSELLOR B: You're right, experience is important . . . . But let's step back a moment. In a very real sense you've had two different jobs for the last four years. One, being a student, a learner, and two, developing your ability to meet and get along with all sorts of people, being a good relater. Let's discuss your track record in these two 'jobs'.

ANAN (pauses): Well . . . OK. But university isn't the real world.

COUNSELLOR B: I'm not sure what you mean. I don't think you're saying that university is an unreal world. So . . .?

ANAN: No, it isn't. I've learned a lot! . . . And I get along well with just about everyone.

COUNSELLOR B: Let's pretend I'm a recruiter. And I say, 'Tell me what kind of learner you are. And then tell me what you're like in building and maintaining interpersonal relationships. Start with either one.' How would you respond?

ANAN: They're not going to ask questions like that! . . . I'm not sure what I'd say.

COUNSELLOR B: Well, just try.

ANAN (hesitatingly): Well . . . I'm a good learner (pauses).

COUNSELLOR B: Meaning?

ANAN (still hesitatingly): Well, I study hard. I love getting a grasp on the fundamental concepts of whatever I'm learning. Maybe that's why I hate exams. So many of my classmates just study for exams. And some of my teachers teach to the exam. I don't like that at all. But I love going deeply into whatever I'm learning.

They go on to deal with Anan's successes in his two main 'jobs' and how he can use these successes as a candidate for jobs. They discuss the culture from which Anan comes, one that emphasises being modest, one where unemployment was very high and one in which even so-called lowly jobs were prized. Anan is a US citizen now. Counsellor B helps him explore the consequences of excessive modesty and Anan's need to develop a self-presentation approach in which he neither oversells or undersells himself: 'In job interviews do you present yourself as a beggar or as an asset? Just tell the truth. If you belittle yourself, you're fudging. My bet is that you hate fudging.'

Make sure that invitations to self-challenge respect clients' values

Help clients clarify their values and make reasonable choices based on them. Respect their autonomy. Be wary of using challenging, even indirectly, to force clients to accept your values. This violates the empowerment value discussed in Chapter 2. In the following example, the client is a 21-year-old woman who has curtailed her social life, her education and her career to take care of her elderly mother who is suffering from incipient Alzheimer's.

CLIENT: I admit that juggling work, home, friends and university is a real challenge for me. I keep feeling that I'm not doing justice to any of them. I am dropping so many balls that it really gets to me. I don't feel like I am on top of anything lately.

COUNSELLOR A: You have every right to have a life of your own. Why not get your mother into a nursing facility? You can still visit her regularly. Then get on with life. That's probably what she wants anyway.

Inviting clients to clarify their values is, of course, legitimate. But this counsellor does little to help the client clarify her values. She makes suggestions without finding out why the client is doing what's she's doing. Counsellor B takes a different approach.

COUNSELLOR B: You're trying to juggle four very important areas of your life – caring for your mother, university, work and social life. That's a tough assignment. It might help to explore what's driving you in all this. It may be helpful to review how you set your priorities.

CLIENT: I've never thought about what drives me to do what I do.

COUNSELLOR B: Well, as you juggle commitments in your life, what values drive you to set priorities?

CLIENT (pauses):   I thought we had values and just, well, did them.

COUNSELLOR B: OK. Let's see if that's the case.

This counsellor challenges her gently to find out what she really wants. Therapists can help clients explore the consequences of the values they hold, but inviting them to take a look at their values is not the same as questioning them. Or you might well invite *clients themselves* to question values that seem to be life-limiting rather than life-enhancing.

The principles outlined here are, of course, guidelines, not absolute prescriptions. In the long run, use your common sense. Put yourself in the client's shoes. Get the client to tell what he or she needs from you. The more flexible you are, the more likely you are to add value to your clients' search for solutions. Box 6.1 summarises ways of making your invitations to self-challenge both wise and appropriately robust.

BOX 6.1   The Wisdom of Challenging

How well do I do each of the following as I try to help my clients?

- Invite clients to challenge themselves.
- Earn the right to invite clients to self-challenge.
- Be tactful and tentative in my invitations without being insipid or apologetic.
- Help clients develop specific self-challenges that hit the mark and make a difference.
- Help clients highlight their strengths rather than their weaknesses.
- Make sure that self-challenge does not become self-demeaning or self-destructive.
- Focus on positive growth and achievements that the client has made.
- Invite clients to clarify and act on their own values.

THE CHALLENGES RELATED TO HELPING CLIENTS MANAGE RELUCTANCE AND RESISTANCE

Helpers inevitably run into clients who are reluctant to engage in the often hard work needed to bring about problem-managing change. Helpers also encounter clients who not only drag their feet in the helping process but, sometimes vigorously, 'push back' against any kind of helping at all or parts of the helping process. This is resistance. In these pages a distinction is made between 'reluctance' and 'resistance' although these two terms are often used interchangeably in the literature and some clients are both reluctant and resistant.

Reluctance: Misgivings about change

The seeds of reluctance are in the client. Obstacles and barriers are often hidden and related to past experiences (Chigwedere, Tone, Fitzmaurice & McDonough, 2012). Managing problem situations and spotting and developing unused opportunities is hard work, and the rewards for that work are not always immediately evident. David, the ex-serviceman struggling with PTSD symptoms, knows that he needs to get back into the community. He talks to Laura about actions he thinks he should take such as re-establishing some kind of relationship with his local church, but he is slow in getting around to doing it. He talks the talk, but he keeps finding reasons for not walking the walk.

Being slow to seek help or accept help when it is offered is an early form of reluctance. Vogel, Wester and Larson (2007) outline the main reasons why troubled people avoid helping in the first place. Here are some common beliefs:

- 'Society looks down on those who seek help' (of course, some members of society do).
- 'The whole experience will be too emotionally painful.'
- 'Counselling probably won't help me very much.' 'I'll have to reveal all my dark secrets.'
- 'My family and friends will see me as odd.'
- 'I'll be embarrassed and feel worse about myself than I do now.'

There are still people who see therapy as a place for 'weak people' and stigma round mental health issues still exists.

For those who do work up the courage to see a helper, reluctance refers to their hesitancy to engage in the work demanded by the tasks of the helping process. Problem management and opportunity development involve a great deal of work. Therefore, there are sources of reluctance in all clients – indeed, in all human beings. A great deal of effort may be involved in trying to rehabilitate or save a failing marriage. Conquering an addiction is hard work. Some people 'give up' smoking dozens of times before finally succeeding. Unused opportunities also provide challenges. Developing unused opportunities means venturing into unknown waters. Although this is a charming idea for some, it strikes something akin to terror in others. Socially shy clients often enough choose living a lonely life rather than taking even small steps towards establishing real friendship. One client who acquired dozens of 'friends' on Facebook and followers on Instagram but never met any of them in person became deeply depressed over her 'make-believe' social life. She referred to herself as an 'internet fraud'.

Clients exercise reluctance in many, often covert, ways. They talk about only safe or low-priority issues, seem unsure of what they want, benignly sabotage the helping process by being overly cooperative, set unrealistic goals and then use them as an excuse for not moving forward, don't work very hard at changing their behaviour and are slow to take responsibility for themselves. They tend to blame others or the social settings and systems of their lives for their troubles and play games with helpers. Or they don't come for counselling in the first place. For instance, Tim is reluctant to join his wife in her sessions with a counsellor. He says that he'll 'think about it', that he doesn't feel 'any real need' to talk to a counsellor, that right now the demands of his job are too pressing and that he can't 'find the time' for the sessions and so forth. Deep down he's afraid of what might happen were he to go. There are many ways clients drag their feet. We need only to reflect on our own experience. Reluctance to change is normal. Reluctance also admits itself in degrees; clients come 'armoured' against change to a greater or lesser degree.

The reasons for reluctance are many. They are built into the human condition. Here is a sampling.

Fear of intensity   If the counsellor uses high levels of tuning in, listening, sharing empathic highlights and probing, and if the client cooperates by exploring the feelings, experiences, behaviours, points of view and intentions related to his or her problems in living, the helping process can be an intense one. This intensity can cause both helper and client to back off. Skilled helpers know that counselling is potentially intense. They are prepared for it and know how to support a client who is not used to such intensity. They certainly know when to back off. They respect the process of therapy and that each client works at a different pace.

Lack of trust   Some clients find it very difficult to trust anyone, even a most trustworthy helper. They have irrational fears of being betrayed. Even when confidentiality is an explicit part of the client–helper contract, some clients are very slow to reveal themselves. They may even ask a lot of questions about what notes you will be writing about them or who you will be talking to about them. A combination of patience, reassurance, encouragement and invitations to self-challenge is demanded of the helper.

Fear of disorganisation   Some people fear self-disclosure because they feel that they cannot face what they might find out about themselves. The client feels that the façade he or she has constructed, no matter how much energy must be expended to keep it propped up, is still less burdensome than exploring the unknown. Such clients often begin well but retreat once they start to be overwhelmed by the data produced in the problem-exploration process. Digging into one's inadequacies always leads to a certain amount of disequilibrium, disorganisation and crisis. But breakthroughs and growth often take place at crisis points. That said, a high degree of disorganisation immobilises the client, whereas very low disorganisation is often indicative of a failure to get at the client's core concerns. By inviting clients to take 'baby steps' that don't end in disaster, counsellors help clients to build confidence.

Shame   Shame is a much-overlooked variable in human living (Bradshaw, 2005; Kaufman, 1989; Lynd, 1958; Miller (n.d.); Nathanson, 1987). Dearing and Tangney (2011) have edited a book that looks at shame from many different points of view. Shame can be an important part of disorganisation and crisis. The root meaning of the verb to shame is 'to uncover, to expose, to wound', a meaning that suggests the process of painful self-exploration. Shame is not just being painfully exposed to another; it is primarily an exposure of self to oneself. In shame experiences, particularly sensitive and vulnerable aspects of the self are exposed, especially to one's own eyes. Shame is often sudden – in a flash, the client sees heretofore unrecognised inadequacies without being ready for such a revelation. Shame is sometimes touched off by external incidents, such as a casual remark someone makes, but it could not be touched off by such insignificant incidents unless, deep down, one was already ashamed. Clients may be paralysed with chronic shame and shame anxiety (Sanderson, 2015). Putting on a 'happy face' or façade can be exhausting for clients. Managing shame, especially internalised shame can be debilitating for clients.

Stewart (2013) describes shame as 'a complex, painful feeling resulting from a strong sense of guilt, unworthiness or disgrace. We feel shame when we are faced with something that draws attention to a discrepancy between what we are and what, ideally, we would like to be.'

A shame experience might be defined as an acute emotional awareness of a failure to *be* in some way. Farber and Sohn (2007) observe that shame is often an obstacle to frank discussions of sexuality: 'Sexuality is the least extensively disclosed theme in psychotherapy and the second least discussed item within marriage.... Even the relative safety and the near-absolute confidentiality of the therapist's office are not sufficient at times to overcome the shame in discussing this most personal issue' (p. 230). Of course, empathy and support help clients deal with whatever shame they might experience. But shame is not limited to issues concerning sexuality. It is often an issue in clients with substance-abuse problems (Potter-Efron, 2011) and PTSD disorders (Herman, 2011).

Gilbert (2009) developed compassionate mind training for individuals who experience high levels of shame and self-criticism. Much has since been written about working more compassionately with clients in a variety of settings. The compassionate mind foundation explains that 'When people hear the word compassion, they tend to think of kindness. But scientific study has found the core of compassion to be courage.'

> A standard definition of compassion is, 'a sensitivity to suffering in self and others with a commitment to try to alleviate and prevent it.' The courage to be compassionate lies in the willingness to see into the nature and causes of suffering – be that in ourselves, in others and the human condition. The challenge is to acquire the wisdom we need to address the causes of suffering in ourselves and others.
>
> Compassion is one of the most important declarations of strength and courage known to humanity. It is difficult and powerful, infectious and influential. It is a universally recognised motivation with the ability to change the world.
>
> Retrieved from: www.compassionatemind.co.uk/about-us

Laura realises early on that David felt deeply ashamed about letting down his comrades, the army and his country. He covered this over with a great deal of bravado, but when he was counselled to accept an honourable discharge, he felt strangely relieved because he knew he 'deserved' to be let go.

The diversity issue makes helping clients deal with reluctance more difficult. Research findings on one population do not automatically transfer to another (Furukowa & Hunt, 2011). Some individuals or even populations may well be glad to share the most intimate details of their personal lives without experiencing any shame or other debilitating emotion. On the other hand, some more conservative cultures abhor the thought of discussing intimate issues. Recall the guidelines for dealing with diversity outlined in Chapter 2.

The cost of change   Some people are afraid to take stock of themselves because they know, however subconsciously, that if they do, they will have to change – that is, surrender comfortable but unproductive patterns of living, work more diligently, suffer the pain of loss, acquire skills needed to live more effectively and so on. For instance, a husband and wife may realise, at some level, that if they see a counsellor, they will have to reveal themselves and that once the cards are on the table, they will have to go through the agony of changing their style of relating to each other. Some clients come with the assumption that counselling is magic and are put off when change proves to be hard work. In cases like this, the counsellor needs to help clients see that the outcomes are worth the effort. It took one client several years to quit smoking, but when she finally did so she told everyone who would listen, 'I just love the sense of freedom I have now. I was a prisoner, but now I'm free. Why did I wait so long?' We know why.

A loss of hope   Some clients think that change is impossible, so why try? A man in his 60s, a participant in a counselling group, complained about constant anxiety. He had given up hope. How could anyone who had been treated as brutally as he was by his father have any hope? Running away from home was just the beginning. He kept running from hope the rest of his life. But, after being challenged by both helper and his fellow participants, he rediscovered hope and, with it, self-responsibility. He no longer focused on the 'scars' inflicted by his father's mistreatment. He no longer focused on the self-inflicted scars of a life lived irresponsibly. He found hope in both the care he experienced in the group and in the life struggles revealed by the other participants. He found hope in community.

This is just a sampling. Each one of us needs only to look at his or her own struggles with growth, development and maturity to add to the list.

Resistance: Reacting to coercion

Clients who resist tend to think that they are being *forced* to do something. They may even want to engage in therapy or in some therapeutic exercise, but feel that their helpers are demanding participation rather than inviting them to participate. They can feel like they are being 'sent' to therapy rather than choosing to go. When Laura suggested that she and David use the feedback surveys, David said no because he thought that she was telling him what he had to do. Later on he told her that at the time he felt that she was more or less saying, 'Be a good boy and fill these surveys out for me.' Of course that was not Laura's intention. She in no way was trying to impose the surveys on him. She knew that there were other collaborative ways of introducing feedback into the helping process.

Reacting to perceived mistreatment Clients who think that they are being mistreated by their helpers in some way tend to resist. Clients who believe that their cultural beliefs, values and norms – whether group or personal – are being violated by the helper can be expected to resist. Resistance is the client's way of fighting back (Dimond *et al.*, 1978; Driscoll, 1984). Spouses who feel forced to come to marriage counselling sessions are often resistant. They resist because they resent what they see as a power play. Tony gets angry when his wife suggests that he come with her to her counselling sessions. Knowing that she has talked this over with her mother, he feels that he is the focus of a conspiracy. They are looking for ways to coerce him to go. 'I don't care what happens, but they're not going to get me' are his sentiments. Of course, some clients see coercion where it does not exist. But because people act on their perceptions, the result is still some form of covert or open fighting back.

Resistant clients, feeling abused, let everyone know that they have no need for help, show little willingness to establish a working relationship and often enough try to con counsellors. They are often resentful, make active attempts to sabotage the helping process or terminate the process prematurely. They can be either testy, argumentative or actually abusive and belligerent towards the therapist. Some will turn up late for sessions or 'have to' leave early. They may not engage in the therapeutic process at all. Resistance to helping is, of course, a matter of degree, and not all resistant clients engage in extreme forms of resistance behaviours.

Involuntary clients Involuntary clients (Brodsky, 2011) – sometimes called 'mandated' clients – are often resisters. A high school student gets into trouble with a teacher and sees being sent to a counsellor as a form of punishment. A felon receives probation on the condition of being involved in some kind of counselling process. A manager accused of sexual harassment keeps his job only if he agrees to a series of counselling sessions. Clients like these are found in schools, especially schools below college level, in correctional settings, in marriage counselling, especially if it is court-mandated, in employment agencies, in welfare agencies, in court-related settings and in other social agencies. But any client who feels that he or she is being coerced or treated unfairly can become a resister. Clients can experience coercion in a wide variety of ways. The following kinds of clients are often resistant:

- Clients who see no reason for going to the helper in the first place.
- Clients who resent third-party referrers (parents, teachers, correctional facilities, social service agencies) and whose resentment carries over to the helper.
- Clients who don't know what helping is about and fear the unknown.
- Clients who have a history of rebelliousness.
- Clients who see the goals of the helper or the helping system as different from their own. For instance, the goal of counselling in a welfare setting may be to help clients become financially independent, whereas some clients may be satisfied with financial dependency.
- Clients who have developed negative attitudes about helping and helping agencies and who harbour suspicions about helping and helpers. They don't trust 'shrinks'.
- Clients who believe that going to a helper is the same as admitting weakness, failure and inadequacy. They feel that they will lose face by going. By resisting the process, they preserve their self-esteem.
- Clients who feel that counselling is something that is being done to them. They feel that their rights are not being respected.
- Clients who feel a need for personal power and find it through resisting a powerful figure or agency. 'I may be relatively powerless, but I still have the power to resist' is the subtext.
- Clients who dislike their helpers but do not discuss their dislike with them.
- Clients who differ from their helpers about the degree of change needed.
- Clients who differ greatly from their helpers – for instance, a poor kid with an older middle-class helper.

Kiracofe and Wells (2007) object to mandated or disciplinary counselling, at least in educational institutions, on both professional and ethical grounds. For instance, they claim that disciplinary counselling muddies the issue of self-responsibility: 'An implied assumption of the mandatory referral is that disruptive behaviour can be managed and changed as a result of regular counselling sessions. This assumption, in effect, removes the responsibility for behaviour change from the student and places it on the counselling process' (p. 263). They offer a set of strategies for judicial action based on disruptive students' readiness for change that are aligned with Prochaska's readiness for change stages outlined in Part III. Student misconduct is not going to go away and both teachers and administrators have been traditionally too ready to pass the buck. Kiracofe and Wells's article calls for a more professional debate and a systemic solution.

Many sociocultural variables – gender, prejudice, race, religion, social class, upbringing, cultural and subcultural blueprints and the like – can play a part in resistance. For instance, a man might instinctively resist being helped by a woman and vice versa. An older black person might instinctively resist being helped by a younger person and vice versa. A person with no religious affiliation might instinctively think that help coming from a minister will be 'pious' or will automatically include some form of proselytising. In the end it's your job to spot resistance and work with the client to determine what is causing it.

Healthy resistance   Of course, resistance can be a healthy sign. It can mean that clients are standing up for their values, rights and fighting back. Koenig (2011) makes an excellent point. Although he is talking about patients who resist the recommendations of medical doctors, what he says applies also to therapy clients. Resistance creates an opportunity for collaborative decision making: 'Through resistance to a treatment recommendation, patients work to negotiate and collaboratively co-construct what counts as an acceptable recommendation' (p. 1105). That is, through resistance clients become agents, negotiating or fighting for what they need.

In practice, of course, a mixture of reluctance and resistance is often found in the same client. If therapy is to become more efficient, then counsellors need to find ways of helping their clients deal with reluctance and resistance as expeditiously as possible.

GUIDELINES FOR HELPING CLIENTS MOVE BEYOND RELUCTANCE AND RESISTANCE

Because both reluctance and resistance are such pervasive phenomena, helping clients manage them is part and parcel of all our interactions with clients (Kottler, 1992). Here are some principles.

Avoid unhelpful responses to reluctance and resistance

Helpers, especially beginning helpers who are unaware of the pervasiveness of reluctance and resistance, are often disconcerted when they encounter uncooperative clients. Such helpers are prey to a variety of emotions – confusion, panic, irritation, hostility, guilt, hurt, rejection, depression. Distracted by these unexpected feelings, they react in any of several unhelpful ways:

- They accept their guilt and try to placate the client.
- They become impatient and hostile and manifest these feelings either verbally or non-verbally.
- They do nothing in the hope that the reluctance or the resistance will disappear.
- They lower their expectations of themselves and proceed with the helping process, but in a half-hearted way.
- They try to become warmer and more accepting, hoping to win the client over by love.
- They blame the client and end up in a power struggle with him or her.
- They allow themselves to be abused by clients, playing the role of a scapegoat.
- They lower their expectations of what can be achieved by counselling.

- They hand the direction of the helping process over to the client.
- They give up.

In short, when helpers engage 'difficult' clients, they experience stress, and some give in to self-defeating 'fight or flight' approaches to handling it.

The source of this stress is not just clients' behaviour; it also comes from the helper's own self-defeating attitudes and assumptions about the helping process. Here are some of them.

- All clients should be self-referred and adequately committed to change before appearing at my door.
- Every client must like me and trust me.
- I am a consultant and not a social influencer; it should not be necessary to place demands on clients or even help them place demands on themselves.
- Every unwilling client can be helped.
- No unwilling client can be helped.
- I alone am responsible for what happens to this client.
- I have to succeed completely with every client.
- I can help every client.
- Even if a client is resistant, I can change them.

These unrealistic beliefs are never spoken, but they can loiter in the background. Effective helpers neither court reluctance and resistance nor are surprised by them.

Psychoanalytic theory and resistance

Stewart (2013) provides a useful summary of the psychoanalytic theory of resistance which states that resistance may be conscious or unconscious on the part of the client. At a conscious level, resistance is the client deliberately withholding information from the helper, and this is relatively simple for the helper to deal with, by skillfully challenging the client. However, when considering unconscious resistance from the client, what causes that resistance might be very significant – disclosure of the shame and guilt that one is engaged in sexual abuse, or in some other criminal activity, can seem like a mountain to the client.

Unconscious resistance may occur at any point during the helping process, as the client confronts something significant which lies beneath the surface. This would appear to be a defence by the unconscious, as to explore it would inevitably mean a challenge between moving towards healing or staying where it is unhealthy to stay. The client's unconscious efforts to thwart the aims and process of helping are sometimes referred to as 'sticking points'. The client does this by blocking unconscious, repressed material from breaking through into the conscious, which can take the form of being unwilling to continue exploring a particular theme, with its thoughts and feelings, perhaps due to anxiety about disclosure or fear of how the helper will react. Due to the client's resistance, access to the unconscious can only be gained by indirect means, the chief of which is free association. Resistance must be overcome if the client is to integrate unconscious material into the conscious and move forward, and this can only be achieved by client and helper working together through the need for resistance. Stewart suggests that overcoming resistance can be helped by:

- The client's need for recovery
- The client's intellectual interest
- Positive transference
- Making the expression of resistance as safe as possible
- Honouring the resistance by careful listening, without discounting what is revealed
- Acknowledging the resistance, not by agreeing with it but by recognising the difficulty the client is experiencing
- Reinforcing that there must be valid reasons for resisting it at this time.

Develop productive approaches to dealing with reluctance and resistance

In a book like this, it is impossible to identify every possible form of reluctance and resistance, much less provide a set of strategies for managing each. Often an awareness of obstacles or potential obstacles can be a good learning opportunity for both the client and helper. For example, identifying barriers to change or reasons behind the client's reluctance may have important meaning that can be explored. However, here are some principles and a general approach to managing reluctance and resistance in whatever forms they take.

Explore your own reluctance and resistance   Examine reluctance and resistance in your own life. How do you react when you feel coerced? Do you dig your heels in? What do you do when you feel you are being treated unfairly? Do you speak up? Do you back down? How do you deal with personal growth and development? Do you run away from them? Do you face them straight on? If you are in touch with the various forms of reluctance and resistance in yourself and are finding ways of overcoming them, you are more likely to help clients deal with theirs.

See some reluctance and resistance as normal   Help clients see that their reluctance and resistance are not 'bad' or odd. After all, yours aren't. Beyond that, help them see the positive side of resistance. It may well indicate that they have fibre. It may be a sign of self-affirmation.

Accept and work with the client's reluctance and resistance   Teyber (2005) talks about 'honouring' the client's resistance. This is a central principle. Start with the client's frame of reference. Accept both the client and his or her reluctance or resistance. Do not ignore it or be intimidated by what you find. Let clients know how you experience it and then explore it with them. Model openness to challenge. Be willing to explore your own negative feelings. The skill of direct, mutual talk (called immediacy), discussed in Chapter 8, is extremely important here. Help clients work through the emotions associated with reluctance and resistance. Avoid moralising. Befriend the reluctance or the resistance instead of reacting to it with hostility or defensiveness.

See reluctance as avoidance   Reluctance is a form of avoidance that is not necessarily tied to client ill will. Therefore, you need to understand the principles and mechanisms underlying avoidance behaviour, which is often discussed in texts dealing with the principles of behaviour (Watson & Tharp, 2007). Some clients avoid counselling or give themselves to it only half-heartedly because they see it as lacking in suitable rewards or even as punishing. If that is the case, then counsellors have to help them search for suitable incentives. Constructive change is usually more rewarding than a miserable status quo, but that might not be the client's perception, especially in the beginning. Find ways of presenting the helping process as rewarding. Talk about outcomes.

Examine the quality of your interventions   Without setting off on a guilt trip, examine your helping behaviour. What are you doing that might seem unfair to the client? In what ways does the client feel coerced? For example, you may have become too directive without realising it. Furthermore, take stock of the emotions that are welling up in you because clients lash back or drag their feet. How are these emotions 'leaking out'? No use denying such feelings. Rather, own them and find ways of coming to terms with them. Do not over-personalise what the client says and does. If you are allowing a hostile client to get under your skin, you are probably reducing your effectiveness. Of course, the client might be resistant, not because of you, but because he or she is under pressure from others to deal with his or her problems. But you take the brunt of it. Find out, if you can.

Be realistic and flexible   Remember that there are limits to what a helper can do. Know your own personal and professional limits. If your expectations for growth, development and change exceed the client's, you can end up in an adversarial relationship. Rigid expectations of the client and of yourself become self-defeating.

Establish a 'just society' with your client   Deal with the client's feelings of coercion. Provide what Smaby and Tamminen (1979) called a 'two-person just society' (p. 509). A just society is based on mutual respect and shared planning. Therefore, establish as much mutuality as is consonant with helping goals. Invite participation. Help clients participate in every step of the helping process and in all the decision making. Share expectations. Discuss and get reactions to helping procedures. Explore the helping contract with your clients and get them to contribute to it.

Help the client search for incentives for moving beyond resistance   Help the client find incentives for participating in the helping process. Use client self-interest as a way of identifying these. Use brainstorming as a way of discovering possible incentives. For instance, the realisation that he or she is going to remain in charge of his or her own life may be an important incentive for a client. Self-determination and autonomy play an important part in the client's willingness to change and engage.

Do not see yourself as the only helper in your client's life   Engage significant others, such as peers, colleagues and family members, in helping the client face reluctance and resistance. For instance, lawyers who belong to Alcoholics Anonymous may be able to deal with a fellow lawyer's reluctance to join a treatment programme more effectively than you can.

Employ reluctant and resistant clients as helpers   If possible, find ways to get a reluctant or resistant client into situations to help others. The change of perspective can help the client come to terms with his or her own unwillingness to work. One tactic is to take the role of the client in the interview and manifest the same kind of reluctance or resistance he or she does. Have the client take the counsellor role and help you overcome your unwillingness to work or cooperate. One person who did a great deal of work for Alcoholics Anonymous had a resistant alcoholic go with him on his city rounds, which included visiting hospitals, nursing homes for alcoholics, prisoners, dosshouses and down-and-out people on the streets. The alcoholic saw through all the lame excuses other alcoholics offered for their plight. After a week, he joined Alcoholics Anonymous himself. Clients can become helpers in group counselling, too.

Hanna, Hanna and Keys (1999; see also Hanna, 2002; Sommers-Flanagan & Sommers-Flanagan, 2006) drew up a list of 50 strategies – some original, many drawn from the helping literature – for counselling defiant, aggressive adolescents. Many of the strategies have wider application to both reluctant and resistant clients of all ages and can be used to put into practice the principles outlined earlier. The authors divide the strategies into three categories: reaching clients, accepting them and relating to them. As you read through their suggestions, it soon becomes clear that they are talking about what helpers should be doing as a matter of course. But their lists are excellent reminders.

Reluctance and resistance create challenges for both clients and helpers. Helping clients overcome, deal with, or come to terms with different forms of unwillingness is often at the heart of helping. Do not be surprised when clients react strongly when invited to challenge themselves. If they react negatively rather than respond, then you have to find ways of helping them work through their emotion-laden reluctance and resistance. If they seem to 'clam up', try to find out what's going on inside. In the following example, the helper has just delivered a brief summary of the main points of the problem situation they have been discussing, gently pointing out the self-destructive nature of some of the client's behaviours.

> **HELPER:**   I'm not sure how all this sounds to you.
>
> **CLIENT:**   I thought you were on my side. Now you sound like all the others. And I'm paying you to talk like this to me!

Even though the helper was tentative in her invitation to self-challenge based on what the client had already said about himself, the client still reacted defensively. Here are two different approaches (A and B) to the client's defensiveness.

HELPER A: All I've done is summarise what you have been saying about yourself. And you know you're doing yourself in. Let's look at each point we've been discussing and see if this isn't the case.

This helper responds with a defensive, judicial approach. He's about to assemble the evidence. This would probably lead to an argument rather than further dialogue. Helper B backs off a bit.

HELPER B: So, I'm sounding harsh and unfair to you . . . . Kind of dumping on you . . . . Let's back up.

This helper backs off without saying that her summary was wrong. She is giving the client some space. It may be that the client needs time to think about what the helper has said. Helper B tries to find a way into a constructive dialogue with the angered client.

Some call clients who are reluctant, resistant and/or slow to tap into the resilience within themselves 'difficult' clients. There is also a tendency to see difficult clients as bad clients. But they are just clients. Wessler, Hankin and Stern (2001) evened the therapy playing field by suggesting that the term 'difficult client' is too one-sided. The therapist often plays a part in the client's 'difficult behaviour': 'When a therapist uses the word "difficult" to describe a client, what he or she really means is: "I am having difficulty working with this person due to either my own emotional issues or a lack of experience working with clients like this." In essence, using the word difficult to describe a client should be a signal to the therapist that he/she needs to grow in some way personally (and interpersonally)' (p. 5). Fair enough, but clients come for help precisely because they are not managing some part of their lives effectively. Their behaviour in the helping sessions is often enough of an indication or an example of poor self-management. It is impossible to be in the business of helping people for long without encountering both reluctance and resistance. The literature is scattered all over the place (Brodsky, 2011; Leahy, 2001; McKay, Abramowitz & Taylor, 2010; Rasmussen, 2002; Westra, 2004; Westra, Aviram, Connors, Kertes & Mariyam, 2011), including the internet (Mitchell, 2006). Predictably, some of the findings and recommendations conflict with one another. You need to use the values outlined in Part I and the skills outlined in Part II of this book to find ways to help clients who, at least at first sight, don't want to be helped.

THE ROLE OF NEGOTIATION IN CHALLENGE

When the word 'negotiation' pops up, what pops into your mind? There are many possibilities. Some people think of the kind of political dialogue that has gone on in places such as Zimbabwe. One side has all the power and does not want to give it up. The other side, duly elected, wants to exercise the governance rights that come with being freely elected. Someone steps in to help them negotiate with each other. Other people think of Company A wanting to buy Company B. Parties from both companies get together and see if they can work out a deal. Often consultants are called in to help with the negotiations. Closer to home we have homeowners faced with foreclosure. They negotiate with their lenders in an attempt to stay in their homes. 'What kind of realistic deal – one that is fair to both sides – can we work out?' is the central question.

All of these are examples of what might be called special-event negotiation. But there are other kinds of negotiation that are part and parcel of the give-and-take of everyday life. Most of us engage in more rounds of negotiation than we realise. Who is going to pick up the children this evening? How do we divide up household tasks? Where should we eat tonight? Should we get a new refrigerator? How should we work out our finances? What do we do about an offensive neighbour? What should we do about a son who has gone off the rails? How do we handle differences in religious observance? In general, working out arrangements with others calls for some degree of negotiation. In dozens of different ways we negotiate in all the social settings of our lives – at home, in our communities, at work, at church, in healthcare settings.

Negotiation in counselling

As we shall see in Part III, helping involves planning. And planning that involves or affects not just the client but others often requires negotiation. When the parties involved or affected by planning are in conflict, negotiation becomes even more important. Furthermore, clients' problem situations often enough focus on conflicts clients have with others. Conflicts are at the heart of marriage counselling and family therapy. Tumi's desire to create a more fulfilling future for herself has led to conflict with her parents, especially her father. The benefits of effective negotiation are clear. The problem is that the ability to negotiate well is one of those life skills people pick up by chance. Some people become reasonably good at it. Many don't. In her failed conversation with her father, Tumi certainly did not consider herself as a negotiator. And her father was not open to negotiation. Counsellors can help clients negotiate fairly in conflict situations and become better negotiators in their daily lives.

A beginners' framework

Fisher, Ury and Patton (1991) have provided us with a basic framework for engaging in what they call 'principled' negotiation. A lot of the popular literature on negotiation focuses on 'winning' and 'getting your own way'. Principled negotiation, on the other hand, underscores the value of fairness. Let's apply the 'rules' of principled negotiation to the conflict between Tumi and her father.

Avoid rigid bargaining positions as the starting point When Tumi talked with her father, in her anxiety she blurted out what she thought she could do for her father's business and the role she would have to play in order to be successful. In doing so, she did her cause no good. Her father probably heard it as a rigid position that came across as an affront to all he had done to build the business. He rejected what he thought was her position out of hand and remarked how 'ungrateful' she was being. Tumi, with some justification, took his response as a rejection of her as a person.

Separate the people from the issue Principled negotiation, in the main, is not about the relationship between the negotiating parties. Rather it is about the issues, problems or concerns of the parties involved. Therefore, it is best to separate the person from the issue. Tumi and her father both left the conversation thinking they had been attacked. Her father's remarks made it clear that he thought she was negotiating about the relationship. He struck back.

Focus on interests rather than positions It would have been better if Tumi had found a way of bringing up her interests – a more engaging career and, perhaps later, a more engaging social life – and of linking her interests to her father's. By talking about what she could do for the dealership, she thought that she was showing concerns for his interests, but it did not come across that way to him. The parties in a negotiation should be able to describe their interests clearly and in a way that does not threaten the other party. Ideally, each party should help the other party explore his or her interests and make it clear that he or she understands these interests.

Search for options or solutions based on mutual interests Solutions for a better future based on a convergence of interests allow both parties to buy in. Tumi assumed a convergence of interests but she really did not understand – and still does not understand – just what her father's interests are. Of course, this is not all her fault since he plays his cards very close to his chest.

Settle on an agreement that has some objectivity to it In some negotiations objective criteria are more readily available than in others. For instance, if a buyer and seller are negotiating the price of a house, the general housing market and local sales provide criteria that are objective even if they are somewhat elastic. A fair price might be a range, but there is some kind of fair price. 'Objective criteria' look different in Tumi's case. Perhaps the same words out of the mouth of a son would have sounded quite different to

Tumi's father; more reasonable. Or if her father were looking for a loan, a lender might have asked him how he was going to reinforce the management structure of the dealership. In such a case, Tumi's ideas, spoken by someone in management, might have clinched the loan.

These, then, are the bare bones of negotiation framework. Fleshed out, they provide an invaluable resource for negotiating fairly or, in a counsellor's case, acting as a catalyst for negotiations in which clients are embroiled. The authors also provide advice for people negotiating with a powerful counterparty (perhaps as in Tumi's case), for dealing with people who refuse to negotiate, and for parties at risk because of a counterparty's 'dirty tricks'. Ury (1991, 2007) has written extensively on using principled negotiation in difficult situations. Fisher and Shapiro (2005) have written a book on managing emotions in order to make them serve rather than impede the negotiation process. Tumi would probably benefit from many of Ury's principles when she has another difficult conversation with her father:

- Stay in control even when emotions run high and you feel under great pressure.
- Find ways of defusing hostility and anger, both your own and the other person's.
- Try to find out what the other person's real rather than stated interests are.
- Find ways of coping with unfair tactics on the part of the other person.
- Look for incentives that will bring the other party back to the table and keep him or her there.
- Search for agreements that meet mutual needs and interests.

Good negotiators and counsellors who try to help clients in negotiation situations need all the communication skills outlined and illustrated in Chapters 3–4. The lack of these skills and their role in developing relationships make principled negotiation impossible. Goodwill is essential, but not enough.

Helping clients negotiate with themselves

Finally, counsellors can adapt the principles outlined earlier (including Ury's getting-past-no principles) to helping clients negotiate with themselves as in Tumi's case. Some of her conflicts are internal, that is, with herself, although there are external consequences. Given her bi- or tri-cultural background, there are, in a sense, two or three Tumis. There is the Tumi who culturally leans towards embracing the beliefs, values and norms of a South African family with its pre-apartheid roots. Second, there is the Tumi who encountered a different South African culture – in some ways more socially interactive – during her visit there. Third, there is the Tumi, born, bred and educated in the United Kingdom, the Tumi who has experienced its culture but who has not entirely bought into it. Carlos can help her negotiate with herself in her search for a different future. It would seem that possibly painful trade-offs lie ahead as we follow Tumi into constructing a future for herself that is in keeping with her key beliefs and values.

THE SHADOW SIDE OF HELPERS

There is an interesting body of literature on the humanity and flaws of helpers (Kottler, 2010) that can be of enormous help to both beginners – because prevention is infinitely better than cure – and old-timers – because you *can* teach old dogs new tricks. Kottler has provided trainees and novices a positive view of what passion and commitment in the helping professions should look like. An awareness of the reasons that you came into the helping profession is also important to consider. The 'wounded healer' is a concept created by Jung stating that the helper is urged to help others because of their own wounds. More recent writings offer a view of celebrating the wounded healer (Martin, 2011; Farber, 2016).

One of the critical responsibilities of supervisors is to help counsellors identify their blind spots and learn from them. Once out of training, skilled helpers use different forums or methodologies to continue this process, especially with difficult cases. They take counsel with themselves, asking, 'What am I missing here?' They take counsel with colleagues. Without becoming self-obsessed, they scrutinise and challenge themselves and the role they play in the helping relationship. Or, more simply, throughout their careers they continue to learn about themselves, their clients and their profession. One way to identify and do something about your own blind spots as a helper is to elicit clear, honest feedback from your clients.

The 'Mum effect'

Initially, some counsellor trainees are quite reluctant to help clients challenge themselves. They become victims of what has been called the 'Mum effect', the tendency to 'keep mum about undesirable messages', to withhold bad news even when it is in the other's interest to hear it (Rosen & Tesser, 1970, 1971; Tesser & Rosen, 1972; Tesser, Rosen & Batchelor, 1972; Tesser, Rosen & Tesser, 1971). In ancient times, the person who bore bad news to the king was sometimes killed. That obviously led to a certain reluctance on the part of messengers to bring such news. Bad news – and, by extension, the kind of 'bad news' involved in invitations to self-challenge – often arouses negative feelings in the challenger, no matter how he or she thinks the receiver will react. If you are comfortable with the supportive dimensions of the helping process but uncomfortable with helping as a social-influence process, you could fall victim to the Mum effect and become less effective than you might otherwise be.

Excuses for not inviting clients to challenge themselves

Reluctance to challenge is not a bad starting position. In my estimation, it is a far better approach than being too eager to challenge. However, all helping, even the most client-centred, involves social influence. It is important for you to understand your reluctance (or eagerness) to challenge – that is, to challenge yourself on the issue of challenging and on the very notion of helping as a social-influence process. When trainees examine how they feel about inviting others to challenge themselves, here are some of the unexplored assumptions they discover:

- I am just not used to challenging others. My interpersonal style has had a lot of the live-and-let-live in it. I have misgivings about intruding into other people's lives.
- If I challenge others, then I open myself to being challenged. I may be hurt, or I may find out things about myself that I would rather not know.
- I might find out that I like challenging others, and the floodgates will open and my negative feelings about others will flow out. I have some fears that deep down I am an angry person.
- I am afraid that I will hurt others, damage them in some way or other. I have seen others hurt by heavy-handed confrontations.
- I am afraid that I will delve too deeply into others and find that they have problems that I cannot help them handle. The helping process will get out of hand.
- If I challenge others, they will no longer like me. I want my clients to like me.

Vestiges of this kind of thinking can persist long after trainees move out into the field as helpers. People in all sorts of people-oriented occupations, including human-service workers and managers, are bedevilled by the Mum effect and come up with their own set of excuses for not giving feedback. Of course, being willing to invite others to challenge themselves responsibly is one thing; having the skills and wisdom to do so is another. Box 6.2 summarises, in question form, how effective you are at self-challenge.

BOX 6.2 **The Shadow Side: Self-Challenge for Helpers**

How well do I do the following?
- Identify the games my clients attempt to play with me without becoming cynical in the process
- Become comfortable with the social-influence dimension of the helping role, with the kind of 'intrusiveness' that goes with helping
- Incorporate invitations to self-challenge into my counselling style without becoming a confrontation specialist
- Develop the assertiveness needed to overcome the Mum effect
- Challenge the excuses I give myself for failing to invite clients to challenge themselves
- Come to grips with my own imperfections and blind spots both as a helper and as a 'private citizen'.

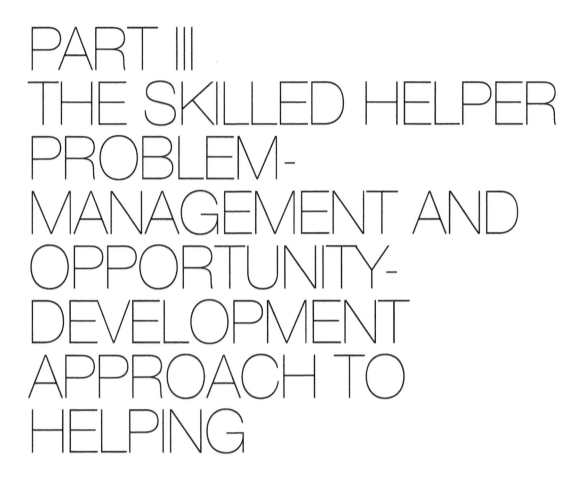

PART III
THE SKILLED HELPER
PROBLEM-
MANAGEMENT AND
OPPORTUNITY-
DEVELOPMENT
APPROACH TO
HELPING

Because all approaches to helping must eventually help clients manage problem situations and develop unused opportunities, it seems logical to start with a flexible, humanistic, broadly based problem-management and opportunity-development model or framework. Of those who write about problem-solving approaches, some use the term explicitly (Bedell & Lennox, 1997; Chang, D'Zurilla & Sanna, 2004; D'Zurilla & Nezu, 1999, 2001; Elias & Tobias, 2002; Nezu, Nezu, Friedman, Faddis & Houts, 1998), whereas others use some form of the process but not the name (Bertolino & O'Hanlon, 2002; Cormier & Nurius, 2003; Hill, 2009). General problem solving has a rich research history spanning some 100 years. The fact that the research is scattered does not belie its importance. Nobel Laureate Herbert Simon and his associates put it nicely:

> "The work of managers, of scientists, of engineers, of lawyers ... is largely work of making decisions and solving problems. It is work of choosing issues that require attention, setting goals, finding or designing suitable courses of action and evaluating and choosing among alternative actions. ... Nothing is more important for the well-being of society than that this work be performed effectively, that we address the many problems requiring attention at the national level ... at the level of business organisations ... and at the level of our individual lives." (1986, p. 1)

Problem solving applied 'at the level of our individual lives', called, variously, social problem solving or applied problem solving or personal problem solving or human problem solving, has an evolving research base (see the research sections in Chang, D'Zurilla & Sanna, 2004; D'Zurilla & Nezu, 1999; Heppner, Witty & Dixon, 2004). The emergence of cognitive-behavioural coaching is also a field gaining momentum in applying the techniques and skills to address problems and issues in individuals' lives (Neenan & Palmer, 2012). Common sense suggests that problem-management models, techniques and skills are important for all of us, because all of us must grapple daily with problems of greater or lesser severity. Heppner's work (for a review and summary see Heppner, Witty & Dixon, 2004) has focused on people's appraisal of their ability to cope with personal problems. Confidence in one's ability to solve problems, the bravery to face up to them and a sense of self-control (especially emotional self-control) can lead in many ways to a richer life. O'Neil (2004), commenting on Heppner and his colleagues' review, says, 'The core of their review is the authors' passion for helping people learn problem solving to improve their lives. Helping others solve problems is a passionate part of our mission as counselling psychologists' (p. 439).

Ask parents whether problem-management skills, like the communication and relationship-building skills detailed in Part II, are important for their children, and they say 'certainly'. But asked where and how their children pick up these skills, they hum and haw. 'Sometimes at home, but perhaps not that much' is a common answer. Parents don't always see themselves as paragons of effective problem solving. 'Maybe at school?' is another half answer in the form of a question. Yet review the curricula of our primary, secondary and tertiary schools and you will find little about problem solving that focuses on problems in living. Some say that formal courses in problem-solving skills are not found in our schools because such skills are picked up through experience. To a certain extent, that's true. However, if problem-management skills are so important, you may well wonder why society leaves the acquisition of these skills to chance. A problem-solving or problem-management mentality should be second nature to us. The world may be the laboratory for problem solving, but the skills needed to optimise learning in this lab should be taught. They are too important to be left to chance.

Because all approaches to therapy must eventually help clients manage problems and develop unused resources, the model or approach of choice in these pages is a flexible, humanistic, broadly based problem-management and opportunity-development model – a model that is straightforward without ignoring the complexities of clients' lives or of the helping process itself. Indeed, because the problem-management and opportunity-development process outlined in this book is embedded in almost all approaches to helping, this model provides an excellent foundation for any 'brand' of helping you eventually choose. This book provides the basics.

THE INGREDIENTS OF SUCCESSFUL THERAPY: A REVIEW

Beginning Part III is a good time to review the ingredients of successful therapy outlined in Chapter 1 to see where we stand. In Part III the problem-management and opportunity-development approach will be presented as the organiser of key ingredients. They all reside, as it were, within the confines of this process:

- *The client and the contextual factors of the client's life.* Clients and their needs are the centrepiece of all aspects of the problem-management helping process. Keeping the client in the driver's seat has been, and remains, one of the imperatives of therapy.

- *The person of the therapist.* Everything we have discussed in Parts I and II relates to the therapist becoming competent in the skills needed to be a consultant and catalyst in the client's efforts to manage problem situations and develop unused opportunities. But the therapist is not the main character in this drama. The client is.

- *The helping relationship.* The client and the therapist are not equal partners in the problem-management process because the client's, not the helper's, problems are the focus. Rather they collaborate. Clients must maintain their autonomy and manage their problem situations. Therapists have a tool kit that helps clients do just that. The more successful counsellors are in helping clients bring out the best in themselves, the more successful they are. Helpers are successful only to the degree that clients are.

- *The therapeutic dialogue between client and helper.* Part II is about the communication skills helpers need to be competent. We have emphasised how important it is for therapists to use their skills to help clients communicate more effectively. These communication skills are at the heart of the therapist's role as consultant to the problem-management process.

- *Two-way feedback between client and helper.* As Duncan and colleagues note, therapy is client-directed and outcome-informed. Session-to-session feedback with respect to both progress towards outcomes and the usefulness of the helping sessions themselves is critical to the problem-management process.

- *The standard problem-management process as a human universal.* It is clear that the standard problem-management model is used, directly or indirectly, in just about every approach to therapy. And, in its basic form, it is readily understood by clients.

- *The model or method of treatment and the assumptions behind it.* It is now clear that the standard problem-management model is also a method of treatment in itself. As presented in these pages, it is an experiential-cognitive-behavioural-emotive model covering the totality of human behaviour.

- *Decision making as a human universal.* Effective decision making is at the heart of problem management. Because problem management is impossible without making decisions, a fuller understanding of the ins and outs and the ups and downs of decision making is essential to both helper and clients. Strategic and tactical decisions may need to be made.

- *The beliefs, values, norms, ethics and morality that drive human behaviour.* This package permeates the totality of human behaviour. Because it is not a 'scientific' package, it introduces a degree of messiness to all human transactions, including that transaction called therapy. But it, too, is at the heart of therapy.

These themes flow through Part III. The primary integrative process is simple – a client successfully managing a problem situation.

CHAPTER 7
AN INTRODUCTION TO THE PROBLEM-SOLVING AND PROBLEM-MANAGEMENT PROCESS

Chapter Contents

- An Overview of the Stages of Problem Management

- Flexibility in the Use of the Problem-Management Process

- Stages of Change and Client Readiness for Change

- Integrative Eclecticism: The Ongoing Search for Best Practice

- 'How Are We Doing?' – Ongoing Evaluation of the Helping Process

- Understanding and Dealing with the Shadow Side of Helping Models

As noted in Chapter 1, all worthwhile helping frameworks, models or processes ultimately help clients ask and answer for themselves four fundamental questions. I repeat them here:

- **What's going on?** 'What are the problems, issues, concerns or undeveloped opportunities I should be working on?' This involves helping clients spell out his or her *current picture*.

- **What does a better future look like?** 'What do I want my life to look like? What changes would help manage my problem situation and develop unused opportunities? What goals do I need to pursue to manage my problem situation?' This involves helping clients paint their *preferred picture*.

- **How do I get there?** 'What do I need to do to make the preferred picture a reality? What plan will get me where I want to go? What actions will get me started on the right path?' The plan outlines the actions clients need to take to create a better future. This is the *way forward*.

- **How do I make it all happen?** 'How do I turn planning and goal setting into the kind of action that leads to the solutions, results, outcomes or accomplishments that have the impact I'm looking for? How do I get going and persevere until I manage my problems and develop my unused opportunities?' The Action Arrow in Figure 7.1 indicates the broad and specific actions clients must take to produce the changes they want. This is the *ongoing challenge of implementation*.

These four questions, turned into three logical 'stages' and an implementation 'arrow' in Figure 7.1, provide the basic framework for the helping process.

FIGURE 7.1   Four key problem-management questions

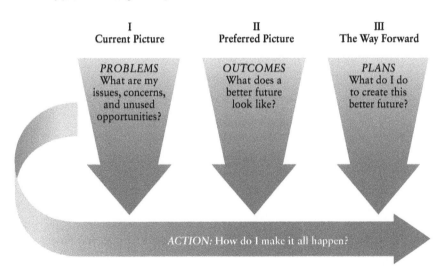

Take the example of workers who leave work, usually temporarily, because of common mental-health problems such as anxiety, depression, stress, adjustment disorder, emotional exhaustion and the like. A study (Lagerveld *et al.*, 2012) was done on roughly 170 such workers to determine what kind of therapy proved to be most successful. One-half of these workers were treated with a standard evidence-based form of cognitive-behavioural therapy (CBT). The other half were treated with a form of CBT that emphasised managing the kinds of problems that came up at work, and also took a problem-management approach to getting back to work. Those who received the work-focused therapy went back to work on the average of 65 days sooner than workers receiving regular CBT. My best bet is that both forms of therapy had a problem-management focus, but the work-focused form of CBT was much more *explicitly* focused on both ameliorating the mental health disorder *and* getting back to work. The second form of therapy dealt more directly with the problem-management factors mentioned in Figure 7.1. It included Action-Arrow components such as homework exercises, including practising stress-reduction techniques, coming up with ways of altering the work conditions that gave rise to some of the mental health problems and drawing up an explicit return-to-work plan. The researchers were not out to prove anything about the problem-management process itself, but it is impossible to prove almost anything about successful therapy without at least implicitly referring to elements of the process. These researchers were quite explicit. Employee assistance programmes (EAPs) are becoming more common in organisations and are focused on supporting the employee back to work with a focus on a graded return to work (for a review of the literature see Beulah, Walker & Fuller-Tyszkiewicz, 2017).

Figure 7.2 takes the four elements of the problem-management process and arranges them in a more detailed and dynamic way.

FIGURE 7.2 The problem-management process

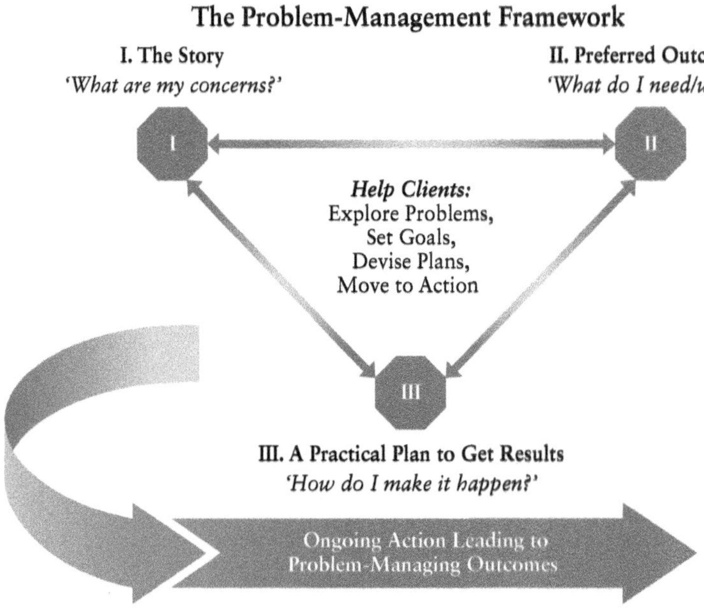

Note that in Figure 7.2 I refer to the problem-management *framework* rather than model and I do so for the following reasons:

- The framework *organises* all the ingredients of successful therapy outlined in Chapter 1.
- It lays out the *geography* of problem management. It helps both clients and therapists know 'where they are' in the flow of the helping process.
- The framework is owned by *both* the client and the helper and therefore promotes dialogue and collaboration.
- While it has an ingrained logic to it, it is *systematic but non-linear*. It is flexible, and it has elastic borders. Clients can move back and forth to stages and tasks they find most helpful. Therapists can invite clients to potentially helpful areas which they are overlooking.
- The framework is, therefore, both *rigorous* and *soft-edged*. It bends with the needs of clients but always remains focused on life-enhancing outcomes.

This theme of flexibility cannot be overstated as many people reject the problem-management process because they experience it as 'rigid' and add that 'ordinary people don't lead their lives that way'. More about that later. Similar graphics will be used at each of the three stages.

AN OVERVIEW OF THE STAGES OF PROBLEM MANAGEMENT

Each of these 'stages' involves three 'tasks' which are mentioned briefly here and are explored in detail in subsequent chapters. This overview is cast in terms of questions that clients can ask themselves as they grapple with their problems.

Stage I: Help clients explore their concerns

In Stage I the tasks are activities that help clients spell out their concerns as clearly as possible with neither too much nor too little detail. These three tasks help clients develop answers to three sets of questions which outline the work that clients need (with the help of their therapists) to do in order to move forward in the problem-management process.

- **Task A. The Story: Problem Situations**. 'What's going on in my life? What are my main concerns? What would I like to focus on?'
- **Task B. The Real Story: New Perspectives**. 'As I look more closely, what's really going on in my life? What new perspectives will help me deal with my concerns?'
- **Task C. The Right Story: Key Issues to Work on**. 'What should I be working on? Which issues, if handled well, will make a real difference in my life?'

The work that is done in any one of these tasks should stimulate actions that lead, eventually, to the client's preferred outcomes.

Stage II: Help clients determine problem-managing outcomes and set goals

In Stage II therapists help clients imagine the kind of future they want in terms of outcomes and goals. The interrelated tasks of Stage II outline three ways in which helpers can partner with their clients with a view to exploring and developing this better future.

- **Task A. Possibilities**. 'What possibilities do I have for a better future? What do I want the future to look like? What do problem-managing outcomes look like? What tasks do I need to focus on?'
- **Task B. Goals/Outcomes**. 'What do I really want and need? What solutions are best for me? Is what I think I want/need really what I want/need? What are my options?'
- **Task C. Commitment**. 'What am I willing to pay for what I want? Do I have the focus needed to follow through with my goals? Is this the right time to pursue these goals?'

Again, the work that is done in any one of these tasks prompts actions that lead to the client's preferred outcomes.

Stage III: Help clients draw up plans to accomplish goals

Stage III also has three interrelated tasks. They are directed at coming up with a realistic plan to achieve the goals that lead to problem-managing outcomes.

- **Task A: Possible Strategies**. 'What are the possible paths to my goals? What kind of actions will help me get what I need and want? How do I move forward?'
- **Task B: Best-Fit Strategies**. 'What strategy or set of strategies is best for me? Which strategies fit my resources?'
- **Task C: Plans to Accomplish Goals**. 'What should my campaign for constructive change look like? How do I organise my strategies to accomplish my goals? What do I need to do first? Second? Third?'

The stages, together with the tasks that make them operative, constitute a logical, but, in practice, not necessarily linear, step-by-step process. Why this is necessarily the case will be considered later in this chapter.

Burnard (2005, p. 127) provides a useful illustration of Egan's three-stage framework in practice, exploring the scenario of June, an occupational therapist working in a small psychiatric day hospital in rural England:

June is an occupational therapist working with a group of young patients in a small psychiatric day hospital in a rural English village. She is approached by one patient, Alice, a girl recently discharged from hospital, where she was treated for anorexia nervosa. Alice says that she wants to talk but is unclear about what her problems are. June uses the three-stage framework and allows Alice to describe everything that is happening to her at the present time. Thus, a picture of Alice's life emerges. Out of this picture, Alice identifies two problem areas: her overdependent relationship with her mother and her lack of self-confidence. June asks her to clarify how she would like the future to be. Alice talks of greater independence from her mother and an enhanced ability to socialise and mix more easily.

Out of their discussion, June and Alice draw up a list of practical, manageable tasks for the immediate future, including:

1 Alice to set aside time to talk to her mother

2 Alice to consider the practicality of finding a flat or bedsitter near her parents' home

3 Alice and June to work out a social-skills training programme for Alice to follow with a group of other hospital day clients

4 Alice to attend a weekend workshop on assertiveness training at a local college.

Implementation: Help clients make it all happen

Clients need to ask themselves, 'How do I turn problem exploration, goal setting and planning into the kind of action that leads to problem-managing and opportunity-developing solutions, results, outcomes or accomplishments?' 'How do I get going and persevere until I make it all happen?' Helping is about change. Change demands effort. Figure 7.3 highlights the importance of results-focused action.

FIGURE 7.3 **The importance of ongoing client action**

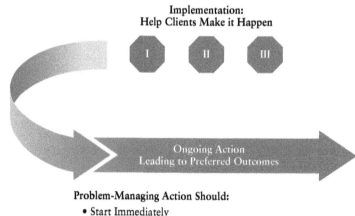

All three stages of the helping model sit on the 'Action Arrow', indicating that clients need to act on their own behalf right from the beginning of the helping process. The Action Arrow is a strong reminder that all three stages of the helping process are about outcomes and the impact these outcomes have on clients' lives.

The bias towards action outlined in Chapter 2 must permeate every stage and every task of the helping process. Stage I is about issues in a client's past and present that call for change. Stages II and III are about planning for change – setting goals and drawing up plans to achieve these goals – not constructive change itself. Stages I, II, III, and their nine tasks, all revolve around planning for change, not change itself. Talking about problems and opportunities, discussing goals and figuring out strategies for accomplishing goals are just so much blah, blah, blah without goal-accomplishing action. Change does not emerge magically from therapy; it is hard work. But, as we shall see in subsequent chapters, each stage and task of the process can promote problem-managing and opportunity-developing action right from the beginning.

The need to incorporate action into planning and planning into action will be emphasised throughout this book. Clients may need to think about how they maintain their momentum to change. The 'little actions' needed to get the change process moving at the very beginning of the helping process will be noted and illustrated. Some clients may be better suited to smaller goals to maintain their motivation levels.

FLEXIBILITY IN THE USE OF THE PROBLEM-MANAGEMENT PROCESS

Obliquity is the title of a book about, broadly speaking, problem management and opportunity development written by the British economist John Kay (2011). His thesis is this: problem management, especially the kind that involves changing human behaviour, is best pursued indirectly rather than linearly. As Kay points out, we rarely know enough about the 'moving parts' of important problems to tackle them head-on. Problem management evolves; it is iterative. People are not really that good at linear thinking, especially when involved in messy problem situations. Emotions add to the confusion. An overly direct and linear change process, he says, blinds people to discovering facts that contradict their assumptions. Therefore, logic and linearity can stand in the way of common sense and the best kind of intuition. The best solutions to problems often emerge as we try to sift through possibilities, while logic and linearity sometimes keep us locked into solutions we prefer rather than ones that will really work. Kay's advice: Don't disregard logic, but use it with caution.

The logic of problem management presented in these pages might suggest to some that change can be pursued in a prescriptive linear or direct fashion. After all, *The Skilled Helper* process talks about 'stages' and 'tasks', and assigns linear coding – I, II, III and A, B, C, respectively – to stages and tasks within each stage. Add in the Action Arrow and there are ten tasks nicely packaged. Indeed, there *is* a kind of linear logic to this process, but this logic should never be overstated because the logic of problem management is useful only to the degree it serves the needs of clients. As Kay notes, don't confuse logic with truth. To sum up, don't be fooled by the logic of the problem-management process outlined in these pages. Don't impose it on clients. Let clients' needs guide you in helping them. Therefore, in subsequent chapters you will be exposed to ten different 'tasks' or 'moves', that is, ten different ways of helping clients move towards life-enhancing outcomes. The trick is to learn to use these 'moves' instinctively and wisely at the service of your clients. That said, a number of points about flexibility need to be made.

Clients start and proceed differently

Any stage or task of the helping process can be the entry point. For instance, Client A might start with something that he tried to do to solve a problem but that did not work – 'I threatened to quit if they didn't give me a leave of absence, but it backfired. They told me to leave.' The starting point is a failed strategy. Client B might start with what she believes she wants but does not have – 'I need a boyfriend who will take me as I am. Joe keeps trying to redo me.' Stage II is her entry point. Client C might start with the roots of his problem situation – 'I don't think I've ever got over being abused by my uncle.' Stage I is the entry point. Client D might announce that she really has no problems but is still vaguely dissatisfied with her life – 'I don't know. Everyone tells me I've got a great life, but something's missing.' The implication here is that she has not been seizing the kind of opportunities that could make her happy. Opportunity rather than problem is the starting point.

Clients engage in each stage and task differently

Take, for example, clients' stories. Some clients spill out their stories all at once. Others 'leak' bits and pieces of their story throughout the helping process. Still others tell only those parts that put them in a good light. Most clients talk about problems rather than opportunities. Because clients do not always present all their problems at once in neat packages, it is impossible to work through Stage I completely before moving on to Stages II and III. It is not even advisable to do so. Some clients don't even understand their problems until they begin talking about what they want but don't have. Others need to engage in some kind of remedial action before they can adequately define the problem situation. That is, action sometimes precedes understanding. If some supposedly problem-solving action is not successful, then the counsellor helps the client learn from it and return to the tasks of clarifying the problem or opportunity and then setting some realistic goals. Take the case of Andreas.

> Andreas, a first-year university student in London, came to the student counselling services with a variety of interpersonal and somatic complaints. He felt attracted to a number of women on his university campus but did very little to become involved with them. After exploring this issue briefly, he said to the counsellor, 'Well, I just have to go out and do it.' Two months later he returned and said that his experiment had been a disaster. He had gone out with a few women, but the chemistry never seemed right. Then he did meet someone he liked quite a bit. They went out a couple of times, but the third time he called, she said that she didn't want to see him anymore. When he asked why, she muttered vaguely about his being too preoccupied with himself and ended the conversation. He felt so miserable he returned to the counselling centre. He and the counsellor took another look at his social life. This time, however, he had some experiences to probe. He wanted to explore this 'chemistry thing' and his reaction to being described as 'too preoccupied with himself'.

Andreas put into practice Weick's (1979) dictum that chaotic action is sometimes preferable to orderly inactivity. Once he acted, he learned a few things about himself. Some of these lessons proved to be painful, but he now had a better chance of examining his interpersonal style much more concretely.

Because the stages and tasks of the process intermingle, clients will often move back and forth between them

Often two or more tasks or even two stages of the process merge into one another. For instance, clients can name parts of a problem situation, set goals and develop strategies to achieve them in the same session. New and more substantial concerns arise while goals are being set, and the process moves back to an earlier, exploratory stage. Helping is seldom a linear event. In discussing a troubled relationship with a friend, one client said something like this:

> Every time I try to be nice to her, she throws it back in my face. So who says being more considerate is the answer? Maybe my problem is that I'm a pushover, not the self-centred brute she makes me out to be. Maybe I'm being a pushover with you and you're letting me do it. Maybe it's time for me to start looking out for my own interests – you know, my own agenda rather than trying to make myself fit into everyone else's plans. I need to take a closer look at the person I want to be in my relationships with others.

Look carefully. In these few sentences the client mentions a failed action strategy, questions a previously set goal, hints at a new problem, suggests a difficulty with the helping relationship itself, offers, at least generically, a different approach to managing his problem and recasts the problem as an opportunity to develop a more solid interpersonal style. Your challenge is to make sense of clients' entry points and guide them through whatever stage or task that will help them move towards problem-managing and opportunity-developing action.

Flexibility is not mere randomness or chaos

Focus and direction in helping are also essential. Letting clients wander around in the morass of problem situations under the guise of flexibility leads nowhere. The structure of the problem-management helping process is the very foundation for flexibility; it is the underlying 'system' that keeps helping from being a set of random events. In the light of the geography metaphor mentioned earlier, the stages and tasks of the problem-management process are orientation devices. At its best, the helping framework is a shared map that helps clients participate more fully in the helping process. They, too, need to know where they are going. Flexibility in clients' behaviour and attitudes needs to be nurtured within the therapeutic relationship. Dryden (2018) states that 'flexibility is the first major feature of [his] clinical practice' (p. vi).

STAGES OF CHANGE AND CLIENT READINESS FOR CHANGE

The problem-management process can be described in terms of the natural stages of change and what clients think, feel and do at each stage. Yankelovich (1992) offered a seven-step process. Prochaska and colleagues (Norcross, Krebs & Prochaska, 2011; Prochaska & DiClemente, 2005; Prochaska & Norcross, 2010), seeing helping as facilitating client change, have developed a five-stage process of both client-mediated and helper-assisted change that many helpers find useful. The five stages are pre-contemplation, contemplation, preparation, action and maintenance. Both models are forms of the problem-management process and both provide insights regarding a client's readiness for change. What follows is my reworked combination of these two models:

1   **Unawareness**. In this stage the person is either unaware that he or she has a problem, or is only vaguely aware, or if aware, has no intention of doing anything about it. Sunil says to his flat neighbours who are complaining about the noise he and his mates make late at night, 'It's your problem, not mine. Take some sleeping pills.' Clarissa's friends get on her case for overeating, even though she has a heart condition, saying, 'With your heart the way it is, eating all that fatty food and smoking heavily is going to kill you, not later but sooner.' Resistance to recognising or dealing with a problem is the hallmark of this stage. There is no readiness for change.

2   **Initial awareness**. In this stage clients become aware of an issue or a set of issues, but readiness for change is still very low. For instance, after a number of disputes over household finances, a couple develop a vague awareness of dissatisfaction with the relationship itself. Or consider Clive. He has received two DUI (Driving under the influence) citations. A third will give him mandated prison time. He's vaguely aware that there are legal consequences lying in wait for him. The thought pops into his head from time to time. He even cuts back on his drinking a bit when he has to drive. So he has some initial awareness of possible legal consequences, but he is still unaware of the fact that he is a problem drinker.

3   **Heightened awareness**. In this stage the person knows that he or she has a problem, thinks seriously about doing something about it, but has yet to make a commitment to take action. Consider William who says, 'I know that smoking is doing me in and I've got to find a way, sooner or later, of giving it up.' He is still ambivalent about change. Although clients in this stage think that the price of change still seems too high, they move beyond mere awareness to some significant consideration of change. But serious motivation for change is still missing.

4   **Preliminary actions**. In this stage the person is on the verge of doing something about his or her problem situation or has already tried, however unsuccessfully, to do something about it. The actions taken are often feeble or symbolic. William says, 'You know, I'm down to eight cigarettes a day. From two packs!' In this stage the person may be doing such things as trying to avoid temptation and some planning, however meagre, for change.

5   **Urgency**. A sense of urgency develops, especially as the underlying problem situation becomes more distressing. Take a married couple who feel the dissatisfaction with their relationship becoming more pronounced. Even small annoyances are now seen in the light of overall dissatisfaction. Or consider when Clive is stopped by an officer for a small infraction – making an illegal turn – and the officer looks up his record and says, 'I've got to breathalyse you.' Clive objects, saying, 'I haven't been drinking at all!' This incident shakes him up. Later he says to himself, 'I came this close to landing in prison.' He finally has a heightened awareness that he is a problem drinker.

6   **Search for remedies**. Clients begin to look for remedies. However implicitly or perfunctorily, they explore different strategies for managing the problem situation. For instance, clients in difficult marriages begin thinking about

complaining openly to their partners or friends, separating, getting a divorce, instituting subtle acts of revenge, having an affair, going to a marriage counsellor, seeing a minister, unilaterally withdrawing from the relationship in one way or another and so forth. The parties may try out one or more of these remedies without evaluating their cost or consequences.

7   **Estimation of costs.** The costs of pursuing different remedies begin to become apparent. Someone in a troubled relationship might say to herself: 'Being open and honest hasn't really worked. If I continue to put my cards on the table, I'll have to go through the agony of confrontation, denial, argument, counter accusations and who knows what else.' Or he might say, 'Simply withdrawing from the relationship in small ways has been painful. What would I do if I were to go out on my own?' Or, 'What would happen to the children?' At this point clients often back away from dealing with the problem situation directly because there is no cost-free or painless way of dealing with it.

8   **Weighing the costs.** Because the problem situation does not go away, it is impossible to retreat completely. And so a more serious weighing of choices takes place. For instance, the costs of confronting the situation are weighed against the costs of merely withdrawing. Often, a kind of dialogue goes on in the client's mind between steps 7 and 8. 'I might have to go through the agony of a separation for the children's sake. Maybe time apart is what we need.'

9   **Rational decision.** An intellectual decision is made to accept some choice and pursue a certain course of action. 'I'm going to bring all of this up with my spouse and suggest we see a marriage counsellor.' Or, 'I'm going to get on with my life, find other things to do, and let the marriage go where it will.'

10   **Rational-emotional decision.** However, a merely intellectual decision is often not enough to drive action. So the heart joins the head, as it were, in the decision. One spouse might finally say, 'I've had enough of this! I'm leaving. It won't be comfortable, but it's better than living like this.' The other might say, 'It is unfair to both of us to go on like this; and it's certainly not good for the children', and this drives the decision to seek help, even if it means going alone. Decisions driven by convictions and emotion are more likely to be translated into action.

11   **Serious action.** In this stage individuals are involved in life-enhancing change and actually put time and effort into modifying their dysfunctional behaviour. Change at this stage tends to be visible and is recognised by others. Modification of the undesirable behaviour to an acceptable standard through systematic effort is the hallmark of action.

12   **Maintenance.** In this stage the person consolidates his or her gains and works to avoid relapse. This stage can go on for a long time, even a lifetime, for instance, for the person who fights the urge to smoke every day. A married couple might continually look for ways to 'reinvent' their marriage. Clive not only stops drinking but also joins Alcoholics Anonymous (AA) to make sure that he stays dry by attending a meeting every day. 'I can't afford another drink.'

13   **Relapse.** Of course, people are prone to relapses. There is a difference between a minor lapse, a relapse and a total collapse into the old way. Clive is out with some friends who have made fun of his being in Alcoholics Anonymous, saying such things as, 'I didn't know they accepted children.' He gets drunk, but his friends take him home. The person can learn from lapses. The next morning Clive says to himself, 'I thought I could go out with my drinking buddies and not drink. How stupid can I get!' A relapse or total collapse can mean moving back to a previous stage or even starting the whole process over again. Clive can't afford this scenario and returns to Alcoholics Anonymous.

If this process is in the back of your mind, it can help you meet clients 'where they are' and tailor the problem-management process to their needs. But remember, this is a conceptual framework to help you work with clients. Becoming preoccupied with a framework is a disservice to clients.

INTEGRATIVE ECLECTICISM: THE ONGOING SEARCH FOR BEST PRACTICE

Every form of therapy deals with clients' experiences, cognitions, internal and external behaviour and emotion. In that sense every form of therapy is a cognitive-behavioural-emotive approach to helping. That is certainly the case with the problem-management process presented in these pages. It is both a process that is inherent in every form of therapy and a valid approach to treatment in and of itself. However, no one approach to therapy will ever be the 'last word' in helping for at least two reasons, perhaps three. First, ongoing research into both human behaviour and the helping process will always either challenge coveted ideas about clients and therapy or complement ideas that have stood the test of time. Second, effective helpers will always be looking for better ways of delivering their services. Third, clients will always expect, knowingly or unknowingly, best practice from their helpers.

Client-focused eclecticism and integration

Many experienced helpers, even when they choose one specific school or approach to helping, often borrow methods and techniques from other approaches. Some helpers, without declaring explicit allegiance to any particular school, stitch together their own approach to helping. This borrowing and stitching is called 'eclecticism' (Corey, 2012; Jensen, Bergin & Greaves, 1990; Lazarus, Beutler & Norcross, 1992; Norcross & Goldfried, 2005; Prochaska & Norcross, 2001). In one study, some 40 per cent of helpers said that eclecticism was their primary approach to helping (Milan, Montgomery & Rogers, 1994). Effective eclecticism, however, must be more than a random borrowing of ideas and techniques from here and there. There must be some integrating framework to give coherence to the entire process; that is, to be effective, eclecticism must be systematic (Corey, 2012; Norcross & Goldfried, 2005).

Cooper and McLeod (2011) and Dryden (2018) see themselves as going a step beyond integrative eclecticism in their 'pluralistic' approach to helping. Pluralistic practice is based on this pluralistic 'perspective', that is, the 'belief that different clients are likely to benefit from different things at different points in time, and that therapists should work closely with clients to help them identify what they want from therapy and how they might get it' (Cooper & McLeod, 2011, p. 12). Practice is based on the pluralistic perspective and focuses on the dialogue between client and helper to identify goals, tasks and methods drawn from a variety of therapeutic orientations. Keeping the client in 'the driver's seat' is central to their approach. Involving the client fully in the clinical decision-making process within therapy is 'practically sound, ethically desirable and liberating for the client' (Dryden, 2018, p. vii).

Their integrating framework consists of the three overlapping domains of goals, tasks and methods of therapy; terms, as you will notice, at the heart of problem management. As I see it, then, Cooper and McLeod, Duncan and colleagues (Duncan, 2011; Duncan *et al.*, 2010), Dryden (2018), and Egan all sit in the same church, but perhaps in different pews.

The problem-management framework as a 'browser'

How do helpers go about borrowing from a range of therapeutic approaches and stitching them together? The problem-management process in this book can be used as a tool – a 'browser', to use an internet term – for mining, organising and evaluating concepts and techniques that work for clients, no matter what their origin. There are examples of this throughout the book.

- **Mining**. First, helpers can use the problem-management model to mine any given school or approach, 'digging out' whatever is useful without having to accept everything that is offered. The philosophy, communication skills, stages and tasks of the model serve as tools for identifying methods and techniques that will serve the needs of clients.

- **Organising**. Second, because the problem-management model is organised by stages and tasks, it can be used to organise the methods and techniques that have been mined from the rich literature on helping. For instance, a number of contemporary therapies have elaborated excellent techniques for helping clients identify blind spots and develop new perspectives on the problem situations they face. As we have seen (Chapters 5 and 6), these techniques are organised around the concepts of 'identifying blind spots' and 'developing new perspectives'.

- **Evaluating**. Because the problem-management model is pragmatic and focuses on outcomes of helping, it can be used to evaluate the vast number of helping techniques that are constantly being devised. The model enables helpers to ask in what way a technique or method contributes to the 'bottom line', that is, to outcomes that serve the needs of clients.

- **Incorporating**. Finally, the best ideas can be incorporated into the helper's ever-evolving framework – replacing outmoded ideas, correcting flawed ideas, enhancing viable ones and generally enhancing the helping process at the service of clients. Every edition of this book has done precisely that. As I mentioned earlier, sometimes people ask me, 'Why are you doing a new edition? It's a good book just as it is.' The question still mystifies me.

- **The client as decision maker**. Duncan and his colleagues, Cooper and McLeod, and I insist on the client as decision maker. Clients have to be intimately involved in all the decisions made throughout the helping process. Perhaps I go further when I talk about 'nudging' and inviting clients to self-challenge (see Chapter 5). Some would see this as 'fudging', while I see it is an essential service to clients.

The problem-management and opportunity-development model can serve these functions because it is an open-systems model, not a closed school. That's why I now refer to it as a framework rather than a model. Although it takes a stand on how counsellors may help their clients, it is open to being corroborated, complemented and challenged by any other framework, approach, model or school of helping. The needs of clients, not the egos of model builders, must remain central to the helping process. Our clients deserve 'best practice', whatever its source.

'HOW ARE WE DOING?' – ONGOING EVALUATION OF THE HELPING PROCESS

In the light of the importance of feedback discussed in Chapter 1, how do helpers use the problem-management and opportunity-development framework to evaluate what is happening with each client? By making each case a 'mini-experiment' in itself. In psychological research there has been a long history of what are called N=1 or single-case research designs both to evaluate practice and to conduct research (Blampied, 2000; Borckardt, Nash, Murphy, Moore, Shaw & O'Neil, 2008; Elliott, 2002; Hilliard, 1993; Kazdin, 2010; Lundervold & Belwood, 2000; Sharpley, 2007). It's not enough to know that helping in general works. We have to know how well it is working in each case. Jay Lebow (2002) puts it this way: 'A clinician can carry out with any individual client a method researchers call the "single-case design" – which is simply a more formal and systematic way of documenting what he or she does anyway' (p. 63). He (like Duncan, 2011) recommends using questionnaires to document the changes that occur, both in therapy and in the client's day-to-day life. Bangert and Baumberger (2005) argue that although N=1 is the most relevant design for practising counsellors, few are adept in using it.

In many helping models, evaluation is presented as the last step in the model. However, if evaluation occurs only at the end, it is too late. As Mash and Hunsley (1993) noted, early detection of what is going wrong in the helping process is needed to prevent failure. They claimed that an early-detection framework should be theory-based, ongoing, practical and sensitive to whatever new perspectives might emerge from the helping process. The problem-management and opportunity-development framework outlined in this chapter fills the bill. It is a tool to check progress throughout the helping process. As we shall see, it provides criteria for helper effectiveness, for client participation and for assessing outcomes.

UNDERSTANDING AND DEALING WITH THE SHADOW SIDE OF HELPING MODELS

This book outlines a framework for helping that is rational, linear and systematic. What good is that, you well might ask, in a world that is often irrational, non-linear and chaotic? One answer is that rational frameworks help clients bring much-needed discipline and order into their chaotic lives, especially when these frameworks are culturally flexible. Effective helpers do not apologise for using such frameworks, but they also make sure that their humanity permeates them. Besides the broad shadow-side themes mentioned earlier, there are a number of specific shadow-side pitfalls in the use of any helping model.

No model or framework

Some helpers 'wing it'. They have no consistent, integrated model of treatment that they have made their own. Some use a version of the problem-management process outlined in these pages but do not seem to know that that is what they are doing. Professional training programmes often offer a wide variety of approaches to helping drawn from the 'major brands' on offer. If helpers-to-be leave such programmes knowing a great deal about different approaches but lacking an integrated approach for themselves, then they need to develop one quickly. The problem-management/opportunity-development framework is a good place to start because it is inevitably at the core of other helping models. But remember, research shows that helpers need to have a method of treatment in which they both believe and are competent and which they share with clients.

Confusing and needless multiplication of helping models

Institute a computer search and you will soon discover that there are dozens, if not hundreds, of methods or treatments or approaches to helping, all of them claiming a high degree of success. While it is important to have a thorough understanding of the disorders you are trying to help clients manage, the thought of multiple models of almost every known psychological disorder is a thought too far. Likewise, while it is important to understand the developmental tasks and challenges of various age groups, having a specific model of therapy for each age group and sometimes subgroups within each major group from childhood through old age is, I might say, a 'stretch'. Include helping approaches around such psychological terms as 'emotions', 'mindfulness', 'motivation', 'strengths' and the like, and it is no wonder the number soars into the hundreds. Don't get me wrong. I am not insinuating that there is nothing of value in what these authors have to say; far from it. But there must be a better way of distilling and organising the research findings and clinical wisdom of our profession.

Fads and forgetfulness

The helping professions are not immune to fads. A fad is an insight or a technique that would have some merit were it to be integrated into some overriding model or framework of helping. Instead it is marketed on its own as the central, if not the only meaningful, intervention needed. A fad need not be something new; it can be the 'rediscovery' of a truth or a technique that has not found its proper place in the helping toolkit. Rachman (2008) puts it well: 'The market for ideas – like the market for shares – always overshoots. Ideas become fashionable and get pushed to their logical conclusions and beyond, as their backers succumb to "irrational exuberance". Then comes the crash' (p. 13). Helpers become enamoured of these ideas and techniques for a while and then abandon them. There will always be 'hot topics' in helping. Note them and integrate whatever you find useful into a comprehensive approach to your clients. The proponents of many new approaches to helping make outrageous claims. Don't ignore them, but take the claims with a grain of salt and test the approach.

The opposite – what might be called 'irrational forgetfulness' – is also a problem. Really good ideas are highlighted for a while, then shoved into a drawer rather than being further developed and incorporated into psychological practice. There is little talk in the helping literature these days about the 'laws of human behaviour' (Watson & Tharp, 2007) based on an understanding of incentives, rewards and punishment. 'Cognitive dissonance' is seldom heard, though this useful concept has recently been resurrected by a popular book (Tavris & Aronson, 2007).

Failure to share the helping model

When it comes to sharing the helping process itself, some counsellors are reluctant to let the client know what the process is all about. Of course, helpers who 'fly by the seat of their pants' can't tell clients what it's all about because they don't know what it's all about themselves. Still others seem to think that knowledge of helping processes is secret or sacred or dangerous and should not be communicated to the client, even though there is no evidence to support such beliefs (Duncan *et al.*, 2010). If the client is to be in the driver's seat, he or she has to have a fundamental grasp of the helping process and be encouraged to make decisions about and within that framework.

Rigid applications of treatment methods

Some helpers buy into a model early on and then ignore subsequent challenges or alterations to the model. They stop being learners. The 'purity' of the model becomes more important than the needs of clients. Other helpers, especially beginners, apply a useful helping model too rigidly. They drag clients in a linear way through the model even though that is not what clients need. All of this adds up to excessive control. Effective models effectively used are liberating rather than controlling.

Chaos in defining competence

In Chapters 1 and 2 we presented some evidence-based suggestions on what a competent helper looks like. This was the short form. The professional long form looks quite different. A Special Section of seven highly academic articles on the *assessment* of helper competence fills most of the pages of an issue of *Professional Psychology: Research and Practice* (2007, 38, 441–537). In these articles the enormous ambition of setting up a professional 'cradle to grave' assessment system covering all helping-related competencies, including 'knowledge, skills, dispositions, self-perceptions, motives and beliefs-attitudes' (Kaslow and associates, 2007, p. 443), is outlined.

At times they present helping almost as an adjunct to the medical profession. But assessing the competence of a gall bladder surgeon is one thing; assessing the competence of a marriage counsellor is quite a different thing. The 15 guiding principles for the assessment of competence are brutally thorough and highly academic. Lichtenberg and his associates (2007) outline some of the challenges to creating a picture of the competent helper and conclude that 'achieving consensus within the [helping] profession and across its diversity of specialties, orientations and models on the necessary competencies for professional practice is a critical first step' (p. 478). Professionally, it seems that we are still at the starting gate. Although there is some kind of broad consensus that helping in the main helps and that there is a set of 'common factors' that contributes to successful helping, practitioners are divided as to just what competence is in helping relationships.

Failure to grow with the profession

I remember the first time I gave a talk to a group of experienced helpers. I soon found out that they knew little about the research going on within the helping professions. I was surprised. Even a bit shocked. But let me start with a caveat. For all I knew, these practitioners may well have been very successful at what they were doing and my shock was more related to my being an academic twit. However, one would think that staying in touch with relevant research in both the theory and practice of helping would be high on the list of helpers who wanted to increase their competence, but this does not seem to be the case. Boisvert and Faust (2006), in a study of over 180 practitioners, found a disconnect between what they think the research says and what it actually says. Many practitioners think that much, if not most, of the research is irrelevant to their practice.

But another study made me think. Cook and her colleagues (Cook *et al.*, 2009) found that 'the greatest influences on psychotherapists' willingness to learn a new treatment were its potential for integration with the therapy they were already providing and its endorsement by therapists they respected. Clinicians were more often willing to continue to use a new treatment when they were able to effectively and enjoyably conduct the therapy and when their clients liked the therapy and reported improvement' (Cook *et al.*, 2009, p. 671). That is, many practitioners may well look sceptically at the current flood of research and then take a more common-sense approach.

The ethics involved in the training of helpers

Finally, but no less in importance, are ethical issues in the training of helpers. Barnett (2008), as editor of a Focus on Ethics section of *Professional Psychology: Research and Practice*, oversees three short articles on this 'hot potato' issue in the training of helpers. Not everyone who is accepted into a doctoral programme in the helping professions turns out to be a winner. Some trainees do not achieve the basic levels of competence required of someone who wants to be a helper. Some trainees are high academic achievers but still lack even initial professional competence. Some trainees arrive with or develop behavioural problems or disorders that stand in the way of becoming effective helpers. Some trainees do not pass the ethical behaviour test.

What to do? I have witnessed the 'hot potato' problem first-hand. Years ago these issues were often ignored. In these days of accountability such issues are difficult (but not impossible) to ignore, so responsibility for doing something about them is shuttled around. That means that some people who should never be helpers slip through the cracks. The articles in Barnett's edited section suggest systemic ways of managing the problem. This very real human problem will, hopefully, be managed better, but, like many human problems, never fully solved. Better selection of candidates is the starting point. But, of course, in selecting candidates we run into the false positives and the false negatives problem in the beginning and possible lawsuits in the middle and end.

CHAPTER 8
STAGE I: HELPING CLIENTS EXPLORE THEIR CONCERNS AND TELL THEIR STORIES

Chapter Contents

- The Wider Use of I-B: Rising to the Challenge

- Task I-C: The Right Story

- Principles for Helping Clients Work on Issues that Make a Difference

- The Wider Use of I-C: Making the Right Choices

A BRIEF INTRODUCTION TO STAGE I

Clients come to helpers because they need help in managing their lives more effectively. Stage I illustrates three ways in which counsellors can help clients understand themselves, their problem situations and their unused opportunities with a view to managing them more effectively. Counsellors help clients (1) tell their stories, (2) reframe their stories, develop new, more useful perspectives and begin thinking about new, more constructive ways of acting, and (3) stay focused on the key issues and concerns that will make a difference in their lives. These three tasks are illustrated in Figure 8.1.

FIGURE 8.1 **The tasks of Stage I**

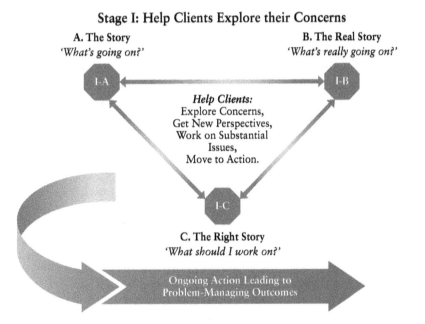

Even though these tasks are described separately, in actual helping sessions, as described in Chapter 7, they are intermingled. The two-headed arrows that connect A, B and C in Figure 8.1 highlight the fact that it is not a question of moving from the first to the second to the third task in any rigid sequential way.

How the tasks of Stage I pervade the entire helping process

These three tasks are not restricted to Stage I for the following reasons:

- *First,* clients don't tell all of their stories at the beginning of the helping process. Often the full story 'leaks out' over time.

- *Second*, new perspectives are needed at every stage of the helping process – telling stories, choosing problem-managing goals, developing plans and implementing programmes. Blind spots can appear at any stage of the helping process. Helpful new perspectives are always welcome.

- *Third*, the word 'right' is important. The entire helping process is a search for value for clients. You can help them ask themselves 'right'-related questions throughout: 'Am I working on the *right* issues? Am I setting the *right* goals? Have I drawn up the *right* plan for accomplishing these goals? Am I implementing my plan in the *right* way?' 'Right' here means what is right for the client, not what fits the helper's theories or preferred approach to treatment: 'Does it fit me, my resources, my personal culture?' Clients are the decision makers, but you can and sometimes should invite them to consider the implications of the decisions they are making.

Client-focused assessment

Stage I of the helping process can be seen as the assessment stage (Hood & Johnson, 2007) – finding out what's going wrong, what opportunities remain undeveloped, what resources are not being used. Client-centred assessment means helping clients understand themselves, find out 'what's going on' with their lives, see what they have been ignoring and make sense from the messiness of their lives. Assessment in this sense is not something helpers do to clients. Rather, it is a kind of practical learning in which both client and helper collaborate. Other forms of assessment such as psychological testing and applying psychiatric diagnostic categories may or may not be useful, but they are beyond the scope of this book.

Linking to action

Linking the problem-management process to action should start early in the helping process. Early gains are a sign that therapy is headed in the right direction and will be successful. Helping clients connect what they learn from their work in A, B and C to the Action Arrow is critical. Right from the beginning, help clients act on what they are learning. Consider Sal, who has been severely burned and whose initial reaction is to withdraw from people. In the light of his despair, he needs what Auerbach, Salick and Fine (2006) call 'engagement', that is, choosing to go on, finding some kind of inner strength, being willing to reach out to people who care and who can help, and being open to finding a way of dealing with the trauma, no matter what its dimensions might be. If you were sitting at Sal's bedside, what would be going through your mind and what might you do to help the patient open up to be helped and become active in the helping process?

Clients do not need 'grand plans' before they can act on their own behalf. In Sal's case, the therapist talked with the burn centre's chaplain who brought one of the centre's previous patients with him. The chaplain has seen it all and the recovered patient has experienced it all. Sal opened up. He talked about all the 'desperate' thoughts racing through his mind. The recovered patient said, 'I spent a lot of time chasing those demons away.' Sal asks, 'Is there a way out of this?' The recovered patient answers, 'Sal, you are the way out of this.' 'Can I see you again?' Sal asks. 'Of course' is the answer. Sal reaches out and touches him. Sal's telling part of his story to a stranger, his request for a return visit and his reaching out are actions, perhaps small actions, but actions nevertheless, and hopefully the beginning of a flow. He's beginning to learn that he cannot take this journey alone. If Sal is to recover his life, there are a lot of things he must do bit by bit over time. Formal and informal helpers can help him step by step.

In Stage I, the current picture, counsellors help clients spell out the issues, concerns, difficulties or problems they are facing. What are the problems, issues, concerns and undeveloped opportunities with which Tumi needs to grapple? As we shall see here and in the chapters that follow, each stage is divided into three interrelated tasks. Like the stages themselves, the tasks are not steps in a mechanistic, 'now do this' sense. In Stage I the tasks are activities that help clients spell out their concerns as clearly as possible with neither too much nor too little detail. These three tasks help clients develop answers to three questions:

1 'What's going on in my life? What are my main concerns?'

2 'As I look more closely, what's really going on in my life? What new perspectives will help me deal with my concerns?'

3 'What should I be working on? Which issues, if handled well, will make a real difference in my life?'

TASK I-A: HELP CLIENTS TELL THEIR STORIES

Denise Sloan (2010) reviews the evidence that links self-disclosure in various settings, including psychotherapy, to psychological well-being. People in general tend to want to talk about themselves when things are good and when things are bad. She goes on to say, 'In addition to facilitating social bonds, self-disclosure also produces a wide variety of health benefits' (p. 212). Strange to say, there is more research on the benefits and perils of therapist self-disclosure than on the pluses and minuses of client self-disclosure. Ethical considerations of boundary crossing and violations have been explored. Danzer (2019) explores some of the negative experiences of disclosure and argues for practitioner training in this area. Perhaps this points to the need of the helping professions to focus more on clients and placing them at the centre than on modalities of treatment. The helping literature does focus attention on clients' narratives, which is a literary rather than a social science term. Most clients do not think in terms of 'life narratives', but they do have practical concerns about self-disclosure. In this chapter we will consider the first task of Stage I (I-A), that is, helping clients tell their stories, and then Tasks B and C.

The importance of helping clients tell their stories well should not be underestimated. As Pennebaker (1995) has noted, 'An important … feature of therapy is that it allows individuals to translate their experiences into words. The disclosure process itself, then, may be as important as any feedback the client receives from the therapist' (p. 3). Much has been written about clients' reluctance to talk about themselves, but Farber, Berano and Capobianco (2004) outline the bright side of client self-disclosure:

> "Most clients feel that therapy is a safe place to disclose, made especially so by the goodness of the thera-peutic relationship; that the disclosure process initially generates shame and anticipatory anxiety but ultimately engenders feelings of safety, pride, and authenticity; that keeping secrets inhibits the work of therapy, whereas disclosing produces a sense of relief from physical as well as emotional tension; that disclosures in therapy facilitate subsequent disclosures to one's therapist as well as to family members and friends; and that thera-pists should actively pursue material that is difficult to disclose." (p. 340)

Of course, other research has shown that fear of self-disclosure is a leading factor in not seeking therapy (Vogel & Wester, 2003). So it is important for you to discern whether the client you are helping is eager to engage in self-disclosure or fears it. Farber and his associates (Farber, Berano & Capobianco, 2004) note that many clients may not only need a helper's encouragement to speak about difficult issues but also welcome and appreciate counsellors' efforts to help them. See Farber's (2006) book *Self-Disclosure in Psychotherapy* and Danzer's (2019) book *Therapist self-disclosure: An evidence-based guide for practitioners* for a comprehensive overview of both client and helper self-disclosure.

Let's turn our attention back to Tumi and Carlos in I-A. We have seen bits and pieces of this case to illustrate issues highlighted in Chapters 3 through 6. However, it would be useful for you to review the basics of the case presented in Chapter 3. In subsequent chapters we will see the case more systematically in terms of the stages and tasks of the helping process.

Carlos knows that if he can help Tumi get a reasonably clear picture of herself, her problems and her unused opportunities, she will have a better chance of doing something about them. Using the communication skills outlined in Part II, he helps Tumi tell her story and review her concerns.

When Carlos begins the session by saying, 'Well, Tumi, what's going on? How can I help?', Tumi responds by saying that she's not there to rehash the accident and its immediate consequences, although she admits that she is still working it through. As she talks, however, she realises that this is not going to be as easy as she thought. Talking about the accident would be relatively easy, but talking about the fact that she has come to realise that she is broadly dissatisfied with the direction of her life seems much more daunting. This is uncharted territory. Furthermore, she is not used to sharing her concerns with anyone, not even with her parents. She also wonders whether she should have chosen a woman as her counsellor. Up to this point she has been able to keep all her problems under control but begins to wonder whether talking about them to a stranger will 'cause the dam to burst'. In the midst of her ruminations Carlos suggests, 'A bit of background about you and your family might help.'

(Continued)

This sounds good to Tumi. It's relatively safe. So through the give-and-take of the conversation the details of the background outlined earlier emerge.

Then in the rest of this session and the next one a week later she moves on to her more immediate concerns. She is worried about her father who has never got over the death of his son, the loss of his career or his exile from his country. He lives in the United Kingdom but has never felt British. His business is faltering because the economy is sputtering and for a couple of years cars have not been selling. As the economy picks up, car sales begin to rise in the industry, but his business for some reason stagnates. He has become more and more dependent on his daughter, although he can't seem to admit this either to himself or to her. And because he does not take care of himself, he has health problems. He does not get check-ups. He became disoriented one day, was taken to the hospital and then released. The doctor said that he might have had a mini-stroke.

Besides worrying about her father, Tumi has her own set of issues. Although in many ways fully British, she feels she has allowed herself to remain a captive of 'old country' cultural norms. During her trip to South Africa she had conversations with young people who seemed to be much more 'culturally free' than she was. In her eyes they seemed to suffer from some social and financial constraints but seemed to know what they wanted. In the United Kingdom she certainly does not feel like an outsider, but she knows that she is not leading a typical 'British life' either. She's not even sure that she wants to. She expresses some hostility towards her two cousins, at one time saying, 'These guys', while shaking her head. From her point of view they have bought into British materialism too quickly. And, in her view, it has not really made them happy.

The young people she met in South Africa seemed to have a rich social life. Not a wild one, but a rich one. She feels that she is missing out on something. These feelings have recently become more intense because she met a man she likes through work and has met him a few times for coffee. She has not told her parents anything about this, because she knows that they would not approve. She feels guilty about this. She has been suffering from insomnia and headaches for the past few months but has always put on such a good face that no one suspects. She talks about all of these things in a very matter-of-fact way.

These are some of the issues Tumi brings up. As she becomes more comfortable with Carlos and with herself as client, she talks more freely. But there are still some hesitancies. Carlos realises that clients' stories don't come tumbling out all at once in a neat package. Stories sometimes emerge or even 'dribble out' over the entire course of the helping relationship. He also wonders whether at some point it would be wise to revisit the accident and the story of her recovery. But she is in the driver's seat.

Clients differ radically in their ability to talk about themselves and their problem situations. Reluctance to disclose oneself within counselling sessions is often a window into the client's inability to share himself or herself with others and to be reasonably assertive in the social settings of everyday life. If this is the case, then one of the goals of the entire counselling process is to help clients develop the skills, confidence and courage they need to share themselves appropriately.

GUIDELINES FOR HELPING CLIENTS TELL THEIR STORIES

These are guidelines, not hard and fast rules. Some of the guidelines and examples here and in subsequent chapters include the kind of 'nudging' and invitations to self-challenge discussed in Chapter 5. Helpers have to make a judgement about invitations to self-challenge based not on their theories but the needs of clients. Clients' needs take precedence over helping models. That said, there are a number of principles that can guide you as you help clients tell their stories. Hanna (2002) has developed a list of 'precursors', which 'taken together form a comprehensive picture of how people change and why they do not' (p. 6). This is Hanna's version of the readiness-for-change list outlined in Chapter 7. His 'precursors' include, on the part of the client, a sense of necessity ('I've got to do something about this'), a willingness to experience anxiety or difficulty, awareness of the main factors in the problem situation, a desire to confront the problem, effort directed towards change, hope for a better future, and social support. Hanna calls these conditions 'regulators of change' in the sense that 'the more they are present in a person, the more quickly change will occur, and in some cases, the deeper the change will be in the psyche of the person' (p. 6). As clients tell their stories, you can listen and probe for these regulators and even help clients develop them. Here, then, is a set of guidelines.

Learn to work with all styles of storytelling

As mentioned in Part II, there are both individual and cultural differences in clients' willingness to talk about themselves. Both affect storytelling. Some clients are highly verbal and quite willing to reveal almost everything about themselves at the first sitting. Take the case of Martina.

Martina, 27, asks a counsellor in private practice for an appointment to discuss 'a number of issues'. Martina is both verbal and willing to talk, and her story comes tumbling out in rich detail. Although the helper uses the skills of attending, listening, sharing highlights and probing, she does so sparingly. Martina is too eager to tell her story.

Although trained as a nurse, Martina is currently working in her uncle's business because of an offer she 'could not turn down'. She is doing very well financially, but she feels guilty because service to others has always been a value for her. And although she likes her current job, she also feels hemmed in by it. A year of study in Europe during college whetted her appetite for 'adventure'. She feels that she is nowhere near fulfilling the great expectations she has for herself.

She also talks about her problems with her family. Her father is dead. She has never got on well with her mother, and now that she has moved out of the house, she feels that she has abandoned her younger brother, who is 12 years younger than she is and whom she loves very much. She is afraid that her mother will 'smother' her brother with too much maternal care.

Martina is also concerned about her relationship with a man who is two years younger than she is. They have been involved with each other for about three years. He wants to get married, but she feels that she is not ready. She still has 'too many things to do' and would like to keep the arrangement they have.

This whole complex story – or at least a synopsis of it – comes tumbling out in a torrent of words. Martina feels free to skip from one topic to another. The way Martina tells her story is part of her enthusiastic style. At one point she stops, smiles and says, 'My, that's quite a bit, isn't it!'

As the helper listens to Martina, he learns a number of things about her. She is young, bright and verbal, and has many resources; she is eager and impatient; some of her problems are probably of her own making; she has some blind spots that could stand in the way of her grappling more creatively with her problems; and she has many unexplored options and many unexploited opportunities. That said, the counsellor surmises that Martina would probably make her way in life, however erratically, with no counselling at all.

Contrast that example with the following one of a man who comes to a local mental-health centre in Durban, South Africa because he feels he can no longer handle his mounting debts nor his nine-year-old son. Martina's story is full of possibilities, whereas Herman's is mainly about limitations. In both content and communication style, they are at opposite ends of the scale.

Herman is referred to the centre by a doctor in a local clinic because of his serious debt problems (he took out an easy access loan which he was then unable to pay back, and resulted in both the departure of his wife and the loss of his home) and the trouble he is having with his son. He has been divorced for about two years and is now living in a housing project on public assistance. After introductions and preliminary formalities have been taken care of, he just sits there and says nothing; he does not even look up. Because Herman offers almost nothing spontaneously, the counsellor uses a relatively large number of probes to help him tell his story. Even when the counsellor responds with empathy (including mentioning how widespread debt problems are in South Africa in general and how steps are being taken at government level to tackle it, so Herman is not alone), Herman volunteers very little. Every once in a while, tears well up in his eyes. When asked about the divorce, he says he does not want to talk about it. 'Good riddance' is all he can say about his former wife, 'she wouldn't stay with me after our finances fell apart'. Gradually, almost torturously, the story gets pieced together. Herman talks mostly about the 'trouble' his son is getting into, how uncontrollable he seems to be getting, and how helpless he [Herman] feels.

Each client is different and will approach the telling of the story in a different way. Some clients will come voluntarily; others will be sent. Some of the stories you will help clients tell will be long and detailed, others short and stark. Some will be filled with emotion; others will be told coldly, even though they are stories of terror. Some stories will be, at least at first blush, single-issue stories – 'I want to get rid of these headaches' – whereas others, like Martina's, will be multiple-issue stories. Some stories will deal with the inner world of the client almost exclusively – 'I hate myself', 'I'm depressed', 'I feel lonely' – whereas others will deal with the outer world, for instance problems with finances, work or relationships. Still others will deal with a combination of inner and outer concerns.

Some clients will tell the core story immediately, whereas others will tell a secondary story first to test your reactions. Some clients will make it clear that they trust you just because you are a helper, but you will read mistrust in the eyes of others, sometimes just because you are a helper. In all these cases, your job is to establish a working relationship with your clients and help them tell their stories as a prelude to helping them manage the problems and take advantage of the opportunities buried in those stories. A story that is brought out into the open is the starting point for possible constructive change. Often the very airing of the story is a solid first step towards a better life.

When clients like Martina pour out their stories, you may let them go on or you may insist on some kind of dialogue. If the client tells the 'whole' story in a more or less non-stop fashion, it will be impossible for you to share highlights relating to every core issue the client has brought up. But you can then help the client review the most salient points in some orderly way. For example, you might want to help the client review the core parts of the story by saying something like this: 'You've said quite a bit. Let's see if I've understood some of the main points you've made. First of all. ...' At this point the highlights you share will let the client know that you have been listening intently and that you are concerned about him or her. With clients like Herman, however, it's a different story. Those who lack the skills needed to tell their stories well or who are reluctant to do so constitute a different kind of challenge. Engaging in dialogue with them can be tough work.

Allegorical storytelling can help

Story telling has been used effectively in helping professions for a number of years. Rhiannon Crawford's text, *Storytelling in Therapy* (2004, pp. 35–36), provides an interesting discussion of how allegorical stories can be used therapeutically within psychotherapy, counselling and helping, to help clients struggling to otherwise engage in dialogue begin to tell their stories. It can be a useful way of getting reluctant clients to reveal their dilemmas and worries without telling the 'real facts' of their predicament at the outset – either they can read a selection of allegorical stories provided by the helper or they can attempt to tell their own. Hammel (2019) focuses on therapeutic storytelling and metaphors, highlighting the importance of stories in encouraging positive change in clients. Consider the following story retold by Gersie (1997). This story follows a common pattern of allegorical stories with a 'trouble' of some kind at its heart. Such stories contribute to their usefulness in therapy or education because difficulties in the management of conflict are often at the core of a client's problems, but this is something they really struggle to disclose:

The Open Door

A newly-married couple arrive in their new home. It is a dark and stormy night. Just as they are about to snuggle into bed, they hear the sound of a door flapping in the wind. They realise that in their hurry to carry the wedding gifts safely indoors, they must have forgotten to shut the door. The groom says to the bride: 'The door has been left open, hasn't it?' When she asks him to close it, he replies in anger: 'Me? Why should I? Can't you go and do it yourself?' She refuses. They haggle, urge and accuse one another for a while but to no avail. Neither of them wants to go downstairs and close the front door. However, as this is their first wedding night, they decide that they must find a solution to their problem. They agree to stay in their room, go to bed and to keep silent. The first one to speak will have to go downstairs to close the front door. They believe that their wager of silence will only last a little while.

One of them surely will say something to end this hassle. But they grossly underestimate the other's stubbornness. They lie there next to each other, eyes closed, determined not to speak. They bring to their battle of wills all the defiance and commitment they can muster.

Well, as it is a dark and stormy night, the flapping door has been noticed by thieves who are doing their rounds. Under the cover of night they creep into the house and take whatever wedding gifts they can lay their hands on. As the couple are still awake, trying their very best not to be the loser of the wager of silence, they can even hear the thieves wander around the house. But still, they manage not to speak. In this way they spend their first wedding night, neither succumbing to the other's will.

When daylight comes, disquieted neighbours notice that the front door of the newly-wedded couple's house is wide open. They talk about what to do. At last, they decide they must go into the house. Stunned at the havoc that the thieves have wrought, they knock on the bedroom door. Terrified at the thought of what might have happened to the couple, they open the door. To their horror they see the newlyweds sitting upright in bed. They look proudly defiant and still refuse to speak. Whatever the neighbours do, they can't get them to talk. In exasperation one of them shakes the man by the shoulders and shouts, 'Talk! Talk!' The young woman cries: 'Please don't hurt him.' Triumphantly the husband croons: 'I won! I won! You have to shut the door.'

What can we deduce from this story? That people become concerned with trivia at the expense of maintaining a focus on more important things? That people may be overly concerned with their place in hierarchies or have a sense that it is unjust for them to have to change when they feel it is others who have initiated the problem? Getting clients to think about how the characters in this allegorical story might address their problems can help encourage clients to think about their own problems and how best to describe them. The hope is that with a situation like this, the disadvantages of the protagonist's behaviour will outweigh the advantages. Moreover, it can be used to illustrate the difficulties that 'all or nothing thinking' can lead to, as well as being overly caught up with 'should statements' – about what the other person 'should do' – or blame.

Start where the client starts

Bearing all this in mind, remember that clients frequently launch into their stories at different starting points. They can start with any stage of the helping process. Join them there. Therefore, 'story' is used in its widest sense. It does not mean, narrowly, 'This is what happened to me, here's how I reacted, and now this is how I feel.' Your job is to stay with your clients no matter where they are, not where you would like them to be. This means that you need an intimate understanding of the 'geography' of helping illustrated by the relatively simple graphics used in this book. Know where the client is before you begin to help them think about where they need to go. Here are a range of clients, each starting at a different point in the helping process.

Stage I: Exploring the Problem Situation. Norman begins by saying, 'The last time I was in therapy, I was in a real mess. I'm still in a mess. I was taking dope; I was belligerent at work; they called me a "difficult" employee. But the managers were really stupid. I had just lost a girlfriend. But maybe that was for the best. She certainly had her problems. Not that I didn't. The match was wrong. I'm back here because I've just been fired. I tackled the dope problem. I don't take any stuff now. I'm clean and it wasn't easy. I was sure that would help me straighten things out.'

Norman worked on a problem, even successfully, but it wasn't the key problem. He probably would have done better to realise that he had a problem relating to people. You can help him start over.

Stage II: Setting Goals. Thad says, 'I don't know whether I want to be a doctor or a politician – or at least a political scientist. I love both, but I can't do both. I mean I have to make my mind up this coming year and choose my university course. I hate being stuck with this kind of decision.'

Thad's starting point is choosing a goal. He has an *approach-approach conflict*. He wants both goals. You can help him weigh the pros and cons of each option.

Stage III: Choosing a Course of Action. Kimberley, a human resources executive for a large company, says, 'I've found out that our chief executive has been involved in some unethical and, I think, immoral behaviour. He's due to retire within the next six months. I don't know whether it's best to bring all this to light or just monitor him till he goes. If I move on him, this could blow up into something big and hurt the reputation of the company itself. If I just monitor him till he goes, he gets away with it. I want to do what's best for the company.'

Kimberley's starting point is a dilemma about which *action strategy* to use. The chief executive is going one way or another. You can help Kimberley search for the strategy that best fits the needs of the institution.

Implementation: The Action Arrow. Themba is having problems sticking to his resolve to restrain himself when one of his neighbours on his condo in Johannesburg 'does something stupid'. He says, 'I know when I speak up [his euphemism for flying off the handle] things tend to get worse. I know I should leave it to others who are more tactful than I am. But they don't move quickly enough – or forcefully enough.'

His starting point is *difficulty in implementing a course of action* to which he has committed himself. You can help Themba find incentives for sticking to his programme.

A Failed Solution. Elizabeth, a single mother living in Somerset in the UK, starts by saying, 'I thought I knew how to handle my son when he reached his teenage years. I knew he might want to try all sorts of crazy things, so I might have to keep the reins pretty tight. And that's what I did. But now things are awful. It's not working. He's out of control. The more I've tried to control him the worse he's got. I don't know what I've done wrong.' Elizabeth has gone all the way through the helping process but has come up empty-handed.

Elizabeth's starting point is a *failed solution*, which has spawned a new problem. You can help Elizabeth take another look at her son's behaviour and come up with solutions that fit his and her needs.

Assess the severity of the client's problems

Clients come to helpers with problems of every degree of severity. James Hicks (2005) has written an award-winning book in clear, straightforward language on the most common signs of mental illness. He provides a service that most books on abnormal psychology do not.

Objectively, problems run from the inconsequential to the life-threatening. Subjectively, however, a client can experience even a relatively inconsequential problem as severe. If a client thinks that a problem is critical, even though by objective standards the problem does not seem to be that bad, then for him or her it is critical. In such a case, the client's tendency to 'catastrophise' – to judge a problem situation to be more severe than it actually is – itself becomes an important part of the problem situation. One of the counsellor's tasks in this case will be to help the client put the problem in perspective or to teach him or her how to distinguish between degrees of problem severity. Howard (1991, p. 194) put it well:

> "In the course of telling the story of his or her problem, the client provides the therapist with a rough idea of his or her orientation towards life, his or her plans, goals, ambitions, and some idea of the events and pressures surrounding the particular presenting problem. Over time, the therapist must decide whether this problem represents a minor deviation from an otherwise healthy life story. Is this a normal, developmentally appropriate adjustment issue? Or does the therapist detect signs of more thorough-going problems in the client's life story? Will therapy play a minor, supportive role to an individual experiencing a low point in his or her life course? If so, the orientation and major themes of the life will be largely unchanged in the therapy experience. But if the trajectory of the life story is problematic in some fundamental way, then more serious, long-term story repair might be indicated. So, from this perspective, part of the work between client and therapist can be seen as life-story elaboration, adjustment, or repair."

Savvy therapists not only gain an understanding of the severity of a client's problem or the extent of the client's unused resources but also understand the limits of helping. What has been this client's highest lifetime level of functioning? What, then, are appropriate expectations? What Howard calls life-story adjustment or repair is not the same as attempting to help clients redo their personalities.

Years ago Mehrabian and Reed (1969) suggested the following formula as a way of determining the severity of any given problem situation. Even though it is not a mathematical formula, it is still useful today.

$$\text{Severity} = \text{Distress} \times \text{Uncontrollability} \times \text{Frequency}$$

The multiplication signs in the formula indicate that these factors are not just additive. Even low-level anxiety, if it is uncontrollable or persistent, can constitute a severe problem; that is, it can severely interfere with the quality of a client's life. In some cases, assessing for possible self-harm or harm to others is called for. The literature on suicide details possible self-harm signs that you need to look out for. You can also review the literature on violence in social relationships for signs of possible impending aggression. Even a casual reading of accounts of outbreaks of social violence such as fired employees gunning down superiors and colleagues tells us how easily signs can be missed.

Continuing efforts are being made to help therapists spot early warning signals. For instance, Cannon and his associates (2008) have come up with a 'new tool' for predicting and therefore possibly preventing psychosis in youths at high clinical risk. They found that a package of risk factors or symptoms – a youth who has an immediate relative with a psychotic disorder, problems in functioning in everyday life, unusual thoughts or suspicions, growing difficulty in social interactions and a history of substance abuse – predicted the likelihood, from 35 to 80 per cent, that the person would have an episode of losing touch with reality within 30 months. Predictably, other members of the medical community did not see the findings as a 'breakthrough' and called for brain scans and genetic tests to diagnose the disease. At any rate, because clients' stories often unfold over time, assessment is not a one-time intervention at the beginning of the helping process but ongoing.

Help clients clarify key issues

To clarify means to discuss problem situations and unused opportunities – including possibilities for the future, goals, strategies for accomplishing goals, plans, implementation issues and feelings about all of these – as concretely as possible. Vagueness and ambiguity lead nowhere. Clarity means helping clients move from the general to the specific – specific experiences, thoughts, behaviours, intentions, points of view and decisions.

Consider this case. Alice's husband has been suffering from severe depression for over a year. One day, after Alice suffers a fainting spell, she, too, talks with a counsellor. At first, feeling guilty about her husband, she is hesitant to discuss her own concerns. In the beginning she says only that her social life is 'a bit restricted by my husband's illness'. With the help of empathic highlights and probing on the part of the helper, her story emerges. 'A bit restricted' turns, bit by bit, into the following, much fuller story. This is a summary. Alice did not say this all at once.

'John has some sort of "general fatigue syndrome" illness that no one has been able to figure out. It's like nothing I've ever seen before. I move from guilt to anger to indifference to hope to despair. I have no social life. Friends avoid us because it is so difficult being with John. I feel I shouldn't leave him, so I stay at home. He's always tired, so we have little interaction. I feel like a prisoner in my own home. Then I think of the burden he's carrying and the roller-coaster emotions start all over again. Sometimes I can't sleep, then I'm as tired as he. He is always saying how hopeless things are and, even though I'm not experiencing what he is, some kind of hopelessness creeps into my bones. I feel that a stronger woman, a more selfless woman, a smarter woman would find ways to deal with all of this. But I end up feeling that I'm not dealing with it at all. From day to day I think I cover most of this up, so that neither John nor the few people who come around see what I'm going through. I'm as alone as he is.'

This is the fuller story spelled out in terms of specific experiences, thoughts, behaviours and feelings. The actions Alice takes – staying at home, covering her feelings up – are part of the problem, not the solution. But now that the story is out in the open, there is some possibility of doing something about it.

In another case, a woman suffering from bulimia is now under psychiatric care, and says that she acted 'a little erratically at times' with some of her classmates in law school. The counsellor, sharing highlights and using probes, helps her tell her story in much greater detail. Like Alice, she does not say all of this at once, but this is the fuller picture of 'a little erratic'.

'I usually think about myself as plain looking, even though when I take care of myself some say that I don't look that bad. Ever since I was a teenager, I've preferred to go it alone, because it was safer. No fuss, no muss and especially no rejection. In university, right from the beginning I entertained romantic fantasies about some of my classmates who I didn't think would give me a second look. I pretended to have meals with those who attracted me and then I'd have fantasies of having sex with them. Then I'd purge, getting rid of the fat I got from eating and getting rid of the guilt. But all of this didn't just stay in my head. I'd go out of my way to run into my latest imagined partner in university. And then I'd be rude to him to "get back at him" for what he did to me. That was my way of getting rid of him.'

She was not really delusional, but gradually her external behaviour with a kind of twisted logic began to reinforce her internal fantasies. However, once her story became 'public' – that is, once she began talking about it openly with her helper – she began to take back control of her life.

Antony and Swinson (2009) in their book *When Perfect Isn't Good Enough* describe the nature of perfectionism and outline key strategies that helping professionals can use with clients to overcome perfectionistic thinking and behaviour. Rhiannon Crawford (2004, p. 44) provides guidance on helping clients who could be said to have an exaggerated sense of perfectionism tell their stories and come to terms with how, though perfectionist tendencies have some advantages, they can also be unhelpful and cause clients to lose control of their lives, as indicated in the following story.

Story: The Perfect Picture

Molly was a professional painter whose work had been exhibited at small galleries. She was so careful about her work that she often discarded canvases that didn't live up to expectation. These perfectionist tendencies had clearly helped in the past to produce some very fine work that had won awards, but there were, however, certain downsides. Her desire to produce a great painting got her so anxious that it interfered with her actual painting. She spent so much time and energy on trying to achieve a masterpiece that she neglected the needs of her family, who were getting increasingly irritated and frustrated with her. She was hypercritical of her art to the point of not seeing what was good about her work and getting satisfaction and pleasure from it. She could always find something that was not perfect in her pictures and then became self-critical and upset. This critical outlook was also turned on the work of fellow artists of whom she became just as critical, and as a result lost several friends. Outside of her painting, her life and activities became quite narrow and unsatisfying, and within her painting itself, her techniques became limited because she was afraid to risk mistakes by experimenting. This in turn dispirited her and her actual output also became so small that she struggled to make ends meet financially. Finally, Molly sought the advice of a professional helper and began to talk through her story and discuss her concerns.

Help clients discuss the context of their concerns

Sometimes helping clients explore the background or context of the concern they bring up helps clarify things. This is a further application of a people-in-systems approach to listening (Conyne & Cook, 2004; Cook, 2012; Egan & Cowan, 1979; Hutchison, 2003). Consider the following case.

> In a management development seminar, Tarik tells his counsellor that he is a manager in a consulting firm. The firm is global, and he works in one of its offices in Southeast Asia. He says that he is already overworked, but now his new boss wants him to serve on a number of committees that will take away even more of his precious time. He is also having trouble with one of his subordinates, himself a manager, who Tarik says is undermining his authority in the wider team.

So far we have a garden-variety story, one that could be repeated thousands of times throughout the world. The counsellor, however, suspects there is more to this. Because the counsellor is Canadian, he wants to learn about Tarik's Middle Eastern culture to get the full picture. He knows that there is an overlay of Western culture in these consulting firms, but he wants to deal with his client as a full person. And so in sharing highlights and by using a few probes, he learns enough about the background of the manager's story to cast a new light on the problem situation. Here is the fuller story that emerges.

> Tarik is not only a manager in the firm, but also a partner. However, he is a newly-minted partner. The structure in these firms is relatively flat, but the culture is quite hierarchical. And so the clients he has been given to work with are, in large part, the 'dogs' of the region. His boss is an American who has been in his present job for only four months. Tarik has heard through the grapevine that he [his boss] is going to stay for only one more year. Because the boss is near retirement, this is his 'fling' in Asia. Though a decent man, he is quite distant and offers Tarik little help. This leads Tarik to believe that his real boss is his boss's boss, whom he can't approach because of company and cultural protocol. The subordinate who is giving Tarik trouble is also a partner. In fact, he has been a partner for several years, but has not been very successful. This man thought that he should have been made the manager of the unit Tarik is now running. He has been engaging in a bit of sabotage behind Tarik's back.

A search for some background quickly takes the client's story out of the 'routine' category. Of course, you should not be looking for background just for the sake of looking. The right kind and amount of background provides both richness and context.

Help clients talk productively about the past

Some schools of psychology suggest that problem situations are not clear and fully comprehended until they are understood in the context of their historic roots. Therefore, helpers in these schools spend a great deal of time helping clients uncover the past and linking themes and patterns from their past. However, if both the client and the helper are on 'the same page' in this regard, therapy can be successful. Others disagree with that point of view. Glasser (2000, p. 23) puts it this way: 'Although many of us have been traumatised in the past, we are not the victims of our past unless we presently choose to be. The solution to our problem is rarely found in explorations of the past unless the focus is on past successes.'

Fish (1995) suggested that attempts to discover the hidden root causes of current problem behaviour may be unnecessary, misguided or even counterproductive. Constructive change does not depend on causal connections in the past. There is evidence to support Fish's contention. Long ago Deutsch (1954) noted that it is often almost impossible, even in carefully controlled laboratory situations, to determine whether event B, which follows event A in time, is actually caused by event A. Trying to connect present complicated patterns of current behaviour with complicated events that took place in the past is an exercise in frustration.

Therefore, asking clients to come up with causal connections between current unproductive behaviour and past events could be an exercise in futility for a number of reasons. First, causal connections cannot be proved; they remain hypothetical. Second, there is little evidence suggesting that understanding past behaviour causes changes in present behaviour. Third, talking about the past often focuses mostly on what happened to clients (their experiences) rather than on what they did about what happened to them (their thoughts, intentions, decisions and behaviours) and therefore interferes with the 'bias towards action' clients need to manage current problems.

This is not to say that a person's past does not influence current behaviour. Nor does it imply that a client's past should not be discussed. Quite often being stuck in the past is a function of rejection and resentment. But the fact that past experiences may well influence current behaviour does not mean that they necessarily *determine* present behaviour. Kagan (1996) has challenged what may be called the 'scarred for life' assumption: 'If orphans who spent their first years in a Nazi concentration camp can become productive adults and if young children made homeless by war can learn adaptive strategies after being adopted by nurturing families' (p. 901), that means that there is hope for us all. As you can imagine, this is one of those issues that members of the helping professions argue about endlessly. Therefore, this is not a debate that is to be settled with a few words here. Here are some suggestions for helping clients talk meaningfully and productively about the past.

Help clients talk about the past to make sense of the present   Many clients come expecting to talk about the past or wanting to talk about the past. There are ways of talking about the past that help clients make sense of the present. But making sense of the present needs to remain centre stage. Thus, how the past is discussed is more important than whether it is discussed. The following man has been discussing how his interpersonal style gets him into trouble. His father, now dead, played a key role in the development of his son's style.

HELPER: So your father's unproductive interpersonal style is, in some ways, alive and well in you.

CLIENT: Until we began talking I had no idea about how alive and well it is. For instance, even though I hated his cruelty, it lives on in me in much smaller ways. He beat my brother. But now I just cut him down to size verbally. He told my mother what she could do and couldn't do. I try to get my mother to adopt my 'reasonable' proposals 'for her own good' – without, of course, listening very carefully to her point of view. There's a whole pattern that I haven't noticed. I've inherited more than his genes.

HELPER: That's quite an inheritance. . . . But now what?

CLIENT: Well, now that I see what's happened, I'd like to change things. A lot of this is ingrained in me, but I don't think it's genetic in any scientific sense. I've developed a lot of bad habits.

It really does not make any difference whether the client's behaviour has been 'caused' by his father or not. In fact, by hooking the present into the past, if he feels in some way that his current nasty style is not his fault, then he has a new problem. Helping is about the future. Now that the problem has been named and is out in the open, it is possible to do something about it. Very often, perhaps most often, problem situations are more about 'bad habits' (Duhigg, 2012) than socio-biological determinism.

Help clients talk about the past to be reconciled to or liberated from it   A potentially dangerous logic can underlie discussions of the past. It goes something like this: 'I am what I am today because of my past. But I cannot change my past. So how can I be expected to change today?'

CLIENT: I was all right until I was about 13. I began to dislike myself as a teenager. I hated all the changes – the awkwardness, the different emotions, having to be as 'cool' as my friends. I was so impressionable. I began to think that life actually must get worse and worse instead of better and better. I just got locked into that way of thinking. That's the same mess I'm in today.

That is not liberation talk. The past is still casting its spell. Helpers need to understand that clients may see themselves as prisoners of their past, but then, in the spirit of Kagan's earlier comments, help them challenge themselves to move beyond such self-defeating beliefs.

The following case provides a different perspective. It is about the father of a boy who has been sexually abused by a priest at the local church. He finds that he can't deal with his son's ordeal without revealing his own abuse by his father. In a tearful session he tells the whole story. In a second interview he has this to say:

> **CLIENT:** Someone said that good things can come from evil things. What happened to my son was evil. But we'll give him all the support he needs to get through this. Although I had the same thing happen to me, I kept it all in until now. It was all locked up inside. I was so ashamed, and my shame became part of me. When I let it all out last week, it was like throwing off a dirty cloak that I'd been wearing for years. Getting it out was so painful, but now I feel so different, so good. I wonder why I had to hold it in for so long.

This is liberation talk. When counsellors help or encourage clients to talk about the past, they should have a clear idea of what their objective is. Is it to learn from the past? Is it to be liberated from it? To assume that there is some 'silver bullet' in the past that will solve today's problem is probably asking too much of the past.

King and Hicks (2007) have shown that discussing lost opportunities and mistaken expectations, and the regrets, disappointments and humiliation associated with them, can prove quite beneficial. Facing up to failures has its unpleasant side, but, as these authors note, 'If contentment were the sole goal of adulthood, examining life's regrettable experiences might seem to have little value' (p. 625). Their research shows that it is possible to learn and grow by reviewing what might have been. 'Recognition of the losses that have led to one's current place in the life story may open one up to a number of valuable and rich experiences, including a paradoxical sense of gratitude for loss itself' (p. 634).

Help clients talk about the past in order to prepare for action in the future   The well-known historian, A. J. Toynbee, had this to say about history: 'History not used is nothing, for all intellectual life is action, like practical life, and if you don't use the stuff – well, it might as well be dead.' As we will soon see, any discussion of problems or opportunities should lead to constructive action, starting with Stage I and going all the way through to implementation. The insights you help clients get from the past should in some way stir them to action. When one client, Christopher, realised how much his father and one of his secondary school teachers had done to make him feel inadequate, he made this resolve: 'I'm not going to do anything to demean anyone around me. You know, up to now I think I have, but I called it something else – wit. I thought I was being funny when I was actually being mean.' Help clients invest the past proactively in the future.

These guidelines are not set in stone. They do not imply that you should never let clients talk about the past unless they do it in a way that fits the guidelines reviewed here. Short (2006) puts it well: 'I don't like to focus on the past or on a person's symptoms, but people shouldn't suffer alone, so I listen to these stories with respect and acceptance' (p. 72). To do otherwise would contribute to what Hansen (2005) calls the 'devaluation of [clients'] inner subjective experiences by the counselling profession' (p. 83). Valuing the subjective experiences of clients is a key factor in counselling and psychotherapy (Feltham, 2010). Furthermore, as mentioned earlier, some approaches to helping include deeper searches into a client's past as an essential part of their approach. Remember what was said about the treatment method in Chapter 1. In the hands of helpers who are competent in orchestrating the key ingredients of successful therapy, any solid approach to treatment can be useful.

Help clients spot unused opportunities

Sometimes clients' existing coping strategies are not as effective as they used to be. It can therefore be useful to discuss the strategies they would usually be drawn to and any alternative strategies they have learned. Highlighting the client's capability, previous coping strategies and what they have managed to do can help them to see opportunities for the future. Note that Martina's story is about both problem situations and opportunities. Many stories are a mixture of both. Early in the history of modern psychology, William James remarked that few people bring to bear more than about 10 per cent of their human potential on the problems and challenges of living. Others since James, although changing the percentages somewhat, have said substantially the same thing, and few have challenged their statements. It is probably not an exaggeration to say that unused human potential constitutes a more serious social problem than emotional disorders, because it is more widespread. People with problems have unused opportunities. People who are relatively problem-free have unused opportunities. If this is the case, then most clients you meet will have unused opportunities that can play a role in helping them manage their problem situation. Pursuing an opportunity can be a way of transcending rather than 'solving' a problem.

Mamello, 23, a university student taking an accounting degree at university in South Africa, came from a strong religious background. He said that he was 'obsessed' by sexual thoughts. When he gave into them he felt very guilty. On a more positive note, he liked the fact his religion put a great deal of emphasis on helping others. He was pursuing a degree in accounting because he believed that it would help him get a decent job, but he did not find the subject matter intellectually stimulating. Working in a bank and attending university did not give him much time for socialising, but he wasn't a big socialiser anyway. Nor did he have time for doing the kind of volunteer work encouraged by his church. He thought he would get to that later. In short, there was a kind of vacuum in his life.

Sensing the vacuum as a possible opportunity, the counsellor asked Mamello how wide his church's focus on helping others extended. Mamello thought for a moment and then replied, 'To the whole world.' In the discussion that followed, Mamello realised that he didn't know much about the world. Developing a 'sense of the world' made sense to him; it was an opportunity. The counsellor doubted that 'sexual obsession' was Mamello's main issue. In fact, Mamello set up a programme for developing a sense of the world for himself that included reading, an occasional lecture, a course in developing-country finance and the luxury of a very occasional conference. He made friends with some of the people he met through these activities and eventually met a like-minded young woman whom he began to date. His 'obsession' disappeared.

Clients are much more likely to talk about problem situations than about unused opportunities. That's a pity because clients can manage many problems better by developing unused opportunities instead of dealing directly with their problems. Here is one example:

Clementine, a single woman in her mid-20s, was arrested when she hacked into a government computer. She was fined and sent to prison, a defeated and demoralised hacker. While in prison, she became friends with Arelia, who one day convinced her to go to a religious service. 'Just this one time', Clementine said. She discovered that the vicar was a man with lots of down-to-earth understanding and 'not too pious'. She liked the service more than she wanted to admit. After a few weeks, she went back to the vicar 'for a bit of advice'. After he found out that she had been a hacker, he rolled his eyes and said, 'Wow, could we make use of you.' She met with him on and off, and they discussed what she'd do 'on the outside'.

After she was released from prison, she helped the vicar set up a computer training programme for disadvantaged children. The fact that she had been a hacker appealed to the children who saw her as 'cool'. They listened to her. She supported herself by working as a computer security consultant. This kept her up to date on the latest hacking techniques, which was still her passion.

How fortunate that the vicar saw talent, however misdirected, rather than depravity. Box 8.1 outlines some of the questions you can help clients ask themselves in order to identify unused opportunities.

| BOX 8.1 | **Opportunity-Finding Questions for Clients** |

Here are some questions counsellors can help clients ask themselves to identify unused opportunities:

- What are my unused skills/resources?
- What are my natural talents?
- What resources are available to me in my environment?
- How could I use some of these to enhance my life?
- Which opportunities would help me transcend my problems?
- What opportunities do I let go by?
- What ambitions remain unfulfilled?
- What could I accomplish if I put my mind to it?
- Which opportunities should I be developing?
- Which role models could I be emulating?

As clients tell their stories, help them begin to search for unused resources

Incompetent helpers concentrate on clients' deficits. Skilled helpers, as they listen to and observe clients, do not blind themselves to deficits, but they are quick to spot clients' resources, whether used, unused or even abused. These resources can become the building blocks for the future. Consider this example:

Sherry, a young woman in her late teens who has been arrested several times for street prostitution, is an involuntary, or 'mandated', client. The charge this time is possession of drugs. She ran away from home in Portsmouth, United Kingdom, when she was 16 and is now living at the other end of the country, in Newcastle. Like many other runaways, she was seduced into prostitution 'by a halfway decent pimp'. Now she is very street wise. She is also cynical about herself, her occupation and the world. She is forced to see a counsellor as part of the probation process. As might be expected, Sherry is quite hostile during the interview. She has seen other counsellors and sees the interview as a game. The counsellor already knows a great deal of the story because of the court record. The dialogue is not easy. Some of it goes like this:

SHERRY: If you think I'm going to talk with you, you've got another think coming. What I do is my business.

COUNSELLOR: You don't have to talk about what you do outside. We could talk about what we're doing here in this meeting.

SHERRY: I'm here because I have to be. You're here either because you're dumb and like to do stupid things or because you couldn't get a better job. You people are no better than the people on the street. You're just more 'respectable'.

COUNSELLOR: So nobody could really be interested in you.

SHERRY: I'm not even interested in me!

COUNSELLOR: So, if you're not interested in yourself, then no one else could be, including me.

Sherry has obvious deficits. She is engaged in a dangerous and self-defeating lifestyle. But as the counsellor listens to Sherry, he spots many different resources. Sherry is a tough, street wise woman. The very virulence of her cynicism and self-hate, the very strength of her resistance to help and her almost unchallengeable determination to go it alone are all signs of resources. Many of her resources are currently being used in self-defeating ways. They are misused resources, but they are resources nevertheless.

Helpers need a resource-oriented mindset in all their interactions with clients. Contrast two different approaches:

> **CLIENT:** I practically never stand up for my rights. If I disagree with what anyone is saying – especially in a group – I keep my mouth shut.
>
> **COUNSELLOR A:** So clamming up is the best policy. . . . What happens when you do speak up?
>
> **CLIENT (pausing):** I suppose that on the rare occasions when I do speak up, the world doesn't fall in on me. Sometimes others do actually listen to me. But I still don't seem to have much impact on anyone.
>
> **COUNSELLOR A:** So speaking up, even when it's safe, doesn't get you much.
>
> **CLIENT:** No, it doesn't.

Counsellor A, sticking to sharing highlights, misses the resource mentioned by the client. Although it is true that the client habitually fails to speak up, he has some impact when he does speak. Others do listen, at least sometimes, and this is a resource. Counsellor A emphasises the deficit. Let's try another counsellor.

> **COUNSELLOR B:** So when you do speak up, you don't get blasted, you even get a hearing. Tell me what makes you think you don't exercise much influence when you speak?
>
> **CLIENT (pauses):** Well, maybe influence isn't the issue. Usually I don't want to get involved. Speaking up gets you involved.

Note that both counsellors try to respond with empathy, but they focus on different parts of the client's message. Counsellor A emphasises the deficit; Counsellor B notes an asset and follows up with a probe. This produces a significant clarification of the client's problem situation. Now not wanting to get involved is an issue to be explored.

The search for resources is especially important when the story being told is bleak. I once listened to a man's story that included a number of bone-jarring life defeats – a bitter divorce, false accusations that led to his dismissal from a job, months of unemployment, serious health concerns, months of homelessness and more. The only emotion the man exhibited during his story was depression. Towards the end of the session, we had this interchange:

> **HELPER:** Just one blow after another, grinding you down.
>
> **CLIENT:** Grinding me down, and almost doing me in.
>
> **HELPER:** Tell me a little more about the 'almost' part of it.
>
> **CLIENT (hesitates):** Well, I'm still alive, still sitting here talking to you.
>
> **HELPER:** Despite all these blows, you haven't fallen apart. That seems to say something about the fibre in you.

At the word 'fibre', the client looked up, and there seemed to be a glimmer of something besides depression in his face. I put a line down the centre of a newsprint pad. On the left side I listed the life blows the man had experienced. On the right I put 'Fibre'. Then I said, 'Let's see if we can add to the list on the right side.'

We came up with a list of the man's resources. His 'fibre' included his musical talent, his honesty, his concern for and ability to talk to others and so forth. After about a half hour, he smiled weakly, but he did smile. He said that it was the first time he could remember smiling in months.

Help clients see problems as an opportunity

Clients don't come with just problems or opportunities. They come with a mixture of both. Although there is no justification for romanticising pain, the flip side of a problem is an opportunity. Here are a few examples:

- Baruti used his diagnosis of AIDS as a starting point for reintegrating himself into his extended family and challenging the members of his family to come to grips with some of their own problems, problems they had been denying for a long time.
- Beatrice used her divorce as an opportunity to develop a new approach to men based on mutuality. Because she was on her own and had to make her own way, she discovered that she had entrepreneurial skills. She started an arts and crafts company.
- Jerome, after an accident, used a long convalescence period to review and reset some of his values and life goals. He began to visit other patients in the rehabilitation centre. This gave him deep satisfaction. He began to explore opportunities in the helping professions.
- Jess used her incarceration for shoplifting – she called it 'time out' – as an opportunity to finish secondary school and get a head start on university.
- A couple mourning the death of their only child started a day-care centre in conjunction with other members of their church.

William C. Miller (1986) talked about one of the worst days of his life. Everything was going wrong at work. Projects were not working out, people were not responding, the work overload was bad and getting worse – nothing but failure all around. Later that day, over a cup of coffee, he took some paper, put the title 'Lessons Learned and Relearned' at the top, and wrote down as many entries as he could. Some hours and seven pages later, he had listed 27 lessons. The day turned out to be one of the best of his life. So he began to keep a daily 'Lessons Learned' journal. It helped him avoid getting caught up in self-blame and defeatism. Subsequently, on days when things were not working out, he would say to himself, 'Ah, this will be a day filled with learnings!' Sometimes helping a client spot a small opportunity, be it the flip-side of a problem or a standalone opportunity, provides enough leverage to put him or her on a more constructive tack.

Indeed, many clients experience positive growth through trauma. Joseph and Linley (2005) highlight the potential of positive growth in individuals who have experienced trauma and adversity, and the importance of cognitive appraisal in adversarial growth. For the helper, working relationally with trauma is an essential part of the work (Walsh, Dillon, Frankland, Kerr, Larsson, Nicholas *et al.,* 2013).

HELP CLIENTS MOVE INTO ACTION RIGHT FROM THE BEGINNING

We return to one of the main themes of this book. Shakespeare, in the person of Hamlet, talks about important enterprises – what he calls 'enterprises of great pith and moment' – losing 'the name of action'. Helping, which is an enterprise 'of great pith and moment', can too often lose the name of action. One of the principal reasons clients do not manage the problem situations of their lives effectively is their failure to act intelligently, forcefully and prudently in their own best interests. A strength of positive psychology is its focus on personal agency and self-regulation (Bandura 2001; Caprara & Cervone, 2003), called a 'bias towards action' in Chapter 2. Self-affirmation and agency can fend off ego depletion effects in the short term (Maranges & Baumeister, 2016).

Help clients see the importance of being proactive

Inactivity can be bad for body, mind and spirit. Consider the following workplace example:

A counsellor at a large manufacturing company in Gauteng, South Africa, realised that inactivity did not benefit injured workers. If they stayed at home, they tended to sit around, gain weight, lose muscle tone and suffer from a range of psychological symptoms such as psychosomatic complaints unrelated to their injuries. Taking a people-in-systems approach (Egan & Cowan, 1979), she worked with management, the unions and doctors to design temporary, physically light jobs for injured workers. In some cases, nurses or physical therapists visited these workers on the job. Counselling sessions helped to get the right worker into the right job. The workers, active again, felt better about themselves. Both they and the company benefited from the programme.

Helping too often entails too much talking and too little action. Here is a brief overview of a case that illustrates almost the magic of action. Marcus's 'helpers' are his sister-in-law and a friend.

Life was ganging up on Marcus. Only recently 'retired' from his job as office manager of a brokerage firm because the managing partner did not think that he would fit into the new e-commerce strategy of the business, he discovered that he had a form of cancer, the course of which was unpredictable. He had started treatment and was relatively pain-free, but he was always tired. He was also beginning to have trouble walking, but the medical specialists did not know why. It may or may not have been related to the cancer. Health-wise, his future was uncertain.

After losing his job, he took a marketing position with a software company. But soon health problems forced him to give it up. Around the same time his daughter was expelled from high school for using drugs. She was sullen and uncommunicative and seemed indifferent to her father's plight. Marcus's wife and daughter did not get along well at all, and the home atmosphere was tense whenever they were together. Discussions with his wife about their daughter went nowhere. To top things off, one of his two married sons announced that he was getting a divorce from his wife and was going to fight for custody of their three-year-old son.

Given all these concerns, Marcus, though very independent and self-reliant, more or less said to himself, 'I've got to take charge of my life or it could fall apart. And I could use some help.' He found help in two people – Sarah, an intelligent, savvy, no-nonsense sister-in-law who was a lay minister of their church, and Sam, a friend of many years who was a doctor in family practice. Sam helped Marcus maintain his self-reliance by helping him find out as much as he could about his illness through the internet. Without becoming preoccupied with his search, Marcus learned enough about his illness and possible treatments to partner with his doctors in choosing therapeutic interventions. He also drew up a living will and gave Sam power of attorney in order to avoid needlessly prolonging his life at the end. Sam also helped him pursue some intellectual interests – art, literature, theatre – that Marcus hadn't had time for because of business.

Here's a man who, with some help from his friends, uses adversity as an opportunity to get more fully involved with life. He redefines life, in part, as good conversations with family and friends. Refusing to become a victim, he stays active. Marcus did die two years later, but he managed to live until he died.

Help clients use the time between sessions productively

If helping proves to be short term for whatever reason, then counsellors must help clients use the time between sessions as productively as possible. 'How can I leverage what I do within the session to have an impact on what the client does the rest of the week?' Or month, as the case may be. This does not deny that good things are happening within the session. On the contrary, it capitalises on whatever learning or change takes place there.

Wosket (2006; see Chapter 2), at the end of each session, asks the client to describe what has happened in the session and where they are. Then she asks the client if there is anything they could do between sessions to move things along before the next session. At the beginning of the next session, she asks the client to review what he or she did between sessions and what impact it had. If the client has done nothing, she asks, non-judgementally, 'If you had thought of acting, what might you have done?' This reinforces the necessity-for-action theme.

Sixty-eight per cent of practising psychologists frequently use between-session assignments with their clients (Kazantzis, Lampropoulos & Deane, 2005) as a way of helping clients act on what they're learning in the sessions (Detweiler-Bedell & Whisman, 2005; Kazantzis, 2000; Scheel, Hanson & Razzhavaikina, 2004; Tompkins, 2005; also, much of the May 2002, Vol. *58, Journal of Clinical Psychology* was devoted to articles dealing with homework). Daitch (2008) believes that homework is so important that she makes homework compliance part of the therapeutic contract: 'From the beginning of therapy, I emphasise the importance of homework, telling clients about research demonstrating that willingness to engage in homework is directly related to the success of therapy' (p. 50). Mahrer and his associates (1994) reviewed the methods helpers use to influence clients to use between-session time productively. Helpers may wish to use behavioural activation techniques with clients, which focus on activity scheduling as an encouragement for clients to engage in activities, goals and a more positive beneficial way of tackling any avoidance they may have. This has become a formal therapy for depression (Veale, 2008).

For suggestions on how to incorporate homework into your helping sessions, see Broder (2000). He not only offers many techniques but discusses why some clients resist the idea of homework and suggests ways of addressing such resistance. For instance, in conjunction with Albert Ellis, the originator of rational emotive behaviour therapy, Broder developed a series of audio tapes dealing with many of the problems clients encounter. Clients use these tapes to further their understanding of what they learned in the therapy session and to engage in activities that will help them resolve their conflicts.

Of course, there is no need to call what the client does between sessions homework. The term 'homework' puts some clients off. It is also too 'teacherish' for some helpers. It sounds like an add-on rather than something that flows organically from what takes place within the helping sessions. But 'flow' is a wide term. The principle behind homework is more important than the name, and the principle is clear. Use every stage and every task of the helping process as a stimulus for problem-managing and opportunity-developing action. Use the term 'homework' if it works for you. 'Assign' it if this works for you and your client. But have a clear picture of why you are assigning any particular task. Don't routinely assign homework for its own sake.

Homework often has a predetermined cast to it. But encouraging clients to act on their own behalf can be a much more spontaneous exercise. Take the case of Jacoline.

> Jacoline, 70, single, was a retired teacher. In fact, she had managed to find ways of teaching even after the mandatory retirement age. But she was ultimately 'eased out'. Given her savings, her pension and general finances, she was ready for retirement financially. But she had not prepared socially or emotionally. She was soon depressed and described life as 'aimless'. She wandered around for a few months and finally, at the urging of a friend, saw a counsellor, someone about her own age. The counsellor knew that Jacoline had many internal resources, but they had all seemed to go dormant. In the second session, he said to her, 'Jacoline, you're allowing yourself to become a wreck. You'd never stand for this kind of behaviour from your students. You need to get on with seizing life again. Tell me what you're going to do. I mean right after you get out of this session with me.' This was a bit of shock treatment for Jacoline. A revived Jacoline looked at him and asked, 'Well, what do you do?' They went on to discuss what life can offer after 70. Her first task, she decided, was to get into community in some way. The school had been her community, but it was gone. She went to the next counselling session with some options.

You can use homework assignments or find other, perhaps more organic, ways of helping clients move to action. Your role demands that you be a catalyst for client action. Box 8.2 summarises some of the main guidelines for doing the work of Task I-A.

BOX 8.2   Guidelines for Stage I

Establish a Working Alliance

- Develop a collaborative working relationship with the client.
- Use the relationship as a vehicle for social-emotional re-education.
- Don't do for clients what they can do for themselves. Keep the client in the driver's seat.

Help Clients Tell their Stories

- Use a mix of tuning in, listening, empathy, probing and summarising to help clients tell their stories, share their points of view, discuss their decisions and talk through what they want to do as concretely as possible.
- Help clients talk productively about the past.
- Use probes when clients get stuck, wander about or lack clarity.
- Understand blocks to client self-disclosure and provide support for clients having difficulty talking about themselves.
- Invite clients to reframe their stories and develop new perspectives.
- Determine clients' willingness to engage in self-challenge.

Build Ongoing Client Assessment into the Helping Process

- Get an initial feel for the severity of clients' problems and their ability to handle them.
- Note client resources, especially unused resources, and help the client work with these resources.
- Understand clients' problems and opportunities in the larger context of their lives.

Help Clients Move to Action

- Help clients develop an action orientation.
- Help clients spot early opportunities for changing self-defeating behaviour or engaging in opportunity-development behaviour.
- Find innovative forms of homework to help clients engage in problem-managing action in their everyday lives.

Establish a Feedback and Evaluation System

- Integrate feedback and evaluation into the helping process.
- Find ways of getting clients to participate in and own the evaluation process.
- Keep an evaluative eye on the entire process with the goal of adding value through each interaction and making each session better.

TASK I-B: THE REAL STORY

As we have seen, the purpose of Stage I is to help clients tell their stories in a way that opens them up to doing something about them. All three interrelated and intermingled tasks – A, B and C – work together to do just that. Take another look at the graphic for Stage I in Figure 8.2.

We have already seen many examples of Task I-B, especially in Chapters 5 and 6 where the communication skills needed to invite clients to self-challenge are outlined. In other words the communication skills illustrated in Chapters 5 and 6 are of the essence of Task I-B. They are joined at the hip. In Task I-B, counsellors use these skills to help clients work through blind spots and develop the kind of new perspectives that lead to new problem-managing and opportunity-developing behaviour. The 'real' story gives an accurate picture of the client's problem situation. If the client says, 'It's never my fault; my spouse is always the cause of our trouble', we most likely do not have the real story. Task I-B skills can be used to help clients uncover hidden concerns, clarify vague issues, add important details, explore clients' hesitancies, see their problems from a

FIGURE 8.2 **The three tasks of Stage I**

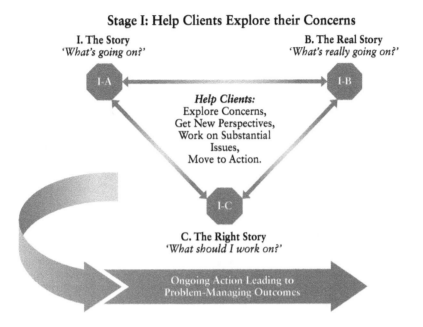

more constructive perspective, add important information and details that are being left out, find unused strengths and resources, and spot and explore opportunities buried in or masked by problem situations. It is essential to re-read Chapters 5 and 6 before moving further into this chapter.

TUMI AND CARLOS IN I-B

The conflict-laden conversation Tumi had with her father left her shocked and disoriented. Here is a snapshot:

> Before her disappointing conversation with her father, Tumi was an excellent participant in the helping process. In some ways it was easy because the discussion focused on opportunities rather than problems. She envisioned new career opportunities and there was a budding relationship with a male friend. After the conversation with her father which both overlooked, new problems emerged. In the sessions that followed the disastrous encounter Tumi was depressed; she found it difficult to talk, she felt that she was trapped, she was reluctant to focus on other possibilities and she resisted Carlos's attempts to engage her in self-challenge. An underground current of resentment towards the 'cultural captivity' imposed on her by her parents surfaced together with the low-grade depression that accompanied it. This depression was exacerbated by the memories she had from her trip to South Africa – young people 'happy and free' – and by the ignored but persistent feelings of vulnerability associated with the car accident. In a sense she and Carlos were back at square one but without the euphoria associated with her intention to create a better future for herself.

Tumi is disappointed and stuck. What can Carlos do to help Tumi move beyond this stumbling point and get back to the work of problem management?

I-B has an aura of challenge or self-challenge about it. It is not something you do to clients. It is something clients engage in with your help. Here are some of the things Tumi and Carlos uncovered as they worked together:

One of the first things that Carlos notes is that Tumi herself has developed a very useful new perspective on her own. While she could have blamed the discontent she was feeling about her life on the car accident, she realises that the accident was a wake-up call. Over the course of the helping encounter, Carlos helps Tumi develop a range of useful new perspectives so that both of them will have a clearer picture of what is going on in Tumi's life and what is bothering her the most. For instance, because she never talks about her mother, Carlos at one point says, 'I'm curious why you never talk about your mother, except indirectly when you say "my parents". She's sort of a missing person.' This helps Tumi realise that she does not see her mother as an 'agent' in her story. Her mother is 'just there', as it were. She hasn't seen this as an issue, but maybe it is.

Carlos also helps Tumi see that while, externally, she gives people the impression that she is assertive, a doer – that's the way she comes across – she seems to endure personal problems rather than wrestle with them. Or in some ways she's a doer and in other ways not. Also because she feels culturally adrift – she describes herself as living between two cultures without becoming her own person in either of them – he wonders aloud how this might be affecting her. For instance, in her view her cousins, having bought into the worst of British consumer culture, are very narcissistic. She knows that her father disapproves, but he has never said anything about it. She wonders more and more about what's going on inside him.

Carlos believes that some of the symptoms Tumi is describing constitute a mild form of depression, though at this point he does not see any value in using the word itself. In one session he asks her whether she sees her insomnia and headaches as symptoms of health problems or reactions to the concerns she is discussing. Tumi thinks that it is the latter but observes, 'Well, this might be the kind of incentive I need to get a physical check-up. I haven't had one in years. I don't want to end up like my father.'

Carlos helps her get in touch with the fact that she describes herself as very duty driven. For instance, even though she does a great deal for her father both at work and at home, she intimates that she has always thought that she should be taking better care of him. She feels some guilt because she is not doing as good a job as she thinks she should do. Tumi begins to realise that she resents the fact that she thinks like this.

Carlos does not just tell Tumi all these things or interpret what she is saying. He does not use Task B skills and activities to 'psych her out'. Rather he acts as a catalyst to help her make problem-managing discoveries for herself.

HELP CLIENTS CHALLENGE THEMSELVES TO PARTICIPATE AS FULLY AS POSSIBLE IN THE HELPING PROCESS

In Chapter 5 we have seen a number of examples of counsellors helping clients engage in different kinds of self-challenge. In this chapter the self-challenge focus is on helping clients get the most out of the helping process. Clients benefit by owning and participating as fully as possible in the helping process. This section focuses on some of the challenges to engagement that clients face. As we have seen, even clients whose goodwill is beyond doubt can have trouble participating for a variety of reasons. Here are some principles you can use to help clients challenge themselves to participate as fully and as intelligently as possible. They are principles and not must-do rules. Use them when they benefit your clients.

Invite clients to own their problems and unused opportunities

It is all too common for clients to refuse to take responsibility for their problems and unused opportunities. Instead, there is a whole list of outside forces and other people who are to blame. Therefore, clients may need to challenge themselves to own the problem situation more fully. Here is the experience of one counsellor who had responsibility for about 150 young men in a youth prison within the confines of a larger central prison.

I believe I interviewed each of the inmates. And I did learn from them. What I learned had little resemblance to what I had found when I read their files containing personal histories, including the description of their crimes. What I learned when I talked with them was that they didn't belong there. With almost universal consistency they reported a 'reason' for their incarceration that had little to do with their own behaviour. An inmate explained with perfect sincerity that he was there because the judge who sentenced him had also previously sentenced his brother, who looked very similar; the moment this inmate walked into the courtroom he knew he would be sentenced. Another explained with equal sincerity that he was in prison because his court-appointed solicitor wasn't really interested in helping him. (L. M. Miller, 1984, pp. 67–68)

Given studies on prison life some of this may be true. But we don't have to go behind prison walls to find this lack of ownership. It is all too common, especially in cases where it is easy to blame someone else.

Take the case of a client who feels that her business partner has been pulling a fast one on her. He's made a deal on his own. She's alarmed, but she hasn't done anything about it so far. Let's say that three different helpers, A, B and C, respond. Consider how their empathic responses differ:

HELPER A: You feel angry because he unilaterally made the decision to close the deal on his terms.

HELPER B: You're angry because your legitimate interests were ignored.

HELPER C: You're furious because you were ignored, your interests were not taken into consideration, maybe you were even financially victimised, and you let him get away with it.

Challenging clients in terms of ownership means helping clients understand that in some situations they may have some responsibility for creating or at least perpetuating their problem situations. Statement C does precisely that – 'you let him get away with it'.

Not only problems but also opportunities need to be seized and owned by clients. As Wheeler and Janis (1980) note, 'Opportunities usually do not knock very loudly, and missing a golden opportunity can be just as unfortunate as missing a red-alert warning' (p. 18). Consider Tess and her brother, Josh.

Tess and Josh's father died years ago. Their mother died about a year ago. She left a small country cottage to both of them. They have been fighting over its use. Some of the fighting has been quite bitter. Issues that were swept under the rug now leap out in all their ugliness. They have never been that close, but up till now they have just had squabbles, not all-out war. Without admitting it, Tess has been shocked by her own angry and bellicose behaviour. But not shocked enough to do anything about it.

Then Josh has a heart attack. Tess knows that this is an opportunity to do something about their relationship. But she keeps putting it off. She even realises that the longer she puts it off, the harder it will be to do something about it. In a counselling session, she says:

TESS: I thought that this was going to be our chance to patch things up, but he hasn't said anything.

COUNSELLOR: So, nothing from his camp. . . . What about yours?

TESS: I think it might already be too late. We're falling right back into our old patterns.

COUNSELLOR: I didn't think that's what you wanted.

TESS (angrily):   Of course that's not what I wanted! . . . That's the way it is.

COUNSELLOR: Tess, if someone put a gun to your head and said, 'Make this work or I'll shoot', what would you do?

(Continued)

> **TESS (after a long pause):** You mean it's up to me . . .
>
> **COUNSELLOR:** If you mean that I'm assigning this to you as a task, then no. If you mean that you can still seize the opportunity no matter what Josh does, well. . . .
>
> **TESS:** I think I'm really angry with myself. . . . I know deep down it's up to me . . . no matter what Josh does. And I keep putting it off. . . . What if he were to die while we're at each other's throats!

Josh, of course, is not in the room. So it's about Tess's ownership of the opportunity. And she senses, now more deeply, that 'missing a golden opportunity can be just as unfortunate as missing a red-alert warning.'

Invite clients to state their problems as solvable

Jay Haley (1976, p. 9) said that 'if therapy is to end properly, it must begin properly – by negotiating a solvable problem'. Or exploring a realistic opportunity, someone might add. It is not uncommon for clients to state problems as unsolvable. This justifies a 'poor-me' attitude and a failure to act.

> **UNSOLVABLE PROBLEM:** In sum, my life is miserable now because of my past. My parents were indifferent to me and at times even unjustly hostile. If only they had been more loving, I wouldn't be in this mess. I am the failed product of an unhappy environment.

Of course, clients will not use this rather stilted language, but the message is common enough. The point is that the past cannot be changed. As we have seen, clients can change their attitudes about the past and deal with the present consequences of the past. Therefore, when a client defines the problem exclusively as a result of the past, the problem cannot be solved. 'You certainly had it rough in the past and are still suffering from the consequences now' might be the kind of response that such a statement is designed to elicit. The client needs to move beyond such a point of view.

A solvable or manageable PROBLEM is one that clients can do something about. Consider a different version of the foregoing unsolvable problem. Kasigo has had a rough childhood, living in poverty in South Africa with her father slowly dying of the HIV virus and her mother very mean to her. She finally went out on her own and her parents didn't seem to care.

> **SOLVABLE PROBLEM:** Over the years I've been blaming my parents for my misery. And I don't want to let my mother off the hook for how she treated me, even though my father was dying. But I still spend a great deal of time feeling sorry for myself. As a result, I sit around and do nothing. I don't make friends, I don't involve myself in the community, I don't take any constructive steps to get a decent job.

This message is quite different from that of the previous client. The problem is now open to being managed because it is stated almost entirely as something the client does or fails to do. The client can stop wasting her time blaming her parents, because she cannot change her mother and her father is now dead; she can increase her self-esteem through constructive action and therefore stop feeling sorry for herself; and she can develop the interpersonal skills and courage she needs to enter more creatively into relationships with others. She can create a different future.

This does not mean that all problems are solvable by the client's direct action. A teenager may be miserable because his self-centred parents are constantly squabbling and seem indifferent to him. He certainly can't solve the problem by making them less self-centred, stopping them from fighting or getting them to care for him more. But he can be helped to find ways to cope with his home situation more effectively by developing fuller social opportunities outside the home. This could mean helping him develop new perspectives on himself and family life, and challenging him to act both internally and externally on his own behalf.

A handy technique that helpers can use is the McKinsey SMART technique to problem solving. This technique ensures that any solution, goal or plans that the helper and clients come up with meet the criteria of being Specific, Measurable, Action oriented, Relevant and Time bound. Planning has been shown to promote goal striving by self-regulation and motivation researchers (see for example, Gollwitzer & Oettingen, 2016). Goal intentions versus the implementation of goal intentions can also influence the outcome or behaviour clients feel able to commit to.

Invite clients to explore their 'problem-maintenance structure'

Pinsof (1995) points out how important it is to explore with clients the 'actions, biology, cognitions, emotions, object relations and self-structures' (p. 7) that keep them mired in their problems. What he calls the 'problem-maintenance structure' (p. 7) refers to the set of factors – including personal, social, organisational, community and political factors – that keeps clients from identifying, exploring and ultimately doing something about their problem situations and unused opportunities. 'You say that you don't like the way you relate to people. Well, what is it that you don't like? And what is it that keeps that style in place? What is it that prevents you from doing something about it?'

> Alexandru, a Romanian immigrant, rejoiced the day he got confirmation of his right to work in the United Kingdom. But the next two years were a let-down. He lived aimlessly, wandering from place to place and from one part-time job to another. All the great plans he had for his life 'in a land of opportunity' disappeared. The lifestyle that he had let himself fall into left him miserable. He finally saw a counsellor who helped him explore not only what had happened, but also the factors that kept him locked into a lifestyle he pretended to like but really hated. This forced him to look at personal, social and cultural factors he had been avoiding. An intelligent and personable university graduate, Alexandru faced all sorts of unused opportunities.

The work of helping clients 'restructure' self-defeating defences, cognitions, patterns of emotional expression, self-focused and outward-focused behaviour, relationships and approaches to the environment (see Magnavita, 2005) begins in Stage I.

Invite clients to move on to the right stage and task of the helping process

We have touched on this already in discussing probing. There is no reason to keep going over the same issue with clients. You can help clients challenge themselves to do the following:

- Clarify problem situations by describing specific experiences, behaviours and feelings when they are being vague or evasive.
- Talk about issues – problems, opportunities, goals, commitment, strategies, plans, actions – when they are reluctant to do so.
- Develop new perspectives on themselves, others and the world when they prefer to cling to distortions.
- Review possibilities, critique them, develop goals and commit themselves to reasonable agendas when they would rather continue wallowing in their problems.
- Search for ways of getting what they want, instead of just talking about what they would prefer.
- Spell out specific plans instead of taking a scattered, hit-or-miss approach to change.
- Persevere in the implementation of plans when they are tempted to give up.
- Review what is and what is not working in their pursuit of change 'out there'.

In sum, you can help clients challenge themselves to engage more effectively in all the stages and tasks of problem management during the sessions themselves and in the changes they are pursuing in their everyday life.

IMMEDIACY: DEALING WITH ISSUES IN THE HELPING RELATIONSHIP ITSELF

Many clients have trouble with interpersonal relationships either as a primary or as a secondary concern. Helping sessions, therefore, constitute a kind of interpersonal lab, as key features of clients' interpersonal styles show up in client–helper interactions. Both helper and client can learn a great deal from these interactions. Some of the difficulties clients have in their day-to-day relationships are reflected in their relationships with their helpers. For instance, if they are compliant with authority figures in their everyday lives, they may be compliant with their helpers. Or they may move to the opposite pole and become aggressive and angry. Therefore, helpers can learn something about a client's interpersonal style (and, of course, their own) by being sensitive to the give-and-take within the helping sessions. Even more important, clients can learn a great deal about their own style. If counselling takes place in a group, the opportunity to learn is even greater. Robert Carkhuff (Carkhuff, 1969a, 1969b; Carkhuff & Anthony, 1979) called the package of skills enabling helpers and clients to explore their relationship at the service of greater interpersonal competence 'immediacy'. Immediacy can include the helper using their own interpretations within the session, such as using here-and-now techniques or their relationship with the client. Within psychotherapy, immediacy has been shown to be effective in developing the relationship to a deeper level and thus helpful for the client in their relationships outside the therapeutic relationship (Hill *et al.*, 2014).

Immediacy is a useful tool for monitoring and managing the working alliance (Hill, Knox & Pinti-Coelho, 2019). Since the quality of the relationship in therapy is one of the best predictors of success (Horvath *et al.*, 2011; Norcross & Lambert, 2011), immediacy as a skill is important for both client and helper. It goes without saying that clients may or may not have this skill, but helpers certainly should. There is an element of challenge in this skill because it is used to repair 'ruptures' (Safran, Muran & Eubanks-Carter, 2011) in the relationship between client and helper. Safran and colleagues define rupture as 'a tension or breakdown in the collaborative relationship between patient and therapist' (p. 224).

Two kinds of immediacy are reviewed here: first, immediacy that focuses on the overall relationship – 'How are you and I doing?' and, second, immediacy that focuses on some particular event in a session – 'What's going on between you and me right now?'

Relationship-focused immediacy

Reviewing your ongoing relationship with the client and helping the client do the same should be taken care of by the feedback systems mentioned earlier. General relationship immediacy refers to your ability to discuss with a client where you stand in your overall relationship with him or her and vice versa. The focus is not on a particular incident but on the way the relationship itself has developed and how it is helping or standing in the way of progress. In the following example, the helper is a 44-year-old woman working as a counsellor for a large company. She is talking to a 36-year-old man she has been seeing once every other week for about two months. One of his principal problems is his relationship with his supervisor, who is also a woman.

COUNSELLOR: If I were to review the feedback we have been giving each other at the end of each session, I'd say that we've developed a good working relationship. I feel we respect each other. We have been able to make demands of each other. There has been a great deal of give-and-take in our relationship. You've got angry with me, and I've got impatient with you at times, but we've worked it out. If you see it more or less the same way, I'm wondering what our relationship has that might be missing in your relationship with your supervisor.

CLIENT: Yes, we do pretty well. . . . My boss? That's another matter. For one thing, you listen to me, and I don't think she does. On the other hand, I listen pretty carefully to you, but I don't think I listen to her at all, and she probably knows it. Frankly, I think she's stupid, and I guess I 'say' that to her in a number of ways even without using the words. She knows how I feel.

The review of the relationship helps the client focus more specifically on important dimensions of his relationship with his supervisor. Now it's out in the open.

In a second example, Angie, a 38-year-old trainer in a counsellor-training programme, is talking to Weijun, 25, one of the trainees. She has not been practising what she preaches regarding mutual feedback.

> **ANGIE:**   Weijun, let's take a moment to reflect and talk a bit about our relationship. I'm a bit bothered about some of the things that are going on between you and me. When you talk to me, I get the feeling that you are being very careful. You talk slowly. And you seem to be choosing your words, sometimes to the point that what you are saying sounds almost prepared. You have never challenged me on anything in the group. When you talk most intimately about yourself, you seem to avoid looking at me. I find myself giving you less feedback than I give others. I've even found myself putting off talking to you about all this. Perhaps some of this is my own imagining. But I have a problem. Maybe we have a problem, but I want to check it out with you.

Angie has let things pile up. Putting things off has only made things worse. She should have put a feedback system in place, but she didn't. Now they are both paying the price.

> **WEIJUN:**   I've been afraid to talk about all this, so I keep putting it off, too. I'm glad that you've brought it up. A lot of it has to do with how I relate to people in authority, even though you don't come across as an 'authority figure'. You don't act the way an authority figure is supposed to act.

In this case, cultural differences play a role. For Weijun, a naturalised American citizen born in China, giving direct feedback to someone in authority is not natural. However, authority is not the issue here. He has some misgivings about her style and the way she conducts the class. He tells Angie that he thinks that her interventions in the training group are too 'unorganised'. He also thinks she plays favourites. He has not wanted to bring these things up because he fears that his position in the programme will be jeopardised. But now that Angie has made the overture, he accepts the challenge. Of course, an immediacy interaction can be initiated by the client, although many clients for obvious reasons would hesitate to do so. Who wants to take on the leader?

Event-focused immediacy

Here-and-now immediacy refers to your ability to discuss with clients what is happening between the two of you at any given moment. It is not the state of the relationship that is being considered, but rather some specific interaction or incident. In the following example, the helper, a 43-year-old woman, is a counsellor in a neighbourhood human services centre. Agnes, a 49-year-old woman who was recently widowed, has been talking about her grief, her loneliness and her financial problems. In the current session she seems to have withdrawn somewhat abruptly, and the interaction has bogged down.

> **COUNSELLOR:**   I'd like to stop a moment and take a look at what's happening right now between you and me.
>
> **AGNES:**   I'm not sure what you mean.
>
> **COUNSELLOR:**   Well, our conversation today started out quite lively, and now it seems rather subdued. I've noticed that the muscles in my shoulders have become tense. I sometimes tense up that way when I feel that I might have said something wrong. It could be just me, but I sense that things are a bit strained between us right now.
>
> **AGNES (hesitatingly):**   Well, a little. . . .

Agnes goes on to say how she resented one of the counsellor's remarks early in the session. She thought that he had intimated that she was lazy. Agnes knows that she isn't lazy. They discuss the incident, clear it up and move on. They could have waited until the feedback process at the end of the session, but that would have meant time misused.

Both kinds of immediacy are at work in the following example. Carl Rogers, the dean of client-centred therapy mentioned earlier, talks about one of his clients. Once more, if a feedback system had been in place, this incident would never have happened. But Rogers's self-involving statement, genuine but quite challenging, helped the client move forward, at least at that moment, but from what Rogers said it did not 'solve' the problem. Note also that Rogers called what he did 'confrontation'.

> I am quite certain, even before I stopped carrying individual cases, I was doing more and more of what I would call confrontation. . . . For example, I recall a client with whom I began to realise I felt bored every time he came in. I had a hard time staying awake during the hour, and that was not like me at all. Because it was a persisting feeling, I realised I would have to share it with him. . . . So with a good deal of difficulty and some embarrassment, I said to him, 'I don't understand it myself, but when you start talking on and on about your problems in what seems to me a flat tone of voice, I find myself getting very bored.' This was quite a jolt to him and he looked very unhappy. Then he began to talk about the way he talked and gradually he came to understand one of the reasons for the way he presented himself verbally. He said, 'You know, I think the reason I talk in such an uninteresting way is because I don't think I have ever expected anyone to really hear me.'. . . We got along much better after that because I could remind him that I heard the same flatness in his voice I used to hear.

But there is another point of view on this entire event. Someone once said, 'Boredom is a self-indictment.' In my opinion, Rogers may have been bored because he restricted himself to responding with empathy to his clients. On principle, he did not ordinarily use probing, summaries and challenging lest he rob them of responsibility. He was a master at understanding clients and responding with empathy. But perhaps this story also points to the direction in which Rogers was moving towards the end of his career – adding the 'spice' of probing and challenging to his interactions with clients (see Moon, 2007). This example once more highlights the importance of a mutual session-by-session feedback system. But, if Rogers had employed such a system, we would not have this charming vignette to teach us a lesson.

Situations calling for immediacy

Part of skilled helping – and, more generally, social-emotional intelligence – is knowing when to use any given communication skill. Immediacy can be useful in the following situations:

- When a session is directionless and it seems that no progress is being made.
- When there is tension between helper and client.
- When trust seems to be an issue.
- When diversity, some kind of 'social distance', cultural differences or widely differing interpersonal styles between client and helper seem to be getting in the way.
- When dependency seems to be interfering with the helping process: 'You don't seem willing to explore an issue until I give you permission to do so or urge you to do so. And I seem to have let myself slip into the role of permission giver and nagger.'

Finally, be sure that you know why you are using either form of immediacy. Talking about your relationship with a client is not an end in itself. The relationship is important but the client's goals are even more important. And, once more, all of these situations could be routinely handled with an ongoing feedback system.

THE WIDER USE OF I-B: RISING TO THE CHALLENGE

Chapter 5 introduces the concept of inviting clients to challenge themselves. Ancient Greek wisdom tells us that 'the unexamined life is not worth living'. But because self-examination leads naturally to self-challenge, it is just as true to say that 'the unchallenged life is not worth living'. However, these bits of wisdom are not science.

They are values; they are choices that people can make. It is not our job to make choices for our clients, but I believe that it is our job to help clients set the scene so that they can make choices. As we shall see in Stage II, clients cannot make reasonable *choices* for a better future without first understanding the *possibilities* for a better future.

I've often thought that helping needs to be different from everyday life if it is to make a difference. That is, therapy in itself is, or should be, a challenging experience. We do our clients a disservice if we water it down. If collaboration with our clients is of the essence of therapy, then they should have a good idea of the resources we bring to the table. This means not just the helping model or approach to treatment, but the fibre and substance of the moves and methods within the problem-management approach.

TASK I-C: THE RIGHT STORY

Help clients work on issues that will add value to their lives

Many clients have a range of issues. Tumi certainly does. In that case help them choose issues that will make a significant difference in their lives. If a client wants to work only on trivial things or does not want to work at all, then it might be better to defer counselling.

> At one point Carlos says to Tumi, 'So there are a number of things you would like to do to reset your life. What's most important for you? If you could work on only one or two things, what would that be?' As they talk, three areas of concern emerge. First, Tumi tends to take things as they are. She is reactive rather than proactive. Except for getting a business degree, she has done nothing about developing a career. She feels she has talents she is not using. In one session she notes, 'Everyone sees me as a good worker. I do all my assigned tasks well and on time. I'm a good example for others there. But I don't really add to the business. There's a lot of things we could do to make the business more viable, but I've left all that to my father. But he's not going to do it. Given what's happening in the automotive industry, we could go out of business.' Furthermore, she is on automatic pilot in her dealings with her parents, doing what she is 'supposed' to do. She gets on with the everyday tasks of life quite well. Her parents have never faulted her for not being a contributor.
>
> Second, she has not come to grips with being a South African-British citizen. She has no social life outside the family and work and has a vague sense of taboo when it comes to developing an intimate relationship with a man. She does not know what kind of social being she is or wants to be. She realises that she has come to hate what she calls her 'cultural neutrality'.
>
> Third, she realises she lacks 'enthusiasm', perhaps her way of saying that she feels depressed much of the time. Carlos is quite hesitant to suggest that she work on her 'depression' directly. She seems to be depressed because she feels that she is going nowhere rather than being unable to go anywhere because she is depressed. His best bet is that it will diminish or disappear once she begins to make headway in the substantive areas of her life.
>
> At one point Tumi says, 'I've often thought that my work life and my social life were going nowhere because I'm depressed. To tell you the truth I think it's the opposite.' This is her way of saying that she has to do something about her work life and her social life, with work life taking precedence.

At the beginning of each session Carlos gets feedback from Tumi as to the impact of the previous session. At the end of the session Carlos gets feedback with respect to how the relationship is going, what she has learned during the session and how she intends to make use of what she has learned as she goes about her life between sessions. As a result Tumi feels like she is getting somewhere.

Helping is expensive both financially and psychologically. It should not be undertaken lightly. Therefore, a word is in order about what might be called the 'economics' of helping: helping clients set priorities. The term 'value' is used to introduce the economics of helping. How can we help our clients get the most out of the helping process? Helpers need to ask themselves, 'Am I adding value through each of my interactions with this client?' Clients need to be helped to ask themselves, 'Am I working on the right things? Am I spending my time well in these sessions and between sessions?' The question here is not 'Does helping help?' but 'Is helping working in this situation? Is it worth it?' There are many ways that we can help clients create value. First of all, they create value by working on the right things, addressing issues that will make some kind of substantive difference in their lives. They also create value through the quality of their participation in the helping process and by making the right decisions. In the end it is their process and they can make it value-added or not.

Consider the case of a 41-year-old depressed man with a failing marriage, a boring, run-of-the-mill job, deteriorating interpersonal relationships, health concerns and a drinking problem. He cannot work on everything at once. Priorities need to be set. The blunt questions go something like this: Where is the biggest payoff? Where should the limited resources of both client and helper be invested? Where to start?

Or take the case of Andrea, a woman in her mid-30s, who has been referred to a neighbourhood mental-health clinic by a social worker. During her first visit, she pours out a story of woe, both historical and current – brutal parents, teenage drug abuse, a poor marriage, unemployment, poverty and the like. Andrea is so taken up with getting it all out that the helper can do little more than sit and listen. Where is Andrea to start? How can the time, effort and money invested in helping provide a reasonable return to her? What are the economics of helping in Andrea's case?

PRINCIPLES FOR HELPING CLIENTS WORK ON ISSUES THAT MAKE A DIFFERENCE

The following principles of getting value from the helping process serve as guidelines for choosing issues to be worked on. These seven principles overlap; more than one may apply at the same time:

- Determine whether or not helping is called for or should be continued.
- If there is a crisis, first help the client manage the crisis.
- Begin with the issue that seems to be causing the client the most pain.
- Begin with issues the client sees as important and is willing to work on.
- Begin with some manageable sub-problem of a larger problem situation.
- Move as quickly as possible to a problem that, if handled, will lead to some kind of general improvement.
- Focus on a problem for which the benefits will outweigh the costs.

Underlying all these principles is an attempt to make clients' initial experience of the helping process rewarding so that they will have the incentives they need to continue to work. These principles are guidelines not a set of step-by-step directives. The outcome is important: clients working on issues that will make a difference in their lives. Examples of the use and abuse of these principles follow.

Determine whether or not helping is called for or should be continued

Relatively little is said in the literature about screening – that is, about deciding whether any given problem situation or opportunity deserves attention. The reasons are obvious. Helpers-to-be are rightly urged to take their clients and their clients' concerns seriously. They are also urged to adopt an optimistic attitude, an attitude of hope, about their clients. Finally, they are schooled to take their profession seriously and are convinced that their services can make a difference in clients' lives. For those and other reasons, the first impulse of the average counsellor is to try to help clients no matter what the problem situation might be.

There is something very laudable in this. It is rewarding to see helpers prize people and express interest in their concerns. It is rewarding to see helpers put aside the almost instinctive tendency to evaluate and judge others and to offer their services to clients just because they are human beings. However, like other professions, helping can suffer from the 'law of the instrument'. A child, given a hammer, soon discovers that almost everything needs hammering. Helpers, once equipped with the models, methods and skills of the helping process, can see all human problems as needing their attention. In fact, in many cases, counselling may be a useful intervention but one in which the costs outweigh the benefits.

It's important that the client–helper dialogue determines whether the client is ready to invest in constructive change or not. And to what degree. Change requires work on the part of clients. If they do not have the incentives to do the work, they might begin and then trail off. If this happens, it's a waste of resources. For instance, Helmut and Gretchen are mildly dissatisfied with their marriage and seem to be looking for a 'psychological pill' that will magically make things better. There seem to be few incentives for the work required to reinvent the marriage. Their dialogue with each other and with the counsellor casts doubt on their readiness for change. Further dialogue needs to focus on whether they want to get involved with the work counselling requires. The counsellor need not make a unilateral decision and end up saying:'I don't think this is going to work.' The decision should emerge from the dialogue between helper and client.

Under the term 'differential therapeutics', Frances, Clarkin and Perry (1984) and Clarkin (2005) discussed ways of fitting different kinds of treatment to different kinds of clients. They also discussed the conditions under which 'no treatment' is the best option.

In the no-treatment category, they included clients who have a history of treatment failure or who seem to get worse from treatment, such as the following:

- Criminals trying to avoid or diminish punishment by claiming to be suffering from psychiatric conditions
- Patients with malingering or fictitious illness
- Chronic non-responders to treatment
- Clients likely to improve on their own
- Healthy clients with minor chronic problems
- Reluctant and resistant clients who try one dodge after another to avoid help.

Although helpers and clients together must make a decision in each case, and some might dispute one or more of the categories proposed, the possibility of no treatment deserves serious attention.

It goes without saying that screening can be done in a heavy-handed way. Statements such as the following are not useful:

- 'Your concerns are actually not that serious.'
- 'You should be able to work that through without help.'
- 'I don't have time for problems as simple as that.'

Whether such sentiments are expressed or implied, they obviously indicate a lack of respect and constitute a caricature of the screening process.

Interrupting treatment – the no-further-treatment option – can do a number of useful things: interrupt helping sessions that are going nowhere or are actually destructive; keep both client and helper from wasting time, effort and money; delay help until the client is ready to do the work required for constructive change; provide a 'breather' period that allows the client to consolidate gains from previous treatments; provide the client with an opportunity to discover that he or she can do without treatment; keep helper and client from playing games with themselves and one another; and provide motivation for the client to find help in his or her own daily life. However, helping professionals' decisions not to treat or to discontinue treatment that is proving fruitless are countercultural and therefore difficult to make.

Practitioners in the helping and human-service professions are not alone in grappling with the economics of treatment. Doctors face clients day in and day out with problems that run from the life-threatening to the inconsequential. Statistics suggest that more than half of the people who come to doctors have nothing physically wrong with them. Doctors consequently have to find ways to screen patients' complaints. I am sure that the best doctors find ways to do so that preserve their patients' dignity.

Effective helpers, because they listen well and are empathic, pick up clues relating to a client's commitment, but they don't jump to conclusions. Empathy, as we have seen, is a two-way street and clients often have their private logic which needs to be understood. Helpers test the waters in various ways. If clients' problems seem inconsequential, they probe for more substantive issues. If clients seem reluctant, resistant and unwilling to work, they challenge clients' attitudes and help them work through their resistance. But in both cases they realise that there may come a time, and it may come fairly quickly, to judge that further effort is uncalled for because of lack of results. It is better, however, to help clients make such a decision themselves or challenge them to do so. In the end, the helper might have to call a halt, but his or her way of doing so should reflect basic counselling values.

If there is a crisis, first help the client manage the crisis

Phillip Kleespies (2009) has put together a book dealing with 'behavioural emergencies'. Crises in clients' lives are usually forms of behavioural emergencies. Kleespies focuses on risk for suicide, violence and victimisation, but also discusses common emergency-related crises such as self-injury, personality disorders and substance abuse, such as being caught in the meth trap. Mendenhall (2007), a medical family therapist, gives a striking account of the crises he faces and defuses in the casualty, trauma units and hospital wards. Although crisis intervention is sometimes seen as a special form of counselling (France, 2005), it can also be seen as a rapid application of the three stages of the helping process to the most distressing aspects of a crisis situation.

PRINCIPLE VIOLATED: Zachary, a student near the end of the second year of a four-year doctoral programme in counselling, gets drunk one night and is accused of sexual harassment by a student whom he met at a party. Knowing that he has never sexually harassed anyone, he seeks the counsel of a faculty member whom he trusts. The faculty member asks him many questions about his past, his relationship with women, how he feels about the programme and so on. Zachary becomes more and more agitated and then explodes: 'Why are you asking me all these silly questions?' He stalks out and goes to a fellow student's house.

PRINCIPLE USED: Seeing his agitation, his friend says, 'Good grief, Zach, you look terrible! Come in. What's going on?' He listens to Zachary's account of what has happened, interrupting very little, merely putting in a word here and there to let his friend know he is with him. He sits with Zachary when he falls silent or cries a bit, and then slowly and reassuringly 'talks Zach down', engaging in an easy dialogue that gives his friend an opportunity gradually to find his composure again. Zach's student friend has a friend in the university's student services department. They call him up, go over, and have a counselling and strategy session on the next steps in dealing with the harassment charges.

The friend's instincts are much better than those of the faculty member. He does what he can to defuse the immediate crisis and helps Zach take the next crisis-management step. I use a compressed version of the problem-management process outlined in this book to help clients defuse crises. In helping clients defuse crises, it is important to focus on the context in which the crisis takes place (Myer & Moore, 2006). Because the client is often only one of the stakeholders, a client-only focus can be simplistic and ineffective.

Burnard (2005, pp. 18–20) provides a useful discussion of crisis counselling and highlights Murgatroyd and Woolfe's (1982) characterisation of crisis as the following:

- **Symptoms of stress** – the person experiences stress both physically and psychologically.
- **Attitude of panic and defeat** – the person feels overcome by the situation and experiences both helplessness and hopelessness.
- **Focus on relief** – the person wants, more than anything, relief from the feeling of being in crisis.
- **Lowered efficiency** – in other areas of their life, apart from the crisis, the person's functioning may be impaired.
- **Limited duration** – because the experience is psychologically painful, it does not last long and can be viewed as an acute experience of limited duration.

Burnard also explains how crisis counselling can be delivered through a variety of means, and that telephone crisis counselling can be quite common. He provides an interesting description of how telephone counselling and helping requires a different range of skills from face-to-face counselling because it has to use entirely verbal means of communication between the two people. Burnard's general guidelines to crisis counselling on the telephone include the following:

- Allow the caller to talk freely. Try not to interrupt them but keep them talking.
- Take the lead from the caller. Explore the issues he or she wants to talk about.
- Once you have established rapport, try to make sure that the caller (or other people in his/her company) are out of direct danger.

- Use occasional 'minimal prompts' to indicate that you are listening ('mmm' or 'yes') but use them sparingly.
- If appropriate, make sure that you have the caller's name and a contact phone number. Make sure the caller knows your name.

According to Burnard, 'Crisis counselling calls for swift action in helping the person to function effectively.' Schwartz (cited by Murgatroyd, 1985) offers some suggestions as to how such action may be initiated. Among other things, Schwartz suggests the following steps that the counsellor may take:

- **Help the person to face up to the crisis** – discourage denial and attempt to help him to be objective.
- **Break up the crisis into manageable doses** – most people can deal with serious problems more easily if they are not overwhelmed by the sheer magnitude of the situation.
- **Avoid false reassurance** – the counsellor should resist the temptation to prematurely assure the person in crisis that 'Everything will work out OK.'
- **Help and encourage the person to help himself** – if the person in crisis can actively use the help of friends or family, this will cut down the dependence on the counsellor and increase decision making.
- **Teach the person in crisis coping skills** – once the immediate danger has passed, the individual needs to develop a repertoire of coping strategies to help ward off future and similar situations.

Burnard also warns us that crisis counselling is demanding work and the urgency of the situation often calls for quick decisions to be made. In such situations it is easy to take over too quickly and for the helper to try to take control of the situation – while this may help in the first instance, such an approach does not help the person in crisis in the longer term. Everly and Lating (2004) note the importance of providing support to people in emergent distress, such as in terrorist attacks, natural disasters or distressing situations. They call this support psychological first aid, describing it 'as physical first aid is to the practice of medicine, psychological first aid is to the practice of psychotherapy'. Using the Johns Hopkins RAPID psychological first aid model they emphasise the importance of the following factors when providing individuals in an emergency with psychological support:

R – Rapport and reflective listening
A – Assessment (appraisal of the situation)
P – Prioritisation (psychological triage)
I – Intervention (for example making efforts to stabilise and mitigate the adverse reactions)
D – Disposition (what to do next, 'where do we go from here?')

Bearing all this in mind, let us return to Tumi and Carlos. When Tumi returned from her encounter with her father, she was in crisis. The world she was trying to create fell apart during that conversation. Carlos knew he had to help her handle the crisis as constructively as possible. During the session he used a great deal of empathy to help her work through her disappointment, hurt and bewilderment. But he also looked for signs of the strength or fibre he thought he had seen in her which would be the foundation of resilience. Even though her future now was one big challenging question mark, his best bet was that an extremely important factor in managing the crisis was a return to the work of creating a better future.

Begin with an issue that seems to be causing the client the most pain

Clients often come for help because they are hurting, even though they are not in crisis. Helping them use their hurt as an incentive to work on their problems, then, is a way of adding value. Their pain also makes them vulnerable. If it is evident that they are open to influence because of their pain, seize the opportunity, but move cautiously. Their pain may also make them demanding. They can't understand why you cannot help them get rid of it immediately. This kind of impatience may put you off, but it, too, needs to be understood. Such clients are like patients in Casualty, each seeing himself or herself as needing immediate attention. Their demands for immediate relief may well signal a self-centredness that is part of their character and therefore part of the broader problem situation. It may be that their pain is, in your eyes, self-inflicted, and ultimately you may have to challenge them on it. But pain, whether self-inflicted or not, is still pain. Part of your respect for clients is your respect for them as vulnerable.

PRINCIPLE VIOLATED: Rob, a man in his mid-20s, comes to a counsellor in great distress because his wife has just left him. The counsellor's first impression is that Rob is an impulsive, self-centred person with whom it would be difficult to live. The counsellor immediately challenges him to take a look at his interpersonal style and the ways in which he alienates others. Rob seems to listen, but he does not return.

PRINCIPLE USED: Rob goes to a second counsellor, who also sees a number of clues indicating self-centred-ness and a lack of maturity and discipline. However, she listens carefully to his story, even though it is one-sided and might well be very complicated. She explores with him the incident that precipitated his wife's leaving. Instead of adding to his pain by making him come to grips with his selfishness, she focuses on what he wants for the future, especially the immediate future. Of course, Rob thinks that his wife's return is the most important part of a better future. She says, 'I assume she would have to be comfortable with returning.' He says, 'Of course.' She asks, 'What could you do on your part to help make her more inclined to want to return?' His pain provides the incentive for working with the counsellor on how he might need to change, even in the short term.

The second helper does not use pain as a club. However guilty he might be, Rob didn't need his nose rubbed in his pain. The counsellor helps Rob use his pain as an incentive to deal with the critical issues of his life. What is Rob willing to do to rid himself of his pain and create the future he says he wants?

Tumi's most intense pain came, not from the collapsing of her plans, but from her father's 'brutal' rejection of her. In her eyes she has been loyal, perhaps even overly loyal, to him, and in return she had been dismissed. She was not angry; she was hurt. Carlos thought that it might be useful to help her understand or rather come to grips with her father's rejection. At one point he asks her, 'What sense can you make of what he did?' – not as a way of ignoring her emotions or condoning what her father did, but as a way of tapping into the psychological strength he knew she had.

Begin with issues the client sees as important and is willing to work on

The frame of reference of the client is a starting point in the search for value. Given the client's story, you may think that he or she has not chosen the most important issues for initial consideration. However, helping clients work on issues that are important in their eyes sends an important message: 'Your interests are important to me.'

PRINCIPLE VIOLATED: A woman comes to a counsellor complaining about her relationship with her boss. She believes that he is sexist. Male colleagues not as talented as she get the best assignments and a couple of them are promoted. After listening to her story, the counsellor has her explore her family background for 'context'. After listen-ing, he believes that she probably has some leftover developmental issues with her father and an older brother that affect her attitude towards older men. He pursues this line of thinking with her. She is confused and feels put down. When she does not return for a second interview, the counsellor tells himself that his hypothesis has been confirmed.

PRINCIPLE USED: The woman seeks out a solicitor who deals with equal-opportunity cases. The solicitor, older and not only smart but wise, listens carefully to her story and probes for missing details. Then he gives her a snapshot of what such cases involve when they go to litigation. Against that background, he helps her explore what she really wants. Is it more respect? More pay? A promotion? Revenge? A different kind of boss? A better use of her talents? A job in a company that does not discriminate? Once she names her preferences, he dis-cusses with her options for getting what she wants. Litigation is not one of them.

The first helper substituted his own agenda for hers. He turned out to be somewhat sexist himself. The second helper accepted her agenda and helped her broaden it. He saw no value in litigation, but he did suggest that her problem situation could be an opportunity to reset her career. He suspected that there were plenty of firms eager to employ people of her calibre.

When Carlos asked Tumi what sense she could make of her father's dismissal of her, he was testing the waters. Was making sense of his rejection important to her or at least important enough to start considering at this time?

TUMI: It's important all right. It's critical, but I haven't been able to make any sense of it on my own. I stopped trying.

CARLOS: Maybe you can use me as a sounding board. And we can go slowly. And we can stop whenever you think it's not useful.

TUMI: All right. Let's try.

CARLOS: Let's say that your father, even though he was put off by what you were saying, did his best to have a real dialogue with you, the kind we're having now. Describe what that could have looked like. Describe what you would have found helpful.

TUMI: Well, he would have listened to me more patiently. And he would have asked me some questions, the way you do, so that he could get a clear idea of what I was trying to say. Even if he didn't agree, he could have tried to find out what was motivating me to talk with him in the first place. He would not have assumed that my intent was to betray him.

Carlos goes on to ask what might have prevented her father from doing a more 'decent' job. He makes it clear that he is not trying to help her excuse her father's behaviour, just to understand it. Tumi begins to see that what Carlos is doing is helping her, not to rehash the misery of the past, but to prepare for the next conversation.

Begin with some manageable sub-problem of a larger problem situation

Large, complicated problem situations often remain vague and unmanageable. Dividing a problem into manageable bits can clarify where value lies. Most larger problems can be broken down into smaller, more manageable sub-problems.

PRINCIPLE VIOLATED: Aaron and Ruth, in their mid-50s, have a 25-year-old son living with them who has been diagnosed as schizophrenic. Aaron is a manager in a manufacturing company that is in economic difficulty. His wife has a history of panic attacks and chronic anxiety. All these problems have placed a great deal of strain on the marriage. They both feel guilty about their son's illness. The son has become quite abusive at home and has been stigmatised by people in the neighbourhood for his 'odd' behaviour. Aaron and Ruth have also been stigmatised for 'bringing him up wrong'. They have been seeing a counsellor who specialises in a 'systems' approach to such problems. They are confused by his 'everything is related to everything else' approach. They are looking for relief but are exposed to more and more complexity. They finally come to the conclusion that they do not have the internal resources to deal with the enormity of the problem situation and drop out.

PRINCIPLE USED: A couple of weeks pass before they screw up their courage to contact a psychiatrist, Fiona, whom a family friend has recommended highly. Although Fiona understands the systemic complexity of the problem situation, she also understands their need for some respite. She first sees the son and prescribes some anti-psychotic medication. His odd and abusive behaviour is significantly reduced. Even though Aaron and his wife are not actively religious, she also arranges a meeting with a rabbi from the community known for his ecumenical activism. The rabbi puts them in touch with an ecumenical group of Jews and Christians who are committed to developing a 'city that cares' by starting up neighbourhood groups. Involvement with one of these groups helps diminish their sense of stigma. They still have many concerns, but they now have some relief and better access to both internal and community resources to help them with those concerns.

The psychiatrist helps them target two manageable sub-problems – the son's behaviour and the couple's sense of isolation from the community. Some immediate relief puts them in a much better position to tackle their problems longer term. There are, indeed, serious family systems issues here, but theories and methodologies should not take precedence over the client's immediate needs.

Carlos did not begin the session by saying something like, 'Well, that didn't work at all, Tumi, so what do you think you should do next?' This would be dumping the whole mess into Tumi's lap. Helping her explore her father's behaviour and contrasting it with what she would have found helpful is a way of taking just a piece of the larger problem situation. That is the approach Carlos took. What would you have done in light of the 'manageable sub-problem' principle?

Move as quickly as possible to a problem that, if handled, will lead to some kind of general improvement

Some problems, when addressed, yield results beyond what might be expected. This is the spread effect.

> **PRINCIPLE VIOLATED:** Larry, a single carpenter in his late 20s, living in Pretoria, South Africa, comes to a community mental-health centre with a variety of complaints, including insomnia, light drug use, feelings of alienation from his family, a variety of psychosomatic complaints, and temptations towards exhibitionism. He also has an intense fear of dogs, something that occasionally affects his work. The counsellor sees this last problem as one that can be managed through the application of an evidence-based behaviour modification methodology. He and Larry spend a fair amount of time in the desensitisation of the phobia. Larry's fear of dogs abates quite a bit and many of his symptoms diminish. But gradually the old symptoms re-emerge. His phobia, though significant, is not related closely enough to his primary concerns to involve any kind of significant spread effect.
>
> **PRINCIPLE USED:** Predictably, Larry's major problems re-emerge. One day he becomes disoriented and bangs a number of cars near his job site with his hammer. He is overheard saying, 'I'll get even with you.' He is admitted briefly to a general hospital's psychiatric ward. The immediate crisis is managed quickly and effectively. During his brief stay, he talks with a psychiatric social worker. He feels good about the interaction, and they agree to have a few sessions after he is discharged. In their talks, the focus turns to his isolation. This has a great deal to do with his lack of self-esteem – 'Who would want to be my friend?' The social worker believes that helping Larry to get back into community may well help with other problems. He has managed this problem by staying away from close relationships with both men and women. They discuss ways in which he can begin to socialise. Instead of focusing on the origins of Larry's feelings of isolation, the social worker, taking an opportunity-development approach, helps him involve himself in mini-experiments in socialisation. As Larry begins to get involved with others, his symptoms begin to abate.

The second helper finds Larry's lack of human contact as a starting point in the search for value. The mini-experiments in socialisation reveal some underlying problems. One of the reasons that others shy away from him is his self-centred and abrasive interpersonal style. When he repeats his question – 'Who would want to be my friend?' – the helper responds, 'I bet a lot of people would… if you were a bit more concerned about them and a bit less abrasive. You're not abrasive with me. We get along fine. What's going on?'

Carlos could have put this principle in practice by asking Tumi, 'Name one thing you could do that would help you, if not the most, then help you a great deal?' Let's say that this led to the following conversation:

> **TUMI:** I'd like to work up enough courage to say to myself that I am going to reach out for a different life, that I'm not going to let what happened shut me down. Right now my overwhelming instinct is to retreat to safety, back into the life I've been living. I need the courage to keep moving. I want to be responsible in whatever I do. But I need the guts not to back down.'

They go on to discuss what a 'courageous' Tumi would look like at this time. Tumi points out that if she had a friendship community made up of the kind of people she met in South Africa, it would be so much easier to stick to her guns.

Focus on a problem for which the benefits will outweigh the costs

This is not an excuse for not tackling difficult problems, but it is a call for balance. If you demand a great deal of work from both yourself and the client, then the expectation is that there will be some kind of reasonable payoff for both of you.

PRINCIPLE VIOLATED: Jewel, a young wife living in Bloemfontein, Free State, South Africa discovers to her horror that her husband Dominick is HIV-positive. Tests reveal that she and her recently born son have not contracted the disease. This helps cushion the shock. But she has difficulty with her relationship with Dominick. He claims that he picked up the virus from a 'dirty needle'. But she didn't even know that he had ever used drugs. The counsellor focuses on the need for the 'reconstruction of the marital relationship'. He tells her that some of this would be painful because it would mean looking at areas of their lives that they had never reviewed or discussed. But Jewel is looking for some practical help in reorienting herself to her husband and to family life. After three sessions, she decides to stop coming.

PRINCIPLE USED: Jewel still searches for help. The doctor who is treating Dominick suggests joining one of the self-help groups for spouses, children and partners of HIV-positive patients available locally. In the sessions, Jewel learns a great deal about how to relate to someone who is HIV-positive. The meetings are very practical. The fact that Dominick is not in the group helps. She begins to understand herself and her needs better. In the security of the group, she explores mistakes she has made in relating to Dominick. Although she does not 'reconstruct' either her relationship with Dominick or her own personality, she does learn how to live more creatively with both herself and her husband. She realises that there will probably be further anguish, but she also sees that she is getting better prepared to face that future.

Reconstructing both relationships and personality, even if possible, is a very costly and chancy proposition. The cost–benefit ratio is out of balance. Once more it may be a question of a helper more committed to his or her theories than the needs of clients. Jewel gets the help she needs from the group and from sessions she and Dominick have with a psychiatric aide. The value or value-seeking mindset that pervades these principles is second nature in effective helpers. Box 8.3 lists some questions you can help clients ask themselves with an aim to adding value by working on the right things.

BOX 8.3   Helping Clients Create Value by Working on the Right Things

Here are some questions related to the search for value that counsellors can help clients ask themselves:

- What problem or opportunity should I really be working on?
- Which issue, if faced, would make a substantial difference in my life?
- Which problem or opportunity has the greatest payoff value?
- Which issue do I have both the will and the courage to work on?
- Which problem, if managed, will take care of other problems?
- Which opportunity, if developed, will help me deal with critical problems?
- What is the best place for me to start?
- If I need to start slowly, where should I start?
- If I need a boost or a quick win, which problem or opportunity should I work on?

When Tumi says that her immediate instinct is to fade back into the safety of the life she has been living, she is doing a quick cost–benefit analysis driven by her hurt and fear. She knows the power of the cultural law or mandate that permeates her thinking and feeling: 'Do nothing that would harm, offend, or even annoy your parents and always place their needs and wants above your own.' She knows that she wants to honour her parents, even as she questions the principle. Carlos knows that he needs to help her negotiate with herself.

THE WIDER USE OF I-C: MAKING THE RIGHT CHOICES

For clients Task I-C means initially choosing which issues to work on. Tumi decides that working directly on her depression makes no sense. She believes that doing something about a career will clear her mind and give her something to strive for. She even thinks that work will help her with her social life. Career and a better social life, in that order, are most likely the answer to her depression. Working on these two issues has value for her. Indeed, value is a cardinal word in therapy. The wider use of Task I-C revolves around value.

So the spirit of I-C moves beyond the clients choosing the right things to work on. In its fullness it contributes to clients' search for meaning. 'Meaning' is one of those words. In the sense that it is being used here it has no basis in science, at least in a narrow understanding of science. When a client says that her life is 'meaningless', we know instinctively what she means, even if we know little about the specifics. Stories in the therapeutic encounter are often enough about the lack of meaning, even though the specifics differ from client to client. Things have meaning to the degree that they relate to our values. So the beliefs-values-norms-ethics-morality package permeates the helping process. It cannot be different, even though the makeup of this package differs from client to client.

Clients don't find value. Rather they *create* value through the choices they make and the way they translate these choices into action and life-enhancing outcomes. Task I-C is not just about choosing the right things to work on. It involves making the right decisions at every step of the helping process.

So the spirit of I-B and I-C permeates the whole of the helping process and involves decision making based on clients' beliefs and values. At their core, B and C are both invitations to self-challenge and a search for value. The principle is this: in every stage and every task collaborate with the client and enlist his or her collaboration in adding value and making a difference – focusing on issues that make a difference, engaging in substantive self-challenge, setting goals that make a difference, coming to grips with commitment to these goals, making plans that go somewhere and engaging in life-enhancing change in everyday life. If you and your client are dabbling in change, then reset the system or forget the whole thing. Box 8.4 provides some broad guidelines for helping your clients get the most value out of therapy.

BOX 8.4	**Broad Guidelines in the Search for Value**

- Help clients focus on issues that have payoff potential for them.
- Maintain a sense of movement and direction in the helping process.
- Avoid unnecessarily extending the problem identification and exploration stage.
- Help clients move to the stages of the helping process that will provide them with most value.
- Remember that clients are making decisions throughout the helping process and can, at times, benefit from your help.
- Encourage clients to act on what they are learning.

Most therapy engagements are relatively short term – say, six to ten sessions. A lot can be accomplished in that period of time, especially if therapy is designed to help clients 'push start' themselves towards more productive or life-enhancing ways of thinking, behaving, dealing with emotions and coping with negative experiences. When our clients leave us, they should be managing their problem situations more effectively or be well on their way. There is also some evidence that longer-term therapy can, in some cases, add even more value.

CHAPTER 9
STAGE II: HELPING CLIENTS DESIGN PROBLEM-MANAGING OUTCOMES AND SET GOALS

Chapter Contents

- What Kind of Change Do Clients Need and How Much?

- Emerging Goals

- Task II-C: Help Clients Commit Themselves – 'What Am I Willing to Pay for What I Want?'

- Help Clients Commit Themselves to a Better Future

- Great Expectations: Encourage Client Self-Efficacy – 'I Can, I Will'

- Stage II and Action

- The Shadow Side of Goal Setting

AN INTRODUCTION TO STAGE II

In many ways Stages II and III, together with the Action Arrow, are the most important parts of the helping model because they are about problem-managing outcomes in an approach to helping that is client-directed and outcome-informed (CDOI). It is here that counsellors help clients develop and implement programmes for constructive change. The payoff for identifying and clarifying both problem situations and unused opportunities lies in doing something about them. Insights are fine only to the degree that they lead directly or indirectly to problem-managing action. The skills helpers need to help clients to do precisely that – engage in constructive change – are reviewed and illustrated in Stages II and III. In these stages, counsellors help clients ask and answer the following two common-sense but critical questions: 'What outcomes do I want?' and 'What do I have to do to get what I want?' Stages II and III are about a better future for our clients.

The three tasks of Stage II

Problems can make clients feel hemmed in and closed off. With respect to the problem situation there is no positive future. Both the present and future look troubled. But, as Gelatt (1989) noted, 'The future does not exist and cannot be predicted. It must be imagined and invented' (p. 255). The interrelated tasks of Stage II outline three ways in which helpers can partner with their clients with a view to exploring, designing and developing this better future.

- **Task II-A – Problem-Managing Possibilities**. 'What possibilities do I have for a better future?' 'What are some of the things I think I want?' 'What about my needs?' 'What would my problem situation look like if it were being managed well?' In helping clients move from problems to solutions, counsellors help them develop a sense of hope.
- **Task II-B – Goals, Outcomes and Impact**. 'What do I really want and need? What outcomes will manage my problem situation?' Here counsellors help clients craft a viable change agenda from among the possibilities. Helping them shape this agenda is one of the central tasks of helping.
- **Task II-C – Commitment**. 'What am I willing to pay for what I want?' Help clients discover incentives for commitment to their change agenda.

Without minimising in any way what counsellors can help their clients accomplish through Stage I skills and interventions – that is, problem and opportunity clarification; the development of new, more constructive perspectives of self, others and the world; the choice of high-leverage issues to work on – the real power of helping lies in assisting clients to set goals and move to accomplish them. However, in actual counselling sessions, Stages I and II are intermingled. Stories lead to the setting of problem-managing goals, there is a return to the story and new perspectives emerge, and then the goals are modified, and, added to this, clients take small or large actions that move them towards problem-managing outcomes, which, in turn, have an impact on the entire process. The cyclical nature of the client's difficulties can be outlined and explained in order to see how the cycle can be broken through collaborative working. Become comfortable in the geography of helping so that you can move with clients in order to help them move forward. Figure 9.1 highlights the three tasks of Stage II. Tasks II-B and II-C are explored later in this chapter.

FIGURE 9.1 The three tasks of Stage II

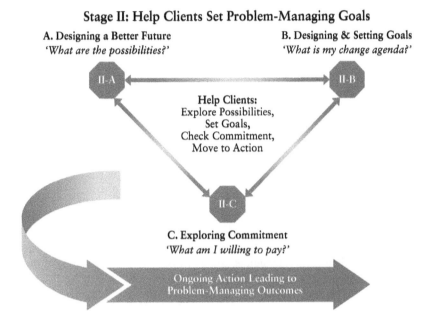

Solution: An ambiguous term

As noted earlier, in many versions of the Standard Problem-Management Model the exploration and clarification of problem situations (the work of Stage I) are followed, almost immediately, by the search for 'solutions', that is, actions that will remedy the problem or develop the opportunity. A more solution-focused and goal-directed approach could be beneficial for the client. After a devastating encounter with a nurse, Derek, a surgeon, finally realises that his I'm-always-right approach to communication is counterproductive. It simply doesn't work. That evening he discusses the encounter with the nurse with his wife. She has heard this story before, but she hears something a bit different. At the end of the conversation she says, 'It sounds like you think that it's time to do something about this.' All he says is, 'Yeah.' Beginning the next day he starts to listen to staff members. He doesn't always agree, but he listens. When he makes decisions, he tries not to shove them down the throats of his co-workers. Within weeks there is a different, more settled, even positive, atmosphere in the operating room. So sometimes this problem-to-solution approach works, but there are some caveats. The problem-to-solution approach ignores the logic of problem management because it leaves out the goals-outcomes-impact package that is at the heart of problem management. It might have been better if he had stopped to think about what the dimensions of a communication style that made sense to him, his colleagues and the hospital should look like. He could then move on to design that style at the service of his profession.

A *goal* is some desired state. Clive, the young man in DUI trouble mentioned earlier, realised that an essential goal was to stop drinking. But a goal is just an idea until it is accomplished. An accomplished goal is an *outcome*, and, as we have seen, therapy is about life-enhancing outcomes for clients. Clive, perhaps driven by the fear of jail time for one more DUI citation, joined Alcoholics Anonymous, conscientiously followed the programme and stopped drinking – an essential outcome. But there is one more important factor or dimension. The outcome must have the desired *impact* on the client's life; that is, it must be a *problem-managing* outcome (or opportunity-developing outcome), which it was in Clive's case. He no longer had to fear another DUI citation as long as he avoided alcohol. In a sense we can say that Clive 'solved' his problem. In many ways, outcomes are more important than actions through which they are achieved. Although Clive chose the Alcoholics Anonymous programme, he could have cut his addiction to alcohol in other ways.

Perhaps it is best to avoid the word 'solution'. At times, managing an issue is a good enough outcome for clients. Mathematical problems have solutions, but problems in living need to be managed rather than solved. Moreover, when it comes to changing human behaviour, the term 'solution' can mean two different things. An outcome with the desired impact is a solution with a big *S* – in Clive's case eliminating the alcohol habit. The actions leading to this outcome – his adherence to the Alcoholics Anonymous programme – constitute a solution with a small *s*. Programmes that lead to outcomes are not outcomes themselves. They should not be confused. When facing a problem situation, some, perhaps many, clients try a variety of solutions-with-a-small-s, that is, action programmes, until they find one that works. This may ultimately be effective; that is, the goal *is* accomplished, but the hit-and-miss process leading to the accomplishment is not very efficient. People don't tend to learn very much from this approach, but they keep trying it because 'it works'. Again, this cyclical nature enables clients to see how they start to work on goals and how outcomes and solutions (with a small s) then feed into more goals and so on.

Therapy: Art or science?

The answer to the question 'Is therapy an art or a science?' is 'both'. It is a product of the social sciences (not the 'hard' sciences such as physics or chemistry) so it is imperative that therapists adapt and tailor its research findings to the needs of clients. One way of saying this is that there is an element of *design* in what we do. Thus the use of the word 'design' rather than just 'set' in relation to goals, in the title of Stage II. Therapists help clients design their future. Design is usually associated with the arts. But there is a movement to incorporate 'design thinking' with problem management (Ambrose & Harris, 2010; Lockwood, 2010), or to incorporate problem-management thinking with design. Ill-defined problems constitute the starting point of design thinking, which moves on to acquiring a deeper understanding of the context of the problem. This kind of thinking highlights creativity in the search for insights and solutions. It often starts with the goal, then moves between the present and the future in the search for creative solutions. The ultimate challenge is to fit the solution to the context.

As you can see, much of design thinking sounds like some of the main themes of the *art* of problem management. Remember what we said about therapy: it needs to be both rigorous and soft-edged. There is both art and science in what we do. There is an art to helping clients explore possibilities for a better future before nailing down one possibility or a particular set. While a lot of the books on design thinking are focused on business (Merholz, Wilkens, Schauer & Verba, 2008) they still provide a good account of the principles underlying such thinking. Stanford University offers a Design-Thinking Boot Camp that is associated with its business school. There are a number of design-thinking programmes for higher education and for educators in general (Bell, 2010). IDEO, a global design firm, relates design thinking to creating a more desirable future in the face of difficult challenges. Sounds like Stage II of the problem-management process. Some see design thinking as nonsense, perhaps because of the way it mixes art and reason, but I see it as a softer-edged contribution to the helping professions that can help produce hard-edged results.

THE ROLE OF HOPE IN THERAPY

Stage II is about yet-to-be-realised outcomes. It's about the future. And so hope, another soft-edged concept or experience that can have a hard-edged impact on therapeutic outcomes, is involved. Hope as part of human experience is as old as humanity. Who of us has not started sentences with 'I hope...'? Who of us has not experienced hope or lost hope? Hope also has a long history as a religious concept. St Paul said, 'Hope that centres around things you can see is not really hope', thus highlighting the element of uncertainty. If you know that tomorrow you will receive an Oscar, you can no longer hope for it. You know it's a sure thing. Hope plays a key role in both developing and implementing possibilities for a better future and is essential in counselling and psychotherapy (O'Hara, 2013). O'Hara writes about the emergence of hope within the helping professions. Helpers can be witnesses to clients' hopelessness and pain, and having an understanding of the importance of hope within this context can be beneficial for both the helper and client.

Rick Snyder, who, as we have seen earlier, has written extensively about the positive and negative uses of excuses in everyday life (Snyder & Higgins, 1988; Snyder, Higgins & Stucky, 1983), became a kind of champion for hope (1994, 1995, 1998; McDermott & Snyder, 1999; Snyder, McDermott, Cook & Rapoff, 1997; Snyder, Michael & Cheavens, 1999). Indeed, he linked excuses and hope in an article titled 'Reality Negotiation: From Excuses to Hope and Beyond' (1989). He died in 2006 and the encomiums he received at the time of his death from his colleagues at the University of Kansas indicated how well he lived what he preached. One colleague, Ray Higgins, summed it up: 'Rick was one of the most courageous and generous people I have known. His seminal work on the psychology of hope grew out of his own 15-year struggle with chronic pain. He was a beloved mentor and life teacher for scores of students and was never so passionate as when he was helping others achieve their goals. A natural leader in life, in his dying he was still showing us the way.'

In psychological terms hope in therapy is sometimes called 'expectancy'. Or, because expectancies can be positive, neutral or negative, the term 'positive-outcome expectancy bias' is used. There is plenty of evidence to show that clients who expect therapy outcomes to be positive have a better chance of achieving positive outcomes. That's why it is important that therapists do their part in establishing a working alliance with clients and get clients aboard the method of treatment to be used. At any rate, hope and expectancy can play an important role in therapy (Reiter, 2010; Westra, Constantino & Aviram, 2011 – an internet search will give you dozens of articles).

The nature of hope

Over the course of history there have been different takes on hope. German philosopher Friedrich Nietzsche's view lies at the negative end when he says that 'hope is the worst of all evils, because it prolongs man's torments'. In a different vein, Gerard Manley Hopkins in his poem *The Wreck of the Deutschland* gives two different views of hope. When a ship is sinking and it seems that any kind of rescue is impossible, he writes sadly:

> *Hope had grown grey hairs,*
> *Hope had mourning on,*
> *Trenched with tears, carved with cares,*
> *Hope was twelve hours gone.*

But later Hopkins talks about a nun aboard the ship who, knowing that all is lost, cries out in resignation to her God – not a cry of despair but of a different kind of hope.

More positive literary portrayals of hope include the famous Ancient Greek myth of Pandora's Box (where Hope flies out after Envy, Crime, Hate and Disease have all been released from the box) and 19th-century American poet Emily Dickinson's poem *Hope*. This opens with the words 'Hope is the thing with feathers, that perches in the soul' and closes with a positive message about hope:

> *I've heard it in the chillest land,*
> *And on the strangest sea;*
> *Yet, never, in extremity,*
> *It asked a crumb of me.*

More subtly, the theme of hope runs as an undercurrent through much literature emerging from troubled political times, including much of the South African literature written about and during the years of apartheid. One example is former South African President Nelson Mandela's autobiography, *The Long*

Walk to Freedom, published in 1994 by Little Brown & Co. The book profiles his early life, coming of age, education and 27 years in prison. Under the apartheid government, Mandela was regarded as a terrorist, and was jailed for his role as a leader of the then-outlawed African National Congress. A classic quote from the book which encapsulates the important role of hope is as follows:

> *"I am fundamentally an optimist. Whether that comes from nature or nurture, I cannot say. Part of being optimistic is keeping one's head pointed towards the sun, one's feet moving forward. There were many dark moments when my faith in humanity was sorely tested, but I would not and could not give myself up to despair. That way lays defeat and death."*

A second example is Njabulo Ndebele's novel *Fools and Other Stories* (first published in 1983), which evokes township life with humour and subtlety, rejecting the image of black South Africans as victims and focusing instead on the complexity and fierce energy of their lives. The novel explores how and why people can survive under such harsh conditions as Apartheid rule, and the role of hope in making this possible is a central theme.

Even in science there are positive views of hope and some research is backing them up. Jerome Groopman (2004), who holds a chair of medicine at Harvard Medical School, in a very moving book on the anatomy of hope, defines it as 'the elevating feeling we experience when we see – in the mind's eye – a path to a better future. Hope acknowledges the significant obstacles and deep pitfalls along that path. True hope has no room for delusion' (p. xiv). His search for a scientific basis for understanding the key role hope plays in dealing with illness takes him to the 'biology' of hope. His book also shows how counselling is at the heart of medical practice.

Snyder, on the other hand, started with the premise that human beings are goal directed and relates hope to the goal-setting process. According to Snyder, hope is the process of:

- Thinking about one's goals – for instance, Abri is determined that she will give up smoking, drinking and soft drugs now that she is pregnant.
- Having the will, desire or motivation to move towards these goals – Abri is serious about her goal because she has seen the damaged children of mothers on drugs, and she is also, at heart, a decent, caring person.
- Thinking about the strategies for accomplishing one's goals – Abri knows that two or three of her friends will give her the support she needs and she is willing to join an arduous 12-step programme to achieve her goal.

Hope is a dimension of the problem-management process. Abri is hopeful. If we say that Abri has 'high hopes', we mean that her goal is clear, her sense of agency (or urgency) is high and that she is realistic in planning the pathways to her goal. Both a sense of agency and some clarity around pathways are required.

Hope, of course, has emotional connotations. But it is not a free-floating emotion. Rather, it is the by-product or outcome of the work of setting goals, developing a sense of agency and devising pathways to the goal. Abri feels a mixture of positive emotions – elation, determination, satisfaction – knowing that 'the will' (agency) and 'the way' (pathways) have come together. Success is in sight even though she knows that there will be barriers – for instance, the ongoing lure of tobacco, wine and soft drugs.

The benefits of hope

Snyder (1995, pp. 357–358) combed the research literature in order to discover the benefits of hope as he defines it. Here is what he found:

> *"The advantages of elevated hope are many. Higher as compared with lower hope people have a greater number of goals, have more difficult goals, have success at achieving their goals, perceive their goals as challenges, have greater happiness and less distress, have superior coping skills, recover better from physical injury, and report less burnout at work, to name but a few advantages."*

It is not suggested here that hope 'cures cancer' or any other malady. There is evidence, however disputed (for instance, Coyne, Stefanek & Palmer, 2007, review 'the conflict between hope and evidence'), that hope has a positive effect on the lives of many people. An article in the *Harvard Heart Letter* (August 2008) highlights the benefits of hope but counsels balance: 'Hope is a powerful force. It can sustain you through personal tragedy or can carry you through the dark tunnel of disease. A sense of realism matters, too, grounding hope before it flits into fantasy' (p. 2).

In summary, counsellors who do not spend a significant part of their time helping clients develop possibilities, clarify goals, devise strategies or pathways and develop the sense of agency needed to bring all of this to fruition are certainly short-changing their clients. Because Stages II and III deal with possibilities, goals, commitment, pathways and overcoming barriers, they could be named 'ways of nurturing hope'.

TASK II-A: HELP CLIENTS DISCOVER POSSIBILITIES FOR A BETTER FUTURE

The goal of Task II-A is to help clients develop a sense of direction by exploring *possibilities* for a better future. I once was sitting alone at the counter of a late-night diner when a young man sat down next to me, even though all the other stools were empty. The conversation drifted to the problems he was having with a friend of his. I listened for a while and then asked, 'Well, if your relationship was just what you wanted it to be, what would it look like?' It took him a bit of time to get started, but eventually he drew a picture of the kind of relationship he could live with. Then he stopped, looked at me, and said, 'You must be a professional.' I believe he thought that I must be a professional because this was the first time in his life that anyone had ever asked him to describe some possibilities for a better future.

Reviewing possibilities for a better future often helps clients move beyond the problem-and-misery mindset they bring with them and develop a sense of hope. It can also help clients understand their problem situations better – 'Now that I am beginning to know what I want, I can see my problems and unused opportunities more clearly.' This is a common example of the intermingled nature of the task of the problem-management process. Let's take a look at Tumi's involvement in Task II-B.

One theme she explores is 'Tumi the doer'. 'Doer' is her code for substantial change. She wants to change from being a passive person who manages the everyday problems of life 'well enough' to a person who reaches out to life. She describes the direction in terms of an article she has read on the path to leadership: 'from observer to participant to player to contributor and, who knows, maybe even leader'. Carlos says, 'Tell me what the new Tumi would look like. Draw me some pictures.' Tumi does precisely that. She says that she would like to draw on her business education and be more assertive at work. 'For instance, the dealership has no business strategy. I could pull one together. I know the numbers better than anyone. And then we could debate it.' She even talks about the possibility of getting an MBA part time and moving out of her father's business. A wilder thought is getting a job with either Honda or Toyota. They're both growing. What could possibly be better than that?

Another area of 'doing' is family and social life. She is dissatisfied with home life. 'I want to move from dutiful daughter to partner. I'm an adult.' The new Tumi wants to be one of the decision makers at home. While she doesn't like the fact that her parents lead such a quiet life – they see it as quiet, while she is beginning to see it as dull – she realises that it's not her job to change them. She also dislikes time spent with her two married cousins. She is turned off by what she sees as their narcissism. She is not sure that she wants to be married, but she wants to find out whether she wants to or not. She certainly does not want a marriage like the marriages of her cousins.

Too many clients are locked in to the present. Even when they try to use their imaginations, they think incrementally. The future they envisage is not much better than the present they dislike. Helpers do a service for their clients when they encourage them to engage in some kind of 'breakaway' thinking.

SKILLS FOR IDENTIFYING POSSIBILITIES FOR A BETTER FUTURE

At its best, counselling helps clients move from problem-centred mode to 'discovery' mode. Discovery mode involves creativity and divergent thinking. Do an internet search on creativity and divergent thinking and you will be overwhelmed by the results. Dean Simonton (2000) reviewed advances in our understanding and use of creativity as part of positive psychology. According to Taylor, Pham, Rivkin and Armor (1998), however, not just any kind of mental stimulation will do. Mental stimulation is helpful to the degree that it:

> *"provides a window on the future by enabling people to envision possibilities and develop plans for bringing those possibilities about. In moving oneself from a current situation towards an envisioned future one, the anticipation and management of emotions and the initiation and maintenance of problem-solving activities are fundamental tasks."* (p. 429)

Your role in helping clients become more creative in their thinking about the future is important, even essential. Exploring new possibilities or different ways of thinking can be a turning point in helping the client tackle their challenges. Uzzi and Spiro (2005) debunk the myth that creativity is the 'brash work of loners' (p. 448). The research shows that creative thinking and acting at its best is a social enterprise. When it comes to therapy, one (the client on his or her own) is not enough. Too many cooks – the client with therapist, friends, relatives and others all providing noisy help – can, predictably, spoil the broth. Helping is a two-person collaborative exercise in creativity. You are truly a catalyst for the client's elusive creative abilities. The research also suggests that small-group therapy, done right, can be powerful.

Trying to imagine a future in which the problem situation is being managed well is not just fantasy or rumination because of its link to the problem situation. If I ask a married couple, 'If you are to stay married, what kind of marriage do you want?', their answer is rooted in what they have but don't want. They are being asked to move beyond the problem situation that they know only too well. They are being asked, to use Simonton's phrase, to 'harness the imagination'. Here are some ways to help clients do precisely that.

Help clients focus on their 'possible selves'

One of the characters in Gail Godwin's (1985) novel *The Finishing School* warns against getting involved with people who have 'congealed into their final selves'. Clients come to helpers, not necessarily because they have congealed into their final selves – if this is the case, why come at all? – but because they are stuck in their current selves. Counselling is a process of helping clients get 'unstuck' and develop a sense of direction. Markus and Nurius used the term 'possible selves' to represent 'individuals' ideas of what they might become, what they would like to become and what they are afraid of becoming' (1986, p. 954). Over the years a great deal of interesting and clinically useful research has been done on the concept of 'possible selves' (Bardach *et al.*, 2010; Carroll, Shepperd & Arkin, 2009; Cross & Markus, 1991, 1994; Eagly, Eastwick & Johannesen-Schmidt, 2009; Meek, 2011; Oyserman, Bybee, Terry & Hart-Johnson, 2004; Robinson, Davis & Meara, 2003; Rossiter, 2007). Although we are using the term as a tool for helping clients imagine a better future for themselves, it is also possible that clients come to us with very limiting or negative possible selves. Consider the case of Ernesto. He was very young, but very stuck for a variety of sociocultural and emotional reasons.

A counsellor first met Ernesto in the casualty department of a large urban hospital in Glasgow, Scotland. He was throwing up blood into a pan. He was a member of a street gang, and this was the third time he had been beaten up in the last year. He had been so severely beaten this time that it was likely that he would suffer permanent physical damage. Ernesto's lifestyle was doing him in, but it was the only one he knew. No thought of any kind of positive possible self crossed his mind. He was in desperate need of a new way of living, a new scenario, a new way of participating in city life. This time he was hurting enough to consider the possibility of some kind of change. The counsellor worked with Ernesto, not by helping him explore the complex sociocultural and emotional reasons he was in this fix, but principally by helping him explore his positive 'possible selves' in order to discover a different purpose in life, a different direction, a different lifestyle.

Remember that identifying and developing an opportunity can help clients manage a problem by transcending rather than 'solving' it. Just under 12 million people with physical challenges live in the United Kingdom. Brenda, a victim of a hit-and-run driver, is one of them. The accident left her with a back condition that cut short her career as a fitness instructor and left her understandably depressed. She was now one of the physically challenged who, as noted by Cartwright, Arredondo and D'Andrea (2004), 'possess strengths that are often overlooked by persons in the dominant cultural group in general and by many counsellors who work with these persons in particular' (p. 24).

Some of Brenda's friends now saw her as 'broken' and shied away from spending time with her. Unfortunately, her counsellor also fell into this category. He was sympathetic, rather than empathic, and expected little from her. Once she realised that this relationship was one of the main sources of her depression, she switched counsellors. Her new counsellor used the notion of possible selves to help Brenda use inner resources to focus on opportunities rather than loss. She found ways of coping with her chronic pain. She had always been interested in design, but never had the time to pursue this interest. Now she wanted to experiment with becoming an interior designer. This was one of her possible selves. She took online courses and purchased design software. She became a successful interior designer, now mentally and imaginatively active, and she did whatever she could physically. She became so engaged in her new career that there was no need to mourn the loss of her previous one. Her new career also brought some new friends. She still lived with her bad back, but transcending was her way of coping.

The second counsellor quickly spotted pools of resilience, together with a range of strengths and talent in Brenda. He helped her tap into the positive resources within her. Possible selves are broader and therefore richer than stark behavioural goals. 'Possible selves encompass not only the goals we are seeking but all the imaginable futures we might occupy' (King & Hicks, 2007, p. 626). The term 'possible self', although psychologically respectable, has a flair to it that can capture clients' imaginations in a way that behavioural goals cannot. Possible selves is an element of self-knowledge that can be used to help the client self-regulate (Bak, 2015).

Help clients tap into their creativity

There has been an enormous amount of research on creativity and creative thinking (Kaufman & Sternberg, 2010) and a parallel literature on how to apply the findings of this research in everyday life (Wolff, 2009). Wolff's book is divided into four parts, each addressing a separate piece of the creative process. Each of these sections is further divided into 25 short chapters. They are:

Dreaming – a number of ways you can put yourself into a more creative frame of mind

Originating – a range of methods for generating new ideas

Varying – dealing with how to take something that already exists and use creative ideas to make it better or different

Adapting – short overviews of the methods others have used to turn possibilities into realities.

If you think your ability to help your clients think and act more creatively could use a boost, read this. Some members of the helping profession look down on such 'how to' writings because they are simplistic or have not been 'proved' to be effective by proper research methodologies. Two things: first, I will use anything I believe will help clients; second, for me proof lies in the ways Wolff has used these to be very creative. The focus is always on what best suits the client's needs.

One of the myths of creativity is that some people are creative and others are not. All of us have some spark of creativity within us. So clients can be more creative than they are. It is a question of finding ways to help them be so. Of course, counsellors cannot help clients be more creative unless they themselves are creative about the helping process itself. Carson and Becker (2004; see also Carson & Becker, 2003), in reviewing a group of articles in a special 2002 issue of the *Journal of Clinical Activities, Assignments & Handouts in Psychotherapy Practice*, edited by L. Hecker (see Hecker & Kottler, 2002; Kottler & Hecker, 2002), suggest that 'being able to access our own creativity at peak levels in an effort to help clients tap their own creative problem-solving abilities (internal and relational) and creative resources is a prerequisite to effective therapy' (p. 111). Clients, they say, should be a source of creativity for helpers and vice versa. Stages II and III help clients tap into their dormant creativity.

A review of the requirements for creativity (see Cole & Sarnoff, 1980; Robertshaw, Mecca & Rerick, 1978, pp. 118–120) shows, by implication, that people in trouble often fail to use whatever creative resources they might have. The creative person is characterised by the following:

- Optimism and confidence (whereas clients are often depressed and feel powerless)
- Acceptance of ambiguity and uncertainty (whereas clients may feel tortured by ambiguity and uncertainty and want to escape from them as quickly as possible)
- A wide range of interests (whereas clients may be people with a narrow range of interests or whose normal interests have been severely narrowed by anxiety and pain)
- Flexibility (whereas clients may have become rigid in their approach to themselves, others and the social settings of life)
- Tolerance of complexity (whereas clients are often confused and looking for simplicity and simple solutions)
- Verbal fluency (whereas clients are often unable to articulate their problems, much less their goals and ways of accomplishing them)
- Curiosity (whereas clients may not have developed a searching approach to life or may have been hurt by being too venturesome)
- Drive and persistence (whereas clients may be all too ready to give up)
- Independence (whereas clients may be quite dependent or counter-dependent)
- Non-conformity or reasonable risk taking (whereas clients may have a history of being very conservative and conformist or may have got into trouble with others and with society precisely because of their particular brand of non-conformity).

A review of some of the principal obstacles or barriers to creativity (see Azar, 1995) brings further problems to the surface. Innovation is hindered by the following:

- Fear – clients are often quite fearful and anxious.
- Fixed habits – clients may have self-defeating habits or patterns of behaviour that may be deeply ingrained.
- Dependence on authority – clients may come to helpers looking for the 'right answers' or be quite counter-dependent (the other side of the dependency coin) and fight efforts to be helped with a variety of games.
- Perfectionism – clients may come to helpers precisely because they are hounded by this problem and can accept only ideal or perfect solutions.
- Problems with social networks – being 'different' sets clients apart when they want to belong.

It is easy to say that imagination and creativity are most useful in Stages II and III, but it is another thing to help clients stimulate their own, perhaps dormant, creative potential. Although there is a very rich body of literature on creativity, including creativity in the helping professions (Carson & Becker, 2003; Carson, Becker, Vance & Forth, 2003; Sternberg, Grigorenko & Singer, 2004), only a small percentage of this creativity seems to find its way into the helping process. The 13 chapters of the edited book *Everyday Creativity* (Richards, 2007) will send your mind racing in search for ways of tapping into your own creativity and helping clients tap into theirs. Perhaps one sign of creativity's increasing importance is the formation of the Association for Creativity in Counselling, which sponsors the *Journal of Creativity in Mental Health*. In the book *Therapy and Beyond* (Milton, 2010) the authors draw on a variety of areas within counselling psychology, including working creatively with clients in a wide variety of settings. This openness, playfulness and creativity within a therapeutic relationship is beneficial for the client to co-construct new meanings and ways of working.

Help clients engage in divergent thinking

Many people habitually take a convergent-thinking approach to problem solving – that is, they look for the 'one right answer' or the one that would be culturally acceptable. Such thinking has its uses, of course. Often enough there is a right answer. However, many of life's problem situations are too complex to be handled by convergent thinking. Such thinking limits the ways in which people use their own and environmental resources.

Divergent thinking, on the other hand, assumes that there is always more than one answer. De Bono (1992) called it 'lateral thinking'. It is related to curiosity, 'a positive emotional-motivational system associated with the recognition, pursuit and self-regulation of novelty and challenge' (Kashdan, Rose & Fincham, 2004, p. 291). In helping, divergent thinking means 'more than one way to manage a problem or develop an opportunity'. Unfortunately, as helpful as it can be, divergent thinking is not always rewarded in our culture and sometimes is even punished. For instance, students who think divergently can be thorns in the sides of teachers. Some teachers feel comfortable only when they ask questions in such a way as to elicit the 'one right answer'. When students who think divergently give answers that are different from the ones expected – even though their responses might be quite useful (perhaps more useful than the expected responses) – the students may be ignored, corrected or punished. Students then may generalise their experience and end up thinking that it is simply not a useful form of behaviour. Consider the following case.

> Quentin wanted to be a doctor, so he enrolled in a preparatory course for medicine. He did well but not well enough to get into medical school. When he received the last notice of refusal, he said to himself, 'Well, that's it for me and the world of medicine. Now what will I do?' When he graduated, he took a job in his brother-in-law's business. He became a manager and did fairly well financially, but he never experienced much career satisfaction. He was glad that his marriage was good and his home life rewarding, because he derived little satisfaction from his work.

Not much divergent thinking went into handling this problem situation. No one asked Quentin what he really wanted. For Quentin, becoming a doctor was the 'one right career'. He didn't give serious thought to any other career related to the field of medicine, even though there are dozens and dozens of interesting and challenging jobs in the field of healthcare.

The case of Caroline, who also wanted to become a doctor but failed to get into medical school, is quite different from that of Quentin.

> Caroline thought to herself, 'Medicine still interests me; I'd like to do something in the health field.' With the help of a medical career counsellor, she reviewed the possibilities. She had never realised that there were so many medical careers other than just medicine. She decided to take whatever courses and practicum experiences she needed to become a nurse. Then, while working in a clinic in the hills of Appalachia – an invaluable experience for her – she managed to get an MA in family-practice nursing by attending a nearby university part time. She chose this speciality because she thought that it would enable her to be closely associated with delivery of a broad range of services to patients and would also enable her to have more responsibility for the delivery of these services.
>
> When Caroline graduated, she entered private practice as a nurse practitioner with a doctor in a small town. As the doctor divided his time among three small clinics, Caroline had a great deal of responsibility in the clinic where she practised. She also taught a course in family-practice nursing at a nearby university and conducted workshops in holistic approaches to preventive medical self-care. Still not satisfied, she began and finished a doctoral programme in practical nursing. She taught at a university and continued her practice. Needless to say, her persistence paid off with an extremely high degree of career satisfaction. Today she is one of two deans in a university of nursing.

A successful professional career in healthcare remained Caroline's aim throughout. A great deal of divergent thinking and creativity went into the elaboration of that aim into specific goals and coming up with the courses of action to accomplish them. But for every success story, there are many more failures. Quentin's case is probably the norm, not Caroline's. For many, divergent thinking is either uncomfortable or too much work.

Use brainstorming adaptively

One way of helping clients think divergently and more creatively is brainstorming. Brainstorming is a simple idea-stimulation technique for exploring the elements of complex situations. Brainstorming in Stages II and III is a tool for helping clients develop both possibilities for a better future and ways of making this future a reality.

There are certain rules that help make this technique work: suspend judgement, produce as many ideas as possible, use one idea as a take-off point for others, get rid of normal constraints to thinking and produce even more ideas by clarifying items on the list. Here, then, are the rules.

Suspend your own judgement, and help clients suspend theirs When brainstorming, do not let clients criticise the ideas they are generating and, of course, do not criticise them yourself. There is some evidence that this rule is especially effective when the problem situation has been clarified and defined, and goals have not yet been set. In the following example, a woman whose children are grown and married is looking for ways of putting meaning into her life.

> **CLIENT:** One possibility is that I could become a volunteer, but the very word makes me sound a bit pathetic.
>
> **HELPER:** Add it to the list. Remember, we'll discuss and critique them later.

Having clients suspend judgement is one way of handling the tendency on the part of some to play a 'Yes, but' game with themselves. That is, they come up with a good idea and then immediately show why it isn't really a good idea, as in the preceding example. By the same token, avoid saying such things as 'I like that idea', 'This one is useful', 'I'm not sure about that idea' or 'How would that work?' Premature approval and criticism cut down on creativity. A marriage counsellor was helping a couple brainstorm possibilities for a better future. When Nina said, 'We will stop bringing up past hurts', Tip, her husband, replied, 'That's your major weapon when we fight. You'll never be able to give that up.' The helper said, 'Add it to the list. We'll look at the realism of these possibilities later on.'

Encourage clients to come up with a wide but focused range of possibilities The traditional principle is that quantity ultimately breeds quality. Some of the best ideas come along later in the brainstorming process. Cutting the process short can be self-defeating. In the following example, a man in a sex-addiction programme has been brainstorming activities that might replace his preoccupation with sex.

> **CLIENT:** Maybe that's enough. We can start putting it all together.
>
> **HELPER:** It doesn't sound like you were running out of ideas.
>
> **CLIENT:** I'm not. It's actually fun. It's almost liberating.
>
> **HELPER:** Well, let's keep on having fun for a while.
>
> **CLIENT (pausing):** Ha! I could become a monk.

Later on, the counsellor, focusing on this 'possibility', asked, 'What would a modern-day monk who's not even a Catholic look like?' This helped the client explore the concept of sexual responsibility from a completely different perspective and to rethink the place of religion and service to others in his life.

However, possibility generation is not an end in itself. Coyne, Clifford and Dye (2007) challenge the quantity-breeds-quality rule, at least in terms of its efficiency. They suggest that *focused* brainstorming does a better job. In counselling that means the helper formulates questions relevant to the client's problems or unused opportunities and then helps the client brainstorm around these more focused issues. For instance, Carlos could have asked Tumi to build a picture of what a good relationship with her father would look like. However, he thought that this might be premature given the disastrous nature of their previous conversation. Furthermore, since it takes two to tango, both parties should be contributing to defining the relationship. So he asks Tumi to brainstorm around what kind of mindset she would like to be in before attempting another 'serious' conversation.

CARLOS: Describe the state of mind you'd like to be in before trying to talk to your father about your future again.

TUMI: Well, I'd like to be composed, you know, in possession of myself. And I guess I'd like to feel, no, *be* confident. I'd like to be sure of myself. Hmm. I'd like to go in without any preconceived expectations about how he should act or what he should say. . . .

As she brainstorms, Tumi realises that she is not just preparing herself for another conversation with her father. Rather she is challenging some of the attitudes she has about herself. For instance, she realises how submissive she is, not so much at work but certainly at home. And 'being in possession of herself' is not arrogance. Rather it is part of her being a mature adult. After the brainstorming sessions, Carlos asks her to draw a picture of her state of mind by choosing two or three of the elements she has identified. Afterwards he helps her explore what she needs to do to develop such a state of mind.

When it comes to how extensive brainstorming should be, use your clinical judgement, your social intelligence, to determine when enough is enough. If a client wants to stop, often it's best to stop.

Help clients use one idea to stimulate others This is called piggybacking. Without criticising the client's productivity, encourage him or her both to develop strategies already generated and to combine different ideas to form new possibilities. In the following example, a client suffering from chronic pain is trying to come up with possibilities for a better future.

CLIENT: Well, if there is no way to get rid of all the pain, then I picture myself living a full life without pain at its centre.

HELPER: Expand that a bit for me.

CLIENT: The papers are filled with stories of people who have been living with pain for years. When they're interviewed, most of them look miserable. They're like me. But every once in a while there is a story about someone who has learned how to live creatively with pain. Very often they are involved in some sort of cause which takes up their energies. They don't have time to be preoccupied with pain.

When one client with multiple sclerosis brought up this possibility: 'I'll have a friend or two with whom I can share my frustrations as they build up', the helper asked, 'What would that look like?' The client replied, 'Not just a complaining session or just a poor-me thing. It would be a normal part of a give-and-take relationship. We'd be sharing both joys and pain of our lives like other people do.'

Help clients let themselves go and develop some 'wild' possibilities When clients seem to be 'drying up' or when the possibilities being generated are quite pedestrian, you might say, 'Okay, now draw a line under the items on your list and write the word "wild" under the line. Now let's see if you can come up with some really wild possibilities.' Later it is easier to cut suggested possibilities down than to expand them. The wildest possibilities often have within them at least a kernel of an idea that will work. In the following example, an older single man who is lonely is exploring possibilities for a better future.

CLIENT: I can't think of anything else. And what I've come up with isn't very exciting.

HELPER: How about getting a bit wild? You know, some crazy possibilities.

CLIENT: Well, let me think. . . . I'd start a commune and would be living in it. . . . And. . . .

Clients often need permission to let themselves go even in harmless ways. They repress good ideas because they might sound foolish. Helpers need to create an atmosphere in which such apparently foolish ideas will be not only accepted but also encouraged. Help clients come up with conservative possibilities, liberal possibilities, radical possibilities and even outrageous possibilities.

That said, brainstorming might not be your client's cup of tea. Or your cup of tea. It's not always necessary or even advisable to use brainstorming explicitly. As a helper, you can keep these rules – which themselves are not set in stone – in mind and then by sharing highlights and using probes, you can get clients to brainstorm, even though they don't know that's what they're doing. A brainstorming mentality, not its ritualistic practice, is useful throughout the helping process. Sir Peter Hall, who directed 30 Shakespeare plays on major stages over 50 years, said that directors should not present the cast with a finished concept on the first day, but rather lead them on a voyage of discovery during the weeks of rehearsal and then edit the findings (Hall, 2005). There is no one right way in the theatre of life either. Helpers serve as guides to clients who are on their own 'voyage of discovery'.

Use future-oriented probes

One way of helping clients invent the future is to ask them, or get them to ask themselves, future-oriented questions related to their current unmanaged problems or undeveloped opportunities. The following questions are different ways of helping clients find answers to the questions 'What do you want?' and 'What do you need?' These questions focus on outcomes – that is, on what will be in place after the clients act.

- **What would this problem situation look like if you were managing it better**? Ken, a college student who has been a 'loner', has been talking about his general dissatisfaction with his life. In response to this question, he said, 'I'd be having fewer anxiety attacks. And I'd be spending more time with people rather than by myself.'

- **What changes in your present lifestyle would make sense**? Cindy, who described herself as a 'bored homemaker', replied, 'I would not be drinking as much. I'd be getting more exercise. I would not sit around and watch the soaps all day. I'd have something meaningful to do.'

- **What would you be doing differently with the people in your life**? Lon, a graduate student at a university near his parents' home, realised that he had not yet developed the kind of autonomy suited to his age. He mentioned these possibilities: 'I would not be letting my mother make my decisions for me. I'd be sharing a flat with one or two friends.'

- **What patterns of behaviour would be in place which are not currently in place**? Bridget, a depressed resident in a nursing home, had this suggestion: 'I'd be engaging in more of the activities offered here in the nursing home.' Rick, who is suffering from lymphoma, said, 'Instead of seeing myself as a victim, I'd be on the web finding out every last thing I can about this disease and how to deal with it. I know there are new treatment options. And I'd also be getting a second or a third opinion. You know, I'd be managing my lymphoma instead of just suffering from it.'

- **What current patterns of behaviour would be eliminated**? Bridget, a resident in a nursing home, added these to her list, 'I would not be putting myself down for incontinence I cannot control. I would not be complaining all the time. It gets me and everyone else down!'

- **What would you have that you don't have now**? Sissy, a single woman who has lived in a housing project for 11 years, said, 'I'd have a place to live that's not rat-infested. I'd have some friends. I wouldn't be so miserable all the time.' Drew, a man tortured by perfectionism, mused, 'I'd be wearing sloppy clothes, at least at times, and like it. More than that, I'd have a more realistic sense of the world and my place in it. The world is messy, it's chaotic much of the time. I'd find the beauty in the chaos.'

- **What accomplishments would be in place that are not in place now**? Ryan, a divorced man in his mid-30s, said, 'I'd have my degree in practical nursing. I'd be doing some part-time teaching. I'd be close to someone that I'd like to marry.'

- **What would an unused opportunity look like if you were to develop it**? Enid, a woman with a great deal of talent who has been given one modest promotion in her company but who feels like a second-class citizen, had this to say: 'In two years I'll be an officer of this company or have a very good job in another firm.'

It is a mistake to suppose that clients will automatically gush with answers. Ask the kinds of questions just listed, or encourage them to ask themselves the questions, but then help them answer them. Many clients don't know how to use their innate creativity. Thinking divergently is not part of their mental lifestyle.

You have to work with clients to help them produce some creative output. Moreover, some clients are reluctant to name possibilities for a better future because they sense that this will bring more responsibility. They will have to move into action mode.

Help clients review exemplars and role models as a source of possibilities

Some clients can see future possibilities better when they see them embodied in others. You can help clients brainstorm possibilities for a better future by helping them identify exemplars or models. By models, I don't mean superstars or people who do things perfectly. That would be self-defeating. In the next example, a marriage counsellor is talking with a middle-aged, childless couple. They are bored with their marriage. When he asked them, 'What would your marriage look like if it looked a little better?' he could see that they were stuck.

> **COUNSELLOR:** Maybe the question would be easier to answer if you reviewed some of your married relatives, friends or acquaintances.
>
> **WIFE:** None of them have super marriages. (Husband nods in agreement.)
>
> **COUNSELLOR:** No, I don't mean super marriages. It's about bits and pieces, smaller things that you could put in your marriage that would make it a little better.
>
> **WIFE:** Well, Fred and Lisa are not like us. They don't always have to be doing everything together.
>
> **HUSBAND:** Who says we have to be doing everything together? I thought that was your idea.
>
> **WIFE:** Well, we always are together. If we weren't always together, we wouldn't be in each other's hair all the time.
>
> **COUNSELLOR:** All right, who else do you know who are doing things in their marriage that appeal to you? Anyone?
>
> **HUSBAND:** You know Ron and Carol do some volunteer work together. Ron was saying that it gets them out of themselves. I bet they have better conversations because of it.

Even though it was a somewhat torturous process, these two people were able to come up with a range of possibilities for a better marriage. The counsellor had them write them down so they wouldn't lose them. At this point, the purpose was not to get the clients to commit themselves to these possibilities but to identify them.

In the following case, the client finds herself making discoveries by observing people she had not identified as models at all.

> Fran, a somewhat withdrawn university student, realises that when it comes to interpersonal competence, she is not ready for the business world she intends to enter when she graduates. She wants to do something about her interpersonal style and a few nagging personal problems. She sees a counsellor in the Office of Student Services. After a couple of discussions with him, she joins a 'lifestyle' group on campus that includes some training in interpersonal skills. Even though she expands her horizons a bit from what the members of the group say about their experiences, behaviours and feelings, she tells her counsellor that she learns even more by watching her fellow group members in action. She sees behaviours that she would like to incorporate into her own style. A number of times she says to herself in the group, 'Ah, there's something I never thought of.' Without becoming a slavish imitator, she begins to incorporate some of the patterns she sees in others into her own style.

Models or exemplars can help clients name what they want more specifically. Models can be found anywhere: among the client's relatives, friends and associates, in books, on television, in history, in movies, among well-publicised charities.

One example which could be used as a model or exemplar to help clients struggling with problems such as unemployment, heavy financial debts or impending house repossession and potential homelessness is the founding of the international Emmaus Movement already alluded to in Chapter 2:

> The first Emmaus Community was founded in Paris in 1949 by Father Henri-Antoine Groues, better known as the Abbé Pierre, a Catholic priest, MP and former member of the French Resistance during the Second World War. As an MP, he fought to provide homes for those who lived on the streets of Paris. One night, a man called Georges was brought to the Abbé Pierre. Georges had been released after 20 years in prison, only to find his family unable to cope with his reappearance. Homeless and despairing, he had tried to commit suicide in the Seine. The Abbé Pierre did not just offer him a place to sleep. He asked for his help. He told Georges of the homeless mothers who came to him for help for them and their children and how he could not cope with the problem on his own. Could Georges join him in his mission to help them?
>
> Georges became the first Emmaus Companion, living with the Abbé Pierre and helping him to build temporary homes for those in need, first in the priest's own garden, then wherever land could be bought or scrounged. He later said; 'Whatever else he might have given me – money, home, somewhere to work – I'd have still tried to kill myself again. What I was missing, and what he offered, was hope and a goal, something to live for.'
>
> (emmaus.org.uk/about-us/history/)

Counsellors can help clients identify models, choose those dimensions of others that are relevant and translate what they see into realistic possibilities for themselves.

CASES FEATURING POSSIBILITIES FOR A BETTER FUTURE

Here are a couple of cases that illustrate how helping clients develop possibilities for a better future had a substantial impact.

The case of Brendan: Dying better

Brendan, a heavy drinker, had extensive and irreversible liver damage, and it was clear that he was getting sicker. But he wanted to 'get some things done' before he died. Brendan's action orientation helped a great deal. Over the course of a few months, a counsellor helped him name some of the things he wanted before he died or on his journey towards death. Brendan in a homework exercise came up with the following possibilities:

- 'I'd like to have some talks with someone who has a religious orientation, like a minister. I want to discuss some of the "bigger" issues of life and death.'
- 'I don't want to die hopeless. I want to die with a sense of meaning.'
- 'I want to belong. You know, to some kind of community, people who know what I'm going through, but who are not sentimental about it. People not disgusted with me because of the way I've done myself in.'
- 'I'd like to get rid of some of my financial worries.'
- 'I'd like a couple of close friends with whom I could share the ups and downs of daily life. With no apologies.'
- 'As long as possible, I'd like to be doing some kind of productive work, whether paid or not. I've been a flake. I want to contribute even if just in an ordinary way.'
- 'I need a decent place to live, maybe with others.'
- 'I need decent medical attention. I'd like a doctor who has some compassion. One who could challenge me to live until I die.'
- 'I need to manage these bouts of anxiety and depression better.'
- 'I want to get back with my family again. I want to hug my dad. I want him to hug me.'
- 'I'd like to make peace with one or two of my closest friends. They more or less dropped me when I got sick. But at heart, they're good guys.'
- 'I want to die in my home town.'

Of course, Brendan didn't name all these possibilities at once. Through empathy and probes, the counsellor helped Brendan name what he needed and wanted, and then helped him stitch together a set of goals from these possibilities (Stage II) and ways of accomplishing them (Stage III). The charity *Dying matters*, set up in 2009, has a variety of useful resources for clients and helpers. The charity aims to encourage us to talk more openly about death and dying, including end of life and palliative care. www.dyingmatters.org/overview/ resources

The Salisbury family case

This case is more complex because it involves a family. Not only does the family as a unit have its wants and needs, but also each of the individual members has his or her own. Therefore, it is even more imperative to review possibilities for a better future so that competing needs can be reconciled.

Michael, the 15-year-old son of William and Katy Salisbury, was hospitalised with what was diagnosed as an 'acute schizophrenic attack'. He had two older brothers, both teenagers, and two younger sisters, one 10 and one 12, all living at home. The Salisburys lived in a large city in the south of England. Although both parents worked, their combined income still left them pinching pennies. They also ran into a host of problems associated with their son's hospitalisation – the need to arrange ongoing help and care for Michael, financial burdens, behavioural problems among the other siblings, marital conflict and stigma in the community ('They're a funny family with a crazy son'; 'What kind of parents are they?'). To make things worse, they did not think the psychiatrist and the psychologist they met at the hospital took the time to understand their concerns. They felt that the helpers were trying to push Michael back out into the community; in their eyes, the hospital was 'trying to get rid of him'. 'They give him some pills and then give him back to you' was their complaint. No one explained to them that short-term hospitalisation was meant to guard the civil rights of patients and avoid the negative effects of longer-term institutionalisation.

When Michael was discharged, his parents were told that he might have a relapse, but they were not told what to do about it. They faced the prospect of caring for Michael in a climate of stigma without adequate information, services or relief. Feeling abandoned, they were very angry with the mental health establishment. They had no idea what they should do to respond to Michael's illness or to the range of family problems that had been precipitated by the episode. By chance, the Salisburys met someone who had worked for the local office of a mental health advocacy and education organisation. This person referred them to an agency that provided support and help.

What does the future hold for such a family? With help, what kind of future can be fashioned? Social workers at the agency helped the Salisburys identify both needs and wants in seven areas (see Bernheim, 1989):

- **The home environment**. The Salisburys needed an environment in which the needs of all the family members were balanced. They didn't want their home to be an extension of the hospital. They wanted Michael taken care of, but they wanted to attend to the needs of the other children and to their own needs as well.
- **Care outside the home**. They wanted a comprehensive therapeutic programme for Michael. They needed to review possible services, identify relevant services and arrange access to those services. They needed to find a way of paying for all this.
- **Care inside the home**. They wanted all family members to know how to cope with Michael's residual symptoms. He might be withdrawn or aggressive, but they needed to know how to relate to him and help him handle behavioural problems.
- **Prevention**. Family members needed to be able to spot early warning symptoms of impending relapse. They also needed to know what to do when they saw those signs, including such things as contacting the clinic or, in the case of more severe problems, arranging for an ambulance or getting help from the police.
- **Family stress**. They needed to know how to cope with the increased stress all of this would entail. They needed forums for working out their problems. They wanted to avoid family blow-ups, and when blow-ups occurred, they wanted to manage them without damaging the social fabric of the family.

- **Stigma**. They wanted to understand and be able to cope with whatever stigma might be attached to Michael's illness. For instance, when taunted for having a 'crazy brother', the children needed to know what to do and what not to do. Family members needed to know whom to tell, what to say, how to respond to inquiries and how to deal with blame and insults.

- **Limitation of grief**. They needed to know how to manage the normal guilt, anger, frustration, fear and grief that accompany problem situations like this.

Bernheim's schema constituted a useful checklist for stimulating thinking about possibilities for a better future. Ideally, all these possibilities would be in place, but that's not the way of the world. The ideal approach is a holistic one, and this is essential within caring professions. The Salisburys first needed help in developing these possibilities. Then they needed help in setting priorities and establishing goals to be accomplished. This is the work of Task II-B.

So there are many things you can do to help clients think more broadly and deeply about problem-managing outcomes. The trick here, as always, is to tailor your interventions to the needs of your clients.

THE POWER OF GOAL SETTING

The following section deals with what clients need to do, both to set problem-managing and opportunity-developing goals and to commit themselves to the accomplishment of these goals. Clients do not have to do all the things discussed here. Rather you have to be ready to help them no matter what their goal-setting needs are. This section will help you put yourself in a position to do so. We begin with an overview of the power of goal setting in therapy and in everyday life.

Goal setting, whether it is called that or not, is part of everyday life. We all do it all the time. See Dörner:

> "Why do we formulate goals? Well, if we didn't have goals, we wouldn't do anything. No one cooks a meal, reads a book, or writes a letter without having a reason, or several reasons, for doing so. We want to get something we want through our actions or we want to prevent or avoid something we don't want. These desires are beacons for our actions; they tell us which way to go. When formalized into goals, they play an important role in problem solving." (1996, p. 49)

Even not setting goals is a form of goal setting. If we don't name our goals, that does not mean that we don't have any. Instead of overt goals, then, we have a set of covert goals. These are our default goals. They may be enhancing or limiting. We don't like the sagging muscles and flab we see in the mirror. But not deciding to get into better shape is a decision to continue to allow the fitness programme to drift.

Because life is filled with goals – chosen goals or goals by default – it makes sense to make them work for us rather than against us. Goals at their best mobilise our resources; they get us moving. They are a critical part of the self-regulation system. If they are the right goals for us, they get us headed in the right direction. There is a massive amount of sophisticated theory and research on goals and goal setting (Karoly, 1999; Locke & Latham, 1984, 1990, 2002, 2017). In their 2002 *American Psychologist* article, Locke and Latham summarise 35 years of empirical research on goal setting. According to this research, helping clients set goals empowers them in the following four ways.

Goals help clients focus their attention

A counsellor at a refugee centre in London described Simon, a victim of torture in a Middle Eastern country, to her supervisor as aimless and minimally cooperative in exploring the meaning of his brutal experience. Her supervisor suggested that she help Simon explore possibilities for a better future instead of focusing on the hell he had gone through. The counsellor started one session by asking, 'Simon, if you could have one thing you don't have, what would it be?' Simon's response was immediate. 'A friend', he said. During the rest of the session, he was totally focused. What was uppermost in his mind was not the torture but the fact that he was so lonely in a foreign country. When he did talk about the torture, it was to express his fear that torture had 'disfigured' him, if not physically, then psychologically, thus making him unattractive to others.

Goals help clients mobilise their energy and direct their effort

Clients who seem lethargic during the problem-exploration phase often come to life when asked to discuss possibilities for a better future. A patient in a long-term rehabilitation programme who had been listless and uncooperative said to her counsellor after a visit from her minister, 'I've decided that God and God's creation, and not pain, will be the centre of my life. This is what I want.' That was the beginning of a new commitment to the arduous programme. She collaborated more fully in doing exercises that helped her manage her pain. Clients with goals are less likely to engage in aimless behaviour. Goal setting is not just a 'head' exercise. Many clients begin engaging in constructive change after setting even broad or rudimentary goals.

Goals provide incentives for clients to search for strategies to accomplish them

Setting goals, a Stage II task, leads naturally into a search for means to accomplish them, a Stage III task. Lonnie, a woman in her 70s who had been described by her friends as 'going downhill fast', decided, after a heart-problem scare that proved to be a false alarm, that she wanted to, as she put it, 'begin living again'. She said that the things that scared her most about almost meeting 'Mr Death' was that she had already died. She searched out ingenious ways of redeveloping her social life, including a low-budget remodelling of her house and taking in two young women from a local university as boarders.

Clear and specific goals help clients increase persistence

Not only are clients with clear and specific goals energised to do something, but they also tend to work harder and longer. An AIDS patient who said that he wanted to be reintegrated into his extended family managed, against all odds, to recover from five hospitalisations to achieve what he wanted. He did everything he could to buy the time he needed. Clients with clear and realistic goals don't give up as easily as clients with vague goals or with no goals at all.

One study (Payne, Robbins & Dougherty, 1991) showed that high-goal-directed retirees were more outgoing, involved, resourceful and persistent in their social settings than low-goal-directed retirees. The latter were more self-critical, dissatisfied, sulky and self-centred. People with a sense of direction don't waste time in wishful thinking. Rather, they translate wishes into specific outcomes towards which they can work. Picture a continuum. At one end is the aimless person; at the other, a person with a keen sense of direction. Your clients may come from any point on the continuum. Taz knows that he wants to become a better supervisor but needs help in developing a programme to do just that. On the other hand, Lola, one of Taz's colleagues, doesn't even know whether this is the right job for her and does little to explore other possibilities. Any given client may be at different points with respect to different issues – for instance, mature in seizing opportunities for education but aimless in developing sexual maturity. Most of us have had directionless periods in one area of life or another at one time or another.

Dealing with clients' bottled-up emotions and tension when goal setting

Burnard (2005, pp. 164–165) provides some invaluable guidance on the importance of helping clients deal with bottled-up emotions and tensions when they are trying to set goals for themselves. He highlights the research conducted by Wilhelm Reich, a psychoanalyst with a particular interest in the relationship between emotions and musculature, and who concluded that 'anger' frequently seemed to be trapped in the shoulder muscles, 'grief' in muscles near the stomach and 'fear' in the leg muscles. Burnard advises helpers to observe signs of muscle tensions in clients, and to encourage them to release the feelings and tensions causing them, as part of the goal-setting process.

TASK II-B: GOALS, OUTCOMES, IMPACT: HELP CLIENTS MOVE FROM POSSIBILITIES TO CHOICES

In Chapter 3 of her book, Wosket (2006) recalls something I said during a lecture she attended. Stage I of the helping model is about failed solutions. People do things in their lives that don't work. Stage II is about solutions as problem-managing goals. Stage III is about solutions as strategies. As you know, I now have reservations about the term 'solution' because of the ambiguities attached to it. Once possibilities for a better future have been developed, clients need to make some choices – that is, they need to choose one or more of those possibilities and turn them into a programme for constructive change. Task II-A is, in many ways, about creativity, getting rid of boundaries, thinking beyond one's limited horizon, moving outside the box. Task II-B is about innovation – that is, turning possibilities into a practical programme for change. Consider the following case.

> Kayla, a black South African woman, was arrested when she went on a rampage in a bank in Johannesburg and broke several windows. She had exploded with anger because she felt that she had been denied a loan mainly because she was black and a single mother. In discussing the incident with her reverend, she comes to see that she has become very prone to anger. Almost anything can get her going. She also realises that venting her anger as she had done in the bank led to a range of negative consequences. But she is constantly 'steamed up' about 'the system'. To complicate the picture, she tends to take her anger out on those around her, including her friends and her two children. The reverend helps her look at four possible ways of dealing with her anger – venting it, repressing it, channelling it or simply giving up and ignoring the things she gets angry at, including the injustices around her. Giving up is not in her makeup. Merely venting her anger seems to do little but make her more angry and it has a number of negative consequences. Repressing her anger, she reasons, is just another way of giving up, and that is demeaning. And she's not very good at repressing anyway. The 'channelling' option needs to be explored.
>
> In the end, Kayla takes a positive approach to dealing with her frustrations. She joins a political action group involved in community organising and community development. She learns that she can channel her anger without giving up her values or her intensity. She also discovers that she is good at influencing others and getting things done. She begins to feel better about herself. The 'system' doesn't seem to be such a fortress any more.

FIGURE 9.2 **The three tasks of Stage II**

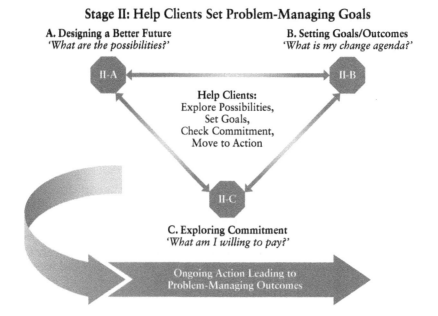

Stage II: Help Clients Set Problem-Managing Goals

A. Designing a Better Future
'What are the possibilities?'

B. Setting Goals/Outcomes
'What is my change agenda?'

II-A

II-B

Help Clients:
Explore Possibilities,
Set Goals,
Check Commitment,
Move to Action

II-C

C. Exploring Commitment
'What am I willing to pay?'

Ongoing Action Leading to
Problem-Managing Outcomes

A new pattern of behaviour in place changes Kayla's life. Figure 9.2 lays out the geography of the goal-setting process once more.

Because goals can be highly motivational, helping clients set realistic goals is one of the most important tasks of the helping process. But remember, a goal is a concept. An accomplished goal is an outcome. If the outcome has a positive impact on the problem situation, then it is a problem-managing or opportunity-developing outcome. Kayla's overall goal of channelling her anger becomes an outcome when she becomes an active participant in a political action group. In her case it is a problem-managing outcome because she replaces aimless venting of anger and all its negative consequences with involvement with a group of community organisers in the pursuit of community-enhancing goals.

FLEXIBLE GUIDELINES IN HELPING CLIENTS SET GOALS FOR THEMSELVES

Practical goals do not usually leap out fully formed. They need to be shaped or, as noted earlier, 'designed'. Effective counsellors add value by engaging clients in the kind of dialogue that will help them design, choose, craft, shape and develop their goals. Goals are specific statements about what clients want and need. The goals that emerge through this client–helper dialogue are more likely to be workable if they have, for the most part, the following characteristics. They need to be:

- Stated as **outcomes** rather than activities – Tumi needs not just to talk to her father, but to have in place an ongoing working relationship based on mutual respect.
- **Specific** enough to be verifiable and to drive action – Tumi needs a clear idea what this relationship would look like. For instance, she sees herself negotiating a different role within the family and the pursuit of a career outside of the family business.
- **Substantive** and challenging – Tumi realises that merely symbolic or incremental changes in her role within the family would not be enough; she needs to be a full partner in the decisions that are being made.
- Both venturesome and **prudent** – Tumi needs to remain respectful of her father's heritage, his personal culture and his role in the family and the business, but still be faithful to her own career and social aspirations.
- **Realistic** in regard to the internal and external resources needed to accomplish them – Tumi has the fibre needed to do her part in refocusing the relationship with her father, but must take into account the fact that her father remains responsible for doing his part. Given her father's personal culture, she believes that she has to negotiate some compromises.
- **Sustainable** over a reasonable time period – Tumi needs to believe that she can handle the impact that a new career and social life will have on her family, especially in view of her father's health problems. Is she ready to deal with the flare-ups that are almost inevitable?
- **Flexible** without being wishy-washy – Tumi needs to understand what is core to a working relationship with her father, such as mutual acceptance, and what is peripheral, such as mood swings.
- **Congruent** with the client's **values** – because Tumi values a more challenging work life and a fuller social life, any accommodation with her father needs to respect these values.
- Set in a reasonable **timeframe** – Tumi believes that substantial progress needs to be made in developing a career and establishing a fuller social life within a year's time.

Just how this package of goal characteristics will look in practice will differ from client to client. There is no one formula – one way is to keep goals SMART (see Chapter 8 for details). From a practical point of view, these characteristics can be seen as 'tools' that counsellors can use to help clients design and shape or reshape their goals. In general, goals with these characteristics are more likely to be turned into problem-managing outcomes with the desired impact on clients' lives. If you listen carefully to clients, they will provide hints or clues or cues as to when any given principle might help. These principles are not a step-by-step programme. Ineffective helpers will get lost in the details of these characteristics. Some might say, 'Clients don't need all this', and they would be right. Helpers need to understand the anatomy of goal setting and decision making in order to be able to respond to any given client-need. Effective helpers will keep these principles in the back of their minds and, in a second-nature manner, turn them into helpful 'sculpting' probes at the right time. The characteristics of fully shaped goals listed earlier take on life through the following flexible principles.

Help clients describe the future they want in outcome or accomplishment language

The goal of counselling, as emphasised again and again, is neither discussing nor planning nor engaging in activities. Helping is about problem-managing outcomes. 'I want to start doing some exercise' is an activity rather than an outcome. 'Within six months I will be running three miles in less than 30 minutes at least four times a week' is an outcome. It is a pattern of behaviour that will be in place by a certain time. If a client says, 'My goal is to get some training in interpersonal communication skills', then she is stating her goal as a set of activities rather than as an accomplishment. But if she says that she wants to become a better listener as a wife and mother, then she is stating her goal as an accomplishment, even though 'better listener' needs further clarification. Goals stated as outcomes provide direction for clients.

You can help clients describe what they need and want by using this 'past-participle' approach – drinking stopped, number of marital fights decreased, anger habitually controlled. Stating goals as outcomes or accomplishments is not just a question of language. Helping clients state goals as accomplishments rather than activities helps them avoid directionless and imprudent action. If a woman with breast cancer says that she thinks she should join a self-help group, she should be helped to see what she wants to get out of such a group. Joining a group and participating in it are activities. She wants support. She wants to feel supported. Clients who know what they want are more likely to work not just harder but also smarter.

Let's return to David, the ex-soldier who has been suffering from a variety of ailments associated with PTSD, and Laura, his therapist. As we have seen, Laura, David's counsellor, has a good relationship with him. She has helped David tell his story and has helped him challenge some of his self-defeating thinking, especially his tendency to blame himself for the deaths of his comrades. She quickly went on to help David focus on what he wanted from life. They moved back and forth between Stages I and II, between problems and possibilities for a better future. Eventually, David began talking about his real needs and wants – that is, what he needed to 'get back to his old self'. Here is an excerpt from their dialogue. It involves Peter, the ex-soldier who has successfully managed his bout with PTSD and is now David's 'buddy'.

DAVID: I've said that I want a more 'normal' social life, but now I've got some second thoughts. You know I get on well with Peter. And you also know that I'm still not totally comfortable with you. I'm comfortable with Peter because he's a soldier. But you represent a different kind of social life; the civilian one. I think we're getting along better, but we're not there yet. . .

LAURA: So even when you say you want a better social life as a civilian, you hesitate to do anything about it because, in a way, it's a different world. Could you describe what you would like that world to look like? Not a total picture and no definite timeframe, but some of bits and pieces; some of the details.

DAVID: Well, I'd like to be seeing women again. I'm not talking about marriage; but some special woman friend who sees me as an ordinary guy.

It is helpful when clients draw 'pictures', as it were, of what they want. The terms 'special woman friend' and 'ordinary guy' are evocative because they are concrete.

At one point, David says that he wants to become 'more disciplined'. He has a part-time job and only the minimum of social life. He's also taking a business course at a local university. The course deals with an overview of business basics. He spends a lot of time on his own and the discipline that he associates with the army has escaped him. In the army he felt productive even when the 'productivity' didn't have a lot of meaning. Almost discipline for the sake of discipline. Laura helps him get more specific.

LAURA: Discipline is a kind of wide area. What do you want to focus on?

DAVID: Well, if I'm going to get more out of life, I'm going to have to put more into it. I need to look at the time I spend sleeping. I've been going to bed whenever I feel like it and getting up whenever I feel like it. It was the only way I could get rid of those thoughts and the anxiety. But I'm not nearly as anxious as I used to be. Things are calming down.

LAURA: So more disciplined means a more regular sleep schedule because there's no particular reason now for not having one.

DAVID: Yeah, sleeping whenever I want is just a bad habit. It's part of my aimlessness. And I can't get things done if I'm asleep.

David goes on to translate 'more disciplined' into more specific problem-managing needs and wants related to school, work and even his appearance. Greater discipline, once translated into specific patterns of behaviour, could have a decidedly positive impact on his life.

The dialogue goes on in the same vein. David talks about possibilities – not just goals, but the possibilities for a better future discussed earlier can run from the vague to the very specific – but he also gets specific as in the previous example. Their conversation moves between II-A, possibilities for a better social future, and II-B, goals; that is, priorities for that future. With Laura's help he begins to design his future in terms of desired outcomes.

Help clients move from broad aims to clear and specific goals

Counsellors often add value by helping clients move from good intentions and vague desires to broad aims and then on to quite specific goals.

Good intentions 'I need to do something about this' is a statement of intent. However, even though good intentions are a good start, they need to be translated into aims and goals. In the following example, the client, Jon, has been discussing his relationship with his wife and children. The counsellor has been helping him see that his 'commitment to work' is perceived negatively by his family. Jon is open to challenge and is a fast learner.

JON: Boy, this session has been an eye-opener for me. I've really been blind. My wife and children don't see my investment – rather, my overinvestment – in work as something I'm doing for them. I've been fooling myself, telling myself that I'm working hard to get them the good things in life. In fact, I'm spending most of my time at work because I like it. My work is mainly for me. It's time for me to realign some of my priorities.

The last statement is a good intention, an indication on Jon's part that he wants to do something about a problem now that he sees it more clearly. It may be that Jon will now go out and put a different pattern of behaviour in place without further help from the counsellor. Or he may benefit from some help in realigning his priorities.

Broad aims A broad aim is more than a good intention. It has content – that is, it identifies the area in which the client wants to work and makes some general statement about that area. Let's return to the example of Jon and his overinvestment in work.

> **JON:** I don't think I'm spending so much time at work in order to run away from family life. But family life is deteriorating because I'm just not around enough. I must spend more time with my wife and children. Actually, it's not just a case of must. I want to.

Jon moves from a declaration of intent to an aim or a broad goal, spending more time at home. But he still has not created a picture of what that would look like.

Specific goals To help Jon move towards greater specificity, the counsellor uses such probes as 'Tell me what "spending more time at home" will look like.'

> **JON:** I'm going to consistently spend three out of four weekends a month at home. During the week I will make every effort to work no more than two evenings.
> **COUNSELLOR:** So you'll be at home a lot more. Tell me what you'll be doing with all this time.

Notice how much more specific Jon's statement is than 'I'm going to spend more time with my family'. He sets a goal as a specific pattern of behaviour he wants to put in place. But his goal as stated deals with quantity, not quality. The counsellor's probe is really an invitation to self-challenge. It's not just the amount of time Jon is going to spend with his family but also the kinds of things he will be doing. Quality time, if you want. Although a client trying to come to grips with work–life balance once said to me, 'My family, especially my children, don't make the distinction between quantity and quality. For them quantity is quality. Or there's no quality without a chunk of quantity.' This warrants further discussion because maybe the family wants a relaxed rather than an intense Jon at home.

Instrumental versus ultimate goals This example brings up the difference between instrumental goals and higher-order or ultimate goals. Jon's ultimate goal is 'a good family life'. Such a goal, once spelled out, will differ from family to family and from culture to culture. Think of your own definition of good family life. Therefore, when Jon says that one of his goals is spending more time at home, he is talking about an instrumental goal. Unless he's there, he can't do things with his wife and children. But although just 'being there' is a goal because it is a pattern of behaviour in place, it is certainly not Jon's ultimate goal. But Jon is not worried about the ultimate goal. When he is there, they have a rich family life together. That's not the problem. However, because instrumental goals are strategies for achieving higher-order goals, it's important to make sure that the client has clarity about the higher-order goal. When you are helping clients design and shape instrumental goals, make sure they can answer the 'instrumental-for-what?' question.

Helping clients move from good intentions to more and more specific goals is a shaping process. Consider the example of a couple whose marriage has degenerated into constant bickering, especially about finances.

> **Good intention.** 'We want to straighten out our marriage.'
> **Broad aim.** 'We want to handle our decisions about finances in a much more constructive way.'
> **Specific goal.** 'We try to solve our problems about family finances by fighting and arguing. We'd like to reduce the number of fights we have and begin making mutual decisions about money. We yell instead of talking things out. We need to set up a month-by-month budget. Otherwise, we'll be arguing about money we don't even have. We'll have a trial budget ready the next time we meet with you.'

Having sound household finances is a fine goal. In fact, it's a goal in itself. Reducing unproductive conflict is also a fine goal. In this case, however, installing a sound, fair and flexible household budget system is also instrumental to establishing peace at home. Declarations of intent, broad goals and specific goals can all drive constructive behaviour, but specific goals have the best chance. Is it possible to get clients to be too specific about their goals? Yes, if they get lost in the planning details, because crafting the goal becomes more important than the goal itself. Remember. We're looking at the anatomy of goal setting. It's up to your clients, with your help, to determine which parts of the goal-setting process make sense for them.

Goal setting and evaluating progress   If the goal is clear and specific enough, the client will be able to determine progress towards the goal. If there is a two-way feedback system in place, client and helper can collaborate routinely on goal clarification. Being able to measure progress is an important incentive. If goals are stated too broadly, it is difficult to determine both progress and accomplishment. 'I want to have a better relationship with my wife' is a very broad goal, difficult to verify. 'I want to socialise more, you know, with couples we both enjoy' comes closer, but 'socialise more' needs more clarity. It is not always necessary to count things to determine whether progress is being made towards a goal, though sometimes counting is helpful. Helping is about living more fully, not about accounting activities. At a minimum, however, desired outcomes need to be capable of being verified in some way. For instance, a couple might say something like 'Our relationship is better, not because we've stopped squabbling; in fact, we've discovered that we like to squabble. But life is better because the meanness has gone out of our squabbling. We accept each other more. We listen more carefully, we talk about more personal concerns, we are more relaxed, and we make more mutual decisions about issues that affect us both.' This couple does not need a scientific experiment to verify that they have improved their relationship.

Help clients establish goals that make a difference

Clients need goals with substance. What do we mean by substance? In counselling, goals have substance to the degree that they make some significant contribution towards managing the original problem situation or developing some opportunity. Goals are not substantive unless they are on target. Consider this case:

> Vittorio ran the family business. His son, Anthony, worked in sales. After spending a few years learning the business and getting an MBA part time at a local university, Anthony wanted more responsibility and authority. His father never thought that he was 'ready'. They began arguing quite a bit, and their relationship suffered from it. Finally, a friend of the family persuaded them to spend time with a consultant-counsellor who worked with small family businesses. He spent relatively little time listening to their problems. After all, he had seen this same problem over and over again – the reluctance and conservatism of the father, the pushiness of the son.

Vittorio wanted the business to stay on a tried-and-true course. Anthony wanted to be the company's marketer, to move it into new territory. After a number of discussions with the consultant-counsellor, they settled on this scenario: A 'marketing department' headed by Anthony would be created. He could divide his time between sales and marketing as he saw fit, provided that he maintained the current level of sales. Vittorio agreed not to interfere. They would meet once a month with the consultant-counsellor to discuss problems and progress. Vittorio insisted that the consultant's fee come from increased sales. After some initial turmoil, the bickering decreased dramatically. Anthony easily found new customers, although they demanded modifications in the product line, which Vittorio reluctantly approved. Both sales and margins increased to the point that they needed another person in sales.

Not all issues in family businesses are handled as easily. In fact, a few years later, Anthony left the business and founded his own. But the goal package they worked out – the deal they cut – made quite a difference both in the father–son relationship and in the business.

Second, goals have substance to the degree that they help clients 'stretch' themselves. As Locke and Latham (1984, pp. 21, 26) noted, 'Extensive research...has established that, within reasonable limits, the... more challenging the goal, the better the resulting performance. ... People try harder to attain the hard goal. They exert more effort. ... In short, people become motivated in proportion to the level of challenge with which they are faced... '. Even goals that cannot be fully reached will lead to high effort levels, provided that partial success can be achieved and is rewarded. Consider the following case:

> A young woman became a quadriplegic because of a road traffic collision. In the beginning, she was full of self-loathing and self-critical – 'The accident was all my fault; I was just stupid.' She was close to despair. Over time, however, with the help of a counsellor, she came to see herself, not as a victim of her own 'stupidity', but as someone who could bring hope to young people with life-changing afflictions. In her spare time, she visited young patients in hospitals and rehabilitation centres, got some to join self-help groups and generally helped people like herself to manage an impossible situation in a more humane way. One day she said to her counsellor, 'The best thing I ever did was to stop being a victim and become a fellow traveller with people like myself. The last two years, though bitter at times, have been the best years of my life.' She had set her goals quite high – becoming an outgoing helper instead of remaining a self-centred victim, but they proved to be quite realistic.

Of course, when it comes to goals, 'challenging' should not mean 'impossible'. There seems to be a curvilinear relationship between goal difficulty and goal performance. If the goal is too easy, people see it as trivial and ignore it. If the goal is too difficult, it is not accepted. However, this difficulty–performance ratio differs from person to person. What is small for some is big for others.

Help clients formulate realistic goals

Setting stretch goals can help clients energise themselves. They rise to the challenge. On the other hand, goals set too high can do more harm than good. Locke and Latham (1984, p. 39) put it succinctly:

> "Nothing breeds success like success. Conversely, nothing causes feelings of despair like perpetual failure. A primary purpose of goal setting is to increase the motivation level of the individual. But goal setting can have precisely the opposite effect if it produces a yardstick that constantly makes the individual feel inadequate."

A goal is realistic if the client has access to the resources needed to accomplish it, the goal is under the client's control and external circumstances do not prevent its accomplishment.

Resources: Help clients choose goals for which the resources are available   It does little good to help clients develop specific, substantive and verifiable goals if the resources needed for their accomplishment are not available. Consider the case of Rory, who has had to take a demotion because of merger and extensive restructuring. He now wants to leave the company and become a consultant.

> **INSUFFICIENT RESOURCES:**   Rory does not have the assertiveness, marketing savvy, industry expertise or interpersonal style needed to become an effective consultant. Even if he did, he does not have the financial resources needed to tide him over while he develops a business.
> **SUFFICIENT RESOURCES:**   Challenged by the outplacement counsellor, Rory changes his focus. Graphic design is an avocation of his. He is not good enough to take a technical position in the company's design department, but he does apply for a supervisory role in that department. He is good with people, is very good at scheduling and planning, and knows enough about graphic design to discuss issues meaningfully with the members of the department.

Rory combines his managerial skills with his interest in graphic design to move in a more realistic direction. The move is challenging, but it can have a substantial impact on his work life. For instance, the opportunity to hone his graphic design skills will open up further career possibilities.

Control: Help clients choose goals that are under their control   Sometimes clients defeat their own purposes by setting goals that are not under their control. For instance, it is common for people to believe that their problems would be solved if only other people would not act the way they do. In most cases, however, we do not have any direct control over the ways others act. Consider the following example:

> Tony, a 16-year-old boy, felt that he was the victim of his parents' inability to relate to each other. Each tried to use him in the struggle, and at times he felt like a ping-pong ball. A counsellor helped him see that he could probably do little to control his parents' behaviour, but that he might be able to do quite a bit to control his reactions to his parents' attempts to use him. For instance, when his parents started to fight, he could simply leave instead of trying to 'help'. If either tried to enlist him as an ally, he could say that he had no way of knowing who was right. Tony also worked at creating a good social life outside the home. That helped him weather the tensions he experienced when at home.

Tony needed a new way of managing his interactions with his parents to minimise their attempts to use him as a pawn in their own interpersonal game. Goals are not under clients' control if they are blocked by external forces that they cannot influence. 'To live in a free country' may be an unrealistic goal for a person living in a totalitarian state because he cannot change internal politics, nor can he change emigration laws in his own country or immigration laws in other countries. 'To live as freely as possible in a totalitarian state' might well be an aim that could be translated into realistic goals.

Tumi may be able to influence her father's attitudes and behaviour, but she cannot *change* his attitudes and behaviour. Only he can do that. Carlos helps her see that she might have to set a pre-goal. She can hardly negotiate with him unless he commits himself to some kind of reasonably open dialogue – 'Father, I know how you feel and maybe even have some idea why you feel the way you do, but I'd still like to talk more openly.' Her pre-goal goal, then, is to get him to commit to that kind of conversation. How to negotiate that kind of commitment is another matter.

Help clients set goals that are prudent

Realistic and prudent are not the same things. A goal may be realistic, that is, it can be accomplished, but it may not be prudent. Although the helping model described in this book encourages a bias towards client action, action needs to be both directional and wise. Discussing and setting goals should contribute to both direction and wisdom. The following case begins poorly but ends well.

> Christopher was a first-year university student in Johannesburg in South Africa who was admitted to a mental health hospital because of some bizarre behaviour at the university. He was one of the DJs for the university radio station. University officials noticed him one day when he put on an attention-getting performance that included rather lengthy dramatisations of grandiose religious themes. In hospital, the counsellors soon discovered that this quite pleasant, likeable young man was actually a loner. Everyone who knew him at the university thought that he had many friends, but in fact he did not. The campus was large, and his lack of friends went unnoticed.
>
> Christopher was soon released from the hospital but returned weekly for therapy. At one point he talked about his relationships with women. Once it became clear to him that his meetings with women were perfunctory and almost always took place in groups – he had imagined that he had a rather full social life with women – Christopher launched a full programme of getting involved with the opposite sex. His efforts ended in disaster, however, because Christopher had some basic sexual and communication problems. He also had serious doubts about his own worth and therefore found it difficult to make a gift of himself to others. He ended up in hospital again.

The counsellor helped Christopher get over his sense of failure by emphasising what Christopher could learn from the 'disaster'. With the therapist's help, Christopher returned to the problem-clarification and new-perspectives part of the helping process and then established more realistic short-term goals regarding getting back 'into the community'. The direction was the same – establishing a realistic social life – but the goals were now more prudent because they were 'bite-size'. Christopher attended socials at a local support group where volunteers provided support and guidance.

Christopher's leaping from problem clarification to action without taking time to discuss possibilities and set reasonable goals was part of the problem rather than part of the solution. His lack of success in establishing solid relationships with women actually helped him see his problem with women more clearly. There are two kinds of prudence – playing it safe is one; doing the wise or even heroic thing is the other. Problem management and opportunity development should be venturesome. They are about making wise and even heroic choices rather than playing it safe.

Help clients set goals that can be sustained

Clients need to commit themselves to goals that have staying power. One separated couple said that they wanted to get back together again. They did so only to get divorced again within six months. Their goal of getting back together again was achievable but not sustainable. Perhaps they should have asked themselves, 'What do we need to do not only to get back together but also to stay together? What would our marriage have to look like to become and remain workable?' In discretionary-change situations, the issue of sustainability needs to be visited early on.

Many Alcoholics Anonymous-like programmes work because of their one-day-at-a-time approach. The goal of being, say, drug-free has to be sustained only over a single day. The next day is a new era. In a previous example, Vittorio and Anthony's arrangement had enough staying power to produce good results in the short term. It also allowed them to reset their relationship and to improve the business. The goal was not designed to produce a lasting business arrangement because, in the end, Anthony's aspirations were bigger than the family business.

Help clients choose goals that have some flexibility

In many cases, goals have to be adapted to changing realities. Therefore, there might be some trade-offs between goal specificity and goal flexibility in uncertain situations. Napoleon noted this when he said, 'He will not go far who knows from the first where he is going.' Sometimes making goals too specific or too rigid does not allow clients to take advantage of emerging opportunities.

Even though he liked the work and even the company he worked for, Jessie felt like a second-class citizen. He thought that his supervisor gave him most of the dirty work and that there was an undercurrent of prejudice against Hispanics in his department. Jessie wanted to quit and get another job, one that would pay the same relatively good wages he was now earning. A counsellor helped Jessie challenge his choice. Even though the economy was booming, the industry in which Jessie was working was in recession. There were few jobs available for workers with Jessie's set of skills.

The counsellor helped Jessie choose an interim goal that was more flexible and more directly related to coping with his present situation. The interim goal was to use his time preparing himself for a better job outside this industry. In six months to a year he could be better prepared for a career in a still healthy economy. Jessie began volunteering for special assignments that helped him learn some new skills and took some crash courses dealing with computers and the internet. He felt good about what he was learning and more easily ignored the prejudice.

Counselling is a living, organic process. Just as organisms adapt to their changing environments, clients' choices need to be adapted to their changing circumstances.

Gollwitzer, Parks-Stamm, Jaudas and Sheeran (2007) explore goal-directedness in terms of flexibility, tenacity and rigidity. These three characteristics relate both to the goal itself and the means taken to accomplish the goal. Flexibility, as we have seen, refers to the client's ability to modify goals while keeping intact the original purpose of the goal. It also refers to the client's ability to change tactics, again within reason, when one course of activity is blocked or proves to be ineffective or inefficient. Tenacity refers to the ability to stick with a goal or the means to achieve the goal even when the going gets rough. Rigidity means sticking with the original formulation of a goal or a set of actions to achieve a reasonable goal, even when the goal itself is proving to be ineffective in managing a problem situation or the action programme is not doing its job. And so Gollwitzer and his associates recommend 'flexible tenacity' in goal pursuit.

Carlos realises that these concepts relate in very practical ways to Tumi's plans for a better future. Her plans will change depending on whether her father relents completely, a little, a lot or not at all. If he doesn't relent at all, she will have to face some very difficult choices. If he relents just a little, she might have to be quite flexible in terms of the size or substance of her goals. One extreme possibility is living and working separately from her parents. Carlos helps her see that being flexible is not just compatible with but essential to the new identity that she is trying to establish for herself.

Help clients choose goals consistent with their values

Although helping is a process of social influence, it remains ethical only if it respects, within reason, the values of the client. Values are criteria we use to make decisions. They are seen as desired qualities of behaviour and are one of the main aspects within acceptance and commitment therapy (Harris, 2008, 2009). Values are seen to reflect how we would like to engage in the world, with people and with ourselves. There are a number of values worksheets that clients may find useful, and helpers may want to invite clients to examine their values before putting some actions into place. It is also important to encourage clients to perform actions that are in keeping with their values.

> The son of Vincente and Consuela is in a coma in hospital after an automobile accident. He needs a life-support system to remain alive. His parents are experiencing a great deal of uncertainty, pain and anxiety. They have been told that there is practically no chance that their son will ever come out of the coma. One possibility is to terminate the life-support system. The counsellor should not urge them to terminate the life-support system if that is counter to their values. She can help them explore and clarify their values. In this case, the counsellor suggests that they discuss their decision with their clergyman. In doing so, they find out that the termination of the life-support system would not be against the tenets of their religion. Now they are free to explore other values that relate to their decision.

Some problems involve a client trying to pursue contradictory goals or values. David, the ex-soldier, came to realise that he wanted to get a degree in business, but he also wanted to make a decent living as soon as possible. The former goal would put him in debt, but failing to get a university education would lessen his chances of securing the kind of job he wanted. The counsellor helps him identify and use his values to consider some trade-offs. David chooses to work part time and go to university part time. He chooses an office job instead of one in construction. Even though the latter pays better, it would be much more exhausting and would leave him with little energy for university.

Help clients establish realistic timeframes for accomplishing goals

Goals that are to be accomplished 'sometime or other' probably won't be accomplished at all. Therefore, helping clients put some timeframes in their goals can add value. Greenberg (1986) talked about immediate, intermediate and final outcomes. Here's what they look like when applied to Janette's problem situation. She has begun to hate her passive lifestyle. She easily lets others take advantage of her. She needs to become more assertive and to stand up for her own rights.

- *Immediate outcomes* are changes in attitudes and behaviours evident in the helping sessions themselves. For Janette, the helping sessions constitute a safe forum for her to become more assertive. In her dialogues with her counsellor, she learns and practises the skills of being more assertive.
- *Intermediate outcomes* are changes in attitudes and behaviours that lead to further change. It takes Janette a while to transfer her assertiveness skills both to the workplace and to her social life. She chooses relatively safe situations to practise being more assertive. For instance, she stands up to her mother more.

- *Final outcomes* refer to the completion of the overall programme for constructive change through which problems are managed and opportunities developed. It takes more than two years for Janette to become assertive in a consistent, day-to-day way.

The next example deals with a young man who has been caught shoplifting. Here, too, there are immediate, intermediate and final outcomes.

Jensen, a 22-year-old on probation for shoplifting, was seeing a counsellor as part of a court-mandated programme. An immediate need in his case was overcoming his resistance to his court-appointed counsellor and developing a working alliance with her. Because of the counsellor's skills and her unapologetic caring attitude that had some toughness in it, he soon came to see her as 'on his side'. Their relationship became a platform for establishing further goals. An intermediate outcome was a change in attitude. Brainwashed by what he saw on television, Jensen thought that his country owed him some of its affluence and that personal effort had little to do with it. The counsellor helped him explore this entitlement attitude. At one point he said, 'Maybe what they say is true. Nobody said that life had to be fair.' True or not, he began to see that work played a key role in most payoffs. There were two significant final outcomes in Jensen's case. First, he made it through the probation period free of any further shoplifting attempts. Second, he acquired and kept a job that helped him pay his debt to the retailer.

Taussig (1987) talked about the usefulness of setting and executing mini goals early in the helping process. The achievement of sequenced mini goals can go a long way towards making a dent in many different kinds of problems.

There is no such thing as a set timeframe for every client. Some goals need to be accomplished now, some soon; others are short-term goals; still others are long-term goals. Consider the case of a priest who had been unjustly accused of child molestation.

- A *'now' goal*: some immediate relief from debilitating anxiety attacks and keeping his equilibrium during the investigation and court procedures
- A *'soon' goal*: obtaining the right kind of legal aid
- A *short-term goal:* winning the court case
- A *long-term goal:* re-establishing his credibility in the community and learning how to live with those who would continue to suspect him.

There is no particular formula for helping all clients choose the right mix of goals at the right time and in the right sequence. Although helping is based on problem-management principles, it remains an art.

Once more, it is not always necessary to make sure that each goal in a client's programme for constructive change has all the characteristics outlined here. For some clients, identifying broad goals is enough to kick-start the entire problem-management and opportunity-development process. They shape the goals themselves. For others, some help in formulating more specific goals is called for. The principle is clear: help clients develop goals that have some sort of agency – if not urgency – built in. In one case, this may mean helping a client deal with clarity; in another, with substance; in still another, with realism, values or timeframe. Box 9.1 outlines some questions that you can help clients ask themselves to assist them in choosing and shaping the most useful goals for them.

WHAT KIND OF CHANGE DO CLIENTS NEED AND HOW MUCH?

Therapy should be client driven. The degree of change sought is in the client's hands. While focusing on trivial issues and insignificant life changes is to be avoided, a complete personality makeover is an unrealistic goal. But consider Charles Colson, Nixon's 'hatchet man', sent to prison in 1974 for obstructing justice.

BOX 9.1   **Questions for Choosing and Shaping Goals**

Help clients ask themselves these kinds of questions to shape their goals:

- Is my goal stated in outcome or results language?
- Is my goal specific enough to drive behaviour?
- How will I know when I have accomplished it?
- If I accomplish this goal, will it make a difference?
- Will it really help manage the problems and opportunities I have identified?
- Does this goal have 'bite' while remaining prudent?
- Is it realistic? Is it doable?
- Can I sustain this goal over the long haul?
- Does this goal have some flexibility?
- Is this goal in keeping with my values?
- Have I set a realistic timeframe for the accomplishment of the goal?

He converted to Christianity and changed his life radically. When he died in 2012, he had written some 30 books; received 15 honorary doctorates for his non-profit work in prison ministry, prisoner rehabilitation and prison reform; had been given the Templeton Prize for an 'exceptional contribution to affirming life's spiritual dimension'; and was awarded the Presidential Citizens Medal. It seems that Colson was high on the list of '100 percenters', people who give their all to any task they undertake. Most change falls somewhere between a teenager upset over a lost girlfriend and the Colsons of the world. Let's see if we can come up with an answer to the question at the start of this section.

Help clients distinguish needs from wants

In answering the question 'How much change do clients need?', perhaps we need to ask another: 'What kind of change does the client need?' In some cases, what clients want and what they need coincide. The lonely person wants a better social life and needs some kind of community to live a more engaging human life. In other cases, what clients want differs from what they need. Goal setting should focus on the package of needs and wants that makes sense for this particular client. Discrepancies must be worked out with the client. Consider the case of Irv:

> Irv, a 41-year-old entrepreneur, collapsed one day at work. He had not had a physical in years. He was shocked to learn that he had both a mild heart condition and multiple sclerosis. His future was uncertain. The father of one of his wife's friends had multiple sclerosis but had lived and worked well into his 70s. But no one knew what the course of the disease would be. Because he had made his living by developing and then selling small businesses, he wanted to continue to do this, but it was too physically demanding. What he needed was a less physically demanding work schedule. Working 60–70 hours per week, even though he loved it, was no longer on the cards. Furthermore, he had always ploughed the money he received from selling one business into starting up another. But now he needed to think of the future financial well-being of his wife and three children. Up to this point, his philosophy had been that the future would take care of itself. It was very wrenching for him to move from a lifestyle he wanted to one he needed.

Involuntary clients often need to be challenged to look beyond their wants to their needs. One woman who voluntarily led a homeless life was attacked and severely beaten on the street. But she still wanted the freedom that came with her lifestyle. When challenged to consider the kinds of freedom she wanted, she admitted that freedom from responsibility was at the core. 'I want to do what I want to do when I want to do it.' It was her choice to live the way she wanted. The counsellor helped her explore the consequences of her choices and tried to help her look at other options. How could she be 'free' and not at risk? Was there some kind of trade-off between what she wanted and what she needed? In the end, of course, the decision was hers.

In the following case, the client, dogged by depression, was ultimately able to integrate what he wanted with what he needed.

Milos had come to the United Kingdom as a political refugee. The last few months in his native land had been terrifying. He had been jailed and beaten. He got out just before another crackdown. Once the initial euphoria of having escaped had subsided, he spent months feeling confused and disorganised. He tried to live as he had in his own country, but the British culture was too invasive. He thought he should feel grateful, and yet he felt hostile. After two years of misery, he began seeing a counsellor. He had resisted getting help because 'back home' he had been 'his own man'.

In discussing these issues with a counsellor, it gradually dawned on Milos that he wanted to re-establish links with his native land but that he needed to integrate himself into the life of his host country. He saw that the accomplishment of both these broad aims would be very freeing. He began finding out how other immigrants who had been here longer than he had accomplished this goal. He spent time in the immigrant community, which differed from the refugee community. In the immigrant community, there was a long history of keeping links to the homeland culture alive. But the immigrants had also adapted to their adopted country in practical ways that made sense to them. The friends he made became role models for him. The more active he became in the immigrant community, the more his depression lifted.

In this case, goals responded to a mixture of needs and wants. If Milos had focused only on one or the other, he would have remained unhappy.

Help clients consider adaptive goals

Collins and Porras (1994) coined the term 'big, hairy, audacious goals' (BHAGs) for 'super-stretch' goals. However, the term fits better into the hype of business than the practicalities of helping. It is true that some clients are looking for big goals. They believe, and perhaps rightly so, that without big goals their lives will not be substantially different. But even clients who choose goals that can be called 'big' in one way or another need a bit-by-bit approach to achieving these goals. It is usually better to take big goals and divide them up into smaller pieces, lest the big goal on its own seems too daunting. The term 'within reasonable limits' will differ from client to client.

Adaptive goals   Although difficult or 'stretch' goals are often the most motivational, this is not true in every case. Some clients choose to make very substantive changes in their lives, but others take a more modest approach. Wheeler and Janis (1980, p. 98) cautioned against the search for the 'absolute best' goal all the time: 'Sometimes it is more reasonable to choose a satisfactory alternative than to continue searching for the absolute best. The time, energy and expense of finding the best possible choice may outweigh the improvement in the choice.' Consider the following case:

Joyce, a near-middle-aged buyer for a large retail chain, centred most of her non-working life on her ageing mother. Joyce had even turned down promotions because the new positions would have demanded more travel and longer hours. Her mother had been pampered by her now-deceased husband and her three children and allowed to have her way all her life. She now played the role of the tyrannical old woman who constantly feels neglected and who can never be satisfied. Although Joyce knew that she could live much more independently without abandoning her mother, she found it very difficult to move in that direction. Guilt stood in the way of any change in her relationship with her mother. She even said that being a virtual slave to her mother's whims was not as bad as the guilt she experienced when she stood up to her mother or 'neglected' her.

> The counsellor helped Joyce experiment with a few new ways of dealing with her mother. For instance, Joyce went on a two-week trip with friends even though her mother objected, saying that it was ill-timed. Although the experiments were successful in that no harm was done to Joyce's mother and Joyce did not experience excessive guilt, counselling did not help her restructure her relationship with her mother in any substantial way. The experiments, however, did give her a sense of greater freedom. For instance, she felt freer to say no to her mother's demands. This provided enough slack, it seems, to make Joyce's life more liveable.

In this case, counselling helped the client fashion a life that was 'a little bit better', although not as good as the counsellor thought it could be. When asked, 'What do you want?' Joyce had in effect replied, 'I want a bit more slack and freedom, but I do not want to abandon my mother.' Joyce's 'new' lifestyle did not differ dramatically from the old. But perhaps it was enough for her. It was a case of choosing a satisfactory alternative rather than the best.

Leahey and Wallace (1988, p. 216) offered the following example of another client in adaptive mode:

> For the last five years, I've thought of myself as a person with low self-esteem and have read self-help books, gone to therapists and put things off until I felt I had good self-esteem. I just need to get on with my life, and I can do that with excellent self-esteem or poor self-esteem. Treatment isn't really necessary. Being a person with enough self-esteem to handle situations is good enough for me.

In some cases, clients will be satisfied with 'surface' solutions such as the elimination of symptoms. For instance, a couple is satisfied with reducing and managing the petty annoyances both of them experience in their relationship. Yet the very structure of the relationship may be problematic because some fundamental inequalities or inequities are built into the relationship. But they don't want to do much about restructuring the relationship in order to avoid the annoyances they experience.

Some helpers, reviewing these examples, would be disappointed. Others would see them as legitimate examples of adapting to, rather than changing, reality. However, all these clients did act to achieve some kind of goal, however minimal. They did something about the way they thought and behaved. And they felt that their lives were better because of it.

Choosing strategic self-limitation   Robert Leahy (1999) relates the kinds of reluctance and resistance to goal setting reviewed earlier under the rubric of 'strategic self-limitation'. Reluctant and resistant behaviours serve the purpose of setting limits on change. All change carries some risk and uncertainty, and these can be distressing in themselves. Putting up barriers to change limits both risk and uncertainty. It is the client's way of saying, 'Enough is enough. I don't want to engage in a change programme that will lead to further effort, stress, failure and regret.' The strategies such clients use are the ordinary ones – attacking the therapist, failing to do homework assignments, emotional volatility, getting mired in a 'this won't work' mentality and so forth. Even though helpers may point out to clients the ways they are engaging in what Leahy calls 'self-handicapping', it is still not their job to push clients to adopt a specific set of goals. There is a huge difference between best possible goals and goals that are possible for this client in this set of circumstances.

The main point, however, is that helping clients cope with the adversities of life does not mean that you are short-changing them. When you help them adapt rather than conquer, you are not failing. Neither are they. When it comes to outcomes, there is no one universal rule of success.

Coping as an important goal

A 2005 article in *The Economist* suggested that then Secretary of State Condoleeza Rice's challenge in the Middle East was to help parties in conflict 'to adjust expectations without squashing hope' (*The Economist*, 3 February, 2005, p. 12). While her statement would not win a prize for forecasting what would happen in the Middle East, what she said is not a bad definition of coping. Choosing an adaptive, rather than a stretch, goal has been associated with coping (Coyne & Racioppo, 2000; Folkman & Moskowitz, 2000; Lazarus, 2000; Snyder, 1999). All human beings cope rather than conquer at times. In fact, in human affairs as a whole, coping probably outstrips conquering. And sometimes people have no other choice. It's cope or succumb. For some, coping has a bad reputation because it seems to be associated with mediocrity. But in many difficult situations helping clients cope is one of the best things helpers can do. The research on coping often comes from research on stress where the two go hand in hand (Frydenberg, 2002).

Coping often has an enormous upside. A young mother with three children has just lost her husband. Someone asks, 'How's she doing?' The response, 'She's coping quite well.' She's not letting her grief get the better of her. She is taking care of the children and helping them deal with their sense of loss. She's moving along on all the tasks that a death in a family entails. At this stage, what could be more positive than that?

Folkman and Moskowitz (2000) see positive affect as playing an important role in coping. And so they ask how counsellors can help clients generate positive affect and sustain it in the face of chronic stress. They suggest three ways:

Positive reappraisal Help clients reframe a situation to see it in a positive light. For instance, Victor, recovering from multiple injuries received in a motorcycle accident, sees the entire rehabilitation process as 'one big daunting glob'. Taken as a whole, it looks undoable. However, the rehabilitation counsellor first helps Victor picture the overall goal of the rehabilitation process. She encourages him to see himself engaging fully in the ordinary tasks of everyday life, even riding a motorcycle. That is, she helps him separate the very desirable end state from the arduous set of activities that will get him there. Victor does not have to cope with the whole thing all at once. He needs to cope with part of it each day. Victor is rebuilding his body. Every day he is doing something to forge a link in the recovery chain. Each week he is helped to see that there is something he can now do that he was not able to do the previous week. Victor has low moments, of course. But he also has moments of positive affect that keep him going.

Problem-focused coping Help clients deal with problems one at a time as they arise. For instance, Agnes is caring for her husband who has multiple sclerosis (MS). There is a certain unpredictability and uncontrollability associated with her husband's disease. However, she does not have to cope with his MS. Rather, each day or each week or each stage brings its own set of problems. In fancy language her counsellor can help her 'pursue realistic, attainable goals by focusing on specific proximal tasks or problems related to caregiving' (Folkman & Moskowitz, 2000, p. 650). Agnes is heartened by the very fact that she faces and deals with each problem as it arises. The sense of mastery and control she experiences is accompanied by positive affect. Even in the face of great stress, she is buoyed enough to move on to the next task or stage with grace.

Infusing ordinary events with positive meaning In one study, Folkman and Moskowitz (2000) asked the participants, all caregivers for people with AIDS, to describe something they did or something they experienced that made them feel good and helped them get through the day. More than 99 per cent of the caregivers interviewed talked about some such event. The point is that even during times of great stress, people note and remember positive events. The events were not 'big deals'. Rather, they were 'ordinary events', such as having dinner with a friend, seeing some flowers in a hospital room or receiving a compliment from someone. But these events, together with the positive affect they produced, helped them get through the day.

What kind of coping skills does the client have? It is easy to suggest that therapists help clients cope with problem situations, but the assumption is that clients have the skills needed to cope, that is, the thoughts and actions people use to handle difficult situations such as confronting a difficult situation directly and trying to change it; distancing oneself from the situation; controlling one's feelings and actions; seeking social support; accepting responsibility for a problem together with efforts to make things right, and similar kinds of behaviour (Rexrode, Petersen & O'Toole, 2008; Roussi, Krikeli, Hatzidimitriou & Koutri, 2007). Even if clients have a repertoire of coping skills, they need flexibility to fit the skill to the situation and alter it when necessary (Cheng, 2001; Kato, 2012). If clients do not have the skills, then helpers can coach them through the difficult situation or, even better, teach them the skills they need. Helping clients manage problem situations by teaching them needed skills is discussed in Chapter 10.

Second-order change goals

The concept of second-order change deals not with substantive change – its degree of problem-managing power – but rather with how big or extensive the substantive change is. Coping is at one end of the continuum, second-order change at the other.

Singhal, Rao and Pant (2006) highlight the differences between first-order and second-order change as follows:

- Adjustments to the current situation versus changing the underlying system
- Motoring on as well as possible versus creating something new
- Change prone to collapse versus change that is designed to endure
- Shoring up or fixing versus transforming
- Change based on old learning or no learning versus change based on new learning
- Current set of values and behaviours staying in place versus a fundamental shift in values and behaviours
- The persistence of an old narrative versus the creation of a new narrative
- Fiddling with symptoms versus attacking causes.

Given these characteristics, it is not surprising that in much of the literature, second-order change is seen, not just as a form of substantial change, but as 'good' or 'real' change. First-order change becomes the 'little brother' or 'distant cousin' to second-order change. The language used is interesting. Second-order change means rolling up our sleeves and resetting the system, while first-order change means tinkering or coping with the system. Second-order change deals with causes, while first-order change deals with symptoms. Second-order change resolves the problem, while first-order change leaves the underlying problem in place and deals mostly with the easily seen manifestations of the problem.

However, I don't think things are that simple. It might be more useful to see change as a continuum with minor change (first-order change) at one end and major change (second-order change) at the other. First-order change has it uses. Sometimes it is the only kind of change possible. Let's return to Tumi and Carlos. If Tumi is to pursue her two goals – a new career and a new social life – the change involved tends to be major. It is second-order change. However, she could choose to pursue minor changes in both her work and social lives, making life itself more liveable or at least more tolerable. Who is to say that the first choice for her is a good choice, while the second is poor? It is Carlos's job to help her review her options and the consequences of each. If she were to talk about nothing but first-order change, he could invite her to review second-order possibilities. If she talks only about second-order change, then it is important for her to know what she is getting herself into. But the choice is hers. Here is another case.

Algis and Rodaina have been married for almost five years. He is 42, she is 34. He is the son of Lithuanian immigrants, she emigrated from Palestine. They are both nominally Catholic, but come from quite different Catholic traditions. Both work. They have no children even though they have always 'intended' to. They find themselves constantly squabbling more and more over a range of issues, some important, many relatively trivial. These constant squabbles are undermining their relationship. Every once in a while it all erupts into a very nasty argument. They are headed for deeper trouble.

During a session with their pastor, he suggests that they should begin to think seriously about having a child. 'You've become too preoccupied with yourselves and your differences. A child will change everything. It will help you get out of yourselves. Love will take the place of strife.' He urges them to see a marriage counsellor.

They do spend a few, at times stormy, sessions with a marriage counsellor. He tries to help them talk with one another more constructively. He teaches them listening and responding skills. He coaches them on how to discuss their grievances with each other fairly and decently. He helps them engage in problem solving around key problems such as finances. There is some progress, but it is inconsistent – one step forward, one step backwards, one step sideways. The prognosis does not look good. Eventually they stop seeing him. 'We're getting nowhere anyway.'

Let's skip what their pastor said for the moment. Looking at their sessions with the counsellor, we can ask ourselves the following questions:

- Were Algis and Rodaina making adjustments to their current situation or were they trying to reset or reinvent their relationship?
- Were they trying to motor on the best they could or were they trying to create something new?
- Were the changes they were making likely to be lasting or were they still in danger of falling back into their old ways?
- Were they striving for incremental improvement or transforming their relationship?
- Were they learning small steps towards making their relationship work or were they learning what a renewed relationship would look like?
- Was their usual set of values still in place or were they working towards a fundamental shift in the values and behaviours?
- Were they creating a new 'narrative' or was the old narrative still in place?
- Were they fiddling with symptoms or dealing with causes?

Helping Algis and Rodaina reduce the frequency and the intensity of their squabbling smacks of first-order change. Helping them take a good look at their current relationship and changing the style and terms of that relationship is closer to second-order change. But it is up to them, with the help of their counsellor, to ask themselves the kind of questions listed earlier and make their own choices.

So how much or what kind of change do clients need? It depends. They are in the driver's seat. They must make the decisions. The more you know about the ins and outs of goal setting and change, the more capable you are of helping them make the life-enhancing decisions that suit them.

EMERGING GOALS

Finally, it is not always a question of designing and setting goals in an explicit way. Rather, goals can naturally emerge through the client–helper dialogue or the client's interaction with his or her environment in everyday life. Often when clients talk about problems and unused opportunities, possible goals and action strategies bubble up. Once clients are helped to clarify a problem situation through a combination of probing, empathic highlights and challenge, they begin to see more clearly what they want and what they have to do to manage the problem. Indeed, some clients must first act in some way before they find out just what they want to do. After goals begin to emerge, counsellors can help clients clarify them and find ways to implement them. However, 'emerge' should not mean that clients wait around until 'something comes up'. Nor should it mean that clients try many different solutions in the hope that one of them will work. These kinds of 'emergence' tend to be self-defeating.

Although goals do often emerge, explicit goal setting is not to be underrated. Taussig (1987) showed that clients respond positively to goal setting even when goals are set very early in the counselling process. A client-centred, 'no one right formula' approach seems to be best. Although all clients need focus and direction in managing problems and developing opportunities, what focus and direction will look like will differ from client to client.

TASK II-C: HELP CLIENTS COMMIT THEMSELVES – 'WHAT AM I WILLING TO PAY FOR WHAT I WANT?'

After reviewing a number of books on human evolution and where the human race seems to be headed, Tickell (2005, p. W5) says with some sorrow, 'If there is optimism about human ability to cope, there is pessimism about the human will to do so.' Thus the necessity of addressing commitment. As mentioned earlier, Task II-C is not really a sequential step but rather a dimension of the goal-setting process. Clients may formulate goals, but that does not mean that they are willing to pay for them. Once clients state what they want and set goals, the battle is joined, as it were. It is as if the client's 'old self' or old lifestyle begins vying for resources with the client's potential 'new self' or new lifestyle. On a more positive note, history is full of examples of people whose strength of will to accomplish some goal has enabled them to do seemingly impossible things.

A woman with two sons in their 20s was dying of cancer. The doctor thought she could go at any time. However, one day she told the doctor that she wanted to live to see her older son get married six months hence. The doctor talked vaguely about 'trusting in God' and 'playing the cards she had been dealt'. Against all odds, the woman lived to see her son get married. Her doctor was at the wedding. During the reception, he said to her, 'Well, you got what you wanted. Despite the way things are going, you must be deeply satisfied.' She looked at him wryly and said, 'But, Doctor, my second son will get married someday.'

Although the job of counsellors is not to encourage clients to heroic efforts, counsellors should not undersell clients, either.

In this task, which is usually interrelated with the other two tasks of Stage II, counsellors help their clients pose and answer such questions as:

- Why should I pursue this goal?
- Is it worth it?
- Is this where I want to invest my limited resources of time, money and energy?
- What competes for my attention?
- What are the incentives for pursuing this agenda?
- How strong are competing agendas?

Again, there is no formula. Some clients, once they establish goals, race to accomplish them. At the other end of the spectrum are clients who, once they decide on goals, stop dead in the water. Furthermore, the same client might speed towards the accomplishment of one goal and drag her feet on another. Or start out fast and then slow to a crawl. The job of the counsellor is to help clients face up to their commitments.

HELP CLIENTS COMMIT THEMSELVES TO A BETTER FUTURE

There is a difference between initial commitment to a goal and an ongoing commitment to a strategy or plan to accomplish the goal. The proof of initial commitment lies in goal-accomplishing action. For instance, one client who chose as a goal a less abrasive interpersonal style began to engage in an 'examination of conscience' each evening to review what his interactions with people had been like that day. In doing so, he discovered, somewhat painfully, that in some of his interactions he actually moved beyond abrasiveness to contempt. That forced him back to a deeper analysis of the problem situation and the blind spots associated with it. Being dismissive of people he did not like or who were 'not important' had become ingrained in his interpersonal lifestyle.

There is a range of things you can do to help clients in their initial commitment to goals and the kind of action that is a sign of that commitment. Counsellors can help clients by helping them make goals appealing, by helping them enhance their sense of ownership and by helping them deal with competing agendas.

Economics: Help clients set goals that are worth more than they cost

Here we revisit the 'economics' of helping. Cost-effectiveness could have been included in the characteristics of workable goals outlined earlier in this chapter, but it is considered here instead because of its close relationship to commitment. Some goals that can be accomplished carry too high a cost in relation to their payoff. It may sound overly technical to ask whether any given goal is 'cost-effective', but the principle remains important. Skilled counsellors help clients budget rather than squander their resources – work, time, emotional energy.

Eunice discovered that she had a terminal illness. In talking with several doctors, she found out that she would be able to prolong her life a bit through a combination of surgery, radiation treatment and chemotherapy. However, no one suggested that these would lead to a cure. She also found out what each form of treatment and each combination would cost, not so much in monetary terms, but in added anxiety and pain. Ultimately she decided against all three because no combination of them promised much for the quality of the life that was being prolonged. Instead, with the help of a doctor who was an expert in hospice care, she developed a scenario that would ease both her anxiety and her physical pain as much as possible.

It goes without saying that another patient might have made a different decision. Costs and payoffs are relative. Some clients might value an extra month of life no matter what the cost.

Because it is often impossible to determine the cost–benefit ratio of any particular goal, counsellors can add value by helping clients understand the consequences of choosing a particular goal. For instance, if a client sets her sights on a routine job with minimally adequate pay, this outcome might well take care of some of her immediate needs but prove to be a poor choice in the long run. Helping clients foresee the consequences of their choices may not be easy. Another woman with cancer felt she was no longer able to cope with the sickness and depression that came with her chemotherapy treatments. She decided abruptly one day to end the treatment, saying that she didn't care what happened. No one helped her explore the consequences of her decision. Eventually, when her health deteriorated, she had second thoughts about the treatments, saying, 'There are still a number of things I must do before I die.' But it was too late. Some reasonable challenge on the part of a helper might have helped her make a better decision.

The balance-sheet method outlined in Chapter 10 is also a tool you can use selectively as a way of helping clients choose best-fit strategies for accomplishing their goals. It can help clients weigh costs against benefits both in choosing goals and in choosing programmes to implement goals.

Incentives: Help clients set appealing goals

Just because goals will help in managing a problem situation or develop an opportunity and are cost-effective does not mean that they will automatically appeal to the client. Setting appealing goals is common sense, but it is not always easy to do. For instance, for many if not most addicts, a drug-free life is not immediately appealing, to say the least.

A counsellor tries to help David work through his resistance to giving up prescription drugs. He listens and is empathic. He also challenges the way David has come to think about drugs and his dependency on them. One day the counsellor says something about 'giving up the crutch and walking straight'. In a flash David sees himself not as a drug addict but as a 'cripple'. A friend of his had lost a leg in a landmine explosion in Iraq. He remembered how his friend had longed for the day when he could be fitted with a prosthesis and throw his crutches away. The image of 'throwing away the crutch' and 'walking straight' proved to be very appealing to David.

An incentive is a promise of a reward. As such, incentives can contribute to developing a climate of hope around problem management and opportunity development. A goal is appealing if there are incentives for pursuing it. Counsellors need to help clients in their search for incentives throughout the helping process. Ordinarily, negative goals – giving up something that is harmful – need to be translated into positive goals – getting something that is helpful. It was much easier for David to commit himself to returning to education than to giving up prescription drugs, because education represented something he was getting. Images of himself with a degree and of holding some kind of professional job were solid incentives. The picture of him 'throwing away the crutch' proved to be an important incentive in cutting down on drug use.

Ownership: Help clients embrace and own the goals they set

Earlier, we discussed how important it is for clients to 'own' the problems and unused opportunities they talk about. It is also important for them to own the goals they set. It is essential that the goals chosen be the client's rather than the helper's or someone else's. Various kinds of probes can be used to help clients discover what they want to do to manage some dimension of a problem situation more effectively.

For instance, Carl Rogers, in a film of a counselling session (Rogers, Perls & Ellis, 1965; also see Moon, 2007), is asked by a woman what she should do about her relationship with her daughter. He says to her, 'I think you've been telling me all along what you want to do.' She knew what she wanted the relationship to look like, but she was asking for his approval. If he had given it, the goal would, to some degree, have become his goal instead of hers. At another time he asks, 'What is it that you want me to tell you to do?' This question puts the responsibility for goal setting where it belongs – on the shoulders of the client. In the following case, the helper challenges a client to take responsibility for setting goals:

> Cynthia was dealing with a solicitor because of an impending divorce. Discussions about what would happen to the children had taken place, but no decision had been reached. One day she came in and said that she had decided on mutual custody. She wanted to work out such details as which residence, hers or her husband's, would be the children's primary one and so forth. The solicitor asked her how she had reached her decision. She said that she had been talking to her husband's parents – she was still on good terms with them – and that they had suggested this arrangement. The solicitor challenged Cynthia to take a closer look at her decision. 'Let's start from zero,' he said, 'and you tell me what kind of living arrangements you want and why.' He did not think that it was wise to help her carry out a decision that was not her own.

Choosing goals suggested by others enables clients to blame others if they fail to reach the goals. Also if they simply follow other people's advice, they often fail to explore the down-the-road consequences.

From compliance to ownership   Commitment to goals can take different forms – compliance, buy-in and ownership. The least useful is mere compliance. 'Well, I guess I'll have to change some of my habits if I want to keep my marriage afloat' does not augur well for sustaining changes in behaviour. But it may be better than nothing. Buy-in is a level up from compliance. 'Yes, these changes are essential if we are to have a marriage that makes sense for both of us. We say we want to preserve our marriage, but now we have to prove it to ourselves.' This client has moved beyond mere compliance. But sometimes, like mere compliance, buy-in alone does not provide enough staying power because it depends too much on reason. 'This is logical' is far different from 'This is what I really want!' Ownership is a higher form of commitment. It means that the client can say, 'This goal is not someone else's, it's not just a good idea; it is mine, it is what I want to do.' Consider the following case:

> A counsellor worked with a manager whose superiors had intimated that he would not be moving much further in his career unless he changed his style in dealing with the members of his team and other key people with whom he worked within the organisation. At first the manager resisted setting any goals. 'What they want me to do is a lot of hogwash. It won't do anything to make the business better' was his initial response. One day, when asked whether accomplishing what 'they' wanted him to do would cost him that much, he pondered a few moments and then said, 'No, not really.' That got him started. He moved beyond resistance.
>
> With a bit of help from the counsellor, he identified a few areas of his managerial style that could well be 'polished up'. Within a few months he got much more into the swing of things. Given the favourable response to his changed behaviour he had received from the people who reported to him, he was able to say, 'Well, I now see that this makes sense. But I'm doing it because it has a positive effect on the people in the department.

(Continued)

It's the right thing to do.' Buy-in had arrived. A year later, he moved up another notch. He became much more proactive in finding ways to improve his style. He delegated more, gave people feedback, asked for feedback, held a couple of managerial retreats, joined a human-resource task force and routinely rewarded his direct reports for their successes. Now he began to say such things as 'This is actually fun.' Ownership had arrived. The people in his department began to see him as one of the best executives in the company. This process took over two years.

The manager did not have a personality transformation. He did not change his opinion of some of his superiors, and he was right in pointing out that they didn't follow their own rules. But he did change his behaviour because he gradually discovered meaningful incentives to do so.

Contracts as commitment devices   Self-contracts – that is, contracts that clients make with themselves – can also help clients commit themselves to new courses of action. Although contracts are promises clients make to themselves to behave in certain ways and to attain certain goals, they are also ways of making goals more focused. It is not only the expressed or implied promise that helps but also the explicitness of the commitment. Consider the following example, in which one of Dora's sons disappears without a trace.

About a month after one of Dora's two young sons disappeared, she began to grow listless and depressed. She was separated from her husband at the time the boy disappeared. By the time she saw a counsellor a few months later, a pattern of depressed behaviour was quite pronounced. Although her conversations with the counsellor helped ease her feelings of guilt – for instance, she stopped engaging in self-blaming rituals – she remained listless. She shunned relatives and friends, kept to herself at work and even distanced herself emotionally from her other son. She resisted developing images of a better future, because the only better future she would allow herself to imagine was one in which her son had returned.

Some strong challenging from Dora's sister-in-law, who visited her from time to time, helped jar her loose from her preoccupation with her own misery. 'You're trying to solve one hurt, the loss of Bobby, by hurting Timmy and hurting yourself. I can't imagine in a thousand years that this is what Bobby would want!' her sister-in-law screamed at her one night. Afterwards, Dora and the counsellor discussed a 'recommitment' to Timmy, to herself, to the extended family and to their home. Through a series of contracts, she began to reintroduce patterns of behaviour that had been characteristic of her before the tragedy. For instance, she contracted to opening her life up to relatives and friends once more, creating a much more positive atmosphere at home, encouraging Timmy to have his friends over and so forth. Contracts worked for Dora because, as she said to the counsellor, 'I'm a person of my word.'

When Dora first began implementing these goals, she felt she was just going through the motions. However, what she was really doing was acting herself into a new mode of thinking. Contracts helped Dora in both her initial commitment to a goal and her movement to action. In counselling, contracts are not legal documents but human instruments to be used if they are helpful. They often provide both the structure and the incentives some clients need.

Even self-contracts have a shadow side. There is no such thing as a perfect contract. Most people don't think through the consequences of all the provisions of a contract, whether it be marriage, employment or self-contracts designed to enhance a client's commitment to goals. And even people of goodwill unknowingly add covert codicils to contracts they make with themselves and others – 'I'll pursue this goal – until it begins to hurt' or 'I won't be abusive – unless she pushes me to the wall.' The codicils are buried deep in the decision-making process and only gradually make their way to the surface.

Obstacles: Help clients deal with competing agendas

Clients often set goals and formulate programmes for constructive change without taking into account competing agendas – other things in their lives that soak up time and energy, such as job, family and leisure pursuits. The world is filled with distractions. For instance, one manager wanted to begin developing computer and internet-related skills, but the daily push of business and a divorce set up competing agendas and sapped his resources. Not one of the goals of his self-development agenda was accomplished.

Programmes for constructive change often involve a rearrangement of priorities. If a client is to be a full partner in the reinvention of his marriage, then he cannot spend as much time 'with the boys'. Or the underemployed blue-collar worker might have to put aside some parts of her social life if she wants a more fulfilling job. She eventually discovers a compromise. A friend introduces her to the job-search possibilities on the internet. She discovers that she can work full time to support herself, do a better job looking for new employment on the internet than by using traditional methods and still have some time for a reasonable social life.

This is not to suggest that all competing agendas are frivolous. Sometimes clients have to choose between right and right. The woman who wants to expand her horizons by getting involved in social settings outside the home still has to figure out how to handle the tasks at home. This is a question of balance, not frivolity. The single parent who wants a promotion at work needs to balance her new responsibilities with involvement with her children. A counsellor who had worked with a two-career couple as they made a decision to have a child helped them think of competing agendas once the pregnancy started. A year after the baby was born, they saw the counsellor again for a couple of sessions to work on some issues that had come up. However, they started the session by saying, 'Are we glad that you talked about competing agendas when we were struggling with the decision to become parents! After the baby was born, we went back time and time again and reviewed what we said about managing competing and conflicting priorities. It helped stabilise us for the last two years.'

Box 9.2 indicates the kinds of questions you can help clients ask themselves about their commitment to their change agendas.

BOX 9.2	**Questions for Evaluating Clients' Commitment to Goals**

Here are the kinds of questions you can help clients ask themselves in order to test their commitment to goals they are setting:

- What is my state of readiness for change in this area at this time?
- How badly do I want what I say I want?
- How hard am I willing to work?
- To what degree am I choosing this goal freely?
- How highly do I rate the personal appeal of this goal?
- How do I know I have the courage to work on this?
- What's pushing me to choose this goal?
- What incentives do I have for pursuing this change agenda?
- What rewards can I expect if I work on this agenda?
- If this goal is in any way being imposed by others, what am I doing to make it my own?
- What difficulties am I experiencing in committing myself to this goal?
- In what way is it possible that my commitment is not a true commitment?
- What can I do to get rid of the disincentives and overcome the obstacles?
- What can I do to increase my level of commitment?
- In what ways can the goal be reformulated to make it more appealing?
- To what degree is the timing for pursuing this goal poor?
- What do I have to do to stay committed?
- What resources can help me? What kind of support do I need?

GREAT EXPECTATIONS: ENCOURAGE CLIENT SELF-EFFICACY – 'I CAN, I WILL'

Clients need to find the motivation to seize their goals and run with them. The more they find their motivation within themselves the better. 'Self-regulation' is the ideal. The counsellor's role in client self-regulation is to help clients choose goals, develop commitment to them and develop a sense of agency and assertiveness (Galassi & Bruch, 1992). Expectations, whether 'great' or not, also play a part in self-regulation. As we have seen, expectancy on the part of clients contributes significantly to successful outcomes. Here we look at client expectations through the lens of 'self-efficacy' (Bandura, 1986, 1989, 1991, 1995, 1997, 2001; Cervone, 2000; Cervone and Scott, 1995; Lightsey, 1996; Locke & Latham, 1990; Maddux, 1995; Schwarzer, 1992). Within the National Health Service (NHS) in the UK there are a number of expert patient programmes to help clients build their self-efficacy through psychoeducation, increased knowledge, greater sense of control and informed social support (Galbraith, 2016). Self-concepts such as self-esteem and self-efficacy, once seen as tried and true, have been questioned by more recent research. It's not that these concepts have been thrown out completely. Indeed research on both continues. Rather the claims made for the uses of self-concepts have been questioned. Other researchers insist that self-concepts or self-views do matter and 'that it is worthwhile and important to develop and implement theoretically informed programs to improve them' (Swann, Chang-Schneider & McClarty, 2007, p. 84).

I tend to cast my lot with those who see self-efficacy is an extremely useful clinical concept when it comes to constructive change. Concepts do not have to be 'pure' from an evidence-based point of view to be clinically useful. What follows will, hopefully, pique your interest and help you relate self-efficacy to helping. You can feast on the vast self-efficacy literature, pro and con, later.

The nature of self-efficacy

As Bandura (1995, p. 2) notes, 'Perceived self-efficacy refers to beliefs in one's capabilities to organise and execute the courses of action required to manage prospective situations. Efficacy beliefs influence how people think, feel, motivate themselves and act.' People's expectations of themselves and can-do beliefs have a great deal to do with their willingness to put forth effort to cope with difficulties, the amount of effort they will expend and their persistence in the face of obstacles. Clients with higher self-efficacy will make bolder choices, moving from adaptation towards more substantial goals. Clients tend to take action when two conditions are fulfilled:

1 ***Outcome expectations.*** Clients tend to act when they see that their actions will most likely lead to certain desirable results or accomplishments. 'I will end up with a better relationship with Sophie.'

2 ***Self-efficacy beliefs.*** People tend to act when they are reasonably sure that they have the wherewithal – for instance, working knowledge, skills, time, stamina, guts and other resources – to successfully engage in the kind of behaviour that will lead to the desired outcomes. 'I have the ability to deal with the conflicts Sophie and I have. I can do this. I'm going to do this.'

Now let's see these two factors operating together in a few examples.

Yolanda, who has had a stroke, not only believes that participation in a rather painful and demanding physical rehabilitation programme will literally help her get on her feet again (an outcome expectation), but she also believes that she has what it takes to inch her way through the programme (a self-efficacy belief). She therefore enters the programme with a very positive attitude and makes good progress.

Yves, on the other hand, is not convinced that an aggressive drug rehabilitation programme will lead to a more fulfilling life (a negative outcome expectation), even though he knows he could 'get through' the programme (a self-efficacy belief). So he says no to the therapist. Even though the therapist has assured him that he is capable of leading a drug-free life, Yves keeps saying to himself, 'Drug-free for what?' He sees being drug-free as an instrumental goal. But he has not yet come up with an attractive ultimate goal.

Xavier is convinced that a series of radiation and chemotherapy treatments would help him (a positive outcome expectation), but he does not feel that he has the stamina and courage to go through with them (a negative self-efficacy expectation). He, too, refuses the treatment.

Outcome expectations and self-efficacy beliefs are factors, not just in helping, but in everyday life. Do an internet search on that term and you will find a rich body of literature covering all facets of life – for instance, applications to education (Lopez, Lent, Brown & Gore, 1997; Multon, Brown & Lent, 1991; Smith & Fouad, 1999; Zimmerman, 1995, 1996), healthcare (O'Leary, 1985; Schwarzer & Fuchs, 1996; Schwarzer & Renner, 2000), physical rehabilitation and health (Altmaier, Russell, Kao, Lehmann & Weinstein, 1993; Bailey, 2017) and work (Donnay & Borgen, 1999).

Helping clients develop self-efficacy

People's sense of self-efficacy can be strengthened in a variety of ways. Lest self-efficacy be seen as a paradigm that applies only to the weak, let's take the case of a very strong manager, let's call him Nick, who wanted to change his abrasive supervisory style but was doubtful that he could do so. 'After all these years, I am what I am', he would say. It would have been silly to merely tell him, 'Nick, you can do it; just believe in yourself.' It was necessary to help him do a number of things to help strengthen his sense of self-efficacy in supervision.

Skills   *Make Sure that Clients have the Skills they Need to Perform Desired Tasks* Self-efficacy is based on ability and the conviction that you can use this ability to get a task done. Nick first read about and then attended some skill-building sessions on such 'soft' skills as listening, responding with empathic highlights, giving feedback that is softer on the person but harder on the problem, and constructive challenging. In truth, he had many of these skills, but they lay dormant. These short training experiences put him back in touch with some things he could do but didn't do. Note, however, that merely acquiring skills does not by itself increase clients' self-efficacy. The way they acquire them must give them a sense of competence. 'I now have these skills and I am positive that I can use them to get this task done.'

Corrective feedback   *Provide Feedback that is Based on Deficiencies in Performance, not on Deficiencies in the Client's Personality* Corrective feedback can help clients develop a sense of self-efficacy because it helps clear away barriers to the use of resources. Because I attended many meetings with Nick, I routinely described the ups and downs of his performance. I'd say such things as, 'Nick, in yesterday's meeting you listened to and responded to everyone's ideas. Let me make a proposal. You don't have to respond, as you did, in a positive way to every suggestion. Crap is still crap. Do some sorting as you listen and respond. Show why good ideas are good and why lousy ideas are bad. Then, whether the ideas are good or bad, everyone learns something.'

When corrective feedback sounds like an attack on clients' personalities, their sense of self-efficacy will suffer. My feedback helped Nick's self-efficacy belief because it pointed out that he could be decent and listen well and still use his excellent critical abilities. People would leave the room enlightened, not angry. When you give feedback, you would do well to ask yourself, 'In what ways will this feedback help increase the client's sense of self-efficacy?'

Positive feedback   *Provide Positive Feedback and Make it as Specific as Corrective Feedback* Positive feedback strengthens clients' self-efficacy by emphasising their strengths and reinforcing what they do well. This is especially true when it is specific. Too often negative feedback is very detailed, whereas positive feedback is perfunctory – 'Nice job.' This and other throwaway phrases probably sound like clichés to the person getting the feedback. Here's one bit of feedback I gave Nick: 'Yesterday, you interrupted Jeff, who was engaging in another one of his monologues. You summarised his main ideas. Then, with a few questions you showed him why only part of his plan was viable. The others were glad you took Jeff on. He learned something. And you saved us all a lot of time.'

The formula for giving specific positive feedback goes something like this. 'Here's what you did. Here's the positive outcome it had. And here's the wider positive impact.' Helping Nick see the value of this pattern of behaviour helped him engage in it more frequently and increased his sense of self-efficacy. 'I can combine the hard stuff and the soft stuff.' Clients need to see feedback as information they need to accomplish a task.

Success as a reinforcer *Invite Clients to Challenge Themselves to Engage in Actions that Produce Positive Results* Even small successes can increase a client's sense of self-efficacy. Success is reinforcing. Often success in a small endeavour will give clients the courage to try something more difficult. 'I can do even more.' Nick began delegating a few minor tasks to some of his direct reports. They handled their assignments very well. When I commented, 'They seem to be doing pretty well', Nick replied, 'I think that I can safely begin to put more on their plate. They like it, and I like seeing them succeed.' Successful delegation increased Nick's sense of supervisory self-efficacy. He could say to himself more assuredly, 'I can delegate without worrying whether or not it's going to get done.' Make sure, however, that the link between success and increased self-confidence is forged. A series of successes on its own does not necessarily increase the strength of a client's self-efficacy beliefs. Success has to be linked to a sense of increased competence.

Models *Help Clients Increase their Own Sense of Self-Efficacy by Learning from Others* I asked Nick to name the best manager in the division. He mentioned a name. 'What's he like?' I asked. Of course Nick talked about how competent this guy was, how effective he was in getting results and how tough he was. Tongue-in-cheek, I remarked, 'But I suppose that he's not very good with people.' Nick exploded. 'Of course he's fair. He's as good at all of this soft stuff as anyone else.' He went on to name ways in which the guy was 'good with people'. Then suddenly he stopped, looked at me, and smiled. 'Caught me, didn't you?' Learning makes clients more competent and increases their self-efficacy. Learning from models is, as we have seen, a bit tricky. Nick had too much pride to think that he could learn very much from others.

Providing encouragement *Support Clients' Self-Efficacy Beliefs Without Being Patronising* We took a brief look at motivational interviewing and encouragement in Chapter 7. However, if your support is meant to increase clients' sense of self-efficacy, it must be real, and what you support in them must be real. Encouragement and support must be tailored to each client in each instance. A supportive remark to one client might sound patronising to another. Had I patronised Nick – 'Give it a try, Nick, I know that you can do it' – I would have failed. My encouragement was, let's say, more subtle and indirect.

Reducing fear and anxiety *Help Clients Overcome their Fears* Fear blocks clients' sense of self-efficacy. If clients fear that they will fail, they will be reluctant to act.

Therefore, procedures that reduce fear and anxiety help heighten their sense of self-efficacy. Deep down, Nick was fearful of two things regarding changing his supervisory style – messing up the business and making a fool of himself. As he tentatively changed some of his supervisory practices, business results held steady. He even noticed that two of his team members seemed to become more productive. Helping him allay his fear of making a fool of himself by being too soft was a bit trickier. His behaviour outside the office came to the rescue. Although he was often an ogre in the office, Nick was very positive when we visited teams out in the field. He was as good at 'rallying the troops' as anyone I have ever seen. And he was real. Discussions about his two different styles helped him get rid of fears that he would make a fool of himself with his direct reports by engaging them instead of driving them.

Admittedly, I was Nick's coach and consultant, not his therapist. In the business world 'challenge' isn't always a bad word. Still, for the most part, I was invitational rather than challenging. I suggested ways of acting. That said, you would probably have to adapt the entire scenario with Nick to the needs and capabilities of your clients. Once more, the principles outlined in this chapter are things that you can do, not things that you must do with your clients. You have to develop your own style as a therapist and no one style is the 'right' style. A good friend of mine is one of the best counsellors I know. Her clients quickly learn that she is totally 'for' them. But she does not tolerate nonsense. If a client is rambling on about things that are not contributing to progress, she does not hesitate to say, 'Tim, I think we've spent too much time on this issue. Let's move on.' That's her style, not necessarily yours or mine. But she is very successful.

STAGE II AND ACTION

The work of formulating goals can in and of itself trigger action. Thinking about a better future often leads to experimenting with ways of making that future a reality. Each task of Stage II has this capability.

The tasks of Stage II as triggers for action

The work of Task A – developing possibilities for a better future – is just what some clients need. It frees them from thinking solely about problem situations and unused resources and enables them to begin fashioning a better future. Once they identify some of their wants and needs and consider a few possible goals, they move into action.

> Francine is depressed because her ageing and debilitated father has been picking on her, even though she has put off marriage in order to take care of him. Some of the things he says to her are quite hurtful. The situation has begun to affect her productivity at work. A counsellor suggests to her that the hurtful things her father says to her are not her father but his illness speaking. This gives her a whole new perspective and frees her to think about other possibilities. Once she spends a bit of time brainstorming answers to the counsellor's question – 'What do you want for both yourself and your father?' – she says things like, 'I'd like both of us to go through this with our dignity intact' and 'I'd like to be living the kind of life he would want me to have if his mind wasn't so clouded.' Once she brainstorms some possibilities for a better arrangement with her father, she needs little further help. Her usual resourcefulness returns. She gets on with life.

For other clients, Task B is the trigger for action. Shaping goals helps them see the future in a very different way. Once they have a clear idea of just what they want or need, they go for it.

> While driving under the influence of alcohol, Nero, a man in his early 20s, had a car accident that took his wife's life. Strangely, Nero is filled with self-pity rather than remorse. The counsellor, at her wit's end, invites him to take a good look at the way he is wrapped up in himself. She says, 'Who's the most decent person you know?' After fudging around a bit, he names Saul, an uncle. 'Describe his lifestyle to me', she urges, 'What makes him so decent?' With some prodding, he describes the lifestyle of this decent man. Then she says, 'Do the description again, but instead of saying "Saul" say "Nero".' Nero sweats, but the session has enormous impact on him. The picture of the contrast between his uncle's lifestyle and his own haunts him for days after. But he begins to stop feeling so sorry for himself; he visits his wife's parents and begs their forgiveness. He begins to see that there are other people in the world besides Nero.

For still other clients, Task C – the search for incentives for commitment – is the trigger for action. Once they see what's in it 'for me' – a kind of positive and productive selfishness, if you will – they move into action.

> Callahan is seeing a consultant because he is very distressed. He owns and runs a small business. A few of his employees have got together and filed a workplace discrimination suit against him. The 'troublemakers' he calls them, meaning a few women, a couple of Hispanics and three African Americans. The consultant finds out that Callahan believes that they are 'decent workers'. In fact, they are more than decent. Callahan tells the counsellor that he is paying them 'scale', but actually he underpays them. Callahan also says that he doesn't expect his supervisors to 'bend over backwards to become their friends'. The truth is that some supervisors – all but two are white males – are sometimes abusive.
>
> The consultant invites Callahan to consider attending an excellent programme on diversity 'before some court orders you to'. A couple of weeks after returning from the programme, he has a session with the consultant. He says that he has never even once considered the advantages of diversity in the workplace. All the term had meant to him was 'a bunch of politicians looking for votes'. Now that he sees the business reasons for diversity, he knows there are a few things he could do, but he still needs the consultant's help and guidance. 'I don't want to look like a soft jerk.' Callahan's newly acquired 'human touch' is far from being soft. He remains a rather rough-and-ready business guy.

Callahan didn't change his stripes overnight, but finding a package of incentives certainly helped him move towards much-needed action. Who knows, the whole situation might have even made a dent in his deeply ingrained prejudices.

The role of 'implementation intentions' in helping clients act

Commitment to goals is not enough. Commitment to goals must be accompanied or followed by commitment to the courses of action needed to accomplish these goals – the work of Stage III. There are a number of inspirational goal-setting diaries and planners that can be purchased, aimed at helping inspire clients to set and keep their goals. Gollwitzer and associates (Achtziger, Gollwitzer & Sheeran, 2008; Bayer & Gollwitzer, 2007; Gollwitzer, 1999; Gollwitzer & Sheeran, 2006; Oettingen & Gollwitzer, 2010; Webb & Sheeran, 2006) have researched a simple way to help clients cope with the common problems associated with translating goals into action – failing to get started, becoming distracted, reverting to bad habits and so forth. Even strong commitment to goals is not enough. Equally strong commitment to specific actions to accomplish goals is required. Good intentions, Gollwitzer points out, don't deserve their poor reputation. Strong intentions – 'I strongly intend to study for an hour every weekday before dinner' – are 'reliably observed to be realised more often than weak intentions' (p. 493):

> *"Implementation intentions are subordinate to goal intentions and specify the when, where, and how of responses leading to goal attainment. They have the structure of 'When situation x arises, I will perform response y!' and thus link anticipated opportunities with goal-directed responses."* (p. 494)

So Gwendolyn, an aide in a nursing home, may say, 'When Enid [a patient] becomes abusive, I will not respond immediately. I'll tell myself that it's her illness that's talking. Then I'll respond with patience and kindness.' Her ongoing goal is to control her anger and other negative responses to patients. However, Gwendolyn keeps pursuing this goal by continually refreshing her strong implementation intentions. Because Enid has been a particularly difficult patient, Gwendolyn needs to refresh her intentions frequently. However, her initial strong intention to substitute anger and impatience with kindness and equanimity means that in most cases her responses are more or less automatic. The environmental cue – patient anger, abuse, lack of consideration and whatever – 'triggers' the appropriate response in Gwendolyn. In a way, poor patient behaviour becomes 'opportunities' for her responses. You can help clients enunciate to themselves strong specific intentions that will help them 'automatically' handle many of the obstacles to goal implementation. For instance, the person trying to manage his or her weight gets the menu in the restaurant and automatically looks for the right kind and amount of food. 'I'll have the vegetarian entrée, thank you.' The research being done on implementation intentions has great pragmatic value with respect to translating goals into accomplishments.

THE SHADOW SIDE OF GOAL SETTING

Despite the advantages of goal setting outlined in this chapter, some helpers and clients seem to conspire to avoid goal setting as an explicit process. It is puzzling to see counsellors helping clients explore problem situations and unused opportunities and then stopping short of asking them what they want and helping them set goals. As Bandura (1990, p. xii) put it, 'Despite this unprecedented level of empirical support [for the advantages of goal setting], goal theory has not been accorded the prominence it deserves in mainstream psychology.' Years ago, the same concern was expressed differently. A US developmental psychologist was talking to a Russian developmental psychologist. The Russian said, 'It seems to me that American researchers are constantly seeking to explain how a child came to be what he is. We in the USSR are striving to discover how he can become what he not yet is' (see Bronfenbrenner, 1977, p. 258).

There are other reasons. *First*, some clients see goal setting as very rational, perhaps too rational. Their lives are so messy and goal setting seems sterile. Both helpers and clients object to this overly rational approach. There is a dilemma. On the one hand, many clients need or would benefit from a rigorous application of the problem-management process, including goal setting. On the other, they resist its rationality and discipline.

They find it alien. *Second,* goal setting means that clients have to move out of the relatively safe harbour of discussing problem situations and of exploring the possible roots of those problems in the past, and move into the uncharted waters of the future. This may be uncomfortable for client and helper alike. *Third*, clients who set goals and commit themselves to them move beyond the victim-of-my-problems game. Victimhood and self-responsibility make poor bedfellows.

Fourth, goal setting involves clients placing demands on themselves, making decisions, committing themselves and moving to action. If I say, 'This is what I want', then, at least logically, I must also say, 'Here is what I am going to do to get it. I know the price and I'm willing to pay it.' Because this demands work and pain, clients will not always be grateful for this kind of 'help'. *Fifth*, although goals are liberating in many respects, they also hem clients in. If a woman chooses a career, then it might not be possible for her to have the kind of marriage she would like. If a man commits himself to one woman, then he can no longer play the field.

There is some truth in the ironic statement: 'There is only one thing worse than not getting what you want, and that's getting what you want.' The responsibilities accompanying getting what you want – a drug-free life, a renewed marriage, custody of the children, a promotion, the peace and quiet of retirement, freedom from an abusing husband – often open up a new set of problems. Even good solutions create new problems. It is one thing for parents to decide to give their children more freedom; it is another to watch them use that freedom. Finally, there is a phenomenon called post-decisional depression. Once choices are made, clients begin to have second thoughts that often keep them from acting on their decisions.

As for action, some clients move into action too quickly. The focus on the future liberates them from the past, and the first few possibilities are very attractive. They fail to get the kind of focus and direction provided by Task B. So they go off half-cocked. Failing to weigh alternatives and shape goals often means that they have to do the process all over again.

Culture plays an important role in goal setting. Wosket (2006) points out that goal setting has cultural implications that helpers too easily overlook:

> "Objections are sometimes legitimately raised about the endorsement of the pursuit of individual over-collective goals that are explicit or implicit in most Eurocentric and Westernized approaches to counselling – the Skilled Helper model included. So here the counsellor has to be careful not to contaminate the client's process with his or her own conscious or unconscious bias towards the reinforcement of predominant cultural norms attached to goal setting. The process of goal setting can still be usefully applied to communal or collective contexts, for instance where the client's allegiance to family or cultural expectations prevails over individual preferences or objectives. Committing to a course of action that honours a sense of duty is a legitimate goal. For instance, the goal of keeping the family together may be a high priority for an Irish Catholic woman and one that, if accomplished, might give her more of a sense of achievement and fulfillment than pursuing the individual goal of leaving an unsatisfying relationship."

Effective helpers know what lurks in the shadows of goal setting both for themselves and for their clients and are prepared to manage their own part of it and help clients manage theirs. The answer to all of this lies in helpers being trained in the entire problem-management process and in their sharing a basic picture of the entire process with the client. Then goal setting, described in the client's language, will be a natural part of the process. Artful helpers weave goal setting, under whatever name, into the flow of helping. They do so by moving easily back and forth among the stages and tasks of the helping process, even in brief therapy.

King and Burton (2003) have written a sobering article on 'the hazards of goal pursuit'. They say that the research, read in one way, suggests that people who pursue goals 'ought to endeavour to achieve and approach goals that only slightly implicate the self; that are only moderately important, fairly easy and moderately abstract; that do not conflict with each other; and that concern the accomplishment of something other than financial gain' (p. 64) – that is, a boring life not worth living. However, there is another way to read the cited research – it is a wonderful compendium of common mistakes made in the pursuit of goals. Read the article and you will discover that just about every negative outcome takes place because of the violation of one or more of the principles outlined in this chapter. It highlights the fact that striving for goals is great, but it's going to cost you. So you better do it right. To be fair, the authors do not suggest avoiding striving for goals just because there are pitfalls along the way. Your job as a therapist is to help clients avoid or deal with the pitfalls. They end by saying, 'Only a hopelessly adolescent psychology of mental functioning would assert that it is best to care about nothing to avoid disappointment.'

CHAPTER 10
STAGE III: PLANNING
THE WAY FORWARD

Chapter Contents

- The Three Tasks of Stage III

- Tumi and Carlos Revisited: Tumi's Goals

- Task III-A: Help Clients Develop Strategies for Accomplishing their Goals

- Principles for Helping Clients Discover Viable Strategies for Accomplishing Goals

- Task III-B: Help Clients Choose Best-Fit Strategies

- Jayden's Amazing Odyssey

- Criteria for Choosing Goal-Accomplishing Strategies

- A Balance-Sheet Method for Choosing Strategies

- Help Clients Link Best-Fit Strategies to Action

- The Shadow Side of Selecting Strategies

- Task III-C: Help Clients Formulate Viable Plans

- Shaping the Plan: Two Cases

- Principles for Humanising the Mechanics of Constructive Change

- Ready-Made Action Programmes

THE THREE TASKS OF STAGE III

In its broadest sense, planning includes all the steps of Stages II and III – that is, it deals with solutions with a big-S and a small-s. In a narrower sense, planning deals with identifying, choosing and organising the strategies needed to accomplish goals. Whereas Stage II is about outcomes – goals or accomplishments 'powerfully imagined' – Stage III is about the activities or the work needed to produce those outcomes. It is about 'implementation intentions' and implementation itself.

When helped to explore what is going wrong in their lives, clients often ask, 'Well, what should I do about it?' That is, they focus on actions they need to take in order to 'solve' things. But, as we shall see, action – though essential – is valuable only to the degree that it leads to problem-managing and opportunity-developing outcomes. Of course, outcomes are valuable only to the degree that they have a constructive impact on the life of the client. The distinction between action, outcomes, results and impact is seen in the following example.

Mosa, a 40-year-old single woman, is making a great deal of progress in controlling her drinking through her involvement with the South African Alcoholics Anonymous programme. She attends Alcoholics Anonymous meetings, follows the 12 steps, stays away from situations that would tempt her to drink and calls fellow Alcoholics Anonymous members when she feels depressed or when the temptation to drink is pushing her hard. The outcome is that she has stayed sober for over seven months. She feels that this is quite an accomplishment. The impact of all this is very rewarding. She feels better about herself, and she has had both the energy and the enthusiasm to do things that she has not done in years – developing a circle of friends, getting interested in church activities and doing a bit of travel.

But Mosa is also struggling with a troubled relationship with a man. In fact, her drinking was, in part, an ineffective way of avoiding the problems in the relationship. She knows that she no longer wants to tolerate the psychological abuse she has been getting from her male friend, but she's afraid of the vacuum she will create by cutting off the relationship. She is, therefore, trying to determine what she wants, almost fearing that ending the relationship might turn out to be the best option.

She has attempted to manage the relationship in a number of ways. For instance, she has become much more assertive with her friend. She now cuts off contact whenever he becomes abusive. And she no longer lets him make all the decisions about what they are going to do together. But the relationship remains troubled. Even though she is doing many things, there is no satisfactory outcome. She has not yet determined what the outcome should be; that is, she has not determined what kind of relationship she would like and if it is possible to have such a relationship with this man. Nor has she determined to end the relationship.

Finally, after one seriously abusive episode, she tells him that she is ending the relationship. She does what she has to do to sever all ties with him (action), and the outcome is that the relationship ends permanently. The impact is that she feels liberated but lonely. The helping process needs to be recycled to help her with this new problem.

Stage III has three interrelated tasks. They are all aimed at problem-managing action on the part of the client.

- **Task III-A: Possible strategies.** Help clients develop possible strategies for accomplishing their goals. 'What kind of actions will help me get what I need and want?'
- **Task III-B: Best-fit strategies.** Help clients choose strategies that are effective, efficient and tailored to their preferences and resources. 'What actions are best for me?'
- **Task III-C: Plans.** Help clients turn strategies into a realistic plan. 'What should my campaign for constructive change look like? What do I need to do first? Second? When should I start?'

Stage III, highlighted in Figure 10.1, adds the final pieces to a client's planning of a programme for constructive change. Stage III deals with the 'game plan'. However, these three tasks constitute planning for action and should not be confused with action itself. Without action, a programme for constructive change is nothing more than a wish list. The implementation of plans is discussed in the next chapter.

FIGURE 10.1 The three tasks of Stage III

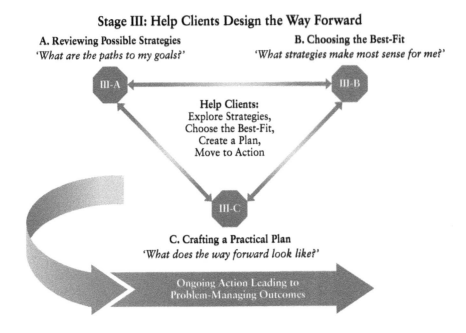

TUMI AND CARLOS REVISITED: TUMI'S GOALS

Before entering into the details of Stage III, let's summarise where Tumi stands at the moment. Then, as we move through Stage III, we can see some of the ways she struggles with the planning process.

After her disastrous conversation with her father, Tumi realised that she was back at Stage I with the added burden of her emotional devastation. She tipped, understandably, into full-blown depression and it was a few weeks before she began to climb out, even with Carlos's help. She came to realise that her excitement about creating a better future blinded her to how deep her father's opposition might be. She did not take the few rehearsals with Carlos for the fated conversation that seriously. She saw Carlos, even when he played the role of an angry and disappointed father, as Carlos, a person she liked and respected. Turning to her mother for help afterwards provided no respite. Although her mother tried to provide Tumi with some comfort, it was clear that she was fully aligned with her husband. Except for Carlos, Tumi felt alone in her misery.

As she regained her equilibrium, Tumi's immediate goal was to set up a second conversation with her father to determine whether he would agree to have a dialogue with her about her future. She needed to know whether he was at all willing to have some kind of reasonable conversation with her about career possibilities and about her social life. If he was unwilling to talk with her about these issues with some kind of openness, then she felt she needed to move to some kind of Plan B. When she finally talked to him about having such a conversation, he said, without rancour, that he thought this issue had been resolved and that they should both get on with their lives.

So she realised that fashioning a better future was something that she would have to do for herself. As mentioned earlier, Carlos thought that she might be suffering from an ongoing low-grade depression. However, he noticed that the crisis itself somehow energised her. She felt a range of negative emotions from time to time, but she no longer seemed depressed. It's as if the crisis itself somehow swept the cobwebs out. She seemed freer and even more determined to reach out for a better life.

With Carlos's help here's what she came up with. She feared that she might eventually have to break away from her parents in one way or another. But she realised that in order to do this she needed some kind of support group – something like the young people she had met in South Africa. Breaking away from her parents would be a huge step. She could begin planning for it now, but in terms of immediate action she needed some kind of community, people who would come to know her, accept her and her aspirations, and provide support for her as she struggled to fashion a different life. With a support community in place she thought that she could tackle the more daunting task of creating a new career for herself, even if this meant moving away from her parents.

Moving out of her home would be daunting because she has come to realise that the roots of the South African culture run deeper in her than she might have thought. On the other hand, the get-up-and-go nature of British culture also appeals to her. Sometimes these two strains work together. But sometimes they clash. The picture that comes to her mind focuses on the young people she met in South Africa. She half flirts with the idea of living in South Africa, but, with Carlos's help, realises that she has been idealising what she discovered during her trip. The upside is that there would be a ready-made community. The downside is that the British part of her could well clash with the South African system. And she heard some negative comments about life in South Africa from the young people she had met, even though they tended to be positive.

Tumi's first goal deals with her social life. 'How do I go about establishing *or* entering a community that has something like the community spirit I experienced in South Africa?' Her second goal deals with her work life. 'What do I need to do to move on to a better career?' Her third goal relates to her current arrangements with her parents. 'How can I prepare myself to leave my parents – whatever that might mean – if this is the price I have to pay in order to pursue these other two goals? But what if my father gets sick? What if the business crashes? What if they threaten to totally reject me?' Tumi has plenty of work to do. Stage III is about the work clients have to do to manage problems and develop unused opportunities.

TASK III-A: HELP CLIENTS DEVELOP STRATEGIES FOR ACCOMPLISHING THEIR GOALS

Strategies are actions that help clients accomplish their goals. This chapter is important precisely because it deals with actions clients must engage in to change their lives. That is why a bias towards action is one of the key values outlined in Chapter 2. Task III-A, developing a range of possible strategies to accomplish goals, is an exercise in liberation. Clients who feel hemmed in by their problems and are unsure of the viability of their goals are liberated by defining the way forward through this process. Clients who begin to see clear pathways to their goals have a greater sense of self-efficacy. 'I can do this.'

Strategy is the art of identifying and choosing realistic courses of action for achieving goals and doing so under adverse conditions, such as war. The problem situations in which clients are immersed constitute adverse conditions; clients often are at war with themselves and the world around them. Helping clients develop strategies to achieve their goals can be a most thoughtful, humane and fruitful way of being with them. This step in the counselling process is another that helpers sometimes avoid because it is too jargon-laden and mechanical. They do their clients a disservice. Clients with goals but no clear idea of how to accomplish them are still at sea.

PRINCIPLES FOR HELPING CLIENTS DISCOVER VIABLE STRATEGIES FOR ACCOMPLISHING GOALS

Once more it is a question of helping clients stimulate their imaginations and engage in divergent thinking. Most clients do not instinctively seek different routes to goals and then choose the ones that make most sense. These principles are similar to the ones used to discover possibilities for a better future in Stage II.

Use brainstorming to stimulate clients' thinking

Brainstorming, discussed in Chapter 9, can play an important role in developing strategies to accomplish goals. People tend to make better decisions if they have an opportunity to choose from among a number of options. But brainstorming in Stage III must be focused, just as it is in Stage II. Tumi's first goal is to establish a social life beyond home and work. Carlos helps her brainstorm ways of doing this. But Tumi suggests that she give herself a couple of weeks. She keeps a pad of paper with her and writes down ideas as they come along. Here are some of the possibilities she came up with:

- Go to select alumni events of her local university.
- Get involved with the alumni association itself as a volunteer.
- Join LinkedIn and Facebook and look into more tailored social networking sites.
- Experiment with a few sessions with a non-denominational church group.
- Start a part-time MBA in order to get involved with people with similar business aspirations.
- Do a two-week stint as a volunteer at a voluntary centre which helps South-African–British young people address cultural worries and uncertainties they might feel.
- Spend two more weeks in South Africa to identify more carefully just what she means by 'community'.
- Check to see what social-focused activities might be available with societies and support groups for South Africans living in Britain.
- See if there are any online South African social networking sites.
- Experiment with some online 'friendships'.
- Volunteer in a local hospital as a way of finding a community of like-minded people.
- Investigate local civic clubs.
- See if there are single women's clubs in town.
- See if there are women's book clubs in town.
- Say yes to fellow workers who have invited her over to their houses for a meal.

Tumi acted on some of these possibilities right away. Remember that the work done in any stage or task can stimulate action, often small actions, that keep the client headed in the right direction. For instance, she joined LinkedIn. She had an interview with the head of alumni relations at her old university and attended one of the alumni events.

Helpers may make suggestions but they have to do it in a way that keeps the client in the driver's seat. Therapists don't make choices for clients either directly or indirectly; rather they help clients make life-enhancing decisions. There are a number of ways of doing this. There is the 'prompt and fade' technique. The counsellor can say, 'Here are a couple of possibilities. ... Let's take a look at them and see whether any of them make sense to you. Or maybe they can kick-start some ideas of your own.' Or, 'Here are some of the things that people with this kind of problem situation have tried. ... How do they sound to you?' The 'fade' part of this technique keeps it from being advice-giving. It remains clear that the client must think these strategies over, choose the right ones, and commit to them.

Elton, a graduate student in counselling psychology, is plagued with perfectionism. Although he is an excellent student, he worries about getting things right. After he writes a paper or practises counselling, he agonises over what he could have done better. This puts him on edge when he practises counselling with his fellow trainees. They tell him that his 'edge' makes them uncomfortable and interferes with the flow of the helping process. One student says to him, 'You make me feel as if I'm not doing the right things as a client.'

Elton realises that 'less is more' – that is, becoming less preoccupied with the details of helping will make him a more effective helper. His goal is to become more relaxed in the helping sessions, free his mind of the 'imperatives' to be perfect and learn from mistakes rather than expending an excessive amount of effort trying to avoid them. He and his supervisor talk about ways he can free himself of these inhibiting imperatives.

SUPERVISOR: What kinds of things can you do to become more relaxed?

ELTON: I need to focus my attention on the client and the client's goals instead of being preoccupied with myself. I'm so focused on myself.

SUPERVISOR: So a basic shift in your orientation right from the beginning will help.

ELTON: Right. . . . And this means getting rid of a few inhibiting beliefs.

SUPERVISOR: Such as. . .?

ELTON: That technical perfection in the helping model is more important than the relationship with the client. I get lost in the details of the model and have forgotten that I'm a human being with another human being.

SUPERVISOR: So 're-humanising' the helping process in your own mind will help. . . . Any other internal behaviours need changing?

ELTON: Another belief is that I have to be the best in the class. That's my history, at least in academic subjects. Being as effective as I can be in helping a client has nothing to do with competing with my fellow students. Competing is a distraction. I know it's in my bones. It might have been all right in high school, but. . .

SUPERVISOR: Okay, so the academic-game mentality doesn't work here. . .

ELTON (interrupting): That's precisely it. Even the practising we do with one another is real life, not a game. You know that a lot of us talk about real issues when we practise.

SUPERVISOR: You've been talking about getting your attitudes right and the impact that can have on helping sessions. Are there things you can do that are not in your head?

ELTON (pauses): I'm hesitating because it strikes me how I'm in my head too much, always figuring me out. . . . On a much more practical basis, I like what Jerry and Philomena do. Before each session with their 'clients' in their practice sessions, they spend 5 or 10 minutes reviewing just where the client is in the overall helping process and determining what they might do in the next session to add value and move things forward. That puts the focus where it belongs, on the client.

SUPERVISOR: So a mini-prep for each session can help you get out of your world and into the client's.

ELTON: Also in debriefing the training videos we make each week. . . . I now see that I always start by looking at my behaviour instead of what's happening with the client. . . . Oh, there's another thing I can do. I can share just what we've been discussing here with my training partner.

SUPERVISOR: I'm not sure whether you bring up the perfectionism issues when you're the 'client' in the practice sessions or in the weekly lifestyle group meetings.

ELTON (hesitating): Well, not really. I'm just coming to realise how pervasive it is in my life. . . . To tell you the truth I think I haven't brought it up because I'd rather have my fellow trainees see me as competent, not perfectionist. . . . Well, the cat is out of the bag with you, so I guess it makes sense to put it on my lifestyle group agenda.

This dialogue, which includes empathy, probes and invitations to self-challenge from the supervisor, produces a number of strategies that Elton can use to develop a more client-focused mentality.

Use frameworks for stimulating clients' thinking about strategies

Helpers can use simple frameworks to formulate questions or probes that help clients develop a range of strategies. Simple frameworks can help. Consider the following case.

James has terminal cancer. He has been in and out of the hospital several times over the past few months, and he knows that he probably will not live more than a year. He would like the year to be as full as possible, and yet he wants to be realistic. He hates being in hospital, especially a large hospital, where it is so easy to be anonymous. One of his goals is to die outside the hospital. He would like to die as peacefully as possible and retain possession of his faculties as long as possible. How is he to achieve these goals?

You can use probes and prompts to help clients discover possible strategies by helping them investigate resources in their lives, including people, models, communities, places, things, organisations, programmes and personal resources.

Individuals   What individuals might help clients achieve their goals? James gets the name of a local doctor who specialises in the treatment of chronic, cancer-related pain. The doctor teaches people how to use a variety of techniques to manage pain. James says that perhaps his wife and daughter can learn how to give simple injections to help him control the pain. A friend of his has mentioned that his father got excellent hospice care and died at home. Also, he thinks that talking every once in a while with a friend whose wife died of cancer, a man he respects and trusts, will help him find the courage he needs.

Models and exemplars   Who is presently doing what the client wants to do? One of James's fellow workers died of cancer at home. James visited him there a couple of times. That's what gave him the idea of dying at home, or at least outside the hospital. He noticed that his friend never allowed himself to engage in poor-me talk. He refused to see dying as anything but part of living. This touched James deeply at the time, and now reflecting on that experience may help him develop the same kind of positive attitudes.

Communities   What communities of people are there through which clients might identify strategies for implementing their goals? Even though James has not been a regular churchgoer, he does know that the parish within which he resides has some resources for helping those in need. A brief investigation reveals that the parish has developed a relatively sophisticated approach to providing various services for the sick. He also does an internet search and discovers that there are a number of self-help groups for people like him.

Places   Are there particular places that might help? James immediately thinks of Lourdes, the shrine to which Catholic believers flock with all sorts of human problems. He doesn't expect miracles, but he feels that he might experience life more deeply there. It's a bit wild, but why not a pilgrimage? He still has the time and also enough money to do it. He also finds a high-tech place – an internet chat room for cancer patients and their caregivers. This helps him get out of himself and, at times, become a helper instead of a client.

Things   What things can help clients achieve their goals? James has read about the use of combinations of drugs to help stave off pain and the side effects of chemotherapy. He has heard that certain kinds of electric stimulation can ward off chronic pain. He explores all these possibilities with his doctor and even arranges for second opinions.

Organisations   James runs across an internet-based organisation that helps cancer patients get social support. He volunteers. In his role as helper, he finds he receives as much help and motivation and solace as he gives.

Tumi, wanting to develop and expand her social life, explores various societies which exist in Britain for South Africans. She is impressed by what she finds on one website: 'Its foci include preservation and advancement of South African arts and culture, development of leaders through fellowships and awards, and encouragement of civic engagement through non-profit capacity building and voter registration.'

Programmes   Are there any ready-made programmes for people in the client's position? James, for example, learns that a new hospice in his part of town has three programmes. One helps people who are terminally ill stay in the community as long as they can. A second makes provision for part-time residents. The third provides a residential programme for those who can spend little or no time in the community. The goals of these programmes are practically the same as James's.

Box 10.1 outlines some questions that you can help clients ask themselves to develop strategies for accomplishing goals.

BOX 10.1 Questions for developing strategies

Here are the kinds of questions you can help clients ask themselves in their search for ways of accomplishing their goals:

- Now that I know what I want, what do I need to do?
- Now that I know my destination, what are the different routes for getting there?
- What actions will get me to where I want to go?
- Now that I know the gaps between what I have and what I want and need, what do I need to do to bridge those gaps?
- How many ways are there to accomplish my goals?
- How do I get started?
- What can I do right away?
- What do I need to do later?

Help clients determine the kind of working knowledge and skills they will need to move forward

People often get into trouble or fail to get out of it because they lack the needed life skills or coping skills to deal with problem situations. When this is the case, helping clients find ways of learning the life skills they need to cope more effectively is an important broad strategy. Indeed, the use of skills training as part of therapy – what Carkhuff years ago (1971) called 'training as treatment' – might be essential for some clients. Challenging clients to engage in activities for which they don't have the skills compounds, rather than solves, the problem. What kinds of working knowledge and skills does a client need to get where he or she wants to go? Consider the following case:

> Jerzy and Zelda fell in love. They married and enjoyed a relatively trouble-free honeymoon period of about two years. Eventually, however, the problems that inevitably arise from living closely together asserted themselves. For instance, they found that they counted too heavily on romantic fervour to help them overcome – or, more often, ignore – difficulties. Once that fervour had cooled, they began fighting about finances, sex and values. They lacked certain critical interpersonal communication skills. Furthermore, their nine-year age difference became problematic because they lacked understanding of each other's developmental needs. Jerzy had little working knowledge of the developmental demands of a 20-year-old woman; Zelda had little working knowledge of the kinds of cultural blueprints that were operative in the lifestyle of her 29-year-old husband. The relationship began to deteriorate. Because they had few problem-solving skills, they didn't know how to handle their situation.

Jerzy and Zelda needed both working knowledge and skills. This is hardly surprising. Lack of requisite interpersonal communication and other life skills is often at the heart of relationship breakdowns.

One marriage counsellor I know does marriage counselling in groups of four couples. Training in communication skills is part of the process. He separates men from women and trains them in tuning in, active listening and responding with empathy. For skills practise, he begins by pairing a woman with a woman and a man with a man. Next he pairs a man and a woman, but not spouses. Finally, spouses are paired, taught a simple version of the problem-management process outlined in this book and then helped to use the skills they have learned to engage in problem solving with each other. In sum, he equips them in two sets of life skills – interpersonal communication and problem solving. This is his way of pursuing the second goal of helping outlined in Chapter 1.

TASK III-B: HELP CLIENTS CHOOSE BEST-FIT STRATEGIES

In Task III-B, clients are in decision-making mode – with all its pitfalls and promises – once more. After brainstorming strategies for accomplishing goals, clients need to choose a strategy or a 'package' of strategies that best fits their situation, resources, personality and preferences, and turn them into some kind of plan for constructive change. Whether these tasks are done with the kind of formality outlined here is not the point. Counsellors, understanding what planning is and what makes it work, can add value by helping clients find ways of accomplishing goals (getting what they need and want) in a systematic, flexible, personalised and cost-effective way.

Once they are helped to develop a range of strategies to implement goals, some clients move forward on their own; that is, they choose the best strategies, put together an action plan and implement it. Others, however, need help in choosing strategies that best fit their situation, and so we add Task III-B to the helping process. It is useless to have clients brainstorm if they don't know what to do with the action strategies they generate.

JAYDEN'S AMAZING ODYSSEY

Let's start with Jayden, a man who was helped to discover two best-fit strategies for achieving emotional stability in his life. With these, he achieved outcomes that surpassed anyone's wildest expectations.

One morning, Jayden, then 18 years old, woke up unable to speak or move. He was taken to a hospital, where catatonic schizophrenia was diagnosed. After repeated admissions to hospitals, where he underwent both drug and electroconvulsive therapy (ECT), his diagnosis was changed to paranoid schizophrenia. He was considered incurable.

A quick overview of Jayden's earlier years suggests that much of his emotional distress was caused by unmanaged life problems and the lack of human support. He was separated from his mother for four years when he was young. They were reunited in a city new to both of them, and there he suffered a great deal of harassment at school because of his 'ethnic' looks and accent. There was simply too much stress and change in his life. He protected himself by withdrawing. He was flooded with feelings of loss, fear, rage and abandonment. Even small changes became intolerable. His catatonic attack occurred in the autumn on the day of the change from daylight saving to standard time. It seemed that this ordinary change was the last straw.

In hospital, Jayden became convinced that he and many of his fellow patients could do something about their illnesses. They did not have to be victims of their own helplessness or of the institutions designed to help them. Reflecting on his hospital stays and the drug and ECT treatments, he later said he found his 'help' so debilitating that it was no wonder that he got crazier. Somehow Jayden, using his own inner resources, managed to get out of the hospital. Eventually, he got a job, found a partner and got married.

One day, after a series of problems with his family and at work, Jayden felt himself becoming agitated and thought he was choking to death. His doctor sent him to the hospital 'for more treatment'. There Jayden had the good fortune to meet Aimee, a psychiatric social worker who was convinced that many of the hospital's patients were there because of lack of support before, during and after their bouts of illness. She helped him see his need for social support, especially during times of stress. She also discovered in her in-patient counselling groups that Jayden had a knack for helping others. Jayden's broad goal was still emotional stability, and he wanted to do whatever was necessary to achieve it. Finding support and helping others cope with their problems, instrumental goals, were his best strategies for achieving the stability he wanted.

Once discharged from the hospital, Jayden got to work. He enrolled Aimee to coach his wife on the best ways to provide support for him at times of stress. He then started a self-help group for ex-patients like himself. In the group, he was a full-fledged participant. But because he also had a deep desire to help others like himself, he developed the self-help group into a network of self-help groups for ex-patients.

This is an amazing example of a client who focused on one broad goal, emotional stability; translated it into a number of immediate, practical goals; discovered two broad strategies – finding ongoing emotional support and helping others – for accomplishing those goals; translated the strategies into practical applications; and by doing all that found the emotional stability he was looking for. Jayden's case is hardly the norm, but it does highlight the power of problem management coupled with a clear sense of self-responsibility.

CRITERIA FOR CHOOSING GOAL-ACCOMPLISHING STRATEGIES

The criteria for choosing goal-accomplishing strategies are like the criteria for choosing goals outlined in Stage II. These criteria are reviewed briefly here through a number of examples. Strategies to achieve goals should be, like goals themselves, specific, robust, prudent, realistic, sustainable, flexible, cost-effective and in keeping with the client's values. The client does not need to know all of this, though it might help, but you do. Let's take a look at a few of these criteria as applied to choosing strategies.

Specific strategies

Strategies for achieving goals should be specific enough to drive behaviour. In the preceding example, Jayden's two broad strategies for achieving emotional stability, tapping into human support and helping others, were translated into quite specific strategies – keeping in touch with Aimee, getting help from his wife, participating in a self-help group, starting a self-help group, and founding and running a self-help organisation. Contrast Jayden's case with Nadine's.

Nadine was admitted to a mental hospital because she had been exhibiting bizarre behaviour in her neighbourhood. She dressed in a slovenly way and went around admonishing the residents of the community for their 'sins'. Her condition was diagnosed as schizophrenia, simple type. She had been living alone for about five years, since the death of her husband. It seems that she had become more and more alienated from herself and others. In hospital, medication helped control some of her symptoms. She stopped admonishing others and took reasonable care of herself, but she was still quite withdrawn. She was assigned to 'milieu' therapy, a euphemism meaning that she was helped to follow the more or less general routine of the hospital – a bit of work, a bit of exercise, some programmed opportunities for socialising. She remained withdrawn and usually seemed moderately depressed. No therapeutic goals had been set, and the non-specific programme to which she was assigned was totally inadequate.

So-called milieu therapy did nothing for Nadine because in no way was it specific to her needs. It was a general programme that was only marginally better than drug-focused standard care. Jayden's strategies, on the other hand, proved to be powerful. They not only helped him gain stability but also gave him a new perspective on life.

Effective strategies

Strategies are effective to the degree that, when implemented, they actually achieve the goal. They can be 'big' strategies such as Jayden's or small as in Nadine's programme. The strategies in Nadine's case did not get the job done. They were too general, but they also lacked bite. Jayden's self-chosen strategies, on the other hand, were both big and effective, especially the strategy of starting and running a self-help organisation. What could be done for Nadine?

A newly hired psychiatrist saw immediately that Nadine needed more than either standard psychiatric or milieu-centred care. He involved her in a new comprehensive social-learning programme, which included cognitive restructuring, social-skills training and behavioural-change interventions based on incentives, shaping, modelling and rewards. Despite a few ups and downs, Nadine responded very well to the new, rather intensive programme. She was discharged within six months and, with the help of an outpatient extension of the programme, remained in the community.

For Nadine this programme proved to be specific, effective, prudent, realistic, sustainable, flexible, cost-effective and in keeping with her values. It was cost-effective in two ways. First, it was the best use of Nadine's time, energy and psychological resources. Second, it helped her and others like her get back into the community and stay there. It was in keeping with her values because, even though some staff members at the hospital had concluded that all she wanted was 'to be left alone', Nadine deep down valued human companionship and freedom. She did better in a community setting.

Realistic strategies

When clients choose strategies that are beyond their resources, they are doing themselves in. Strategies are realistic when they can be carried out with the resources the client has, are under the client's control and are unencumbered by obstacles. Jayden's strategies would have appeared unrealistic to most clients and helpers. But this highlights an important point. Just as we should invite clients to review stretch goals in their search for life-enhancing outcomes, so we should not underestimate what actions clients are capable of taking to move beyond their problem situations. In the following case, Desmond moves from unrealistic to realistic strategies for accomplishing his goals.

> Desmond was in a halfway house after leaving a mental hospital. From time to time he still had bouts of depression that would incapacitate him for a few days. He wanted to get a job because he thought that it would help him feel better about himself, become more independent and manage his depression better. He applied for jobs in a rather random way and was constantly turned down after being interviewed. He simply did not yet have the kinds of resources needed to put himself in a favourable light in job interviews. Moreover, he was not yet ready for a regular, full-time job.

On his own, Desmond does not do well in choosing strategies to achieve even modest goals. But here's what happened next.

> A local university received funds to provide outreach services to halfway houses in the metropolitan area. The university programme included finding companies that were willing, on a win-win basis, to work with halfway-house residents. A counsellor from the programme helped Desmond get in contact with companies that had specific programmes to help people with psychiatric problems. He found two that he thought would fit his needs. Some of the best workers in these companies had a variety of disabilities, including psychiatric problems. After a few interviews, Desmond got a job in one of these companies that fitted his situation and capabilities. The entire work culture was designed to provide the kind of support he needed.

Of course, there is a difference between realism and allowing clients to sell themselves short. Substantive strategies that make clients stretch for a valued goal can be most rewarding. Jayden's case is an exceptional example of that.

Strategies in keeping with the client's values

Make sure that the strategies chosen are consistent with the client's values. Let's return to the case of the priest who had been unjustly accused of child molestation.

> In preparing for the court case, the priest and his solicitor had a number of discussions. The solicitor wanted to do everything possible to destroy the accusers' credibility. He had dug into their pasts and dredged up some dirt. The priest objected to these tactics. 'If I let you do this,' he said, 'I descend to their level. I can't do that.' The priest discussed this with his counsellor, his superiors and another solicitor. He stuck to his guns. They prepared as strong a case as possible, but one based on facts without any sleaze.
>
> After the trial was over and he was acquitted, the priest said that his discussion about the lawyer's preferred tactics was one of the most difficult issues he had to face. Something in him said that, because he was innocent, any means to prove his innocence was allowed. Something else told him that this was not right. The counsellor helped him clarify and challenge his values but made no attempt to impose either his own or the lawyer's values on his client.

Tumi wonders what package of strategies will give the best route towards getting into community. She realises how many of her strategies involve getting in touch with her South African roots. She wonders whether this is her way of moving away from what could be called her cultural 'neutrality'. She realises that some of her depressive feelings come from feeling 'bland'. Her South African roots seem to have more potential to give her life some colour than what mainstream British culture has to offer. But this gives her another idea. Would it be possible for her to live with a British family for a while? Perhaps with a family or extended family with lots of life and driven by more 'noble' values than those driving her cousins? Perhaps an Asian or Indian rather than a traditional white British family? Box 10.2 outlines the kinds of questions you can help clients ask themselves in order to choose best-fit strategies.

BOX 10.2 Questions on best-fit strategies

Here are some questions you can help clients ask themselves to determine which strategies will best fit their situation:

- Which strategies will be most useful in helping me get what I need and want?
- Which strategies are best for this situation?
- Which strategies best fit my resources?
- Which strategies will be most economical in the use of resources?
- Which strategies are most powerful?
- Which strategies best fit my preferred way of acting?
- Which strategies best fit my values?
- Which strategies will have the fewest unwanted consequences?

Sample, then choose

Some clients find it easier to choose strategies when they first sample some of the possibilities. Consider this case:

> Two business partners were in conflict over ownership of the firm's assets. Their goals were to see justice done, to preserve the business and, if possible, to preserve their relationship. A colleague helped them sample some possibilities. Under her guidance, they discussed with a solicitor the process and consequences of bringing their dispute to the courts, they had a meeting with a consultant-counsellor who specialised in these kinds of disputes and they visited an arbitration firm.

In this case, the sampling procedure had the added effect of giving them time to let their emotions simmer down. They agreed to go the consultant-counsellor route.

Of course, some clients could use strategy sampling as a way of putting off action. That was certainly not the case with Jayden. His attending the meeting of a self-help group after leaving the hospital was a form of strategy sampling. Although he was impressed by the group, he thought that he could start a group limited to ex-patients that would focus more directly on the kinds of issues he and other ex-patients were facing. As we have seen earlier, Tumi instinctively moves into strategy sampling after her brainstorming. She finds that she is much more ready to explore than she might have imagined.

A BALANCE-SHEET METHOD FOR CHOOSING STRATEGIES

Balance sheets in general deal with the economics of an enterprise. In therapy, the balance-sheet method can help clients come to grips with the economics of problem management and opportunity development. The methodology could be used for any key decision related to the helping process – whether to get help in the first place, to work on one problem rather than another or to choose this rather than that goal. Balance sheets deal with the acceptability and unacceptability of both benefits and costs. A balance-sheet approach, applied to choosing strategies for achieving goals, poses questions such as the following:

- What are the benefits of choosing this strategy? For myself? For significant others?
- To what degree are these benefits acceptable? To me? To significant others?
- In what ways are these benefits unacceptable? To me? To significant others?
- What are the costs of choosing this strategy? For myself? For significant others?
- To what degree are these costs acceptable? To me? To significant others?
- In what ways are these costs unacceptable? To me? To significant others?

The balance-sheet method can be used whenever clients need to make an important decision, for instance, setting a goal.

Consider Karen. She is married, has three teenage children and works in the accounting department of a retailer. She has finally admitted that she is an alcoholic because her condition has become almost impossible to hide. She thinks that she could just stop drinking. After several failed attempts, she admits that she does not know how to stop drinking and seeks help. One possible strategy is a one-month residential programme at an alcoholic treatment centre with a high success rate. This possibility appeals to her, but she wonders if she is being self-indulgent. However, because choosing this strategy would be a serious decision, the counsellor, Joan, helps Karen use the balance sheet to weigh possible costs and benefits. After all, this will be costly, but it will also affect her husband, her children, her workplace and, of course, herself – 'What will people think of me? What if I fail?' After filling out a version of the balance sheet outlined earlier, Karen and Joan, her counsellor, discuss Karen's findings. Karen concludes, 'All in all, it seems like the residential programme is a good idea. There is something much more substantial about it than the outpatient programme. I'm scared, but I think it's what will help me best.' Joan helps her work out a plan for finding ways to address the pain she is causing her family and workplace.

If you use the balance sheet in any of its forms, take a practical and flexible approach. Do not use it with every client to work out the pros and cons of every course of action. If you do use it, do so because the client and you think it will help and, even then, tailor it to the needs of the client. One of the best ways to use the balance sheet is not to use it directly at all. Keep it in the back of your mind whenever clients are making decisions. Use it as a filter to listen to clients. Then turn relevant parts of it into probes to help clients focus on issues they may be overlooking. 'How do you think that this decision will affect your husband?' is a probe that originates in the balance sheet. 'Is there any downside to that strategy?' might help a client who is being a bit too optimistic. No formula.

HELP CLIENTS LINK BEST-FIT STRATEGIES TO ACTION

Some clients are filled with great ideas for getting things done but never seem to do anything. They lack the discipline to evaluate their ideas, choose the best and turn them into action. Often this kind of work seems too tedious to them, even though it is precisely what they need. Consider the following case:

Clint came away from the doctor feeling depressed. He was told that he was in the high-risk category for heart disease and that he needed to change his lifestyle. He was cynical, very quick to anger and did not readily trust others. Venting his suspicions and hostility did not make them go away, however; it only intensified them. Therefore, one critical lifestyle change was to change this pattern and develop the ability to trust others.

He developed three broad goals: reducing mistrust of others' motives, reducing the frequency and intensity of such emotions as rage, anger and irritation, and learning how to treat others with consideration. Clint read through the common strategies used to help people pursue these broad goals (see Williams, 1989). They included the following:

- Keeping a hostility log to discover the patterns of cynicism and irritation in one's life
- Finding someone to talk to about the problem, someone to trust

- 'Thought stopping', catching oneself in the act of indulging in hostile thoughts or in thoughts that lead to hostile feelings
- Talking sense to oneself when tempted to put others down
- Developing empathic thought patterns – that is, walking in the other person's shoes
- Learning to laugh at one's own silliness
- Using a variety of relaxation techniques, especially to counter negative thoughts
- Finding ways of practising trust
- Developing active-listening skills
- Engaging in assertive rather than aggressive behaviour
- Putting things in context, seeing each day as one's last or contrasting the seriousness of one's problems with those of people with real, life-limiting problems
- Practising forgiving others without being patronising or condescending.

Clint prided himself on his rationality (though his 'rationality' was one of the things that got him into trouble). So, as he read down the list, he chose strategies that could form an 'experiment', as he put it. He decided to talk to a counsellor (for the sake of objectivity), keep a hostility log (data gathering) and use the tactics of thought stopping and talking sense to himself whenever he felt that he was letting others get under his skin. The counsellor noted to himself that none of these necessarily involved changing Clint's attitudes towards others. However, he did not invite Clint to challenge himself at this point. His best bet was that through 'strategy sampling' Clint would learn more about his problem, that he would find that it went deeper than he thought. Clint set himself to his experiment with vigour.

Clint chose strategies that fitted his values. The problem was that the values themselves needed reviewing. But Clint did act, and action gave him the opportunity to learn.

THE SHADOW SIDE OF SELECTING STRATEGIES

The shadow side of decision making is certainly at work in clients' choosing strategies to implement goals. Early on Goslin (1985, pp. 7, 9) described pitfalls in decision making that subsequent research has, as mentioned in Chapter 1, proved to be all too prevalent.

> *"In defining a problem, people dislike thinking about unpleasant eventualities, have difficulty in assigning values to alternative courses of action, have a tendency towards premature closure, overlook or undervalue long-range consequences and are unduly influenced by the first formulation of the problem. In evaluating the consequences of alternatives, they attach extra weight to those risks that can be known with certainty. They are more subject to manipulation when their own values are poorly thought through. A major problem for individuals is knowing when to search for additional information relevant to decisions."*

In choosing a course of action, clients often fail to evaluate the risks involved and determine whether the risk is balanced by the probability of success.

Three pitfalls

Gelatt, Varenhorst and Carey (1972) suggested three ways in which clients may try to deal with the factors of risk and probability: wishful thinking, playing it safe and avoiding the worst outcome. Clients often indulge in these ways of thinking and acting without reflecting on what they are doing or considering unintended downside consequences. Thus, they lie in the 'shadows'.

Wishful thinking   In this case, clients choose a course of action that might (they hope) lead to the accomplishment of a goal regardless of risk, cost or probability. For instance, Jenny wants her ex-husband to increase the amount of support he is paying for the children. She tries to accomplish this by constantly nagging him and trying to make him feel guilty. She doesn't consider the risk (he might get angry and stop giving her anything), the cost (she spends a great deal of time and emotional energy arguing with him) or the probability of success (he does not react favourably to nagging). The wishful-thinking client operates blindly, engaging in some course of action without taking into account its usefulness. At its worst, this is a reckless approach. Clients who 'work hard' and still 'get nowhere' may be engaged in wishful thinking, persevering in using means they prefer but that are of doubtful efficacy. Effective helpers find ways of challenging wishful thinking. 'Jenny, it might be useful to review what you've been doing to get Tom to pay up and how successful you've been.'

Playing it safe   In this case, the client chooses only safe courses of action, ones that have little risk and a high degree of probability of producing at least limited success. For instance, Liam, a manager in his early 40s, is very dissatisfied with the way his boss treats him at work. His ideas are ignored, the delegation he is supposed to have is pre-empted and his boss does not respond to his attempts to discuss career development. His goals centre on his career. He wants to let his boss know about his dissatisfaction and he wants to learn what his boss thinks about him and his career possibilities. These are instrumental goals, of course, because his overall goal is to carve out a more promising career path. However, he fails to bring these issues up when his boss is 'out of sorts'. On the other hand, when things are going well, Liam doesn't want to 'upset the applecart'. He drops hints about his dissatisfaction, even joking about them at times. He tells others in hope that word will filter back to his boss. During formal appraisal sessions he allows himself to be intimidated by his boss. However, in his own mind, he is doing whatever could be expected of a 'reasonable' man. He does not know how safe he is playing it. What might you say to Liam at this juncture?

Avoiding the worst outcome   In this case, clients choose means that are likely to help them avoid the worst possible result. They try to minimise the maximum danger, often without identifying what that danger is. Crissy, dissatisfied with her marriage, sets a goal to be 'more assertive'. However, even though she has never said this either to herself or to her counsellor, the maximum danger for her is to lose her partner. Therefore, her 'assertiveness' is her usual pattern of compliance, with some frills. For instance, every once in a while she tells her husband that she is going out with friends and will not be around for supper. Without her knowing it, he actually enjoys these breaks. At some level of her being, she realises that her absences are not putting him under any pressure, but she continues to be 'assertive' in the same way. She never sits down with her husband to review where they stand with each other because that might be the beginning of the end. At the beginning of one session, the counsellor says, 'What if some good friend were to say to you, "Bill has you just where he wants you." How would you react?' Crissy is startled, but she comes away from the session with a much more realistic view of what her strategy is achieving – or not achieving.

Striking a balance

In the ideal case, the authors say, clients choose strategies for achieving goals that balance risks against the probability of success. This 'combination' approach is the most difficult to apply, for it involves the right kind of analysis of problem situations and opportunities, choosing goals with the right edge, being clear about one's values, ranking a variety of strategies according to these values and estimating how effective any given course of action might be. Even more to the point, it demands challenging the blind spots that might distort these activities. But these are precisely problem-management tasks that you should be prepared to help clients do – at least clients who are up to it.

TASK III-C: HELP CLIENTS FORMULATE VIABLE PLANS

The logic is this. After identifying and choosing strategies to accomplish goals, clients need to organise these strategies into a plan. In this task, counsellors help clients come up with the plan itself, that is, the sequence of actions – what should I do first, second and so forth – to turn the goal into an outcome.

However, the execution of these tasks – and all the tasks of the problem-management process – is often much messier. Therapists need to understand where their clients are in the geography of helping, and what they are struggling with in order to know how to intervene.

The case of Bernard: No plan of action

The lack of a plan – that is, a clear step-by-step process to accomplish a goal – keeps some clients mired in their problem situations. Consider the case of Bernard, a vice president of a large Cape Town corporation.

Bernard was a go-getter. He was very astute about business and had risen quickly through the ranks. Christopher, the president of the company, was in the process of working out his own retirement plans. From a business point of view, Bernard was the heir apparent. But there was a glitch. Christopher was far more than a good manager; he was a leader. He had a vision of what the company should look like 5 to 10 years down the line. Early on, he saw the power of the internet and used it wisely to give the business a competitive edge.

Although tough, Christopher related well to people. People constituted the human capital of the company. He knew that products and people kept customers happy. He also took to heart the results of a millennium survey of one million employees in South Africa. One of the sentences in the summary of the survey results haunted him – 'People join companies but leave supervisors.' In the 'war for talent', he couldn't afford supervisors who alienated their team members.

Bernard was quite different. He was a 'hands-on' manager, meaning, in his case, that he was slow to delegate tasks to others, however competent they might be. He kept second-guessing others when he did delegate, reversed their decisions in a way that made them feel put down, listened poorly and took a fairly short-term view of the business – 'What were last week's figures like?' He was not a leader but an 'operations' man. His direct reports called him a micromanager.

One day, Christopher sat down with Bernard and told him that he was considering him as his successor down the line, but that he had some concerns. 'Bernard, if it were just a question of business acumen, you could take over today. But my job, at least in my mind, demands a leader.' Christopher went on to explain what he meant by a leader and to point out the things in Bernard's style that had to change.

So Bernard did something that he never thought he would do. He began seeing a coach. Teresa had been an executive with another company in the same industry but had opted to be a consultant for family reasons. Bernard chose her because he trusted her business acumen. That's what meant most to him. They worked together for over a year, often over lunch and in hurried meetings early in the morning or late in the evening. And, indeed, he valued their dialogues about the business.

Bernard's ultimate aim was to become president. If getting the job meant that he had to try to become the kind of leader his boss had outlined, so be it. Because he was very bright, he came up with some inventive strategies for moving in that direction. But he could never be pinned down to an overall programme with specific milestones by which he could evaluate his progress. Teresa pushed him, but Bernard was always 'too busy' or would say that a formal programme was 'too stifling'. That was odd, because formal planning was one of his strengths in the business world.

Bernard remained as astute as ever in his business dealings. But he merely dabbled in the strategies meant to help him become the kind of leader Christopher wanted him to be. Bernard had the opportunity of not just correcting some mistakes, but also developing and expanding his managerial style. But he blew it. At the end of two years, Christopher appointed someone else president of the company.

Bernard never got his act together. He never put together the kind of change programme needed to become the kind of leader Christopher wanted as president. Why? Bernard had two significant blind spots that the consultant did not help him overcome. First, he never really took Christopher's notion of leadership seriously. So he wasn't really ready for a change programme. He thought the president's job was his and that business acumen alone would win out in the end. Second, he thought he could change his management style at the margins, even though more substantial changes were called for.

Teresa never challenged Bernard as he kept 'trying things' that never led anywhere. Maybe things would have been different if she had said something like, 'Come on, Bernard, you know you don't really buy

Christopher's notion of leadership. But you can't just give lip service to it. Christopher will see right through it. We're just messing around. You don't want a programme because you don't believe in the goal. Let's do something or call these meetings off.' If she had challenged him like this, Bernard probably would have said, 'I think I need a different consultant.' In a way she was a co-conspirator because she, too, relished their business discussions. When Bernard didn't get the job, he left the company, leaving Teresa to ponder her success as a consultant but her failure as a coach.

How plans add value to clients' change programmes

Some clients, once they know what they want and some of the things they have to do to get what they want, get their act together, develop a plan and move forward. Other clients need help. Because some clients (and some helpers) fail to appreciate the power of a plan, it is useful to start by reviewing the advantages of planning.

Not all plans are formal. 'Little plans', whether called such or not, are formulated and executed throughout the helping process. Tess, an alcoholic who wants to stop drinking, feels the need for some support. She contacts Lou, a friend who has shaken a drug habit, tells him of her plight and enlists his help. He readily agrees. Objective accomplished. This 'little plan' is part of her overall change programme. Change programmes are filled with setting 'little objectives' and developing and executing 'little plans' to achieve them.

Formal planning usually focuses on the sequence of the 'big steps' clients must take in order to get what they need or want. Clients are helped to answer the question, 'What do I need to do first, second and third?' A formal plan in its most formal version takes strategies for accomplishing goals, divides them into workable steps, puts the steps in order and assigns a timetable for the accomplishment of each step. Formal planning, provided that it is adapted to the needs of individual clients, has a number of advantages.

Plans help clients develop needed discipline   Many clients get into trouble in the first place because they lack discipline. Planning places reasonable demands on clients to develop discipline. Desmond, the halfway-house resident discussed earlier in this chapter, needed discipline and benefited greatly from a formal job-seeking programme. Indeed, ready-made programmes such as the 12-step programme of Alcoholics Anonymous are in themselves plans that demand or at least encourage self-discipline.

Plans keep clients from being overwhelmed   Plans help clients see goals as doable. They keep the steps towards the accomplishment of a goal 'bite-size'. Amazing things can be accomplished by taking bite-size steps towards substantial goals. Jayden, the ex-psychiatric patient who ended up creating a network of self-help groups for ex-patients, started with the bite-size step of participating in one of those groups himself. He did not become a self-help entrepreneur overnight. It was a step-by-step process that proved to be messy at times – two steps forward and one back.

Formulating plans helps clients search for more useful ways of accomplishing goals – that is, even better strategies   Simon Johnson was an alcoholic. When Mr Johnson's wife and children, working with a counsellor, began to formulate a plan for coping with their reactions to his alcoholism, they realised that the strategies they had been trying were hit-or-miss. With the help of an Alcoholics Anonymous self-help group, they went back to the drawing board. Mr Johnson's drinking had introduced a great deal of disorder into the family. Planning would help them restore order.

Plans provide an opportunity to evaluate the realism and adequacy of goals   This is an example of the 'dialogue' that should take place among the stages of the helping process. When Walter, a middle manager who had many problems in the workplace, began tracing out a plan to cope with the loss of his job and with a lawsuit filed against him by his former employer, he realised that his initial goals – getting his job back and filing and winning a countersuit – were unrealistic. His revised goals included getting his former employer to withdraw the suit and getting into better shape to search for a job by participating in a self-help group of managers who had lost their jobs.

Plans make clients aware of the resources they will need to implement their strategies   When Dora was helped by a counsellor to formulate a plan to pull her life together after the disappearance of her younger son, she realised that she lacked the social support needed to carry out the plan. She had retreated from friends and even relatives, but now she knew she had to get back into community. Normalising her life demanded ongoing social involvement and support. A goal of finding the support needed to get back into community was added to her constructive-change programme.

Formulating plans helps clients uncover unanticipated obstacles to the accomplishment of goals   Ernesto, a soldier who had accidentally killed an innocent bystander during his stint in Afghanistan, was seeing a counsellor because of the difficulty he was having returning to civilian life. Only when he began pulling together and trying out plans for normalising his social life did he realise how ashamed he was of what had happened to him in the military. He felt so flawed because of it that it was almost impossible to involve himself intimately with others. Helping him deal with his shame became one of the most important parts of the healing process.

Formulating plans will not solve all our clients' problems, but it is one way of making time an ally instead of an enemy. Many clients engage in aimless activity in their efforts to cope with problem situations. Plans help clients make the best use of their time. Finally, planning itself has a hefty shadow side. For a good review of the shadow side of planning, see Dietrich Dörner's book *The Logic of Failure* (1996, pp. 153–183).

SHAPING THE PLAN: TWO CASES

Plans need 'shape' to drive action. A formal plan identifies the activities or actions needed to accomplish a goal or a subgoal, puts those activities into a logical but flexible order and sets a timeframe for the accomplishment of each key step. Therefore, a plan should include the answers to these three simple questions:

- What are the concrete things that need to be done to accomplish the goal or the subgoal?
- In what sequence should these be done? What should be done first, what second, what third?
- What is the timeframe? What should be done today, tomorrow, next month?

If clients choose goals that are complex or difficult, then it is useful to help them establish subgoals as a way of moving step-by-step towards the ultimate goal. For instance, once Jayden decided to start an organisation of self-help groups composed of ex-patients from mental hospitals, there were a number of subgoals he needed to accomplish before the organisation would become a reality. His first step was to set up a test group. This instrumental goal provided the experience needed for further planning. A later step was to establish some kind of charter for the organisation. 'Charter in place' was one of the subgoals leading to his main goal.

In general, the simpler the plan the better. However, simplicity is not an end in itself. The question is not whether a plan or programme is complicated but whether it is well shaped and designed to produce results. If complicated plans are broken down into subgoals and the strategies or activities needed to accomplish them, they are as capable of being achieved, if the timeframe is realistic, as simpler ones.

The case of Harriet: The economics of planning

Harriet, an undergraduate student at a small university, wants to become a counsellor. Although the university offers no formal programme in counselling psychology, with the help of an advisor she identifies several undergraduate courses that would provide some of the foundation for a degree in counselling. One is called Social Problem-Solving Skills; a second, Effective Interpersonal Communication Skills; a third, Developmental Psychology: The Developmental Tasks of Late Adolescence and Early Adulthood. Harriet takes the courses as they come up. Unfortunately, Social Problem-Solving Skills is the first course. The good news is that it includes a great deal of practice in the skills. The bad news is that it assumes competence in interpersonal communication skills. Too late she realises that she is taking the courses out of optimal sequence. She would be getting much more from the courses had she taken the communication skills course first.

Harriet also volunteers for the dormitory peer-helper programme run by the Centre for Student Services. The Centre's counsellors are very careful in choosing people for the programme, but they don't offer much training. It is a learn-as-you-go approach. Harriet realises that the developmental psychology course would have helped her enormously in this programme. It would have helped her understand both herself and her peers better. She finally realises that she needs a better plan. In the next semester, she drops out of the peer counsellor programme. She sits down with one of the Centre's psychologists, reviews the school's offerings with him, determines which courses will help her most and determines the proper sequencing of these courses. He also suggests a couple of courses she could take in a local community college. Harriet's opportunity-development programme would have been much more efficient had it been better shaped in the first place.

The case of Bernard revisited

Let's see what planning might have done for Bernard, the vice president who needed leadership skills. In this fantasy, Bernard, like Scrooge, gets a second chance.

What does Bernard need to do? To become a leader, Bernard decides to reset his managerial style with his subordinates by involving them more in decision making. He wants to listen more, set work objectives through dialogue, ask subordinates for suggestions and delegate more. He knows he should coach his direct reports in keeping with their individual needs, give them feedback on the quality of their work, recognise their contributions and reward them for achieving results beyond their objectives.

In what sequence should Bernard do these things? Bernard decides that the first thing he will do is call in each subordinate and ask, 'What do you need from me to get your job done? How can I add value to your work? And what management style on my part would help you most?' Their dialogue around these issues will help him tailor his supervisory interventions to the needs of each team member. The second step is also clear. The planning cycle for the business year is about to begin, and each team member needs to know what his or her objectives are. It is a perfect time to begin setting objectives through dialogue rather than simply assigning them. Bernard therefore sends a memo to each of his direct reports, asking them to review the company's strategy and business plan, and the strategy and plan for each of their functions, and to write down what they think their key managerial objectives for the coming year should be. He asks them to include 'stretch' goals.

What is Bernard's timeframe? Bernard calls in each of his subordinates immediately to discuss what they need from him. He completes his objective-setting sessions with them within three weeks. He puts off further action on delegation until he gets a better reading on their performance. This is a rough idea of what a plan for Bernard might have looked like and how it might have improved his chaotic and abortive effort to change his managerial style – on the condition, of course, that he was convinced that a different approach to management and supervision made personal and business sense. Box 10.3 is a list of questions you can use to help clients think systematically about crafting a plan to get what they need and want.

BOX 10.3 **Questions on planning**

Here are some questions you can help clients ask themselves in order to come up with a viable plan for constructive change:

- Which sequence of actions will get me to my goal?
- Which actions are most critical?
- How important is the order in which these actions take place?
- What is the best timeframe for each action?
- Which step of the programme needs substeps?
- How can I build informality and flexibility into my plan?
- How do I gather the resources, including social support, needed to implement the plan?

PRINCIPLES FOR HUMANISING THE MECHANICS OF CONSTRUCTIVE CHANGE

Some years ago I lent a friend of mine an excellent, though somewhat detailed, book on self-development. About two weeks later he came back, threw the book on my desk and said, 'Who would go through all of that!' I retorted, 'Perhaps someone really interested in self-development.' That was the righteous, not the realistic, response. Planning in the real world seldom looks like planning in textbooks. Textbooks do provide useful frameworks, principles and processes, but they are seldom implemented exactly as they are outlined. Most people are too impatient to do the kind of planning just outlined. One of the reasons for the dismal track record of discretionary change mentioned in Chapter 2 is that even when clients do set realistic goals, they lack the discipline to develop reasonable plans. The detailed work of planning is too burdensome.

Therefore, Stages II and III of the helping process together with their six tasks need a human face. If helpers skip the goal-setting and planning steps clients need, they short-change them. On the other hand, if they are pedantic, mechanistic or awkward in their attempts to help clients engage in these steps – failing to give these processes a human face – they run the risk of alienating the people they are trying to serve. Clients might well say, 'I'm getting a lot of boring garbage from him.' Here, then, are some principles to guide the constructive-change process.

Build a planning mentality into the helping process right from the start

A constructive-change mindset should permeate the helping process right from the beginning. Helpers need to see clients as self-healing agents capable of changing their lives, not just as individuals mired in problem situations. Even while listening to a client's story, the helper needs to begin thinking of how the situation can be remedied and through probes find out what approaches to change clients are thinking about – no matter how tentative these ideas might be. As mentioned earlier, helping clients act in their real world right from the beginning of the helping process helps them develop some kind of initial planning mentality. If helping is to be solution-focused, thinking about strategies and plans must be introduced early. When a client tells of some problem, the helper can ask early on, 'What kinds of things have you done so far to try to cope with the problem?'

> Cora, a battered spouse, did not want to leave her husband because of the kids. Right from the beginning, the helper saw Cora's problem situation from the point of view of the whole helping process. While she listened to Cora's story, without distorting it, she saw possible goals and strategies. Within the helping sessions, the counsellor helped Cora learn a great deal about how battered women typically respond to their plight and how dysfunctional some of those responses are. She also learned how to stop blaming herself for the violence and to overcome her fears of developing more active coping strategies. At home she confronted her husband and stopped submitting to the violence in a vain attempt to avoid further abuse. She also joined a local self-help group for battered women. There she found social support and learned how to invoke both police protection and recourse through the courts. Further sessions with the counsellor helped her gradually change her identity from battered woman to survivor and, eventually, to doer. She moved from simply facing problems to developing opportunities.

Constructive-change scenarios like this must be in the helper's mind from the start, not as preset programmes to be imposed on clients but as part of a constructive-change mentality.

Adapt the constructive-change process to the style of the client

Setting goals, devising strategies and making and implementing plans can be done formally or informally. Kirschenbaum (1985) challenged the notion that planning should always provide an exact blueprint for specific actions, their sequencing and the timeframe. He suggested that helpers consider these three questions:

- How specific do the activities have to be?
- How rigid does the order have to be?
- How soon does each activity have to be carried out?

Kirschenbaum (p. 492) suggested that, at least in some cases, being less specific and rigid about actions, sequencing and deadlines can 'encourage people to pursue their goals by continually and flexibly choosing their activities'. That is, flexibility in planning can help clients become more self-reliant and proactive. There is a continuum. Some clients actually like the detailed work of devising plans; it fits their style. Consider the following two cases:

> Gitta sought counselling as she entered the 'empty nest' period of her life. Although there were no specific problems, she saw too much emptiness as she looked into the future. The counsellor helped her see this period of life as a normal experience rather than a psychological problem. It was a developmental opportunity and challenge (see Raup & Myers, 1989). It was an opportunity to reset her life. After spending a bit of time discussing some of the maladaptive responses to this transitional phase of life, they embarked on a review of possible scenarios. Gitta loved brainstorming, getting into the details of the scenarios, weighing choices, setting strategies and making formal plans. She had been running her household this way for years. So the process was familiar even though the content was new.

Gitta readily embraced the detailed work needed to come up with a good plan. But she might be the exception. The distribution is skewed towards the 'I hate all this detail and won't do it' end of the continuum. Rigid planning strategies can lead to frequent failure to achieve short-term goals. Consider the case of Yousef.

> Yousef was a single parent whose son had an intellectual disability. He was challenged one day by a colleague at work. 'You've let your son become a ball and chain and that's not good for you or him!' his friend said. Yousef smarted from the remark, but eventually – and reluctantly – sought counselling. He never discussed any kind of extensive change programme with his helper, but with a little stimulation from her he began doing little things differently at home. When he came home from work especially tired and frustrated, he had a friend in the block of flats stop by. This helped him to refrain from taking his frustrations out on his son. Then, instead of staying cooped up over the weekend, he found simple things to do that eased tensions, such as going to the zoo and to the art museum with a woman friend and his son. He discovered that his son enjoyed these pastimes immensely despite his limitations. In short, he discovered little ways of blending caring for his son with a better social life. His counsellor had a constructive-change mentality right from the beginning but did not try to engage Yousef in overly formal planning activities.

Of course, a slipshod approach to planning – 'I will have to pull myself together one of these days' – is also self-defeating. We need only look at our own experience to see that such an approach can be fatal.

Overall, counsellors should help clients embrace the kind of rigour in planning that make sense for them in their situations. There are no formulas; there are only client needs, planning skills and common sense. Some things need to be done now, some later. Some clients need more slack than others. Sometimes it helps to spell out the actions that need to be done in quite specific terms; at other times it is necessary only to help clients outline them in broad terms and leave the rest to their own sound judgement. If therapy is to be brief, help clients start doing things that lead to their goals. Then, in a later session, help them review what they have been doing, drop what is not working, continue what is working, add more effective strategies and put more organisation in their programmes. If you have a limited number of sessions with a client, you can't engage in extensive goal setting and planning. 'What can I do that will add most value?' is the ongoing challenge in brief therapy.

Outline a plan for the client and then help the client tailor it to his or her needs

The more experienced helpers become, the more they learn about the elements of programme development, and the more they come to know what kinds of programmes work for different clients. They build up a stockpile of useful programmes and know how to stitch pieces of different programmes together to create new programmes. And so they can use their knowledge and experience to fashion a plan for any clients who lack the skills or the temperament to pull together a plan for themselves. Of course, their objective is not to foster dependence but to help clients grow in self-determination. For instance, they can first offer a plan as a sketch or in outline form rather than as a detailed programme. Helpers then work with clients to fill out the sketch and adapt it to their needs and style. Consider the following case:

> Katrina, a woman who dropped out of high school but managed to get a high school equivalency diploma, was overweight and reclusive. Over the years she had restricted her activities because of her weight. Sporadic attempts at dieting had left her even heavier. Because she was chronically depressed and had little imagination, she was not able to come up with any kind of coherent plan. Once her counsellor understood the dimensions of Katrina's problem situation, she pulled together an outline of a change programme that included such things as blame reduction, the redefinition of beauty, decreasing self-imposed social restrictions, cognitive restructuring activities aimed at lessening depression. She also provided information about obesity and suggestions for dealing with it drawn from healthcare sources. She presented these in a simple format, adding detail only for the sake of clarity. She added further detail as Katrina got involved in the planning process and in making choices.

Although this counsellor pulled together elements of a range of already existing programmes, counsellors are, of course, free to make up their own programmes based on their expertise and experience. The point is to give clients something to work with, something to get involved in. The elaboration of the plan emerges through dialogue with the client and in the kind of detail the client can handle.

Another useful example is supplied by Finlay (2004, pp. 194–196) in the case of Dowie:

> Dowie is a 52-year-old unemployed, married man living in Darlington in the UK. He lacks motivation and drive. He doesn't want to do anything other than lie at home in bed all day. As his extreme inactivity and passivity become entrenched in habit, his functioning deteriorates. His family despairs and don't know how to help. They turn to the GP, who calls in an occupational therapist to advise.
>
> The occupational therapist, Kevin, observes how seemingly intractable Dowie's inactivity has become. He asks Dowie if he wants this for the rest of his life. Dowie denies this, saying he wishes he had the energy to do things but he doesn't. Kevin explains the value and importance of doing some level of activity every day to prevent Dowie from going on a downward spiral. Dowie agrees to a treatment contract. He'll give Kevin's ideas one month, and if he hasn't improved significantly by then, he is free to withdraw from therapy.
>
> Kevin therefore devises the following plan for Dowie to work with, which has the long-term aim of encouraging productive activity and the specific aim of developing a range of regular daily activities and leisure interests which take account of Dowie's former interest in sport:
>
> | Week 1 | – Plan activity programme with Kevin. |
> | | – Help cook family meal on one occasion. |
> | | – Visit sports centre with friends whom he has not seen for several years, to decide preferred activity for the week. |
> | Week 2 | – Help cook family meal on two occasions. |
> | | – Go with wife to shop for weekly groceries. |
> | | – Sports centre activity with Kevin. |
> | | – Go into town for coffee. |
> | Week 3 | – Help cook family meal on two occasions and help clear up afterwards. |
> | | – Meet Kevin at the sports centre having found own way there. |
> | | – Go with wife to shop for weekly groceries. |
> | | – Go to see a local football match. |
> | | – Visit pub one evening for a drink and meal with wife/family. |

(Continued)

Week 4   – Cook family meal on own.
    – Go with wife to shop for weekly groceries.
    – Help to cook and clear up after at least one other meal.
    – Meet Kevin at the sports centre and go there alone at least once.
    – Visit pub at least one evening.
    – Have another family outing, e.g. bingo, drive into the country.

Kevin has managed to creatively engage Dowie in treatment with a well-graded activity programme which achieved the right level of stimulation and pressure, and appropriately drew on Dowie's past interests and current motivations. By the end of the month Dowie is a changed person who enjoys doing things with his family again and makes an effort to get out of the house at least once a month.

The ultimate test of the effectiveness of plans lies in the problem-managing and opportunity-developing action clients engage in to get what they need and want. There is no such thing as a good plan in and of itself. Life-enhancing outcomes, not planning or hard work, are the final arbiter.

Help clients develop contingency plans

If the future is uncertain, it pays to have a broad range of options open. There is no use investing a great deal of time and energy in a goal or in a programme to accomplish a goal that will have to be changed because the client's world changes. Therefore, help clients choose one or more backup goals to take care of such eventualities. In this way, clients have direction, but they also have contingency. If the world changes, then the client can choose the goal that best fits the circumstances at the time. So choosing a goal or a programme to achieve a goal is not necessarily a once-and-forever decision. The client says to herself, 'I'll stick with this goal until I see that it is no longer viable. Or until a better goal emerges.' Having viable options helps you kill, or at least put on the back burner, an option that is no longer working. Backup plans provide freedom and flexibility. They also keep clients from falling into the status quo decision-making trap outlined earlier. Consider Linda's case.

Linda is a young woman working for a computer firm in Mexico. She was born and raised in Iraq. She has made a tortuous journey through South and Central America as an illegal immigrant. Her journey included prostitution and a range of harrowing, even life-threatening, experiences. The upside of all this is that she has learned to live by her wits. After returning from an illegal trip to the United States, she has one goal – to live there permanently. She takes counsel with a friend of hers, a solicitor in Mexico, telling him of her plan to live as an illegal in the United States. Both intelligent and socially savvy, she feels that she can pull it off. Her solicitor friend, knowing that her ultimate goal is to live permanently in the United States, helps her review a range of instrumental goals – goals in themselves but steps towards helping her achieve her ultimate goal. They discuss possibilities. Options other than living by her wits as an illegal immigrant include obtaining political refugee status, becoming a green card holder, marrying a US citizen, marrying a foreigner who is most likely to get a green card, and being included in the quota of immigrants allowed permanent resident status because they have essential skills such as those needed in booming technology industries. A plan would be needed to pursue each of these. Linda's future is certainly filled with risk and uncertainty. She has to choose an instrumental goal that she thinks offers the best possibility for achieving her ultimate goal, but after her discussion she has a range of fall-back options.

If at times goals need to be changed – 'If I don't get into medical school, then the nurse-practitioner route is still attractive' – it is also true that strategies for achieving goals might have to change. Contingency plans answer the question, 'What will I do if the plan of action I choose is not working?' They help make clients more effective tacticians. We make contingency plans because we live in an imperfect world. Contingency plans are needed, especially when clients choose a high-risk programme to achieve a critical goal. Having backup plans also helps clients develop more responsibility. If they see that a plan is not working, then they have to decide whether to try the contingency plan. Backup plans need not be complicated. A counsellor might merely ask, 'If that doesn't work, then what will you do?'

READY-MADE ACTION PROGRAMMES

In these pages we have focused mainly on clients with messy problems in living. Therapists help such clients explore problem situations, identify desired outcomes, devise action programmes to achieve these outcomes and move on to implement the plans they have made. That is, we have focused on the basics of problem management. However, there are by some counts hundreds of ready-made therapy and well-being programmes that expand and complement basic therapeutic skills. In the last edition of this book I discussed some of them, but it is impossible to do justice to these programmes within the confines of this text. So I will name and describe them here briefly. If you are in a therapist training programme, they will be part of the curriculum.

Ready-made therapeutic interventions: Evidence-supported treatments (ESTs)

Researchers together with practitioners have designed evidence-based programmes to treat a whole host of mental health problems. Though different terminology has been used, we will refer to them as evidence-supported treatments (ESTs). These interventions have been validated by rigorous research. Step-by-step manuals have been developed to be used in both training and clinical settings. Take phobias. Any number of ESTs *have* been developed to treat almost *every* type of phobia. David Barlow (Allen, McHugh & Barlow, 2008; Antony & Barlow, 2010; Barlow, 2008; Barlow, Ellard *et al.*, 2011; Barlow, Farchione *et al.*, 2011; DeAngelis, 2008a, 2008b; Ehrenreich, Buzzella & Barlow, 2007; McHugh & Barlow, 2012; Barlow, 2014; Barlow, Farchione *et al.*, 2018) is a pioneer in the area of evidence-based practice. Many ESTs are simple, step-by-step processes easily learned by both therapist and client to deal with, say, anxiety. But they can also be relatively complex.

An example of the more complex is Barlow and his associates' (Barlow, Ellard *et al.*, 2011; Barlow, Farchione *et al.*, 2011) new step-by-step protocol for the treatment of a variety of disorders, including depression, anxiety and phobias. He claims that the protocol they developed takes three or four basic concepts that seem to be present in all successful treatments for these emotional disorders and puts them together as a single, unified, 'transdiagnostic' set of principles that clinicians could adapt to anyone sitting in front of them. The seven modules of the protocol are psychoeducation, motivational enhancement to help clients engage in treatment, emotional awareness training including present-focused emotional awareness training, cognitive appraisal and reappraisal, modifying emotion-driven behaviours and emotional avoidance, exposure to actual emotional experience, and relapse prevention. Barlow said that this evidence-based protocol gives practitioners greater treatment flexibility than most manuals allow. You begin to see why evidence-based treatments need deeper consideration than what can be presented here.

As you might imagine, there has also been a backlash against the evidence-based treatment movement, not because many ESTs are not useful 'in their place', but because of professional disagreements and professional politics about where that 'place' is and the nature and scope of the evidence-based practice movement itself. Also ESTs tend to deal with isolated symptoms rather than the kind of problems in living with which clients are struggling. There is no ready-made step-by-step programme therapists can use to help a distressed married couple, one of whom is bipolar, who come from two different cultural backgrounds and who are having disputes over finances and how to raise their three children. Is it useful to use relevant ESTs as part of the treatment? Certainly. It is not a question of either-or, that is, either the common factors approach to therapy or an evidence-based practice approach. Rather a both-and (not either-or) approach based on the needs of the client is called for. The 'ingredients of successful therapy' approach taken here in no way opposes the use of ESTs. Use whatever helps clients manage the problem situations of their lives.

However, dealing with the very complex ready-made programme debate within the helping professions is beyond the remit of this book. The basics outlined in this book are needed by therapists on both sides of the debate. There are many hotly debated questions. What relevance does the medical model have to psychotherapy? Where should the emphasis of the helping professions be placed – on the client or on the treatment? To what degree is therapy influenced by economics and third-party payers? How does the probability associated with human behaviour differ from the kind of probability dealt with in the 'hard' sciences? It's a challenging time to be moving into the helping professions. Welcome to the profession and its debates.

General well-being programmes: Nutrition, exercise and stress reduction

Some programmes that contribute to general well-being can be used as adjuncts to all approaches to helping. There are ready-made programmes that can help people in general improve the quality of their lives by eating well (Booth, 1994; Ogden, 2010; Somov, 2008; Taubes, 2011; Wansink, 2011), exercising (Azar, Ball, Salmon & Cleland, 2010; DeAngelis, 2002; Hays, 1999; Johnson, Addamo, Raj, Borkoles, Wyckelsma, Cyarto *et al.*, 2016; Landro, 2010; Nieman, 2010; Ratey & Hagerman, 2008; Servan-Schreiber, 2004) and reducing stress (Benson, 1975; Benson & Proctor, 2010; Davis, Eshelman & McKay, 2008; Melbourne Academic Mindfulness Interest Group, 2006; Monash Academic Mindfulness Interest Group, 2006). All well-being programmes demand self-regulation, something that is sorely needed by many clients. There are also social reasons for using such programmes. Researchers have indicated that if people were to eat properly, exercise regularly, and reduce and manage stress in their lives, our national healthcare bill would be reduced by over 30 per cent. Clients who manage stress well have a better chance of dealing with problem situations. Changing Unhealthy Habits (a supplement to the Mayo Clinic Health Letter, February, 2007) is typical of the practical science-based literature that forms the basis of general well-being programmes. The Harvard Medical School also publishes a wide range of special reports on mental health, including stress management. This literature reviews the research and packages the results in practical ways to appeal to both practitioners and clients. At any rate there is a very rich literature on both ready-made and well-being programmes (for instance, go to www.mindful.org to find hundreds of articles on mindfulness listed by year of publication – what did we do before internet search engines?). Anyway, the literature is yours to devour.

The three stages of the problem-management process constitute planning for life-enhancing change. But talk is not change. Change calls for action; that's why we have discussed the various ways the stages and tasks of the problem-management process should stimulate action on the part of clients. Endless sessions that do no more than discuss problems and 'consider' changes are a lot of blah, blah, blah. Introducing a feedback system into therapy is one of the best ways of assuring that talk leads to action. So we move on to the last chapter which deals formally with implementation. Hopefully we have been talking about implementation throughout this book.

CHAPTER 11
HOW TO IMPLEMENT AND MAKE IT ALL HAPPEN

Chapter Contents

INTRODUCTION TO IMPLEMENTATION

The Action Arrow of the helping model in Figure 11.1 highlights the difference between planning and action. Stages I, II, III and their nine tasks all revolve around planning for change, not change itself. However, the need to incorporate action into planning and planning into action has been emphasised throughout this book. That is, the 'little actions' needed to get the change process moving right from the start have been noted and illustrated. We now take a more formal look at results-producing action and how to help clients identify obstacles to action and find ways to move beyond them.

FIGURE 11.1 **The Action Arrow and change**

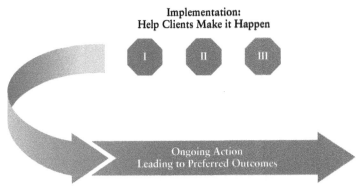

Implementation:
Help Clients Make it Happen

I   II   III

Ongoing Action
Leading to Preferred Outcomes

Problem-Managing Action Should:
- Start Immediately
- Continue Throughout the Helping Process
- Lead to Client's Preferred Outcomes

In a book called *True Success*, Tom Morris (1994) lays down the conditions for achieving success. As you will note, they are all part of the problem-management process. They include the following:

- Determining what you want – that is, a goal or a set of goals 'powerfully imagined'
- Focus and concentration in preparation and planning
- The confidence or belief in oneself to see the goal through – that is, self-efficacy
- A commitment of emotional energy
- Being consistent and persistent in the pursuit of the goal
- The kind of integrity that inspires trust and gets people pulling for you
- A capacity to enjoy the process of getting there.

The first two of these conditions refer to Stages II and III of the helping process, while the other five refer to implementing what has been imagined and planned. The role of the counsellor is to help clients engage in these kinds of internal and external behaviours in the interest of goal accomplishment.

Some clients, once they have a clear idea of what to do to handle a problem situation or develop some opportunity, go ahead and do it, whether or not they have a formal plan. They need little or no further support and challenge from their helpers. They either find the resources they need within themselves or get support and challenge from the significant others in the social settings of their lives. However, other clients choose goals and come up with strategies for implementing them, but are, for whatever reason, stymied when it comes to action. Most clients fall between these two extremes.

Discipline and self-control – dimensions of self-responsibility – play an important role in implementing change programmes. Kirschenbaum (1987) found that many things can contribute to not getting started or to giving up: low initial commitment to change, weak self-efficacy, poor outcome expectations, the use of self-punishment rather than self-reward, depressive thinking, failure to cope with emotional stress, lack of consistent self-monitoring, failure to use effective habit-change techniques, giving in to social pressure, failure to cope with initial relapse and paying attention to the wrong things, for instance focusing on the difficulty of the change process rather than the attractiveness of the outcome. Clearly, this kind of thinking and behaviour is the opposite of what Morris recommends.

We have seen that self-determination and self-control are essential for action. Kanfer and Schefft (1988, p. 58) differentiated between two kinds of self-control. In *decisional* self-control, a single choice terminates a conflict. For instance, a woman decides to leave an abusive spouse and goes through with it. In *protracted* self-control, continued resistance to temptation is required. For instance, it is not enough for a client with severe health problems to begin a demanding nutritional, exercise and stress-reduction programme. She also has to remain vigilant and committed day in and day out. Each time a temptation to backslide arises she has to renew her resolve. It helps enormously if she develops the attitude that temptations are learning opportunities and not just battles to be fought. She needs to find ways to make the struggle itself tolerable or even rewarding. One client would eat a carrot when she was tempted to give into nutritional temptation. As she munched, she said to herself, 'I'm not enjoying this as much as a rabbit would, but it's not bad.'

Most clients need both kinds of self-control to manage their lives better. A client's choice to give up alcohol completely (decisional self-control) needs to be complemented by the ability to handle inevitable longer-term temptations. Protracted self-control calls for a preventive mentality and a certain degree of street smarts. It is easier for the client who has given up alcohol to turn down an invitation to go to a bar in the first place than to sit in a bar all evening with friends and refrain from drinking.

TUMI MOVES INTO ACTION

Let's review some of the plans Tumi has formulated both on her own and during her discussions with Carlos and then, in the course of this chapter, see how things work out as she tries to implement these plans. The title of this section is somewhat unfair because, to some, it might indicate that Tumi has only been talking with Carlos. The truth is that she has engaged in many 'small actions' that have been, on her part, signs of the 'bias towards action' mentioned in Chapter 2. These smaller actions have oriented her in the right direction; they have been small steps to a better future. Tumi's case demonstrates clearly that formulating and implementing a change programme is not an exercise in precision engineering. Human beings and their problem situations are generally too messy for that. We have already seen that Tumi, perhaps more than most, has a bias towards action. However, we have also seen that she, like most, can be blown off course. Her disastrous conversation with her father almost sidetracked her completely. But Tumi is resilient. Her aspirations empower her.

One of Tumi's top priorities is to do something about her social life. She wants some version of what she experienced during her stay in South Africa. There she found a ready-made community or series of communities. Now she has to create her own. Carlos asks her whether establishing a close relationship with a man would be part of the picture. This is something that did not happen in South Africa. She says that she wants to play that by ear: 'I'd rather see that happen in the context of some kind of larger community. The relationship with Jim didn't work out, but it was too separate or private anyway. I want some kind of community first, not just a one-to-one relationship.' If Tumi's quest for community involves a decision to leave her parents' home and live on her own (decisional self-control), it would be essential for her to understand the degree of protracted self-control she would need to manage feelings of separation, guilt and initial loneliness as she builds a different kind of life for herself.

The two-way feedback process focusing on progress towards goals and usefulness of the therapy sessions has proved enormously helpful for her. At one point Carlos says something like this:

CARLOS: It might be helpful to step back and take a look at the overall picture. As you have noted, the feedback process at the beginning and ending of each session has proved to be very useful. Now let's see where we stand overall. Let's look at the bigger picture.

TUMI: Give me 10 minutes to prepare. I like the idea.

They reconvene. Here are the highlights. Tumi felt that she was on the right track. Her immediate goal of developing a community of friends and colleagues as the basis of a solid social life was still her top priority. Geography would probably stand in the way of a social life with a South African flavour. There were no South-African–British communities nearby. However, South African cultural values could still influence her choice of friends and social activities. She was still experimenting with the best ways of getting 'into community'. Her ideal – a community like the ones she experienced in South Africa – might be, well, just that, an ideal, partly because of her tendency to idealise what she had experienced during her trip.

Tumi's second goal related to career but had changed a bit. 'Preparing myself for a more fulfilling career in the business world' took the place of moving into a more significant managerial role in her father's business. She was thinking about an MBA as a way of moving forward on that goal. She had also made contact with a group called 'Women in Business'. Her current quasi-managerial role at the dealership and her career aspirations made her a good candidate for that group.

Tumi wasn't sure whether 'normalising' her relationship with her parents was a goal because it was not co-owned by them. Normalising was something that the three of them would have to do together and her father's 'case-closed' mentality militated against any kind of cooperation. In her narrative her mother remained a shadow figure.

Tumi finishes by talking about her 'moods'. Emotionally, she says, she has been 'all over the place'. When she is busy getting things done that move her towards her goals, she feels great, sometimes exhilarated. When she is working at the dealership, her affect tends to be flat. She does her work and does it well. Although she feels some degree of satisfaction in being 'professional', the work no longer has the same meaning. Her aspirations of creating a greater managerial role for herself have disappeared partly because the business seems to have stalled. Given her father's health problems, they might even have to sell the business at a depressed price. So work at the dealership has a dead-end feel to it, and this depresses her. 'When I get depressed,' she says, 'I have to work hard to dig myself out of it.'

In light of this picture, filled as it is with hope, sadness and challenge, let's take a look at the work clients need to do to move into action and accomplish their goals.

HELP CLIENTS MOVE FROM PLANNING TO ACTION: PRINCIPLES OF EFFECTIVE IMPLEMENTATION

When it comes to client action, Norcross, Krebs and Prochaska (2011) urge caution: 'Beware treating all patients as though they are in action' (p. 294) because most arrive not ready for action. This causes a dilemma because the sooner clients begin to act on their own behalf the more likely are they to succeed. Your job is to help clients bridge this gap. But, as Johancen-Walt (2010) notes, progress in therapy is often an 'accumulation of small changes, plateaus and regressions' (p. 50) and patience on the part of both client and helper is essential.

In the implementation phase, strategies for accomplishing goals need to be complemented by tactics and logistics. A *strategy* is a practical plan or programme to accomplish some objective. *Tactics* is the art of adapting a plan to the immediate situation. This includes being able to change the plan on the spot to handle unforeseen complications. *Logistics* is the art of being able to provide the resources needed for the implementation of a plan in a timely way. Here is a simple case illustrating all three.

During the summer, Rebecca wanted to take an evening course in statistics so that the first semester of the following academic year would be lighter. Having more time would enable her to act in one of the university plays, a high priority for her. But she didn't have the money to pay for the course, and at the university she planned to attend prepayment for summer courses was the rule. Rebecca had counted on paying for the course from her summer earnings, but she would not have the money until later. Consequently, she did some quick shopping around and found that the same course was being offered by a community college not too far from where she lived. Her tuition fee there was minimal, because she was a resident of the area the college served.

In this example, Rebecca keeps to her overall plan (strategy). However, in light of an unforeseen circumstance, the demand for prepayment, she adapts her plan (a tactic) by locating another resource (logistics). Because many well-meaning and motivated clients are simply not good tacticians and are not good at finding the resources they need, counsellors can add value by using the following principles to help them engage in focused and sustained goal-accomplishing action.

Help clients overcome procrastination

At the other end of the spectrum are clients who keep putting action off. The 'knowing doing gap' (Kegan & Lahey, 2010; Pfeffer & Sutton, 2000) has been with us from time immemorial and will probably remain with us till the Earth disappears. In Chapter 9, I described how 'competing agendas' can stand in the way of change. Kegan and Lahey take this concept further. They talk about how clients' 'hidden commitments' stand in the way of change. For instance, a principal thinks that she should get out of her office and into classrooms more often, but she never finds the time. What hidden commitments might keep her from changing her behaviour? Well, she might be afraid of what she will find in any given classroom. But what hidden commitment stands in the way? The school has a 'comfortable' faculty culture that she might disrupt. Or she might be afraid of going into maths and science classrooms because maths and science are not her forte. She could be embarrassed if asked a maths question. What's her hidden commitment? Authority figures should stay on the pedestal. This is important for order in the institution. We all have hidden commitments that keep us from changing. So do our clients. We need to challenge ours and help clients become aware of and challenge theirs.

There are many other reasons for procrastination (Fernie, Bharucha, Nikcevic, Marino & Spada, 2017; Ferrari, 2010; Ferrari, Johnson & McCowan, 1995; Pychyl, 2010; Sirois & Pychyl, 2016). Each person has his or her set of factors that create what Kegan and Lahey call their personal 'immunity to change'. Many clients procrastinate because they focus on the short-term pain of moving into action even when they can clearly see the long-term benefits of doing so. Take the case of Eula.

> Eula, disappointed with her relationship with her father in the family business, decided that she wanted to start her own. She thought that she could capitalise on the business skills she had picked up in school and in the family business. Her goal, then, was to establish a small software firm that created products for the family-business market.
>
> But a year went by and she still did not have any products ready for market. A counsellor helped her see two things. First, her activities – researching the field, learning more about family dynamics, going to information technology seminars, getting involved for short periods with professionals such as accountants and lawyers who did a great deal of business with family-owned firms, drawing up and redrafting business plans and creating a brochure – were helpful, but they did not produce products. The counsellor helped Eula see that at some level of her being she was afraid of starting a new business. She had a lot of half-finished products. Over-preparation and half-finished products were signs of that fear. So she ploughed ahead, finished a product and brought it to market on the internet. To her surprise, it was successful. Not a roaring success, but it meant that the cork was out of the bottle. Once she got one product to market, she had little problem developing and marketing others.

Eula certainly was not lazy. She was very active. She did all sorts of useful things. But she let herself become a victim of what Andreou (2007) calls 'second-order' procrastination. Second-order procrastination is procrastinating on implementing a solution to procrastination itself. Eula avoided getting around to accomplishing the most critical actions – creating and marketing products.

Procrastination is not a problem for Tumi. She does not tend to put things off except when the situation calls for her to be assertive with someone else. For instance, when she volunteers to work with the alumni group at her college as a way of developing a community of friends and associates, she is welcomed but given clerical and administrative tasks that she can do by working alone. In mentioning this to Carlos, she says in a rather resigned voice, 'It's not exactly what I thought it would be.' And this was probably an understatement. Carlos replies, 'I wonder if there's a way of turning your volunteering into a win for them *and* a win for yourself.' It turns out that Tumi had not told her contact at the alumni association what *she* wanted to get out of volunteering. 'I didn't want to seem selfish.' She catches herself and then begins to talk with Carlos about how much her 'selflessness' has pervaded her life, especially in her relationship with her parents. They have a good session on how to capitalise on her discovery – or perhaps awakening. She hates selfishness when she sees it, for instance, in her cousins, but realises that her brand of selflessness is not the antidote to selfishness. Afterwards she has a session with the director of alumni relations and easily finds work involving interactions with others.

The opposite of procrastination is a sense of urgency that leads to timely problem-managing action. Kotter (2008) suggests that change, and this applies to personal change, does not start, continue or 'stick' without a sense of urgency. But he distinguishes between true and false urgency. The former means doing the right things in a timely way. False urgency refers to lots of activity, even frenzied activity, that goes nowhere. It looks like urgency but isn't the real thing. Except when she gets depressed, Tumi is always busy. But is she efficient, that is, is she busy in the right way about the right things?

Finally, and we might say 'of course', some analysis of the research on procrastination (Partnoy, 2012) suggests that procrastination is not all that bad. Delaying decisions and actions gives clients time to think more carefully about the consequences of acting, especially the consequences of acting too quickly. So Partnoy suggests that there is good procrastination and bad – but perhaps this is something that most of us already know.

Help clients avoid imprudent action

For some clients, the problem is not that they refuse to act but that they act imprudently. Rushing off to try the first 'strategy' that comes to mind is often imprudent.

Elmer injured his back and underwent a couple of operations. After the second operation he felt a little better, but then his back began troubling him again. When the doctor told him that further operations would not help, Elmer was faced with the problem of handling chronic pain. It soon became clear that his psychological state affected the level of pain. When he was anxious or depressed, the pain always seemed much worse.

Elmer was talking this through with a counsellor. One day he read about a pain clinic located several hundred miles away. Without consulting anyone, he signed up for a six-week programme. Within 10 days he was back, feeling more depressed than ever. He had gone to the programme with extremely high expectations because his needs were so great. The programme was a holistic one that helped the participants develop a more realistic lifestyle. It included activities that focused on such things as nutrition, stress management, problem solving and quality of interpersonal life. Group counselling was part of the programme and training was part of the group experience. For instance, the participants were trained in behavioural approaches to the management of pain.

The trouble was that Elmer had arrived at the clinic, which was located on a converted farm, with unrealistic expectations. He had bought a 'packaged' programme without studying the package carefully. Because he had expected to find marvels of modern medicine that would magically help him, he was extremely disappointed when he found that the programme focused mainly on reducing and managing rather than eliminating pain.

Elmer's goal was to be completely free of pain, but he failed to explore the realism of his goal. A more realistic goal would have centred on the reduction and management of pain. Elmer's counsellor failed to help him avoid two mistakes – setting an unrealistic goal and, in desperation, acting on the first strategy that came along. Obviously, action cannot be prudent if it is based on flawed assumptions – in this case, Elmer's assumption that he could be pain-free.

Although Tumi was chastened by her father's outburst and his summary dismissal of a second overture on her part – 'That issue has been settled' – she gradually regained a degree of self-confidence. The idea of building a better future for herself slowly re-energised her. At one point she tells Carlos that now that she has a much clearer picture of what she wants to do, she has more or less decided to tell her mother what her picture of the future is. She knows that her mother will tell her father, but she (Tumi) won't have to deal with his reactions. 'I think that planning my future is the right thing to do and that I have nothing to hide.'

Carlos asks her to explore the 'more or less' part of her decision. In their discussion it becomes clear to Tumi that 'more or less' means a number of things. It means not telling her father directly. It means that she is not sure that this is the most 'moral' way of acting. It means that she has not adequately explored the possible fallout from such action on her part. At the end of the session Tumi says that she has to 'rethink' how to be both honest *and* prudent in her dealing with her parents.

Help clients identify possible obstacles to and resources for implementing plans

Years ago Kurt Lewin (1969) codified common sense by developing what he called 'force-field analysis'. In ordinary language, this is simply a review by the client of the major obstacles to and the major facilitating forces for implementing action plans. The slogan is 'forewarned is forearmed'.

Obstacles The identification of possible obstacles or restraining forces to the implementation of a programme helps forewarn clients.

> Raul and Maria were a childless couple living in a large city. They had been married for about five years and had not been able to have children. They finally decided that they would like to adopt a child, so they consulted a counsellor familiar with adoptions. The counsellor helped them work out a plan of action that included helping them examine their motivation, reviewing their suitability to be adoptive parents, contacting an agency and preparing themselves for an interview. After the plan of action had been worked out, Raul and Maria, with the help of the counsellor, identified two possible obstacles or pitfalls: the negative feelings that often arise on the part of prospective parents when they are being scrutinised by an adoption agency, and the feelings of helplessness and frustration caused by the length of time and uncertainty involved in the process.

The assumption here is that if clients are aware of some of the 'wrinkles' that can accompany any given course of action, they will be less disoriented when they encounter them. Identifying possible obstacles is, at its best, a straightforward census of likely pitfalls rather than a self-defeating search for every possible thing that could go wrong.

Obstacles can come from within the clients themselves, from others, from the social settings of their lives and from larger environmental forces. Once an obstacle is spotted, counsellors can help clients identify ways of coping with it. Sometimes simply being aware of a pitfall is enough to help clients mobilise their resources to handle it. At other times a more explicit coping strategy is needed. For instance, the counsellor arranged two role-playing sessions with Raul and Maria in which she assumed the role of the examiner at the adoption agency and took a 'hard line' in her questioning. These rehearsals helped them stay calm during the actual interviews. The counsellor also helped them to locate a mutual-help group of parents working their way through the adoption process. The members of the group shared their hopes and frustrations and provided support for one another. In short, Raul and Maria were trained to cope with the restraining forces they might encounter on the road towards their goal.

Facilitating forces In a more positive vein, counsellors can help their clients identify unused resources that facilitate action.

> Nora found it extremely depressing to go to her weekly dialysis sessions. She knew that without them she would die, but she wondered whether it was worth living if she had to depend on a machine. The counsellor helped her see that she was making life more difficult for herself by letting herself think such discouraging thoughts. He helped her learn how to think thoughts that would broaden her vision of the world instead of narrowing it down to herself, her discomfort and the machine. Nora was a religious person and found in the Bible a rich source of positive thinking. She initiated a new routine: The day before she visited the clinic, she began to prepare herself psychologically by reading from the Bible. Then, as she travelled to the clinic and underwent treatment, she meditated slowly on what she had read.

In this case, the counsellor helped Norah substitute positive thinking, an underused resource, for poor-me thinking. Brainstorming resources that can counter obstacles to action can be very helpful for some clients. Helping clients brainstorm facilitating forces raises the probability that they will act in their own interests. They can be simple things. George was avoiding an invasive diagnostic procedure. After a brainstorming session, he decided to get a friend to go with him. This meant two things. Once he asked for his friend's help, he 'had to go through with it'. Second, his friend's very presence distracted him from his fears.

Obstacles can pop up anytime. Neither we nor our clients are in charge of the way the world turns. Tumi is no exception.

While Tumi was clear about what she wanted, she was not as adept in dealing with obstacles. She was making headway in creating a social life for herself and she was also carrying out her plans for a different career or at least preparing for a different career. One strategy that was working well was her membership in the Women at Work group. She attended meetings that featured either speakers or members who shared their experiences. She really liked meetings in which they broke up into smaller groups. She met women like herself wanting to get a different job or fashion a new career for themselves. These women helped Tumi think things through. She was also a contributor. She found that her managerial experience enabled her to help others plan their moves.

Then an obstacle with a capital O appeared. Her father told her and her mother that the automobile company was closing the dealership. Tumi would be out of a job. Even though she knew that this would eventually happen, the timeframe for the closing gave her a jolt. The dealership was going to close within two months. The second blow came when he revealed that he had lost almost two-thirds of his pension money in the market. It seems that he placed his money with a broker who, though honest, took too many risks. Up to this point Tumi knew little or nothing about her father's finances. As far as she knew, he owned the company and they lived a comfortable life. She had been receiving a nominal salary because it had been more or less understood that the sale of the dealership would provide her and her mother a living if her father were to die. Her salary covered all her expenses and she put the modest surplus in a savings account. Because of her undergraduate business degree she knew a lot about accounting and finance but never thought about money. Fashioning a new career for herself was about fulfilment and freedom, not about money. The dealership was meant to be part of her and her mother's saving programme. The settlement from the car company would be modest. Their financial world was collapsing.

Tumi called Carlos, told him briefly what had happened and scheduled an emergency session. When they met, Tumi seemed unexpectedly composed to him. He thought that she might be very depressed and that their session might have a 'help me, I'm falling into the abyss' feeling about it. But Tumi wanted to get down to work. In a sense the sky had fallen, but it was time to figure out what she needed to do. She said that she had been thinking about how her father's news had changed things. There was good news and bad news, she said. In two months she would have no job, but that meant that the pathway to a new job and career was wide open. The economy was falling into a recession that could be deep, but she trusted her ability to find, not just anything, but work that fitted some of her aspirations. As to developing a cadre of friends and associates, this was now more important than ever. It even had a name – networking. She had to continue building a network and begin working it.

Here was a woman who had taken to heart goal one of the overall goals of the helping process – she had been learning how to apply the problem-management process to problems and opportunities on her own. There are opportunities hidden in almost every problem situation. But the latest turn of events brought her face to face with an issue she had been avoiding.

Her deeper fear was for her father directly and indirectly for her mother. Tumi thought that this financial debacle might crush him. Now the question was clear: How could she fashion a new life for herself without abandoning her parents? She knew that she could not just leave them, but she also knew that she had the will and the strength to reset her relationship with them. She could be both a daughter and an independent agent. So now she had three broad goals – a new social life, a new career path and a new relationship with her parents. Each of these goals involved second-order change. Taken together they constituted, for her, massive second-order change, but they intersected, they fed into one another. Each made the others, paradoxically, easier. Some problem situations cannot be solved or even managed. They must be transcended. Each goal would require a great deal of work, but she felt up to it. The bad news about the economy had liberated her and made her start thinking seriously about key issues that she had been pushing to the back of her mind – resetting her relationship with her parents.

Tumi at this moment did not know exactly what resetting her relationship with her parents would look like or how to accomplish it. Perhaps it would be a by-product of her pursuit of her other two goals. She was confident that she could work it out. She had an exciting, if arduous, project. And Carlos was her consultant.

Help clients find incentives and rewards for sustained action

Clients avoid engaging in action programmes when the incentives and the rewards for *not* engaging in the programme outweigh the incentives and the rewards for doing so. The counsellor in this case thinks that he is justified in taking a tough confrontational approach to helping.

Miguel, a police officer on trial for use of excessive force with a young offender, had a number of sessions with a counsellor that handled police health insurance. During the sessions, the counsellor learned that although this was the first time Miguel had run foul of the law, it was in no way the first expression of a brutal streak within him. He was a bully on the beat and a despot at home, and had run-ins with strangers when he visited bars with his friends. During the trial, witnesses recalled instances of these behaviours.

Up to the time of his arrest, he had got away with all of this, even though his friends had often warned him to be more cautious. His badge had become a licence to do whatever he wanted. His arrest and now the trial shocked him. Before, he had seen himself as invulnerable; now, he felt very vulnerable. The thought of being an ex-cop in prison understandably horrified him. He was found guilty, was suspended from the force for several months and received probation on the condition that he continued to see the counsellor.

Beginning with his arrest, Miguel had modified his aggressive behaviour a great deal, even at home. Of course, fear of the consequences of his aggressive behaviour was a strong incentive to change. The next time, the courts would show no sympathy. The counsellor took a tough approach to this tough cop. He confronted Miguel for 'remaining an adolescent' and for 'hiding behind his badge'. He called the power Miguel exercised over others 'cheap power'. He challenged the 'decent person' to 'come out from behind the screen'. He told Miguel point-blank that the fear he was experiencing was probably not enough to keep him out of trouble in the future. After probation, the fear would fade and Miguel could easily fall back into his old ways. Even worse, fear was a 'weak man's' crutch.

On a more positive note, the counsellor saw in Miguel's expressions of vulnerability the possibility of a much more decent human being, one 'hiding' under the tough exterior. The real incentives, he suggested, came from the 'decent guy' buried inside. He had Miguel paint a picture of a 'tough but decent' cop, family man and friend. He had Miguel come up with 'experiments in decency' – at home, on the beat, with his buddies – to get first-hand experience of the rewards associated with decency.

The counsellor was not trying to change Miguel's personality. Indeed, he didn't believe in personality transformations. But he pushed him hard to find and bring to the surface a different, more constructive set of incentives to guide his dealings with people. The new incentives had to drive out the old. This counsellor's approach seems to run up against a lot that has been said about responsible helping. What is your view? If you were Miguel's counsellor, what approach would you take?

The incentives and rewards that help a client get going on a programme of constructive change in the first place may not be the ones that keep the client going.

Dwight, a man in his early 30s who was recovering from an accident at work that had left him partially paralysed, had begun an arduous physical rehabilitation programme with great commitment. Now, months later, he was ready to give up. The counsellor asked him to visit the children's ward. Dwight was both shaken by the experience and amazed at the courage of many of the children. He was especially struck by one teenager who was undergoing chemotherapy. 'He seems so positive about everything', Dwight said. The counsellor told him that the boy was tempted to give up, too. Dwight and the boy saw each other frequently. Dwight put up with the pain. The boy hung in there. Three months later, the boy died. Dwight's response, besides grief, was, 'I can't give up now; that would really be letting him down. I've got to keep my part of the bargain.'

Dwight's partnership with the teenager proved to be an excellent incentive. It helped him renew his resolve. Although the counsellor joined with Dwight in celebrating his newfound commitment, he also worked with Dwight to find 'backup' incentives for those times when current incentives seem to lose their power.

Constructive-change activities that are not rewarded tend over time to lose their vigour, decrease, and even disappear. This process is called extinction. It was happening with Luigi.

> Luigi, a middle-aged man, had been in and out of mental hospitals a number of times. He discovered that one of the best ways of staying out was to use some of his excess energy helping others. He had not returned to the hospital once during the three years he worked at a soup kitchen. However, finding himself becoming more and more manic over the past six months and fearing that he would be re-hospitalised, he sought the help of a counsellor.
>
> Luigi's discussions with the counsellor led to some interesting findings. He discovered that, whereas in the beginning he had worked at the soup kitchen because he wanted to, he was now working there because he thought he should. He felt guilty about leaving and also thought that doing so would lead to a relapse. In summary, he had not lost his interest in helping others, but his current work was no longer interesting or challenging. As a result of his sessions with the counsellor, Luigi began to work for a group that provided housing for the homeless and the elderly. He poured his energy into his new work and his manic episodes subsided.

The lesson here is that incentives cannot be put in place and then be taken for granted. They need tending.

Help clients develop action-focused self-contracts

Earlier we discussed self-contracts as a way of helping clients commit themselves to what they want – that is, their goals. Self-contracts are also useful in helping them both initiate and sustain problem-managing action and the work involved in developing opportunities. Self-contracts and agreements with others focus clients' energies. Sherman and her associates (2008) point out the obstacles to getting family, spouses, partners and friends to provide support for veterans with PTSD. Family members shy away for a number of reasons: no one has enlisted their help, they live too far away, they have unchallenged beliefs such as 'what goes on behind closed doors is not to be discussed', they are reluctant to make an effort to understand the veteran and they fear being exposed to upsetting information. Spouses and partners have misgivings about engaging in formal programmes, feel hopeless about the veteran's ability to improve, become resigned to being lifelong caregivers and feel that most of their attention should be given to their children. Perhaps the main problem with social support is that it does not happen automatically. Involved parties – client, helper and others – have to make it happen. In some sense of the term relevant parties need to be *enrolled*. Karlan (2008) demonstrates the power of commitment contracts. His website (www.stickK.com) allows people to set a goal, determine the stakes for not pursuing the goal, choose a referee to determine if progress is being made and get supporters' help in staying on target. Public commitment works. If you share your change agenda 'with the world', it is easier to move forward and harder to give up. Transparency helps. The stickK system tends to work because it provides incentives that work with most people. The principles Karlan outlines – goal setting, putting stakes at risk, an objective referee and transparency – can, with some adaptation, be used in therapy.

In the following case, several parties had to commit themselves to the provisions of a commitment contract.

> A 12-year-old boy was causing a great deal of disturbance by his outbursts in class, which included verbal jousting with his friends and profanities. The apparent purpose of the disruptions was to position himself among his friends. He seemed to want to cultivate a reputation for being unafraid of the teachers and principal. The punishments handed down by them were dwarfed by what he saw as the admiration of his friends. After the teacher discussed the situation with the school counsellor, the counsellor called a meeting of all the stakeholders – the boy, his parents, the teacher and the principal. The counsellor offered a simple contract. When the boy disrupted the class, he would spend the next day working by himself under the direction of a teacher's aide. This would take him away from his friends. The day after, he would return to the classroom. There would be no further punishment. Concurrently, the counsellor would work with him on what 'leadership' behaviour in the classroom might look like.

The first month, the boy spent a fair number of days with the teacher's aide. The second month, however, he missed only two days, and the third month only one. The truth is that he really wanted to be in school with his classmates. That's where the action was. And so he paid the price of self-control to get what he wanted. He also began to discover more constructive forms of leadership behaviour. For instance, on occasion he challenged what the teacher was saying about a particular topic. Sometimes this led to a very lively classroom debate. Even the teacher thought that the boy's behaviour was responsible and added value.

The counsellor had suspected that the boy found socialising with his classmates rewarding. But now he had to pay for the privilege of socialising. Reasonable behaviour in the classroom was not too high a price. This was more than just a self-contract. Other stakeholders were involved. Getting others involved increases the likelihood that progress towards the goal will be made. The more you know about the power of incentives, the more clients will benefit.

SOCIAL SUPPORT AND THE IMPORTANCE OF CHALLENGE

As we have seen, planning includes helping clients identify the resources, both internal and environmental, they need to pursue goals. One of the most important resources is social support (Barker & Pistrang, 2002; Seeman, 1996; Taylor, 2007; Taylor and associates, 2004), although, surprisingly enough, research to verify the usefulness of social support is skimpy (Cruza-Guet and associates, 2008; Hogan, Linden & Najarian, 2002; Roehrle & Strouse, 2008), highlighting once more the not infrequent necessity of common sense to outpace 'science'. Lakey (2010) contends that despite the need for an understanding of social support on the part of helpers, the helping professions 'still lack sufficient understanding of social support processes to create effective, new interventions' (p. 177). The starting point for understanding social support is the client and his or her relationship with the support provider. The kind and quality of the relationship has, perhaps, the most influence when it comes to social support (Lakey, 2010). So-called objectively supportive people or actions are actually so only if they are perceived to be so by the client. *How* people provide support is also critical in the eyes of the recipient. Sometimes 'supportive' people, especially those with 'good intentions', wonder why they are being shunned by those they are trying to support.

Yet most practitioners see social support as a key element in problem-managing change.

> "Social support has... been examined as a predictor of the course of mental illness. In about 75% of studies with clinically depressed patients, social-support factors increased the initial success of treatment and helped patients maintain their treatment gains. Similarly, studies of people with schizophrenia or alcoholism revealed that higher levels of social support are correlated with fewer relapses, less frequent hospitalisations, and success and maintenance of treatment gains." (Basic Behavioral Science Task Force of the National Advisory Mental Health Council, 1996, p. 628)

While helpers themselves can provide a great deal of support, still, if clients are to pursue goals 'out there' in their real lives, their main support should also be out there. Unfortunately, such support may not always be easy to find (Putnam, 2000). In much of Western society, the supply of 'social capital' – both informal social connectedness and formal civic engagement – has fallen. We belong to fewer organisations that conduct meetings, know our neighbours less, meet with friends less frequently and even socialise with our families less often. Yet this is the environment in which clients must do the work of constructive change.

In a study on weight loss and maintaining the loss (Wing & Jeffery, 1999), clients who enlisted the help of friends were much more successful than clients who took the solo path. This is called 'social facilitation' and is quite different from dependence. Social facilitation is energising, whereas dependence is often limiting and depressing. Therefore, a culture of social isolation does not bode well for clients. Of course, all of this reinforces what we already know through common sense. Who among us has not been helped through difficult times by family and friends?

When it comes to social support, there are two categories of clients. First, there are those who lead an impoverished social life. The objective with this group is to help them find social resources, to get back into community in some productive way. But what about clients who do have people they can turn to? Well, as Putnam points out, even when clients, at least on paper, have a social system, they may not use it very effectively. This provides counsellors with a different challenge – that is, helping clients tap into those human resources in a way that helps them manage problem situations more effectively. Consider this example.

> Casey, a bachelor whose job involved frequent travel literally around the world, fell ill. He had many friends, but they were spread around the world. Because he was neither married nor in a marriage-like relationship, he had no primary caregiver in his life. He received excellent medical care, but his psyche fared poorly. Once out of the hospital, he recuperated slowly, mainly because he was not getting the social support he needed. In desperation, he had a few sessions with a counsellor, sessions that proved to be quite helpful. The counsellor challenged him to 'ask for help' from his local friends. He had underplayed his illness with them because he didn't want to be a 'burden'. He discovered that his friends were more than ready to help. But because their time was limited, he, with some hesitancy, 'grafted' onto his rather sparse hometown social network some very caring people from the local church. He was fearful that he would be deluged with piety, but instead he found people like himself. Moreover, they were, in the main, socially intelligent. They knew how much or how little care to give. In fact, most of the time their care was simple friendship.

Casey was likeable. But what about those who are less likeable? The National Advisory Mental Health Council study just mentioned showed that people who are highly distressed and therefore most in need of social support may be the least likely to receive it because their expressions of distress drive away potential supporters. Who among us has not avoided at one time or another a distressed friend or colleague? Therefore, distressed clients can be helped to learn how to modulate their expressions of distress. Who wants to help whiners? On the other hand, potential supporters can learn how to deal with distressed friends and colleagues, even when these friends and colleagues let themselves become whiners.

Because getting 'into community' is one of Tumi's major goals, Carlos gives Tumi an article on social support and culture (Kim, Sherman & Taylor, 2008). Tumi is struck by the differences in social support in collectivistic versus individualistic societies. She feels that she straddles the two and often enough loses out on the advantages of both while being burdened by the disadvantages of both. She and Carlos have a good 'Who *am* I?' conversation. Tumi realises how alone she has been, even though she hasn't felt lonely. Her social isolation may not be debilitating, but it isn't helping either. She longs for something more. She also needs more social support if she is to pursue her rather demanding agendas.

Challenging relationships

Support without challenge can be hollow, just as challenge without support can be abrasive. Ideally, the people in the lives of clients provide a judicious mixture of encouragement and challenge.

> Harry, a man in his early 50s, was suddenly stricken with a disease that called for immediate and drastic surgery. He came through the operation quite well, even getting out of the hospital in record time. For the first few weeks he seemed, within reason, to be his old self. However, he had problems with the drugs he had to take following the operation. He became quite sick and took on many of the mannerisms of a chronic invalid. Even after the right mix of drugs was found, he persisted in invalid-like behaviour. Whereas right after the operation he had 'walked tall', he now began to shuffle. He also talked constantly about his symptoms and generally used his 'state' to excuse himself from normal activities.

At first Harry's friends were in a quandary. They realised the seriousness of the operation and tried to put themselves in his place. They provided all sorts of support. But gradually they realised that he was adopting a style that would alienate others and keep him out of the mainstream of life. Support and encouragement were essential, but not enough. They used a variety of ways (some included a bit of dark humour) to invite Harry to challenge himself to stay on the road to recovery. They mocked his 'invalid' movements, engaged in serious one-to-one talks, turned a deaf ear to his discussion of symptoms and routinely included him in their plans.

Harry did not always react graciously to his friends' challenges, but in his better moments he admitted that he was fortunate to have such friends. He died three years later, but because of the challenges of his friends, he lived quite a full life until the end. Counsellors can support clients in their search for people willing to provide a judicious mixture of encouragement and challenge.

Tumi confesses that the only challenging relationship she has is her relationship with Carlos. Her relationship with her father is dysfunctional, not challenging in a positive sense. Her relationship with her mother is bland and trying to improve it is not on her (Tumi's) agenda. She does not look to her mother for support. But Carlos points out two things. First, she is not alone in her social isolation; many others are in the same position, lacking anyone in whom they can confide. Second, Carlos notes, one of her top priorities – to create a community of friends and associates for herself – is designed to remedy this situation. Tumi thinks for a moment and then says, 'In South Africa the young people I met talked quite freely among themselves about many things – their aspirations, their discontent with needless social strictures, the problems they have with society and with the regime and so forth. I found these discussions full of substance and very satisfying. But they did not talk very openly about their personal problems or the more intimate details of their lives such as their own relationships and their views on religion.' Carlos says, 'But they weren't "bowling alone" in Putnam's sense, were they?' Tumi laughs, 'Of course not. But now I'm getting a much better sense of the kind of "community" of friends I would like to have. And I need people outside of this counselling relationship with whom I can discuss the important issues of my life. I want confidants.'

Two-way feedback

Let's revisit feedback, identified in Chapter 1 as one of the key ingredients of successful therapy (Lambert, 2010a). Feedback on progress towards problem-managing outcomes at the beginning of each therapy session and on the quality and value of the interactions during therapy at the end of each session is a principal contributor to implementation. There is no place to hide for either the client or the helper. If therapy is ultimately defined by life-enhancing outcomes, then two-way feedback within the session is crucial. Feedback helps both client and therapist engage in course correction. Dörner's (1996) research found that successful project managers reviewed their progress, looked for unanticipated and unintended consequences, and corrected course often. The same could be said of clients and their helpers.

Feedback from significant others in clients' everyday lives also goes far in helping them start acting on their own behalf and persevere even when the going gets rough. Gilbert (1978, p. 175), in his book on human competence, claimed that 'improved information has more potential than anything else I can think of for creating more competence in the day-to-day management of performance'. Feedback is certainly one way of providing both encouragement and challenge. If clients are to be successful in implementing their action plans, they need adequate information about how well they are performing. If goals and the path to these goals are clear, clients will know whether they are making progress or not. But sometimes clients need a more objective view of their progress. The purpose of feedback is not to pass judgement on clients' performance but rather to provide information, guidance, support and challenge to help them move forward. There are two kinds of feedback:

> **Confirmatory feedback.** Through confirmatory feedback, significant others – such as helpers, relatives, friends and colleagues – let clients know that they are on course, that is, moving successfully through the steps of an action programme towards a goal.

> **Corrective feedback.** Through corrective feedback, significant others let clients know that they have wandered off course and specify what they need to do to get back on.

Corrective feedback, whether from helpers or people in the client's everyday life, should incorporate the following principles:

- Help clients give feedback to themselves.
- Give feedback in the spirit of caring.
- Remember that mistakes are opportunities for growth.

- Use a mix of both confirmatory and corrective feedback.
- Be concrete, specific, brief and to the point.
- Focus on the client's behaviours rather than on more elusive personality characteristics.
- Help clients see whether their behaviour is helping or hindering goal accomplishment.
- Help clients explore the impact and implications of the behaviour.
- Avoid negative language arising from impatience ('Gosh, that was a stupid thing to do').
- Provide feedback in moderate doses. Overwhelming the client defeats the purpose of the entire exercise.
- Engage the client in dialogue. Invite the client not only to comment on the feedback but also to expand on it. Lectures don't usually help.
- Help the client discover alternative ways of doing things. If necessary, make suggestions.
- Help clients explore the upside of changing and the downside of not changing.

The spirit of these 'rules' should also govern confirmatory feedback. Very often people give very detailed corrective feedback and then just say 'nice job' when a person does something well. All feedback provides an opportunity for learning. Consider the following statement from a father talking to his son, who stood up for the rights of a friend who was being bullied by some of his high school classmates:

> 'Paul, I'm proud of you. You stood your ground even when they turned on you. They were mean. You weren't. You gave your opinion calmly, but forcefully. You didn't apologise for what you were saying. You were ready to take the consequences. It's easier now that a couple of them have apologised to you, but at the time you didn't know they would. You were honest to yourself. And now the best of them appreciate it. It made me think of myself. I'm not sure that I would have stood my ground the way you did (he pauses), but I'm more likely to do so now.'

Although not as brief, this is much more powerful than 'I'm proud of you, son.' Being specific about behaviour, together with pointing out the impact of the behaviour, turns positive feedback into a learning experience. Of course, one of the main problems with feedback is finding people in the client's day-to-day life who see the client in action enough to make it meaningful, who care enough to give it and who have the skills to provide it constructively.

Tumi realises that she does not yet have people in her life who could give her this kind of feedback. At work she has received a lot of indirect feedback that she is doing a good job, but nothing more personal than that. And her days at the auto dealership are numbered. She muses on the fact that she does not get direct feedback from Carlos. He helps her provide feedback to herself, but she wonders whether getting direct feedback from Carlos would be some kind of violation of the counselling method he is following. Box 11.1 outlines the kinds of questions you can help clients ask themselves as they implement change programmes.

BOX 11.1   Questions on Implementing Plans

Here are the kinds of questions you can help clients ask themselves in their search for ways of implementing their plans:

- Now that I have a plan, how do I move into action?
- What kind of self-starter am I? How can I improve?
- What obstacles lie in my way? Which are critical?
- How can I manage these obstacles?
- How do I keep my efforts from flagging?
- What do I do when I feel like giving up?
- What kind of support will help me keep going?
- What role does hope play in my search for a better life?
- What's my track record with life-enhancing change?

The checklist

A lot of jokes have been made about people who let checklists, often ignored, rule their lives. One obsessive artist even made a list of his lists. Gawande (2010) showed how the use of the checklist reduced the number of medical errors in hospitals and saved thousands of lives. In his book he tries to show the value of checklists in many other areas of life. Although he has his critics (Howard, 2010) and the overuse of checklists can be stultifying, they can be very useful in therapy. To-do lists can help clients move into action, stay the course and even change the course when necessary. Howard rightly cautions that checklists can stand in the way of creativity: 'if [clients] are thinking about a checklist, they may not be focused on solving the problem' (p. A21). What he is really saying, however, is that the misuse or overuse of any methodology is often self-defeating. In therapy, a to-do list reminds clients of the importance of action and progress. Clients who stay in the driver's seat use to-do lists rather than become captives of them.

THE SHADOW SIDE OF IMPLEMENTING CHANGE

Change programmes have a large shadow side. There are many reasons why clients fail to act on their own behalf. Three are discussed here: helpers who do not have an action mentality, client inertia and client entropy. As you read about these common phenomena, recall what was said about 'implementation intentions' earlier. They can play an important role in managing the shadow-side obstacles outlined here.

Helpers as reluctant agents of change

Driscoll (1984, pp. 91–97) discussed the temptation of helpers to respond to the passivity of their clients with a kind of passivity of their own, a 'sorry, it's up to you' stance. This, he claimed, is a mistake.

> "A client who refuses to accept responsibility thereby invites the therapist to take over. In remaining passive, the therapist foils the invitation, thus forcing the client to take some initiative or to endure the silence. A passive stance is therefore a means to avoid accepting the wrong sorts of responsibility. It is generally ineffective, however, as a long-run approach. Passivity by a therapist leaves the client feeling unsupported and thus further impairs the already fragile therapeutic alliance. Troubled clients, furthermore, are not merely unwilling but generally and in important ways unable to take appropriate responsibility. A passive countermove is therefore counterproductive, for neither therapist nor client generates solutions, and both are stranded together in a muddle of entangling inactivity." (p. 91)

To help others act, helpers must be agents and doers in the helping process, not mere listeners and responders. The best helpers are active in the helping sessions. They keep looking for ways to enter the worlds of their clients, to help them become more active in the sessions, to help them own more of the constructive change process, to help them see the need for action – action in their heads and action outside their heads in their everyday lives. And they do all this while espousing the client-centred values outlined in Chapter 2. Although they don't push reluctant clients too hard, thus turning reluctance into resistance, neither do they sit around waiting for reluctant clients to act.

Client inertia: Reluctance to get started

Inertia is the human tendency to put off problem-managing action. I sometimes say to clients who I suspect are prone to inertia something like this, 'The action programme you've come up with seems to be a sound one. The main reason that sound action programmes don't work, however, is that they are never tried. Don't be surprised if you feel reluctant to act or are tempted to put off the first steps. This is quite natural. Ask yourself what you can do to get by that initial barrier.' The sources of inertia are many, ranging from pure sloth to paralysing fear. Understanding what inertia is like is easy. We need only look at our own behaviour. The list of ways in which we avoid taking responsibility is endless. We'll examine several of them here: passivity, learned helplessness, disabling self-talk and getting trapped in vicious circles.

Passivity One of the most important ingredients in the generation and perpetuation of the 'psychopathology of the average' is passivity, the failure of people to take responsibility for themselves in one or more developmental areas of life or in various life situations that call for action. Passivity takes many forms: doing nothing – that is, not responding to problems and options; uncritically accepting the goals and solutions suggested by others; acting aimlessly; and becoming paralysed – that is, shutting down or becoming violent, blowing up (see Schiff, 1975).

> When Zelda and Jerzy first noticed small signs that things were not going right in their relationship, they did nothing. They noticed certain incidents, mused on them for a while and then forgot about them. They lacked the communication skills to engage each other immediately and to explore what was happening. Zelda and Jerzy had both learned to remain passive before the little crises of life, not realising how much their passivity would ultimately contribute to their downfall. Endless unmanaged problems led to major blow-ups until they decided to end their marriage.

Passivity in dealing with little things can prove very costly. Little things have a way of turning into big things.

Learned helplessness Seligman's (1975, 1991) concept of 'learned helplessness' and its relationship to depression is an important one (Garber & Seligman, 1980; Peterson, Maier & Seligman, 1995). Some clients learn to believe from an early age that there is nothing they can do about certain life situations. There are degrees in feelings of helplessness – from mild forms of 'I'm not up to this' to feelings of total helplessness coupled with deep depression. Learned helplessness, then, is a step beyond mere passivity.

Bennett and Bennett (1984) saw the positive side of helplessness. If clients' problems are indeed out of their control, then it is not helpful for them to have an illusory sense of control, unjustly assign themselves responsibility and indulge in excessive expectations. Somewhat paradoxically, they found that challenging clients' tendency to blame themselves for everything actually fostered realistic hope and change.

The trick is helping clients learn what is and what is not in their control. A man with a physical disability may not be able to do anything about the disability itself, but he does have some control over how he views his disability and his power to pursue certain life goals despite it. The opposite of helplessness is 'learned optimism' (Seligman, 1998) and resourcefulness. If helplessness can be learned, so can resourcefulness. Indeed, increased resourcefulness is one of the principal goals of successful helping. Optimism, however, is not an unmixed blessing; nor is pessimism always a disaster (Chang, 2001). Although optimists do live longer and enjoy greater success than pessimists, pessimists are better predictors of what is likely to happen. The price of optimism is being wrong a lot of the time. Perhaps we should help our clients be hopeful realists rather than optimists or pessimists.

Disabling self-talk Inviting clients to challenge their dysfunctional self-talk was discussed earlier. Clients often talk themselves out of things, thus talking themselves into passivity. They say to themselves such things as 'I can't do it', 'I can't cope', 'I don't have what it takes to engage in that programme; it's too hard' and 'It won't work.' Such self-defeating conversations with themselves get people into trouble in the first place and then prevent them from getting out. Helpers can add great value by helping clients challenge the kind of self-talk that interferes with action.

Vicious circles Pyszczynski and Greenberg (1987) developed a theory about self-defeating behaviour and depression. They said that people whose actions fail to get them what they want can easily lose a sense of self-worth and become mired in a vicious circle of guilt and depression.

> "Consequently, the individual falls into a pattern of virtually constant self-focus, resulting in intensified negative affect, self-derogation, further negative outcomes, and a depressive self-focusing style. Eventually, these factors lead to a negative self-image, which may take on value by providing an explanation for the individual's plight and by helping the individual avoid further disappointments. The depressive self-focusing style then maintains and exacerbates the depressive disorder." (p. 122)

It does sound depressing. One client, Amanda, fits this theory perfectly. She had aspirations of moving up the career ladder where she worked. She was very enthusiastic and dedicated, but she was unaware of the 'gentleman's club' politics of the company in which she worked and didn't know how to 'work the system'. She kept doing the things that she thought should get her ahead. They didn't. Finally, she got down on herself, began making mistakes in the things that she usually did well and made things worse by constantly talking about how she 'was stuck', thus alienating her friends. By the time she saw a counsellor, she felt defeated and depressed. She was about to give up. The counsellor focused on the entire 'circle' – low self-esteem producing passivity producing even lower self-esteem – and not just the self-esteem part. Instead of just trying to help her change her inner world of disabling self-talk, he also helped her intervene in her life to become a better problem solver. Small successes in problem solving led to the start of a 'benign' circle – success producing greater self-esteem leading to greater efforts to succeed.

Disorganisation   Tico lived out of his car. No one knew exactly where he spent the night. The car was chaos, and so was his life. He was always going to get his career, family relations and love life in order, but he never did. Living in disorganisation was his way of putting off life decisions. Ferguson (1987, p. 46) painted a picture that may well remind us of ourselves, at least at times.

> "When we saddle ourselves with innumerable little hassles and problems, they distract us from considering the possibility that we may have chosen the wrong job, the wrong profession, or the wrong mate. If we are drowning in unfinished housework, it becomes much easier to ignore the fact that we have become estranged from family life. Putting off an important project – painting a picture, writing a book, drawing up a business plan – is a way of protecting ourselves from the possibility that the result may not be quite as successful as we had hoped. Setting up our lives to insure a significant level of disorganisation allows us to continue to think of ourselves as inadequate or partially-adequate people who don't have to take on the real challenges of adult behaviour."

Many things can be behind this unwillingness to get our lives in order, like defending ourselves against a fear of succeeding.

Driscoll (1984, pp. 112–117) has provided us with a great deal of insight into this problem. He described inertia as a form of control. He says that if we tell some clients to jump into the driver's seat, they will compliantly do so – at least until the journey gets too rough. The most effective strategy, he claimed, is to show clients that they have been in the driver's seat all along: 'Our task as therapists is not to talk our clients into taking control of their lives, but to confirm the fact that they already are and always will be.' That is, inertia, in the form of staying disorganised, is itself a form of control. The client is actually successful, sometimes against great odds, at remaining disorganised and thus preserving inertia. Once clients recognise their power, then we can help them redirect it.

Entropy: The tendency of things to fall apart

Entropy is the tendency to slow down and give up action that has been initiated. Kirschenbaum (1987), in a review of the research literature, uses the term 'self-regulatory failure', and further research looks at the cognitive neuroscience of self-regulatory failure (Wagner & Heatherton, 2016). Programmes for constructive change, even those that start strong, often dwindle and disappear. All of us have experienced problems trying to implement programmes. We make plans and they seem realistic to us. We start the steps of a programme with a good deal of enthusiasm. However, we soon run into tedium, obstacles and complications. What seemed so easy in the planning stage now seems quite difficult. We become discouraged, flounder, recover, flounder again and finally give up, rationalising to ourselves that we did not want to accomplish those goals anyway.

False hopes   Under the rubric of 'false hopes of self-change', Polivy and Herman (2002) suggest that this scenario occurs all too frequently. Perhaps it is even the norm in self-change programmes such as dieting, which they use as their point of reference. At the centre of the false-hope syndrome, they say, are the clients' unrealistic expectations. They refer to things like New Year's Eve resolutions. Most of us can immediately think of many of our own resolutions that fell by the wayside. Fletcher (2003), Lowe (2003) and Snyder and Rand (2003) all quite vigorously challenge Polivy and Herman's findings and even the concept of 'false hopes'.

They say that the authors paint an overly pessimistic picture of self-change programmes, especially dieting. That makes *a priori* sense if we consider outcome research in helping. When it comes to counselling, if we start with the premise that helping does help, then the kind of pessimism that Polivy and Herman suggest must be wrong. Right? Well, let's take a look.

We have already seen that hope and expectancy, on the part of both client and helper, are key ingredients in successful therapy. But substantive change is hard work. Even 'true hope' can grow grey hairs in the face of adversity. That said, we should be able to help clients spot 'false hopes' in their search for problem-managing outcomes. Expectancy is an ally only when it is realistic. We therapists will run across both true hopes and false hopes in our practice, but we will encourage the former and help clients challenge the latter. Even if the work of Polivy and Herman is as flawed as its critics say – and by the way, how could something so flawed end up in the *American Psychologist*? – there is something about it that rings true.

Discretionary change   The track record of discretionary change – change that is not forced in one way or another – on the part of both individuals and institutions is poor. This is my read of individuals (including myself), companies, institutions and countries. The change may not actually be discretionary, but it is seen, at whatever level of consciousness, as discretionary. If we think we don't have to change, then often we do not, even though we say we want to. In my work with institutions, I talk about the Okavango–Kalahari phenomenon. When the waters from the highlands in the north flood into the Okavango Delta in Botswana, it becomes an ecological wonderland. But somehow those waters disappear into the Kalahari Desert, though hydrologists don't know exactly how. I ask the managers, 'Does this sound like any of your change programmes?' They laugh. 'Where's that management development programme you started so vigorously two years ago?' 'In the Kalahari!' shouts one. I'm not sure that I have the Okavango–Kalahari hydrology right, but the challenge of discretionary change will always be with us. As you sit with clients, how much of the change being discussed is discretionary? 'Forewarned is forearmed' is realism, not pessimism.

The decay curve   Phillips (1987, p. 650) identified what he called the 'ubiquitous decay curve' in both helping and in medical-delivery situations. Attrition, non-compliance and relapse are the name of the game. A married couple trying to reinvent their marriage might eventually say to themselves, 'We had no idea that it would be so hard to change ingrained ways of interacting with each other. Is it worth the effort?' Their motivation is on the wane. Wise helpers know that the decay curve is part of life and help clients deal with it. With respect to entropy, a helper might say, 'Even sound action programmes begun with the best of intentions tend to fall apart over time, so don't be surprised when your initial enthusiasm seems to wane a bit. That's only natural. Rather, ask yourself what you need to do to keep yourself at the task.'

Brownell and her associates (1986) provided a useful caution. They drew a fine line between preparing clients for mistakes and giving them 'permission' to make mistakes by implying that mistakes are inevitable. Preparation, yes; permission, no. They also made a distinction between 'lapse' and 'relapse'. A slip or a mistake in an action programme (a lapse) need not lead to a relapse – that is, giving up the programme entirely. Consider Graham, a man who has been trying to change what others see as his 'angry interpersonal style'. Using a variety of self-monitoring and self-control techniques, he has made great progress in changing his style. On occasion, he loses his temper, but never in any extreme way. He makes mistakes, but he does not let an occasional lapse end up in relapse.

RESILIENCE: PEOPLE'S ABILITY TO HOLD THEMSELVES TOGETHER, BOUNCE BACK, AND GROW

As to the reality of resilience, let me offer a case.

Juliana was a headstrong girl right from the start. High school was a bit tumultuous, but the seeds of really significant problems were sown during her college years. There she learned both the pleasures and the misery of drugs. Because her friends were 'druggies', she chose boyfriends who were also playing with drugs and who could accommodate her headstrong nature. Predictably, boyfriends came and went. The drugs were a constant. After college she stuck to this lifestyle. New boyfriends and jobs came and went.

Her parents loved her dearly and did everything they could to help her. She played them like a harp. At times she would give hints that she was tired of her lifestyle, and their hopes were raised. Then she plunged back into her old ways with a vengeance. Her parents were always there for her. In a sense, this was part of the problem situation. Their financial and social support allowed her to continue in her unhealthy ways. After some sessions with a counsellor, her parents decided to cut her loose. She had to leave the house and make her own way financially. This ripped them apart but they did not know what else to do.

Off Juliana went. The ensuing picture was not pretty at all. It almost seemed that she was going to get even worse as a way of getting back at her parents. To their horror, she ended up in jail. But jail seemed to be the turning point. After getting out, she all but quit taking drugs. She got a number of jobs, but her headstrong nature still asserted itself. She moved from job to job either because she could not stand the people at work or they could no longer put up with her. She was really shaken up when her father lost his job. By then she had re-established some kind of minimal relationship with her family. She began to see a counsellor again. He soon recognised a number of Juliana's inner resources. Headstrong, yes, but a woman with guts, too. A woman who could not seem to establish reasonable relationships with others – especially men – but also a woman with a keen understanding of human nature. In spite of all the messy years she had not lost her spark, and her rather substantial inner resources were hidden but intact.

Juliana finally nailed down a job she liked, was promoted, was headhunted by another company but stayed with the original one because she got a better position in that company with better pay. She established a home for her two children who had been farmed out to relatives. She subscribed to and promoted the values, such as self-discipline and decency in interpersonal relationships, that her children had learned in their foster homes. She re-established full contact with her family. She became a caring companion to the man with whom she lived. In short, she successfully rejoined the community she had abandoned.

The counsellor played a catalytic role in this process of renewal, but Juliana did the work. He encouraged her to tap into the wellspring of resilience or hardiness (Khoshaba & Maddi, 2004; Maddi, 2002 & 2013) or growth-through-adversity (Joseph & Linley, 2005) inside her, and she did. She moved from self-loathing to a non-indulgent form of self-esteem. Success in one area of life (work) spread to others (interpersonal relationships). Like many converts, she even became a crusader with her children, relatives and friends for hard work, self-discipline and the total avoidance of self-pity. The point is that even in the most difficult cases, there is probably some residue of resilience. Tapping into it is the challenge.

Will Juliana stay the course? No one can say for sure, but her actions and accomplishments so far have a sense of permanency to them, which is not always the case. So there is, as you might expect, a literature on helping clients stay the course (Bosworth & Oddone, 2005; Christensen, 2004; Cockell, Zaitsoff & Geller, 2004; Colan, 2003; Meichenbaum & Turk, 1987; Witkiewitz & Marlatt, 2005). The literature on terminating psychotherapy also has some helpful guidelines (Murdin, 2015). Juliana made do with her own revived inner strengths and with the social support she received, mainly from family members. She was lucky because she came from a family of good communicators. Too many people who would like to provide support are ineffective interpersonal communicators. They either do it poorly or their support remains buried inside (Cohen, Underwood & Gotlieb, 2000; Goldsmith, 2004).

Help clients tap into their resilience

Although buried under despair, resilience is found even in some of the most desperate clients. There has been a mini-explosion of theory and research about resilience (Alvord & Grados, 2005; Bonanno, 2004, 2005; Flach, 1997; T. Kelley, 2005; Linley & Joseph, 2005; Litz, 2005; Maddi, 2005; Reivich & Shatté, 2002; Tedeschi & Kilmer, 2005; Tugade & Fredrickson, 2004), and the American Psychological Association has even launched a 'resilience initiative' (Kersting, 2003, 2005; Newman, 2005). Newman defines resilience as 'the human ability to adapt in the face of tragedy, trauma, adversity, hardship and ongoing significant life stressors' (p. 227). Resilience is also the ability to stay mentally healthy or return to mental health during times of adversity. For a summary of basic common sense about resilience you might well read 'Building your resilience' (American Psychological Association Help Centre, retrieved 1 July, 2012, at www.apa.org/topics/resilience)

or Padesky and Mooney's (2012) four-step model to building resilience. Glicken (2006) first takes a stab at cataloguing the attributes of resilience, then, realising that research and 'science' have such a long way to go in this area, ends up by letting examples of resilience speak eloquently for themselves.

Outcome versus process resilience

The ability to bounce back is an essential life capability. Holaday and McPhearson (1997) have compiled a list of common factors that influence resilience. Although they focused on severe-burn survivors, their discussion of resilience applies to all of us and our clients. They distinguish between outcome resilience and process resilience. Whereas resilience in general is the ability to overcome or adapt to significant stress or adversity, *outcome resilience* implies a return to a previous state. This is 'bounce back' resilience. Dora goes through the trauma of divorce, but within a few months she bounces back. Her friends say to her, 'You seem to be your old self now.' She replies, 'Both older and wiser.' *Process resilience*, on the other hand, represents the continuous effort to cope that is a 'normal' part of some people's lives. The burn survivors in Holaday and McPhearson's study would say such things as, 'Resilience? It's my spirit and it's the reason I'm here', '[Resilience] is deep inside of you, it's already there, but you have to use it' and 'To do well takes a lot of determination, courage and struggling, but it's your choice' (p. 348).

You can encourage both kinds of resilience in clients. Let's start with outcome resilience. Kerry finds himself in a financial mess because of a tendency to be a spendthrift and because of a few poor financial decisions. He seeks out a financial counsellor who understands the dynamics of resilience. He helps Kerry review the mistakes that have been his downfall and guides him along the sometimes painful path to recovery. Although Kerry makes a couple more mistakes, he gradually works his way out of the mess. It takes more than two years. Along the way he is tempted more than once to declare bankruptcy, but the counsellor helps him review the financial consequences. The ads inviting people to declare bankruptcy don't mention the downside. He gets depressed at times but talks it through with his counsellor. Once he is back on his feet, Kerry spends a bit more time with the counsellor on prevention strategies. A society in which the media focus on, and even idolise, the super-rich is filled with temptations to pursue easy money. Kerry puts himself on a strict budget and things stabilise. It's not difficult for him to walk the financial straight and narrow because the mess has been too painful to repeat. He prides himself on being financially stable.

Process resilience is another matter. Oscar finds that controlling his anger is a constant struggle. He has to keep finding the process-resilience resources within himself needed to keep plugging away. And then there is Nadia, a middle-aged single woman suffering from chronic fatigue syndrome. She has to dig deep within herself every day to find the will to go on. Like many people suffering from this condition, she wants to do her best and even make a good impression (Albrecht & Wallace, 1998). On the days she's successful in pulling herself together, the people she meets cannot believe that she is ill. For her, running into this kind of disbelief is a two-edged sword. On the one hand, her affliction is so painful that she wonders how intelligent people could possibly not notice. On the other hand, she realises that working hard at showing her best face to the world and often enough succeeding in doing so is a victory.

Factors contributing to resilience

Holaday and McPhearson (1997) suggest that core factors that influence resilience include social support, cognitive skills and psychological resources. Certain personality characteristics or dispositions protect people from stress and contribute to 'bounce back'. They include an internal locus of control, empathy, curiosity, a tendency to seek novel experiences, a high activity level, flexibility in new situations, a sense of humour, the ability to elicit positive regard from others, accurate and positive self-appraisal, personal integrity, a sense of self-protectiveness, pride in accomplishments and a capacity for fun. Here are some examples:

- *Social support* got one burn victim going. He said, 'I wanted to give up, but my wife would have none of it. She made me get out of the hospital bed and learn to walk again.' As we have seen, your job is to help clients identify, create and tap into social support.

- The ability to use *fantasy and hope* helps some clients spring back. Fantasy can distract clients from their misery and therefore use whatever resources they have to move forward. One client, in misery because one of his best friends 'stole' the girl to whom he was engaged, told me, 'A long time ago I learned how to deal with chronic back pain by distracting myself from it. I used fantasy a lot and it helped. The pain right now is psychological and it's worse. I'm almost addicted to my pain. I want to find a way to use fantasy again.' And we have already seen the power of hope. One marine who lost both his legs said, 'I'll run again.' And he did.

- A *'belligerent style'* (Zimrin, 1986), rather than a passively enduring, accepting or yielding style, often contributes more to resilience. One of my clients, a 'pleasant' woman in her early 40s, lost her husband to another woman. She moved from being 'pleasant' to being very assertive. She did not run rough-shod over the rights of others, but she did fight for her own. Some of her friends found it hard to interact with the 'new' Geraldine, but her new interpersonal style helped her create a new life.

- Some clients find resilience in newfound ability to *discuss feelings*. One burn survivor said, 'Sometimes I still choose to feel sorry for myself and have a bad day, and that's OK.'

- Another useful coping strategy for some is *avoiding self-blame* and using the *energy of anger* to cope with the world rather than damage the self. One client, who had been severely burned as a child, said, 'When I was little, I wanted the scars to go away, but now I don't care about them anymore. They're part of me. I've stopped apologising for myself.'

- The way clients exercise *personal control* in their lives and how they *interpret* their experiences can contribute to their resilience. One client who fell off the wagon and got drunk for a couple of days said, 'It's a glitch, not a pattern. I can expect a glitch now and again. Glitches can be dealt with. Patterns are damaging.' He was no longer a drunk. For the most part he controlled alcohol rather than vice versa. 'I'm certainly not a drunk but sometimes I'm no better than a lot of others.'

As these examples attest, resilience is not always a 'pretty picture'. Different theoreticians and researchers continue to name different sets of factors that contribute to resilience (Van Vliet, 2008). But there is, at least not yet, no 'scientific' set of such factors. But the growing literature (and life itself) suggests that there is a range of 'resilience levers' in every client. Your job is to help clients discover and pull them together in order to bounce back. Resilience is 'deep inside' your clients. It's part of their self-healing nature. The communication skills described and illustrated earlier are essential for helpers. With them, therapists help clients tap into the pool of resilience found, to a greater or lesser extent, in and around every human being.

Post-traumatic growth

There is a growing literature on 'post-traumatic growth' (Calhoun & Tedeschi, 2006; Joseph, 2009; Joseph & Linley, 2008; Tedeschi & Calhoun, 2004), which is related to outcome resilience but goes beyond it. For instance, Phillips and Daniluk (2004), in exploring the stories of seven adult women who had experienced sexual abuse as children, found that a 'strong sense of resiliency and growth was a persistent theme that wove itself throughout the interviews' (p. 181). One of the women said: 'I wouldn't wish the pain of child abuse on anybody, but I realise that if I hadn't been abused or been through hell like that, I might never have known how unlimited the human spirit is around finding its way through impossible odds. I wouldn't have missed the experience of learning that for the world' (p. 182). Bogar and Hulse-Killacky (2006), in a study of ten women who had been sexually abused as children, discovered what they call 'resiliency determinants' (interpersonally skilled, competent, high self-regard, spiritual, and helpful life circumstances) and 'resiliency processes' (coping strategies, refocusing and moving on, active healing and achieving closure) that facilitated resiliency in these women's adult lives. Park, Lechner, Antoni and Stanton (2009) have edited a book that demonstrates how medical illness can lead to positive life change.

Post-traumatic growth research that focuses on children who have been abused sexually, physically and/ or psychologically is socially and culturally tricky. There is no need to review the huge controversy over such research that erupted at the beginning of this century. But we can take Stephen Joseph's (2009) advice to heart: 'Therapists should be aware of the potential for positive change in their clients following adversity. But, importantly, we need to be careful not to inadvertently imply that there is anything inherently positive in trauma. ... Tedeschi and Calhoun (2004) make it clear that personal growth after trauma should be viewed as originating not from the event, but from within the person themselves through the process of their struggle with the event and its aftermath' (p. 341). So some clients have the ability to seize the horror of abuse or torture or almost any kind of disorder and somehow use it as a stimulus for growth. We can be glad that there is such a thing as post-traumatic growth and that we can help clients in their struggle to benefit from it.

GETTING ALONG WITHOUT A HELPER: A STRIKING CASE

I know people who have remained 'in therapy' for years, but I don't – or perhaps don't want to – understand why. I do understand the following possible approaches to therapy by clients:

- The counsellor helps clients with their plans for constructive change and then clients, using their own initiative and resources, take responsibility for the plans and pursue them on their own.
- Clients continue to see a helper regularly in the implementation phase until the desired changes are 'in place'. Then they keep them in place by using their own internal and external resources.
- Clients, after spending some time with a helper, join some kind of self-help group to get the kind of support they need to continue a change programme successfully. This may be complemented by an occasional one-to-one session with the helper.
- Clients continue to see a helper occasionally, as the need arises.
- Some clients, with debilitating psychological conditions such as bipolar or addiction disorders, find it necessary to tap into therapy throughout their lives.

In the end, however, most clients need to get on with their lives without a helper. Part of the shadow side of helping is the fact that some helpers enter into a covert conspiracy with their clients to maintain the relationship. In effect, talking takes the place of life-enhancing outcomes. In such cases the co-dependent helping relationship becomes the problem rather than the solution.

As indicated earlier, many client problems are managed or coped with, not solved. Consider the following, very real case of a woman who certainly did not choose not to change. Quite the contrary. Her case is an amazing example of a no-formula approach to developing and implementing a programme for constructive change.

Vicky readily admits that she has never fully 'conquered' her illness. Some 20 years ago, she was diagnosed with manic-depressive disorder (now called 'bipolar disorder'). The picture looked something like this: she would spend about six weeks on a high; then the crash would come, and for about six weeks she'd be in the pits. After that she'd be normal for about eight weeks. This cycle meant many trips to the hospital. Some seven years into her illness, during a period in which she was in and out of the hospital, she made a decision. 'I'm not going back into the hospital again. I will so manage my life that hospitalisation will never be necessary.' This non-negotiable goal was her manifesto.

Starting with this declaration of intent, Vicky moved on, in terms of Task B of Stage II, to spell out what she wanted: (1) she would find ways to channel the energy of her 'highs'; (2) she would consistently manage or at least endure the depression and agony of her 'lows'; (3) she would not disrupt the lives of others by her behaviour; (4) she would not make important decisions when either high or low. Vicky, with some help from a rather non-traditional counsellor, began to do things to turn those goals into reality. She used these broad goals to provide direction for everything she did.

Vicky learned as much as she could about her illness, including cues about crisis times and how to deal with both highs and lows. To manage her highs, she learned to channel her excess energy into useful – or at least non-destructive – activity. Some of her strategies for controlling her highs centred on the phone. She knew instinctively that controlling her illness meant not just managing problems but also developing opportunities. During her free time, she would spend long hours on the phone with a host of friends, being careful not to overburden any one person. Phone marathons became part of her lifestyle. She made the point that a big phone bill was infinitely better than a stay in hospital. She called the phone her 'safety valve'. She went so far as to set up her own phone-answering business and worked very hard to make it a success.

She would also do whatever she had to do to tire herself out and get some sleep, for she had learned that sleep was essential if she was to stay out of the hospital. This included working longer shifts at the business. She made exercise an important part of her daily routine. She developed a cadre of supportive people, including her husband. She took special care not to overburden him. She made occasional use of a drop-in crisis centre but preferred avoiding any course of action that reminded her of the hospital.

It must be noted that the central driving force in this case was Vicky's decision to stay out of the hospital. Her determination drove everything else. Urgency became central to Vicky's life. Her case exemplifies the spirit of action that ideally characterises the implementation stage of the helping process. Here is a woman who, with occasional help from a counsellor, took charge of her life and turned her bipolar disorder into an asset. She set some simple goals and devised a set of simple strategies for accomplishing them. She never looked back. And she was never hospitalised again. Some will say that she was not 'cured' by this process. But her goal was not to be cured but to lead as normal a life as possible. Some would say that her approach lacked elegance. Perhaps, but it certainly did not lack results. She seized life.

CHOOSING NOT TO CHANGE

Some clients who seem to do well in analysing problems, developing goals and even identifying reasonable strategies and plans end up by saying – in effect, if not directly – something like this: 'Even though I've explored my problems and understand why things are going wrong – that is, I understand myself and my behaviour better, and I realise what I need to do to change – right now I don't want to pay the price called for by action. The price of more effective living is too high.'

The question of human motivation seems almost as enigmatic now as it must have been at the dawning of the history of the human race. So often we seem to choose our own misery. Worse, we choose to stew in it rather than endure the relatively short-lived pain of behavioural change. Helpers can and should invite clients to challenge themselves to search for incentives and rewards for managing their lives more effectively. They should also help clients understand the consequences of not changing. But in the end, it is the client's choice.

The shadow side of change stands in stark contrast to the case of Vicky. Savvy helpers are not magicians, but they do understand the shadow side of change, learn to see signs of it in each individual case and, in keeping with the values outlined in Chapter 2, do whatever they can to invite clients to challenge themselves to deal with the shadow side of themselves and the world around them. Box 11.2 summarises some of the main principles to be followed in helping clients manage change in their lives.

BOX 11.2   Action-Arrow Guidelines for Implementing Change

Here are some guidelines for helping clients develop a bias for problem-managing and opportunity-developing action as they strive to implement their plans:

- Understand how widespread both inertia and entropy are and how they are affecting this client.
- Help clients become effective tacticians.
- Help clients form 'implementation intentions', especially when obstacles to goal attainment are foreseen.
- Help clients avoid both procrastination and imprudent action.
- Help clients develop contingency plans.
- Help clients discover and manage obstacles to action.
- Help clients discover resources that will enable them to begin acting, to persist and to accomplish their goals.
- Help clients find the incentives and the rewards they need to persevere in action.
- Help clients acquire the skills they need to act and to sustain goal-accomplishing action.
- Help clients develop a social support and challenge system in their day-to-day lives.
- Prepare clients to get along without a helper.
- Come to grips with the fact that helpers need to become agents of change in their own lives.
- Face up to the fact that not every client wants to change.

REVISITING THE 'POWER OF BASICS' OF SUCCESSFUL THERAPY

This book is not the last word on therapy. It is a contemporary book on therapy. It does not address the fads of the helping professions. Rather it focuses on the basics of successful therapy and makes every attempt to describe them logically and clearly. The message is this. Become an expert in the basics and then spend the rest of your career augmenting them with whatever you find best in clinical research and practice. Choose whatever approach to therapy you want but make sure the basics permeate its structure and its delivery. Here are some final words on the basics.

- **The Client.** Never forget that helping is first and foremost about the client. Everything the helping industry creates should serve the client's needs. In professional disputes, let client needs be the arbiter. Befriending diversity is key to therapeutic success.

- **The Therapist.** Make sure that these basics permeate your life and not just your practice. Helping is not theatre; be genuine. Subordinate the excesses of your profession to the needs of your clients. You don't have a success rate. Clients do.

- **The Helping Relationship.** Make the interactions with each client a learning event and then invest whatever knowledge and wisdom you gain in the next client. Collaboration is not just another word; it is at the heart of the helping relationship.

- **Communication Skills.** Prize them. Develop them. Make them second nature. Use them every day in both your public and private life. Teach them to your children. Make dialogue your default communication position.

- **Feedback.** Do your clients a favour by making feedback a part of every session – feedback on between-session progress and feedback on the helpfulness of each session. Get feedback from clients but don't short-change clients by denying them the opportunity to challenge themselves.

- **The Treatment Approach.** Understand the role your approach to treatment plays in the total helping process. While it is not the most important part of helping, your understanding of and commitment to it is important. You should choose an approach that you can communicate with relative ease to your clients. Helping is not something you do to your clients. It's a journey you take together.

- **Problem Management.** You can choose your version of the problem-management process outlined in these pages as your mode of treatment. But remember that every treatment approach, either directly or indirectly, involves the basics of problem management. Problem management is not an add-on. It should permeate your life.

- **Decision Making.** Become an expert in the dynamics and shadow side of decision making because you are making decisions throughout the helping process and you are a coach to clients in the decisions they are making. You will be better prepared to do this if you incorporate the wisdom of decision making in your everyday life.

- **The Beliefs-Values-Norms-Ethics-Morality Factors.** This set of factors permeates everything we do in life and therefore permeates the entire helping process. It constitutes the heart of both social and personal culture. Beliefs and values drive behaviour. It is crucial that you know how these factors influence your own life and that clients know how they drive behaviour in their lives. These factors are the source of some of the major certainties and uncertainties of life. Ethics in the helping professions is often taught as an add-on. Don't be deceived.

Each of these ingredients brings its own set of uncertainties to therapy. Uncertainties bedevil the social sciences. They bedevil the practices that flow from the social sciences such as social work and therapy. Science looks for certainties. Therapy deals with uncertainties on a daily basis. Get comfortable with becoming a professional juggler.

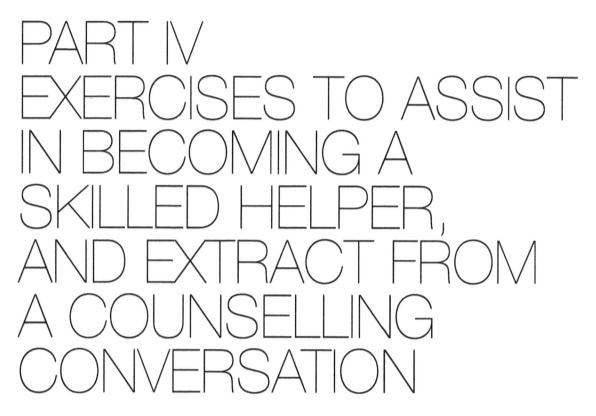

PART IV
EXERCISES TO ASSIST
IN BECOMING A
SKILLED HELPER,
AND EXTRACT FROM
A COUNSELLING
CONVERSATION

Part IV offers a range of helping and counselling skills exercises and activities in Chapter 12, together with an extract from a counselling/helping conversation in Chapter 13.

In Chapter 12, the first set of exercises is for the individual working on their own, the second set is pairs' activities and the third set is group activities.

Chapter 13 provides an annotated extract of counsellor/helper–client discussion. It is offered as an example of *one* way in which a counselling or helping conversation may be conducted. It is not claimed to be *typical* of counselling or helping (although many of the interventions used by the counsellor are used by *many* counsellors). It is offered as an illustration of some counselling interventions and as the focus of possible discussion about the hows and whys of counselling and helping. Many of the interventions illustrated in this sample were discussed earlier in this book.

CHAPTER 12
COUNSELLING SKILLS EXERCISES

Chapter Contents

- Introduction

- Exercises

- Conclusion – Counselling Skills and the Helper

INTRODUCTION

This chapter offers a range of counselling skills exercises and activities. The first set is for the individual working on his or her own, the second set is pairs' activities and the third set is group activities. The second and third group may be used in combination by a group of colleagues working together to enhance their counselling skills. Each exercise should be worked through slowly and plenty of time allowed for processing or discussing the activity afterwards.

As we noted in the last chapter, a useful format for a compelling skills training session is as follows:

- Identification of how the group wants to spend the time
- A theory input and some examples of good counselling practice, either 'live' or shown on video or film
- Using a variety of exercises to develop counselling skills
- Evaluation activities.

The following exercises will serve as the 'exercises to develop counselling skills'. Built into each of the pairs and group exercises is the means to evaluate learning at the end of each activity. It is recommended that the evaluation procedure is followed fairly closely so that the maximum amount of learning may be gained from each exercise. No claims are made that the list of exercises is exhaustive of all possible exercises, and many more may be gleaned from the literature. Many exercises may also be developed by group members themselves.

The 'pairs' format is particularly useful. In this, the group breaks into pairs, each member of which spends some time in the role of 'counsellor' and of 'client'. After a period of practising specific counselling skills, the partners swap roles. This format can be used on a regular basis for practising counselling and may be combined with receiving feedback on skills development from the partner.

All of the work done individually, in pairs or in a group must be followed up quickly by real-life experience. Thus the counsellor must learn to develop the 'conscious use of self' referred to throughout this book. In this way, the helper can make full use of any learning gained by putting it into practice, in real counselling situations. Like all skills, counselling skills must be reinforced if they are to become a regular part of the person's repertoire of behaviour.

EXERCISES

Exercise No. 1

Aim of the exercise   To clarify beliefs and values, prior to undertaking counselling.

Process of the exercise   Write out in a free style a paper which expresses your current set of values and beliefs about human beings, counselling and about yourself. Do not try to make the paper 'academic' in any way and do not worry about style or presentation. Once you have written the paper, consider whether or not it highlights any ambiguities or contradictions in your construing of the world. If so, consider whether or not you will attempt to resolve those contradictions. Consider, also, ways in which your beliefs and values affect your work and your attitude towards counselling. You may or may not choose to show the paper to someone else and have them comment on it.

Exercise No. 2

Aim of the exercise   To consider aspects of yourself and your work that will help or hinder your counselling.

Process of the exercise   'Brainstorm' onto a sheet of paper all those aspects of yourself and your work that you bring to your counselling work. Include in your list those aspects of yourself and your work that you anticipate will cause difficulties. Allow yourself to think and write quickly. Once the list has become fairly lengthy, organise it into 'pluses' and 'minuses'. Consider, then, the degree to which one list is longer than the other and the implications of that. Consider, also, what you intend to do about the 'minuses'.

Exercise No. 3

Aim of the exercise   To enable a continuous means of personal evaluation to be maintained.

Process of the exercise   Keep a journal from the point of taking up counselling. Use the following headings to order the journal:

- Recent skills developed
- Recent problems encountered and problem-solving methods used
- New references to books and journals noted
- Aspects of personal growth.

Journals may usefully be kept by all members of a group working together on developing counselling skills. At each meeting of the group, time can be set aside to discuss journal entries.

Exercise No. 4

Aim of the exercise   To develop 'conscious use of self'.

Process of the exercise   Set aside a time each day when you notice what it is you do and how you do it. Notice patterns of behaviour, speech, proximity to others, use of touch, hand and arm gestures, social skills and so on. Try out new behaviour and new counselling skills as they develop. Allow this time to develop and lengthen until you become more aware of how you react and interact.

Exercise No. 5

Aim of the exercise   To develop the ability to 'notice'.

Process of the exercise   Noticing (sometimes called 'staying awake' or 'conscious awareness') involves setting aside time each day to notice everything that is going on around you. Notice sounds, smells, colours, activity, objects and so on. Allow this period of noticing to develop and lengthen. Use the activity, particularly, when you are with other people.

Exercise No. 6

Aim of the exercise   To develop observational skills, 'conscious use of self' and the ability to 'notice'.

Process of the exercise   Spend 20 minutes each evening, sitting in the same place and at the same time. Allow your attention to focus only on those things that you see, hear, smell or feel outside of yourself. Do not attempt to evaluate what comes in through your senses, but only notice them. Regular use of this activity (akin to certain types of meditation) will improve your ability to keep your attention 'out' and will improve your observational skills.

Exercise No. 7

Aim of the exercise   To experience physical changes in the body, to become more aware of the body and to relax physically.

Process of the exercise   Find a place that is quiet and warm in which you can lie down for about half an hour, undisturbed. Once you have lain down take three deep breaths. Then allow your attention to focus on the muscles in your face. Let them relax. Then focus your attention on the muscles in your shoulders and upper arms. Let them relax. Focus your attention on the muscles in your lower arms and hands. Stretch out your fingers, then let your arms relax. Then put your attention on the muscles in your chest and stomach. Let those muscles relax. Then focus on the muscles in your legs and stretch your feet forward. Then let all the muscles in your legs relax. Then notice how all the muscles in your body are relaxed. Allow yourself to notice what it feels like to be relaxed. Notice, too, parts of the body that you find difficult to relax. After about 10 minutes, stretch gently, allow yourself to sit up and then, slowly, stand up. Notice the difference in the way you feel before and after the activity.

   This exercise may also be used as a stress-reduction activity with clients who find it difficult to relax. It can also be dictated onto an audio recording for use as a means of deep relaxation.

Exercise No. 8

Aim of the exercise   To identify personal strengths and weaknesses in terms of counselling interventions.

Process of the exercise   Consider Heron's (2001) 'Six category intervention analysis':

- Prescriptive interventions: giving advice, offering suggestions
- Informative interventions: offering information

- Confronting interventions: challenging
- Cathartic interventions: helping the client to express emotion
- Catalytic interventions: 'drawing out' the client
- Supportive interventions: encouraging, validating the client.

Identify the two categories that you feel you are least skilled in using at the moment. Then consider the two categories that you are most skilled in using at the moment. Consider the implications of your assessment and anticipate ways that you can enhance your deficiencies.

Exercise No. 9

Aim of the exercise   To plan future objectives.

Process of the exercise   Write down a list of the counselling skills or aspects of counselling that you need to improve upon. Make each of them a specific, behavioural objective and ones that are attainable. Then determine how you will meet those objectives.

Exercise No. 10

Aim of the exercise   To experience problems associated with listening.

Equipment required/environmental considerations   The pair should sit facing each other in chairs of equal height. It is helpful if the room is comfortably warm and free from distractions and interruptions.

The process of the exercise   The pair divide themselves into A and B. A talks to B on any subject for four minutes and B does not listen! After the four minutes, roles are reversed and B talks to A, who does not listen! After the second round, the pair discuss the activity.

Evaluation procedure   At the end of the exercise each person should report to the other what they disliked and what they liked about the activity. They may also comment on what they will be able to carry over from it into the 'real' counselling situation.

Exercise No. 11

Aim of the exercise   To experience problems with the non-verbal aspects of listening.

Equipment required/environmental considerations   The pair should sit facing each other in chairs of equal height. It is helpful if the room is comfortably warm and free from distractions and interruptions.

The process of the exercise   The pair divide themselves into A and B. A talks to B for four minutes about any topic and B listens but contradicts the first four aspects of the SOLER behaviours. Thus B does not sit squarely in relation to A. They fold their arms and their legs. They lean away from their partner and make no eye contact with them. After four minutes, roles are reversed and B talks to A, while A listens but offers contradictory behaviours. After the second four minutes, the pair discuss the exercise.

Evaluation procedure   At the end of the exercise each person should report to the other what they disliked and what they liked about the activity. They may also comment on what they will be able to carry over from it into the 'real' counselling situation.

Exercise No. 12

Aim of the exercise   To experience effective listening and to enhance listening skills.

Equipment required/environmental considerations   The pair should sit facing each other in chairs of equal height. It is helpful if the room is comfortably warm and free from distractions and interruptions.

The process of the exercise   The pair divide themselves into A and B. A talks to B for four minutes about any topic and B listens, observing the SOLER behaviours. Thus they sit squarely in an open position. They lean slightly towards their partner and maintain good eye contact. They also relax and do nothing but listen. It is important that this is not a conversation but a listening exercise. After four minutes, roles are reversed and B talks to A, who listens appropriately. After the second four minutes the pair discuss the exercise and compare it with the previous two.

Evaluation procedure   At the end of the exercise each person should report to the other what they disliked and what they liked about the activity. They may also comment on what they will be able to carry over from it into the 'real' counselling situation.

Exercise No. 13

Aim of the exercise   To practise effective listening and to evaluate the effectiveness of the listening.

Equipment required/environmental considerations   The pair should sit facing each other in chairs of equal height. It is helpful if the room is comfortably warm and free from distractions and interruptions.

The process of the exercise   The pair divide themselves into A and B. A talks to B for four minutes on any topic. B listens and periodically 'recaps' what A has said, to A's satisfaction. After four minutes, roles are reversed and B talks to A, who listens and periodically recaps. After a further four minutes, the pair discuss the exercise.

Evaluation procedure   At the end of the exercise each person should report to the other what they disliked and what they liked about the activity. They may also comment on what they will be able to carry over from it into the 'real' counselling situation.

Exercise No. 14

Aim of the exercise   To discriminate between open and closed questions.

Equipment required/environmental considerations   The pair should sit facing each other in chairs of equal height. It is helpful if the room is comfortably warm and free from distractions and interruptions. A pencil and paper are needed for this activity.

The process of the exercise   Both partners jot down the following sequence: O,O,C,C,O,C,O,C. Then the pair divide themselves into A and B. A then asks questions of B on any of the following topics:

- Current issues at work
- Recent holidays
- The current political situation.

The questions are asked in the sequence noted (i.e. 'open question, open question, closed question, closed question' and so on) until they have all been asked. Then the pair swap roles and B asks questions of A, in that sequence and on one of those topics.

Evaluation procedure At the end of the exercise each person should report to the other what they disliked and what they liked about the activity. They may also comment on what they will be able to carry over from it into the 'real' counselling situation.

Exercise No. 15

Aim of the exercise To practise 'funnelling' in questioning.

Equipment required/environmental considerations The pair should sit facing each other in chairs of equal height. It is helpful if the room is comfortably warm and free from distractions and interruptions.

The process of the exercise The pair divide themselves into A and B. A then asks questions of B on any subject they wish, starting with a very broad open question and slowly allowing the questions to become more specific and focused. After four minutes, the pair swap roles and B asks questions of A, moving from the general to the particular.

Evaluation procedure At the end of the exercise each person should report to the other what they disliked and what they liked about the activity. They may also comment on what they will be able to carry over from it into the 'real' counselling situation.

Exercise No. 16

Aim of the exercise To practise 'reflection' and 'selective reflection'.

Equipment required/environmental considerations The pair should sit facing each other in chairs of equal height. It is helpful if the room is comfortably warm and free from distractions and interruptions.

The process of the exercise The pair divide themselves into A and B. A talks to B about any subject and A uses only reflection or selective reflection to encourage them to continue. This should be carried on for about six minutes. After six minutes, roles are reversed and B talks to A who uses only reflection or selective reflection as a response. For details of these two techniques, see the chapter on client-centred counselling skills (Chapter 2).

Evaluation procedure At the end of the exercise each person should report to the other what they disliked and what they liked about the activity. They may also comment on what they will be able to carry over from it into the 'real' counselling situation.

Exercise No. 17

Aim of the exercise To practise a range of client-centred counselling skills.

Equipment required/environmental considerations The pair should sit facing each other in chairs of equal height. It is helpful if the room is comfortably warm and free from distractions and interruptions.

The process of the exercise The pair divide themselves into A and B. A then begins to 'counsel' B but restricts themselves only to the following types of interventions:

- Open or closed questions
- Reflections or selective reflections
- Checking for understanding
- Empathy-building statements.

The counselling session should continue for at least ten minutes, then both partners change roles for a further ten minutes. There should be no sense of play-acting or role-playing about the exercise. Both partners should counsel on 'real' issues and thus develop realistic skills. This exercise, like the previous one, is very difficult because both parties are 'in the know'.

Evaluation procedure   At the end of the exercise each person should report to the other what they disliked and what they liked about the activity. They may also comment on what they will be able to carry over from it into the 'real' counselling situation.

Exercise No. 18

Aim of the exercise   To experience being asked a wide range of questions.

Equipment required/environmental considerations   The pair should sit facing each other in chairs of equal height. It is helpful if the room is comfortably warm and free from distractions and interruptions.

The process of the exercise   The pair divide themselves into A and B. A then asks a wide range of questions, on any topic at all, for five minutes and B does not respond to them or answer them. After five minutes, roles are reversed and B asks questions of A, who does not respond to them. It is important for both partners to notice how they feel about asking and being asked very personal questions.

Evaluation procedure   At the end of the exercise each person should report to the other what they disliked and what they liked about the activity. They may also comment on what they will be able to carry over from it into the 'real' counselling situation.

Exercise No. 19

Aim of the exercise   To notice the difference between being asked questions and making statements.

Equipment required/environmental considerations   The pair should sit facing each other in chairs of equal height. It is helpful if the room is comfortably warm and free from distractions and interruptions.

The process of the exercise   The pair divide themselves into A and B. A sits and makes a series of statements, on any topic, to B for five minutes. B listens to the statements but does not respond to them. After five minutes, roles are reversed and B makes a series of statements to A who only listens. Afterwards, the pair discuss the perceived differences between how this exercise felt and how the previous one felt. They discuss, also, the relative merits of questions and statements with regard to counselling.

Evaluation procedure   At the end of the exercise each person should report to the other what they disliked and what they liked about the activity. They may also comment on what they will be able to carry over from it into the 'real' counselling situation.

Exercise No. 20

Aim of the exercise   To explore personal history.

Equipment required/environmental considerations   The pair should sit facing each other in chairs of equal height. It is helpful if the room is comfortably warm and free from distractions and interruptions.

The process of the exercise   The pair divide themselves into A and B. A talks to B for 10 minutes and reviews their life history to date. Any aspects may be included or left out but some sort of chronological order should be aimed at. After 10 minutes, roles are reversed and B reviews their biography to date, while A listens but does not comment.

Evaluation procedure   At the end of the exercise each person should report to the other what they disliked and what they liked about the activity. They may also comment on what they will be able to carry over from it into the 'real' counselling situation.

Exercise No. 21

Aim of the exercise   To explore 'free association'.

Equipment required/environmental considerations   The pair should sit facing each other in chairs of equal height. It is helpful if the room is comfortably warm and free from distractions and interruptions.

The process of the exercise   The pair divide themselves into A and B. A sits and verbalises whatever comes into their head, whilst B sits and listens only. Everything possible should be verbalised but A should note the things that they do not verbalise. This process continues for three minutes, after which the pair swap roles and B attempts 'free association' accompanied by A's attention and listening. Afterwards the pair discuss the implications of the activity for themselves and for their counselling practice.

Evaluation procedure   At the end of the exercise each person should report to the other what they disliked and what they liked about the activity. They may also comment on what they will be able to carry over from it into the 'real' counselling situation.

Exercise No. 22

Aim of the exercise   To self-evaluate.

Equipment required/environmental considerations   The pair should sit facing each other in chairs of equal height. It is helpful if the room is comfortably warm and free from distractions and interruptions.

The process of the exercise   The pair divide themselves into A and B. A then considers and verbalises all the positive and negative aspects of their counselling practice to date. Negative considerations should be made first. When A has finished, B goes through the same process. Afterwards, the pair consider the implications of their evaluations for their counselling practice.

Evaluation procedure   At the end of the exercise each person should report to the other what they disliked and what they liked about the activity. They may also comment on what they will be able to carry over from it into the 'real' counselling situation.

Exercise No. 23

Aim of the exercise   To receive feedback on counselling skills.

Equipment required/environmental considerations   The pair should sit facing each other in chairs of equal height. It is helpful if the room is comfortably warm and free from distractions and interruptions.

The process of the exercise   The pair divide themselves into A and B. A then offers B both positive and negative feedback as to how they perceive the other's counselling skills. Negative comments should be made first. Then B offers A feedback on their counselling skills. Afterwards both partners consider the implications of this feedback for their counselling practice and compare it with their own self-evaluation.

Evaluation procedure   At the end of the exercise each person should report to the other what they disliked and what they liked about the activity. They may also comment on what they will be able to carry over from it into the 'real' counselling situation.

Exercise No. 24

Aim of exercise   To increase the listening and attending skills of group members.

Number of participants   Any number between 5 and 20.

Time required   Between 1 and 1½ hours.

Equipment required/environmental considerations   The group should sit in chairs of equal height and in a circle. It is helpful if the room is comfortably warm and does not contain too many distractions.

The process of the exercise   The group holds a discussion on any topic. One ground rule applies throughout the exercise: once the first person has spoken, before anyone else contributes to the discussion, they must first summarise what the person before them has said, to that person's satisfaction. After half an hour, the group discusses the activity.

Evaluation procedure   Learning from the exercise is evaluated by two 'rounds'. First, each person in turn says what they did not like about the exercise. Then, each person in turn says what they did like about the activity. A third round can be used to establish how each person will use the learning gained, in the future.

Variations on the exercise

1   The facilitator chooses a topic for discussion, e.g.:
   - qualities of the effective counsellor
   - how we can become better counsellors
   - how this group is developing.
2   The larger group can break into small groups of four or five to carry out the exercise and then have a plenary session back in the larger group.

Exercise No. 25

Aim of exercise   To practise asking questions in a group and to experience being asked questions.

Number of participants   Any number between 5 and 20.

Time required   Between 1 and 1½ hours.

Equipment required/environmental considerations   The group should sit in chairs of equal height and in a circle. It is helpful if the room is comfortably warm and does not contain too many distractions.

The process of the exercise   Each person, in turn, spends five minutes in the 'hot seat'. When occupying the hot seat, they may be asked questions, on any subject, by any member of the group. If they wish not to answer a particular question, they may say 'pass'. At the end of the person's five minutes in the hot seat, they nominate the next person to occupy it, until all members of the group have had a five-minute turn.

Procedure   Learning from the exercise is evaluated by two 'rounds'. First, each person in turn says what they did not like about the exercise. Then, each person in turn says what they did like about the activity. A third round can be used to establish how each person will use the learning gained in the future.

Variations on the exercise

1   The time in the hot seat may be varied from 2 to 10 minutes depending upon the size of the group and the time available.
2   A large group may be split up into smaller groups.
3   With a group in which members know each other very well, the 'pass' facility may be abandoned.

Exercise No. 26

Aim of exercise   To experience clear communication within the group.

Number of participants   Any number between 5 and 20.

Time required   Between 1 and 1½ hours.

Equipment required/environmental considerations   The group should sit in chairs of equal height and in a circle. It is helpful if the room is comfortably warm and does not contain too many distractions.

The process of the exercise   The group holds a discussion on any topic, and observes the following ground rules:

- Speak directly, using 'I' rather than 'you', 'we' or 'one'.
- Speak directly to others, using the first person.
- Stay in the present.
- Avoid theorising about what is going on in the group.

Either the facilitator acts as guardian of the ground rules or the group monitors itself.

Evaluation procedure   Learning from the exercise is evaluated by two 'rounds'. First, each person in turn says what they did not like about the exercise. Then, each person in turn says what they did like about the activity. A third round can be used to establish how each person will use the learning gained in the future.

Variations on the exercise   No topic is chosen by or for the group: the material for discussion evolves out of what is happening in the 'here and now'.

Exercise No. 27

Aim of exercise   To experience participation in a 'leaderless' group and to consider the dynamics of such an activity.

Number of participants   Any number between 5 and 20.

Time required   Between 1 and 1½ hours.

Equipment required/environmental considerations   The group should sit in chairs of equal height and in a circle. It is helpful if the room is comfortably warm and does not contain too many distractions. An object to use as a 'conch' is required.

The process of the exercise   The group has a discussion on any topic. In order to speak, however, members must be in possession of the 'conch': an object which signifies that, at that moment, the person holding it is leading the group. Other people who wish to speak must non-verbally negotiate for possession of the conch. After about half an hour, the group drops the 'conch' rule and freely discusses the activity.

Evaluation procedure   Learning from the exercise is evaluated by two 'rounds'. First, each person in turn says what they did not like about the exercise. Then, each person in turn says what they did like about the activity. A third round can be used to establish how each person will use the learning gained in the future.

Variations on the exercise

1   The facilitator chooses a topic for the group to discuss.
2   A rule may be introduced whereby each person may only make one statement when in possession of the 'conch'.

Exercise No. 28

Aim of exercise   To practise using client-centred counselling interventions in a group.

Number of participants   Any number between 5 and 20.

Time required   Between 1 and 1½ hours.

Equipment required/environmental considerations   The group should sit in chairs of equal height and in a circle. It is helpful if the room is comfortably warm and does not contain too many distractions.

The process of the exercise   The group members are only allowed to:

- Ask questions of each other
- Practise reflections
- Offer empathy-building statements
- Check for understanding of each other.

After half an hour, the group discusses the exercise, having dropped the rule about types of interventions.

Evaluation procedure   Learning from the exercise is evaluated by two 'rounds'. First, each person in turn says what they did not like about the exercise. Then, each person in turn says what they did like about the activity. A third round can be used to establish how each person will use the learning gained in the future.

Variations on the exercise

1   One group member is invited to facilitate a general discussion with the group using only: (a) questions, (b) reflections, (c) empathy-building statements or (d) checking for understanding. Afterwards, the group offers that person feedback on their performance.
2   Group members, in turn, facilitate a discussion using only the aforementioned types of interventions, for periods of 10 minutes each.

Exercise No. 29

Aim of exercise   To explore silence in a group context.

Number of participants   Any number between 5 and 20.

Time required   Between 1 and 1 ½ hours.

Equipment required/environmental considerations   The group should sit in chairs of equal height and in a circle. It is helpful if the room is comfortably warm and does not contain too many distractions.

The process of the exercise   The group facilitator suggests to the group that they sit in total silence for a period of five minutes. When the five minutes are over, the group discusses the experience.

Evaluation procedure   Learning from the exercise is evaluated by two 'rounds'. First, each person in turn says what they did not like about the exercise. Then, each person in turn says what they did like about the activity. A third round can be used to establish how each person will use the learning gained in the future.

Variations on the exercise   The group may sit in silence with their eyes closed.

Exercise No. 30

Aim of exercise   To explore a variety of facets of counselling.

Number of participants   Any number between 5 and 20.

Time required   Between 1 and 1½ hours.

Equipment required/environmental considerations   The group should sit in chairs of equal height and in a circle. It is helpful if the room is comfortably warm and does not contain too many distractions. A large sheet of paper or a black- or whiteboard is required for this activity.

The process of the exercise   The group carries out a 'brainstorming' activity. One member of the group acts as 'scribe' and jots down on a large sheet of paper or a black- or whiteboard all comments from the group on one of the following topics. No contributions are discarded and group members are to be encouraged to call out any associations they make with the topic:

- Qualities of an effective counsellor
- Problems/difficulties of this group
- Activities for improving counselling skills
- Qualities of the ineffective counsellor
- Skills required for effective counselling
- Problems that helpers are likely to encounter in counselling.

Evaluation procedure   Learning from the exercise is evaluated by two 'rounds'. First, each person in turn says what they did not like about the exercise. Then, each person in turn says what they did like about the activity. A third round can be used to establish how each person will use the learning gained in the future.

Exercise No. 31

Aim of exercise   To receive feedback from other group members.

Number of participants   Any number between 5 and 20.

Time required   Between 1 and 1½ hours.

Equipment required/environmental considerations   The group should sit in chairs of equal height and in a circle. It is helpful if the room is comfortably warm and does not contain too many distractions.

The process of the exercise   Each member of the group, in turn, listens to other members of the group offering them positive feedback, i.e. things they like about that person. The feedback is given in the form of a 'round', with each person in turn offering feedback until every group member has spoken. The group member receiving feedback is not allowed to 'respond' to the comments but must listen in silence.

Evaluation procedure   Learning from the exercise is evaluated by two 'rounds'. First, each person in turn says what they did not like about the exercise. Then, each person in turn says what they did like about the activity. A third round can be used to establish how each person will use the learning gained in the future.

Variations on the exercise   With a group where members know each other very well, a round of negative feedback may be offered to each group member, if they require it. This activity should be handled with care.

Exercise No. 32

Aim of exercise   To carry out a peer and group evaluation.

Number of participants   Any number between 5 and 20.

Time required   Between 1 and 1½ hours.

Equipment required/environmental considerations   The group should sit in chairs of equal height and in a circle. It is helpful if the room is comfortably warm and does not contain too many distractions.

The process of the exercise   The group identifies six criteria for evaluating members of the group, e.g.:

- Contribution to activities
- Self-disclosure
- Contribution of new ideas to the group, etc.

Then each group member silently jots down their own evaluation of themselves under these six headings. When all members have finished, each reads out their notes to the rest of the group and invites feedback from other group members on those six criteria. The process is repeated until all group members have both verbalised their evaluation and received feedback from other group members.

Evaluation procedure   Learning from the exercise is evaluated by two 'rounds'. First, each person in turn says what they did not like about the exercise. Then, each person in turn says what they did like about the activity. A third round can be used to establish how each person will use the learning gained in the future.

Variations on the exercise   The feedback from the group may be offered systematically: each group member, in turn, working round the group, offers the individual feedback on their performance.

Exercise No. 33

Aim of exercise   To explore a spontaneous and leaderless group activity: the 'Quaker' group.

Number of participants   Any number between 5 and 20.

Time required   Between 1 and 1½ hours.

Equipment required/environmental considerations   The group should sit in chairs of equal height and in a circle. It is helpful if the room is comfortably warm and does not contain too many distractions.

The process of the exercise   The group has no topic for discussion and no leader. Group members are encouraged to verbalise what they are feeling and what they are thinking as those thoughts and feelings occur, but there is no obligation for anyone else to respond to the statements offered. The group may fall into silence at times and at others be very noisy. The group exercise should be allowed to run for at least three-quarters of an hour. After that period, group members can freely discuss how it felt to take part in the activity.

Evaluation procedure   Learning from the exercise is evaluated by two 'rounds'. First, each person in turn says what they did not like about the exercise. Then, each person in turn says what they did like about the activity. A third round can be used to establish how each person will use the learning gained in the future.

Variations on the exercise   A topic may be chosen for the group to consider, but no direction is offered by the group facilitator, and group members make statements about the topic as and when they choose.

CONCLUSION – COUNSELLING SKILLS AND THE HELPER

These are a range of counselling and helping skills exercises that have been used by the writer in a variety of contexts to help in the development of counselling and interpersonal skills. They can be modified and adapted to suit the specific needs of particular groups of helpers. Often, too, as we have noted, the best exercises are those that you devise yourself: the group that learns to identify its particular needs and then develop exercises to explore a particular skill can quickly become an autonomous learning group.

Learning to practise as a helper and counsellor can be an exciting and challenging process. It is hoped that this book has offered some signposts towards directions in which counselling expertise may be gained by the helper. The rest is up to the individual or the group.

CHAPTER 13 EXTRACT FROM A COUNSELLING CONVERSATION

This annotated extract of counsellor–client discussion is offered as an example of *one* way in which a counselling or helping conversation may be conducted. It is not claimed to be *typical* of counselling or helping (although many of the interventions used by the counsellor are used by *many* counsellors). It is offered as an illustration of some counselling interventions and as the focus of possible discussion about the hows and whys of counselling. Most of the interventions illustrated in this sample were discussed earlier in this book.

The conversation described here is free-ranging and exploratory in nature. Conversations that took place later might be more focused. The early stages of counselling are often 'ground-clearing' in nature: they allow the client to open up and to begin to explore a range of issues. Often the 'real' issues don't emerge until the client has been allowed to 'wander' a little through a number of issues.

COUNSELLOR: Hello, how can I help?[1]

CLIENT: Well, I don't know really. I just need to talk some things through. I don't really know where to start.[2]

COUNSELLOR: Tell me a little bit about yourself.[3]

CLIENT: I'm 32, married with two small children. I work as a nursing assistant in a small cottage hospital. We've been married for 10 years and... things ... aren't working out...[4]

COUNSELLOR: Things aren't working out...[5]

---

[1] Broad, opening question, perhaps *too* broad.
[2] Client has problems answering it, so...
[3] Counsellor asks a more specific question. The question allows the client to begin to talk about himself.
[4] After brief biographical details, the client alludes to problems.
[5] Client offers straight *reflection*.

CLIENT: Well, not properly. Me and my wife are unhappy with the way things are at the moment.

COUNSELLOR: What's your wife's name?[6]

CLIENT: Jane. She *says* she's happy enough but I don't really think we communicate very well.

COUNSELLOR: Jane says she's happy enough. . .[7]

CLIENT: She hasn't actually *said* that but I always get the impression that things are alright for her. On the other hand, we don't talk very much to each other. We sort of live parallel lives, I think.

COUNSELLOR: What do you *need* to talk about?[8]

CLIENT: Almost everything! How we feel about each other and the children. Our relationship. . . sex. Everything really.[9]

COUNSELLOR: Was there a time when you *did* talk to each other?[10]

CLIENT: Yes. We *always* used to talk. . . When we first got married, we talked about everything we did. We had no secrets from each other and we used to go out about twice a week and we couldn't stop talking. Now we can't really *start!*

COUNSELLOR: When did you stop?[11]

CLIENT: We just drifted into it, I suppose. . . you know how it is. . .

COUNSELLOR: There was nothing, particular, that stopped you. . .?[12]

CLIENT: Well, yes, there was. I. . . I had an affair a couple of years ago. I met this girl at work and we got quite serious for a while. I ended up telling Jane and she was, obviously, very upset – so was I – and we talked about it all. . . She reckoned she forgave me. . . I'm not sure she has. . .[13]

COUNSELLOR: You're not sure she forgave you. . .[14]

CLIENT: No. I know she hasn't. She brings it up, sometimes, when we have an argument. She sort of throws it in my face. She *hated* Sarah. . . I suppose I can't blame her. I suppose I would hate it if *Jane* had an affair. . .

COUNSELLOR: Would you?[15]

CLIENT: (Laughs, nervously). I was just wondering about that! It sounds awful, but sometimes I wish she *would* have an affair. That would sort of even things up. It would make things a bit more balanced.

COUNSELLOR: It would make you feel better?[16]

---

[6] Counsellor encourages the client to *personalise* the relationship.

[7] Counsellor offers a *selective reflection* and picks up on the tone of voice and emphasis offered by the client.

[8] This is a slightly confronting and challenging question.

[9] Client's response suggests that the intervention may have been too direct. His response suggests that *everything* needs to be talked about.

[10] As a result, the counsellor 'backs off' a little and asks a more general question about communication.

[11] Now, the counsellor returns to a very specific and challenging question.

[12] Counsellor, picking up on non-verbal behaviour, persists in trying to focus the conversation.

[13] Considerable disclosure on the part of the client and first indication of what may be at the *heart* of some of the problems.

[14] Counsellor offers a *reflection* on the issue of forgiveness.

[15] A challenge from the counsellor. The client's statement is checked and seems to strike a chord.

[16] A slightly judgemental response from the counsellor.

CLIENT: I suppose so. I feel really guilty about what happened with Sarah.[17]

COUNSELLOR: What *did* happen?[18]

CLIENT: Well, we talked about setting up together. At one stage, I was going to leave Jane and move in with Sarah.

COUNSELLOR: Did you discuss that with Jane?

CLIENT: No, not at all. Me and Sarah used to talk about it a lot. Sarah wasn't married or anything – she was only young. . . 18. . . and she reckoned we could live together and that it would all work out. . .

COUNSELLOR: So what happened?[19]

CLIENT: She gave me an ultimatum. Either I told Jane that I was leaving her or *she* would leave. . .

COUNSELLOR: And you chose to stay with Jane?

CLIENT: Yes. I told Sarah that I wasn't going to leave her and the children. I *couldn't* leave. . . it would have been the end of things. . .

COUNSELLOR: What's happening now. . .?[20]

CLIENT: I'm feeling upset. . . I'm a bit embarrassed I think. . . (begins to cry).

COUNSELLOR: It's OK if you cry . . . you're allowed to have feelings. . .[21]

CLIENT: I just. . . bottled them up a bit, I suppose. . . I just sort of froze after we finished and I went back home. . . I just couldn't settle back down with Jane. I felt guilty. . .[22]

COUNSELLOR: And how are you feeling now?[23]

CLIENT: Still guilty. . . I *wish* I hadn't messed things up at home. It wasn't fair to Jane or the children. . .

COUNSELLOR: Or to you?

CLIENT: No, I suppose not. Though I *chose* to go out with Sarah. . . no one made me do it![24]

COUNSELLOR: Why did you?

CLIENT: Because I liked her. She had a sense of humour and she liked me. We got on well together and everything. It just sort of happened. . .

COUNSELLOR: But you *chose* to go out with her?[25]

CLIENT: Yes, I can remember that. I can remember the day when I made that decision. . .[26]

---

[17] Client's response may be in direct response to the counsellor's slightly judgemental tone. Counsellor notes this and moves on.

[18] Counsellor invites the client to be specific about the relationship.

[19] Again, the counsellor looks for *specifics* and helps the client to focus on the discussion.

[20] At this point, the client looks at the floor and his tone of voice and facial colour change. The counsellor notes these non-verbal changes and asks the client what is happening.

[21] Counsellor 'gives permission' to the client.

[22] Client identifies a mixture of feelings.

[23] Counsellor brings the client to the 'present time'. It might be possible to return to the feelings 'in the past', later in the counselling session. At this point, though, the counsellor has made a decision to return to the present.

[24] Client accepts 'responsibility' for the relationship.

[25] Counsellor persists with the 'responsibility' issue, perhaps a little too much.

[26] On the other hand, it leads the client to a *specific* remembrance.

COUNSELLOR: Can you describe it?[27]

CLIENT: I was at work and she came on duty. We talked a bit over coffee and everything and she kept looking at me and smiling. I can remember . . . it was 3.30 . . . and I said . . . (begins to cry again) . . . I asked her if she would go out with me . . .

COUNSELLOR: That was a tough decision?[28]

CLIENT: It was horrible, looking back! I should never have said it. . . I fancied her. . . I thought I loved her at the time. . .

COUNSELLOR: Did you love her?[29]

CLIENT: Yes! That's the problem. . . I did love her. . .

COUNSELLOR: What's happening now. . .?[30]

CLIENT: I feel sort of angry. . .

COUNSELLOR: Who with?

CLIENT: Sarah. . . (goes quiet). . . me . . .

COUNSELLOR: You're angry with yourself. . .[31]

CLIENT: With both of us. We were like adolescents! She *was* adolescent, sort of. . .

COUNSELLOR: And you were older. . .[32]

CLIENT: I suppose I should have known better. I *was* older.

COUNSELLOR: And because you were older, you were supposed to be in control?

CLIENT: I suppose it doesn't work quite like that, does it? I suppose we were both responsible in some ways for what happened.

COUNSELLOR: What was happening at home, with Jane?[33]

CLIENT: Nothing much. We were getting on OK. The children were quite small and Jane was caught up with them. She gave up work around that time and gave all her time to them.

COUNSELLOR: Leaving you out?[34]

CLIENT :   (Grins) That's awful, isn't it? Yes, I suppose I felt left out. . . Sarah was there at the right – the *wrong* time. . . and we just. . .

COUNSELLOR: How do you feel about Sarah now? If you met her again. . .?[35]

CLIENT: I wouldn't want to. It wouldn't work, now. We wouldn't have much in common any more. I've changed. . .

---

[27] Counsellor invites client to offer a 'literal description' of the events of the time. Sometimes such invitations lead to further cathartic (emotional) release.

[28] Counsellor offers an 'empathy-building' statement. If it is 'right', the client will agree.

[29] Challenging and confronting question on the part of the counsellor.

[30] Again, the counsellor notes non-verbal changes and invites the client to verbalise what is happening.

[31] Counsellor offers a mixture of *reflection* and empathy *building*.

[32] Counsellor finishes the client's sentence.

[33] Counsellor changes tack and asks about the 'home' situation.

[34] Counsellor seems to respond to an *unspoken* thought and to the client's non-verbal behaviours.

[35] Counsellor checks 'present time' feelings.

COUNSELLOR: You *and* Jane have changed?

CLIENT: Yes, I think so.

COUNSELLOR: Does it all date back to when you were going out with Sarah?

CLIENT: Not completely. It goes back further than that.

COUNSELLOR: Let me just check where we've got to so far. You feel that you and Jane aren't communicating and, on the one hand, you feel that this dates back to when you met Sarah. On the other, you feel that it goes back much further. . .?[36]

CLIENT: Yes, that's it, so far. I guess a lot of it has to do with things that happened way back. . . Those things are going to be more difficult to talk about. . .

COUNSELLOR: Well, we can make a start. . .[37]

Key issues demonstrated in this extract

- The counsellor 'takes the lead' from the client and 'follows' him.
- The counsellor listens, not only to the words that the client uses but also to the non-verbal signals.
- The counsellor clarifies what he or she does not understand or follow.
- The counsellor is prepared to challenge issues raised by the client.
- The counsellor, by his or her approach, indicates that *anything* can be talked about and that *feelings* can be expressed.

CONCLUSION

This book has covered a wide range of aspects of counselling and helping skills. In essence, there are few laws of counselling and the helper/counsellor functions best when they encourage the client to find his or her own way through.

The key aim of helping and counselling should be to listen to and understand the client's point of view, and effective listening is the bedrock of achieving this. As human beings we all develop a sort of personal theory about the world, and it is that theory which guides us. The client's personal theory is the key to the helper understanding what it is that the client does in their life and the direction in which they want their life to go.

---

[36] The counsellor offers a summary of what has been talked about so far. In this respect, the counsellor is checking *for understanding*.

[37] The counsellor indicates an openness to listening to 'anything' and quietly gives the client permission to talk further and deeper.

References

ABRAMSON, P. R., Cloud, M. Y., Keese, N. & Keese, R. (1994, Spring). How much is too much? Dependency in a psychotherapeutic relationship. *American Journal of Psychotherapy*, 48, 294–301.

ACHTZIGER, A., Gollwitzer, P. M. & Sheeran, P. (2008). Implementation intentions and shielding goal striving from unwanted thoughts and feelings. *Personality and Social Psychology Bulletin*, 34(3), 381–393.

ACKERMAN, S. J. & Hilsenroth, M. J. (2003). A review of therapist characteristics and techniques positively impacting the therapeutic alliance. *Clinical Psychology Review*, 23, 1–33.

ADAIR, J. (2010). *Decision making and problem solving strategies* (2nd ed.). London: Kogan Page.

ADLER, R. B., Proctor, R. F. & Towne, N. (2007). *Looking out, looking in* (12th ed.). Belmont, CA: Wadsworth.

ALBRECHT, F. & Wallace, M. (1998). Detecting chronic fatigue syndrome: The role of counselors. *Journal of Counseling and Development*, 76, 183–188.

ALTMAIER, E. M., Russell, D. W., Kao, C. F., Lehmann, T. R. & Weinstein, J. N. (1993). Role of self-efficacy in rehabilitation outcome among chronic low back pain patients. *Journal of Counseling Psychology*, 40, 335–339.

ALVORD, M. K. & Grados, J. J. (2005). Enhancing resilience in children: A proactive approach. *Professional Psychology: Research and Practice*, 36, 238–245.

AMBROSE, G. & Harris, P. (2010). *Basics design 08: Design thinking*. Worthing, UK: Ava Publishing.

America in the Middle East: Night turns into day? (2005). *The Economist*. www.economist.com/leaders/2005/02/03/night-turns-into-day

ANDREOU, A. (2007). Environmental preservation and second-order procrastination. *Philosophy & Public Affairs*, 35(3), 233–248.

ANGUS, L. & Kagan, F. (2007). Empathic relational bonds and personal agency in psychotherapy: Implications for psychotherapy supervision, practice, and research. *Psychotherapy: Theory, Research, Practice, Training*, 44(4), 371–377.

ANGUS, L. E. & Greenberg, L. S. (2012). *Working with narrative in emotion-focused therapy: Changing stories, healing lives*. Washington, DC: American Psychological Association Books.

ANGUS, L. E. & McLeod, J. (Eds.). (2004). *The handbook of narrative and psychotherapy: Practice, theory and research*. Thousand Oaks, CA: Sage.

ANTONY, M.M. & Swinson, R.P. (2009). *When perfect isn't good enough: Strategies for coping with perfectionism* (2nd ed.). Oakland, CA: New Harbinger Publications Inc.

ARGYRIS, C. (1980). *Inner contradictions of rigorous research*. New York: Academic Press.

ARGYRIS, C. (1999). *On organizational learning* (2nd ed.). Cambridge, MA: Blackwell.

ARGYRIS, C. & Schön, D. A. (1974). *Theory in practice: Increasing professional effectiveness*. San Francisco, CA: Jossey-Bass.

ARIELY, D. (2010a). *Predictably irrational: The hidden forces that shape our decisions* (Rev. ed.). New York: HarperCollins.

ARIELY, D. (2010b). *The upside of irrationality: The unexpected benefits of defying logic at work and at home*. New York: HarperCollins.

ARKOWITZ, H. & Westra, H. A. (Eds.). (2008). *Motivational interviewing in the treatment of psychological problems*. New York: The Guilford Press.

ARNETT, J. J. (2000, May). Emerging adulthood: A theory of development from the late teens through the twenties. *American Psychologist, 55*, 469–480.

ARNOLD, E. C., & Boggs, K.U. (2020). *Interpersonal relationships: Professional communication skills for nurses* (8th ed.). Missouri: Elsevier Inc.

ASPINWALL, L. G. & Staudinger, U. M. (Eds.). (2003). *A psychology of human strengths: Fundamental questions and future directions for a positive psychology*. Washington, DC: American Psychological Association Books.

AUERBACH, C. F., Salick, E. & Fine, J. (2006). Using grounded theory to develop treatment strategies for multi-contextual trauma. *Professional Psychology: Research and Practice, 37*, 367–373.

AZAR, B. (1995). Breaking through barriers to creativity. *Monitor, 26*(8), 1, 20.

AZAR, D., Ball, K., Salmon, J. & Cleland, V. J. (2010). Physical activity correlates in young women with depressive symptoms: A qualitative study. *International Journal of Behavioral Nutrition and Physical activity, 7*(3). doi.org/10.1186/1479-5868-7-3

BACH, P. & Moran, D. (2008). *ACT in practice: Case conceptualization in acceptance and commitment therapy*. Oakland, CA: New Harbinger.

BACHELOR, A., Laverdière, O., Gamache, D. & Bordeleau, V. (2007). Clients' collaboration in therapy: Self-perceptions and relationships with client psychological functioning, interpersonal relations, and motivation. *Psychotherapy: Theory, Research, Practice, Training, 44*, 175–192.

BAILEY, R. (2017, July). Physical activity after stroke: Exploring self-efficacy, self-regulation, social support and outcome expectations. *The American Journal of Occupational Therapy, 33*(2), 129–141, DOI: 10.1080/07380577.2018.1558326

BAK, W. (2015). Possible selves: Implications for psychotherapy. *International Journal of Mental Health Addiction, 13*(5), 650–658.

BANDURA, A. (1986). *Social foundations of thought and action: A social cognitive theory*. Englewood Cliffs, NJ: Prentice Hall.

BANDURA, A. (1989). Human agency in social cognitive theory. *American Psychologist, 44*, 1175–1184.

BANDURA, A. (1990). *Foreword to E. A. Locke & G. P. Latham (1990), A theory of goal setting and task performance*. Englewood Cliffs, NJ: Prentice Hall.

BANDURA, A. (1991). Human agency: The rhetoric and the reality. *American Psychologist, 46*, 157–161.

BANDURA, A. (Ed.). (1995). *Self-efficacy in changing societies*. New York: Cambridge University Press.

BANDURA, A. (1997). *Self-efficacy: The exercise of control*. New York: Freeman.

BANDURA, A. (2001). Social cognitive theory: An agentic perspective. *Annual Review of Psychology, 52*, 1–26.

BANDURA, A. (2006). Toward a psychology of human agency. *Perspectives on Human Science, 1*, 164–180.

BANGERT, A. W. & Baumberger, J. P. (2005). Research and statistical techniques used in the *Journal of Counseling and Development* 1990–2001. *Journal of Counseling and Development, 83*, 480–487.

BARBER, J. P., Muran, J. C., McCarthy, K. S. & Keefe, R.J. (2013). Research on psychodynamic therapies. In M. J. Lambert (Ed.). *Bergin and Garfield's handbook of psychotherapy and behavior change* (6th ed.) (pp. 443–494). New York: John Wiley & Sons, Inc.

BARDACH, S. H., Gayer, C. C., Clinkinbeard, T., Zanjani, F. & Watkins, J. F. (2010, May). The malleability of possible selves and expectations regarding aging. *Educational Gerontology, 36*(5), 407–424.

BARKER, C. & Pistrang, N. (2002). Psychotherapy and social support: Integrating research on psychological helping. *Clinical Psychology Review*, 22, 361–379.

BARLOW, D. H., Ellard, K. K., Fairholme, C. P., Farchione, T. J., Boisseau, C. L., Allen, L. B. *et al.* (2011). *The unified protocol for transdiagnostic treatment of emotional disorders: Client workbook*. New York: Oxford University Press.

BARLOW, D. H., Farchione, T. J., Fairholme, C. P., Ellard, K. K., Boisseau, C. L., Allen, L. B. *et al.* (2011). *The unified protocol for transdiagnostic treatment of emotional disorders: Therapist guide*. New York: Oxford University Press.

BARLOW, D. H. (2014). *Clinical handbook of psychological disorders: A step-by-step treatment manual* (5th ed.). New York: The Guilford Press.

BARLOW, D. H., Farchione, T. J., Sauer-Zavala, S., Latin, H. M., Ellard, K. K., Bullis, J. R. *et al.* (2018).*Unified protocol for transdiagnostic treatment of emotional disorders, second edition, therapist guide*. New York: Oxford University Press.

BARNETT, J. E. (Ed.). (2008). Focus on ethics. *Professional Psychology: Research and Practice*, 39, 589–599.

BARNETT, J. E. (2011). Psychotherapist self-disclosure: Ethical and clinical considerations. *Psychotherapy*, 48, 315–321.

BARON, J. (2001). *Thinking and deciding* (3rd ed.). New York: Cambridge University Press.

BARRETT-LENNARD, G. T. (1981). The empathy cycle: Refinement of a nuclear concept. *Journal of Counseling Psychology*, 28, 91–100.

BASIC BEHAVIORAL SCIENCE TASK FORCE OF THE NATIONAL ADVISORY MENTAL HEALTH COUNCIL. (1996). Basic behavioral science research for mental health: Family processes and social networks. *American Psychologist*, 51, 622–630.

BATSON, C. D. (2011). *Altruism in humans*. New York: Oxford University Press.

BAUMEISTER, R. F., Gailliot, M., DeWall, C. N. & Oaten, M. (2006, December). Self-regulation and personality: How interventions increase regulatory success, and how depletion moderates the effects of traits on behavior. *Journal of Personality*, 74, 1773–1801.

BAYER, C. & Gollwitzer, P. M. (2007). Boosting scholastic test scores by willpower: The role of implementation intentions. *Self and Identity*, 6, 1–19.

BAYNE, R., Jinks, G., Collard, P. & Horton, I. (2008) *The counsellor's handbook: A practical A-Z guide to integrative counselling and psychotherapy* (3rd ed.). Andover, UK: Cengage Learning EMEA.

BEDELL, J. R. & Lennox, S. S. (1997). *Handbook for communication and problem-solving skills training: A cognitive-behavioral approach*. New York: Wiley.

BEDI, R. P. (2006). Concept mapping the client's perspective on counseling alliance formation. *Journal of Counseling Psychology*, 53(1), 26–35.

BEDI, R. P., Davis, M. D. & Arvay, M. A. (2005). The client's perspective on forming a counseling alliance and implications for research on counselor training. *Canadian Journal of Counseling*, 39, 71–85.

BELL, S. (2010). "Design thinking" and higher education. *Inside Higher Education*. Retrieved from www.insidehighered.com/views/2010/03/02/design-thinking-and-higher-education

BENISH, S., Imel, Z. E. & Wampold, B. E. (2007). The relative efficacy of bona fide psychotherapies for treating post-traumatic stress disorder: A meta-analysis of direct comparisons. *Clinical Psychology Review*, 28, 746–759.

BENNETT, M. I. & Bennett, M. B. (1984). The uses of hopelessness. *American Journal of Psychiatry*, 141, 559–562.

BENSON, H. (1975). *The relaxation response*. New York: Avon.

BENSON, H. & Proctor, W. (2010). *Relaxation revolution: Enhancing your personal health through the science and genetics of mind body healing.* New York: Scribner.

BERENSON, B. G. & Mitchell, K. M. (1974). *Confrontation: For better or worse.* Amherst, MA: Human Resource Development Press.

BERK, M. & Parker, G. (2009). The elephant on the couch: Side effects of psychotherapy. *Australian and New Zealand Journal of Psychiatry, 43,* 787–794.

BERKING, M., Orth, U., Wupperman, P., Meier, L. L. & Caspar, F. (2008). Prospective effects of emotion-regulation skills on emotional adjustment. *Journal of Counseling Psychology, 55,* 485–494.

BERNAL, G. & Domenech Rodriguez, M. M. (Eds.). (2012). *Cultural adaptations: Tools for evidence-based practice with diverse populations.* Washington, DC: American Psychological Association Books.

BERNE, E. (1961). *Transactional analysis in psychotherapy: A systematic individual and social psychiatry. New York:* Grove Press. doi.org/10.1037/11495-000

BERNE, E. (1964). *Games people play.* New York: Grove Press.

BERNHEIM, K. F. (1989). Psychologists and the families of the severely mentally ill: The role of family consultation. *American Psychologist, 44,* 561–564.

BERTOLINO, B. & O'Hanlon, B. (2002). *Collaborative, competency-based counseling and therapy.* Boston, MA: Allyn & Bacon.

BEULAH, J., Walker, A. & Fuller-Tyszkiewicz, M. (2017). Evaluating the effectiveness of employee assistance programmes: A systematic review. *European Journal of Work and Organizational Psychology, 27*(1), 1–15.

BEUTLER, L. E., Malik, M., Alimohamed, S., Harwood, T. M., Talebi, H., Noble, S. *et al.* (2004). Therapist variables. In M. J. Lambert (Ed.), *Bergin and Garfield's handbook of psychotherapy and behavior change* (5th ed., pp. 227–306). New York: Wiley.

BIESANZ, J. C. & Human, L. J. (2010). The cost of forming more accurate impressions: Accuracy motivated perceivers see the personality of others more distinctively but less normatively. *Psychological Science, 24,* 589–594.

BISWAS-DIENER, R. & Dean, B. (2007). *Positive psychology coaching: Putting the science of happiness to work for your clients.* Hoboken, NJ: Wiley.

BLAMPIED, N. M. (2000). Single-case research designs: A neglected alternative. *American Psychologist, 55,* 960.

BOGAR, C. B. & Hulse-Killacky, D. (2006, Summer). Resiliency determinants and resiliency processes among female adult survivors of childhood sexual abuse. *Journal of Counseling & Development, 84,* 318–327.

BOGG, T. & Roberts, B. W. (2004). Conscientiousness and health-related behaviors: A meta-analysis of the leading behavioral contributors to morality. *Psychological Bulletin, 130,* 887–919.

BOHART, A. C. & Tallman, K. (2010). Clients: The neglected common factor in psychotherapy. In B. Duncan, S. Miller, B. Wampold, & M. Hubble (Eds.), *The heart and soul of change: Delivering what works* (2nd ed., pp. 83–111). Washington, DC: American Psychological Association Books.

BOHART, A. C. & Tallman, K. (1999). *How clients make therapy work: The process of active self-healing.* Washington, DC: American Psychological Association.

BOISVERT, C. M. & Faust, D. F. (2006). Practicing psychologists' knowledge of general psychotherapy research findings. *Professional Psychology: Research and Practice, 37,* 708–716.

BONANNO, G. A. (2004). Loss, trauma, and human resilience. *American Psychologist, 59,* 20–28.

BONANNO, G. A. (2005). Clarifying and extending the construct of adult resilience. *American Psychologist, 60,* 265–267.

BOOTH, D. A. (1994). *The psychology of nutrition*. New York: Taylor and Francis.

BORCKARDT, J. J., Nash, M. R., Murphy, M.D., Moore, M., Shaw, D. & O'Neil, P. (2008). Clinical practice as natural laboratory for psychotherapy research: A guide to case-based time-series analysis. *American Psychologist, 63*, 77–95.

BORDIN, E. S. (1979). The generalizability of the psychoanalytic concept of the working alliance. *Psychotherapy: Theory, Research and Practice, 16*, 252–260.

BORNSTEIN, R. F. & Bowen, R. F. (1995). Dependency is psychotherapy: Toward an integrated treatment approach. *Psychotherapy, 32*, 520–534.

BOSWORTH, H. B. & Oddone, E. Z. (2005). *Patient treatment adherence: Concepts, interventions, and measurement*. Mahwah, NJ: Lawrence Erlbaum.

BRADSHAW, J. (2005). *Healing the shame that binds you*. Deerfield Beach, FL: HCI.

BRAMMER, L. (1973). *The helping relationship: Process and skills*. Englewood Cliffs, NJ: Prentice Hall.

BREMNER, R. H., Koole, S. L. & Bushman, B. J. (2011, June). "Pray for those who mistreat you": Effects of prayer on anger and aggression. *Personality and Social Psychology Bulletin, 37*, 830–837.

BRENNER, S. (2003, June 19). *Persons and genomes: Genetics and the human sciences*. Talk given at the London School of Economics and Political Science, London, UK.

BRICKER, D., Glat, M. & Stover, S. (2007, January/February). Avoiding clinical drift. *Psychotherapy Networker*, pp. 25–26.

BRODER, M. S. (2000). Making optimal use of homework to enhance your therapeutic effectiveness. *Journal of Rational-Emotive & Cognitive Behavior Therapy, 18*, 3–18.

BRODSKY, S. L. (2011). *Therapy with coerced and reluctant clients*. Washington, DC: American Psychological Association Books.

BRONFENBRENNER, U. (1977, July). Toward an experimental ecology of human development. *American Psychologist*, 513–531.

BROOKS, A. C. (2012, March 3–4). Social science with a soul. *Wall Street Journal*, p. A13.

BROWN, C. & Augusta-Scott, T. (2006). *Narrative therapy: Making meaning, making lives*. Thousand Oaks, CA: Sage.

BROWNELL, K. D., Marlatt, G. A., Lichtenstein, E. & Wilson, G. T. (1986). Understanding and preventing relapse. *American Psychologist, 41*, 765–782.

BUCHANAN, M. (2007). The science of subtle signals. *Strategy Business, 48*, 1–10.

BUCHANAN, M. (2009). Secret signals: Does a primitive, non-linguistic type of communication drive people's interactions? *Nature, 457*, 528–530.

BURGOON, J. K., Guerrero, L. K. & Floyd, K. (2009). *Nonverbal communication*. Boston, MA: Pearson.

BURKARD, A. W., Knox, S., Groen, M., Perez, M. & Hess, S. A. (2006). European American therapist self-disclosure in cross-cultural counseling. *Journal of Counseling Psychology, 50*, 324–332.

BURKE, B. L., Dunn, C. W., Atkins, D. C. & Phelps, J. S. (2004). The emerging evidence base for motivational interviewing: A meta-analytic and qualitative inquiry. *Journal of Cognitive Psychotherapy, 18*, 309–322.

BURNARD, P. (2005) *Counselling Skills for Health Professionals* (4th ed.). Andover: Cengage Learning EMEA.

BYSTEDT, S., Rozental, A., Andersson, G., Boettcher, J. & Carlbring, P. (2014). Clinicians' perspectives on negative effects of psychological treatments. *Cognitive Behaviour Therapy, 43*(4), 319–331.

CALHOUN, L. G. & Tedeschi, R. G. (Eds.). (2006). *The handbook of posttraumatic growth*. Mahwah, NJ: Lawrence Erlbaum.

CANARY, D. J., Cody, M. J. & Manusov, V. L. (2008). *Interpersonal communication: A goals based approach* (4th ed.). Boston, MA: Bedford/ St. Martin's.

CANNON, T. D., Cadenhead, K., Heinssen, R., Cornblatt, B., Woods, S. W., Addington, J. *et al.* (2008). Prediction of psychosis in youth at high clinical risk: A multisite longitudinal study in North America. *Archives of General Psychiatry*, 65, 28–37.

CAPRARA, G. V. & Cervone, D. (2003). A conception of personality for a psychology of human strengths: Personality as an agentic, self-regulating system. In L. G. Aspinwall & U. M. Staudinger (Eds.), *A psychology of human strengths* (pp. 61–74). Washington, DC: American Psychological Association Books.

CARKHUFF, R. R. (1969a). *Helping and human relations: Vol. 1. Selection and training*. New York: Holt, Rinehart & Winston.

CARKHUFF, R. R. (1969b). *Helping and human relations: Vol. 2. Practice and research*. New York: Holt, Rinehart & Winston.

CARKHUFF, R. R. (1971). Training as a preferred mode of treatment. *Journal of Counseling Psychology*, 18, 123–131.

CARKHUFF, R. R. (1987). *The art of helping* (6th ed.). Amherst, MA: Human Resource Development Press.

CARKHUFF, R. R. & Anthony, W. A. (1979). *The skills of helping: An introduction to counseling*. Amherst, MA: Human Resource Development Press.

CARR, A. (2004). *Positive psychology: The science of happiness and human strengths*. New York: Brunner-Routledge.

CARROLL, P. J., Shepperd, J. A. & Arkin, R. M. (2009). Downward self-revision: Erasing possible selves. *Social Cognition*, 27(4), 550–578.

CARSON, D. K. & Becker, K. W. (2003). *Creativity in psychotherapy: Reaching new heights with individuals, couples, and families*. Binghamton, NY: Haworth Clinical Practice Press.

CARSON, D. K. & Becker, K. W. (2004). When lightning strikes: Reexamining creativity in psychotherapy. *Journal of Counseling & Development*, 82, 111–115.

CARSON, D. K., Becker, K. W., Vance, K. E. & Forth, N. L. (2003, March). The role of creativity in marriage and family therapy practice: A national online study. *Contemporary Family Therapy*, 25, 89–109.

CARTER, C. L. (2006, March–April). Transformers. *Alliance*, pp. 4–7.

CARTON, J. S., Kessler, E. A. & Pape, C. L. (1999, Spring). Non-verbal decoding skills and relationship well-being in adults. *Journal of Nonverbal Behavior*, 23, 91–100.

CARTWRIGHT, B., Arredondo, P. & D'Andrea, M. (2004). Dignity, development, & diversity. *Counseling Today*, pp. 24–26, 32.

CERVONE, D. (2000). Thinking about self-efficacy. *Behavior Modification*, 24(1), 30–56.

CERVONE, D. & Scott, W. D. (1995). Self- efficacy theory and behavioral change: Foundations, conceptual issues, and therapeutic implications. In W. O'Donohue & L. Krasner (Eds.), *Theories of behavior therapy: Exploring behavior change* (pp. 349–383). Washington, DC: American Psychological Association Books.

CHABRIS, C.F. & Simons, D.J. (2010). *The invisible gorilla: And other ways our intuitions deceive us*. New York: Crown Archetype.

CHANG, E. C. (Ed.). (2001). *Optimism and pessimism: Implications for theory, research, and practice*. Washington, DC: American Psychological Association Books.

CHANG, E. C. (Ed.). (2008). *Self-criticism and self-enhancement: Theory, research, and clinical implications*. American Psychological Association. doi. org/10.1037/11624-000

CHANG, E. C., D'Zurilla, T. J. & Sanna, L. J. (Eds.). (2004). *Social problem solving: Theory, research, and training*. Washington, DC: American Psychological Association Books.

CHENG, C. (2001). Assessing coping flexibility in real-life and laboratory settings: A Multi-method approach. *Journal of Personality and Social Psychology, 80,* 814–833.

CHIGWEDERE, C., Tone, Y, Fitzmaurice, B. & McDonough, M. (2012). *Overcoming obstacles in CBT.* London: SAGE Publishers Inc.

CHRISTENSEN, A. J. (2004). *Patient adherence to medical treatment regimens: Bridging the gap between behavioral science and biomedicine.* New Haven: Yale University Press.

CHURCHLAND, P. S. (2011). *Braintrust: What neuroscience tells us about morality.* Princeton, NJ: Princeton University Press.

CLARKSON, P. (2003). *The therapeutic relationship* (2nd ed.). London, UK: Whurr Publishers.

Changing unhealthy habits. Essential step to a healthier life. Supplement to Mayo Clinic Health Letter. (2007, February). *Mayo Clinic Health Letter,* pp. 1–8.

CIARROCHI, J., Forgas, J. R, & Mayer, J. D. (Eds.). (2006). *Emotional intelligence in everyday life* (2nd ed.). Psychology Press/ Erlbaum (UK) Taylor & Francis.

CIARROCHI, J. & Mayer, J. D. (2007). The key ingredients of emotional intelligence interventions: Similarities and differences. In J. Ciarrochi & J. D. Mayer (Eds.), *Improving emotional intelligence: A practical guide* (pp. 144–156). Philadelphia, PA: Psychology Press.

CLAIBORN, C. D. (1982). Interpretation and change in counseling. *Journal of Counseling Psychology, 29,* 439–453.

CLARK, A. J. (2007). *Empathy in counseling and psychotherapy: Perspectives and practices.* Mahwah, NJ: Lawrence Erlbaum.

CLARK, J. (2003a). *Practitioners' experienced knowledge: Creating space for understanding in cross-cultural clinical practice.* Unpublished doctoral dissertation. Toronto, ON: University of Toronto.

CLARK, J. (2003b). Reconceptualizing empathy for culturally competent practice. In W. Shera (Ed.), *Emerging perspectives on anti-oppressive practice.* Toronto, ON: Canadian Scholars Press, 247–263.

CLARK, A. (2010a, Summer). Empathy: An integral model in the counseling process. *Journal of Counseling and Development, 88,* 348–356.

CLARK, A. (2010b). Empathy and sympathy: Therapeutic distinctions in counseling. *Journal of Mental Health Counseling, 32,* 95–101.

CLARKIN, J. F. (2005). Differential therapeutics. In J. C. Norcross & M. R. Goldfried (Eds.), *Oxford series in clinical psychology. Handbook of psychotherapy integration* (p. 343–361). New York: Oxford University Press.

COCKELL, S. J., Zaitsoff, S. L. & Geller, J. (2004). Maintaining change following eating disorder treatment. *Professional Psychology: Research and Practice, 35,* 527–534.

COFFMAN, S. J., Martell, C. R., Dimidjian, S., Gallop, R. & Hollon. (2007). Extreme non-response in cognitive therapy: Can behavioral activation succeed where cognitive therapy fails? *Journal of Consulting and Clinical Psychology, 75(4),* 531–541.

COHEN, S., Underwood, L. & Gotlieb, B. (Eds.) (2000). *Measuring and intervening in social support.* New York: Oxford University Press.

COLAN, L. J. (2003). *Sticking to it: The art of adherence.* Dallas, TX: Cornerstone Leadership Institute.

COLE, H. P. & Sarnoff, D. (1980). Creativity and counseling. *Personnel and Guidance Journal, 59,* 140–146.

COLLINS, J. C. & Porras, J. I. (1994). *Built to last: Successful habits of visionary companies.* New York: Harper Business.

COLLINS, S., Arthur, N. & Wong-Wylie, G. (2010, Summer). Enhancing reflective practice in multicultural counseling through cultural auditing. *Journal of Counseling and Development, 88,* 340–347.

CONSTANTINE, M. G. & Sue, D. W. (Eds.). (2008). *Strategies for building multicultural competence in mental health and educational settings*. Hoboken, NJ: John Wiley & Sons.

CONYNE, R. & Cook, E. E. (Eds.). (2004). *Ecological counseling: An innovative approach to conceptualizing person-environment interaction*. Alexandria, VA: American Counseling Association.

COOK, E. P. (Ed.). (2012). *Understanding people in context: The ecological perspective in counseling*. Washington, DC: American Counseling Association Books.

COOK, J. M., Schnurr, P. P., Biyanova, T. & Coyne, J. C. (2009, May). Apples don't fall far from the tree: Influences on psychotherapists' adoption and sustained use of new therapies. *Psychiatric Services, 60*, 671–676.

COOPER, M., Norcross, J. C., Raymond-Barker, B., & Hogan, T. P. (2019). Psychotherapy preferences of laypersons and mental health professionals: Whose therapy is it? *Psychotherapy, 56*(2), 205–216.

COOPER, M. & McLeod, J. (2011). *Pluralistic counseling and psychotherapy*. Thousand Oaks, CA: Sage.

COPLAN, A. & Goldie, P. (Eds.). (2012). *Empathy: Philosophical and psychological perspectives*. New York: Oxford University Press.

COREY, G. (2008). *Theory and practice of counseling and psychotherapy* (8th ed.). Belmont, CA: Cengage Brooks/Cole.

COREY, G. (2012). *The art of integrative counseling* (3rd ed.). Belmont, CA: Cengage Brooks/Cole.

COREY, M.S., & Corey, G. (2016). *Becoming a helper*. Boston, MA: Cengage Learning

CORMIER, S. & Nurius, P. S. (2003). *Interviewing and change strategies for helpers: Fundamental skills and cognitive-behavior interventions* (5th ed.). Belmont, CA: Wadsworth/Thomson Learning.

CORSINI, R. J. (2011). Turning the tables on the client: Making the client the counselor. In H. G. Rosenthal (Ed.), *Favorite counseling and therapy techniques* (2nd ed., pp. 87–91). New York: Routledge/Taylor & Francis Group.

COSTANZO, M. (1992). Training students to decode verbal and nonverbal clues: Effects on confidence and performance. *Journal of Educational Psychology, 84*, 308–313.

COVEY, S. R. (1989). *The seven habits of highly effective people*. New York: Simon & Schuster. (Fireside edition, 1990).

COYNE, J. C. & Racioppo, M. W. (2000). Never the twain shall meet? Closing the gap between coping research and clinical intervention research. *American Psychologist, 55*, 655–664.

COYNE, K. P., Clifford, P. G. & Dye, R. (2007, December). Breakthrough thinking from inside the box. *Harvard Business Review*, 70–78.

COYNE, J. C., Stefanek, M. & Palmer, S. C. (2007). Psychotherapy and survival in cancer: The conflict between hope and evidence. *Psychological Bulletin, 133*, 367–394.

CRANO, W. D. (2000, March). Milestones in the psychological analysis of social influence. *Group Dynamics, 4*, 68–80.

CRAWFORD, R., Brown, B. & Crawford, P. (2004). *Storytelling in Therapy*. Andover: Cengage Learning EMEA.

CRITS-CHRISTOPH, P., Baranackie, K., Kurcias, J. S., Beck, A. T., Carroll, K., Perry, K. et al. (1991). Meta-analysis of therapist effects in psychotherapy outcome studies. *Psychotherapy Research, 1*, 81–91.

CRITS-CHRISTOPH, P., Connolly Gibbons, M. B, Crits-Christoph, K., Narducci, J., Schamberger, M. & Gallop, R. (2006). Can therapists be trained to improve their alliances? A pilot study of alliance-fostering therapy. *Psychotherapy Research, 13*: 268–281.

CROSS, S. E. & Markus, H. (1991). Possible selves across the life-span. *Human Development, 34*, 230–255.

CROSS, S. E. & Markus, H. R. (1994). Self-schemas, possible selves, and competent performance. *Journal of Education Psychology, 86*, 423–438.

CROSS, T. L., Bazron, B. J., Dennis, K. W. & Isaacs, M. R. (1989). *Towards a culturally competent system of care: A monograph on effective services for minority children who are severely emotionally disturbed.* Washington, DC: Georgetown University Child Development Center.

CRUZA-GUET, M., Spokane, A. R., Caskie, G. I. L., Brown, S. C., & Szapocznik, J. (2008). The relationship between social support and psychological distress among Hispanic elders in Miami, Florida. *Journal of Counseling Psychology, 55*(4), 427–441.

CUIJPERS, P., van Straten, A. & Warmerdam, L. (2007, April). Behavioral activation treatments of depression: A meta-analysis. *Clinical Psychology Review, 27*, 318–326.

CUMMINGS, N. A. (1979). Turning bread into stones: Our modern anti-miracle. *American Psychologist, 34*, 1119–1129.

CUMMINGS, N. A. (2000). *The first session with substance abusers.* San Francisco, CA: Jossey-Bass.

DAHLSGAARD, K., Peterson, C. & Seligman, M. (2005). Share virtue: The convergence of valued human strength across culture and history. *Review of General Psychology, 9,* 203–213.

DAITCH, C. (2008, September/October). Practice makes perfect: There's no shortcut to lasting change. *Psychotherapy Networker,* pp. 48–52.

DANIEL, J. H., Roysircar, G., Abeles, N. & Boyd, C. (2004). Individual and cultural diversity competence: Focus on the therapist. *Journal of Clinical Psychology, 25*(4), 255–267.

DANIELS, J. & D'Andrea, M. (2007, June). In search of radical thinkers: Beyond the culture of niceness. *Counseling Today,* pp. 49, 51.

DANZER, G.S. (Ed.). (2019). *Therapist self-disclosure: An evidence-based guide for practitioners.* New York: Routledge

DARCY, M., Lee, D. & Tracey, T. (2004). Complementary approaches to individual differences using paired comparisons and multidimensional scaling: Applications to multicultural counseling competence. *Journal of Counseling Psychology, 51*(2), 139–150.

DAVIS, M., Eshelman, E. R. & McKay, M. (2008). *The relaxation and stress reduction workbook.* (6th ed.). Oakland, CA: New Harbinger Publications.

DeANGELIS, T. (2002, July/August). If you do just one thing, make it exercise. *Monitor on Psychology,* pp. 49–51.

DeANGELIS, T. (2005, October). Putting people in their places. *Monitor on Psychology,* pp. 34–35.

DEARING, R. L. & Tangney, J. P. (Eds.). (2011). *Shame in the therapy hour.* Washington, DC: American Psychological Association Books.

De BONO, E. (1992). *Serious creativity: Using the power of lateral thinking to create new ideas.* New York: Harper Business.

DECETY, J. (Ed.). (2012). *Empathy: From bench to bedside.* Cambridge, MA: MIT Press.

DeFIFE, J. A. & Hilsenroth, M. J. (2011, June). Starting off on the right foot: Common factor elements in early psychotherapy process. *Journal of Psychotherapy Integration, 21*, 172–191.

DETWEILER-BEDELL, J. B. & Whisman, M. A. (2005). A lesson in assigning homework: Therapist, client, and task characteristics in cognitive therapy for depression. *Professional Psychology: Research and Practice, 36*, 219–223.

DEUTSCH, M. (1954). Field theory in social psychology. In G. Lindzey (Ed.), *The handbook of social psychology (Vol. 1).* Cambridge, MA: Addison-Wesley.

DEWANE, C. (2008, September/October). The ABCs of ACT - Acceptance and commitment therapy. *Social Work Today, 8*, 36.

DEVITO, J.A. (2011). *The interpersonal communication book*. Harlow, UK: Pearson.

DEVITO, J.A. (2013). *Essentials of human communication* (8th ed.). Harlow, UK: Pearson.

DIENER, E. & Biswas-Diener, R. (2008a). *Happiness: Unlocking the mysteries of psychological wealth*. Hoboken, NJ: Wiley.

DIENER, E. & Biswas-Diener, R. (2008b). *Rethinking happiness: The science of psychological wealth*. Malden, MA: Blackwell.

DILLON, C. (2003). *Learning from mistakes in clinical practice*. Belmont, CA: Brooks/Cole.

DIMOND, R. E., Havens, R. A. & Jones, A. C. (1978). A conceptual framework for the practice of prescriptive eclecticism in psychotherapy. *American Psychologist, 33*, 239–248.

DIXON, J., Durrheim, K. & Tredoux, C. (2005, October). Beyond the optimal contact strategy. *American Psychologist, 60*, 697–711.

DONNAY, D. A. C. & Borgen, F. H. (1999). The incremental validity of vocational self-efficacy: An examination of interest, self-efficacy, and occupation. *Journal of Counseling Psychology, 46*, 432–447.

DORN, F. J. (Ed.). (1986). *The social influence process in counseling and psychotherapy*. Springfield, IL: Charles C. Thomas.

DÖRNER, D. (1996). *The logic of failure: Why things go wrong and what we can do to make them right*. New York: Holt.

DRISCOLL, R. (1984). *Pragmatic psychotherapy*. New York: Van Nostrand Reinhold.

DRUCKERMAN, P. (2012). *Bringing up bébé: One American mother discovers the wisdom of French parenting*. New York: Penguin.

DRYDEN, W. (2018). *Flexibility-based cognitive behaviour therapy: Insights from 40 years of practice*. Oxon: Routledge.

DUFF, C. T. & Bedi, R. P. (2010). Counselor behaviors that predict therapeutic alliance: From the client's perspective. *Counseling Psychology Quarterly, 23*(1), 91–110.

DUHIGG, C. (2012). *The power of habit: Why we do what we do in life and business*. New York: Random House, Inc.

DUNCAN, B. L. (2010). *On becoming a better therapist*. Washington, DC: American Psychological Association Books.

DUNCAN, B. L. (2011, May–June). What therapists want. *Psychotherapy Networker*, pp. 40–43, 47, 62.

DUNCAN, B. L., Miller, S. & Sparks, J. (2004). *The heroic client: A revolutionary way to improve effectiveness*. San Francisco, CA: Jossey-Bass.

DUNCAN, B. L., Miller, S. D., Wampold, B. E. & Hubble, M. A. (Eds.). (2010). *The heart and soul of change: Delivering what works in therapy* (2nd ed.). Washington, DC: American Psychological Association Books.

DUNCAN, B. L. & Sparks, J. (2010). *Heroic clients, heroic agencies: Partners for change. A manual for client-directed, outcome-informed clinical services and implementation* (2nd ed.). HSCP Press. Retrieved from www.heartandsoulofchange.com

DYKENS, E. M. (2006). Toward a positive psychology of mental retardation. *American Journal of Orthopsychiatry, 76*, 185–193.

D'ZURILLA, T. J. & Nezu, A. M. (1999). *Problem-solving therapy: A social competence approach to clinical intervention* (2nd ed.). New York: Springer.

D'ZURILLA, T. J., & Nezu, A. M. (2001). Problem-solving therapies. In K. S. Dobson (Ed.), *The handbook of cognitive-behavioral therapies* (2nd ed., pp. 211–245). New York: The Guilford Press.

EAGLY, A. H., Eastwick, P. W. & Johannesen-Schmidt, M. (2009, April). Possible selves in marital roles: The impact of the anticipated division of labor on the mate preferences of women and men. *Personality and Social Psychology Bulletin, 35*, 403–414.

EGAN, G. (2010). *The skilled helper*, (9th ed.). Pacific Grove, CA: Cengage Learning Brooks/Cole.

EGAN, G. (2013) *The skilled helper: A problem-management and opportunity-development approach to helping* (10th ed.). Monterey, CA: Brooks/Cole Cengage Learning.

EGAN, G. & Cowan, M. A. (1979). *People in systems: A model for development in the human service professions and education*. Monterey, CA: Brooks/Cole.

EGAN, G. & Reese, R. (2018). *Exercises in Helping Skills: A manual to accompany The Skilled Helper*. Boston, USA: Cengage Learning.

ELIAS, M. J. & Tobias, S. E. (2002). *Social problem solving interventions in the schools*. New York: The Guilford Press.

ELLIOTT, R. (2002). Hermeneutic single-case efficacy design. *Psychotherapy Research, 12*, 1–21.

ELLIOTT, R., Bohart, A. C., Watson, J. C. & Greenberg, L. S. (2010). Empathy. *Psychotherapy, 48*(1), 43–49.

ELLIOTT, R., Bohart, A. C., Watson, J. C. & Greenberg, L. S. (2011). Empathy. In J. C. Norcross (Ed.), *Psychotherapy relationships that work* (2nd ed., pp. 132–152). New York: Oxford University Press.

ELLIS, A. (1984). Must most psychotherapists remain as incompetent as they are now? In J. Hariman (Ed.), *Does psychotherapy really help people?* Springfield, IL: Charles C. Thomas.

ELLIS, A. (2004). *Rational emotive behavior therapy: It works for me – it can work for you*. Amherst, NY: Prometheus.

ELLIS, A. & Ellis, D. J. (2011). *Rational emotive behavior therapy*. Washington, DC: American Psychological Association Books.

ERSKINE, R.G. (2015). Relational patterns, therapeutic presence: concepts and practice of integrative psychotherapy. London: Routledge

EUBANKS-CARTER, C., Muran, J. C. & Safran, J. D. (2010). Alliance ruptures and resolution. In J. C. Muran & J. P. Barber (Eds.), *The therapeutic alliance: An evidence-based guide to practice* (pp. 74–94). New York: The Guilford Press.

EVERLY, G. S. Jr. & Lating, J. M. (2004). *Personality-guided therapy for posttraumatic stress disorder*. Washington, DC: American Psychological Association Books.

FARBER, B. A. (2006). *Self-disclosure in psychotherapy*. New York: The Guilford Press.

FARBER, B. A., Berano, K. C. & Capobianco, J. A. (2004). Clients' perceptions of the process and consequences of self-disclosure in psychotherapy. *Journal of Counseling Psychology, 51*, 340–346.

FARBER, B. A. & Doolin, E. M. (2011). Positive regard and affirmation. In J. C. Norcross (Ed.), *Psychotherapy relationships that work* (2nd ed., pp. 168–186). New York: Oxford University Press.

FARBER, B. A. & Sohn, A. (2007). Patterns of self-disclosure in psychotherapy and marriage. *Psychotherapy: Theory, Research, Practice, and Training, 44*, 226–231.

FARBER, S.K. (2016). *Celebrating the wounded healer psychotherapist: Pain, post-traumatic growth and self-disclosure*. Abingdon, UK: Routledge.

FARIS, R. & Ennett, S. (2011, sourced October 11). Adolescent aggression: The role of peer group, status motives, peer aggression, and group characteristics. *Social Networks*. Retrieved from i2.cdn.turner.com/cnn/2011/images/10/10/findings.from.the.wheatley.school.pdf

FARIS, R. & Felmlee, D. (2011). Status struggles: Network centrality and gender segregation in same- and cross-gender aggression. *American Sociological Review, 76*(1), 48–73.

FARMER, R. F. & Nelson-Gray, R. O. (2005). *Personality-guided behavior therapy*. Washington, DC: American Psychological Association Books.

FARRELLY, F. & Brandsma, J. (1974). *Provocative therapy*. Cupertino, CA: Meta Publications.

FARROW, T. & Woodruff, P. (Eds.). (2007). *Empathy in mental illness*. New York: Cambridge University Press.

FAUTH, J. & Williams, E. N. (2005). The in- session self-awareness of therapist-trainees: Hindering or helpful? *Journal of Counseling Psychology, 52,* 443–447.

FELTHAM, C. (2010). *Critical thinking in counselling and psychotherapy.* London: SAGE Publications Ltd.

FERGUSON, T. (1987, January-February). Agreements with yourself. *Medical Self-Care,* 44–47.

FERRARI, J. R. (2010). *Still procrastinating? The no regrets guide to getting it done.* New York: Wiley.

FERRARI, J. R., Johnson, J. L. & McCowan, W. G. (1995). *Procrastination and task avoidance: Theory, research, and treatment.* New York: Springer.

FERNIE, B.A., Bharucha, Z., Nikcevic, A.V., Marino, C. & Spada, M.M. (2017). A metacognitive model of procrastination. *Journal of Affective Disorder, 210,* 196–203.

FINLAY, L. (2004) *The Practice of Psychosocial Occupational Therapy* (3rd ed.). Andover: Cengage Learning EMEA.

FINN, S. E. (2005). How psychological assessment taught me compassion and firmness. *Journal of Personality Assessment, 84,* 29–32.

FISH, J. M. (1995, Spring). Does problem behavior just happen? Does it matter? *Behavior and Social Issues, 5,* 3–12.

FISHER, R. & Shapiro, D. (2005). *Beyond reason: Using emotions as you negotiate.* New York: Penguin Books.

FISHER, R., Ury, W. & Patton, B. (Eds.). (1991). *Getting to yes: Negotiating agreement without giving in.* New York: Penguin Books.

FLACH, F. (1997). *Resilience: How to bounce back when the going gets tough.* New York: Hatherleigh Press.

FLETCHER, A. M. (2003). Renewed hope for self-change. *American Psychologist, 58,* 822– 823.

FOLKMAN, S. & Moskowitz, J. T. (2000). Positive affect and the other side of coping. *American Psychologist, 55,* 647–664.

FORD, D. (2008). *Why good people do bad things: How to stop being your own worst enemy.* New York: HarperCollins.

FORREST, G. G. (2010). *Self-disclosure in psychotherapy and recovery.* Lanham, MD: Jason Aronson.

FOWERS, B. J. & Davidov, B. J. (2006). The virtue of multiculturalism: Personal transformation, character, and openness to the other. *American Psychologist, 61,* 581–594.

FOWERS, B. J. & Davidov, B. J. (2007). Dialogue as the interplay of otherness and shared humanity. *American Psychologist, 62,* 705–706.

FRAGA, E. D., Atkinson, D. R. & Wampold, B. E. (2004). Ethnic group preferences for multicultural counseling competencies. *Cultural Diversity and Ethnic Minority Psychology, 10*(1), 53–65.

FRANCE, K. (2005). Crisis intervention. In G. P. Koocher, J. C. Norcross & S. S. Hill, III (Eds.), *Psychologists' desk reference* (2nd ed., pp. 245– 249). New York: Oxford University Press.

FRANCES, A., Clarkin, J. & Perry, S. (1984). *Differential therapeutics in psychiatry.* New York: Brunner/Mazel.

FRANKEL, S. A. (2007). *Making psychotherapy work: Collaborating effectively with your patients.* Madison, CT: Psychosocial Press.

FREIRE, P. (1970). *Pedagogy of the oppressed.* New York: Seabury.

FRIEDMAN, H. S. & Martin, L. R. (2011). *The Longevity Project.* New York: Hudson Street Press.

FRYDENBERG, E. (2002). *Beyond coping: Meeting goals, visions and challenges.* New York: Oxford University Press Inc.

FURUKOWA, E. & Hunt, D. J. (2011). Therapy with refugees and other immigrants experiencing shame: A multicultural perspective. In R. L. Dearing & J. P. Tangney (Eds.), *Shame in the therapy hour*. Washington, DC: American Psychological Association Books.

GALASSI, J. P. & Bruch, M. A. (1992). Counseling with social interaction problems: Assertion and social anxiety. In S. D. Brown & R. W. Lent (Eds.), *Handbook of counseling psychology*. New York: Wiley.

GALBRAITH, V. (2016). Developing Resilience and Self-Care. In B. Douglas, R. Woolfe, S. Strawbridge, E. Kasket & V. Galbraith (Eds). *Handbook of Counselling Psychology* (4th ed). London: Sage.

GALOTTI, K. M. (2002). *Making decisions that matter: How people face important life choices*. Mahwah, NJ: Lawrence Erlbaum.

GARBER, J. & Seligman, M. (Eds.). (1980). *Human helplessness: Theory and applications*. New York: W. H. Freeman.

GAWANDE, A. (2010). *The checklist manifesto: How to get things right*. New York: Picador.

GELATT, H. B. (1989). Positive uncertainty: A new decision-making framework for counseling. *Journal of Counseling Psychology, 36*, 252–256.

GELATT, H. B., Varenhorst, B. & Carey, R. (1972). *Deciding: A leader's guide*. Princeton, NJ: College Entrance Examination Board.

GELLER, S. M. & Greenberg, L. S. (2012). *Therapeutic presence: A mindful approach to effective therapy*. Washington, DC: American Psychological Association Books.

GELSO, C. J. (2009). The real relationship in a postmodern world: Theoretical and empirical explorations. *Psychotherapy Research, 19*, 253–264.

GELSO, C. J. (2011). Emerging and continuing trends in psychotherapy: Views from an editor's eyes. *Psychotherapy, 48*, 182–187.

GERSIE, A. (1997). *Reflections on therapeutic storymaking: The use of stories in groups*. Jessica Kingsley.

GIANNETTI, E. (1997). *Lies we live by: The art of self-deception*. New York and London: Bloomsbury.

GILBERT, P. (2009). *The compassionate mind*. London: Constable & Robinson.

GILBERT, P. & Leahy, R.L. (2007). *The therapeutic relationship in cognitive behavioral psychotherapies*. Hove, UK: Routledge.

GILBERT, T. F. (1978). *Human competence: Engineering worthy performance*. New York: McGraw Hill.

GIVENS, D. (2008). *The non-verbal dictionary of gestures, signs & body language cues*. Spokane, Washington: Center for Nonverbal Studies Press.

GLASSER, W. (2000). *Reality therapy in action*. New York: HarperCollins.

GLICKEN, M. D. (2006). *Learning from resilient people: Lessons we can apply to counseling and psychotherapy*. Thousand Oaks, CA: Sage.

GODWIN, G. (1985). *The finishing school*. New York: Viking.

GOLDSMITH, D. J. (2004). *Communicating social support*. New York: Cambridge University Press.

GOLDSTEIN, H. (1994). Ethnography, critical inquiry and social work practice. In E. Sherman & W. J. Reid (Eds.), *Qualitative research in social work* (pp. 42–51). New York: Columbia University Press.

GOLEMAN, D. (1985). *Vital lies, simple truths: The psychology of self-deception*. New York: Simon & Schuster.

GOLEMAN, D. (1995). *Emotional intelligence*. New York: Bantam Books.

GOLEMAN, D. (1998). *Working with emotional intelligence*. New York: Bantam Books.

GOLEMAN, D. & Boyatzis, R. (2008, September). Social intelligence and the biology of leadership. *Harvard Business Review*, 74–81.

GOLLWITZER, P. M. (1999). Implementation intentions strong effects of simple plans. *American Psychologist, 54,* 493–503.

GOLLWITZER, P. M., Parks-Stamm, E. J., Jaudas, A. & Sheeran, P. (2007). Flexible tenacity in goal pursuit. In J. Shah & W. Gardner (Eds.), *Handbook of motivation science* (pp. 325–341). New York: The Guilford Press.

GOLLWITZER, P. M. & Sheeran, P. (2006). Implementation intentions and goal achievement: A meta-analysis of effects and processes. *Advances in Experimental Social Psychology, 38,* 249–268.

GOLLWITZER, P.M. & Oettingen, G. (2016). Planning promotes goal striving. In K.D. Vohs & R.F. Baumeister (Eds.), *Handbook of self-regulation, third edition: Research, theory and applications* (pp. 223–246). New York: The Guilford Press.

GOODMAN, L. A., Liang, B., Helms, J. E., Latta, R. E., Sparks, E. & Weintraub, S. R. (2004). Training counseling psychologists as social justice agents: Feminist and multicultural principles in action. *The Counseling Psychologist, 32*(6), 793–837.

GORDON, M. (2007). *Roots of empathy: Changing the world child by child.* Toronto, ON: Thomas Allen.

GOSLIN, D. A. (1985). Decision making and the social fabric. *Society, 22,* 7–11.

GREEN, J. W. (1995). *Cultural awareness in the human services* (2nd ed.). Toronto: Allyn & Bacon.

GREENBERG, L. S. (1986). Change process research. *Journal of Consulting and Clinical Psychology, 54,* 4–9.

GROOPMAN, J. (2004). *The anatomy of hope: How people prevail in the face of illness.* New York: Random House.

GROSS, J. J. (2014). *Handbook of emotion regulation.* New York: The Guilford Press

GUISINGER, S. & Blatt, S. J. (1994). Individuality and relatedness: Evolution of a fundamental dialectic. *American Psychologist, 49,* 104–111.

HAGEDORN, W. B. (2011, April). Using therapeutic letters to navigate resistance and ambivalence: Experiential implications for group counseling. *Journal of Addictions & Offender Counseling, 31,* 108–126.

HALEY, J. (1976). *Problem solving therapy.* San Francisco, CA: Jossey-Bass.

HALL, E. T. (1977). *Beyond culture.* Garden City, NJ: Anchor Press.

HALL, L. E. (2005). *Dictionary of multicultural psychology: Issues, terms, and concepts.* Thousand Oaks, CA: Sage.

HALLECK, S. L. (1988). Which patients are responsible for their illnesses? *American Journal of Psychotherapy, 42,* 338–353.

HAMILTON, R. A., Del Castillo, D. M. & Stiles, W. B. (2007). Book review: Self-disclosure in psychotherapy. *Psychology, Theory, Research, Practice, Training, 44,* 361–362.

HAMMEL, S. (2019) *Handbook of therapeutic storytelling.* Abingdon, UK: Routledge.

HAMMOND, J. S., Keeney, R. L. & Raiffa, H. (1999). *Smart choices: A practical guide to making better decisions.* Boston, MA: Harvard Business School Press.

HANDELSMAN, M. M., Knapp, S. & Gottlieb, M. C. (2009). Positive ethics: Themes and variations. In C. R. Snyder & S. J. Lopez (Eds.). *Oxford handbook of positive psychology* (2nd ed., pp. 105–113). New York: Oxford University Press.

HANNA, F. J. (2002). *Therapy with difficult clients: Using the precursors model to awaken change.* Washington, DC: American Psychological Association Books.

HANNA, F. J., Hanna, C. A. & Keys, S. G. (1999). Fifty strategies for counseling defiant, aggressive adolescents: Reaching, accepting, and relating. *Journal of Counseling and Development, 77,* 395–404.

HANSEN, N., Pepitone-Arreola-Rockwell, F. & Greene, A. F. (2000). Multicultural competence: Criteria and case examples. *Professional Psychology: Research and Practice, 31,* 652–660.

HANSEN, J. T. (2005). The devaluation of inner subjective experiences by the counseling profession: A plea to reclaim the essence of the profession. *Journal of Counseling and Development, 83,* 406–415.

HARE-MUSTIN, R. & Marecek, J. (1986). Autonomy and gender: Some questions for therapists. *Psychotherapy, 23,* 205–212.

HARFORD, T. (2008). *The logic of life: The rational economics of an irrational world.* New York: Random House.

HARPER, R. (2004). *Personality-guided therapy in behavioral medicine.* Washington, DC: American Psychological Association Books.

HARRIS, R. (2008). *The happiness trap.* London: Robinson.

HARRIS, R. (2009). *ACT made simple: An easy-to-read primer on acceptance and commitment therapy.* Oakland, CA: New Harbinger Publications ltd.

HARVARD BUSINESS ESSENTIALS. (2006). *Decision making: Five steps to better results.* Boston, MA: Harvard Business School Press.

HARVARD HEART LETTER. (2008, August). *Balancing hope and reality in heart failure. 18* (12), 2.

HASTIE, R. & Dawes, R. (2001). *Rational choice in an uncertain world: The psychology of judgment and decision making.* California: Sage Publications.

HATCHER, S. L., Favorite, T. K., Hardy, E. A., Goode, R. L., Deshetler, L. A. & Thomas, R. M. (2005). An analogue study of therapist empathic process: Working with difference. *Psychotherapy: Theory, Research, Practice, Training, 42,* 198–210.

HAYES, S. C. (2007, September/October). Hello darkness: Discovering our values by confronting our fears. *Psychotherapy Networker, 31,* 46–52.

HAYES, S. C. (2008). Climbing our hills: A beginning conversation on the comparison of acceptance and commitment therapy and traditional cognitive behavioral therapy. *Clinical Psychology: Science & Practice, 5,* 286–295.

HAYES, S. C. & Smith, S. (2005). *Get out of your mind and into your life: The new acceptance and commitment therapy.* Oakland, CA: New Harbinger.

HAYES, S. C., Strosahl, K., & Wilson, K. G. (1999). *Acceptance and Commitment Therapy: An experiential approach to behavior change.* New York: The Guilford Press.

HAYS, K. F. (1999). *Working it out: Using exercise in psychotherapy.* Washington, DC: American Psychological Association Books.

HAYS, P. A. (2007). *Addressing cultural complexities in practice: Assessment, diagnosis, and therapy.* Washington, DC: American Psychological Association Books.

HAYS, P. A. (2008). *Addressing cultural complexities in practice: Assessment, diagnosis, and therapy* (2nd ed.). American Psychological Association. doi.org/10.1037/11650-000

HAYS, P. A. (2009). Integrating evidence-based practice, cognitive-behavior therapy, and multicultural therapy: Ten steps to culturally competent practice. *Professional Psychology: Research and Practice, 40*(4), 354–360.

HECKER, L. L. & Kottler, J. A. (2002). Growing creative therapists: Introduction to the special issue. *Journal of Clinical Activities, Assignments, & Handouts in Psychotherapy Practice, 2*(2), 1–4.

HEFFERNAN, M. (2011). *Willful blindness: Why we ignore the obvious at our peril.* New York: Walker.

HEINSSEN, R. K. (1994, June). *Therapeutic contracting with schizophrenic patients: A collaborative approach to cognitive-behavioral treatment.* Paper presented at the 21st International Symposium for the Psychotherapy of Schizophrenia, Washington, DC.

HEINSSEN, R. K., Levendusky, P. G. & Hunter, R. H. (1995). Client as colleague: Therapeutic contracting with the seriously mentally ill. *American Psychologist, 50,* 522–532.

HELLER, K., Swindle, R., Pescosolido, B. & Kikuzawa, S. (2000). Responses to nervous breakdowns in America over a 40-year period: Mental health policy implications. *American Psychologist, 55,* 740–749.

HENRETTY, J. R. & Levitt, H. M. (2010). The role of therapist self-disclosure in psychotherapy: A qualitative review. *Clinical Psychology Review, 30,* 63–77.

HEPPNER, P. P. & Claiborn, C. D. (1989). Social influence research in counseling: A review and critique (monograph). *Journal of Counseling Psychology, 36,* 365–387.

HEPPNER, P. P. & Frazier, P. A. (1992). Social psychological processes in psychotherapy: Extrapolating basic research to counseling psychology. In S. D. Brown & R. W. Lent (Eds.), *Handbook of counseling psychology.* New York: Wiley.

HEPPNER, P. P., Witty, T. E. & Dixon, W. A. (2004). Problem-solving appraisal and human adjustment: A review of 20 years of research using the problem solving inventory. *The Counseling Psychologist, 32,* 344–428.

HERMAN, J. L. (2011). Posttraumatic stress disorder as a shame disorder. In R. L. Dearing; & J. P. Tangney, (Eds.), *Shame in the therapy hour* (pp. 261–275). Washington, DC: American Psychological Association Books.

HERON, J. (2001). *Helping the client: A creative practical guide* (5th ed.). London: SAGE Publications Ltd.

HICKS, J. W. (2005). *50 signs of mental illness: A guide to understanding mental health.* New Haven: Yale University Press.

HIGGINSON, J. G. (1999). Defining, excusing, and justifying deviance: Teen mothers' accounts for statutory rape. *Symbolic Interaction, 22,* 25–44.

HIGHLEN, P. S. & Hill, C. E. (1984). Factors affecting client change in counseling. In S. D. Brown & R. W. Lent (Eds.), *Handbook of counseling psychology* (pp. 334–396). New York: Wiley.

HILL, C. E., Gelso, C. J., Chui, H., Spangler, P. T., Hummel, A., Huang, T. *et al.* (2014). To be or not to be immediate with clients: the use and perceived effects of immediacy in psychodynamic/interpersonal psychotherapy. *Psychotherapy Research, 24*(3): 299–315.

HILL, C. E., Knox, S. & Pinti-Coelho, K. G. (2019). Self-disclosure and immediacy. In J. C. Norcross & M. J. Lambert (Eds.), *Psychotherapy relationships that work: Vol. 1. Evidence-based therapist contributions.* New York: Oxford University Press.

HILL, C. E., Thompson, B. J., Cogar, M. C. & Denman, D. W., III. (1993). Beneath the surface of long-term therapy: Therapist and client report of their own and each other's covert processes. *Journal of Counseling Psychology, 40,* 278–287.

HILL, C. E. (2009). *Helping skills: Facilitating exploration, insight, and action* (3rd. ed.). Washington, DC: American Psychological Association Books.

HILL, P. L., Turiano, N. A., Hurd, M. D., Mroczek, D. K. & Roberts, B. W. (2011). Conscientiousness and longevity: An examination of possible mediators. *Health Psychology, 30*(5), 536–541.

HILLIARD, R. B. (1993, June). Single-case methodology in psychotherapy process and outcome research. *Journal of Consulting & Clinical Psychology, 61,* 373–380.

HOCH, S. & Kunreuther, H. C. (2004). *Wharton on decision making.* New York: Wiley.

HODGES, S. D. (2005). Is how much you understand me in your head or mine? In B. F. Malle & S. D. Hodges (Eds.), *Other minds: How humans bridge the divide between self and others* (pp. 298–309). New York: The Guilford Press.

HOGAN, B. E., Linden, W. & Najarian, B. (2002). Social support interventions: Do they work? *Clinical Psychology Review, 22,* 381–440.

HOLADAY, M. & McPhearson, R. W. (1997, May/June). Resilience and severe burns. *Journal of Counseling and Development, 75,* 346–356.

HOLLIS, J. (2007). *Why good people do bad things: Understanding our darker selves.* New York: Gotham.

HOOD, A. & Johnson, R. (2007). *Assessment in counseling: A guide to the use of psychological assessment procedures.* Alexandria, VA: American Counseling Association.

HOPKO, D. R., Lejuez, C. W., LePage, J. P., Hopko, S. D. & McNeil, D. W. (2003). A brief behavioral activation treatment for depression. *Behavior Modification, 27,* 458–469.

HORVATH, A. O., Del Re, A. C., Fluckiger, C. & Symonds, D. (2011). Alliance in individual therapy. In J. C. Norcross (Ed.), *Psychotherapy relationships that work: Evidence-based responsiveness* (2nd ed., pp. 25–69). New York: Oxford University Press.

HOSKING, G. & Walsh, I. R. (2005). *The WAVE report: Violence and what to do about it.* Croydon, UK: WAVE Trust.

HOUSER, R. F., Feldman, M., Williams, K. & Fierstien, J. (1998, July). Persuasion and social influence tactics used by mental health counselors. *Journal of Mental Health Counseling, 20,* 238–249.

HOWARD, G. S. (1991). Culture tales: A narrative approach to thinking, cross-cultural psychology, and psychotherapy. *American Psychologist, 46,* 187–197.

HOWARD, P. K. (2010, January 21). Problems with protocols. *Wall Street Journal,* p. A21.

HOWELL, W. S. (1982). *The empathic communicator.* Belmont, CA: Wadsworth.

HOYLE, R. H. (Ed.). (2010). *Handbook of personality and self-regulation.* Malden, MA: Blackwell.

HOYT, W. T. (1996). Antecedents and effects of perceived therapist credibility: A meta-analysis. *Journal of Counseling Psychology, 43,* 430–447.

HUBBLE, M. A., Duncan, B. L. & Miller, S. D. (Eds.). (1999). *The heart & soul of change: What works in therapy.* Washington, DC: American Psychological Association Books.

HUNNICUTT-FERGUSON, K., Hoxha, D. & Gollan, J. (2012). Exploring sudden gains in behavioral activation therapy for major depressive disorder. *Behaviour Research and Therapy.*

HUNTER, R. H. (1995). Benefits of competency-based treatment programs. *American Psychologist, 50,* 509–513.

HUTCHISON, E. D. (2003). *Dimensions of human behavior: The changing life course* (2nd ed.). Thousand Oaks, CA: Sage.

ICKES, W. (1993). Empathic accuracy. *Journal of Personality, 61,* 587–610.

ICKES, W. (1997). Introduction. In W. Ickes (Ed.), *Empathic accuracy* (pp. 1–16). New York: The Guilford Press.

ICO. (2018). Information commissioner's annual report and financial statements 2017–2018. Open Government License. Cheshire: ICO.

INCE, S. (2009). *Positive psychology: Harnessing the power of happiness, strength, and mindfulness.* Harvard Medical School Special Health Report. International bright young things. (2009, January 3). *Economist,* 58–60.

IVEY, A. E., Ivey, M. B., Zalaquett, C. P. & Quirk, K. (2012) *Essentials of intentional interviewing: Counseling in a multicultural world* (2nd ed.). Belmont, CA: Cengage Learning.

JACOBS, M. (2012). *The presenting past: The core of psychodynamic counselling and therapy* (4th ed.). Maidenhead, UK: Open University Press.

JACOBSON, N. S., Dobson, K. S., Truax, P. A., Addis, M. E., Koerner, K., Gollan, J. K. *et al.* (1996) A component analysis of cognitive-behavioral treatment for depression. *Journal of Consulting and Clinical Psychology, 64,* 295–304.

JANSE, P. D., De Jong, K., Van Dijk, M. K., Hutschemaekers, G. J. M. & Verbraak, M. J. P. M. (2017) Improving the efficiency of cognitive-behavioural therapy by using formal client feedback. *Psychotherapy Research*, 27(5), 525–538.

JEFFREY, N. A. (2004, September 3). Very interesting—Me, that is. *Wall Street Journal*, pp. W1, W7.

JENCIUS, M. (2010, June). A resourceful look at social justice. *Counseling Today*, pp. 26–27.

JENSEN, J. P., Bergin, A. E. & Greaves, D. W. (1990). The meaning of eclecticism: New survey and analysis of components. *Professional Psychology: Research and Practice*, 21, 124–130.

JOHANCEN-WALT, K. (2010, June). Patience for recovery: Encouraging clients to stay the course of treatment. *Counseling Today*, pp. 48–50.

JOHNSON, L., Addamo, P. K., Raj, I. S., Borkoles, E, Wyckelsma, V., Cyarto, E. *et al.* (2016). An acute bout of exercise improves the cognitive performance of older adults. *Journal of Aging and Physical Activity*, 24(4), 591–598.

JOHNSTON, E. R. (2015). South African clinical psychology's response to cultural diversity, globalisation and multiculturalism: a review. *South African Journal of Psychology*, 45(3), 375–385.

JOHNSTONE, L., & Dallos, R. (Eds.). (2006). *Formulation in psychology and psychotherapy: Making sense of people's problems*. London: Routledge.

JOSEPH, S, (2009). Growth following adversity: Positive psychological perspectives on posttraumatic stress. *Psychological Topics*. 18, 335–344.

JOSEPH, S. (2013). *What doesn't kill us: a guide to overcoming adversity and moving forward*. London: Piatkus.

JOSEPH, S. & Linley, P. A. (2005). Positive adjustment to threatening events: An organismic valuing theory of growth through adversity. *Review of General Psychology*, 9, 262–280.

JOSEPH, S. & Linley, A. (2008). *Trauma, recovery and growth: Positive psychological perspectives on posttraumatic stress*. New Jersey: Wiley and Sons Inc.

KAGAN, J. (1996). Three pleasing ideas. *American Psychologist*, 51, 901–908.

KAHNEMAN, D. (2012). *Thinking, fast and slow*. New York: Farrar, Straus, and Giroux.

KAHNEMAN, D., Lovallo, D. & Sibony, O. (2011, June). Before you make that big decision. *Harvard Business Review*, 51–59.

KANFER, F. H. & Schefft, B. K. (1988). *Guiding therapeutic change*. Champaign, IL: Research Press.

KARLAN, D. (2008, October 22). How to make a decision and then stick to it. *Financial Times*, p. 11.

KAROLY, P. (1999). A goal systems- self- regulatory perspective on personality, psychopathology, and change. *Review of General Psychology*, 3, 264–291.

KARPMAN, S. B. (1968). Fairy tales and script drama analysis. *Transactional Analysis Bulletin*, 7(26), 39–43.

KARPMAN, S. B. (2014). *"A game free life" – the definitive book on the drama triangle and compassion triangle by the originator and author*. San Francisco, CA: Drama Triangle Publications.

KASHDAN, T. B., Rose, P. & Fincham, F. D. (2004). Curiosity and exploration: Facilitating positive subjective experiences and personal growth opportunities. *Journal of Personality Assessment*, 82, 291–305.

KASLOW, N. J., Rubin, N. J., Bebeau, M. J., Leigh, I. W., Lichtenberg, J. W., Nelson, P. D. *et al.* (2007). Guiding principles and recommendations for the assessment of competence. *Professional Psychology: Research and Practice*, 38, 441–451.

KATO, T. (2012). Development of the coping flexibility scale: Evidence for the coping flexibility hypothesis. *Journal of Counseling Psychology*, 59, 262–273.

KAUFMAN, G. (1989). *The psychology of shame*. New York: Springer.

KAUFMAN, J. C. & Sternberg, R. J. (Eds.). (2010). *The Cambridge handbook of creativity*. Cambridge University Press.

KAY, J. (2011). *Obliquity: Why our goals are best achieved indirectly*. New York: Penguin Press.

KAZANTZIS, N. (2000). Power to detect homework effects in psychotherapy outcome research. *Journal of Consulting & Clinical Psychology, 68*, 166–170.

KAZANTZIS, N., Lampropoulos, G. L. & Deane, F. P. (2005). A national survey of practicing psychologists' use and attitudes towards homework in psychotherapy. *Journal of Consulting and Clinical Psychology, 73*, 742–748.

KAZDIN, A. E. (2006, January). Arbitrary metrics: Implications for identifying evidence-based treatments. *American Psychologist, 61*, 42–49.

KAZDIN, A. E. (2010). *Single-case research designs: Methods for clinical and applied settings* (2nd ed.). New York: Oxford University Press.

KEGAN, R. & Lahey, L. L. (2010). *Immunity to change: How to overcome it and unlock the potential in yourself and your organization*. Boston, MA: Harvard Business Press.

KELLEY, T. M. (2005). Natural resilience and innate mental health. *American Psychologist, 60*, 265.

KELLY, A. E. & Rodriguez, R. (2007). Do therapists self-disclose more to clients with greater symptomatology? *Psychotherapy: Theory, Research, Practice, Training, 44*, 470–475.

KELLY, E. W., Jr. (1994). *Relationship-centered counseling: An integration of art and science*. New York: Springer.

KELLY, E. W., Jr. (1997, May/June). Relationship-centered counseling: A humanistic model of integration. *Journal of Counseling and Development, 75*, 337–345.

KENNEDY, A. (2008, May). Impressing the need for empathy. *Counselling Today*, pp. 1, 30–31.

KENNY, M. E., Horne, A. M., Orpinas, P. & Reese, L. E. (2009). *Realizing social justice: The challenge of preventive interventions*. Washington, DC: American Psychology Association Books.

KERSTING, K. (2003). Lessons in resilience. *Monitor on Psychology*, pp. 30–31.

KERSTING, K. (2005, April). Resilience: The mental muscle everyone has. *Monitor on Psychology*, pp. 32–33.

KHOSHABA, D. M. & Maddi, S. R. (2004). *HardiTraining: Managing stressful change* (5th ed.). Irvine, CA: Hardiness Institute.

KIÀI KITAOKA, S. (2005). Multicultural counseling competencies: Lessons from assessment. *Journal of Multicultural Counseling and Development, 33*, 37–47.

KIM, B. S. K., Hill, C. E., Gelso, C. J., Goates, M. K., Asay, P. A. & Harbin, J. M. (2003). Counselor self-disclosure, East Asian American client adherence to Asian cultural values, and counseling process. *Journal of Counseling Psychology, 53*, 15–25.

KIM, H. S., Sherman, D. K. & Taylor, S. E. (2008). Culture and social support. *American Psychologist, 63*, 518–526.

KING, L. A. & Burton, C. M. (2003). The hazards of goal pursuit. In E. C. Chang & L. J. Sanna (Eds.), *Virtue, vice, and personality: The complexity of human behavior* (pp. 53–69). Washington, DC: American Psychology Association Books.

KING, L. A. & Hicks, J. A. (2007). Whatever happened to "what might have been"? Regrets, happiness, and maturity. *American Psychologist, 62*, 625–636.

KIRACOFE, N. M. & Wells, L. (2007). Mandated disciplinary counseling on campus: Problems and possibilities. *Journal of Counseling and Development, 85*, 259–267.

KIRSCHENBAUM, D. S. (1985). Proximity and specificity of planning: A position paper. *Cognitive Therapy and Research*, 9, 489–506.

KIRSCHENBAUM, D. S. (1987). Self-regulatory failure: A review with clinical implications. *Clinical Psychological Review*, 7, 77–104.

KIRSCHENBAUM, H. (2009). *The life and work of Carl Rogers*. Alexandria, VA: American Counseling Association Foundation.

KLEESPIES, P. M. (Ed.). (2009). *Behavioral emergencies: An evidence-based resource for evaluating and managing risk of suicide, violence, and victimization*. Washington, DC: American Psychological Association. doi.org/10.1037/11865-000

KLEIN, G. (1998). *Sources of power: How people make decisions*. Cambridge, MA: MIT Press.

KLEIN, G. (2008, June). Naturalistic decision making. *Human Factors*, 50, 456–460.

KLEIN, G. (2011). *Streetlights and shadows: Searching for the keys to adaptive decision making*. Cambridge, MA: Bradford Books, MIT Press.

KNAPP, H. (2007). *Therapeutic communication: Developing professional skills*. Thousand Oaks: Sage.

KNAPP, M. L. & Hall, J. A. (2010). *Nonverbal communication in human interaction* (7th ed.). Belmont, CA: Wadsworth, Cengage Learning.

KNAPP, S. & VandeCreek, L. (2007). When values of different cultures conflict: Ethical decision making in a multicultural context. *Professional Psychology: Research and Practice*, 38, 660–666.

KNAPP, S. J. (Ed.). (2012). *APA handbook of ethics in psychology. Vol. 1: Moral foundations and common themes. Vol. 2: Practice, teaching, and research*. Washington, DC: American Psychology Association Books.

KNOX, R., & Cooper, M. (2015). *The therapeutic relationship in counselling and psychotherapy*. London: SAGE Publications Ltd.

KOENIG, C. J. (2011, April). Patient resistance as agency in treatment decisions. *Social Science & Medicine*, 72, 1105–1114.

KOHUT, H. (1978). The psychoanalyst in the community of scholars. In P. H. Ornstein (Ed.), *The search for self: Selected writings of H. Kohut*. New York: International Universities Press.

KOLDEN, G. G., Klein, M. H., Wang, C.-C. & Austin, S. B. (2011). Congruence/genuineness. In J. C. Norcross (Ed.), *Psychotherapy relationships that work* (2nd ed., pp. 187–202). New York: Oxford University Press.

KOTTER, J. P. (2008). *A sense of urgency*. Boston, MA: Harvard Business School Press.

KOTTLER, J. A. (1992). *Compassionate therapy: Working with difficult clients*. San Francisco, CA: Jossey-Bass.

KOTTLER, J. A. (2010). *On being a therapist* (4th ed.). San Francisco, CA: Jossey-Bass.

KOTTLER, J. A. & Hecker, L. L. (2002). Creativity in therapy: Being struck by lightning and guided by thunderstorms… *Journal of Clinical Activities, Assignments, & Handouts in Psychotherapy Practice*, 2(2), 5–22.

LAGERVELD, S. E., Blonk, R. W. B., Brenninkmeijer, V., Wijngaards-de Meij, L. & Schaufeli, W. B. (2012). Work-focused treatment of common mental disorders and return to work: A comparative outcome study. *Journal of Occupational Health Psychology*, 17, 220–234.

LAKEMAN, R. (2014). Unknowing: A potential common factor in successful engagement and psychotherapy with people who have complex psychosocial needs. *International Journal of Mental Health Nursing*. onlinelibrary.wiley.com/doi/abs/10.1111/inm.12067

LAKEY, B. (2010). Social support: Basic research and new strategies for intervention. In J. E. Maddux & J. P. Tangey (Eds.), *Social psychological foundations of clinical psychology* (pp. 177–194). New York: The Guilford Press.

LAMBERT, M. J. (2010a). *The prevention of treatment failure: The use of measuring, monitoring, and feedback in clinical practice.* Washington, DC: American Psychology Association Books.

LAMBERT, M. J. (2010b). Yes, it is time for clinicians to routinely monitor treatment outcome. In B. L. Duncan, S. D. Miller, B. E. Wampold & M. A. Hubble (Eds.), *The heart and soul of change. Delivering what works* (2nd ed., pp. 239–266). Washington, DC: American Psychology Association Books.

LANDRO, L. (2010). The hidden benefits of exercise: Even moderate physical activity can boost the immune system and protect against chronic diseases. *Wall Street Journal.* The informed Patient Section. Retrieved from wsj.com/articles/SB10001424052748704350304574638331243027174

LANG, P. J. (1995, May). The emotion probe: Studies of motivation and attention. *American Psychologist, 50,* 372–385.

LA ROCHE, M. J. & Maxie, A. (2003). Ten considerations in addressing cultural differences in psychotherapy. *Professional Psychology: Research and Practice, 34*(2), 180.

LAZARUS, A. A. (1993, Fall). Tailoring the therapeutic relationship, or being an authentic chameleon. *Psychotherapy, 30,* 404–407.

LAZARUS, A. A., Beutler, L. E. & Norcross, J. C. (1992). The future of technical eclecticism. *Psychotherapy, 29,* 11–20.

LAZARUS, R. S. (2000). Toward better research on stressing and coping. *American Psychologist, 55,* 665–673.

LAZZARI, C., Egan, S. J. & Rees, C. S. (2011, January). Behavioral activation treatment for depression in older adults delivered via videoconferencing: A pilot study. *Cognitive and Behavioral Practice, 18,* 555–565.

LEAHEY, M. & Wallace, E. (1988). Strategic groups: One perspective on integrating strategic and group therapies. *Journal for Specialists in Group Work, 13,* 209–217.

LEAHY, R.L. (2001). *Overcoming resistance in cognitive therapy.* New York: The Guilord Press.

LEAHY, R.L., Tirch, D., & Napolitano, L.A. (2011). *Emotional regulation in psychotherapy: A practitioner's guide.* New York: The Guilford Press.

LEAHY, R. L. (1999). Strategic self-limitation. *Journal of Cognitive Psychotherapy, 13,* 275–293.

LEBOW, J. (2002, September/October). Learning to love assessment. *Psychotherapy Networker,* pp. 63–65.

LEE, C. C. (Ed.). (2007). *Counseling for social justice* (2nd ed.). Alexandria, VA: American Counseling Association Foundation.

LEE, S.A. (2020). Coronavirus Anxiety Scale: A brief mental health screener for COVID-19 related anxiety. *Death Studies.* Advanced online publication. doi.org/10.1080/07481187.2020.1748481

LEHRER, J. (2009). *How we decide.* Boston, MA: Houghton, Mifflin, Harcourt Mariner Books.

LEIGH, J.W. (1998). *Communicating for cultural competence.* Needham Heights, MA: Allyn & Bacon.

LEUNG, A. K., Maddux, W. W., Galinsky, A. D. & Chiu, C. (2008, April). Multicultural experience enhances creativity. *American Psychologist, 63,* 181.

LEWIN, K. (1969). Quasi-stationary social equilibria and the problem of permanent change. In W. G. Bennis, K. D. Benne, & R. Chin (Eds.), *The planning of change.* New York: Holt, Rinehart & Winston.

LEWIS, J. A., Lewis, M. D., Daniels, J. A. & D'Andrea, M. J. (2010). *Community counseling: A multicultural-social justice perspective* (4th ed.). Belmont, CA: Brooks/ Cole.

LEWIS, K. L. & Hodges, S. D. (2011). Empathy is not always as personal as you may think: The role of stereotypes in empathic accuracy. In J. Decety (Ed.), *Empathy: From bench to bedside* (pp. 73–84). Cambridge, MA: MIT Press.

LICHTENBERG, J. W., Portnoy, S. M., Bebeau, M. J., Leigh, I. W., Nelson, P. D., Rubin, N. J. et al. (2007). Challenges to the assessment of competence and competencies. *Professional Psychology: Research and Practice*, 38, 474–478.

LIGHTSEY, O. R., Jr. (1996, October). What leads to wellness? The role of psychological resources in well-being. *The Counseling Psychologist*, 24, 589–735.

LILIENFELD, S. O. (2007). Psychological treatments that cause harm. *Perspectives on Psychological Science*, 2, 53–70.

LIN, Y. (2002). Taiwanese university students' perspectives on helping. *Counseling Psychology Quarterly*, 15, 47–58.

LINEHAN, M.M. (2014). *DBT skills training manual* (2nd ed.). New York: The Guilford Press.

LINLEY, P. A. & Joseph, S. (2005). The human capacity for growth through adversity. *American Psychologist*, 60, 262–264.

LITZ, B. T. (2005). Has resilience to severe trauma been underestimated? *American Psychologist*, 60, 262.

LOCKE, E. A. & Latham, G. P. (1984). *Goal setting: A motivational technique that works*. Englewood Cliffs, NJ: Prentice Hall.

LOCKE, E. A. & Latham, G. P. (1990). *A theory of goal setting and task performance*. Englewood Cliffs, NJ: Prentice Hall.

LOCKE, E. A. & Latham, G. P. (2002). Building a practically useful theory of goal setting and task motivation: A 35-year odyssey. *American Psychologist*, 57, 705–717.

LOCKE, E.A. & Latham, G.P. (2017). *New developments in goal setting and task performance*. New York: Routledge.

LOCKWOOD, T. (2010). *Design thinking: Integrating innovation, customer experience, and brand value*. New York: Allworth Press.

LOPEZ, F. G., Lent, R. W., Brown, S. D. & Gore, P. A. (1997). Role of social-cognitive expectations in high school students' mathematics-related interest and performance. *Journal of Counseling Psychology*, 44, 44–52.

LOPEZ, S. (Ed.). (2008). *Positive psychology: Exploring the best in people. Vol 1. Discovering human strengths*. Westport, CT: Greenwood Publishing Company.

LOPEZ, S. J. & Snyder, C. R. (2003). *Positive psychological assessment: A handbook of models and measures*. Washington, DC: American Psychological Association Books.

LOWE, M. R. (2003). Dieting: False hope or falsely accused? *American Psychologist*, 58, 819–820.

LOWENSTEIN, L. (1993). Treatment through traumatic confrontation approaches: The story of S. *Education Today*, 43, 198–201.

LUBORSKY, L., Crits-Christoph, P., McLellan, A. T., Woody, G., Piper, W., Liberman, B. et al. (1986). The nonspecific hypothesis of therapeutic effectiveness: A current assessment. *American Journal of Orthopsychiatry*, 56, 501–512.

LUNDERVOLD, D. A. & Belwood, D. A. (2000, Winter). The best kept secret in counseling: Single-case experimental designs. *Journal of Counseling and Development*, 78, 92–102.

LUNNEN, K. M., Ogles, B. M. & Pappas, L. N. (2008). A multi-perspective comparison of satisfaction, symptomatic change, perceived change. *Professional Psychology: Research and Practice*, 39, 145–152.

LUOMA, J. B., Hayes, S. C. & Walser, R. D. (2007). *Learning Act: An acceptance and commitment therapy skills training manual for therapists (Context / Nhp Context / Nhp)*. Oakland, CA: New Harbinger.

LYND, H. M. (1958). *On shame and the search for identity*. New York: Science Editions.

MADDI, S. R. (2002). The story of hardiness: Twenty years of theorizing, research, and practice. *Consulting Psychology Journal*, 54, 173–185.

MADDI, S. R. (2005). On hardiness and other pathways to resilience. *American Psychologist, 60,* 261–262.

MADDI, S. R. (2013). *Hardiness: turning stressful circumstances into resilient growth.* New York: Springer.

MADDUX, J. E. (Ed.). (1995). *Self-efficacy, adaptation, and adjustment: Theory, research, and application.* New York: Plenum.

MADIGAN, S. (2011). *Narrative therapy.* Washington, DC: American Psychology Association Books.

MAGNAVITA, J. J. (2005). *Personality-guided relational psychotherapy: A unified approach.* Washington, DC: American Psychological Association.

MAHRER, A. R. (1993, Fall). The experiential relationship: Is it all-purpose or is it tailored to the individual client? *Psychotherapy, 30,* 413–416.

MAHRER, A. R., Gagnon, R., Fairweather, D. R., Boulet, D. B. & Herring, C. B. (1994). Client commitment and resolve to carry out post- session behaviors. *Journal of Counseling Psychology, 41,* 407–414.

MALLINCKRODT, B. (1996). Change in working alliance, social support, and psychological symptoms in brief therapy. *Journal of Counseling Psychology, 43,* 448–455.

MANTHEI, R. & Miller, J. (2000). *Good counseling: A guide for clients.* Auckland, NZ: Pearson Education.

MANUSOV, V. (2005). *The sourcebook of nonverbal measures: Going beyond words.* Mahwah, NJ: Lawrence Erlbaum.

MANUSOV, V. & Patterson, M. L. (Eds.). (2006). *The Sage handbook of non-verbal communication.* Thousand Oaks, CA: Sage.

MARANGES, H.M., & Baumeister, R.F. (2016). Self-control and ego depletion. In K.D. Vohs & R.F. Baumeister (Eds.), *Handbook of self-regulation, third edition: research, theory and applications* (pp. 42–61). New York: The Guilford Press.

MARCH, J. G. (1994). *A primer on decision making: How decisions happen.* New York: The Free Press.

MARTIN, J. (1994). *The construction and understanding of psychotherapeutic change.* New York: Teachers College Press.

MARTIN, P. (2011). Celebrating the wounded healer. *Counselling Psychology Review,* 26(1), 10–19.

MARTINEZ-LEWI, L. (2008). *Freeing yourself from the narcissist in your life.* New York: Tarcher/Penguin.

MASH, E. J. & Hunsley, J. (1993). Assessment considerations in the identification of failing psychotherapy: Bringing the negatives out of the darkroom. *Psychological Assessment, 5,* 292–301.

MASLOW, A. H. (1968). *Toward a psychology of being* (2nd ed.). New York: Van Nostrand Reinhold.

MASSIMINI, F. & Delle Fave, A. (2000, January). Individual development in a biocultural perspective. *American Psychologist, 55,* 24–33.

MAST, M., & Ickes, W. (2007). Empathic accuracy: Measurement and potential clinical applications. In T. Farrow & P. Woodruff (Eds.), *Empathy in mental illness* (pp. 408–427). New York: Cambridge University Press.

MAYER, J. D. & Salovey, P. (1997). What is emotional intelligence? In P. Salovey & D. Sluyter (Eds.), *Emotional development and emotional intelligence: Educational implications* (pp. 3–31). New York: Basic Books.

MAYER, J. D., Roberts, R. D. & Barsade, S. G. (2008). Human abilities: Emotional intelligence. *Annual Review of Psychology, 59,* 507–536.

McCARTHY, W. C. & Frieze, I. H. (1999). Negative aspects of therapy: Client perceptions of therapists' social influence, burnout, and quality of care. *Journal of Social Issues, 55*(1), 33–50. doi.org/10.1111/0022-4537.00103

McCARTHY, W. C. & Frieze, I. H. (2002, Spring). Negative aspects of therapy: Client perceptions of therapists' social influence, burnout, and quality of care. *Journal of Social Issues, 55*, 33–50.

McCRAE, R. R. & Costa, P. T., Jr. (1997, May). Personality trait structure as a human universal. *American Psychologist, 52*, 509–516.

McDERMOTT, D. & Snyder, C. R. (1999). *Making hope happen.* Oakland/San Francisco: New Harbinger Press.

McKAY, D., Abramowitz, J. S. & Taylor, S. (Eds.). (2010). *Cognitive-behavioral therapy for refractory cases: Turning failure into success.* Washington, DC: American Psychology Association Books.

McKENZIE, K. S. & Hoyle, R. H. (2008). The Self-Absorption Scale: Reliability and validity in non-clinical samples. *Personality and Individual Differences, 45*, 726–731.

McMILLEN, C., Zuravin, S. & Rideout, G. (1995). Perceived benefit from child sexual abuse. *Journal of Consulting and Clinical Psychology, 63*, 1037–1043.

McNEILL, B. & Stolenberg, C. D. (1989). Reconceptualizing social influence in counseling: The elaboration likelihood model. *Journal of Counseling Psychology, 36*, 24–33.

McNULTY, J. K. & Fincham, F. D. (2012, February–March). Beyond positive psychology? Toward a contextual view of psychological processes and well-being. *American Psychologist, 67*, 101–110.

McWHIRTER, E. H. (1996). *Counseling for empowerment.* Alexandria, VA: American Counseling Association.

MEE-LEE, D., McLellan, A. T., Miller, S. D. (2010). What works in substance abuse and dependence treatment. In B. L. Duncan, S. D. Miller, B. E. Wampold & M. A. Hubble (Eds.). *The heart and soul of change: Delivering what works in therapy* (2nd ed., pp. 393–417). Washington, D. C.: American Psychological Association Books.

MEEK, R. (2011). The possible selves of young fathers in prison. *Journal of Adolescence, 34*(5), 941–949.

MEHRABIAN, A. (1972). *Non-verbal communication.* Chicago, IL: Aldine-Atherton.

MEHRABIAN, A. (1981). *Silent messages: Implicit communication of emotions and attitudes* (2nd ed.). Belmont, CA: Wadsworth.

MEHRABIAN, A. & Reed, H. (1969). Factors influencing judgments of psychopathology. *Psychological Reports, 24*, 323–330.

MEICHENBAUM, D. & Turk, D. C. (1987). *Facilitating treatment adherence: A practitioner's guidebook.* New York: Plenum Press.

MELBOURNE ACADEMIC MINDFULNESS INTEREST GROUP. (2006). Mindfulness-based psychotherapies: A review of conceptual foundations, empirical evidence, and practical considerations. *Australian and New Zealand Journal of Psychology, 40*, 285–294.

MENDENHALL, T. (2007, May/June). Crisis land. *Psychotherapy Networker*, pp. 32–39.

MERHOLZ, P., Wilkens, T., Schauer, B. & Verba, D. (2008). *Subject to change: Creating great products and services for an uncertain world.* Sebastopol, CA: O'Reilly Media Inc.

MICHAEL, K. D., Curtin, L., Kirkley, D. E., Jones, D. L. & Harris, R., Jr. (2006). Group-based motivational interviewing for alcohol use among college students: An exploratory study. *Professional Psychology: Research and Practice, 37*, 629–634.

MIKULINCER, M. & Shaver, P. R. (Eds.). (2012). *The social psychology of morality: Exploring the causes of good and evil.* Washington, DC: American Psychology Association Books.

MILAN, M. A., Montgomery, R. W. & Rogers, E. C. (1994). Theoretical orientation revolution in clinical psychology: Fact or fiction? *Professional Psychology: Research and Practice, 4*, 398–402.

MILLER, G. A., Galanter, E. & Pribram, K. H. (1960). *Plans and the structure of behavior.* New York: Holt, Rinehart & Winston.

MILLER, L. M. (1984). *American spirit: Visions of a new corporate culture.* New York: Morrow.

MILLER, M. (n.d.). *Shame and Psychotherapy.* Retrieved December 30, 2008, from http://www.columbiapsych.com/articles/ shame-and-psychotherapy

MILLER, S. D., Duncan, B. L., Brown, S. R. & Chalk, M. B. (2006). Using formal client feedback to improve retention and outcome: Making ongoing, real-time assessment feasible. *Journal of Brief Therapy, 5,* 5–22.

MILLER, S. D., Hubble, M. A., Duncan, B. L. & Wampold, B. E. (2010). Delivering what works. In B. L. Duncan, S. D. Miller, B. E. Wampol, & M. A. Hubble (Eds.), *The heart and soul of change. Delivering what works* (2nd ed., pp. 421–429). Washington, DC: American Psychological Association Books.

MILLER, W. C. (1986). *The creative edge: Fostering innovation where you work.* Reading, MA: Addison-Wesley.

MILLER, W. R. & Rollnick, S. (1995). What is motivational interviewing? *Behavior and Cognitive Psychotherapy, 23,* 325–334.

MILLER, W. R. & Rollnick, S. (Eds.). (2002). *Motivational interviewing: Preparing people for change.* New York: The Guilford Press.

MILLER, W. R. & Rollnick, S. (2004). Talking oneself into change: Motivational interviewing, stages of change, and therapeutic process. *Journal of Cognitive Psychotherapy, 18,* 299–308.

MILTON, M. (Ed.) (2010). *Therapy and beyond: Counselling psychology contributions to therapeutic and social issues.* Chichester: Wiley Blackwell.

MITCHELL, C. (2006). *Resistant clients: We've all had them; here's how to help them.* Sourced at www.psychotherapy.net/article/ resistantclients.

MONASH ACADEMIC MINDFULNESS INTEREST GROUP. (2006). Mindfulness-based psychotherapies: A review of conceptual foundations, empirical evidence and practical considerations. *Australian and New Zealand Journal of Psychiatry, 40(4),* 285–294.

MOON, K. (2007). A client-centered review of Rogers with Gloria. *Journal of Counseling and Development, 85,* 277–283.

MOORE, S. R. & Gelso, C. J. (2011). Recollections of a secure base in psychotherapy: Considerations of the real relationship. *Psychotherapy, 48,* 368–373.

MORRIS, T. (1994). *True success: A new philosophy of excellence.* New York: Grosset/ Putman.

MOSS, K., Scogin, F., Di Napoli, E. & Presnell, A. (2012, February). A self-help behavioral activation treatment for geriatric depressive symptoms. *Aging Mental Health, 16,* 625–635.

MOYERS, T. B., Miller, W. R. & Hendrickson, S. M. (2005). How does motivational interviewing work? Therapist interpersonal skill predicts client involvement within motivational interviewing sessions. *Journal of Consulting and Clinical Psychology, 73,* 590–598.

MULTON, K. D., Brown, S. D. & Lent, R. W. (1991). Relation of self-efficacy beliefs to academic outcomes: A meta-analytic investigation. *Journal of Counseling Psychology, 38,* 30–38.

MURAN, J. C. (Ed.). (2006). *Dialogues on difference: Studies of diversity in the therapeutic relationship.* Washington, DC: American Psychological Association Books.

MURAN, J. C. & Barber, J. P. (Eds.). (2010). *The therapeutic alliance: An evidence-based guide to practice.* New York: The Guilford Press.

MURDIN, L. (2015). *Managing difficult endings in psychotherapy.* Abingdon, UK: Routledge.

MURGATROYD, S. & Woolfe, R. (1982). *Coping with crisis: Understanding and helping people in need.* New York: Joanna Cotler Books.

MURGATROYD, S. J. (1985). *Counselling and helping.* New York: Routledge.

MURPHY, P. M., Cramer, D. & Lillie, E. J. (1984). The relationship between curative factors perceived by patients in their psychotherapy and treatment outcome: An exploratory study. *British Journal of Medical Psychology, 57,* 187–192.

MURPHY, S. N. (2006, August). Harnessing emotional intelligence. *Counseling Today,* pp. 14–15.

MYER, R. A. & Moore, H. B. (2006). Crisis in context theory: An ecological model. *Journal of Counseling and Development, 84,* 139–147.

MYERS, D. & Hayes, J. A. (2006). Effects of therapist general self-disclosure and counter-transference disclosure on ratings of the therapist and session. *Psychotherapy: Theory, Research, Practice, Training, 43,* 173–185.

NATHANSON, D. (Ed.). (1987). *The many faces of shame.* New York: The Guilford Press.

NEEDLEMAN, J. (2007). *Why can't we be good?* New York: Tarcher/Penguin.

NEENAN, M. & Palmer, S. (2012). *Cognitive behavioural coaching in practice: An evidence based approach.* Hove, UK: Routledge.

NELSON-JONES, R. (2005). *Practical counseling & helping skills* (5th ed.). Thousand Oaks, CA: Sage Publications.

NEWMAN, R. (2005). APA's resilience initiative. *Professional Psychology: Research and Practice, 36,* 227–229.

NEZU, A. M., Nezu, C. M., Friedman, S. H., Faddis, S. & Houts, P. S. (1998). *Helping cancer patients cope. A problem-solving approach.* Washington, DC: American Psychological Association.

NIEMAN, D. C. (2010). *Exercise testing and prescription: A health-related approach* (7th ed.). New York: McGraw Hill.

NORCROSS, J. C. (2010). The therapeutic relationship. In B. L. Duncan, S. D. Miller, B. E. Wampold & M. A. Hubble (Eds.), *The heart and soul of change: Delivering what works* (2nd ed., pp. 113–141). Washington, DC: American Psychology Association Books.

NORCROSS, J. C. (Ed.). (2011a). Evidence-based therapy relationships. *Psychotherapy, 48*(1), 98–102.

NORCROSS, J. C. (Ed.). (2011b). *Psychotherapy relationships that work: Evidence-based responsiveness* (2nd ed.). New York: Oxford University Press.

NORCROSS, J. C. & Goldfried, M. R. (Eds.). (2005). *Handbook of psychology integration.* New York: Oxford University Press.

NORCROSS, J. C., Krebs, P. M. & Prochaska, J. O. (2011). Stages of change. In J. C. Norcross (Ed.), *Psychotherapy relationships that work* (2nd ed., pp. 279–300). New York: Oxford University Press.

NORCROSS, J. C. & Lambert, M. J. (2011). Evidence-based therapy relationships. In J. C. Norcross (Ed.), *Psychotherapy relationships that work* (2nd ed., pp. 3–21). New York: Oxford University Press.

NORCROSS, J. C. & Wampold, B. E. (Eds.). (2011). Adapting psychotherapy to the individual patient. *Journal of Clinical Psychology, 67*(2).

NORENZAYAN, A. & Heine, S. J. (2005). Psychological universals: What are they and how can we know? *Psychological Bulletin, 131,* 763–784.

OETTINGEN, G. & Gollwitzer, P. M. (2010). Strategies of setting and implementing goals. In J. E. Maddux & J. P. Tangney (Eds.), *Social psychological foundations of clinical psychology* (pp. 114–135). New York: The Guilford Press.

OGDEN, J. (2010). *The psychology of eating* (2nd ed.). New York: Wiley-Blackwell.

O'HARA, D. (2013). *Hope in counselling and psychotherapy.* London: SAGE publications ltd.

OKIISHI, J., Lambert, M. J., Nielsen, S. L. & Ogles, B. M. (2003). Waiting for supershrink: An empirical analysis of therapist effects. *Clinical Psychology and Psychotherapy, 10,* 361–373.

O'LEARY, A. (1985). Self-efficacy and health. *Behavior Research and Therapy, 23,* 437–451.

O'NEIL, J. M. (2004). Response to Heppner, Witty and Dixon: Inspiring and high-level scholarship that can change people's lives. *The Counseling Psychologist, 32,* 439–449.

ORLINSKY, D. E. & Howard, K. I. (1987, Spring). A generic model of psychotherapy. *Journal of Integrative and Eclectic Psychotherapy, 6,* 6–27.

ORLINSKY, D. E. & Rønnestad, M. H. (2005). *How psychotherapists develop: A study of therapeutic work and professional growth.* Washington, DC: American Psychological Association Books.

ORLINSKY, D. E., Rønnestad, M. H. & Willutzki, U. (2004). Fifty years of process outcome research: Continuity and change. In M. J. Lambert (Ed.), *Bergin and Garfield's handbook of psychotherapy and behavior change* (5th ed., pp. 307–390). New York: Wiley.

OYSERMAN, D., Bybee, D., Terry, K. & Hart-Johnson, T. (2004). Possible selves as roadmaps. *Journal of Research in Personality, 38,* 130–149.

PADESKY, C. & Mooney, K.A. (2012). Strengths-based cognitive–behavioural therapy: A four-step model to build resilience. *Clinical Psychology and Psychotherapy, 19,* 283–290.

PARÉ, D. & Lysack, M. (2004). The willow and the oak: From monologue to dialogue in the scaffolding of therapeutic conversations. *Journal of Systemic Therapies, 23,* 6–20.

PARK, C. L., Lechner, S. C., Antoni, M. H. & Stanton, A. L. (Eds.). (2009). *Medical illness and positive life change: Can crisis lead to personal transformation?* Washington, DC: American Psychological Association Books.

PARTNOY, F. (2012). *Wait: The art and science of delay.* New York: PublicAffairs.

PATTERSON, K., Grenny, J., McMillan, R. & Switzler, A. (2004). *Crucial confrontations: Tools for resolving broken promises, violated expectations, and bad behavior.* New York: McGraw Hill.

PAYNE, E. C., Robbins, S. B. & Dougherty, L. (1991). Goal directedness and older-adult adjustment. *Journal of Counseling Psychology, 38,* 302–308.

PAYNE, M. (2006). *Narrative therapy.* Thousand Oaks, CA: Sage.

PEASE, A. & Pease, B. (2006). *Body language.* New York: Random House Digital.

PEDERSEN, P., Crethar, H. & Carlson, J. (2008). *Inclusive cultural empathy: Making relationships central in counseling and psychotherapy.* Washington, DC: American Psychological Association.

PENNEBAKER, J. W. (1995). Emotion, disclosure, and health: An overview. In J. W. Pennebaker (Ed.), *Emotion, disclosure, and health* (pp. 3–10). Washington, DC: American Psychological Association.

PENTLAND, A. (2010, May–June). To signal is human. *American Scientist, 98,* 204–210.

PENTLAND, A. (with Heibeck, T.) (2008). *Honest signals: How they shape our world.* Cambridge, MA: MIT Press.

PERRIN, P. B., Heesacker, M., Pendley, C. & Smith, M. B. (2010). In J. E. Maddux & J. P. Tangney (Eds.), *Social psychological foundations of clinical psychology* (pp. 441–460). New York: The Guilford Press.

PERVIN, L. A. (1996). *The science of personality.* New York: Wiley.

PETERSON, C. (2006). *A primer in positive psychology.* New York: Oxford University Press.

PETERSON, C., Maier, S. F. & Seligman, M. E. P. (1995). *Learned helplessness: A theory for the age of personal control.* New York: Oxford University Press.

PETERSON, C. & Seligman, M. E. P. (2004). *Character strengths and virtues: A classification handbook.* New York: Oxford University Press/ Washington, DC: American Psychological Association.

PETERSON, C., Seligman, M. E. P. & Vaillant, G. E. (1988). Pessimistic explanatory style as a risk factor for physical illness: A thirty-five-year longitudinal study. *Journal of Personality and Social Psychology, 55*, 23–27.

PFEFFER, J. & Sutton, R. I. (2000). *The knowing - doing gap: How smart companies turn knowledge into action.* Boston, MA: Harvard Business School Press.

PHILIPPOT, P., Feldman, R. & Coats, E. (Eds.). (2003). *Nonverbal behavior in clinical settings.* New York: Oxford University Press.

PHILLIPS, A. & Daniluk, J. C. (2004). Beyond "survivor": How childhood sexual abuse informs the identity of adult women at the end of the therapeutic process. *Journal of Counseling & Development, 82*, 177–184.

PHILLIPS, E. L. (1987). The ubiquitous decay curve: Service delivery similarities in psychotherapy, medicine, and addiction. *Professional Psychology: Research and Practice, 18*, 650–652.

PINSOF, W. M. (1995). *Integrative problem-centered therapy: A synthesis of family, individual, and biological therapies.* New York: Basic Books.

PLUTCHIK, R. (2001). *Emotions in the practice of psychotherapy: Clinical implications affect theories.* Washington, DC: American Psychological Association.

PLUTCHIK, R. (2003). *Emotions and life: Perspectives from psychology, biology, and evolution.* Washington, DC: American Psychological Association.

POLIVY, J. & Herman, C. P. (2002). If at first you don't succeed: False hopes of self-change. *American Psychologist, 57*, 677–689.

PONTEROTTO, J. G., Casas, J. M., Suzuki, L. A. & Alexander, C. M. (Eds.). (2010). *Handbook of multicultural counseling* (3rd ed.). Thousand Oaks, CA: Sage.

POPE, K. S., Sonne, J. L. & Greene, B. (2006). *What therapists don't talk about and why: Understanding taboos that hurt us and our clients.* Washington, DC: American Psychological Association.

POPE-DAVIS, D. B., Coleman, H. L. K., Liu, W. M. & Toporek, R. L. (Eds.). (2004). *Handbook of multicultural competence for counseling and psychology.* Thousand Oaks, CA: Sage Publications.

POTTER-EFRON, R. T. (2011). Therapy with shame-prone alcoholic and drug-dependent clients. In R. L. Dearing & J. P. Tangney (Eds.), *Shame in the therapy hour.* Washington, DC: American Psychological Association Books.

PROCHASKA, J. O. & DiClemente, C. C. (2005). *The transtheoretical approach.* In J. C. Norcross & M. R. Goldfried (Eds.). *Oxford series in clinical psychology. Handbook of psychotherapy integration* (pp. 147–171). Oxford: Oxford University Press. doi.org/10.1093/med: psych/9780195165791.003.0007

PROCHASKA, J. O. & Norcross, J. C. (2001). Stages of change. *Psychotherapy: Theory, Research, Practice, Training, 38*(4), 443–448. doi.org/10.1037/0033-3204.38.4.443

PROCHASKA, J. O. & Norcross, J. C. (2010). *Systems of psychotherapy: A transtheoretical analysis* (7th ed.). Pacific Grove, CA: Brooks/Cole.

PSYCHOLOGICAL SOCIETY OF SOUTH AFRICA. (2007). *South African professional conduct guidelines in psychology.* Johannesburg: PsySSA.

PUTNAM, R. D. (2000). *Bowling alone.* New York: Simon & Schuster.

PUTNAM, R. D. (2007). *E Pluribus Unum*: Diversity and community in the twenty-first century. The 2006 Johan Skytte prize lecture. *Scandinavian Political Studies, 30*(2), 137–174.

PYCHYL, T. A. (2010). *The procrastinator's digest.* Dartford, UK: Xlibris.

PYSZCZYNSKI, T. & Greenberg, J. (1987). Self-regulatory preservation and the depressive self-focusing style: A self-awareness theory of depression. *Psychological Bulletin, 102*, 122–138.

QUALLS, S. H. & Abeles, N. (2000). *Psychology and the aging revolution: How we adapt to long life*. Washington, DC: American Psychological Association.

RACHMAN, G. (2008, October 7). Conservatism overshoots its limit. *Financial Times*, p. 13.

RASHOTTE, L. S. (2006). Social influence. *Blackwell Encyclopedia of Sociology*, 9, 4426–4429.

RASMUSSEN, P. R. (2002). Resistance: The fear behind it and tactics for reducing it. *Journal of Individual Psychology*, 58(2), 148–159.

RASMUSSEN, P. R. (2005). *Personality-guided cognitive-behavioral therapy*. Washington, DC: American Psychological Association Books.

RATEY, J. & Hagerman, E. (2008). *Spark: The revolutionary new science of exercise and the brain*. New York: Little Brown.

RATTS, M., Toporek, R. & Lewis, J. A. (2010). *ACA advocacy competencies: A social justice framework for counselors*. Alexandria, VA: American Counseling Association.

RAUP, J. L. & Myers, J. E. (1989). The empty nest syndrome: Myth or reality? *Journal of Counseling & Development*, 68, 180–183.

RAYLE, A. D. (2006). Mattering to others: Implications for the counseling relationship. *Journal of Counseling and Development*, 84, 483–487.

REIS, B. F. & Brown, L. G. (2006). Preventing therapy dropout in the real world: The clinical utility of videotape preparation and client estimate of treatment duration. *Professional Psychology: Research and Practice*, 37, 311–316.

REITER, M. D. (2010). Hope and expectancy in solution-focused brief therapy. *Journal of Family Psychotherapy*, 21, 132–148.

REIVICH, K. & Shatté, A. (2002). *The resilience factor: 7 keys to finding your inner strength and overcoming life's hurdles*. New York: Broadway Books.

RENNIE, D. L. (1994). Clients' deference in psychotherapy. *Journal of Counseling Psychology*, 41, 427–437.

REXRODE, K. R., Petersen, S. & O'Toole, S. (2008). The ways of coping scale: A reliability generalization study. *Educational and Psychological Measurement*, 68, 262–280.

RHULE, D. (2005). Take care to do no harm. *Professional Psychology: Research and Practice*, 36, 618–625.

RICHARDS, R. (Ed.). (2007). *Everyday creativity and new views of human nature: Psychological, social, and spiritual perspectives*. Washington DC: American Psychological Association.

RICHMOND, V. P. & McCroskey, J. C. (2000). *Non-verbal behavior in interpersonal relations* (4th ed.). Needham Heights, MA: Allyn & Bacon.

RICHMOND, V., McCroskey, J. & Hickson, M. (2012). *Non-verbal behavior in interpersonal relations* (7th ed.). Needham Heights, MA: Allyn & Bacon.

RIGGIO, R. E. & Feldman, R. S. (2005). *Applications of non-verbal communication (Claremont symposium on applied social psychology)*. Mahwah, NJ: Lawrence Erlbaum.

RISO, L. P., Du Toit, P. L., Stein, D. J. & Young, J. E. (Eds.). (2007). *Cognitive schemas and core beliefs in psychological problems: A scientist-practitioner guide*. Washington, DC: American Psychological Association.

RISTANTO, A. & Caltabiano, M.L. (2019). Psychological support and well-being in post-bariatric surgery patients. *Obesity Surgery*, 29(2), 739–743.

ROBERTS, B. W., Walton, K. E. & Bogg, T. (2005). Conscientiousness and health across the life course. *Review of General Psychology*, 9, 156–168.

ROBERTSHAW, J. E., Mecca, S. J. & Rerick, M. N. (1978). *Problem-solving: A systems approach*. New York: Petrocelli Books.

ROBINSON, B. S., Davis, K. L. & Meara, N. M. (2003). Motivational attributes of occupational possible selves for low-income rural women. *Journal of Counseling Psychology, 50*, 156–164.

ROEHRLE, B. & Strouse, J. (2008). Influence of social support on success of therapeutic interventions: A meta-analytic review. *Psychotherapy: Theory, Research, Practice, Training, 45*, 464–476.

ROFFMAN, A. E. (2004, Summer). Is anger a thing-to-be-managed? *Psychotherapy: Theory, Research, Practice, Training, 41*, 161–171.

ROGERS, C. R. (1951). *Client-centered therapy.* Boston, MA: Houghton Mifflin.

ROGERS, C. R. (1957). The necessary and sufficient conditions of therapeutic personality change. *Journal of Consulting Psychology, 21*, 95–103.

ROGERS, C. R. (1965). *Client-centered therapy: Its current practice, implications and theory.* Boston, MA: Houghton, Mifflin.

ROGERS, C. R. (1975). Empathic: An unappreciated way of being. *The Counseling Psychologist, 5*, 2–10.

ROGERS, C. R. (1980). *A way of being.* Boston, MA: Houghton Mifflin.

ROGERS, C. R., Perls, F. & Ellis, A. (1965). *Three approaches to psychotherapy 1* [Film]. Orange, CA: Psychological Films, Inc.

ROGERSON, M. D., Gottlieb, M. C., Handelsman, M. M., Knapp, S. & Younggren, J. (2011, October). Non-rational processes in ethical decision making. *American Psychologist, 66*, 614–623.

ROLLNICK, S. & Miller, W. R. (1995). What is motivational interviewing? *Behavioural and Cognitive Psychotherapy, 23*, 325–334.

ROLLNICK, S., Miller, W. R. & Butler, C. C. (2008). *Motivational interviewing in healthcare: Helping patients change behavior.* New York: The Guilford Press.

ROSEN, S. & Tesser, A. (1970). On the reluctance to communicate undesirable information: The MUM effect. *Sociometry, 33*, 253–263.

ROSEN, S. & Tesser, A. (1971). Fear of negative evaluation and the reluctance to transmit bad news. *Proceedings of the 79th Annual Convention of the American Psychological Association, 6*, 301–302.

ROSENGREN, D. B. (2009). *Building motivational interviewing skills: A practitioner workbook.* New York: The Guilford Press.

ROSSITER, M. (2007). Possible selves in adult education. *New Directions for Adult and Continuing Education, 114*, 87–94.

ROTTENBERG, J. & Johnson, S. (Eds.). (2007). *Emotion and psychopathology: Bridging affective and clinical science.* Washington, DC: American Psychological Association.

ROUSSI, P., Krikeli, V., Hatzidimitriou, C. & Koutri, I. (2007). Patterns of coping, flexibility in coping and psychological distress in women diagnosed with breast cancer. *Cognitive Therapy and Research, 31*, 97–109.

RUSCIO, J. (2005). *Critical thinking in psychology: Separating sense from nonsense* (2nd ed.). Belmont, CA: Wadsworth.

SAFRAN, J. D., Muran, J. C. & Eubanks-Carter, C. (2011). Repairing alliance ruptures. In J. C. Norcross (Ed.), *Psychotherapy relationships that work* (2nd ed., pp. 224–238). New York: Oxford University Press.

SALMON, L. (2017). The four questions: A framework for integrating an understanding of oppression dynamics in clinical work and supervision. In R. Allen & S.S. Poulsen (Eds.), *Creating cultural safety in couple and family therapy: supervision and training.* Switzerland: Springer.

SALOVEY, P. & Mayer, J. D. (1990). Emotional intelligence. *Imagination, Cognition, and Personality, 9*, 185–211.

SALOVEY, P., Rothman, A. J., Detweiler, J. B. & Steward, W. T. (2000, January). Emotional states and physical health. *American Psychologist, 55*, 110–121.

SANDERSON, C. (2015). *Counselling skills for working with shame*. London: Jessica Kingsley.

SATEL, S. (1996). Psychiatric apartheid. *Wall Street Journal*, A14.

SHAPIRO, F. (1995). *Eye movement desensitization and reprocessing: Basic principles, protocols and procedures* (1st ed.). New York: The Guilford Press.

SCHEEL, M., Hanson, W. & Razzhavaikina, T. (2004). The process of recommending homework in psychotherapy: A review of therapist delivery methods, client acceptability, and factors that affect compliance. *Psychotherapy: Theory, Research, Practice, Training, 41*, 38–55.

SCHIFF, J. L. (1975). *Cathexis reader: Transactional analysis treatment of psychosis*. New York: Harper & Row.

SCHRAAGEN, J. M., Militello, L. G., Ormerod, T. & Lipshitz, R. (2008). *Naturalistic decision making and metacognition*. Burlington, VT: Ashgate Publishing.

SCHUMAN, D. L., Slone, N. C., Reese, R. J. & Duncan, B. (2015) Efficacy of client feedback in group psychotherapy with soldiers referred for substance abuse treatment. *Psychotherapy Research, 25*(4), 396–407.

SCHWARTZ, R. S. (1993). Managing closeness in psychotherapy. *Psychotherapy, 30*, 601–607.

SCHWARZER, R. (Ed.). (1992). *Self-efficacy: Thought control of action*. Bristol, PA: Taylor & Francis.

SCHWARZER, R. & Fuchs, R. (1996). Self-efficacy and health behaviors. In M. Conner & P. Norman (Eds.), *Predicting health behavior: Research and practice with social cognition models* (pp. 163–196). Buckingham, UK: Open University Press.

SCHWARZER, R. & Renner, B. (2000). Social-cognitive predictors of health behavior: Action self-efficacy and coping self-efficacy. *Health Psychology, 19*, 487–495.

SCOTT, N. E. & Borodovsky, L. G. (1990). Effective use of cultural role taking. *Professional Psychology: Research and Practice, 21*, 167–170.

SEEMAN, T. E. (1996, September). Social ties and health: The benefits of social integration. *Annals of Epidemiology, 6*, 442–451.

SEIKKULA, J. & Trimble, D. (2005). Healing elements of therapeutic conversation: Dialogue as an embodiment of love. *Family Process, 44*, 461–473.

SELIGMAN, M. E. & Csikszentmihalyi, M. (2000). Positive psychology: An introduction. *American Psychologist, 55*, 5–14.

SELIGMAN, M. P. (1975). *Helplessness: On depression, development, and death*. San Francisco, CA: Freeman.

SELIGMAN, M. P. (1991). *Learned optimism*. New York: Knopf.

SELIGMAN, M. P. (1998). *Positive psychology network concept paper*. Retrieved November 20, 2005, from www.psyche.upenn.edu/seligman/ppgrant.htm

SELIGMAN, M. P. (2004). *Authentic happiness: Using the new positive psychology to realize your potential for lasting fulfillment*. New York: Free Press.

SELIGMAN, M. P., Steen, T. A., Park, N. & Peterson, C. (2005). Positive psychology progress: Empirical validation of interventions. *American Psychologist, 60*, 410–421.

SERVAN-SCHREIBER, D. (2004, July/August). Run for your life. *Psychotherapy Networker*, pp. 47–51, 67.

SHALLCROSS, L. (2010, June). Counselors taking a stand. *Counseling Today*, pp. 28–35.

SHARPLEY, C. F. (2007). So why aren't counselors reporting *n* = 1 research designs? *Journal of Counseling and Development, 85*, 349–356.

SHERMAN, M. D., Blevins, D., Kirchner, J., Ridener, L. & Jackson, T. (2008). Key factors involved in engaging significant others in the treatment of Vietnam veterans with PTSD. *Professional Psychology: Research and Practice, 39*, 443–450.

SHERWOOD, J. & Glidewell, J. (1973). Planned renegotiation: A norm-setting OD intervention. In J. Jones & J. Pfeiffer (Eds.), *The 1973 annual handbook for group facilitators* (pp. 195–202). La Jolla, CA: University Associates.

SHORT, D. (2006, January–February). Erickson's legacy. *Psychotherapy Networker*, pp. 71–75.

SIEGEL, R. D. & Allison, S. M. (2009). *Positive psychology: Harnessing the power of happiness, personal strength, and mindfulness.* Boston, MA: Harvard Medical School Special Health Report.

SIMON, H. A., Dantzig, G. B., Hogarth, R., Piott, C. R., Raiffa, H., Schelling, T. C., Shepsle, K.A., Thaler, R., Tversky, A & Winter, S. (1986). *Report of the research briefing panel on decision making and problem solving.* Washington, DC: National Academy Press.

SIMONTON, D. K. (2000). *Origins of genius: Darwinian perspectives on creativity.* New York: Oxford University Press.

SIMONTON, D. K. & Baumeister, R. F. (2005). Positive psychology at the summit. *Review of General Psychology, 9,* 99–102.

SINGHAL, A., Rao, N. & Pant, S. (2006). Entertainment-education and possibilities for second-order social change. *Journal of Creative Communications, 1,* 267–283.

SIROIS, F. M. & Pychyl, T. A. (Eds.). (2016). *Procrastination, health, and well-being.* London: Elsevier.

SLATTERY, J. M. & Park, C. L. (2011). *Empathic counseling: Meaning, context, ethics, and skill.* Pacific Grove, CA: Brooks/Cole.

SLOAN, D. M. (2010). Self-disclosure and psychological well-being. In J. E. Maddux & J. P. Tangney (Eds.), *Social psychological foundations of clinical psychology* (pp. 212–225). New York: The Guilford Press.

SMABY, M. & Tamminen, A. W. (1979). Can we help belligerent counselees? *Personnel and Guidance Journal, 57,* 506–512.

SMITH, E. R. & Mackie, D. M. (2000). *Social psychology* (2nd ed.). Philadelphia, PA: Psychology Press.

SMITH, P. L. & Fouad, N. A. (1999). Subject matter specificity of self-efficacy, outcome expectancies, interests, and goals: Implications for the social-cognitive model. *Journal of Counseling Psychology, 4,* 461–471.

SMITH, T. B., Domenech Rodriguez, M. M. & Bernal, G. (2011). In J. C. Norcross (Ed.), *Psychotherapy relationships that work* (2nd ed., pp. 316–335). New York: Oxford University Press.

SMITH, S. D., Reynolds, C., Rovnak, A. & Thibault, P. J. (2010). Face-to-face communication and body language. In D. Matsumoto (Ed.), *APA handbook of interpersonal communication* (pp. 17–56). Washington, DC: American Psychological Association Books.

SNYDER, C. R. (1989). Reality negotiation: From excuses to hope and beyond. *Journal of Social and Clinical Psychology, 8,* 130–157.

SNYDER, C. R. (1995). Conceptualizing, measuring, and nurturing hope. *Journal of Counseling and Development, 73,* 355–360.

SNYDER, C. R. (1998). A case for hope in pain, loss and suffering. In J. H. Harvey, J. Omarzy & E. Miller (Eds.), *Perspectives on loss: A sourcebook.* Washington, DC: Taylor & Francis.

SNYDER, C. R. (Ed.). (1999). *Coping: The psychology of what works.* New York: Oxford University Press.

SNYDER, C. R. & Higgins, R. L. (1988). Excuses: Their effective role in the negotiation of reality. *Psychological Bulletin, 104,* 23–35.

SNYDER, C. R., Higgins, R. L. & Stucky, R. J. (1983). *Excuses: Masquerades in search of grace.* New York: Wiley.

SNYDER, C. R. & Lopez, S. J. (Eds.). (2005). *Handbook of positive psychology* (2nd ed.). New York: Oxford University Press.

SNYDER, C. R. & Lopez, S. J. (2006). *Positive psychology: The scientific and practical explorations of human strengths.* Thousand Oaks, CA: Sage.

SNYDER, C. R., McDermott, D., Cook, W. & Rapoff, M. (1997). *Hope for the journey:*

Helping children through the good times and the bad. New York: Basic Books.

SNYDER, C. R., Michael, S. T. & Cheavens, J. (1999). Hope as a psychotherapeutic foundation for non-specific factors, placebos and expectancies. In M. A. Huble, B. Duncan & S. Miller (Eds.), *Heart and soul of change*. Washington, DC: American Psychological Association.

SNYDER, C. R. & Rand, K. L. (2003). The case against false hope. *American Psychologist, 58,* 820–821.

SOMMERS-FLANAGAN, J. & Sommers-Flanagan, R. (2006). *Tough kids, cool counseling: User-friendly approaches with challenging youth*. Alexandria, VA: American Counseling Association.

SOMOV, P. G. (2008). *Eating the moment: 141 mindful practices to overcome overeating one meal at a time*. Oakland, CA: New Harbinger.

STEPHANY, K. (2015). *Cultivating empathy: Inspiring health professionals to communicate more effectively*. Sharjah, UAE: Bentham Science Publishers.

STERNBERG, R. J. (Ed.). (2002). *Why smart people can be so stupid*. New Haven, CT: Yale University Press.

STERNBERG, R. J. (2003, March). Responsibility: One of the other three Rs. *Monitor on Psychology*, p. 5.

STERNBERG, R. J., Grigorenko, E. L. & Singer, J. L. (Eds.). (2004). *Creativity: From potential to realization*. Washington, DC: American Psychological Association.

STEWART, R. E., Chambless, S. & Chambless, D. (2008). Treatment failures in private practice: How do psychologists proceed? *Professional Psychology: Research and Practice, 39,* 176–181.

STEWART, W. (2013) *An A-Z of Counselling Theory and Practice* (5th ed.). Andover: Cengage Learning EMEA.

STRONG, S. R. (1968). Counseling: An interpersonal influence process. *Journal of Counseling Psychology, 15,* 215–224.

STRONG, S. R. (1991). Social influence and change in therapeutic relationships. In C. R. Snyder & D. R. Forsyth (Eds.), *Handbook of social and clinical psychology: The health perspective* (pp. 540–562). New York: Pergamon Press.

STRONG, S. R. & Claiborn, C. D. (1982). *Change through interaction: Social psychological processes of counseling and psychotherapy*. New York: Wiley.

STRONG, S., Yoder, B. & Corcoran, J. (1995). Counseling: A social process for encouraging personal powers. *The Counseling Psychologist, 23,* 374–384.

STUART, R. B. (2004). Twelve practical suggestions for achieving multicultural competence. *Professional Psychology: Research and Practice, 35,* 3–9.

STUEBER, K. R. (2010). *Rediscovering empathy: Agency, folk psychology, and the human sciences*. Cambridge, MA: Bradford Books, MIT Press.

SUE, D. W, & Sue, D. (1990). *Counseling the culturally different: Theory and practice* (2nd ed.). New York: Wiley.

SWANN, W. B., Chang-Schneider, C. & McClarty, K. L. (2007, February-March). Do people's self-views matter? Self-concept and self-esteem in everyday life. *American Psychologist, 62,* 84–94.

SYKES, C. J. (1992). *A nation of victims*. New York: St. Martin's Press.

TAUBES, G. (2011). *Why we get fat: And what to do about it*. New York: Knopf.

TAUSSIG, I. M. (1987). Comparative responses of Mexican Americans and Anglo-Americans to early goal setting in a public mental health clinic. *Journal of Counseling Psychology, 34,* 214–217.

TAVRIS, C. & Aronson, E. (2007). *Mistakes were made (but not by me): Why we justify foolish beliefs, bad decisions, and hurtful acts*. Orlando, FL: Harcourt.

TAYLOR, S. E. (2007). Social support. In H. S. Friedman & R. C. Silver (Eds.), *Foundations of health psychology* (pp. 145–171). New York: Oxford University Press.

TAYLOR, S. E., Pham, L. B., Rivkin, I. D. & Armor, D. A. (1998). Harnessing the imagination: Mental stimulation, self-regulation, and coping. *American Psychologist, 53*, 429–439.

TAYLOR, S. E., Sherman, D. K., Kim, H. S., Jarcho, J., Takagi, K. & Dunagan, M. S. (2004). Culture and social support: Who seeks it and why? *Journal of Personality and Social Psychology, 87*, 354–362.

TEDESCHI, R. G. & Calhoun, L. G. (2004). Posttraumatic growth: Conceptual foundations and empirical evidence. *Psychological Inquiry, 15*, 1–18.

TEDESCHI, R. G. & Kilmer, R. P. (2005). Assessing strengths, resilience, and growth to guide clinical interventions. *Professional Psychology: Research and Practice, 36*, 230–237.

TESSER, A. & Rosen, S. (1972). Similarity of objective fate as a determinant of the reluctance to transmit unpleasant information: The MUM effect. *Journal of Personality and Social Psychology, 23*, 46–53.

TESSER, A., Rosen, S. & Batchelor, T. (1972). On the reluctance to communicate bad news (the MUM effect): A role play extension. *Journal of Personality, 40*, 88–103.

TESSER, A., Rosen, S. & Tesser, M. (1971). On the reluctance to communicate undesirable messages (the MUM effect): A field study. *Psychological Reports, 29*, 651–654.

TEYBER, E. (2005). *Interpersonal process in therapy: An integrative model* (5th ed.). Belmont, CA: Wadsworth/Thomson Learning.

THALER, R. & Sunstein, C. (2008). *Nudge: Improving decisions about health, wealth, and happiness*. New Haven, CT: Yale University Press.

The British Psychological Society. (2018). *Code of ethics and conduct*. Leicester, UK: BPS.

THOMPSON, S. & Thompson, N. (2008). *The critically reflective practitioner*. Basingstoke, UK: Palgrave Macmillan.

TICKELL, C. (2005). A review of books in human evolution and where the human race seems to be headed. *Financial Times*, p. W5.

TIEDENS, L. Z. & Leach, C. W. (2004). *The social life of emotions*. New York: Cambridge University Press.

TINSLEY, H. E. A., Bowman, S. L. & Barich, A. W. (1993). Counseling psychologists' perceptions of the occurrence and effects of unrealistic expectations about counseling and psychotherapy among their clients. *Journal of Counseling Psychology, 40*, 46–52.

TOMPKINS, M. A. (2005). Six steps to improve psychotherapy homework compliance. In G. P. Koocher, J. C. Norcross & S. S. Hill, III. (Eds.), *Psychologists' desk reference* (2nd ed., pp. 319– 324). New York: Oxford University Press.

TRACEY, T. J. (1991). The structure of control and influence in counseling and psychotherapy: A comparison of several definitions and measures. *Journal of Counseling Psychology, 38*, 265–278.

TREVINO, J. G. (1996, April). Worldview and change in cross-cultural counseling. *Counseling Psychologist, 24*, 198–215.

TROUT, J. D. (2009). *Why empathy matters: The science and psychology of better judgment*. New York: Penguin.

TUGADE, M. M. & Fredrickson, B. L. (2004). Resilient individuals use positive emotions to bounce back from negative emotional experiences. *Journal of Personality and Social Psychology, 86*, 320–333.

TURSI, M. M. & Cochran, J. L. (2006). Cognitive-behavioral tasks accomplished in a person-centered relational framework. *Journal of Counseling and Development, 84*, 387–396.

TYLER, F. B., Pargament, K. I. & Gatz, M. (1983). The resource collaborator role: A model for interactions involving psychologists. *American Psychologist, 38*, 388–398.

URY, W. (1991). *Getting past no: Negotiating your way from confrontation to cooperation*. New York: Bantam Books.

URY, W. (2007). *The power of a positive no.* New York: Bantam Books.

UZZI, B. & Spiro, J. (2005, September). Collaboration and creativity: The small world problem. *American Journal of Sociology, 111,* 447–504.

VAILLANT, G. E. (2000, January). Adaptive mental mechanisms: Their role in a positive psychology. *American Psychologist, 55,* 89–98.

Van DELLEN, M. R. & Hoyle, R. H. (2010). Regulatory accessibility and social influences on state self-control. *Personality and Social Psychology Bulletin, 36*(2), 25–263.

Van DELLEN, M. R., Hoyle, R. H. & Miller, R. (2012, February). The regulatory easy street: Self-regulation below the self-control threshold does not consume regulatory resources. *Personality and Individual Differences, 52*(8), 898–902.

VAN DER KOLK, B. (2015). *The body keeps the score: Mind, brain and body in the transformation of trauma.* London: Penguin Random House UK

Van HECKE, M. L. (2007). *Blind spots: Why smart people do dumb things.* Amherst, NY: Prometheus Books.

Van RIJN, B. (2015). *Assessment and case formulation in counselling and psychotherapy.* London: Sage Publications.

VANSTEENKISTE, M. & Sheldon, K. M. (2006). There's nothing more practical than a good theory: Integrating motivational interviewing and self-determination theory. *British Psychological Society, 45,* 63–82.

Van VLIET, J. (2008). Shame and resilience in adulthood: A grounded theory study. *Journal of Counseling Psychology, 55,* 233–245.

VEACH, P. M. (2011). Reflections on the meaning of clinician self-reference: Are we speaking the same language? *Psychotherapy, 48,* 349–358.

VEALE, D. (2008). Behavioural activation for depression. *Advances in Psychiatric Treatment, 14,* 29–36.

VOGEL, D., Wester, S. R. & Larson, L. M. (2007). Avoidance of counseling: Psychological factors that inhibit seeking help. *Journal of Counseling & Development, 85,* 410–422.

VOGEL, L. & Wester, S. R. (2003). To seek help or not to seek help: The risks of self-disclosure. *Journal of Counseling Psychology, 50,* 351–361.

WAGNER, D. D. & Heatherton, T.F. (2016). The cognitive neuroscience of self-regulatory failure. In K.D. Vohs & R.F. Baumeister (Eds.), *Handbook of self-regulation, third edition: research, theory and applications* (pp. 111–130). New York: The Guilford Press.

WAHLSTEIN, D. (1991). Nonverbal behavior and self-presentation. *Psychological Bulletin, 110,* 587–595.

WALSH, Y., Dillon, S., Frankland, A., Kerr, C., Larsson, P., Nicholas, H. & Sugg, M. (2013). *Working relationally with trauma: A discussion.* P. James (Ed.). Leicester, UK: The British Psychological Society.

WAMPOLD, B. E. (2010a). *The basics of psychotherapy: An introduction to theory and practice.* Washington, DC: American Psychological Association Books.

WAMPOLD, B. E. (2010b). The research evidence for the common factors models: A historically situated perspective. In B. L. Duncan, S. D. Miller, B. E. Wampold & M. A. Hubble (Eds.), *The heart and soul of change: Delivering what works in therapy* (2nd ed., pp. 49–81). Washington, DC: American Psychological Association Books.

WAMPOLD, B. E. (2011). *Qualities and actions of effective therapists* [DVD]. Washington, DC: American Psychological Association Books.

WAMPOLD, B. E. & Brown, G. S. (2005). Estimating therapist variability: A naturalistic study of outcomes in managed care. *Journal of Consulting and Clinical Psychology, 73,* 914–923.

WANG, Y. W., Davidson, M. M., Yakushko, O. F., Savoy, H. B., Tan, J. A. & Bleier, J. K. (2003). The scale of ethnocultural empathy: Development, validation, & reliability. *Journal of Counseling Psychology, 50,* 221–234.

WANSINK, B. (2011). *Mindless eating: Why we eat more than we think*. New York: Bantam.

WATSON, D. L. & Tharp, R. G. (2007). *Self- directed behavior* (9th ed.). Belmont, CA: Wadsworth.

WATTS, D. J. (2011). *Everything is obvious, once you know the answer*. New York: Crown Business.

WEBB, T. L. & Sheeran, P. (2006). Does changing behavioural intentions engender behavior change? A meta-analysis of the experimental evidence. *Psychological Bulletin, 132*, 249–268.

WEI, M. & Ku, T. (2007). Testing a conceptual model of working through self-defeating patterns. *Journal of Counseling Psychology, 54*, 295–305.

WEICK, K. E. (1979). *The social psychology of organizing* (2nd ed.). Reading, MA: Addison-Wesley.

WEINRACH, S. G. & Thomas, K. R. (1996). The counseling profession's commitment to diversity sensitive counseling: A critical reassessment. *Journal of Counseling and Development, 74*, 472–477.

WEITZ, S. (1974). *Nonverbal communication: Readings with commentary*. New York: Oxford University Press.

WELFEL, E. R. (2013). *Ethics in counseling and psychotherapy* (5th ed.). Belmont, CA: Cengage Brooks/Cole.

WESSLER, R., Hankin, S. & Stern, J. (2001). *Succeeding with difficult clients: Applications of cognitive appraisal therapy*. New York: Academic Press.

WEST, R. & Turner, L. H. (2009). *Understanding interpersonal communication: Making choices in changing times*. Belmont, CA: Wadsworth.

WESTRA, H. (2004). Managing resistance in cognitive behavioral therapy: The application of motivational interviewing in mixed anxiety and depression. *Cognitive Behavioral Therapy, 33*(4), 161–175.

WESTRA, H. A., Aviram, A., Connors, L., Kertes, A. & Mariyam, A. (2011, June 20). Therapist emotional reactions and client resistance in cognitive behavioral therapy. *Psychotherapy*. Advanced Online Publication.

WESTRA, H. A., Constantino, M. J. & Aviram, A. (2011, July). The impact of alliance ruptures on client outcome expectations in cognitive behavioral therapy. *Psychotherapy Research, 21*, 472–481.

WHEELER, D. D. & Janis, I. L. (1980). *A practical guide for making decisions*. New York: Free Press.

WHITE, M. (2007). *Maps of narrative practice*. New York: W. W. Norton.

WILLIAMS, R. (1989, January–February). The trusting heart. *Psychology Today*, pp. 36–42.

WILSON, J. Q. (1993). *The moral sense*. New York: Free Press.

WING, R. R. & Jeffery, R. W. (1999). Benefits of recruiting participants with friends and increasing social support for weight loss and maintenance. *Journal of Consulting and Clinical Psychology, 67*, 132–138.

WITKIEWITZ, K. & Marlatt, G. A. (2005). Emphasis on interpersonal factors in a dynamic model of relapse. *American Psychologist, 60*, 341–342.

WOLFF, J. (2009). *Creativity now: Get inspired, create ideas, and make them happen now*. Harlow, UK: Pearson Prentice-Hall Business.

WONG, Y. J. (2006). Strength-centered therapy: A social constructionist, virtues-based psychotherapy. *Psychotherapy, 43*, 133–146.

WOOD, T. T. (2009). *Interpersonal communication: everyday encounters* (6th ed.). Belmont, CA: Wadsworth.

WORTHINGTON, R. L., Soth-McNett, A. M. & Moreno, M. V. (2007). Multicultural counseling competencies research: A 20-year content analysis. *Journal of Counseling Psychology, 5*(4), 351–361.

WOSKET, V. (2006). *Egan's skilled helper model: Developments and applications in counselling*. London: Brunner-Routledge.

YANKELOVICH, D. (1992, October 5). How public opinion really works. *Fortune*, 102–108.

YEH, Y. & Hayes, J. A. (2011). How does disclosing countertransference affect perceptions of the therapist and the session? *Psychotherapy*, 48, 322–329.

YUN, K. A. (1998). Relational closeness and production of excuses in events of failure. *Psychological Reports*, 83, 1059–1066.

ZAKI, J., Bolger, N. & Ochsner, K. (2008). It takes two: The interpersonal nature of empathic accuracy. *Psychological Science*, 19, 399–404.

ZIMMERMAN, B. J. (1995). Self-efficacy and educational development. In A. Bandura (Ed.), *Self-efficacy in changing societies* (pp. 202–231). New York: Cambridge University Press.

ZIMMERMAN, B. J. (1996, April). *Measuring and mismeasuring academic self-efficacy: Dimensions, problems, and misconceptions.*

Symposium presented at the meeting of the American Educational Association, New York.

ZIMRIN, H. (1986). A profile of survival. *Child Abuse and Neglect*, 10, 339–349.

ZOELLICK, R. (2009, January 26). It is time to herald the age of responsibility. *Financial Times*, p. 11.

ZUR, O. (2015). *Power in psychotherapy and counseling*. Online Publication by the Zur Institute. Retrieved from www.zurinstitute.com/power-in-therapy/

ZUR, O. (2008). Re-thinking the "power differential" in psychotherapy: Exploring the myth of therapists' omnipotence and patients' fragility. *Voice: The Art and Science of Psychotherapy*, 44(3), 32–40.

ZUR, O., Williams, W. H., Lehavot, K. & Knapp, S. (2009). Psychotherapist self-disclosure and transparency in the internet age. *Professional Psychology: Research and Practice*, 40, 22–30.

Appendix – Useful Weblinks

The following resources are provided for information purposes and do not necessarily constitute a recommendation.

ABUSE, RAPE AND SELF-HARM/SELF-INJURY SERVICES

Association of Child Abuse Lawyers (ACAL), PO Box 974A, Surbiton, KT1 9XF.
Tel: 0208 390 4701 (10 a.m.–l p.m. and 2 p.m.–4 p.m. Tuesdays and Thursdays only)
Website: www.childabuselawyers.com
Description: Practical support for survivors and professionals working in the field of abuse. Can recommend a solicitor with some understanding of childhood abuse cases, and site contains some useful links and information.

Self Injury Support, PO Box 3240, Bristol, BS2 2EF.
Text support: 0117 927 9600
Website: www.selfinjurysupport.org.uk
Description: A national voluntary organisation that supports women in emotional distress. Particularly helps women who harm themselves (often called self-injury). Provides talks and training courses to professionals, runs and supports self-help groups, and produces information and publications about self-injury.

ChildLine UK
Tel: 0800 1111.
Website: www.childline.org.uk
Description: UK's free, 24-hour helpline for children and young people in trouble or danger. The lines can be busy so please keep trying.

ChildLine South Africa
Tel: 08000 55 555 (24 hour)
Website: www.childlinesa.org.za/
Description: Childline is an effective non-profit organisation that works collectively to protect children from all forms of violence and to create a culture of children's rights in South Africa.

Kidscape, 2 Grosvenor Gardens, London, SW1W 0DH.
Tel: 0207 730 3300.
Parent Advice Line: 020 7823 5430.
(Monday–Wednesday, 9:30 a.m.–2:30 p.m.)
Website: www.kidscape.org.uk
Description: Registered charity committed to keeping children safe from harm or abuse. Kidscape is the only national children's charity that focuses upon preventative policies – tactics to use before any abuse takes place. Kidscape has practical, easy-to-use material for children, parents, teachers, social workers, police and community workers.

Mothers of Sexually Abused Children (MOSAC), 141 Greenwich High Road, London, SE10 8JA.
Helpline: 0800 980 1958 (Monday, Thursday and Friday 10.00 a.m.–2.00 p.m., Tuesday and Wednesday 10 a.m.–6 p.m.)
Website: www.mosac.org.uk
Description: A voluntary organisation supporting all non-abusing parents and carers whose children have been sexually abused. Provides support, advice, information and counselling following the discovery of sexual abuse.

National Association for People Abused in Childhood (NAPAC), CAN Mezzanine, 7–14 Great Dover Street, London, SE1 4YR.
Helpline: 0808 801 0331 (Monday, Wednesday and Friday 10.00 a.m.–4.00 p.m., Tuesday and Friday, 2 p.m.–9 p.m.)
Email: support@napac.org.uk
Website: www.napac.org.uk
Description: National charity providing support and information for people abused in childhood. Freephone support line for adults who suffered any type of abuse. Support and information pack and booklets free to download from their website.

NSPCC (National Society for the Prevention of Cruelty to Children),
Weston House, 42 Curtain Road,
London, EC2A 3NH.
Helpline: 0808 800 5000.
Website: www.nspcc.org.uk
Description: The UK's leading charity specialising in child protection and the prevention of cruelty to children. Website contains a directory of international organisations.

People Opposing Woman Abuse (POWA) in South Africa
Head Office: Berea
Postal Address: PO Box 93416, Yeoville 2143, Johannesburg.
Tel: 011 642 4345/6.
Fax: 011 484 3195.
Email: info@powa.co.za
Website: www.powa.co.za
Description: POWA's uniqueness as an organisation is in providing both services to survivors and engaging in advocacy using a feminist and intersectional analysis. Their work is rooted in the belief that change can only be said to be effective when women's lives are directly improved through our interventions. They also believe that there is no single route to change, and thus constantly seek new and creative approaches in our programming to achieve the change we seek.

Rape Crisis South Africa
Crisis Line: 021 447 9762 (24 hour)
Email: info@rapecrisis.org.za
Website: rapecrisis.org.za
Description: Rape Crisis has a vision of a South African criminal justice system that supports and empowers rape survivors in all of its interventions. Until such time as this vision becomes a reality they aim to provide that support and empowerment.

ADDICTION SERVICES

Al-Anon Family Groups UK and Eire,
57B Great Suffolk Street, London, SE1 0BB.
Tel: 0800 0086 811
Website: www.al-anonuk.org.uk/
Description: Provides understanding, strength and hope to anyone whose life is, or has been, affected by someone else's drinking.

Alcohol Change UK, 27 Swinton Street, London, WC1X 9NW.
Tel: 0203 907 8480.
Email: contact@alcoholchange.org.uk
Website: www.alcoholchange.org.uk/
Description: National agency on alcohol misuse. Works to reduce the incidence and costs of alcohol-related harm, and to increase the range and quality of services available to people with alcohol-related problems.

Alcoholics Anonymous, PO Box 1,
10 Toft Green, York, YO1 7NJ.
Helpline: 0800 9177 650.
Email: help@aamail.org
Website: www.alcoholics-anonymous.org.uk
Description: Offers advice and support to alcoholics. In the UK and Ireland, look for 'Alcoholics Anonymous' in any telephone directory. For Alcoholics Anonymous South Africa, visit www.aasouthafrica.org.za

European Association for the Treatment of Addiction (EATA), 6 Errol Street, London, EC1Y 8SE, UK.
Tel: 0808 278 9885 / 0203 131 6690
Email: secretariat@eata.org.uk
Website: www.eata.org.uk
Description: A charity working to help ensure people with substance dependencies get the treatment they need.

Gamblers Anonymous UK, The Wellness Centre, 45 Montrose Avenue, Intake, Doncaster, DN2 6PL.
Tel: 0330 094 0322
Website: www.gamblersanonymous.org.uk/
Description: A fellowship of men and women who have joined together to do something about their own gambling problem and to help other compulsive gamblers do the same.

Narcotics Anonymous (UK), 202 City Road, London, EC1V 2PH.
Helpline UK: 0300 999 1212
Email: helpline@ukna.org
Website: www.ukna.org
Description: A fellowship of men and women for whom drugs had become a major problem. They meet regularly to help each other stay clean. The only requirement for membership is the desire to stop. Details of meetings throughout the UK.

Narcotics Anonymous South Africa
Website: www.na.org.za/
    Description: Narcotics Anonymous (NA) is a non-profit fellowship of men and women for whom drugs had become a major problem. They are recovering addicts who meet regularly to help each other stay clean.

Talk to FRANK (National Drugs Helpline)
Helpline: 0300 123 6600.
Email: frank@talktofrank.com.
Website: www.talktofrank.com
    Description: Free confidential drugs information and advice 24 hours a day.

Internet resources
DrugWise
The UK's leading independent centre of expertise on drugs. Its aim is to inform policy development and reduce drug-related risk.
Website: www.drugwise.org.uk/

The Way
Confronting addiction. Links to organisations offering help with addictions.
Website: www.theway.uk.com

ADOPTION SERVICES

CoramBAAF Adoption and Fostering Academy, Coram Campus, 41 Brunswick Square, London, WC1N 1AZ.
Tel: 020 7520 0300.
Email: advice@corambaaf.org.uk
Website: www.corambaaf.org.uk/
    Description: CoramBAAF, based in London and with offices in Wales, Scotland and England, is the leading membership organisation for agencies and individuals concerned with adoption, fostering and work with children and families. It is also a major publisher, training provider and family finder.

Office of National Statistics: Adoption Contact Register.
Tel: 0300 123 1837.
Email: adoptions@gro.gsi.gov.uk
Website: www.gov.uk/adoption-records/
the-adoption-contact-register
    Description: The Adoption Contact Register is kept by the Registrar General, and contains a record of every person who has been adopted through a court in England or Wales. The website gives information on applying for adoption certificates, receiving information on original birth details, and making contact with adopted people and their relatives.

COUNSELLING AND PSYCHOTHERAPY SERVICES

Association for Family Therapy and Systemic Practice in the UK, 7 Executive Suite, St James Court, Wilderspool Causeway, Warrington, Cheshire, WA4 6PS.
Tel: 01925 444414.
Website: www.aft.org.uk/
    Description: Aims to develop the profession and to establish standards for training and registration through the UK Council for Psychotherapy.

British Association for Behavioural and Cognitive Psychotherapies (BABCP), Imperial House, Hornby Street, Bury, Lancashire, BL9 5BN.
Tel: 0330 320 0851.
Email: babcp@babcp.com
Website: www.babcp.org.uk/
    Description: A multi-disciplinary interest group for people involved in the practice and theory of behavioural and cognitive psychotherapy. Produces a range of publications including pamphlets on anxiety, depression, schizophrenia, PTSD, general health, OCD, agoraphobia, learning disability, insomnia, chronic fatigue syndrome, eating disorders, understanding CBT, sexual dysfunction, chronic pain, conduct disorder and bipolar disorders.

British Association for Counselling and Psychotherapy, BACP House, 15 St John's Business Park, Lutterworth, Leicestershire, LE17 4HB.
Tel: 01455 883300.
Email: bacp@bacp.co.uk
Website: www.bacp.co.uk
    Description: The association's aims are to promote understanding and awareness of counselling throughout society, increase the availability of trained and supervised counsellors, and maintain and raise standards of training and practice. It produces a range of publications and a quarterly counselling journal. The United Kingdom Register of Counsellors (UKRC) is part of the British Association for Counselling and Psychotherapy.

Website listing psychotherapists throughout South Africa: **www.therapist-directory.co.za/ therapists-south-africa/**

College of Sexual and Relationship Therapists (CORST), PO Box 13686, London, SW20 9ZH.
Tel: 0208 106 9635
Email: info@cosrt.org.uk
Website: www.cosrt.org.uk/
Description: Promotes the education and training of clinicians and therapists working in the fields of sexual and couple relationships, sexual dysfunction and sexual health, and raises public awareness of sexual and relationship therapy.

British Psychological Society (BPS),
St Andrews House, 48 Princess Road East, Leicester, LE1 7DR.
Tel: 0116 254 9568.
Fax: 0116 227 1314.
Email: info@bps.org.uk
Website: www.bps.org.uk
Description: Aims to encourage the development of psychology as a scientific discipline and an applied profession, to raise standards of training and practice in the application of psychology, and to raise public awareness of psychology and increase the influence of psychological practice in society.

Psychological Society of South Africa.
Email: info@psyssa.com
Website: www.psyssa.com/
Description: The Psychological Society of South Africa (PsySSA) is the professional body representing psychologists in South Africa. PsySSA was formed in January 1994, out of various bodies then existing and representing psychology in South Africa (such as OASSA, PASA, and Psychologists Against Apartheid). PsySSA was structured as a transformed entity to deal with the changing dispensation and can speak authoritatively on behalf of the discipline on matters concerning the mental health and psychosocial well-being of all South Africans.

Psychoanalytic Psychotherapy in South Africa
The professional journal, *Psycho-analytic Psychotherapy in South Africa* (PPSA) is a non-profit journal, established in 1992 by Trevor Lubbe, a child psychoanalytic psychotherapist and Tony Hamburger, a clinical psychologist, both now based in Johannesburg, South Africa.
The objective of the PPSA journal is to act as a vehicle for psychoanalytic thinking in order to develop psychoanalytic psychotherapy in areas of theory, clinical practice, training and research. The PPSA journal is Department of Education accredited for research subsidy purposes: ISSN 1023-0548. It is a peer reviewed journal.
Website: www.ppsajournal.co.za/

Relate: The relationship people, Premier House, Carolina Court, Lakeside, Doncaster, DN4 5RA
Helpline: 0300 100 1234
Email: relate.enquiries@relate.org.uk
Website: www.relate.org.uk
Description: UK's largest and most experienced relationship counselling organisation. Whether you are having problems getting on with your partner, your kids, your siblings or even your boss – Relate can help. Local branches can be found by entering a postcode on the website.

The Institute of Counselling, Clinical and Pastoral Counselling,
40 St Enoch Square, Glasgow, G1 4DH.
Tel: 0141 204 2230
Email: admin@instituteofcounselling.org.uk
Website: www.instituteofcounselling.org.uk
Description: The College of Counselling is the accredited distance learning college of the Institute of Counselling. The College offers a wide range of tutor-supported distance and online courses, specialising in counselling skills training.

DIVORCE, MEDIATION AND LONE PARENT SERVICES

Gingerbread, 54–74 Holmes Road, London, NW5 3AQ.
Helpline: 0808 802 0925.
Email: info@gingerbread.org.uk
Website: www.gingerbread.org.uk
Description: Provides information about support for lone parent families.

National Family Mediation (NFM),
1st Floor, Civic Centre,
Paris St, Exeter, EX1 1JN.
Tel: 0300 4000 636.
Fax: 01392 911 240.
Website: www.nfm.org.uk/
Description: NFM is a network of over 60 local not-for-profit Family Mediation Services in England and Wales, offering help to couples, married or unmarried, who are in the process of separation and divorce. They are committed to providing mediation to everyone who needs it in all communities.

EATING DISORDER SERVICES

Beat, Unit 1 Chalk Hill House, 19 Rosary Road, Norwich, Norfolk, NR1 1SZ.
Adult Helpline: 0808 801 0677
Over 18 years of age.
Helpline email service: help@beateatingdisorders.org.uk
Youthline: 0808 801 0711. Up to and including 18 years of age.
Email: fyp@beateatingdisorders.org.uk
Website: www.beateatingdisorders.org.uk
Description: Help on all aspects of eating disorders, including anorexia nervosa, bulimia nervosa, binge eating disorder and related eating disorders.

National Centre for Eating Disorders,
54 New Road, Esher, Surrey, KT10 9NU.
Tel: 0845 838 2040.
Website: www.eating-disorders.org.uk
Description: Effective solutions for eating disorders such as compulsive eating, unsuccessful dieting and bulimia. Counselling, training and information.

The Priory Hospital, Eating Disorder Unit, Priory Lane, Roehampton, London, SW15 5JJ.
Tel: 0800 280 8109.
Website: www.priorygroup.com
Description: In addition to offering treatment for eating disorders, The Priory Hospital offers treatment for other psychiatric conditions, including anxiety, depression and schizophrenia, alcoholism, drug abuse and stress-related disorders.

LOSS AND BEREAVEMENT SERVICES

Child Death Helpline Barclay House, 37 Queen Square, London, WC1N 3BH.
Tel: 0800 282 986.
Email: contact@childdeathhelpline.org
Website: www.childdeathhelpline.org.uk
Description: A helpline for all those affected by the death of a child. Provides local contacts.

Cruse Bereavement Care,
Unit 0.1, One Victoria Villas, Richmond, Surrey, TW9 2GW.
Tel: 0208 939 9530. Helpline: 0808 808 1677.
Email: info@cruse.org.uk
Helpline: helpline@cruse.org.uk
Website: www.cruse.org.uk/

Description: Offers help and counselling for bereaved people as well as a range of useful publications.

The Lullaby Trust, 34 New House, 67-68 Hatton Garden, London, EC1N 8JY.
Tel: 0808 802 6869 (general enquiries).
Helpline: 0808 802 6868.
Website: www.lullabytrust.org.uk/
Description: Offers a range of support leaflets for bereaved families. Also produces a series of leaflets, books, posters, fact files and videos for parents, students, carers, health professionals and anyone interested in knowing more about cot death.

Miscarriage Association, Head Office, 17 Wentworth Terrace, Wakefield, WF1 3QW.
Tel: 01924 200795 (admin).
Helpline: 01924 200799.
Email: info@miscarriageassociation.org.uk
Website: www.miscarriageassociation.org.uk/
Description: Offers support to those who have suffered the loss of a baby in pregnancy. Has 50 support groups across the UK, where people can meet and share their experiences and feelings. Produces leaflets, factsheets and podcasts and works to raise awareness and sensitivity among healthcare professionals through lectures, workshops and articles in professional journals. Site contains a useful list of links to related sites and helpful books.

SANDS (Stillbirth and Neonatal Death Society), Victoria Charity Centre, 11 Belgrave Road, London, SW1V 1RB.
Tel: 020 7436 7940.
Helpline: 0808 164 3332.
Email: helpline@sands.org.uk
Website: www.sands.org.uk/
Description: Provides support for parents and families whose baby is stillborn or dies soon after birth.

The Compassionate Friends for Bereaved Parents, Kilburn Grange, Priory Park Road, London, NW6 7UJ
Tel: 0345 120 3785. Helpline: 0345 123 2304.
Email Information and Support: info@tcf.org.uk
Helpline: helpline@tcf.org.uk
Website: www.tcf.org.uk

Description: Offers understanding, support and encouragement to others after the death of a child or children.

MENTAL HEALTH SERVICES

Association for Post-Natal Illness,
145 Dawes Road, Fulham, London, SW6 7EB.
Helpline: 0207 386 0868.
Email: info@apni.org
Website: www.apni.org
Description: Provides support to mothers suffering from post-natal illness. Aims to raise public awareness of the illness and to encourage research into its cause.

Fellowship of Depressives Anonymous (FDA),
FREEPOST NEA5373,
Beverley, HU17 9BR.
Description: FDA is a UK nationwide self-help organisation made up of individual members and groups that meet locally on a regular basis for mutual support. For more information about the group visit: webhealth.co.uk/support-groups/depression-fellowship-of-depressives-anonymous/

Bipolar UK, 11 Belgrave Road, London, SW1V 1RB.
Tel: 0333 323 3880.
Email: info@bipolaruk.org
Website: www.bipolaruk.org/
Description: Bipolar UK works to enable people affected by bipolar to take control of their lives.

Mind, 15–19 Broadway, Stratford
London, E15 4BQ.
Tel: 0208 519 2122 Fax: 0208 522 1725
(Mind Cymru Tel: 029 2039 5123)
Email: supporterrelations@mind.org.uk
Website: www.mind.org.uk
Description: Mind is the leading mental health charity in England and Wales. It works to create a better life for everyone with experience of mental distress. Also publishes a wide range of books, factsheets, booklets and reports.

The ME Association, 7 Apollo Office Court,
Radclive Road, Gawcott, Bucks., MK18 4DF.
Helpline: 0344 576 5326.
Email meconnect@meassociation.org.uk
Website: www.meassociation.org.uk
Description: Informing and supporting those affected by myalgic encephalopathy (ME), chronic fatigue syndrome and post-viral fatigue syndrome.

The Mental Health Foundation, Colechurch House, 1 London Bridge Walk, London, SE1 2SX.
Tel: 020 7803 1100.
Website: www.mentalhealth.org.uk/
Description: Comprehensive website on mental health (and mental illness). Carries out vital work in supporting people with mental health problems. Information on a wide range of specific mental health issues from attention deficit disorder to obsessive compulsive disorders to eating disorders to stress to self-harm, etc.

Name Index

Subject Index